- ☐ TRIGGERING   Why are you writing this paper? What brought it on? What are you trying to do? What will this piece of writing do for the writer and for the reader?

- ☐ GATHERING   Where are you going to turn for material? What do you already know, and how can you learn more? What opportunities will you have for drawing on personal experience, taking a firsthand look, talking to insiders, or consulting authoritative sources?

- ☐ SHAPING   How are you going to lay out your material? How does it add up — what is the point? How are you going to proceed — what is your strategy?

- ☐ REVISING   As you read your first draft, where does it say what you are trying to say, and where does it fall short? Can the reader follow your train of thought, or do you need to reshuffle parts of your paper? Do you need to do more to show connections between ideas?

- ☐ EDITING   Where should the wording be more pointed or more vivid? Which sentences need work because they are wordy, roundabout, or confused? Did you check spelling and punctuation to make sure your writing is ready-to-print?

> *"I discovered there is a great difference between the expression of an opinion and the formation of an idea."*
> STUDENT PAPER

The Writer's Agenda

THE WADSWORTH WRITER'S GUIDE AND HANDBOOK

Writing well is the art of clear thinking and honest feeling.
DONALD HALL

All good writers speak in honest voices and tell the truth.
KEN MACRORIE

If you really want to get a message across, you have to treat the reader as a separate person, not just as a wall to bounce your feelings off.
ELIZABETH COWAN NEELD

The Writer's Agenda

THE WADSWORTH WRITER'S GUIDE AND HANDBOOK

Hans P. Guth
San Jose State University

WADSWORTH PUBLISHING COMPANY
A DIVISION OF WADSWORTH, INC.   BELMONT, CALIFORNIA

Sponsoring Editor: Steve Rutter
English Editor: Angela M. Gantner
Production Editor: Michael G. Oates
Interior and Cover Design: James Chadwick
Print Buyer: Barbara Britton
Copy Editor: Betty Duncan-Todd
Photo Researcher: Bonnie Trach
Technical Illustrator: Alice Harmon
Compositor: Graphic Typesetting Service, Los Angeles, California
Interior Photographs: pp. 4, 242 © Margaretta K. Mitchell; p. 132 © 1983 Elena Sheehan; p. 322 © Bonnie Trach, 1988; p. 456 © David Wakely, 1988.
Cover Photograph and Title Page: "Washington State Coastline," copyright © Art Wolfe

Printed in the United States of America   34

1 2 3 4 5 6 7 8 9 10---93 92 91 90 89

Library of Congress Cataloging in Publication Data

Guth, Hans Paul
    The writer's agenda : the Wadsworth writer's guide and handbook
Hans P. Guth.
        p.   cm.
    Includes index.
      ISBN 0-534-09636-0
        1. English language—Rhetoric.   2. English language—
Grammar—1950–   I. Title.
PE1408.G937   1988
808'.042—dc19   88-21115
                                                                CIP

Brief Contents

Detailed Contents

Part Three   WRITING AND THINKING

Part Four   THE WRITER'S TOOLS

Part Five SPECIAL ASSIGNMENTS

A CONCISE HANDBOOK

PREFACE

To the Instructor

The Writer's Agenda is designed to help students discover the incentives, the strategies, and the rewards of writing. It is a book for teachers who are part of a revolution of changing expectations: We expect our students to write more and to write better, and they do. Everywhere in recent years, the teaching of composition has become a more positive, a more productive, and a more humane enterprise. Focus on the "making of meaning" is replacing a one-sided preoccupation with the making of mistakes. Emphasis on how student writers succeed is balancing our concern with why they fail.

The Writer's Agenda aims at a new synthesis of what is best in current theory and research and in current practice. The following assumptions have guided the writing of this book:

(1) *A writing text should focus on how successful student writing takes shape.* This book guides the student through five overlapping and inter-related stages in the process of writing: triggering (what brings it on?); gathering (how do we mobilize our sources?); shaping (what strategies help us focus and organize our material?); revising (what kind of second thoughts produce genuine rethinking and rewriting?); and editing (what does it take to make our writing acceptable to a large cross section of educated readers and fit for print?).

(2) *A writing text should bridge the gap between theory and practice.* The heart of this book is its sequence of gradually more demanding writing tasks, each set in motion by a purpose, fueled by exploration and dis-covery, and shaped by a strategy right for the task. A wealth of realistic samples and student models involves students in the actual stuff of writ-ing: rough notes, trial outlines, search strategies, preliminary drafts. Repeatedly, the book takes students from journal entries, brainstorming notes, or preliminary collections of material to a finished paper.

(3) *A writing text should move from experience to exposition.* Writing focused on personal experience helps students break through the cliché barrier, to go beyond dutiful generalities; it makes them discover the roots of purposeful writing in concrete experience, authentic observation, and personal commitment. At the same time, student writers need to forge the link between firsthand experience and larger issues of general concern. They need to test their ideas through reading, through joining in the public dialogue, and through searching out expert opinion. Often our agenda is to help students move from the subjective to the objective, showing them how to preserve the freshness and authentic purpose of personal writing as they move to the more expository modes.

(4) *A writing text should bridge the gap between the parts and the whole.* We need to help students respond to the word that is right for the purpose, to the sentence that effectively makes its point. We need to provide the missing link between grammar and composition: *a writer's grammar* that balances correction after the fact with productive sentence work of all kinds, including sentence recognition, sentence expanding, sentence combining, sentence imitation, and sentence revision.

(5) *A writing text should aim at a maximum of student involvement.* It should not just talk about writing but frequently provide questions for discussion, provide the impetus and instructions for group work, and promote a writing workshop format for class activities. It should help students think of instructor, author, and student as part of a community of writers (frequently using *we* rather than *you* or *they* when talking about how writers work or what writers need to do).

(6) *A writing text should set realistic standards of literacy.* We need standards that apply across the curriculum and in many fields of writing. We should provide productive, workable guidance to help our students meet them.

Building on these assumptions, *The Writer's Agenda* tries to provide a true teaching text that helps the instructor translate into classroom work the best current thinking about composition and that can serve as a common center in a multisection course. The book is divided into six parts:

WHY AND HOW WE WRITE   After the initial overview of what to expect in a college composition class, major chapters guide the student through the process of triggering, gathering, shaping, and revising. The aim is to take students beyond the traditional modes to help them discover the needs and motives that activate true writing; to show how prewriting and invention techniques help a writer work up the material that fuels substantial papers; and to demonstrate the focusing and shaping strategies that help writers to push toward a thesis and work out a pattern that is right for the task.

FROM EXPERIENCE TO EXPOSITION   This central section of the book takes students from autobiography and description (focus on personal experience and observation) through standard expository patterns (focus on laying out a subject) to writing from sources (focus on synthesizing and evaluating material from the writer's reading). The aim is to show how authentically observed detail brings writing to life, how we adapt familiar patterns to make them serve our purpose, and how often writing is part of an ongoing dialogue—a pattern of statement and counter-statement.

WRITING AND THINKING   This section of the book focuses on the kind of thinking that gives shape to effective argument and persuasion. The chapter on definition looks at clearly defined key terms as a necessary first step toward straight thinking. The chapter on reasoning looks at the thought patterns (induction, arguing from principle, pro and con) that help a writer structure an effective argument. The chapter on persuasion looks at the appeals to emotion and shared values that at times reinforce and at other times militate against logical argument.

THE WRITER'S TOOLS   These chapters promote the student's grasp and appreciation of the writer's tools: the right word, the well-built sentence, the well-developed paragraph. The right word is defined as the word right for the purpose: clear, concrete, and at times imaginative, steering clear of clichés, jargon, and sexist language. The well-built sentence is promoted in a sentence-building chapter with an exceptional mix of sentence recognition, sentence combining, and sentence imitation. The paragraph is taught as a composition in miniature, with special attention to what gives it substance, shape, and direction.

SPECIAL ASSIGNMENTS   The research paper chapter stresses the purposes and strategies that make research techniques meaningful while at the same time it tries to provide exceptionally clear and helpful guidance to the mysteries of documentation. The chapter on writing about literature deals with critical writing as a means of enhancing the student's response to imaginative literature. The final chapter in this section deals with the writing of essay tests as one of the survival skills of the college student.

A CONCISE HANDBOOK   The handbook aims at providing graphic, pointed, positively worded help with familiar writing problems. It tries to translate grammarians' terminology into plain English for those students who are most in need of help.

Some special features of the book:

□ The Writing Workshop strand provides activities geared for group work and is intended as a more exploratory, participatory alternative to conventional classroom work.

□ Mindful that "the sound should seem an echo to the sense," instructions on matters of style often mirror what they teach, combining precept and example. ("*The beginning* of a sentence can pull a key idea out for special attention. . . . More often, however, the most emphatic position in the sentence is *the end*." "Use italics and other attention-getters *sparingly*.")

This book owes a special debt to the language scholars and rhetoricians who inspired me as mentors and colleagues; to composition faculties around the country who have shared with me their problems and ephiphanies; and to friends and colleagues who have worked with me on such enterprises as the Young Rhetoricians' Conference, dedicated to the upgrading of composition as an academic subject and to promoting among composition teachers a new sense of solidarity and common purpose. My greatest debt is to my students at San Jose State, whose writing appears everywhere in this volume, and whose curiosity, wit, and gift for language have cheered me over the years.

HANS GUTH

ACKNOWLEDGMENTS

The author and the editors of this book wish to acknowledge gratefully the contributions of reviewers and consultants to this work.

Reviewers

David L. Açkiss
Missouri Southern State College

Peter W. Adams
Essex Community College

Richard P. Batteiger
Oklahoma State University

Paul Belgrade
Millersville University

Kathleen L. Bell
Old Dominion University

Robert Bomboy
Bloomsburg University

Bruce E. Coad
Mountain View College

Peggy Cole
Arapahoe Community College

Linda R. Eastburn
Linn-Benton Community College

Lisa Ede
Oregon State University

Paul D. Farkas
Metropolitan State College

Kim M. Flachmann
California State University, Bakersfield

Judith G. Gardner
University of Texas at San Antonio

Ronald K. Giles
East Tennessee State University

Jan Haag
California State University, Sacramento

Jack Hibbard
St. Cloud State University

Roger B. Horn
Charles County Community College

Jan Kirkpatrick
Southwest Missouri State University

Mary Libertin
Shippensburg University of Pennsylvania

Timothy C. Miller
Millersville University

Dennis Moore
University of North Carolina

Barbara Nicholls
Ashland Community College

David H. Roberts
Samford University

Duane H. Roen
University of Arizona

Glenn C. Rogers
Morehead State University

Judy R. Rogers
Morehead State University

David E. Schwalm
Arizona State University

Richard J. Siciliano
Charles County Community College

Dene Kay Thomas
University of Idaho

Edna M. Troiano
Charles County Community College

Nancy Walker
Southwest Missouri State University

Robert G. Wilborn
Southwest Missouri State University

Consultants

Jim Farrelly
University of Dayton

Gwen Gong
Texas A & M University

Shirley Marney
Oklahoma State University

Theodore Otteson
University of Missouri-Kansas City

Bonnie Salim
Oklahoma State University

David W. Smit
Kansas State University

William Stull
University of Hartford

Tom Waldrep
University of South Carolina

Special thanks go to Rebecca E. Burnett of Carnegie Mellon University and Janet Constantinides of the University of Wyoming for their assistance and helpful suggestions in Chapter 7 (Word Processing).

The Writer's Agenda

THE WADSWORTH WRITER'S GUIDE AND HANDBOOK

INTRODUCTION:

To the Student

The aim of a writing course is to help you use language more effectively for your own purposes. Whether we are part-time writers or professionals, whether we write for pleasure or reward—as writers we share a common agenda: We write to discover what we know and to see what we can learn. We think a subject through and lay it out for the reader. We write to make a difference—to have an impact on what our readers think and do.

How do you become a better writer? Like becoming a good carpenter or a good violinist, becoming a good writer is partly a matter of honing your skills and partly a matter of developing the right habits and the right attitude. To become a more confident writer, keep in mind advice like the following:

- *Cultivate the writing habit.* A sometime writer is like a weekend athlete who works out with much puffing and stiff joints. Plan to spend more time with pen or pencil, at the typewriter, or with your word processor. Take class notes; write notes to yourself and others. Scribble scratch outlines. Copy quotable quotes and astonishing facts. Consider starting a journal in which you record impressions, experiences, and ideas. Write a running commentary in the margin of books and articles (your own copies only); start a reading log. To learn to write, write.

- *Think of your writing as work in progress.* A finished paper does not arrive readymade like a package in the mail. Writing is a creative process. You need to allow time for a subject to come into focus, for following up leads, and for hunting down promising sources. You need to allow for false starts and second thoughts. Whenever you can, talk to others about your writing, consulting with your classmates concerning plans for papers, comparing notes on current work. Ponder feedback from your classmates and your instructor. Allow time for revision—for rewriting and rethinking.

□ *Make your writing serve your own purpose.* To be effective, your writing has to be something you want or need to do. Look for subjects that arouse your curiosity, your enthusiasm, or your indignation. Try to find the personal angle in assigned topics, relating them to your own experience or to the lives of people you know well. Discover the incentives and rewards of writing—the satisfaction of explaining something difficult, of setting the record straight, of making people listen to your side of a controversy.

□ *Carry over what you learn into work in other fields.* The writing and thinking habits you develop should serve you well in other courses, in your major, and in a future career. No matter what your field, you should know how to work up a subject—to explore its ins and outs, to search for relevant material. You should be able to lay out material—to work out a logical order that fits your subject, a plan that your audience can follow. You should be able to synthesize—to make sense of a mass of details and to reconcile conflicting evidence. You should become audience-conscious—respond to the needs and respect the limitations of your listeners and readers.

We write to inform and persuade others, but we also write to learn. As we write, we fill in gaps in our information; we clear up confusions in our minds. We discover what we think. The test of a successful piece of writing is that it does something for both the writer and the reader. Think of a writing class as an opportunity to learn—about language, about yourself, and about others.

THE WRITING WORKSHOP

Learning from Experience

What has been your previous experience as a writer? How much writing have you done, and what kind? For a group of your classmates or the class as a whole, prepare a report on one writing assignment, or one piece of writing, that proved exceptionally successful, difficult, or instructive. Compare notes with other members of the group on their own previous experiences as writers. In your report, cover points like the following:

- What was the assignment? What were you trying to do?
- Where did you turn for material? What kind of material did you use?
- Did your paper have an overall point or key idea?
- What was the plan? How did you organize your material?
- What kind of audience did you have in mind?
- What was especially satisfying or difficult about the project?
- What reactions or feedback did you receive?
- What did the experience teach you about writing?

Part One

WHY AND HOW WE WRITE

When you walk through the doors of a writing class, you are likely to carry with you some familiar questions about the **goals** of the course: Why should you become a better writer? How do people learn to write? What standards will apply to your writing? Once you have some preliminary answers to these questions, you can focus on the basic task that confronts every writer: how to get from a blank sheet of paper or an empty screen to a finished piece of writing. Good writing is the result of a process that moves through overlapping stages. These are not distinct like the making, slicing, and packaging of cheese; a writer, like a cook, is often doing several things at the same time. The first stage is **triggering:** To set the process in motion, we need a purpose—something we need or want to do. We need a reason to write—something the writing will do for us and for the reader. The next stage is **gathering:** To have material to work with, we need to mobilize our resources—to draw on our memory, on firsthand investigation, or on our reading. This second stage overlaps with the third: **shaping.** To have something to say, we need to synthesize our material—to funnel observations into conclusions, to chart a course through the relevant facts, to organize our thinking in a rough first draft. One draft leads to another: To do justice to the task, we allow time for **revising.** We make time for second thoughts and changes in strategy before we finally edit and proofread, looking at our writing through the reader's eyes. As we repeatedly go through the process that produces the finished paper, we become more aware of **the writer's options:** We learn by watching how other writers operate—by studying their procedures and learning the secrets of the trade.

1

PREVIEW

Your Goals as a Writer

Real writing is a decoding of the garble and static of inner speech, an effort to make meanings personal, connected, and accessible to self.   William Strong

Writing is usually communication with others. And yet the essential transaction seems to be with oneself, a speaking to one's best self.   Peter Elbow

"That's not what I meant" is the saddest sentence in the English language. The ability to communicate—to mean what you say and to say what you mean—is the result of a balance between content and form.   Dolores laGuardia

WHY LEARN TO WRITE? The written word is all around us. Business, education, and politics feed on a constant stream of print—newsletters, questionnaires, circulars, abstracts, promotional brochures. Work increasingly means paperwork—memos, letters, reports, records, schedules, minutes, agendas. Forests are cut down to yield the paper for the newspapers, newsmagazines, general-interest magazines, technical journals, and books that keep us informed and entertained.

Both in school and in a future career, you will be judged in part by your ability to put ideas down on paper. Often your writing tasks will have immediate practical value. Essay tests, lab reports, reading journals, or term papers are part of the job description of anyone who wishes to succeed as a student. In the world of work, you may be writing a letter of application, a marketing plan, a note to an angry customer, a fund-raising appeal, or a request for rezoning. Whatever the task, the competitive edge will often be with those who know what they want to say and who say it well.

The rewards of writing, however, are not wholly practical. Good writing has its own built-in incentives:

☐ *Writing is the art of making up your mind.* Working up a subject for your paper gives you a chance to sort things out and see them fall into place. When you seriously take on a current issue—the family, careers, women's sports, the homeless, toxic waste—you go beyond a superficial first impression. You explore the subject; you think the matter through. Writing is a process of discovery: You move beyond prejudice and hearsay to see for yourself.

☐ *Writing gives you a chance to be heard.* It is frustrating to keep quiet when others hold forth on divorce, the military, or comparable worth. We need to express ourselves, to state our own point of view. It is satisfying to participate in a dialogue, to contribute to an ongoing debate. It is good for the ego to have written something that others quote and remember.

☐ *Writing gives you a chance to influence others.* It teaches you to reckon with the reactions of an audience: when to back off and when to come on strong; where to look for areas of agreement; how to overcome objections. You will feel satisfaction when you can correct a misunderstanding or set the record straight. You will be pleased when your solution to a problem is taken seriously or when you can help a good cause prevail.

Questions for Discussion What is the extent of your daily exposure to or interaction with the written word? From memory, can you reconstruct a rough *reader's log* of all contacts with the written word during a recent week? Be sure to include exposure to signs, directions, forms, personal mail and junk mail, newspapers (what sections?), magazines, textbooks, manuals, maps, billboards, and the like.

WRITING AS A CREATIVE PROCESS

You become a better writer the way you become better at other challenging and rewarding tasks: You learn through practice, by trial and error. You watch what others do, and you learn from their successes and failures. At first, you may stumble or miss your cues, but you gradually develop the confidence of the pro. You learn as much as you can from instruction and guided practice. You learn by studying what has worked well for others. You learn to watch for signposts that steer you away from dead ends and false turns in the road.

To profit from the instruction and practice in this book, you need to think of writing as something that takes time—that takes shape gradually, like a vase on the potter's wheel. For most writers, a well-written paper does not suddenly come together in a burst of inspiration. In writing a paper, you need to get involved in the topic. You need to work up the material. You need to get the material into shape. The guidelines in this book will ask you to take a typical piece of writing through five overlapping stages: (1) triggering, (2) gathering, (3) shaping, (4) revising, and (5) editing.

Triggering Something has to set the process of writing in motion. (You need to push the "On" button.) To write with conviction, you have to discover the purposes that drive successful writing. People write best when they tackle a topic that they care about, that they can get involved in personally. For instance, you are likely to write with conviction when you

- □ explain something that has confused or bothered you in the past;
- □ challenge a stereotype about a group to which you belong (Italians, Southerners, Mormons, fraternity brothers, jocks);
- □ tell the inside story of something that has been kept from the public;
- □ enlist support for a cause to which you are committed.

When you write on an assigned subject, try to find the personal angle—the tie-in with your own experience or convictions. It should not surprise us, for instance, that an author who writes eloquently about physical fitness had parents who smoked and drank and had fatal health problems as a result. Health and fitness became an urgent personal issue in the writer's life, a part of her personal agenda. You are likely to write best when you can similarly write as the eyewitness, the insider, or the advocate.

Gathering A successful paper has to go through a stage of exploration and discovery. You need to work up the subject—to gather material, to look at the evidence. Whether your subject is diet fads or movies about the Vietnam War, do not just ask yourself, "What do I think?" Ask, "What do I think after taking a good look?" Have you had any experience with diet fads? Who among family or friends is a dieter? What have you read on the subject? Where would you turn for recent articles or advice? Study and practice the techniques—brainstorming, note taking, using interviews, searching for sources—that help writers work up a rich fund of material for their writing.

Shaping Even while gathering your material, you will be trying to get it into shape. Early in the process, you are likely to draw up a scratch outline to help you lay out what you are collecting. You will need to bring your subject into focus—perhaps by asking some key question. (What is the real issue?) You will be pushing toward tentative conclusions—and gradually toward some overall conclusion. (How does it all add up?) You will be sorting out your examples or your evidence, trying to set up categories that will give you a handle on the subject. For instance, you might be writing a paper on parenting, asking how working couples share the responsibility for child care. After checking your own observation, comparing notes with others, and reading on the subject, you conclude that men have been slow to face up to the demands made on a working parent's time. However, you also conclude that different men react differently. In fact, you set up three major categories for a father's behavior, going from those least likely to those most likely to shoulder their share of the burden. You might first identify the traditional "taskmaster," who interacts with children mainly to admonish and set tasks. You might then go on to the "permissive" father, who means well but often provides little guidance and discipline. Finally, you might describe the concerned, sharing father of the enlightened future. You are getting your material under control; your paper is taking shape.

Revising Few writers produce a well thought-out piece of writing at one sitting. Good writing moves through several stages, from informal notes through a rough first draft (or drafts) to a final version. Much published writing has been reworked and rewritten in response to feedback from friends, colleagues, editors, or reviewers. Allow time for revision: Fill in examples or additional evidence where needed. Expand or adjust your major categories if they leave out too much or if they seem to slice your subject the wrong way. Rearrange or reshuffle material for a better flow—for instance, from the safe and familiar to the new. Fill in the missing links needed to steer the reader's attention in the right direction. This is the time for second thoughts—*before* your readers discover the gaps in your evidence or the holes in your argument.

Editing Editing is the fine-tuning that makes sure your words and sentences say what you mean. All through your writing, but especially in final editing, you will be looking for the right word. (Do you mean *fortunate*—lucky, or *fortuitous*—totally accidental? Was a character you describe really *silent* or merely *taciturn*—disinclined to idle chatter?) Final editing is your chance to shorten *due to the fact that* to *because* and *in this modern day and age* to *today*. You recast awkward sentences so that they tell the reader clearly who does what. Make sure to allow time for final proofreading for spelling, punctuation, or usage problems (*as* or *like*, *who* or *whom*).

Questions for Discussion Do you recognize the five stages of the writing process sketched out here? Which seems most familiar or easy to handle, which least? What is your own typical procedure when you write?

GOALS FOR COLLEGE WRITING

What standards will your work have to meet? Colleges and universities publish standards of proficiency in written composition that divide roughly into two major categories. Standards for the *larger elements* of writing call for a clear focus on a workable subject, a well thought-out central idea or thesis, a clear plan, paragraphs that make and support a point, and links or transitions that blink on like signal lights to guide the reader from one point to the next. Standards for *effective written English* call for language that is right for serious discussion. They call for accurate words, vivid and fresh language, well-built sentences, functional punctuation, and correct spelling.

The Larger Elements

To meet college-level standards, your writing should show that you have taken your subject seriously. To evaluate your own writing, use a mental checklist like the following:

- *You respect the intelligence of your audience.* You are not just repeating what everybody knows; you are not relying on hearsay or first impressions. Instead, you have looked at a range of examples: You have examined conflicting evidence or contradictory testimony.

- *You honor your implied contract with the reader.* In much of the writing you do (other than reports, directions, and instructions), you will be taking a stand. You are entitled to your opinion—if you are willing to support it. When you write about discipline in schools, this might be the main point you want to make: "To judge from my own experience, discipline has broken down in our public schools." Or perhaps, "Our schools are regimented places where students are trained to answer questions 'True' or 'False' instead of asking questions of their own." Whatever your position, the reader is entitled to a follow-up that provides striking examples from your own observation, candid testimony of friends and relatives, thought-provoking quotations from insiders, or facts and figures from recognized authorities.

- *Your writing follows a plan.* You have worked out a strategy for presenting your material. Your paper has a game plan that you could map or chart for your reader. You have laid out your material in a pattern that fits the subject and serves your purpose.

◻ *You anticipate the reader's needs.* You have thought about what your readers need to have explained, what new or provocative points need to be defended or prepared for. You have provided early hints or a preview of the drift of your paper to help your readers get their bearings. Directional signals, or transitions, steer the attention of your readers from point to point.

Effective Written English

Your writing will have to show your command of **edited written English**—the kind of English that readers expect in prose used to inform, explain, argue, or persuade. Standard written English is a common medium—a language of "larger communication"—in a society marked by linguistic diversity. For many bilingual students, aiming at effective written English means strengthening their hold on the patterns of their second language. For many other students, effective written English means shifting from the dialect of home or neighborhood to the standard English of school and office. For everyone, it means shifting from the comfortable patterns of unbuttoned informal speech to the more formal, more businesslike patterns of serious writing.

Writing is more carefully worked out and more lasting than casual talk. The spoken word you can immediately back up or take back; the written word has to stand on its own. The tone of your writing should show that you are taking your subject and your reader seriously. In the following pair, the first sentence is too informal for serious discussion:

TOO INFORMAL: At times, even today's highly competitive students seem to suspect that getting to the top of the heap is not all that it is cracked up to be.

BETTER: At times, even today's highly competitive students seem to suspect that those climbing to the top of the corporate ladder pay a price.

The right level is between two extremes: Do not write a roundabout, hyperformal English that is cut off from the natural rhythms of the spoken language. The best modern prose is *moderately formal*—formal without being stiff or pompous. The following passage is an example of effective modern prose that is never too far removed from plain talk. (Note words and phrases like *picture phone, whisked, cheap, come and gone.*)

Looking Back at the Future

The future was to have been a wondrous time, with a picture phone in every home and an atomic-powered car or a personal airplane in every garage. Conveyor-belt sidewalks were to have whisked us through space-age cities while atomic power plants generated clean energy so cheap there would be no need to meter it. But the future, as envisioned a generation ago, has come and gone. Picture phones, atomic cars, and moving sidewalks have all died on the drawing board. Nuclear energy is here, but it has not exactly lived up to its expectations.   John Flinn, *San Francisco Examiner*

In writing and editing your papers, you will work on several major features of acceptable written English:

WORDS   Writing uses a fuller range of vocabulary than informal talk, with more attention to exact shades of meaning. The right word is right for the purpose. It carries the needed information, calls up the right picture in the reader's mind, or brings the desired attitudes into play. Watch specific, accurate words turn a colorless general sentence into vivid description:

> GENERAL: In the redwood parks, visitors are struck by the awesome beauty of nature's largest trees.
> SPECIFIC: In the redwood parks, thick reddish-brown trunks extend upward toward the sky. Lacy greenery from the uppermost parts of the trees lets the sunlight sift through onto the paths below.

Much editing aims at trite phrases, or clichés (*suffice it to say, last but not least*), wordy tags (*the fact of the matter is*), and self-important jargon (*parameters, prioritize, self-actualization*).

SENTENCES   Good sentences make us want to say "Well put!" or "Well said!" A well-built sentence may be short and to the point:

> His son spent money as if he were trying to see the bottom of the mint.   Alice Walker

Or a well-built sentence may be long, filling in details, carrying considerable information without static that would drown out the message:

> Writing is like a pet that sometimes sits around and mopes and sometimes growls and snaps, but that can be a great companion, and, with care and patience, do some amazing tricks.   Alan Ziegler

Effective writers use the full register of sentence resources. You can expand your own sentence repertory through various kinds of sentence work. Sentence combining exercises start with simple building blocks and show you how to combine them in increasingly more sophisticated sentences:

> SIMPLE: Sam was waiting.
>   He was wrapped in a quilt on the wagon seat.
> COMBINED: Sam was waiting, *wrapped in a quilt on the wagon seat.*
>   William Faulkner

Sentence imitation exercises provide model sentences for different kinds of sentence structure. You then write sentences of your own that follow closely the structure of the originals while bringing your own imagination (and sense of humor) into play:

MODEL: Curiosity, like all other desires, produces pain as well as pleasure.

IMITATION: Taking a bus, like all public transportation, saves money but wastes time.

Final editing is your last chance to catch sentences that are awkwardly put together, with badly matching parts. Often such a sentence seems to set up one pattern but then switches to another:

MIXED: The typical background of women who get abortions are two-thirds white and more than half childless. (The background . . . *are?* The background . . . are . . . *white?*)

CONSISTENT: Of the women who get abortions, *two thirds are white,* and more than half are childless.

Much final editing aims at expressions where usage differs for informal talk and serious writing (*like* I said/*as* I said, between you and *I/* between you and *me.*)

PUNCTUATION Punctuation helps regulate the flow of words on the page. The right punctuation prevents misreading in a sentence like the following:

CONFUSING: *Discouraged by their poor performance in school children* may lose the incentive to learn.

CLEAR: *Discouraged by their poor performance in school,* children may lose the incentive to learn.

To apply punctuation rules, you need to recognize sentence parts and kinds of sentences. For example, you need to recognize and reconnect the sentence fragments that occur as afterthoughts in much stop-and-go conversation.

FRAGMENTS: They got married in Mazatlán. *Early last spring. Without telling anyone.*

COMPLETE: They got married in Mazatlán last spring without telling anyone.

The rules that govern college writing tend to be more conservative than those of popular or journalistic prose. For instance, a traditional rule calls for a semicolon instead of a comma when two complete statements are spliced together without an added link like *and* or *but:*

COMMA SPLICE: Computers are beginning to talk, eventually they will learn to think.

REVISED: Computers are beginning to talk; eventually they will learn to think.

SPELLING Readers are not likely to take your discussion of nuclear wastes seriously if you misspell *nuclear.* If you expect to be heard, you cannot afford to misspell *definite, similar, receive, believe, separate, category, occurred,* or *perform.* If you confuse *it's* and *its,* your readers may not trust you to verify other matters big and small: names (Johnson, Jonson, Johnston?), statistics, exact wording of quotations. Careful final proofreading for punctuation and spelling is not just a courtesy to the reader; it is a survival skill for writers who want to get a fair hearing.

Remember: As a writer, you learn from mistakes. But you learn as much or more from good examples. You make progress by building on what you are doing right. Make sure you improve your writing by observation, imitation, and practice—and not just by correcting what has already gone wrong. Look for positive models, constructive guidance, and practical hints. Discover the pleasure writers feel when they are doing something difficult well.

Questions for Discussion Which of the standards for effective writing make the most sense to you and which the least? Which do you think are easiest and which hardest for you to meet?

EXERCISE 1   *A Sample Paper*

The following paper is a revision prepared after the student writer received comments and advice on a first draft. How well does the writing meet basic requirements for a successful student paper? Answer questions like the following:

- Did the writer take the topic seriously? How can you tell?
- What is the main point? Where is it stated or reinforced?
- What is the plan? How has the writer organized the material?
- Where did the writer turn for material or support?
- Does the paper offer anything new or thought-provoking to the reader?
- Who would make a good reader for this paper?

A Good Move

Moving tears up our roots. It pulls us away from a place that holds memories, and it denies us the comfort of a single place we can always call home. Taking the first step into a new house, we are instantly aware of the cold and dark of a house with the electricity shut off, the musty odor of dust trapped in shut-up rooms, the missing handle on the door of an old refrigerator, and the many other features that will need cleaning or repair. Nevertheless, the experience of moving offers compensating rewards and fringe benefits. I do not believe that families always suffer as the result of relocating frequently; instead, moving on is often the right move, a fresh start.

Circumstances have often forced my mother, my sister, and me to move into houses in poor shape, with such drawbacks as flooded yards, no heat or air conditioning, and a neighborhood where breaking into cars was a favorite leisure-time activity of the younger set. However, the three of us found that moving is a chance to start afresh and make the new surroundings over in our own image. Lack of funds may have allowed us only one can of paint at a time, but gradually the gray little house with peeling paint would turn into a white cottage, with blue trim on the shutters. Later we would fence the backyard with lumber abandoned by the previous owner, patch the roof that leaked buckets of water, reconstruct the sagging bathroom floor, and prune scraggly greenery into respectable bushes and trees.

Sometimes a house holds painful memories. It is hard to shake these off in the surroundings where the events occurred; it is best to move on. My mother was once married to an abusive man who treated the whole family disgracefully, allowing only his cronies into the house, constantly dazed by narcotics or alcohol. One day he ran off, leaving us thousands of dollars in debt. My mother found a job, sold everything except one car, and began the slow climb out of debt. When we were finally able to move out of that house, we left everything behind—the people, the neighborhood, the whole experience. The place does not exist for us anymore. I am glad I do not have to call that house my home.

A bonus of moving is the opportunity to leave behind people who remember our faults. This chance at a new identity is the best thing about being a newcomer in a school. All through junior high school, I was overweight, and I remember being very introverted and self-conscious. When we moved to another school district, I made it my personal crusade to lose weight. I observed the injunctions of my diet book the way a monk observes the monastery rules. I tried hard to be outgoing, and I became a slimmer, more sociable version of my former self.

Benjamin Franklin said that moving three times is as bad as a fire. Was he right?

When I mentioned to a friend recently that I had lived in six houses in ten years, he looked amazed. All his life he had lived in the same house. He knew his neighbors' family history, had gone to a school down the block, and was now attending a local college with childhood friends. He asked me if I regretted not having a permanent place to call home. I had just been about to ask him if he felt deprived of the new faces and the challenges that come with making a new beginning.

WRITING TOPICS 1 *Taking a Stand*

Which of the following topics can you relate to your own observation, experience, or reading? Choose a topic on which you are willing to take a stand. Write a paper in which you present and support your point of view. Include a title. Write for the concerned general reader.

1. Is prejudice on the decline? (Or is it merely taking more contemporary and perhaps more subtle forms?)

THE WRITING WORKSHOP

Work in Progress

The writing topics that conclude this chapter offer you a range of topics for a first paper. What will guide your choice? After you have chosen your topic, prepare a *planning report* for presentation to a group of your classmates or to the class as a whole. Listen and respond to the reactions of the group; take their feedback into account as you write and revise your paper. Make your planning report answer four basic questions:

- ☐ (Purpose) *Why* are you choosing the topic you have selected? Does it have a personal meaning for you?
- ☐ (Sources) *What* are you going to use? Where are you going to turn for material?
- ☐ (Plan) *How* are you going to proceed? How are you going to focus and organize your material? What is going to be your major point?
- ☐ (Audience) *Who* would be the ideal reader for your paper? What do you expect of your audience, and what do you expect to do for them?

2. Does physical fitness "build character"? (Is exercise or athletic competition good merely for the body or also for the mind or the soul?)

3. Are public manners breaking down? (Minor annoyances produce assaults; people fight over parking spaces; public facilities are vandalized or covered with graffiti. Are we turning into a nation of bullies and louts?)

4. Do the media create an unfavorable image of American business? (What picture of people in business would visitors from outer space form if they knew them only from watching television?)

5. Have Americans lost the sense of home? (Is it true that American families move so often or split up so easily that many young Americans have lost a sense of belonging? What, for you, is the meaning of "home"?)

6. Do you believe in ceremonies? (Some people believe in graduation exercises, traditional weddings, church holidays. Others consider them artificial and old-fashioned. Where do you stand?)

7. Do current movies glorify war? (Is there a common denominator or recurrent message in recent movies about war?)

8. Does current popular entertainment tend to demean or belittle women?

(Do you agree with this frequently heard charge? Why or why not?)

9. Do you consider the police your friend or your enemy? (In an emergency or in a difficult situation, would you expect the police to be on your side?)

10. Does current popular entertainment glorify youth and create an unfavorable image of age? (Are older people made to seem irrelevant or unwanted?)

2

TRIGGERING

Discovering Your Purpose

There is nothing to writing. All you do is sit down at a typewriter and open a vein. Red Smith

What axe you have to grind is very important—and you have to take it into account as you structure your argument. Susan Jacoby

The most time-consuming part is at the very beginning. Everything comes out in fragments and then it either starts to string together or it doesn't—and I have to start again. Gretel Ehrlich

STAKING OUT A SUBJECT As you begin to write, you need to feel "This is worth doing" or "This is something I want to do." To make sure you write with a sense of purpose, consider the three starter questions that help set a piece of writing in motion: What am I writing about? What am I trying to accomplish? Who is my reader?

The first of these questions is crucial, since a topic is not likely to catch fire if writer and subject are mismatched. You are writing on an ideal topic if you know more and care more about your subject than your reader. Your task then is to communicate your knowledge and your concern. A basic survival skill for writers is to choose a subject on which they can write with conviction. True, much writing for a class, as in the outside world, starts with an assignment; the agenda is to make the assignment your own. Try to find a personal angle; discover a side of the topic that brings it to life for you.

Consider advice like the following when choosing a subject or shaping an assigned topic:

☐ *Stake out a subject limited enough for a close-up view.* Often you will have to narrow a general area to a workable specific topic. A short paper could

19

barely scratch the surface when dealing with the causes, effects, and future of divorce. Instead, you may want to focus on a part of this subject that means something special to you: disillusionment in the early years of marriage, the emotional aftermath of divorce, the economics of divorce, custody fights, relating to a substitute father, the "children of divorce." Papers that take on too much are like the pictures by an amateur photographer who stays too far away from the people being photographed, leaving them too small and blurry to become real.

☐ *Beware of broad general subjects.* Like a wagon train in the Mojave Desert, your readers are likely to get lost trying to traverse the vast stretches of a subject like "American Education Today." The following titles stake out areas that make possible a better focused, more instructive kind of paper:

> Busing: The Long Way to School
> Spanish Spoken Here
> Testing, Testing, Testing
> My Teacher the Computer
> Mainstreaming the Disabled Student

☐ *Choose a topic that you can relate to your own observation, experience, or reading.* Look for the tie-in with firsthand observation whenever you can. "Mainstreaming the Disabled" will be a good topic for you if you can use, for instance, the story of a young woman living next door to you who drives a car that is specially equipped so she can work the gas pedal with her left foot and the brake with her left hand. It will be a good topic if you can draw on personal experiences like the following:

> It is hard for most people to put themselves in the place of a physically handicapped person. I remember a simulation I did for a roommate. He is an Occupational Therapy major, and for one of his classes he had to care for a disabled person. I consented to spend a day relying on a wheelchair. Our first problem was getting to school: What to do with the wheelchair after my roommate put me inside the car?
>
> Interestingly enough, I was on crutches for six weeks last winter. I felt uncomfortable with people always staring at me wherever I went. As a result, I tended to avoid going places unless I had to. I began noticing everyone else who was on crutches around the school, and, as in a secret club, a smile usually flashed between us. . . .

Often, an ideal topic will let you draw on a good mix of firsthand observation and relevant reading or viewing. Read newspaper and magazine articles with an eye toward using them as possible sources. In your paper on the disabled, draw on a recent newspaper article about the insurance difficulties that make some restaurant owners try to bar people in wheelchairs. Draw on a recent magazine article about special watches, typewriters, and computers for the blind.

☐ *Choose a subject on which your readers are likely to welcome information, explanation, or advice.* What do junk foods do to our health? Do most young people have to settle for dreary and monotonous work? What is the best way to exercise? What causes vandalism—and how can it be stopped? Is there a way to stop acid rain? Writing that tries to answer such questions finds an audience because many readers care about health, careers, safety, and the quality of life.

Some subjects create special interest or excitement because they are on the cutting edge of current research (computers that can talk, apes that are taught to use sign language or to punch out messages on a computer). Other subjects have a special urgency for the concerned reader (rape prevention, subway crime).

☐ *Whenever you can, write on a subject that has a personal meaning for you.* Sometimes you will explore a subject totally new to you and become fascinated by it as you go along. But usually you have a headstart if the subject brings into play some strong personal interest or commitment. The student author of the following passage wrote about divorce with conviction:

Divorce can best be described as the death of a relationship. A union that may once have been based on love, companionship, warmth, and understanding is gone. In its place have appeared contempt, loneliness, coldness, and a breakdown in communication. Both people involved feel confused, pressured, and guilty. Their emotional stability is shattered. Suddenly, divorced people are thrown back into the single life, at a time when they feel like social outcasts. They no longer fit into their married friends' lives, yet single friends are often nonexistent. Emotional turmoil is not the only problem divorced people face. All too soon they are involved in court battles. (Who gets the car, the house, the children . . . the dog?) The money that had been saved for the children's college educations now goes for lawyers' fees. There once were two together, and now there are two apart. The divorced person has just lived through the hardest experience in life.

Questions for Discussion When was the last time you read an article or a book that you found exceptionally helpful, fascinating, or enlightening? What was the subject? Why did the writing hold your interest?

EXERCISE 1   *The Personal Résumé*

Prepare an informal *personal résumé* that can serve as a guide to possible subjects for your writing. Under each of the following headings, discuss two or three items (chosen from or similar to those listed) that are especially meaningful to you.

THE WRITING WORKSHOP

A Poll of Student Attitudes

What are live issues for today's college students? What academic, social, or political topics do they read and talk about? For what kind of writing would they make a good audience? Work with a group to plan an informal survey of students on your campus. What do they care about? What are they apathetic about? Have respondents rank and comment briefly on three topics with which they are most concerned. Chart the strategy for your survey. (How, for example, are you going to reach a representative sample?) Synthesize your findings in a *group report*. What generalizations do the results of your survey justify? Make use of short verbatim quotations to give your report an authentic flavor.

- *Roots:* family—ethnic origin or cultural background; parents' work or occupations; relatives or siblings who played a special role in your life; important or traumatic childhood events; important settings.
- *Schooling:* favorite subjects or special hurdles; memorable teachers, good or bad; high points or low points; social or racial mix of students; school spirit or tensions, conflicts, problems.
- *Friends:* getting along with peers; special friendships or antagonisms; friendships that have changed or developed over the years.
- *Interests:* sports—challenges or disappointments; reading—favorite authors or subjects; hobbies or crafts—special skills or experience; travel—memorable trips or places; movie or television viewing habits—likes or dislikes.
- *Work:* chores and part-time jobs; the first real job; current career interests.

Two sample entries

Interests: "Sweet Sixteen": getting asked to the annual Sadie Hawkins dance, visions of Saturday night in the backseat of a baby-blue Chevy—you may remember all of these, but I surely missed out on them. Instead, I was sitting at home alone, watching another episode of *Saturday Night Live* while munching on all-new sour-cream-and-onion chips and washing them down with Coca-Cola. I was overweight, wore big-bell jeans and steel-rimmed glasses. Those days, thank God, are gone. Now I enjoy running five miles every other day, working out with weights, eating plain yogurt, and washing it down with a cool Hansen's all-natural-berry drink, while wearing casual wear and contact lenses.

Work: The summer after I graduated from high school, I along with several other girls from my school went as apprentices to a small organic farm on the coast of Maine. The farmer offered training in agriculture, a place to pitch a tent, and two meals a day in return for free labor. Our group learned how to plant, cultivate, harvest, and sell crops. Over lunch we talked about how to be self-sufficient on a farm; we examined other alternatives to conventional ways of making a living.

EXERCISE 2   *Narrowing the Topic*

Look at the following sets of possible subjects for papers. For each set, do the following:

- Rank the topics in rough order from the most general to the most specific. (Which are clearly too *broad* for a short paper?)
- From all or most of the sets, select one topic each that might make a good topic for you. How could you relate it to your own observation, experience, or reading? What special meaning or interest does it have for you?

1. Gadgets We Don't Need
    Technology and Its Side Effects
    Wanted: An Uncomplicated Car
    The Automated Workplace

2. My Career as a Test Taker
    Coping with the Commute
    Anxiety in Modern Life
    The Stressful City

3. Our Vanishing Wildlife
    Birds of the City
    Into the Wilderness
    Our Endangered Planet

4. Math Anxiety
    Great Mathematicians
    Math for the Woman Student
    Math: Aptitude or Attitude?

5. The Urban Wasteland
    An Ideal Neighborhood
    A Block Like Any Other
    Does Modern Architecture Have a Soul?

6. New Frontiers for Women
    Escape from the Pink Ghetto
    Wimp or Macho
    The Small Sexist Phrases of Every Day

WHY WE WRITE

When we respond to an effective piece of writing, we sense that the writer wrote with a purpose. Something got the writing started and kept it going—there was a spark that lit the fire. The writer was curious or indignant about something. The writer had a point to prove or an axe to grind. Or the writer took seriously the job of informing or instructing the reader. When the spark is missing, we are left with the dry sticks. When writing lacks a sense of purpose, it becomes drudgery for both writer and reader.

In practice, we do not select a subject first and then decide what to do with it. Choosing a subject and discovering our purpose go hand in hand. We write on a subject because we want to prove a point, clear up confusion, or make a plea. What we are trying to do, or what we should do, becomes clearer to us as we explore the subject.

Modes: Means to an End

What purposes are going to activate your own writing? When people ask you to explain your purpose, they may be looking for two different kinds of answers. We can ask two basic questions about a writer's purpose:

□ *What kind of writing are you going to do?* You may write to tell a story, to give readers a vivid accounting of events (narration). You may write to take them to a scene or to make them see objects or people (description). You may write to explain or instruct—to make your readers understand a process or an idea (exposition). You may write to convince—to change the reader's mind (argument).

☐ *What is the motive behind your writing?* You tell the story of an incident—an unjustified speeding ticket, a violent altercation in a parking lot, a rape trial—in order to make your readers see the events from your point of view. (Your purpose is to make your readers see your side of the story.) You may describe Yellowstone Park in the early spring in order to relive the experience. (Your purpose is to experience again the pleasure or elation of the trip and to share it with your readers.) You write a paper that explains the workings of prejudice as you have observed it at school and at work. (You felt the need to understand better a subject that had puzzled you for a long time.) You argue in favor of a new law aimed at drunk drivers. (The project needs the reader's vote or support.)

Seen from this point of view, narration, description, exposition, or argument are the means to a further end. We call these broad traditional categories the **modes of discourse.** Classifying a project according to the traditional categories can help you clarify in your own mind what you are trying to do. Remember, however, that the traditional modes focus our attention on the what and how rather than on the underlying why. (*Why* are you telling this story? *Why* are you describing this scene?)

NARRATION **Narration** tells the story of events. It focuses on what people say and do, telling us when, where, who, what, and why. You are likely to use narration in *autobiographical* writing, in papers taking stock of personal experience. You may be telling the story of a backpacking trip, of a neighborhood party that turned ugly, of a tragic accident, or of false arrest.

The following passage is a sample of autobiographical narrative:

Almost every detail of that night stands out very clearly in my memory. I even remember the name of the movie we saw because its title impressed me as being so patly ironical. It was a movie about the German occupation of France, starring Maureen O'Hara and Charles Laughton and called *This Land Is Mine.* I remember the name of the diner we walked into when the movie ended: it was the "American Diner." When we walked in the counterman asked what we wanted and I remember answering with the casual sharpness which had become my habit: "We want a hamburger and a cup of coffee, what do you think we want?" I do not know why, after a year of such rebuffs, I so completely failed to anticipate his answer, which was, of course, "We don't serve Negroes here." This reply failed to discompose me, at least for the moment. I made some sardonic comment about the name of the diner and we walked out into the streets. James Baldwin, *Notes of a Native Son*

Like other first-rate autobiographical narrative, this passage sets the scene. It seizes on revealing details that have a special meaning for the author. It tells us not only what people do and say but also what they think and feel.

Three Ways to Look at Purpose

TRADITIONAL KINDS OF WRITING	A MODERN VIEW OF THE WRITER'S AIMS	THE WRITER'S MOTIVES
Narration: telling the story of events	*Expressive writing:* exploring personal experience; expressing personal attitudes and emotions (Focus on the *Self*)	to give directions to give instructions to give advice
Description: describing people, places, and objects		to clarify confusion to correct misconceptions to set the record straight to talk back to the stereotype
Exposition: explaining; sharing information or ideas	*Informative Writing:* sharing information and ideas (Focus on *Reality*)	to bear witness to register a grievance to come to terms with the past to share joy or grief
Argument: convincing by appealing to logic and evidence	*Persuasive Writing:* winning over the reader by logical or emotional appeals (Focus on the *Audience*)	to report events to share data to present a theory to argue a position
Persuasion: convincing by appealing to emotions and shared values		to pay tribute where due to expose wrongdoing to sound a warning to enlist support to clear someone's name to champion a cause to correct abuses
		to promote a product to advance a policy to gain employment
		to entertain to console to inspire to build morale

DESCRIPTION **Description** is the record of close firsthand observation. Your aim may be to describe an object or a piece of machinery in such a way that we can visualize it, understand it, and put it to use. Or your aim may be to describe a scene—a wilderness area, a rush-hour traffic jam—in order to make us share in the sights and sounds and in the feelings the scene inspires.

The following passage, from a bird-watcher's account, is an example of description based on careful firsthand observation:

Clouds are streaming off the ocean, and the metal legs of the tripod are cold against my hands as I set up the spotting scope. I'm out for birds, and the lagoon is thick with them. Grebes and canvasbacks, buffleheads and mergansers work the shallow water for fish, and coots honk and dodge like little black taxicabs in the reeds along the shore.

Across the lagoon, a great blue heron flaps and glides along the shoreline, scouting a likely feeding station. Its thin, improbable legs trail out behind—tools of the trade, in tow from one fishing spot to the next. It lands now, gracefully, delicately for a bird the height of a six-year-old child. Herons are all stilts and feathers and this old giant—which looks as if it could wrap its wings around a Honda—is likely no heavier than a wailing human newborn. Fiddling with the scope until the bird fills my vision, I find it transfixed, surveying the shallows for frogs or cruising fish.   William E. Poole, "For the Birds," *San Francisco Chronicle*

This passage shows several key features of first-rate descriptive writing: It uses specific, exact names for the birds (and for features of the landscape). It shows that the author has an eye for striking, characteristic detail (the thin, "improbable" trailing legs of the bird that is all "stilts and feathers"). It uses words that call up for us authentic sights, sounds, and motions ("honk and dodge," "flaps and glides"). It employs vivid, imaginative comparisons ("like little black taxicabs").

EXPOSITION **Exposition** "sets forth," or lays out, information and ideas. Its aim is to inform, to explain, to instruct. You may be writing to show what the frog's eye tells the frog's brain (and what we can learn from frogs about human vision). You may be writing to show what makes Japanese production techniques superior to American ones. You may be writing to sort out career interests of today's college students. Much exposition aims at making us see how things work, how they compare, or how they fit into a pattern.

The following passage, written by a scientist for a general audience, is an example of exposition:

The importation of plants is the primary agent in the modern spread of species, for animals have almost invariably gone along with the plants, quarantine being a comparatively recent and not completely effective innovation. The United States Office of Plant Introduction alone has introduced almost 200,000 species and varieties of plants from all over the world. Nearly half of the 180 or so major insect enemies of plants in the United States are accidental imports from abroad, and most of them have come as hitchhikers on plants. In new territory, out of reach of the restraining hand of the natural enemies that kept down its numbers in its native land, an invading plant or animal is able to become enormously abundant. Thus it is no accident that our most troublesome insects are introduced species.   Rachel Carson, *Silent Spring*

This passage traces an important process (the spread, in modern times, of species, and especially insect species, beyond their natural habitat). It uses authoritative factual information; it shows the author's ability to translate technical information into striking everyday language (many undesirable insects came to this country as "hitchhikers" on plants).

ARGUMENT   **Argument** is the use of systematic, step-by-step reasoning to prove a point. We try to structure an argument in such a way that a reader examining the evidence and following our reasoning will reach the same conclusions that we did. A writer may be systematically examining cause-and-effect relationships to prove a connection between government policies and recessions. Or a writer may weigh the pros and cons of a proposed immigration law to help readers reach a balanced conclusion.

The following passage from a student paper on gun control is an example of systematic argument:

In a recent year, 65 percent of the murders, 63 percent of the robberies, and 24 percent of the aggravated assaults involved guns. A government commission found that parts of the country with the highest level of gun ownership have the highest incidence of gun-related violence. When stronger gun control laws are enacted, robberies and homicides tend to decrease. When Massachusetts enacted a stricter gun control law, homicides decreased an unbelievable 55 percent during the two following years. Our rate of violent crimes is 100 percent higher than that of Great Britain, which has stricter gun control laws, and it is 200 percent higher than that of Japan, which outlaws private ownership of handguns. All the available evidence shows that the easy availability of handguns in this country is one of the main causes of violent crime.

This passage shows several features of systematic argument. The writer has collected relevant evidence; she presents an array of facts and figures; she draws conclusions.

Some important kinds of writing do not fit well into the fourfold scheme. For instance, logical argument is often highly persuasive but it is different from other kinds of persuasion.

PERSUASION   **Persuasion** is the kind of writing that most directly aims at results. Persuasive writers want to change our minds, but they also want us to take action. They want a vote, a sale, a change in our habits. Persuasive writing goes beyond logical argument to appeal to our emotions and to shared values. It often stirs our compassion or indignation; it may appeal strongly to our sense of fairness or to self-interest. Persuasive writers know how to break down resistance, how to present a case in the best light. (When persuasion exploits the reader's prejudices and weaknesses, it becomes propaganda and manipulation.)

The following plea for support is a sample of effective persuasive writing:

EXTINCTION—IT'S FOREVER. One quarter of all species of animals and plants on earth may disappear in the next thirty years because of our destruction of their habitat. The rate of extinction is increasing enormously as forests are destroyed and other wild areas are lost. Organisms that evolved over hundreds of millions of years will be gone forever. The complex interdependence of all creatures, from the largest animals to the smallest plants, is being shattered. We face a crisis with profound implications for the survival of all life. Unfortunately, little is being done to save our planet's natural heritage. The ark is sinking. We need the help of every concerned citizen to conserve the diversity of life on earth. Help save the endangered species.

This passage illustrates some key features of effective persuasion: It makes a strong, direct, memorable plea for the reader's help. It uses strong emotional language to create alarm, fear, or a sense of loss: *destruction, extinction, forever, shattered*. It uses words with rich positive overtones that appeal powerfully to the reader's values: *interdependence, survival, heritage, diversity*.

In practice, the traditional modes overlap. Writers often use them in combination. To help us understand the "new poor" (exposition), a writer may tell the story of a woman who lost her job, her health, and her place to live (narration). Effective argument often dramatizes the issue by vivid accounts of people and events, by using the story of a representative individual as a case history.

Questions for Discussion From your reading of nonfiction or current newspapers and magazines, can you describe some memorable examples of narration, description, exposition, argument, or persuasion? What made them stand out? What helps you classify them?

The Writer's Motives

To narrate, to describe, to inform, to argue, to persuade—these are the broad general purposes that help us identify kinds of writing. To understand why writers actually write, we have to go beyond these broad general labels. We ask about an example of description or argument: What triggered it? What brought it on? We look for the writer's personal motives or specific need. To ensure that your own writing is worth reading, you need to feel in starting a paper: "On this subject, *I* have something to say. This is something *I* want or need to do."

What are some of the motives that activate successful writing? The strength of much autobiographical writing is that the events being told have a personal meaning for the author. People often write eloquently when they write to *register a grievance* or when they write about a recurrent problem they have had to confront. The following passage, by a student of Japanese descent, shows the force of autobiographical writing that expresses strong personal feelings:

I, personally, am very sensitive to verbal reactions. There is always the question, "What are you?" The mere fact of being questioned makes me stiffen with resentment at the ignorance of those who felt that they had to ask. There have been times when I have been completely at a loss for words on how to reply. I could answer, "American," "Japanese," and "Japanese-American," but somehow I feel unnatural and placed in an awkward situation. I do not consider myself totally American, because of obvious visible differences, nor do I think of myself as Japanese, since I was not brought up with the strict traditions and culture. Being thought of as a member of a minority makes me slightly uncomfortable, and responding to that question has made me sometimes regret my existence.

In writing an autobiographical paper, you may be telling your story *to bear witness*: You may have been present at the arrest of a friend, getting into trouble for what the officers considered interference. By giving an honest, faithful account of the events, you may be trying to show what you learned about the rationality or irrationality, the humanity or brutality of police procedures. Or you may write *to talk back to a stereotype*. Most of us learn to shrug off the barbs aimed at an ethnic, religious, or regional group to which we belong. We put up with remarks about the emotionalism of Italians, the rigidity of Germans, or the megalomania of Texans. But we may reach the point where we feel like saying, "I have heard just about enough of that. I would like to speak to that if I may." For instance, after listening to a class discussion of stereotypes, a student may write a paper about growing up in a large Italian family, with its special family occasions, family quarrels, and religious traditions. This paper is likely to come from the heart; it will have the strength of a personal vindication. The following article by an Italian-American educator has the personal drive and conviction of writing that talks back to a stereotype.

Vincent S. Romano
THE GODFATHER IMAGE PERSISTS

A recent research study has confirmed what Americans of Italian origin already know: negative stereotyping of Italian Americans pervades the U.S. media. A team affiliated with Columbia and George Washington Universities studied prime-time television programs during a recent season. Among the major findings:

- Negative portrayals of Italian Americans outnumber positive ones by two to one.

☐ Television portrays one out of six Italian-American characters as criminals.

☐ Viewers could conclude, judging from TV presentations, that most Italian Americans hold low-status jobs and are unable to speak English correctly.

☐ Italian Americans who are not portrayed as villains or criminals are generally pictured as lovable, laughable dimwits.

Television fails to provide positive role models for Italian-American children. Television is not the only culprit. Newspapers and magazines have portrayed Italian Americans negatively for years. As early as 1881, inflammatory newspaper articles led to the lynching of 11 Italians in New Orleans. Though not as blatant today, coverage of the Italian-American community is still often biased.

The print media continue to use words such as *Mafia* and *Cosa Nostra* as synonyms for organized crime. Despite studies showing that organized crime is not the province of any single racial, ethnic, or religious group, the popular misconception—the "Godfather" image—persists.

In 1980, a Pennsylvania Crime Commission study found that Italian-American involvement in organized crime is negligible. Only a year later, the National News Council, a prestigious media watchdog group, concluded that the press sustains and perpetuates the stereotype of Italian Americans as gangsters.

Even school textbooks are not free from stereotypes, omissions, and inaccuracies. They generally fail, for example, to mention that William Paca, a signer of the Declaration of Independence, was Italian—and that explorer John Cabot was in fact Giovanni Caboto.

Equally destructive are textbook distortions and inaccuracies. One eleventh grade social studies book treats organized crime as an Italian-American invention. The same book suggests that Italian Americans sympathized with the Axis powers in World War II. This obvious falsehood is an insult to the hundreds of thousands of men and women of Italian descent who loyally served in the U.S. armed forces during the War.

There are 20 million Americans of Italian descent who are proud of their family-oriented values, their hard work, and their achievements. They are weary of being unfairly maligned. They want to be an equal part of the American mosaic, maintaining their cultural roots while participating fully and fairly in the economic and social fabric of American life. They want no more. They will accept no less.   *NEA Today*

This article is rooted in the author's personal experience but discusses the issue in general terms and uses examples and evidence accessible to the general reader. In much forceful argument and persuasion, we sense a similar personal interest or commitment.

What motives will activate your writing as you move from personal experience to issues of general interest? Much informative writing is set in motion by a need to clear up confusion or to correct misunderstanding.

On a subject you know well—sports, diets, country music, child custody—you may listen to other people and say: "No, that is not the way it is at all!" You will feel the urge to set the record straight. The following passage is from a paper that aims at correcting a misunderstanding:

> Human beings have used food additives since ancient times to keep meat from spoiling or fat from turning rancid. They used salting, sugar curing, and smoking to keep their food edible. Today, health food advocates object to the addition of chemical preservatives to such common delights as T.V. dinners, cooking pouch entrees, frozen prepared potatoes, and ready-to-bake doughs. We are told that such chemicals are not as "natural" as the methods used in earlier times. What we have to realize is that salt, sugar, and smoke are not wonder substances that magically preserve food. The sodium and chloride in salt chemically bind water so that it cannot interact with the air to initiate spoilage.

We often decide to embark on a systematic argument when an important issue has generated more heat than light. For instance, a discussion of changing immigration laws easily gets bogged down in ethnic prejudices, old allegiances, and ulterior motives. We may decide to clarify the options by tracing the consequences of different possible courses of action. By examining statistics and precedents, by systematically studying causes and effects, we may set up the projections that would help a voter make an intelligent choice.

Persuasion puts the premium on results. In persuasive writing, the writer's purposes are often more obvious (or the ulterior motives more transparent) than in other kinds of writing. The writer's aim may be to persuade us to correct abuses (fleecing of the elderly, overcrowding in prisons); to condemn evildoers (as in an exposé of bribes or collusion in high places); or to support a good cause (a peace initiative, opportunities for the disabled).

Questions for Discussion Have you recently read a piece of writing that took a strong stand or made a strong plea? What was the writer's agenda?

Remember: It is hard to find readers for writing that was done grudgingly, as a dutiful exercise. To interest your readers in a subject, you first have to find your own interest in it; you have to discover your purpose. You will write best when you write in order to explain something new, register a grievance, correct a misunderstanding, clear up confusion, justify a preference, or guide the reader's choices. Your writing is likely to carry conviction when you write to expose negligence, promote a good cause, or protest against injustice. Find your reason for writing; give your readers a reason to read.

EXERCISE 3   *The Reason for Writing*

Study the following writing samples to determine the author's purpose. For each sample, answer the following questions:

☐ Does the excerpt represent one of the major *kinds* of writing—narration, description, exposition, argument, persuasion? (Defend your choice.)

☐ What were the author's more specific or more personal *motives* in this passage? Or, what more specific needs was the writer trying to meet? (Be prepared to compare and discuss reaction with your classmates.)

1. *From a book about the great railroads of Europe and Asia:*

Venice, like a drawing room in a gas station, is approached through a vast apron of infertile industrial flatlands, crisscrossed with black sewer troughs and stinking of oil, the gigantic sinks and stoves of refineries and factories, all intimidating the delicate dwarfed city beyond. The graffiti along the way are professionally executed as the names of the firms. . . . The lagoon with its luminous patches of oil slick, as if hopelessly retouched by Canaletto, has a yard-wide tidewrack of rubble, plastic bottles, broken toilet seats, raw sewage, and that bone white factory froth the wind beats into drifts of foam. The edges of the city have succumbed to industry's erosion, and what shows are the cracked back windows and derelict posterns of water-logged villas, a few brittle Venetian steeples, and farther in, but low and almost visibly sinking, walls of spaghetti-colored stucco and red roofs over which flocks of soaring swallows are teaching pigeons to fly.   Paul Theroux, *The Great Railway Bazaar*

2. *From a book on the skills and crafts needed for rural living:*

There's a lot more to building than just hammering nails, but it's a good place to start. These are some useful things to know: To drive a nail, hold the nail in your left hand (if you're right-handed), and tap directly on the head of it a few times with the hammer to set it. Hold the nail at a slight angle—it is less likely to bend and it makes a stronger joint. Then, take away your left hand and hammer it the rest of the way in. It's most important to hammer directly on the nail head, so that the nail doesn't bend. This sounds simple and it is, but it requires developing coordination and a sense of the hammer, its weight and its force. It is best to hold the hammer near the end of the handle. This gives you more leverage and, therefore, more force.   Jeanne Tetrault and Sherry Thomas, *Country Women*

3. *From an article about the future of Social Security:*

The demographic shift most important to long-term deficits is the dramatic decline in fertility rates for members of the Baby Boom generation. Much more than any increase or decrease in longevity, fertility rates affect the eventual age distribution of a population. In recent years the American fertility rate has ticked up slightly, but it is still close to the record low, reached in 1976, of 65.8 live births per 1,000 women of childbearing age. The low fertility rate guarantees that the median age of the American population will rise dramatically in the years ahead—barring, of course, an enormous increase in immigration. As the population ages, the demands on the budget will become extreme.   Philip Longman, "Justice Between Generations," *Atlantic*

4. *From an editorial on drug traffic:*

Illegal drugs are not some mysterious and uncontrollable plague seeping north from the tropics. They are commodities that are imported because there is an American market for them. The surest way to stop the illegal drug trade is to make that market dry up. This is where the prevailing drug-control strategy is hypocritical. It exempts from all blame the one class of people ultimately responsible for this brutal business: American drug users. Every time an American does a line of coke, he or she is directly subsidizing murder across the hemisphere. It doesn't matter if the user is a legislative aide to a compassionate congressman or an inner-city pimp. As Colombian drug lord Roberto Suarez Gomez boasts, his fortune came entirely from "the depravity of the *Yanquis*."   "The Dope Dilemma," *The New Republic*

EXERCISE 4   *A Student Editorial*

What was the author's purpose when she wrote the following editorial for a student newspaper? What was her agenda or key motive? How does she set her editorial in motion? Where does she state her main point? What are major sections or major stages in her argument? How effectively does she reach a student audience?

Maria J. Gunter
THE PRESS PASS AND COMPASSION

Journalists are hard of heart, nose and head, according to many people. They worship bylines and headlines, clambering over people's feelings and lives to make it to the top.

"It's the press," the secretary whispers, hand covering the phone. "Should I say you're not in?" The pesticide industry executive ponders for a moment, then winks and says, "I'm gone for the day." After the secretary hangs up the receiver, the boss says, "Doesn't matter anyway. Those damn scribblers will put whatever they want."

Across town, a man lies on the ground, groaning in agony, his life's blood forming in pools on the gravel. His wife, uninjured by the now-dead sniper, stands nearby, screaming at reporters to stand back.

In the state capital, a defeated politician sits in his office, wandering the path to the polls over and over again in his mind, while a reporter conducts an interview.

The reporter asks questions that seem to imply the politician's very hopes and dreams belong in another era.

In each situation the reporter seemed an enemy or an intruder to the people involved. It's not surprising. Journalists prod, probe, and pry for a living. They are salaried tellers of tales, but unfortunately, much news is unhappy, and those stories often hurt the subjects.

However, journalists also feel bad when they must ask the hard questions of the injured, the bereaved, and the defeated. Reporters see more than most human beings' share of certain things: mangled cars and airplanes, drowned children, young ambition slain by the assassin's bullet, to name but a few.

At such scenes, journalists often wear their hearts on their sleeves. Tear-stained notes mark the print reporter's feelings, while a radio announcer on the scene may sound his concern via a husky voice during the newscast.

Compassion and empathy do not forestall the journalist's duty to record current events for all to know. Reporters must provide readers the history of today so they'll be aware of what's going on in the world, but also so they can share the feelings of others. Knowing what another mother feels like, whether she's two states or two continents away, helps to foster an understanding of other people, whether it's joy over a child's recovery from illness or shared sorrow in the child's death.

When a tot drowns in a back yard pool, it's rough to ask the parents how long they left the boy or girl alone, why there was no enclosure around the swimming area, and whether the child knew how to swim. But it has to be done. It is news, and it may well prevent another drowning by alerting others parents to the dangers involved when toddlers and water mix.

Less tragic but still difficult circumstances also present challenges for reporters, who serve as the public's representative in places the public cannot or does not go. When something's amiss, whether in city hall, student government, or the church business office, journalists serve as surrogate eyes and ears for other citizens. It's a professional and civic duty to study the situation and report on it, no matter how reticent officials are to discuss the matter, and reticent is a true understatement.

To go where few ever go, to report the facts and to keep one's sanity—that's the duty of all reporters, and it's one few would willingly relinquish, despite the lousy pay, fierce competition, and ulcer-producing environment.

There's no better feeling than to find out and expose fraud, to tell a story of smile-invoking good times, or to write of a life well lived. It makes up by far for the sleepless election nights and ambulance chasing.   *Spartan Daily*

WRITING TOPICS 2   *Writing with a Purpose*

Under the following headings, find a topic on which you can write with conviction. Write a paper in which you can say something that you strongly feel needs to be said. Make sure you can relate your topic to your own experience, observation, or reading. Choose an assignment from the following:

1. *Talking Back to the Stereotype:* Have you or people close to you ever reacted negatively to being stereotyped? Write a paper in which you show first what the stereotype is. Then contrast it with the truth it distorts or obscures. The stereotype you attack may be ethnic or racial (Irish, Oriental, Mexican); regional (Texan, Californian, Southerner, redneck, Yankee); occupational (the jock, the cop, the politician, the bureaucrat); sexual (the woman driver, "just a housewife," the chauvinist male); religious or cultural (Mormon, Jewish); or other.

2. *Paying Tribute Where Due:* Have you ever felt about a group of people that their contribution is often slighted or overlooked? Is there for you a group of unsung heroes or neglected heroines? You might choose a group like firefighters, police officers, social workers, or farmers; you might choose a type like the single parent, the working mother, or the stepfather or stepmother. Show how the merits of the group are slighted. Give it the recognition it deserves.

3. *Writing to Challenge Neglect:* Have you ever felt the need to expose a striking example of waste, callousness, or neglect? You might want to write about litter in public places, a neighborhood allowed to decay, heedless destruction of natural beauty, or a striking example of callousness toward the unfortunate. Support your charge; if you can, point toward a remedy.

4. *Setting the Record Straight:* Are you concerned about a serious case of public ignorance? Have you recently become disturbed by a striking example of misinformation or misrepresentation? Write to show what is wrong and to set the record straight. Possible topics might range from the truth about your readers' water supply to the truth about illegal immigration. Make sure you have details, facts, or evidence that will convince a fair-minded reader.

5. *"My Turn":* For years, the "My Turn" column in *Newsweek* has given freelance writers an opportunity to discuss a current issue from a personal point of view. Is there a current issue, or a topic in the news, that has touched your life or the lives of people close to you? Write on a current issue that has a personal meaning for you. Possible topics might include sexual violence and the single woman, the institutionalization of the elderly, or the dearth of day care.

6. *Championing the Good Cause:* Many readers feel that they have already been too often the object of pleas for their support of worthy causes. Is there a cause in which you are seriously involved? Write a paper in which you try to break through the crust of apathy. Possible topics might include Amnesty International, the Sierra Club, the arts, or world hunger. Make

sure your appeal goes beyond familiar slogans or generalized good intentions.

Your instructor may ask you to prepare a brief *planning report* on why you chose your topic, what you are trying to do, and how. If you can, profit from the preliminary reactions of your classmates or your instructor to your plan.

TARGETING THE AUDIENCE

Writing is meant to be read; it is a transaction between the writer and the reader. How consciously we take aim at the reader varies for different kinds of writing. We can place them on a spectrum from self-expression (or **expressive writing**) to the deliberate influencing of others (or persuasion). In autobiographical writing, for instance, you express personal attitudes and emotions. You may be writing mainly to come to terms with your own experience—although you may expect the reader to sympathize with your feelings. In persuasive writing, at the opposite end of the scale, you will be writing mainly to win the audience over to your side. You will need to size up your readers—are they friendly? hostile? neutral? You will need to work out the strategies that will change the reader's mind or the reader's ways.

Professional writers have a lively awareness of their audience, an awareness that results from years of feedback from editors, reviewers, critics, and plain readers. The experienced writer knows when the reader is likely to say: "What does this mean?" "Where is the evidence to back this up?" "I don't see how this fits in."

Who Is the Reader?

How do you envision your intended reader? Your answer to this question will help shape what you do and how you proceed.

THE CRITICAL READER

Much of the writing you will do in college will aim at an imaginary educated reader. We call such readers "critical readers," but not because they necessarily tend toward negative criticism (although many of them do). Critical readers are thinking readers; they look for a thoughtful, well worked-out piece of writing rather than glib talk. They care about issues of public interest and are open to new ideas. They try to look fairly at arguments and evidence and to rise above bias or prejudice. To get a hearing from a critical audience, we need to avoid name calling, slanted evidence, and cheap shots of all kinds. We do without insults (*redneck, bleeding-heart liberal*), sexist language ("just like a woman") and racial or ethnic slurs. Critical readers like to feel that we are inviting them to "reason together."

THE LAY AUDIENCE In informative writing, we play the role of the expert (or the popularizer) who explains specialized information to a lay audience. We assume a receptive audience that likes to be kept up to date on new developments—for instance, in science or medicine. We shed light on matters that interest or worry our readers but that they lack time to research or think through on their own: security systems for cars, changing career opportunities, new treatments for mental illness. Our responsibility is to show patience with the needs of the outsider: We provide necessary background, explain technical terms to the uninitiated, and present new ideas one step at a time. We try to present a balanced view, showing that we have consulted different (and perhaps disagreeing) authorities.

THE IN-GROUP AUDIENCE When we write for an in-group, we write for a limited audience that shares a common interest or believes in a common cause. Groups that share a common purpose include unions, Rotarians, art associations, *Star Trek* aficionados, Elvis Presley fan clubs, and the like. Writers will find such a group a willing audience if they know the history and the lore of the group, if they can show their commitment to its shared values. A writer writing for an in-group audience of movie buffs, for instance, is likely to speak with affection of legendary early stars from Buster Keaton and Charles Chaplin to Ginger Rogers and Fred Astaire; of the great foreign directors from Truffaut and Fellini to Fassbinder; of the great critics, such as Pauline Kael. At the same time, in-group readers are likely to be sticklers for accuracy; they will expect the writer to get the facts right concerning such movie classics as *Gone with the Wind* or *Psycho* or *Citizen Kane*.

SPECIAL AUDIENCES Much writing targets a special audience identified by age, sex, occupation, religion, or ethnic background (or by a combination of these). Much advertising, for instance, singles out a particular range of customers and works on their special needs or vulnerability. Manufacturers of children's clothes may deliberately aim their advertising at affluent working mothers who feel uneasy about spending much time away from their children and who compensate by buying them "the best."

When you aim your own writing at a particular age group or occupational group, you will have to take into account differences like the following:

□ Many young people have only recently staged their rebellion against parental control; they are less likely than older people to applaud calls for discipline, supervision, "cracking down," law and order.

□ Social workers and teachers will tend to favor spending to alleviate social problems (for instance, money to shelter the homeless or to provide child care). However, property owners or operators of small business tend to be suspicious of "throwing money at a problem," of initiatives that would raise their taxes.

When you share the outlook of your intended audience, you can create a sense of solidarity by appealing to shared values. Your readers may respond warmly if you eloquently voice their grievances or aspirations. When the interests of the audience differ from yours, you confront questions of strategy. Are you going to humor the prejudices of the group? Or are you going to tackle disagreement head on? Are you going to be blunt and aggressive, hoping to shake the audience out of its apathy? Effective writers know how to keep from alienating an audience needlessly while yet challenging ideas it holds dear.

Questions for Discussion If you were preparing an *audience profile* for a magazine editor trying to reach people like you, what interests and values would you stress? What likes and dislikes would you include?

Setting the Tone Your relationship with your intended audience will help set the tone of your writing. You will not want to be too chummy, but not too distant either. The right tone creates mutual respect between writer and reader; it shows that you are taking your subject and your audience seriously. The following passage takes up an issue of urgent importance to the writer; she makes her readers feel that their attitudes and behavior matter.

FORMAL: This new freedom, particularly among women, to use language to describe rather than distort reality is slowly being translated into action. From the etiquette books of colonial times to as recently as the 1970 *New Seventeen Book of Etiquette*, females have been carefully instructed in the art of passivity. For centuries, feminine politeness meant fussiness of language and "fellowship" in behavior. When feminists of the 1970's unleashed the rhetoric of women's equality, they did not mince words. In fact, at times they intentionally drew from a "shock vocabulary," partly to counteract the stereotype of fussy feminine language but mainly, I think, because strong issues demand strong words.   Judy Mednick, "A Woman's World of Words," *California English*

The key terms in this passage carry serious weight: *freedom, distort, reality, passivity, stereotype.* (*Fussy,* used sarcastically, is one of the few words borrowed from informal talk.)

Leavening touches of informality can put the audience in a relaxed and receptive mood; they assure us that a writer is not going to be pompous or self-righteous. However, the more informal the tone, the less we expect the writer to tackle an urgent issue. In the following passage, on the subject of finding the perfect deli sandwich, the author is winking at us, signaling to us to relax and be entertained.

INFORMAL: I left Friday night on the red-eye. By the time I got into Manhattan, it was noon Saturday, the temperature was 33 degrees and the line outside the deli was half an hour long. People stood with their hands in their pockets, hopping up and down. . . . Inside, the place was jammed. Salamis dangled from the ceiling like stalactites at Carlsbad Caverns. The air had dozens of smells in it, all of them worth smelling. Customers sat at long tables back to back, dining-hall style, talking with their mouths full. Nobody bawled them out. . . . The waiter took my order and the fellow's next to me, deposited two cheesecakes at the next table and filled a coffee cup, all in the same breath. Three minutes later, the sandwich arrived. It was warm as a baby and looked a foot high. The bread had been baked that very morning. The whole thing was held together by two oversized toothpicks that did not have any of those silly plastic ruffles on them. Wow.   Steve Rubenstein, "Once a Week," *San Francisco Chronicle*

Here we are close to informal and even slangy talk: *red-eye, jammed, bawl out, wow.* The comparisons are extravagant and funny: salamis like "stalactites"; the sandwich "warm as a baby."

Remember: The tone of your writing makes the audience imagine a person—angry, self-righteous, reserved, outgoing, relaxed. We call the personality reflected in a piece of writing the **persona** of the writer. The stance you take in a paper may be that of the friendly critic, the concerned citizen, the angry victim. Whatever it is, be sure it suits your purpose and sets up the right relationship with the reader.

EXERCISE 5   *Writer and Audience*

Different styles of communication set up different kinds of relationships between the writer and the audience. We can often place a piece of writing somewhere on a scale between two poles. The following are some examples:

AUTHORITATIVE: The writer speaks as the authority, expert, or boss.
COOPERATIVE: The writer speaks to co-workers, fellow voters, or equals.

DIRECT: A blunt, matter-of-fact style heads straight for the point.
DIPLOMATIC: The writer puts the reader in a receptive mood and is careful not to ruffle feathers or hurt feelings.

FORMAL: The writer words things carefully for the record or for public consumption.
INFORMAL: The writer adopts a casual, relaxed, conversational style.

IMPERSONAL: The writer concentrates on the matter at hand, adopting a neutral, objective tone.
PERSONAL: The writer creates a friendly, warm feeling or lets personal emotions show.

Study the *memos* in the following pairs. How do the two versions in each pair differ? What relationship does each version set up between the writer and the audience? What are the advantages and disadvantages of the contrasting styles?

PAIR 1: Please rewrite the attached job description for the new position in our department. As now worded, the qualifications required of the candidate will discourage applicants who expect scope for personal initiative.

The attached job description spells out well the requirements for the new position in our department. However, the tone should be modified somewhat in order to encourage applicants who want to show personal initiative.

PAIR 2: The committee needs to have a meeting next week to discuss final revision of our new guidelines. I suggest meeting at 9 AM in the downstairs conference room.

Next week seems like a good time to have a final look at our new guidelines. Let me know if you can join the rest of the committee at 9 AM in the downstairs conference room.

PAIR 3: At the last few meetings we've all had a chance to speak our piece. At our next session we should really knock our heads together to come up with something that we can all be comfortable with and that we can stand behind.

Our last few meetings have allowed ample discussion of conflicting views. At our next meeting, it is essential that we reach a consensus and formulate a position that we can all support.

PAIR 4: I am sorry to say that this report cannot go out in its present form. Whatever the merits of the contents, the numerous spelling errors and garbled sentences create an impression of hurry and carelessness that we cannot afford in our dealings with the public.

This is without doubt the sloppiest report I have ever read. Whoever wrote it should return the college diploma and ask for tuition back. Where did this person learn how to spell? Really!

EXERCISE 6   *The Range of Styles*

For each of the following brief writing samples, answer the questions below:

- What would be the ideal reader for this passage? What kind of audience did the writer have in mind?
- What is the tone of the passage? What attitude does it show toward the subject, and how? How formal or informal is the passage? (Point to specific evidence.)

1.   Iacocca reveals more about the American automobile industry and its life-style than he perhaps intends. When he was feuding with Henry Ford, the word went around the company that it was unhealthy to be a friend of Iacocca's. So the company masseur, who came to Iacocca's house every Sunday, didn't show, and the chief stewardess of the company fleet got demoted because she was too friendly. Company masseur? Chief stewardess of the company fleet? We taxpayers were supporting that style. And at the same time, the industry was so inept as to give the whole inexpensive end of the automobile spectrum to the Japanese. Reading Iacocca, you conclude that only self-restraint on the part of the Japanese and protectionist noises from Washington kept the Japanese from taking 80 percent of the American automobile market instead of 25 percent.   Adam Smith, "Unconventional Wisdom," *Esquire*

2.   Dr. Bem ran a series of experiments on college students who had been categorized as masculine, feminine, or androgynous. In three tests of the degree of nurturance—warmth and caring—the masculine men scored painfully low (painfully for anyone stuck with a masculine man, that is). In one of those experiments, all the students were asked to listen to a "troubled talker"—a person who was not neurotic but simply lonely, supposedly new in town and feeling like an outsider. The masculine men were the least supportive, responsive or humane. "They lacked the ability to express warmth, playfulness and concern," Bem concluded. (She's giving them the benefit of the doubt. It's possible the masculine men didn't express those qualities because they didn't possess them.)   Amy Gross, "The Appeal of the Androgynous Man," *Mademoiselle*

3.   Many veterans shunned the VA altogether. Widely regarded with firm distrust, it was and still is generally perceived as an uncaring bureaucracy staffed with lifers more interested in pushing their pencils and shuffling their papers than in treating the Vietnam veterans trickling in through the door, looking for help. In addition, the thousands of GIs with "bad-paper" discharges—more often than not shoved at them out of sheer spite for their "attitude"—are barred by law from obtaining treatment of any kind from the VA, even if they suffer service-connected health problems: wounds received in active combat, Agent Orange exposure, delayed stress, and the like.   Larry Heinemann, "Just Don't Fit," *Harper's*

EXERCISE 7   *The Ideal Reader*

Study closely one recent issue of a publication that aims at a distinct audience. Prepare a portrait of the imaginary ideal reader for a publication like the following: *Sports Illustrated, Popular Science, The Wall Street Journal, The New Yorker, Ms., McCall's, New York, The New Republic, Rolling Stone.* What common background or shared interests do the editors assume? Do they cater to shared likes and dislikes? Do they appeal to shared values? (Is there any "outgrouping"—that is, are any groups treated as outsiders?) Use detailed evidence or illustrations.

WRITING TOPICS 3   *Meeting the Needs of the Audience*

Write a short paper in which you pay special attention to the needs of your audience. Write as an insider who serves as a guide to the newcomer or outsider. Choose an assignment from the following:

1. Take a visitor behind the scenes of a day-care center, laundry, McDonald's, or similar operation.
2. Introduce a beginner to bird-watching, fishing, tennis, hiking, or similar activity.
3. Help initiate a new member of a co-op, a military academy, a health club, or similar institution.
4. Help break in a new employee as a dishwasher, usher, cashier, janitor, or the like.
5. Provide orientation for a new student of voice, piano, acting, or the like.

Think about the needs of your readers. Do several or all of the following:

- □ Create the setting.
- □ Sum up the purpose or goals.
- □ Include striking or revealing details.
- □ Describe selected key operations.
- □ Provide essential explanations.

(Your instructor may ask you to present your paper as an oral report, to be followed by *questions* and reactions from your classmates.)

WRITING TOPICS 4   *Knowing Your Audience*

The school authorities in a local high school have collaborated with the police to place undercover narcotics agents in classes to mingle and make friends with the students. After six weeks of investigation, fifteen students have been arrested on charges of selling cocaine or marijuana. They have been taken in handcuffs to Juvenile Hall, where most of them still remain several weeks later. School officials defend their action by explaining that it was necessary to crack down and provide a deterrent to other students. Many of the parents involved are furious, complaining that their children face expulsion and permanent damage to their future careers.

In presenting your views on the situation, *choose your audience* as follows:

1. If, on the whole, you *approve* of the police action, write a letter defending it to the parents of the arrested students.

2. If, on the whole, you *disapprove* of the police action, write a letter attacking it to the school officials.

3. If you prefer *not* to take sides, write a letter to the students at the school, telling them what you think they should learn from the events.

Try to make your letter persuasive for the audience you have chosen.

3

GATHERING

Exploring Your Subject

*What people do—and what people say—continues to take
me by surprise with its wonderfulness, or its quirkiness, or
its drama, or its humor, or its pain. Who could invent all
the astonishing things that really happen? Therefore I
increasingly find myself saying to writers and students: "Trust
your material."* William Zinsser

*No matter how satisfying, writing is a part-time job. Some
of the time you are inside making words, but some of the
time you have to be out there facing life, confronting the
forces, feeling the currents, coming to some understanding
of what it means to be human.* Patrick Bedard

MOBILIZING YOUR SOURCES The writer's task is to move from a blank sheet
of paper (or a blank screen) to a finished piece of writing. Where does
the material come from that fills the page? How does a writer gather the
material for a paper, for a magazine article, for a chapter in a book? A
writer has to learn to explore a topic, to work up a subject. When you
work up a subject, you mobilize resources you already have, and you
turn for help to outside sources. You allow time for exploration and
discovery. Skipping this **prewriting** stage is like trying to bake the bread
without kneading the dough or to build a fire with only a few sticks.

The Range of Sources Learn to draw on the full range of sources that should fuel your
writing. Draw on the sources that will help you satisfy the reader who
asks: "What makes you think so? How do you know?"

PERSONAL EXPERIENCE Ask: "Where has this topic touched my own experience?" Suppose you are writing a paper about changes in how our society treats the disabled. Ask yourself: "What people with physical disabilities have I known? What do I remember about them? What were their problems? How did they cope with them?" Be prepared to take a close look at these people: What were their individual histories, their daily routines, their grievances and aspirations?

CURRENT OBSERVATION A good writer is first of all a good observer. Learn to trust your own eyes and ears. Your finished paper should show that you are the kind of person who notices things: the growing number of students getting around the campus in wheelchairs, the specially equipped vans some of them use, the wheelchair ramps that bypass stairs in front of new buildings, and other signs of a growing awareness in our society of people with special needs.

CURRENT MEDIA COVERAGE A good writer is an alert reader and viewer. Has the topic you are exploring been in the news? Has it recently been the subject of articles in newsmagazines or other periodicals? If, for instance, you are writing about the fitness craze, what current articles have you read about running, aerobics, or diets? Do you recall striking examples, case histories, or revealing statistics? Do you remember warnings by medical authorities or advice from gurus of the fitness movement?

PAST READING AND VIEWING Ask: "What books have I read, or what plays and movies have I seen, that would provide background for my topic?" In writing about industrial robots in tomorrow's automated factories, you may want to quote from a science fiction story about robots, perhaps a story by a writer like Isaac Asimov. In writing about the absence of a social "safety net" in early capitalism, you may want to refer to the picture of the late nineteenth-century British proletariat as sketched by Charles Dickens or to the condition of immigrant laborers in Chicago meat-packing plants as recorded by Upton Sinclair.

SYSTEMATIC RESEARCH Even for shorter papers, scan the current newspaper for relevant material. Read one or more background articles. Do some informal interviewing. The more extensive your project, the more likely you are to embark on a serious search. Before you write on prison reform, for example, you are likely to look for a range of up-to-date and authoritative sources. You may want to study official statistics; you may want to compare the testimony of former inmates, the opinions of law enforcement officers, and the findings of recognized authorities.

Remember that a paper worth reading does not merely present the author's opinion. It presents opinions that are anchored in observation, experience, or exploration.

Questions for Discussion Viewers and readers often follow the media coverage of a topic of special interest to them. Have you recently followed the coverage of an issue or controversy over a period of time? Why do you care? What have you learned? What would you tell readers to bring them up to date on the topic?

Prewriting Techniques

Writers develop their own ways of working up a subject. They jot down rough ideas, collect clippings or photocopies, take systematic notes, use scratch outlines. They write notes to themselves, collect note cards in a shoe box, or start a preliminary file on their word processor. The traditional term for this process of hunting down and squirreling away information and ideas is **invention**—not in the sense of creating something entirely new but of creatively and imaginatively mobilizing the writer's resources.

Study and practice the following techniques for generating material:

BRAINSTORMING

Brainstorming is the process of jotting down, in very rough unsorted form, the ideas and associations that a topic brings to mind. When you brainstorm, one idea leads to another. Jog your memory for relevant material: observations, incidents, data, slogans, headlines, remarks. Get a preliminary idea inventory down on paper. Worry later about how a statement will sound or how well an example will fit. Right now, let things come to the surface. Work up a rich fund of material for later use.

Successful brainstorming brings to the surface the striking images and revealing details needed to bring a subject to life. Look at the following example of brainstorming on the subject of the macho male:

PREWRITING: BRAINSTORMING

Macho: Big, muscular, unfeeling, rough—harsh, moves to kill. (Sylvester Stallone: I hate what he promotes.) Negative impression. Hard craggy faces with mean eyes that bore holes in you.

Men who have to prove themselves through acts of violence. The man who is disconnected from his feelings, insensitive to women's needs—cannot express himself in a feeling manner.

The word seems to have negative connotations for me because I work part-time in a bar. I am forever seeing these perfectly tanned types who come on to a woman. As a child, macho meant a strong male type who would take care of me—paternal, warmth in eyes. John Wayne: gruff, yet you feel secure knowing someone like this was around.

Crude, huge—the body, not the heart—tendency to violence always seems close to the surface. Looks are very important. Craggy face. Bloodshed excites them. Arnold Schwarzenegger muscles, gross.

Tend to dominate in relationships—desire for control. "Me Tarzan—you Jane."

In the following paper, the author of the brainstorming sample has sorted out her material and formulated the conclusions it suggests. Compare the paper with the brainstorming notes.

WRITING SAMPLE: SECOND DRAFT

Misconceptions of Macho

"Macho"—the word makes me see yet another prototype of the muscular tanned male walk through the doors of the establishment where I work. He glides past me, lean and smooth. Dressed to kill, not a hair out of place, he lets his eyes dart this way and that, trying to zero in on his female prey of the evening. Suddenly, some woman catches his eye. He saunters over, makes some unintelligible remark, and the courting dance has begun.

The stereotype of the macho is the tough man who proves his maleness through acts of violence or through dominant behavior. Sylvester Stallone as Rambo creates the stereotypical image, complete with mayhem, blood, guts, and brute strength. The price the macho pays is that he is incapable of expressing himself in a caring, feeling manner. He is insensitive to a woman's needs. He may be the strongest, toughest, most handsome, and best-at-everything kind of person in the world, but he lacks emotional qualities that would link him with the rest of humanity.

Macho is as much a state of mind as a matter of physical appearance. A macho male can be a five-foot-tall, ninety-eight pound weakling and still have that condescending attitude toward women, looking down on her as if she were nothing more than a vehicle put here by God for his own pleasure. As a woman who works in the bar and restaurant business, I have seen this scenario played out many times: A lone woman comes into a bar, perhaps to meet a friend, and finds that she is fair game. The macho male will invade her space immediately; he will not be put off even with a blunt "Get lost!" He thinks all women are little Barbie dolls equipped to satisfy his every whim. This man operates from a "Me Tarzan, you Jane" mentality. His desire to dominate and control is too great to allow any real intimacy to develop.

Yet I remember that when I was a child the image of the strong male held different associations for me. The macho ideal of my childhood was more of a gentle giant. Though tall, strong, and gruff in his John Wayne manner, he was not afraid to show emotion in his "manly" way. Yes, he was tough. But he was never openly condescending towards women, because roles were still definitely defined. He took charge of his wife and family, but he was paternal and at the same time respectful. He had that Jimmy Stewart twinkle of warmth that I remember seeing in the old movies. He represented security, he inspired trust, and he seemed open and genuine. These qualities are missing in today's macho male.

Questions for Discussion If you are a female reader, does this paper express views similar to your own? If you are a male reader, does the paper make you feel angry or defensive? Why or why not?

READING NOTES Learn to look at your reading with the writer's eye. Many professional writers keep a file of clippings and jottings that stores information, statistics, provocative comments, and revealing sidelights on topics in which they have a tentative interest. In reading a newspaper or newsmagazine, an experienced writer will often decide, "Let me write this down" or "I should make a photocopy of this page."

Suppose you are working on a paper that will explore the cult of the star athlete. You should be able to glean material like the following from a few days' reading of current newspapers and magazines.

PREWRITING: READING NOTES

Inflated salaries

- ❑ A *Time* article listed players signed to million-dollar-a-year contracts during the last year. Even such figures pale compared with the earnings of athletic superstars like quarterback Steve Young, who garnered a $40 million lifetime contract from the now defunct USFL and then went on to sign another $5 million contract in the NFL.
- ❑ Sports columnist Glen Dickey said that the signing of baseball great Jack Clark by the New York Yankees meant "a resumption of the giddy free-agent bidding that has sent player salaries through the roof."

The other side of the star system

- ❑ Arthur Ashe, first male black athlete to win the Wimbledon tennis tournament said in a widely quoted article in the *New York Times:* "For every star earning millions there are six or seven others making $20,000 or $30,000." Many others have their careers cut short by injuries. Most high school athletes never make it to the pros.

Parallel patterns in college athletics

- ❑ G. Ann Uhlir, dean at Texas Woman's University, says about women in college sports: "Opportunities for elite women athletes have improved, but total participation slots available for women have declined."

With notes such as these, you are well on the way toward a paper that will contrast the glamorous image of the star athlete created by the media with the sobering realities facing the rank and file. How formally you identify your sources will depend on the kind of paper you are writing. (On informal identification of sources, see Chapter 11, "READ/ WRITE: Writing from Sources." On full identification and description of sources in a formal research paper, see Chapter 18, "THE RESEARCH PAPER: From Search to Documentation.")

JOURNAL WRITING Many professional writers use **journals,** diaries, or logs to record impressions from day to day or from week to week. The entries in your journal might deal with family occasions, jobs, childhood memories, friendships, trips, personal problems, current reading, public events, or TV shows and movies. Journal entries are often personal and informal; they often mingle the important and the trivial, the ordinary and the unusual. Often, a writer will use such entries as raw materials for more formal, more structured kinds of writing. A candid snapshot, a vivid incident, or a passage of soul-searching in your journal can be the starting point for a paper.

A journal entry like the following could form the basis for a paper about the work ethic or about the needy.

PREWRITING: JOURNAL ENTRY

When I was sixteen years old, I worked for the Pope, in a manner of speaking. My first job was that of a part-time receptionist at the St. John rectory. The rectory, a Spanish-style building, white-washed and topped with a red tile roof, was the nerve center of the parish. As one of three part-time receptionists, I needed tact and courtesy, decent communication skills, and a basically friendly outlook toward the rest of humanity. My duties included answering the telephone and writing messages; stuffing, sealing, and organizing mountains of envelopes; running errands; closing the church at night; and often helping with the dishes. It wasn't a bad job for a sixteen-year-old. I also had free access to the refrigerator and baked goods. I performed my job with a happy-go-lucky attitude, but I was often troubled and surprised by the number of people who were in need of food and shelter. Before I worked at the rectory, I thought I had been living in a prosperous middle-class parish.

INTERVIEWS A good writer is likely to be a good listener. Often, you can learn much by talking to people close to your subject. If you are writing about how Americans like work, you might start by asking people you know. The quickest way to find out how ice cream is made may be to talk with the manager of a small ice cream plant in your neighborhood.

A good interviewer knows how to draw people out and how to lead them on. People turn eloquent when they can tell a sympathetic listener their grievances or when they can share their interest in a specialty or a hobby. Often the strategy of a good interviewer is to start with nonthreatening, factual questions motivated by genuine curiosity or by a genuine interest in the person being interviewed. Gradually, the interviewer can approach the more "loaded" questions that are likely to arouse or provoke—for instance, questions that touch on a sore point, on a favorite cause or hobby, on a damaging rumor or accusation, or on a long-standing grievance or complaint. If you are writing on the problems of the elderly, you may approach an interview with a *prepared set of questions* like the following:

- □ What did you do before you retired?
- □ How or why did you retire?
- □ What do you like most about retirement?
- □ What do you like least about retirement?
- □ What do you think about mandatory retirement?
- □ How is retirement different from what you expected?
- □ If you could turn the clock back twenty years, what would you do differently?
- □ Do young people today live in a different world?

Sometimes, you may write up the results of an interview in a *question-and-answer* format. In the following sample, a successful writer and editor comments candidly on her own writing habits.

WRITING SAMPLE: INTERVIEW

From an interview with Amy Gross

QUESTION: Where do you spend most of your writing time?
ANSWER: In revision.
QUESTION: Once you've done a draft, do you put the piece away?
ANSWER: No, I just sit there suffering, imagining what would happen if this were a lead, if that were a lead. I stare and stare, and now that I have a word processor, instead of retyping and retyping, I read and reread. I always wish that I had the time to put something away. I assume that time is the best editor.
QUESTION: Do you ever get stuck?
ANSWER: Always. And then I eat a lot; I used to gain five pounds an article. I'd go to the refrigerator, walk around; I'd feel it was hopeless, there was no point, why was I writing? I'd think I was stupid: I hated the sound of my own voice. And then I'd write some more.

But when I wrote my last piece, the first one I had done in a year, I felt tremendously excited. The writing—three quarters of it, anyway—is throwing stuff out. I would look at what I'd written and get ill at the boring, banal stuff my brain had done. I would sit there hating myself and what I had written. Then I would start to see the thread and how it linked the different beads of sections. It was thrilling to me, and I felt alive, engaged. Then I felt once again that I was temperamentally a writer. Writing is often sitting there waiting for my brain to make connections that I don't know.

You will often draw on interviews as part of a mix that may blend material from your experience and from a range of oral and printed sources. However, you may also devote a whole paper to the results of a fruitful interview. Study and discuss the following **interview paper** as a possible model:

WRITING SAMPLE: INTERVIEW PAPER

Picking Up Garbage

Gabriel was born the youngest of thirteen children. He grew up in the old country and has been in the United States for three years. Every morning he goes to his job in the waste land-fill area. When I ask him about his work, he says: "I used to pick up papers in the area. Everybody starts out with that job. Some people are able to save some money that way. Then they go back to the old country, drink and relax for a few months, and then, when they run out of money, come back here. They will always be picking up papers. I don't want to go back. I drive a truck now, and I crush the garbage. I save money."

I ask him about the place where he lives. He is not living with family. "It is a small place with fifteen people living there. I feel bad because we all sleep together in two rooms. I am the first one to go to work in the morning. So when my alarm goes off at 5:30 AM, everybody is disturbed. I feel bad that everybody wakes up because of the noise from my alarm. But what can I do? I have to work."

Gabriel spends little time at the place where he "lives." He usually works more than five days and goes to school four evenings a week. What does he like least about his job? He says that he does a lot of thinking while he drives the truck. "You know that the American people throw out many things. Much of it is good stuff. I see toys that are brand new. I see radios that are not broken. I see many things that I would like to send to people in my own country. But I cannot pick up any of the things. There is a rule. The driver is not allowed to get out of the truck."

I assume that the company is trying to protect the drivers' health by not letting them handle items from the garbage cans. But Gabriel says that the rule is intended for the driver's safety: Once a driver who climbed out of the truck to pick up something was run over by another driver who did not see him.

"A few times," Gabriel says, "I have taken the chance of losing my job. I got out and picked up a tape recorder once. I brought it home, and it worked perfectly. The Americans throw away so many things like that. It's like throwing away money. Americans are very rich. The people in my country are very poor. Every day I see good things thrown away, and it breaks my heart to crush them. I am destroying what my people could use."

I am looking at the job of the garbage collector from a different perspective since I talked to Gabriel. I used to think that the filth and the smell would bother me most about the job. I found that what bothers Gabriel most is the idea of looking at "waste" all day.

Questions for Discussion Does the person who was interviewed for this paper become real for you? Why or why not?

FREE ASSOCIATION Free association and stimulus-response writing are meant to help writers overcome writing blocks. If a blank sheet of paper has a paralyzing effect on you, you may need limbering-up exercises that make writing seem more natural. In true **freewriting,** you merely keep writing without stopping, putting down all ideas or images that come to mind. You push ahead filling the page. Later you may return to what you have written for ideas that seem worth following up.

In more focused free-association writing, you start with a definite stimulus. You may begin with a word like *old* or *adolescent* or *fear,* writing down the whole train of thoughts, memories, and associations set in motion by the word. The following train of association was started in one writer's mind by the word *old:*

PREWRITING: FREE ASSOCIATION

Old

Watching in the mirror for wrinkles. Bags under the eyes. Likely to break a hip— not enough calcium in the bones. No one wants the old people—shunt them off into nursing homes. Stench of ammonia; people sitting silently in wheelchairs. "Pneumonia is the elderly's best friend." Alzheimer's. Sitting by the phone—the children are gone and hardly ever call. America the country of the young. No room for the old in a Pepsi-Cola commercial.

The following writing sample uses most of this material in a finished paragraph:

WRITING SAMPLE: FINISHED PARAGRAPH

Old

I don't want to get old. No one wants to age, but aging is inevitable. Time gives us wrinkles, a bent posture, and fragile bones. It makes us insecure, forgetful, and fearful. The elderly can easily become a burden to the families they once provided for and protected. The children who once vied for their parents' attention are now so consumed with their own affairs that they hardly ever visit. For many elderly people, the stench of ammonia in the hospital-like atmosphere of a nursing home is worse than death. To some, it signifies loneliness, cruelty, and abandonment. With all the turmoil involved in the aging process, it is no wonder that we are becoming a nation of frightened adults, forever searching for that magical youth serum from the elusive fountain of youth.

CLUSTERING **Clustering** is a kind of free-association writing taught by Gabriele Rico in her book *Writing the Natural Way.* When clustering, a writer starts with a central stimulus word that becomes the core of the cluster. Different lines of association then branch out from the center. A network of images and thoughts takes shape that the writer then turns into a finished piece of writing. In clustering, the image-making, shaping, creative right brain can assert itself, overcoming the usual dominance of the analytical, linear left brain. The ideas called up by the clustering technique often arrange themselves into a satisfying pattern. Here is a sample cluster and the writing sample based on it:

PREWRITING: CLUSTERING

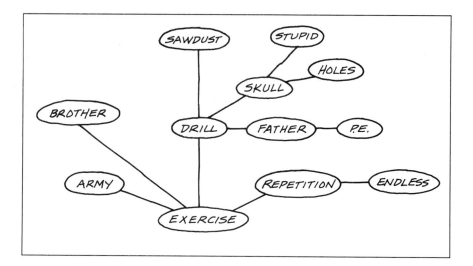

WRITING SAMPLE: FINISHED PARAGRAPH

Drill

Drill to me is a nightmare. I never minded arithmetic or grammar drills in school; I could do them, and they gave me a sense of security. But I can't think of those drills without a crowd of images bursting forth. I see my father bending close to my face saying with horrible enunciation: "Can't-you-drill-that-into-your-thick-skull?" At the same time I see an overlaid image of a real drill, drilling into plywood and showering sawdust everywhere. And I see, too, my brother in green, marching endlessly, with the drill sergeant barking orders at him. For good reason, the word *drill* rhymes with *kill*.

Remember: The techniques for working up material range from open and creative to focused and systematic. As you work up a subject, you need to keep your exploration open enough, so that you can discover important new material. But you also need to push your investigation in a definite direction.

THE WRITING WORKSHOP

Learning from Interviews

What can a writer learn from interviews? Work with a group to conduct interviews that would shed light on a subject of current debate. Coordinate strategy: Discuss the line of questioning the interviewers are going to use. Make plans for synthesizing the results and presenting them to the class. Sample topics:

☐ How well is the wave of new immigrants being assimilated? What is their background? What do they see as key differences between the old country and the new? What opportunities and what obstacles do they encounter in their adopted country? What could be done to help new immigrants become integrated into American society?

☐ Has the American public become blasé about corruption? (When questioned about scandals besetting his administration, the mayor of New York said, "Regrettably, corruption is endemic in our society"; there are "scandals everywhere.") Conduct interviews with a cross section of the public to determine voter opinions concerning the extent or seriousness of the problem, its causes and possible solutions.

☐ What is the nature of the current wave of religious feeling among young people? How is it different from old-fashioned or conventional religion? Plan interviews with people in a position to know: born-again students, cult members, counselors, ministers, professors of religious studies.

EXERCISE 1 *Brainstorming*

As a brainstorming exercise, jot down any ideas, memories, observations, or associations that come to mind on one of the following topics:

fitness	marijuana	Disneyland
beauty contests	public transport	rape prevention
health diets	game shows	drunk drivers
guns		

Keep writing—do not stop to think. Leave the sorting out of material for a later stage.

EXERCISE 2   *Taking Notes*

Examine several issues of newspapers and newsmagazines to study the coverage of a topic currently in the news. Take *detailed notes:* Summarize information, jot down striking details, condense key statistics, quote provocative comments by experts or insiders. Choose a topic like the following:

1. *The Congested Future:* traffic problems and solutions
2. *Women's Sports:* toward equality?
3. *Health Alert:* a health hazard currently in the news
4. *Call the Police:* police work in today's communities
5. *Troubled Youth:* young people in trouble with the law
6. *To Build or Not to Build:* development pro and con
7. *Schools in the Red:* supporting your local schools
8. *Domestic Violence:* battered wives or abused children
9. *Red Tape:* regulation and deregulation
10. *Crisis Coverage:* a crisis currently in the news

(Your instructor may ask you to work out a general conclusion and organize your material in a structured paper as you move on to study the next stage of the writing process.)

EXERCISE 3   *Starting a Journal*

Start a journal. Write in it regularly to record observations, thoughts, memories, or notes on current viewing and reading. Include the kind of detail that would provide promising raw material for future papers:

☐ graphic details on a *setting* where events take place
☐ capsule portraits of *people*
☐ dramatic highlights of *events*
☐ striking *quotations:* what people actually said
☐ your candid *reactions* or feelings (*how* you reacted, and also *why*)

EXERCISE 4   *Sampling Student Opinion*

Interview several students to sample student opinion on topics like the following:

☐ the politics of the student newspaper
☐ support for intercollegiate athletic competition

- □ part-time work while in college
- □ sexual harassment on campus
- □ support for minority students
- □ grading practices
- □ security on campus
- □ a current crisis or grievance

Ask questions that would bring out information about the students' backgrounds, their firsthand experience with the topic, major factors or events that shaped their opinions, their estimates of possible options or solutions, and the like.

EXERCISE 5 *Exploring Through Interviews*

Write a paper based on an interview that takes you *outside* your own familiar world. For instance, interview

- □ a police officer working in a high-crime neighborhood
- □ a security guard for a posh apartment complex
- □ the owners of a mom-and-pop grocery store
- □ an illegal immigrant
- □ a member of a religious cult
- □ a guard in a correctional institution
- □ a nurse or technician in a psychiatric ward
- □ a clerk in an adult bookstore

EXERCISE 6 *Stimulus Words*

From the following list, choose a word or phrase that is rich in meaning for you. Make sure it calls up memories or starts a train of thought. Let the word stimulate a flow of ideas and details from experience, hearsay, reading, or viewing. Do two things:

- □ Get your ideas and details down on paper by *free-association* writing or by *clustering* (letting your ideas branch out from the word as a central core).
- □ Write a substantial paragraph or longer passage in which you arrange your material in some kind of logical order or in a pattern that makes sense to you.

| rivals | sex education | alcohol |
| vandals | illness | the shore |

divorce	the city	independence
cheating	veterans	winning
the team	enemies	losing
accidents	the ballpark	jealousy
fights	gym	the farm
church	holidays	camp

THE STRUCTURED SEARCH

Experienced writers often develop techniques for systematic exploration of a subject. They answer a set of questions that cover different dimensions of the topic; they systematically fill in a number of slots. We call such a set of questions, or such a framework for systematic search and discovery, a **discovery frame**. Suppose you are writing a paper to define *affirmative action*. You might ask yourself a set of questions like the following: What does the dictionary say? Is there a legal or official definition (used by campus hiring committees, for instance)? Where and how have I seen it treated in the media? Where has the subject come up in my own experience? What is the history or historical background of the term? What are some related or similar terms (*antidiscrimination, equal opportunity*), and how are they different? What is the common denominator in the different examples or case histories I have encountered? Answering such questions will give you plenty of material to work with, while at the same time the sequence of questions already points to a tentative plan of organization for the finished paper. You are working up material for your paper in a structured, organized way.

The Journalistic Formula

A familiar example of a discovery frame is the traditional journalistic formula for news reports:

- *Who* was involved?
- *What* happened?
- *When* and *where* did it happen?
- *Why* did things happen as they did?
- *How* did things happen or how were they done?

Often the lead sentence of a news report will answer all of these questions, telling us who, what, when, where, why, and how:

Late last night, 400 chanting protesters were arrested by riot police at the Las Manes testing grounds after they tried to storm the main gate to protest the resumption of nuclear tests.

The reporter can then go on to answer each of the questions in greater detail in subsequent paragraphs.

Using Discovery Frames Use discovery frames to guide your search for material. Work with the sample frames provided in this book; then use them as models when you construct similar frames for the systematic exploration of other topics. Suppose you have been asked to write a paper on a current trend. Is it a passing fad? Or does it reflect some lasting, long-range change in our society? A discovery frame like the following can help you produce a paper that may start with surface symptoms or general impressions but that will go *beyond* them. For your preliminary collection of material on the fitness fad, you might write responses to questions in the following five categories:

PREWRITING: DISCOVERY FRAME

The Fitness Fad

1. *Surface Symptoms:* Where do you see telltale signs of the current fitness craze? What signs do you see in your neighborhood or on campus? How is it reflected in current advertising and, more generally, in the media? (For instance, how aware are you of runners on streets and highways, of ads for exercise bikes and rowing machines and running shoes, of health clubs and aerobics classes?)

2. *Firsthand Exposure.* Are you yourself a participant or merely an observer? Have you had a chance to take a close-up view at people seriously involved? (For instance, do you have close friends or family members who have taken up running, weight lifting, or aerobic dancing? What do they do? What do they say?)

3. *Background Facts:* In your studies or reading, what facts have you encountered concerning the physical benefits of popular kinds of activity or exercise? What do the experts say about such benefits as weight control, stress reduction, or the prevention of heart disease? What are the comparative advantages of different kinds of activity? (For instance, is it true that one hour of running produces the same health benefits as three hours of walking?)

4. *Deeper Causes:* What are some of the underlying causes of the cult of physical fitness? What are revealing slogans, or what are key ideas in the mystique that surrounds it? (For instance, what is a "natural high"? Are we observing a reaction against a mechanized and plastic culture and a return to physical and biological basics? Is keeping in shape a natural ideal for the me generation?)

5. *Doubts or Second Thoughts:* What warnings by medical authorities have you read about the dangers of the fitness craze? What do doctors say about the need for stress tests and for medical supervision in general?

As you gather material under these five headings, you may conclude that the current fitness movement is more than a fad; it is part of a search for physical and mental health that for many has become a kind of substitute religion. It feeds on powerful built-in psychological incentives and rewards. The discovery frame you used already suggests a workable strategy for the paper that will support this conclusion: Your paper is likely to move from amusing surface impressions to a close look at what the movement means in practice and finally to an exploration of its underlying causes and the needs that it serves. The more ambitious your writing project, the more you will profit from a discovery frame guiding your search for material.

Questions for Discussion If you were writing on the fitness topic, how would you fill in the slots in the discovery frame? Which of the questions do you think would lead you to promising material? Should there be additional slots for other dimensions of the topic?

The questions that help you discover material will vary from one paper to another. Questions like the following will help you work up material for some familiar writing tasks:

COMPARISON AND CONTRAST:	How are two things alike? How are they different?
PROCESS:	What is the purpose of the process? What materials or equipment are needed? What are the major steps? What is the end result?
PRO AND CON:	What are the arguments in favor? What are the opposing arguments? What is reasonable common ground?

Remember: Working up material and organizing it are not distinct separate stages. You will continue to work up material and feed it into your paper after you start the actual writing. As your first draft takes shape, you may feel the need for additional examples. You may remember a relevant quotation and stop to look it up; you may notice a gap in your evidence and search for supporting facts and figures. When a project gains momentum, the different phases of the writing process blend and overlap.

WRITING TOPICS 5   *Using a Discovery Frame*

Observers of the American scene have often speculated about key traits in the American national character. Prepare a *preliminary collection* of material on the role one of these traits plays in American life as you know it. Americans have often prided themselves on or been criticized for traits like the following:

rugged individualism	naiveté
Yankee ingenuity	deadpan humor
being a good neighbor	the bonanza mentality
optimism	good will
the work ethic	informality

Choose *one* of these traits that has a special meaning for you. What evidence do you see of it? Is it a thing of the past? Has it always been a myth? Has it changed? Has something else taken its place? Work up preliminary material for a paper that would answer these or similar questions. Write two or three paragraphs under each of the following headings, or under those you consider most applicable:

1. *The Media:* What role does a traditional belief in optimism or goodwill, for instance, play in newspaper stories, *Reader's Digest* articles, popular television programs, or movies? What kind of news story or entertainment reflects the traditional belief? What evidence of any countertrend or current change might a careful media watcher detect?

2. *Traditional Lore:* What role did the traditional idea play in official pronouncements? For instance, have you encountered traditional ideas about the work ethic in political speeches, campaign literature, graduation oratory, or high school textbooks? Is the trait you are investigating reflected in American folklore or symbolized by any American folk heroes?

3. *Personal Experience:* Has the traditional trait influenced people in your own family? For instance, do you have relatives who incline toward optimism or positive thinking? Are you an optimist? Or has there been a strong opposite tendency in your family or personal history?

4. *Current Observation:* For instance, how informal is the life around you compared with what you know about life in other times and places? How informal is the style of neighbors, friends, and fellow students? How do they act and talk? How formal or informal are their customs, ceremonies, living arrangements?

5. *Previous Reading and Study:* Have you read any books in which faith in individualism, for instance, came in for a searching look? Have you ever taken a course that traced or questioned the trait you are studying? Where, for example, have you encountered the bonanza mentality (the hope of striking it rich) as a major theme of a novel or play?

Your instructor may ask you to work out a general conclusion and organize your material in a structured paper as you move on to the next stages of the writing process.

4

SHAPING

Working Out a Plan

Good writing imposes some kind of human order on chaos. Frank D'Angelo

We write to find out what we think. Even when doing something as simple as writing in a journal—intellectual doodling—you're figuring out things. Writing is a way of laying things out. You write to find out what you think, what you know, and what you don't know. Larry Heinemann

There is excitement in the very act of composition. Some of you know this at first hand—a deep satisfaction when the thing begins to take shape. Catherine Drinker Bowen

PLANNING AND DRAFTING How does a paper take shape? Sooner or later, we need to push beyond the stage of exploration and discovery; we need to organize our thinking. Even while we are taking notes or conducting an interview, we ask ourselves: "What does this prove? How does this fit in? What use am I going to make of this?" We do not just accumulate information; like a tax accountant feeding data into a computer, we set up a system that will make the material accessible, that will help us retrieve the material and put it to use. Even while gathering the material for a paper, you will start sorting it out. You will be working out a strategy for putting it to use; you will map out the route that will take you and your readers from the beginning to the end.

What is going to be your strategy for laying out your material? How will you chart a course that your readers can follow without becoming discouraged by detours and dead ends? Allow time for the answers to these questions to take shape. Give your ideas a chance to sort themselves out. Many writers try out different patterns or strategies in their minds till they hit on the one that seems natural for the subject or tailor-made for what they are trying to do. They shuffle pages or note cards, arranging them in tentative patterns. They scratch one trial outline and do another.

Once you have a tentative master plan worked out in your mind (or on paper), you can start your rough draft. Often a writer will already have bits and pieces or whole sections roughed out before the grand design for a paper or article has really taken shape. You may push ahead, following your tentative outline until you have completed a continuous first draft. Or you may draft key sections of a paper first, attending later to introduction and conclusion or to especially difficult parts.

Remember that a well-organized paper has pulled together material that was at first confusing or contradictory. It has funneled evidence into conclusions that you can support. The finished paper moves through stages that you can outline and that will make sense to the reader.

Questions for Discussion When you write, how much tentative putting together of sentences and paragraphs goes on in your head? When you start putting words on paper or on the screen, do you push ahead with one continuous first draft? Or do you work with bits and pieces that combine later?

MOVING TOWARD A THESIS
Although not applicable in all kinds of writing, a powerful tool for organizing related material is the unifying **thesis,** or central idea. When you state your thesis, you take a stand. In one sentence (or sometimes in two or three related sentences), you stake out a claim. You answer the central question your paper raises; you sum up your solution to the problem it has identified. In effect, you tell your reader: "This is what I have found. This is what I think. This is what I mean to show."

A thesis does not merely map out a topic; it sums up what you have to say:

TOPIC: Attitudes of young Americans toward work
THESIS: Young Americans today rarely find work in which they can take personal pride.

TOPIC: The treatment of youth in American advertising
THESIS: American advertising promotes a cult of youth that makes older people seem irrelevant and unwanted.

How do you move toward a unifying thesis? Often, you will start with a tentative idea, a working hypothesis—something you want to prove or hope to find. You then adjust your thinking in the light of what you discover as you explore your subject; you fine-tune your tentative thesis to fit the facts. For instance, you may be writing about the image of the family in current television entertainment. A close look at current programming may confirm your original theory: The idyllic nuclear family of *Leave It to Beaver* days—a breadwinner, a homemaker, siblings, and a dog—is largely gone. On the other hand, you find that some of the spirit of the earlier programs survives: We still encounter the long-suffering, patient parent and the naïve but smart-alecky teenager, for instance. Your final thesis may be that the physical makeup of the television family has changed, but that some of its sentimental clichés remain.

With other projects, you may start closer to the beginning. Exploring the subject of math anxiety, for example, you may truly need to start with an open mind: Is it a myth? If not, what accounts for it? Does it affect male and female students differently? What is the cure? Remember that to write an honest paper you have to leave your tentative ideas open to revision. You have to make your conclusions fit the evidence, gradually making up your own mind.

Raising the Issue

One way to arrive at a unifying thesis is to raise a key question that your paper will answer. Be alert to a central question that may emerge as you study an intriguing subject or as you become interested in a controversy.

> KEY QUESTION: Some critics charge that the true Olympic spirit has been killed by the onslaught of commercialism. Does this charge seem to be true?
>
> KEY QUESTION: Heroes in comic books used to look "all-American," fair-complexioned, white; villains used to look foreign, "ethnic." Has this pattern changed?

Often, the introduction to an article raises such a key question by challenging a familiar point of view:

Speedway

1982, the violent death of driver Gordon Smiley at Indianapolis started a cascade of objections to motor racing. In *Time*, Tom Callahan deplored the whole Indy enterprise: "Some 450,000 people," he wrote, "will perch or picnic at the Speedway on Sunday. Nobody knows how many of them are ghouls spreading their blankets beside a bad intersection." . . . George Vecsey, in the sports pages of *The New York Times*, suggested that the Indy race is becoming too dangerous to be regarded as a sport.

Key question   *Were these people right?* Is the Indy 500 a sporting event, or is it something else? And if something else, is it evil or benign?   Paul Fussell, *Atlantic*

The more pointed your key question, the more likely it is to unify your paper. Avoid questions like "What are *some* of the features that make daytime television drama successful?" Use more focused questions like "What are the *key features* . . .?" or "What is *the most important* ingredient of . . .?"

TOO OPEN: What are some of the stereotypes about police officers that current crime shows perpetuate?

POINTED: Do crime shows on television perpetuate the stereotype of vindictive police officers who take the law into their own hands?

Finding the Common Thread

A thesis emerges naturally from a body of material when we encounter various examples that point in the same direction. At first, they may seem isolated examples, but we come to see that they are part of a pattern. Suppose a reporter is investigating problems in the workplace caused by the influx of workers who are part of a new wave of immigration. Repeatedly, he or she encounters situations like the following:

PREWRITING: INVESTIGATOR'S NOTES

Culture Shock

Coworkers are upset because a newcomer never shows interest in what they say, either by facial expressions or the occasional "I see" or "Oh" that they expect. (In the new employee's homeland, a good listener shows politeness by remaining sober-faced and silent.)

A bank starts a promotional campaign focused on "friendly tellers." It runs into trouble because several of the tellers are foreign-born Filipino women who feel that overly friendly behavior makes them seem like "loose women."

Part of being friendly in a typical American office is to participate in chitchat about sports (football, baseball). Newcomers unfamiliar with the finer points of such sports often feel left out.

These and similar observations point to a common pattern: Problems arise not because there is something wrong with the person but because a culture gap exists. The thesis that pulls together these various related observations might read like this:

THESIS: Misunderstandings between recent immigrants and their coworkers often result not from personality problems but from cultural differences.

In the finished article, this thesis might appear after an introduction that dramatizes the issue by recounting a striking example of cross-cultural misunderstanding. The body of the article would then trace the common thread in many at first random observations.

Reconciling Opposites Obviously, the material for a paper does not always point in one direction. (A writer's life would be easier if it did!) Often a thesis takes shape as we try to reconcile different opinions, as we balance conflicting claims and demands. Opinion on a subject may have moved from one extreme to the other, and we try to find middle ground. For example, many people are disheartened by the shortcomings of both traditional and modern marriage. On the one hand, many found traditional marriage stifling and authoritarian. On the other hand, for many, modern marriages proved traumatic, frustrating, and short. The following outline starts with the thesis that aims at finding middle ground; the rest of the outline shows the weighing of opposite extremes that led up to a balanced conclusion.

PREWRITING: TENTATIVE OUTLINE

Does Your Marriage Have a Future?

TRIAL THESIS: The ideal marriage of the future will combine the best and avoid the worst of the marriages of the past.

(Stage One) The traditional marriage of the past
- lifelong commitment (divorce as a scandal)
- man as head of household/woman as helpmate
- man as breadwinner/woman as homemaker

(Stage Two) The short-term marriage of the present
- provisional commitment (frequent divorce)
- contested responsibilities
- independent careers for women
- children as inconvenience

(Stage Three) The "hybrid" marriage of the future
- permanent commitment (beyond "me-first")
- joint decisions
- planned parenthood
- shared domestic duties

Formulating Your Thesis Your thesis is the weightiest part of your paper, and you will want to give it special thought, the way you would to a pledge you sign or a resolution you put before a group. Consider the following guidelines:

- *Make your thesis add up what you have found.* Your thesis should do justice to what your investigation has uncovered, to what your reading and thinking has led you to believe. Suppose you have observed students in wheelchairs on your campus. You have seen ramps and special elevators being built. You have watched a blind instructor demonstrate a special computer that helps her read and write. You have read about how schools cope with laws requiring them to mainstream students with special needs. Everything you have observed and read will funnel into your thesis.

THESIS: Everywhere, students with physical disabilities are playing a more visible and independent role.

☐ *Try presenting your thesis early in your paper.* The early thesis helps your readers find their bearings; it keeps them from grumbling, "What is this all about?" Often your reader will be ready for your main point after a brief introduction that raises the issue or brings the topic into focus:

The Flip Side of the Coin

introduction What do people envision when they hear about the "Americanizing" influence of education? Most likely, they envision a youngster who can barely speak English but who, after a few years of school, speaks fluent American and shares all the tastes and dislikes of his peers. This stereotype is not always true, though. *Many young Americans continue to speak a second language on the playground and at home, and they retain many of the ways of their own group.*

thesis

Often, the conclusion of such a paper circles back to the beginning: It echoes or reinforces the thesis in some way. Note that no law requires a writer to state a strong thesis early in a paper. In dealing with a much-debated or emotion-laden subject, you may decide to start with a pointed question and take the reader along in the search for the answer. Such a paper may lead up to a **final thesis** stated as a well-earned conclusion; it may state the main point when the reader is ready to agree. (See Chapters 12 and 13 for the use of the final thesis in definition and argument.)

☐ *Think of your thesis as a promise to the reader.* A good thesis serves as a program for the paper as a whole. It creates the expectations that the rest of your paper will satisfy. Suppose your thesis reads as follows:

THESIS: Nineteenth-century American fiction often lacks strong female characters.

To keep your promise to the reader, you would have to look at several striking examples. Key paragraphs in your paper might center on examples like the following:

first example In Mark Twain's *Huckleberry Finn*, the aunt is left behind, and the story revolves around the boy, his father, and Jim, the runaway slave. . . .

second example In Melville's *Moby Dick*, we follow Ishmael and the all-male crew of the whaling ship in pursuit of the White Whale. . . .

third example In Cooper's Leatherstocking novels, we move in a frontier world of hunters and scouts and braves. . . .

THE WRITING WORKSHOP

Writing a Review

In a well-focused movie review, a reviewer will often make a central point that becomes the thesis of the review. We then expect the rest of the review to support that central point. The thesis may sum up the reviewer's *evaluation* of the film—a judgment of its value or appeal. Or the thesis may crystallize the reviewer's *interpretation*—stating a point essential to our understanding of the meaning or intention of the movie. The following passage sums up the central point of a review unified by a strong central thesis:

> *Rambo* is not just one more guts-and-glory series of impossible exploits. It's a statement of political beliefs, genuinely held or cynically utilized. America lost the Vietnam War but could not have lost it fairly: Americans don't lose fairly fought wars. They must have been betrayed—by elements in the government and the public that are still manipulating and betraying. The Vietnam experience bred a corps of veterans who are stalwart, long-suffering, deeply resentful. (Of course *Rambo* was made before the many recent moves to restore veterans' morale.) If given the chance, they can and will prove that history is not a closed book.   Stanley Kauffmann, *The New Republic*

Find a recent review unified by a strong central thesis. For presentation to a small group or your class as a whole, prepare a report that answers the following questions:

- What is the central point or thesis of the review? Where is it stated; where is it echoed or reinforced? (Does the reviewer express any reservations or qualifications that would modify or complicate the central point? Where?)
- How does the reviewer follow up the central thesis? What kind of details support it? Which details are especially telling or effective, and why?

(Your instructor may ask you to write a similar review of a current box-office success, unifying your review around a central thesis.)

□ *Experiment with making your thesis a preview of your overall plan.* An effective thesis often hints at the outline of the paper; it maps out the itinerary that the reader is to follow:

THESIS: Contrary to the stereotype of student apathy, political opinion on campus is a three-ring circus featuring the aggressive young conservative, the well-meaning liberal, and the activist radical left.

(Comment: The reader will expect key sections illustrating each of these three categories.)

Questions for Discussion How good are you at summing up basic claims or assumptions in pointed statements? Can you sum up in two or three statements key ideas or basic tenets of a group to which you belong, a political movement with which you sympathize, or a scientific movement that you have studied?

Remember: Your thesis may appear early in your finished paper, but it often does not take final shape until late in the process of drafting and revision. After you finish your first draft, you may decide to go back to your thesis to add an essential if or but. You may decide to tone down a negative judgment that seems too harsh on second thought. Many writers have to write their way through the material at least once before they can be sure what they think.

EXERCISE 1   *Thesis and Support*

Study and evaluate each of the following statements as the possible thesis for a short paper. Answer the following questions about each:

□ What kind of support does the thesis need? What kind of follow-up does it make you expect? What would it take to make you respect or accept the writer's point of view?
□ If you were writing on the same subject, how would you change the thesis to make it reflect your own point of view? On what grounds would you quarrel with the original? *Rewrite* three or more of the statements to make them reflect your own point of view.

1. The American nightmare is that someday every car in the world will be made by Toyota.
2. The self-service gas station points toward a future where service to the customer will be increasingly hard to find.

3. The typical amusement park has become an artificial wonderland of plastic smiles, faked nostalgic settings, and regimented crowds.

4. A woman attacked in the streets should be allowed to use a gun in self-defense.

5. The great whales have become a symbol of wildlife threatened with extinction by heedless humanity.

6. The last thing we expect on the evening news is pictures of normal, happy people.

7. Institutional food is better than its reputation.

8. Young people hate to be identified as members of a minority—as someone who is different and likely to be a "problem."

9. Fear of violence restricts the activities of many Americans.

10. Earlier immigrants were eager to assimilate; many new immigrants are proud of their separate identity.

EXERCISE 2   *Working Toward a Thesis*

The following is one student's preliminary collection of material for a paper on the topic "Is Prejudice on the Decline?" What thesis do you think might emerge from this unsorted, unedited material? What general conclusion might it suggest?

Our country recently celebrated its first national holiday honoring a black American. The newspapers and the television news were full of this momentous event. The president of the United States gave a speech in which he paid tribute to the great Martin Luther King. The bitterness of King's struggle seemed to be ancient history.

South African blacks look to America for support in their struggle. It is easy for Americans to take sides. Students finally have a cause in South African apartheid. We seem not to understand the immoral position of South African whites—as if white Americans never shared those feelings of superiority.

Several of my son's close friends are black. This makes me happy and eases the conscience of a liberal mother who feels bad that she brought up her son in a predominantly white neighborhood. One night my son and I watch a situation comedy about a liberal white woman who dates a black man and then feels very self-conscious about it. She wonders if she is prejudiced. My son says he can't relate to that at all. He never even thinks about his black friends being black.

He tells me the people he and all his friends (including his black friends) really hate are Asians. "They live in these big, fancy houses up on the hill and they've got Mercedes lined up on the streets. It really makes me sick. They don't even speak English."

I begin to see special reports on television about the new prejudice against Asians. The local newspaper reports Asians are the new minority. I make an effort to help these recent Americans. I eat in Vietnamese restaurants. I buy flowers at a little stand run by a Vietnamese family. I hire a Vietnamese gardener when I can spare the money. When he first comes, we go around the yard and I point out how I like shrubs and vines cut. He is interested in my herbs which are very different than those the Vietnamese use. We get through the language barrier nicely. I feel good to be giving him work. When he comes back two weeks later, I notice my four-month-old kitten playing in the freshly trimmed branches. This cat is my favorite pet of all time. He has the personality of a puppy. I remember a horrible joke about how many ways there are to wok a cat. I know it's dumb; I know it's prejudiced. But, then again, I don't really know anything about the Vietnamese culture. I don't know for a fact they don't eat cats. I go outside and very nonchalantly pick up the cat and bring him inside.

EXERCISE 3   *Formulating a Thesis*

Select five of the following subjects. For each, formulate a *thesis* that you could support in a short paper. Look back over observations, experiences, and readings that are relevant to each topic you have chosen. What conclusions do they justify? Make sure that your thesis does not merely map out an area or raise a question but takes a stand. For each thesis you formulate, be prepared to do the following:

- Explain how you would *support* or defend your thesis.
- Listen to and try to answer *questions* or objections from your classmates. Do these questions make you modify or strengthen your thesis?

1. Parents in current situation comedy
2. Toys as a reflection of American values
3. Changing images of women in current American movies
4. The family in current television commercials
5. Newspaper coverage of crime
6. The typical or average student on your campus
7. Teachers' attitudes toward minority students
8. Adolescents in current television commercials
9. Changing images of native Americans in current movies or television programs
10. Idealism on campus—passé or alive
11. The decline of good manners
12. The arts—frills or essentials
13. Beauty pageants
14. Guns for self-defense
15. Pornography in the campus bookstore

GETTING ORGANIZED   Composition is a Latin word that means "putting it together." The difference between the first raw collection of material and a finished piece of writing is like the difference between noise and music or between piles of construction materials and the finished house. The most creative stage of writing is to organize what was at first shapeless, to lay out the material in an order that makes sense. When you organize a paper, you work out the structure, the design, that is to writing what the blueprint is to the house, the story line to the story, the layout to the full-page ad, or the architect's vision to St. Peter's Square.

Your Organizing Strategy   A successful paper has a strategy that gives it shape and direction. It has a master plan or grand design that you could map out for your reader: "First I pinpoint the problem . . . then I anticipate familiar misconceptions . . . then I zero in on the root cause . . . which leads me to a promising solution." A successful organizing strategy creates a momentum that carries the reader from the beginning to the conclusion. It sets up a pattern of expectations: Your readers will be ready for your next point before you get there.

How do you develop an organizing strategy that will work for you? Pushing toward a unifying thesis and shaping the overall pattern go hand in hand. Often your thesis and your plan of organization will take shape together as you try to do justice to your material. Often your thesis will begin to crystallize as you start to get your material under control, as the pieces of the puzzle start to fall into place. Contrary to what "Writing-Made-Easy" books imply, there is no simple one-size-fits-all way of organizing a paper—but there are basic organizing strategies that writers again and again adapt to their own use.

CHRONOLOGY   Some papers more or less write themselves; the subject seems to come with a built-in pattern for the writer to follow. In much how-to writing—directions, instructions—the nature of the task guides the writer. For example, you may move from the choice of flour and other ingredients through the steps that produce good pasta. **Chronology**—step-by-step progression in time—may also guide writing projects that are more ambitious. Isaac Asimov once said that as a science writer he liked to start from the original mistaken notions, move forward to the questions they left unanswered, then explore some of the answers given by early scientists, and finally arrive at the modern theory that best fits the available facts.

EXEMPLIFICATION   Helpful as chronology is, part of your agenda as a writer is to become weaned from it—to modify it to suit your purpose, to move from chronological to logical order. Some other organizing strategies also stay very close to the way we chart our way in the world, to basic ways of organizing experience. We often get a handle on what is happening around us by grouping together parallel examples—examples that all point in the same direction. When these are funneled into a thesis that sums up the pattern, they provide the substance of the basic **thesis-and-support** paper that starts with the general point and then backs it up with a convincing array of examples. For instance, one student wrote about the gentrification (or yuppification) of what had been a tranquil rural riverfront. The writer complained that for the new owners the small creatures living in this habitat were not wildlife to be cherished but the target of "pest control." In the body of the paper, a series of observations that had shaken the writer over a period of time furnished the examples backing up his indictment. Different sections of the paper described the new residents' warfare against the beavers (who might damage trees), the muskrats (who might nest in the styrofoam used to float boat docks), the groundhogs (who might burrow in the high-priced riverfront), and the owls (whose hoots might disturb the new residents in their slumber).

Exemplification—laying down a barrage of convincing examples to substantiate a central point—often combines with other strategies to shape a piece of writing. In a column titled "An Educational Wait," columnist Jeff Greenfield starts by describing his harried, pressured mood—thinking about deadlines, a trip, shopping—as he sat in a hospital waiting room, waiting for word on his wife's knee operation. The first major example of what he observed, setting up a pattern to be repeated later in the column, reads in part like this:

A young boy, not more than four years old, his eyes alive with mischievous good humor, kept racing back and forth, to the distraction of his mother. He would have gone a lot farther, but he kept having to maneuver his wheelchair past a lot of obstacles. . . .

Then I remembered one of the chores that had put me in a rotten mood: I had to plan a shopping trip to buy a bicycle for my daughter. . . .

We are not surprised that a second major example points in the same direction—and that it again sets up a *contrast* between other people's real problems and his own superficial worries.

A few moments later, a family gathering assembled in the lobby: two middle-age couples and an older woman. From their urgent conversation, it was clear that the older woman's husband had been rushed into surgery. . . .

I thought about how angry I was at the quality of the cable reception on our bedroom TV set.

As the columnist continues this pattern of the misfortune of others contrasted with his own petty worries, many of his readers will be ready to agree with his central point: Affluent Americans live in a culture that makes them oblivious to the suffering of others, that makes them lose their sense of gratitude.

SETTING UP A SCALE   Some organizing strategies are especially effective in moving a paper forward, in getting the reader ready for the next step. Readers are predisposed to follow along as a writer moves from the least to the most desirable alternative, from the least to the most likely hypothesis, from the simple economy model to the elegant specialty version for the connoisseur. Our minds are used to moving up or down a scale; we are used to sorting things out by rating them, ranking them on a scale.

Suppose a baseball fan, in trying to champion his favorite sport, has become interested in the issue of violence in sports. He arranges his supporting material under three major headings:

- ☐ Boxing is an extreme example of a *violent sport*. Although sportswriters talk about a boxer's skill, spectators come to see a slugger; they want to see the knockout.
- ☐ Football is a violent sport *masked as a contest of skill*. Although it is called a contact sport, it is really a collision sport.
- ☐ Baseball is the *most civilized* of the major spectator sports. Although there are injuries in baseball, the spectator's attention is focused on the skill, the strategy, the beauty of the sport.

PROBLEM TO SOLUTION   Perhaps the most effective strategy for capturing and steering the reader's attention is to move from problem to solution, from an urgent question to a needed answer. If the strategy is successful, the reader, instead of feeling like a captive audience being preached at, can feel like an active participant in the search.

In the following overview of a paper that goes from problem to solution, note the italicized links, or **transitions,** that lead the reader from one step to the next.

WRITING SAMPLE: PROBLEM TO SOLUTION

Overworked and Underpaid

thesis   Day-care workers will remain underpaid unless not only parents but government agencies and employers assume their part of the responsibility.

basic problem   Day-care workers who care for preschoolers in a good program do much the same work as kindergarten teachers but are likely to be paid much less. . . .

misunderstanding corrected   *Contrary to what one might expect,* substandard salaries are not limited to financially strapped centers in poor neighborhoods. In the brightly painted, profit-making centers that dot suburban highways the pay can be just as low. . . .

key question   Why are the wages of day-care workers so low? *For one thing,* the job has

traditional cause

traditionally been considered woman's work. *In the past,* older women seeking only to supplement their husband's incomes were not deterred by the paltry wages. . . .

first current cause

Today, the basic economics of running a center put the squeeze on wages. *In the first place,* many centers must meet state-mandated teacher-student ratios and still charge fees that parents can afford. . . .

second current cause

In the second place, large day-care chains attract customers by clean classrooms, cheery decor, and impressive toys and playground equipment. Their ability to provide these attractions depends on their ability to keep wages very low. . . .

possible solutions

What is the answer? To raise salaries, day-care centers need higher fees from parents, or increased state aid, or contributions from corporations helping pay for day care for the children of their employees.

partial answer

Certainly, some parents could afford to pay higher fees. . . .

objection

However, in most families the cost of child care takes an enormous chunk out of the family income. . . .

second alternative

As a result, parents have concentrated their efforts on getting state legislatures to provide increased support. . . .

recent development

Only recently have large corporations faced the need of helping their employees provide for satisfactory care. . . .

Question for Discussion In a well-organized paper, the writer often keeps us moving forward by using connections that we are ready to make, such as rich—poor, then—now, expectation—reality, private—public, or professional—amateur. Where and how does the writer of the day-care paper use such links to help organize the paper?

Later chapters of this book will ask you to study and put to use other classic organizing strategies that writers employ to bring order out of confusion:

- tracing a process
- comparison and contrast
- classification
- analyzing cause and effect
- weighing the pro and con

Remember that you do not take down a workable plan of organization ready-made from a rack. Instead, you work out the pattern that fits the task, that helps you make your point. You make sure it takes your audience in the right direction. Often you will adapt or combine classic organizing strategies to make them serve your purpose.

From Trial Outline to Final Outline

Writers again and again employ organizing strategies that mirror the way our minds process information. But writers differ greatly in the procedures they employ while doing the sorting and charting that produces an organized paper. Some do most or all of their outlining in their heads; some work with minimal scratch outlines; some write their first draft from an exact detailed point-by-point outline they have prepared. (And some write step by step to specifications prepared by someone else.)

In your own writing, you are likely to find that flexible working outlines, frequently updated and adjusted like the timetable for a satellite launch, are indispensable. Your first scratch outline may simply consist of a few scribbled key words. But soon you are likely to need a more detailed working outline to guide you in the process of gathering and sorting out material.

A working outline is not like the architect's finished blueprint for a house, where every door, hallway, sink, and kitchen cabinet are already in place. Think of your working outline as a **trial outline**—a first rough sketch that helps you see how things might fit together and how they might have to be shifted around. Suppose you are writing a paper on the roots of the regulations that ensnarl us in our overregulated society. Your first trial outline may predictably focus on the role of government and Big Brother agencies:

- □ regulation by legislation:
     speed limit
     seat belts/air bag
- □ regulation by government agencies:
     HEW: sexual imbalance in college sports
     special traffic lanes

As you explore the subject further, you may decide to add to your outline a third category that is sometimes overlooked:

- □ regulation as the result of citizen initiatives:
     nonsmoking sections in restaurants

As your paper assumes more definite shape, your trial outline may develop into a final outline in which all divisions and subdivisions are clearly worked out. A final outline is often a well worked-out chart, a detailed guide to the organization of a finished paper. The more substantial your paper, or the more ambitious your project, the more you may need a detailed outline that allows you to check the flow of your discussion or argument.

Suppose you are studying the appeals advertisers use to attract the consumer. You conclude that again and again ads and commercials promise to make the customer's wishful thinking come true. In your trial outline, you group together those examples that seem to illustrate a similar kind of wishful thinking. You set up tentative categories like the following:

PREWRITING: TRIAL OUTLINE

- □ attracting the other sex:
  toothpaste commercials
  deodorants (?)
  fashions
- □ status seeking:
  car commercials
  real estate ads
- □ the easy way:
  push-button appliances

As you look over your trial outline, you decide that ads for deodorants do not fit well under your "wishful thinking" heading. Such ads do not really promise to make us attractive; they promise to make us less offensive. They play on our fear of rejection. In your finished outline, you include a second major section devoted to ads that exploit such basic fears and anxieties. Using traditional outline format, your finished outline might look like this. (See Chapter 6 for more on the format of formal outlines.)

PREWRITING: FORMAL OUTLINE

The Art of Advertising

THESIS: Much American advertising appeals to a few ulterior motives and basic anxieties.

I. Ulterior motives
    A. Attracting the other sex
        1. Toothpaste commercials
        2. Cigarette ads
    B. Status seeking
        1. Car commercials
        2. Real estate ads
    C. Looking for the easy way
        1. Commercials for push-button appliances
        2. Commercials for "miracle" cleansers
II. Basic anxieties
    A. The fear of rejection
        1. Deodorant commercials
        2. Commercials for antidandruff shampoos
    B. The fear of disaster
        1. Life insurance advertising
        2. Accident insurance advertising

Remember: A successful paper has a plan. You have worked out a structure that you can chart or outline. You have developed a rationale

THE WRITING WORKSHOP

A Planning Report

Our personal experience seems miscellaneous as it happens from day to day. But often when we look back years later, we notice a pattern. For instance, have you gone through several stages or phases in your attitude toward parents, school, relatives, church, police, sports, camping, or immigrants?

Choose one of these or a similar topic. Write a planning report sketching out how a paper tracing several stages or phases would shape up. Share your report with members of a small group or with your class as a whole: Explain or defend your plan; respond to the queries and comments of your fellow writers.

Use the following preliminary report by a student writer as a possible model.

Empty Rituals—Vain Ceremonies?

stage 1   I have been on several sides of the argument over ritual and ceremony. As a child, like most children, I happily dressed up for special occasions and went through the familiar rituals of special holidays. Each Thanksgiving and each Christmas followed the same prescribed pattern.

stage 2   In high school, however, I soon adopted the view that most public ceremonies were meaningless charades carried on by mindless idiots. They showed people's inability to think for themselves, their tendency to operate on automatic pilot in accordance with some prescribed pattern set up by society. It seemed that no intelligent people really listened to commencement speeches or to the speakers at dedication ceremonies and the like. When my parents got very upset about the modernizing of traditional worship services at their church, my brother and I failed to see what the big fuss was about.

stage 3   Lately, I have started to take traditional ceremonies more seriously. Several of my friends want traditional weddings in order to make the event and the commitment seem *important*. I have been to funeral services that make the family feel someone *cares* and that give people a chance to express their fond memories and their sense of loss. I know many people just go through the motions, but others get some real personal satisfaction or meaning from the ceremonies in which they participate.

that you can explain to yourself and to your readers. In reading a well-planned paper, your readers begin to sense early where your paper is headed (though they may also be in for some well-planned surprises). They read with a sense of direction; they can follow your discussion or argument without having to ask themselves: "Where are we now? Where do we go from here?"

EXERCISE 4 *Sorting Out Advice*

The following are miscellaneous pieces of well-meant advice designed to help a newcomer do a good job. How would you organize these? Sort them out under several major headings. Be prepared to explain and defend your scheme of organization.

1. Build a reputation for meeting deadlines.
2. Leave personal problems at home; don't bring them to the shop or office.
3. Don't badmouth the company or the employer.
4. Develop regular attendance habits—be there.
5. Be willing to follow regulations and procedures.
6. Don't be a complainer; be a fixer—build a reputation as someone who fixes things that are wrong.
7. Show your ability to do a conscientious job on your own, without supervision.
8. Learn to sound pleasant and receptive on the telephone.
9. Show your pride in a job well done.
10. Learn to turn down the requests of customers or other employees without alienating them.
11. Learn to cooperate with management without seeming insincere or overeager.
12. Be willing to adopt the style of the workplace in matters of dress and hairstyle.
13. Learn to make independent suggestions without seeming to contradict or criticize management.
14. Try to do without alibis and excuses.
15. Be willing to go beyond the minimum effort required of employees.
16. Make fellow employees feel good about their jobs or place of work.
17. Doublecheck your work.
18. Do not "rip off" the company or employer.
19. Keep your temper.
20. Be conscientious in keeping required records.

EXERCISE 5 *A Paper with a Plan*

Study the organizing strategy of the following student paper. How did the writer organize his material? Answer questions like the following:

☐ Where does the writer start?

☐ What course does the paper take?

☐ Is there a thesis, and if so, how does the writer lead up to it?

☐ What explains the major divisions of the paper?

☐ What explains their order?

☐ What are major clues—key phrases, key sentences—that steer the reader in the right direction?

☐ How does the writer conclude his discussion or clinch his argument?

Crime Begins at Home

The American daily newspaper has become a chronicle of local crime: the gas station holdup, the attempted rape, investors swindled out of their life savings, the burglary that turns into a murder as the owner of the apartment returns home at an inopportune time, the child-molestation case, the "drug-related killing," and assorted muggings, shopliftings, and petty thefts.

Who is to blame? The view that crime is the result of deficiencies in our society seems to have fallen into some disrepute in recent years. Those who pay the emotional and financial price for the surging crime rate are understandably reluctant to blame themselves for their own suffering. However, the search for causes must ultimately lead us back to ourselves and our communities. We teach our children, and, for the most part, our children learn.

The major cause for the frightening crime rate in our society is that in many walks of life breaking the law has become accepted or is at least condoned. Teachers of inner-city or minority children have long been concerned about the lack of positive role models for their students. The children's model of success is the man who owns the big car and wears flashy clothes. In Oakland a few years ago, thousands of young people gawked at the pomp and circumstance of the funeral procession honoring the kingpin of the city's drug trade, with a convoy of Rolls Royces following him to his grave.

Disrespect for the law is by no means confined to the "underclass." Scoffing at the law is common among blue-collar workers of the traditional working class. In the honkytonks in Oklahoma, just across the Texas border from the town where I grew up, factory and construction workers gathered on Saturday night to get roaring drunk, with knifings not uncommon. Theft of production equipment from the worksites was a common problem, but certainly the families or neighbors of the thieves never testified.

White-collar society has its own repertory of acceptable crimes. In a recent survey, most middle-class people admitted that they would cheat on their income tax returns when they felt they could get away with it. Defense contractors bestow lavish gifts and privileges on the government officials and Armed Forces personnel with whom they do business. Interest-free loans and favored investments reward those who control access to the taxpayer's money.

As a juvenile hall counselor, my sister worked with scores of young offenders. She found that with few exceptions these children were not anomalies or untamed creatures who attack law-abiding society from the outside. As children usually will, they had taken on the values of the families and communities that nurtured them. If children see everywhere that money, no matter how ill-gotten, is the true mark of success, they will develop their own value system accordingly.

WRITING TOPICS 6 *Getting Organized*

From the following topics, choose one that has a special meaning for you. Work up detailed material, relating the topic to your own observation, experience, and viewing or reading. Structure your material and prepare a detailed *working outline:*

□ Include a thesis that sums up your general conclusion and sets a general direction for the paper.
□ Set up major divisions or categories. (If you wish, include hints of details or examples to be used, putting them in parentheses.)
□ Be prepared to explain the overall strategy of your paper to your classmates.
□ After you strengthen your thesis and revise your outline as necessary in response to your classmates' or your instructor's comments, use your revised outline as your guide in writing a first draft.

1. *O What a Feeling:* how car commercials sell cars
2. *You've Come a Long Way:* career opportunities for women
3. *Details at Eleven:* the predictable television news
4. *The Computer Invasion:* how computers are changing our lives
5. *The Throw-It-Away Society:* how products become obsolete
6. *I Know the Type:* victims of prejudice
7. *A Tale of More Than Two Cities:* different faces of the city
8. *The Fractured Family:* sources of friction in the modern family
9. *That's Not Funny:* objectionable humor or offensive jokes
10. *A Partygoer's Guide:* a guide to social occasions for young adults

5

REVISING

From Notes to Final Draft

The question of revision is closely allied with that of inspiration. There may be inspired writers for whom the first draft is just right. But anyone who is not certifiably a Milton had better assume that the first draft is a primitive thing. John Kenneth Galbraith

My revisions aren't necessarily the best ones that could be made—or the only ones. They're mainly matters of carpentry: fixing the structure and the flow. . . . Most rewriting is a process of juggling elements that already exist. William Zinsser

Remember: It is no sign of weakness or defeat that your manuscript ends up in need of major surgery. This is a common occurrence in all writing, and among the best writers. Strunk and White

TIME FOR REVISION Most published writing has gone through several drafts, and some of it has been extensively reworked and rewritten. (A textbook like this one has usually gone through several rewrites and many last-minute adjustments.) As a student, you will do some of your writing under pressure in class, trying to go from rough notes to a final draft in a very short time. But except for such in-class writing, you will have to allow for the revising and rethinking of an early draft. Now is the time for second thoughts—time to capitalize on the strong points and shore up the weak points of a paper.

Writers vary in how they draft and revise their writing. Some write a fairly rapid first draft, pushing on to get down their main points and leaving details of phrasing to be polished later. Other writers toil over a first draft line by line, trying to get the phrasing right from the beginning, with much crossing out and scribbling on a cluttered page, with passages circled and moved by arrows to a better place. Many writers have discovered **word processing** as their answer to the clutter and recopying of much old-style revision: The word processor allows them to delete, add, and reshuffle material on the screen—*before* a revised clean copy is printed out.

Feedback from the Reader

Often a professional writer sends a trial draft to an editor, reviewer, or agent for feedback: reactions, warnings, advice. As a student writer, you may be asked to rework a first draft in response to comments from your instructor or your peers. Feedback from readers alerts you to blocked lines of communication. A key term may mean one thing to you and another to the reader. You may have ignored a side of the argument that is vivid in the reader's mind. From signals you give early in the paper, the reader may expect you to head in one direction, while you are actually heading in another. These snags are a normal part of trying to communicate. They send us back to the keyboard for the rewriting that will help us get the message through.

The more experienced you become as a writer, the more you will monitor your writing from the reader's point of view. You will *anticipate* the likely reactions of your readers. What will make them pay attention, and what will make them lose interest? What will make them smile, and what will make them frown? Looking at a first draft through the reader's eyes, you spot passages that need follow-through. You notice weak examples or missing links. You review your overall plan and discover awkward backtrackings and detours. Now is the time to fill in, take out, and reshuffle material as needed.

Rewriting and Rethinking

Revision is likely to deal with big as well as little matters. Some of it deals with matters of packaging—comparable to making a cereal box more attractive, more colorful, and easier to open. But much revision deals with matters of substance—comparable to putting less sugar or more raisins in the cereal. Often, we find that we have to do some real rethinking as well as rewriting.

Suppose you are writing a paper on the topic of overregulation. What set your paper in motion was your annoyance at too much bureaucratic meddling: no-smoking ordinances, compulsory seatbelts, compulsory retirement, licenses required for food vendors or promotional events on campus. On second thought, you decide to include a final section on *necessary* regulation, where you admit the need for the testing and licensing of new medications and the like. The outline of your first draft may look roughly as follows:

OUTLINE: FIRST DRAFT

Our Overregulated Society

I. Unnecessary regulation
    A. No-smoking ordinances
    B. Compulsory seatbelts
    C. Licenses for student entrepreneurs
    D. Compulsory retirement
II. Necessary regulation
    A. Traffic laws
    B. Health codes for food handlers
    C. Government testing of new drugs

On rereading your draft, you decide that it has two weaknesses: The first part reads too much like miscellaneous personal grievances. And the second part, intended to make you sound reasonable, actually undercuts the main point of your argument. You then decide on a major reshuffling of your material: You will take a reasonable stance from the beginning, granting the need for regulation in such areas as public health. You work out a strategy that will leave your readers at the end with the questions about debatable regulation that you want them to ponder.

OUTLINE: SECOND DRAFT

Our Overregulated Society

I. Clearly necessary regulation
    A. Traffic laws
    B. Health codes for food handlers
    C. Government testing of new drugs
II. Clearly unwanted regulation
    A. Job restrictions because of sex
    B. Job restrictions because of age
III. Debatable regulation
    A. No-smoking ordinances
    B. Compulsory seatbelts or airbags

Questions for Discussion What experience have you had with revision that goes beyond details? Have you ever experienced a major change of direction or change of heart in writing or revising a paper?

A PAPER FROM START TO FINISH The following pages trace the history of a student paper from the initial notetaking, through a first draft and the instructor's comments, to a fairly substantial revision.

Getting Started Here is a brief account of what set the paper in motion:

SUBJECT The original assignment had asked students to write about their observations of Americans at work. The writer chose this subject from a list of possible topics because it was close to his own experience and interests. He himself had held various part-time jobs, and both his family and his friends often talked about what happened at work. Early in the process, he narrowed this general subject area to a more specific topic: people's *attitudes* toward work. In his experience, people differed a great deal in how seriously they took their work and in how much effort they invested in it.

PURPOSE The author's general purpose was to write an informative paper about the attitudes of Americans at work—to take stock of his observations and show a general pattern that his readers could compare with what they had seen themselves. However, he had a more personal motive: He had been at times amused, annoyed, or angered by co-workers who did less than their share and depended on their colleagues to take up the slack. The writer here had a chance to vent some of the frustration he had experienced in trying to get shirkers to do their share of the work.

AUDIENCE The writer had in mind an audience of his own generation. He was thinking of young people who wonder how they will fare in the world of work and who are interested in sharing experiences on the subject. He assumed that at least some of his contemporaries might have experienced reactions and frustrations similar to his own.

From Notes to Outline Here, from an early stage in the history of the paper, are the student's *working notes:*

PREWRITING: WORKING NOTES

Constant refrain heard around the house when I was younger (mainly from my mother): "Finish the job. Do it right. Take pride in what you do."

Things people say: "I owe, I owe, so off to work I go." "I am doing it strictly for the money." "I love the work, but there is no money in it."

My restaurant job: some waiters/waitresses really put themselves into their jobs—always on their feet: extra glass of water, more bread, return change. Last dishwasher a real loser: piles of dishes always left for the next shift, "clean" dishes with chunks of food. Filthy silverware. Replacement: good worker.

Dad's job: engineer. Seldom brings home any work? Likes his work though. Always talks about people doing "useful work."

"Work ethic"? It really depends. Example, Fred: checked sales of magazines off magazine racks in supermarkets. Turned in reports—didn't even go to the stores! (Mention Amos: drifter, half of the time unemployed.)

Other side of the coin: dedicated physicists, scientists. Einstein. Computer wiz putting in fourteen hours a day.

Who else? Ellen has semiconductor job. Ask her about it—attitudes of workers?

As the student writer sorted out these notes, "That depends" began to stand out as the keynote. There seemed to be a true range of attitudes, from the dedicated to the lackadaisical. In the following *trial outline,* his overall plan is beginning to take shape:

PREWRITING: TRIAL OUTLINE

— truly dedicated (scientists, computer specialists)
— conscientious nine-to-five (Dad's engineering job, Ellen)
— strictly for the money (dishwasher, magazine checker)

The First Draft In his first draft, the writer expanded his scheme to include four categories instead of three. Read his first draft. Then study the comments the instructor wrote in the margin. Can you see the point of each comment?

WRITING SAMPLE: FIRST DRAFT

Is the Work Ethic Extinct?

put this later when you give reasons for different attitudes) (start with a striking example?)

The work ethic is an ideal that has never been embraced by the entire working population. Our attitude toward work is shaped in large part by what we observe our own parents' attitude toward work to be. If their attitude is "I owe, I owe, so off to work I go," we may also absorb the same attitude. If the parents' aim is to do as little work as possible for the most amount of money, their children may also adopt this philosophy. My own parents taught me to take pride in my work, and no matter how hard I try, I cannot shake this attitude.

GOOD OVERVIEW— but very dry (add a graphic touch or two)

To judge from my own experience, there are approximately four different attitudes that people have toward their work. One would be that of true lifelong devotion. Another would be sincere devotion for eight hours a day, five days a week. The third would be indifference, not really caring one way or the other. The last would be the attitude of people who deliberately do as little work as possible for the most amount of money.

we need some examples of real-life people and actual tasks here

provide stronger link? tell us more about his work

GOOD – do more of this kind of detail

again good real-life example

Some people are totally absorbed in their work. A dedicated scientist may spend long hours thinking about an experiment, new data, or a challenged hypothesis. When taking physics and chemistry, I was told that in order to understand a scientific concept I should think about it continuously. Today's computer programmers and communication engineers also work long hours, driven by ambition and taking pride in what they do.

The rank and file of the workforce includes a large number of people who do creditable work while on the job. My father is an engineer, and I know that his work requires hard work and concentration for eight hours a day, five days a week. An acquaintance of mine works in a semiconductor plant. She takes pride in her work and in being asked to help out in different production areas.

I have had some first-hand observations of people who basically do not care. A dishwasher in the restaurant where I work part-time used to send out plates that still had chunks of food baked on to them, and he invariably left a pile of unfinished work for the next shift. The glasses he sent out were cloudy, and the silverware often hardly looked appetizing.

Finally, there is the worker who milks the job for whatever it offers without feeling obligated to offer anything in return. I used to know someone who worked as a magazine checker. His job was to make the rounds of various supermarkets at the end of the week to count how many magazines had been sold and how many were left. It was his policy to make up approximate numbers, often not even visiting the store.

Is the work ethic a thing of the past? The answer depends on the examples we look at. In my family, it is not a thing of the past. But with some people I have known, the work ethic has gone into a total eclipse.

Questions for Discussion If you had contributed to **peer criticism** of the paper, would your comments have been similar to the instructor's? What other comments or suggestions would you have made?

The Second Draft The second draft of the work ethic paper follows the instructor's editorial suggestions fairly closely. It builds on a first draft that had a workable overall plan and usable material. But the second draft buttresses its points with added specific details, and it brings out more vividly and forcefully both the central idea and some of its ramifications. Check how the author's revision has accomplished the following:

- □ used the *introduction* to bring the subject into focus and to bring it to life;
- □ provided a clear *overview* with graphic touches;
- □ provided detailed follow-up with authentic *examples* from the author's reading, personal observation, and employment history;

□ provided effective *transitions* that show the logical connection between one point and the next;

□ added a new *conclusion*.

REVISION: SECOND DRAFT

Is the Work Ethic Extinct?

The work ethic is an ideal that has never been embraced by the entire working population. Some people take a job only when they absolutely need it in order to help them pay their bills. ("I owe, I owe, so off to work I go.") Also, there have always been people who drift aimlessly from job to job. A friend of mine will take almost any job and work at it for a short while, then collect unemployment insurance until it dries up, then take another job. He continues this cycle with amazing regularity. When we ask whether the work ethic is still alive, we should disregard the drifter and take a look at workers who know they need a job and are not likely to move frequently from one job to another.

To judge from my experience, the attitudes of workers towards their jobs cover the whole range. Workers range from people who are obsessed with their work (the workaholics), through people who do the job from 9 to 5 (the rank and file), to people who do as little work as possible for the most amount of money (the shirkers).

Some people are totally absorbed in their work. A dedicated scientist may spend most of his or her waking hours thinking about an experiment, new data, or a challenged hypothesis. I remember a book about the Manhattan Project, responsible for the construction of the atom bomb during World War II. Many of the scientists involved worked long hours from early in the morning till late at night. I remember a story about one of them who was too preoccupied with the work to remember having eaten breakfast in the morning. Today, we read about computer programmers and communications engineers who work late into the night—young men and women dedicated to their work, driven by ambition, and taking pride in what they do.

Obviously, such total dedication and intense ambition are exceptional. The rank and file includes a large number of people who do creditable work while on the job. I know many people who devote eight hours a day, five days a week to doing the best job they are capable of. My father is an engineer who will do his required work, do the necessary background research, and help a fellow worker who comes to him with a problem. His work requires a great deal of concentration eight hours a day, five days a week, but the rest of his time he has to himself. An acquaintance of mine works in a semiconductor plant. She takes pride in her work and in being asked to help out in different production areas when her experience and advice are needed.

These people illustrate the basic element in the work ethic, which is the satisfaction in a job well done. Not all of the people who share this satisfaction have jobs that are glamorous or highly paid. The dishwasher in the restaurant where I work part-time would not consider sending out dirty plates, greasy silverware, or cloudy glasses.

Unfortunately, many people do not care about the quality of their work. The previous dishwasher I worked with sent out plates that had chunks of food on them, and he invariably left a pile of unfinished work for the next shift. I have known waiters who considered it an imposition to be asked for a glass of water by a customer. People with this kind of attitude are often workers trapped in a job they do not like or want, and they continue strictly from economic necessity.

Finally, there is the worker who milks the job for whatever money or privileges it offers without feeling obligated to offer anything in return. I used to know a person who worked as a magazine checker. His job was to make the rounds of various supermarkets at the end of the week to count how many magazines had been sold and how many were left. His reports would tell the distributor how many copies of *Popular Mechanics, Good Housekeeping,* and *True Adventure* had been sold to eager readers. It was his policy to make up approximate numbers, often not even visiting a store while pretending he had been there. With people like him, the work ethic has gone into a total eclipse.

What accounts for such differences in attitude? Previous generations vividly remembered hardship and poverty. To them, hard work was the way to banish the spectre of poverty and deprivation. Often, our attitudes toward work are influenced by early training and the example of our parents. I will never forget the constant refrain I heard around the house when I was young: "Finish the job. Do it right. Any job worth doing is worth doing well." My parents taught me to take pride in my work, and I cannot shake this attitude, even when it might be convenient for me to care less and enjoy myself more.

Questions for Discussion What does the new conclusion add to the paper? Does it change your overall reaction to the paper?

Final Revision In much professional writing, a third and perhaps fourth rewrite is not uncommon. Given a chance for final revision, the author of the work ethic paper might decide that some of the "job descriptions" in the paper are still too general and colorless. Here is a rewrite of the passage dealing with the author's father (in the fourth paragraph):

My father is a *metallurgical engineer working for a company that produces marine turbines and similar gear. He works out and checks the specifications for the metals used—their strength, their ability to withstand corrosion, their capability of being welded, and so forth.* He will do his required work, do the necessary background research, and help a fellow worker who comes to him with a problem.

Remember: Develop your own system of drafting and revising. Give your papers a chance to develop, to take shape. Do not hand in as your finished product a paper written at the last minute without sufficient preparation, without time to plan and think.

STRATEGIES FOR REVISION Each paper has its own life cycle. Your strategies for revision will vary from one writing project to the next. Often, however, guidelines like the following will help you strengthen the final version of a paper:

☐ *Get your paper off to a good start.* Is the title vivid and pointed enough to attract the reader's attention? Does the introduction bring the issue into focus? Does it make the subject come to life for the reader? Contrast the following weak, colorless opening for a paper with the revised version.

WEAK: **Attitudes Toward Divorce**

The attitude toward divorce has changed drastically in recent years. As the number of people who become divorced increases, divorce ceases to be a shock and becomes a familiar everyday experience. Generally, divorce has become socially acceptable in our society. . . .

REVISED: **Breaking Up**

I was married at eighteen and separated at twenty. At the age of twenty-one, I joined the ranks of countless fellow Americans. The label *divorced* was not one that I accepted easily. It is, however, a label that is more and more widely applied, with the divorce rate doubling in the last twenty years. Four or five out of ten couples who pledge their love to each other in holy matrimony will end by battling each other in the divorce courts. What has happened in our society to create this state of affairs?

☐ *Strengthen your thesis.* Is there a pointed statement of the central idea of your paper? Is there a helpful preview or hint of what your paper is going to do? Revise thesis statements that are too open-ended, that do not take a stand:

WEAK: For people to become part of a clan, *certain characteristics* are necessary; some will be more important than others.

REVISED: If people are to feel part of a clan, they need a strong sense of solidarity and elders who symbolize the values and loyalties of the group.

☐ *Strengthen your overall plan.* For a short paper, can you sum up your general plan in a three-point or four-point program? Or is your paper organized around a clear contrast of then and now, of insider and outsider, or of mainstream culture and minority culture? In a paper weighing pros and cons, have you clearly lined up advantages and disadvantages, leading the reader to a balanced conclusion?

It is not too late to *rethink* your overall plan—to shuffle major sections for a more logical or more natural sequence. Suppose you have started a paper on ethnic humor by explaining and illustrating the new etiquette for the telling of ethnic jokes: People should not tell jokes to put down others; they should tell jokes only about their own ethnic group. People of British extraction will tell British jokes; people of German extraction will tell German jokes. (World's shortest book: *Four Centuries of German Humor.*) In your second section, you have contrasted the new etiquette with the offensive ethnic jokes—Polish jokes, Italian jokes, Arab jokes— of the past. In a third section, however, you have claimed that some jokes about other ethnic groups are meant to be affectionate rather than cutting or demeaning.

On second thought, you decide that the order of your paper is anti-climactic—it presents a provocative new idea first and then seems to backtrack and lose its punch. It is like a humorous story in which the punch line appears too early. In your revision, you might reshuffle your major sections to *lead up* to the main point, going from the undesirable to the desirable:

REVISED:

Humor Is No Laughing Matter

I. Truly offensive jokes about other ethnic groups.
II. Affectionate jokes about other ethnic groups
III. The new etiquette: jokes about one's own nationality

☐ *Provide a stronger follow-through for key points.* Build up supporting details and examples. In a first draft, you will often move on too fast—raising one general idea and then going on to the next. Anticipate the comments of the reader who says: "Not so fast! Follow this up. Take a closer look. Show us what this means." The following passage, from a paper about the lack of role models for today's youth, moves too quickly from point to point:

TOO GENERAL: Young people today have no one to look up to. They are living in a time in our nation's history without true heroes. The only heroes young people see are in the movies. There is a big gap between the heroic figures in our history textbooks and the so-called "leaders" on our national scene. Because of the lack of true leadership, young people today easily follow false prophets, becoming involved in gangs or religious cults. . . .

By now there is already a backlog of questions in the reader's mind: What kind of heroes do young people see in the movies? What would be a good example of a textbook hero—and of a "so-called" current leader (and why are we inclined to be disappointed in the latter)? What do gangs offer or promise their followers? What is a good example of a religious cult that attracts young people? Remember that revision is your chance to answer the unanswered questions in the reader's mind.

☐ *Fill in the missing links.* Show connections; provide a bridge or transition from point to point. The following excerpts are from a paper with poorly marked turns:

WRITING SAMPLE: FIRST DRAFT

Stereotypical Males

The reruns of serials that in my youth filled television screens during the daytime mirrored perfectly the traditional ways of stereotyping the American male. *This stereotyping started in childhood.* From *The Little Rascals* to *Dennis the Menace*, it was always the boys (and never the girls) who got into mischief (and who had all the fun). . . .

These bad boys had to grow up to be men. From *I Love Lucy* to *The Dick Van Dyke Show*, the man was the stereotypical breadwinner who worked outside the home, while the housewife stayed home to cook and care for the children. . . .

Another favorite of the old serials was the professional man—the doctor, lawyer, or teacher giving everyone sage advice. . . .

Another old standby was the kindly old grandfather or uncle who was grouchy on the surface at times but who really has a heart of gold. . . .

can you give more of a PREVIEW ?

prepare reader for CONTRAST

weak link— show LOGICAL connection?

Look at the way the revised version provides the missing links:

WRITING SAMPLE: REVISION

The Cartoon Male

The reruns of serials that in my youth filled television screens during the daytime mirrored perfectly the traditional ways of stereotyping the American male. *This stereotyping started in childhood and followed the male into manhood and old age.* From *The Little Rascals* to *Dennis the Menace*, it was always the boys (and never the girls) who got into mischief (and who had all the fun). . . .

Paradoxically, these bad boys grew up to be the men *who were the traditional providers and heads of their households.* From *I Love Lucy* to *The Dick Van Dyke Show,* the man was the stereotypical breadwinner who worked outside the home, while the housewife stayed home to cook and care for the children. . . .

Closely related to the father responsible for the well-being of the family was the wise professional who represented a father image. He was the doctor, lawyer, or teacher giving everyone sage advice. . . .

At the end of his career, we would see the stereotypical male as the kindly old grandfather or uncle who under a sometimes grouchy surface carried a heart of gold. . . .

☐ *Leave your reader with a strong final impression.* A first draft often simply seems to run down, without a final pulling together of important points. Sometimes, the writer at the end backs away from the issue, suddenly turning cautious. Replace a weak ending with a conclusion that has the courage of your convictions.

THE WRITING WORKSHOP

Revising the First Draft

Share a first draft of a paper with a group of your classmates. Ask them for candid oral or written comments. What help or guidance do their comments provide for a revision of your draft? Write a summary and evaluation of the feedback you received. Ask the group to answer questions like the following:

☐ In their opinion, what is your paper trying to do, and how successful is it?

☐ What are strong points of the paper?

☐ What are weak points?

☐ What specific suggestions for improvement do your readers have?

☐ How did they personally react to your paper, and why?

☐ What kind of audience do they think would react best? What kind is likely to react negatively, and why?

Remember: The revising stage is a time for second thoughts. When you see your tentative ideas on paper, you have a chance to decide how well they hold up. You can decide to take a stronger stand or to tone down a negative judgment. You can take into account objections that you may have overlooked. A first draft is for the writer what a tryout on the road is for people in the theater: a chance to discover strong points but also weaknesses that cry out for repair.

EXERCISE 1   *Peer Review*

Study the following first draft of a student paper. Prepare suggestions that would help the student writer revise the paper and prepare a final draft. (In this printed version of the student's draft, obvious spelling errors and punctuation problems have been corrected, but problems like poor sentence structure and awkward wording have not.)

Remember some general guidelines for peer review: Balance *positive and negative* criticism. A good editor identifies strengths (and helps the writer build on them) and weaknesses (and helps the writer overcome them). Pay attention to the *larger elements* as well as more limited points—examine overall purpose, content, and organization of the paper. Try to make *specific suggestions* for improvement. For instance, several readers of this sample paper thought that the three problems listed at the beginning were awkwardly labeled. After reading the whole paper, how would you label them more clearly and consistently?

Here is a brief *checklist* of features you might comment on:

1. Has the writer focused on a limited subject? What was the writer's purpose, and does the paper accomplish it? Who would make a good audience for this paper?

2. Does the paper get off to a good start? How effective are its title and introduction?

3. Is there a central idea or thesis? Does it provide a preview for the rest of the paper? Is there a clear plan, and does the writer help the reader see it?

4. Are the different parts of the paper well developed? Are key points supported with specific details? (Where is there strong supporting material? Where is the supporting material weak? How could it be strengthened?)

5. How well does the paper convey its message? Where is expression effective—clear and vivid? Where is it awkward or confusing?

6. How effective is the conclusion?

WRITING SAMPLE: FIRST DRAFT

#98869

As a consequence of our striving for better technology and efficiency, Americans are becoming severely dissatisfied with their job environment and organization. This businesslike drive for profit and speed causes three serious problems for the American worker: lack of loyalty, lack of praise, and lack of knowing you are needed.

Lack of loyalty is caused primarily by the very impersonal interaction that goes on between employee and boss. I started a job at a company where I was referred to as "98869." I stayed for only a short while and then quit. I felt no loss at leaving anybody behind, because they were just faces with numbers attached to them. No one ever bothered me. (It was more efficient that way!)

Another major problem that causes dissatisfaction is the lack of praise for a job well done. After I quit my first job, I took a job as an assistant legal secretary. Each day I had to prepare wills, depositions, and basically run the office. Little by little I became more annoyed by my constant lack of any kind of praise. Then one day one of the partners in the law firm called me from a phone in the city courtroom. He needed me to prepare some things and bring them to court. I had half an hour. As he proceeded to tell me all the things that were needed, I had one hand on the typewriter, one on the copier, and one getting ready my car keys. When I arrived downtown with one minute to spare, the lawyer said, "I wish I could have looked this over before I went in there!" Not once did he thank me for my help. I felt that no matter what I did my work would not be appreciated.

In my next job, as a bookkeeper/organizer, I realized what the lack of knowing that you are needed could do. When I began this job, I enjoyed each day. I could use my organizing skills and keep everyone on schedule. Each employee had his or her own section, and I would organize it the best way possible. I received much praise from these employees and was told they couldn't do without me.

Sure! About six months later I was introduced to my replacement. It sat there with its lights blinking and little typed words flowing across the screen. It had a rainbow-colored apple (with a bite taken out of it) on its front. "It's our new computer," said the woman I knew only as the "computer lady." "It can do everything. Everyone will be able to write and read messages on it, and it organizes things beautifully." After this, it wasn't long before I felt inadequate. The computer could do in thirty seconds what used to take me an hour. These feelings of inadequacy really affected my self-confidence.

These three problems cause many workers like me to keep looking, hoping that some day a job will come along that offers a chance of personal loyalty, accomplishment and pride, and the feeling of being valued.

GUIDELINES FOR FINAL EDITING

Final editing is your chance for fine-tuning of features that you have already worked on from the beginning of your writing and rewriting. In final editing, you focus on *diction*—finding the right word; *sentence structure*—building sentences that effectively make your point; and *mechanics*—making sure your sentences look right on the page. Your task is to improve features of your writing that might come between you and the reader. You aim at **edited written English**—English that is ready for print, English that will be acceptable to a large cross section of readers.

The search for the right word is always part of the writer's agenda. Some words delay or distract readers, making them wade through wordy expressions (*because of the fact that* instead of *because*) or making them wince at clichés ("We are all in this together"). Some words say only approximately what you mean, or they bring the wrong attitudes and associations (**connotations**) into play. In your early drafts, you may have referred to *techniques* used by advertisers. In final editing, you may decide that this word will mislead your readers, making them think of such technical matters as layout or use of repetition. You may decide that the word you want is *appeals*—the way advertisers appeal to hidden motives, the way they activate our hopes and fears. (See Chapter 15 for more on the right word.)

An equally important part of the writer's agenda is the search for the sentence that effectively makes its point. Well-built sentences cut through the fog. They tell us clearly who does what or what goes with what. In much editing, we try to improve sentences that are disjointed, rewriting them to make them reflect accurately the relation between ideas:

CHOPPY: Benjamin Franklin is everyone's favorite patriot. He is the kindly uncle of the American Revolution.

COMBINED: Benjamin Franklin is everyone's favorite patriot, *the kindly uncle of the American Revolution.*

In much editing, we try to improve sentences that are poorly focused, mixed, or off balance:

MIXED: Television shows about caring and sharing families have left the screen and *are showing mainly comic or exaggerated situations.* (Who is showing what?)

IMPROVED: Television shows about caring and sharing families have left the air; *current programs* show us mainly comic or exaggerated situations.

OFF BALANCE: *Stoner* is a street word referring to people who get stoned, dress in jeans, who have long hair that looks uncombed, and mainly Caucasian.

IMPROVED: *Stoner* is a street word for people (usually Caucasian) who *get* stoned, *dress* in jeans, and *have* long hair that looks permanently uncombed.

(See Chapter 16 for more on the well-built sentence.)

Many writers and editors have checklists or style sheets for a last-minute check of mechanics. The following is such an **editor's checklist,** listing ten high-priority items that you should look for in final editing and proofreading of your papers. Allow time for a final search for these "must-check" items:

Handbook Key   *1a*

(1) Correct sentence fragments. Sentence fragments mirror the afterthoughts and asides of informal stop-and-go conversation. ("My friends would wear baggies. *Loose-fitting pants, usually a size too big."*) Many sentence fragments are isolated words or phrases that lack the subject and complete verb needed to turn them into complete sentences.

FRAGMENT: At the last moment.   (Who did what at the last moment?)
COMPLETE: The mayor filed for reelection *at the last moment.*

Other sentence fragments do have a subject and a verb, but they start with a subordinator (subordinating conjunction) or a relative pronoun. They need to be hooked up to a main clause.

FRAGMENT: If the proposal succeeds.   (If it succeeds, then what?)
COMPLETE: Front Street will become a mall *if the proposal succeeds.*

FRAGMENT: Whose plane disappeared over the Pacific. (Whose plane?)

COMPLETE: She admired Amelia Earhart, *whose plane disappeared over the Pacific.*

1c **(2) Correct comma splices.** A comma splice uses only a comma to splice together two related statements. (There is no coordinator like *and* or *but*, no subordinator like *if* or *whereas*.) Use a semicolon instead of the comma:

COMMA SPLICE: We scratched the dog act, the poodle was ill.

SEMICOLON: We scratched the dog act; the poodle was ill.

Comma splices also result when only a comma appears between two statements joined by *therefore* or *however*. These and similar conjunctive adverbs require a semicolon:

COMMA SPLICE: Peking seemed drab and bureaucratic, Shanghai *however* seemed lively and sophisticated.

SEMICOLON: Peking seemed drab and bureaucratic; Shanghai, *however*, seemed lively and sophisticated.

4 **(3) Correct faulty agreement.** Agreement requires matching forms for subject and verb: The *train stops* here (singular); the *trains stop* here (plural). Blind agreement results when the verb agrees with part of a wedge that came between it and the subject:

FAULTY: The credibility of *these witnesses are* open to question.

REVISED: *The credibility* of these witnesses *is* open to question. (What is open to question? Their credibility *is*.)

7b **(4) Correct dangling or misplaced modifiers.** A modifier is left dangling when it points to something that has been left out of the sentence. (A modifier is misplaced when it seems to point to the wrong thing.)

DANGLING: *Repossessed for nonpayment,* David claimed that the terms of the contract had not been met. (What was repossessed?)

REVISED: When *his car* was repossessed for nonpayment, David claimed that the terms of the contract had not been met.

5a **(5) Correct vague or confusing pronoun reference.** Pronouns like *she* or *they* or *this* serve as shorthand references to people and things, but they need to point clearly to what they stand for. Avoid loose pronoun reference; especially, avoid shifts in the way you refer to a typical or representative person:

SHIFT: *The typical woman* today does not expect Prince Charming to take care of *their* every need. (We are looking at *one* typical woman.)

REVISED: *The typical woman* today does not expect Prince Charming to take care of *her* every need.

5b   *Note:* Avoid being caught on the horns of the pronoun dilemma: A traditional rule required the singular *he* after indefinite pronouns like *everybody, anyone, somebody,* and *one.* ("*Everyone* who runs for public office exposes *his* private life to scrutiny.") Where the **generic** *he* would seem to exclude women, we today expect the unbiased *he or she.* ("*Everyone* who runs for public office exposes *his or her* private life to scrutiny.") When several *he or she* and *his or her* references in a row make a sentence awkward, try to convert the whole sentence to the unbiased plural:

UNBIASED: *All candidates* for public office expose *their* private lives and the private lives of people close to *them* to scrutiny.

10d   **(6) Correct faulty parallelism.** Sentences are parallel when several equal or similar sentence parts appear in a row, joined by a word like *and* or *or* or *but.* ("People were obsessed with *spies, conspiracies,* and *plots.*") But sometimes the second or third element in such a sequence snaps out of the pattern that the writer set up:

FAULTY: A rainy day makes people feel *tired, lazy,* and *in a gloomy mood.*

PARALLEL: A rainy day makes people feel *tired, lazy,* and *gloomy.*

20   **(7) Check for missing capital letters.** Capital letters, like apostrophes, do not show in speech and are therefore easily overlooked. Capitalize names of days, months, places, states, ships, schools. Especially, capitalize the names of nationalities and languages: *Mexican, Spanish, Italian, Canadian, Australia, Japanese, American.*

CAPITALS: The opera singer from Laurel, Mississippi, ended her 32-year career with a stunning farewell performance of Verdi's *Aida* at New York City's Metropolitan Opera.

19b   **(8) Use the apostrophe for the possessive of nouns.** The **possessive** tells us *whose:* my *brother's* keeper, the *world's* safest airport; the *coach's* unexpired contract, the *cat's* meow. Remember the basic rule of thumb: apostrophe and *s* if you are talking about one; *s* and apostrophe if you are talking about several:

	SINGULAR	PLURAL
Whose?	a *friend's* BMW my *brother's* nose one *country's* history a *week's* wage	the *tenants'* cars my *brothers'* noses other *countries'* problems two *months'* salary

Check for some often misspelled possessives: *today's* world, *yesterday's* newspaper, *tomorrow's* election. Check for unusual plurals: the *men's* locker room, *women's* rights, the *children's* hour.

19a **(9) Distinguish between it's and its.** Use *it's* only when it's short for *it is: it's* too late, *it's* a plane, *it's* illegal. *Its* is a key exception to the rule that possessives require an apostrophe: the band and *its* instruments (whose?); the rifle and *its* parts.

17 **(10) Proofread carefully for spelling to catch the unforgivables.** Never misspell the following: *receive, believe, separate, definite, similar, athlete, perform, basically, probably, used to, a lot, writing, occurred.*

Remember: As software for word processing becomes more sophisticated, a computer may be able to flag for you familiar editing problems in the areas of word choice, sentence structure, and mechanics. Nevertheless, except with outright spelling errors, you will still have to decide which of several options is right for what you are trying to say (*their* or *there*?). Successful writers have often programed their own mental computers to flag for them whatever in their writing might delay, confuse, or alienate the reader. Often good writers are their own best editors.

6

THE WRITER'S OPTIONS

Beginnings, Middles, and Ends

There's a great satisfaction in taking the actual facts insofar as you can get them and turning this material into something that is as engrossing as fiction, and in some cases more so, when you succeed.   Tom Wolfe

Keep thinking and rewriting until you say what you want to say.   William Zinsser

BEGINNINGS AND ENDINGS As you become a more confident writer, you develop your sense of the writer's options. You become aware of the range of possibilities, of the strategies other writers have tried. How do they attract and hold the reader? How do they set up expectations that they then satisfy? How do they keep the reader moving in the right direction? How do they leave the reader with a strong final impression?

Titles A good title beckons to the reader. Like the marquee of a movie theater, your title signals to the reader: "Spend some time—it will be worth your while." Effective titles stake out the subject. (Increasingly, writers include in their titles the kind of key word that helps a computer retrieve publications relevant to a particular topic.) But good titles also hint at the writer's point of view; they set the tone. To compete successfully for the reader's attention, an effective title often has a dramatic or humorous touch:

COLORLESS: A Look at Jogging
DRAMATIC: Run for Your Life

101

Often an effective title has a rhythm or pattern that makes us remember it. It may use a striking image or a play on words:

> Aerodynamics: Cheating the Wind
> The Art of Teaching Science
> Looking for a Job Is a Job
> Questioning Quotas
> Good News for Bad Backs

Improve on titles that merely place a colorless, impersonal label on your general subject. Make sure your title sounds like your personal choice and reflects your personal point of view:

> WEAK: Business Success
> BETTER: Red Ink, Black Ink
>   The Customer Is Rarely Right
>   The Creative Use of Credit

Introductions

A good introduction captures the readers' interest and leads them into the heart of the subject. An effective introduction brings the subject into focus and makes it come to life. It may relate the subject to something the reader already knows or cares about. Above all, it heads directly for the central issue or the central idea to be treated in the paper.

A weak introduction merely restates the familiar or belabors the obvious. An introduction like the following reads as if a key word had been punched into a computer, calling up predictable associations:

PREDICTABLE:

A Nation of Immigrants

America has traditionally been a land of immigrants. The pilgrims came to these shores in search of religious freedom. The Statue of Liberty greeted the "huddled masses" that came from Ireland, Italy, or Russia to escape famine, poverty, or persecution. . . .

To improve on such an introduction, try approaching the subject from a new, more personal perspective:

MORE PERSONAL:

A Flood of Immigrants

Everywhere in American life, we see evidence of successive waves of immigration. When I took my first job, the owners of the restaurant where I worked were Hungarian immigrants. Of their twenty-two employees, four were from Central or South America, two from Taiwan, and one from India. Within a block of where I now live, Vietnamese and other South-East Asian immigrants run a quick-lunch place, a shoe repair shop, and a cleaner's. Today with unemployment always around the corner, many Americans facing competition from immigrants ask: *Is it time to close the open door?*

You will seldom write a paper requiring more than one short introductory paragraph. (A long, roundabout introduction may cause the reader to wonder: "Where are we headed? What is this all about?") Study the following examples of effective introductions. Look at how each writer dramatizes the issue and leads directly to the thesis or central idea of the paper.

☐ *Start with a striking example.* To bring your subject to life, select one vivid example to catch the attention or arouse the indignation of the reader:

Test-Tube Food

Extrusion is the method of chopping or powdering foodstuffs and then reforming them to make them look whole. A striking example of extruded products is a foot-long rod of hard-cooked egg used by many caterers, restaurants, and institutions that want to bypass the cost of shelling real eggs. One of these rods enables a busy chef to cut seventy-five perfect center slices. Amazingly, the yolks of these high-tech eggs do not slip out of their white rims. Unfortunately, the slices have a rubbery texture and a vaguely sulfurous aftertaste. *Everywhere today, we encounter processed foods that have been adapted to give them eternal shelf life, to make them more profitable, and to destroy their original texture and taste.*

☐ *Start with an event currently in the news.* Relate your general subject to widely publicized recent events; show that it is the subject of current public concern:

Programed for Failure

A few weeks ago, Malcolm Hyde, a graduate of Oakmont High School, sued the Oakmont Unified School District for having failed to teach him to read and write. Malcolm had been one of the estimated twenty to thirty percent of the students in our public schools who "mark time or drop out." For the parents of such children, it is not enough to be content when a student "passes" and "stays out of trouble." *Parents of educationally deprived youngsters must start taking a direct interest in what happens in the classroom from day to day.*

☐ *Relate your subject to firsthand personal experience.* Show that your subject is not just of academic interest to you; show that it has a personal meaning:

A Thicket of Regulations

Shortly after my eighteenth birthday, my father died of hypertension. At that time, medication that would have controlled his illness was available in Canada but banned in the United States by the Federal Drug Administration. Less than one year after his death it was made available through a belated clearance by the agency. *Every year, promising experimental drugs are delayed because of a maze of bureaucratic regulations and the horrendous cost of extensive testing and trial use.*

☐ *Start with striking symptoms or outward signs of a current trend.* Use telltale signs of current developments to lead the reader into an analysis of key features or underlying causes:

Patriotism Back in Style

Across the land, people are turning out in record numbers for holidays such as Flag Day and the Fourth of July. High school students are again entering patriotic essay contests sponsored by service organizations. ROTC programs, once scorned, are making a comeback on college campuses. *Old-time patriotism is coming back into style.*

☐ *Use a striking quotation as the keynote for the rest of your paper.* Set your paper in motion by quoting an eyewitness, authority, or insider:

Be Happy in Your Work

"64,000 hours are at stake!" That is what Richard Bolles, author of *What Color is Your Parachute?*, tells readers trying to choose a profession. His figure represents the number of hours that an average person will work during a lifetime. *In spite of such warnings, many people drift into kinds of work that they dislike.*

☐ *Use a striking contrast to lead up to your key point.* For instance, use a *then-and-now* contrast to point up a change:

We Are What We Wear

The late sixties was the height of the love affair between the media and youth. Movies, magazines, pop music, and advertising extolled the teenage girl—a long-haired, blank-faced disco-dancing adolescent wearing a mini-skirt and thin as a stick. Today, most women no longer want to look like teenagers. The new ideal is the woman with both a career and a family. She's in her thirties or forties; she has character—you can see it in her face. *The media are struggling toward a new image of the mature woman, wearing a classic suit.*

☐ *Use striking facts or statistics to dramatize the issue:*

Growing Up a Little Faster

According to one recent survey, seven out of ten children of divorced parents had not seen their real father in more than a year. *The traditional practice of awarding custody of children to the mother left a whole generation of children of divorce without the natural father as a model and a guide.*

☐ *Use your introduction to set the tone.* For instance, alert your readers that you will treat your subject with a humorous touch:

Captain of My Own Ship

Worker dissatisfaction has been with us for a long time. There must have been days when stone-age hunters felt weary as they set out on the trail of another mammoth, when Napoleon's soldiers balked at the scheduling of yet another battle, or when Columbus's sailors cringed at the thought of more days out at sea. In the past, however, most of the employed had no choice of how or where they worked. Education was limited, and most people were more or less confined to the same geographical location for a lifetime. *Today people have more freedom to choose the kind of work they want to do; they have more freedom to move on when they are dissatisfied.*

Questions for Discussion Which of these introductions make you want to read on? Which fail to arouse your interest?

Avoid weak or ineffective introductions:

☐ *Repeating the assignment* (often word for word).
☐ *A perfunctory dictionary definition* (unless you bring in a definition to argue with it or to bring out something important that is often overlooked): "*Webster's Dictionary* [which one?] defines *discrimination* as 'prejudiced or prejudicial outlook, action, or treatment.'"
☐ *A dutiful summary:* "Computers have changed our lives in many important ways. They have brought about a revolution in communications, bookkeeping, and entertainment. . . ."
☐ *Puffing up the subject:* "Bird-watching is a wonderful hobby. I have spent countless hours of untold pleasure watching the ways and antics of birds. . . ."
☐ *Complaints or apologies:* "Many contradictory opinions abound on the subject of the perfect interview. I find it hard to give a candidate for a job meaningful advice in a paper of 500 words. . . ."

Conclusions A good conclusion pulls together the different strands of a paper and leaves the reader with a strong final impression. Avoid a lame restatement, in almost identical words, of points already made. Instead of merely repeating, *reiterate*—repeat with added emphasis, with added conviction. In addition, an effective conclusion will often

☐ pull together and highlight *essential points* when an argument has moved through several steps;
☐ spell out the *implications* of what has been said for the reader personally or for society;
☐ *circle back* to the beginning by fulfilling an expectation created earlier in the paper. For instance, the writer may sum up the answer to a question raised in the title or introduction. Or the writer may return to a symbolic incident or key example used at the start of the paper.

Here are some examples of what you might do in an effective conclusion:

□ *Use a final anecdote to reinforce the central idea.* Close with an incident or situation that gives dramatic form to your main point:

From an article on the growing pains of third-world countries:

. . . My Nigerian friend looked out over the congested traffic as we sat in the stalled car. "Money," he said suddenly. "When we don't have it, it bothers you. When you get it, it worries you." He had summed up the story of his country, caught between ancient poverty and sudden wealth.

□ *Make striking details serve as symbols of an idea or a trend.* For example, hobbies or styles of dress may symbolize more general attitudes:

From a paper on prevailing conservative trends on campus:

. . . In the shopping area across from the main entrance to the campus, head shops have been replaced by stores that sell roller skates and running shoes. Conservative styles of dress are coming back: tweed sports jackets and skirts. Some of the students dress up to go to the library.

□ *Use a strong final quotation to reinforce your main point.* Quote an authority or insider who has stated your point in a striking or memorable way:

From a paper on commercialism and the artist:

. . . Some of the world's leading artists and performers have managed to solve this age-old dilemma: how to reach a large audience without pandering to popular taste. Toward the end of her career, the great gospel singer Mahalia Jackson was asked about several albums she had done for a "commercial" label. She said: "All my life, I have sung for my supper as well as for the Lord."

□ *Conclude with a suggestion for remedial action.* Give your readers realistic pointers on what they can *do:*

From an article on prison reform:

. . . If the leading citizens in a community would make it a point to visit their state prison, talk with the warden, then return to their communities with a better understanding of actual down-to-earth prison problems, they would have taken one of the most important and most effective steps toward a solution of our crime problem.   Erle Stanley Gardner, "Parole and the Prisons—An Opportunity Wasted," *Atlantic*

Avoid ineffective conclusions like the following:

□ The well-meaning *platitude:* "Making our neighborhoods safe will require the vigilance of every concerned citizen."

□ The *silver lining:* "Humanity in the past has survived earthquakes, famines, and the plague. And after all, we have already lived with the threat of nuclear war almost half a century."

▫ The *panacea:* "The restoration of old-fashioned discipline in our schools will make juvenile delinquency a thing of the past."
▫ The *sidestepped question:* "Death is sometimes more merciful than a life of suffering. But who decides, and on what grounds? These are moral questions, and, as with all moral questions, the answers will have to come with time."
▫ The *lame afterthought:* "Of course, if we burn more coal rather than rely on nuclear power, we will further pollute our atmosphere. This is a problem for the engineers of the future to resolve."

EXERCISE 1   *What's in a Title?*

React briefly to the following *book titles.* How effective is each title? What kind of book does it seem to promise? What seems to be the writer's agenda? What do you think would be a good audience or an ideal reader for each book?

Strategies for Women at Work
Easy Basics for Good Cooking
Our Bodies, Ourselves
Computer Programing for the Compleat Idiot
Number: The Language of Science
Make Your Money Grow
A Place Called School
Nuclear War, Nuclear Peace
Lost Worlds of Africa
The Marital Arts

EXERCISE 2   *Studying Leads*

Find three recent magazine articles whose *titles* and *introductions* you consider exceptionally effective. Explain how they attract the reader's attention and what strategy they use to lead the reader into the subject.

EXERCISE 3   *Evaluating Introductions*

Study the following *titles* and *introductions.* Which are effective, and how? Which are weak, and why? Answer questions like the following:

▫ What function does the title serve? How does it attract the reader's attention?

□   How does the introduction lead up to the key issue or central thesis? What method or strategy does it illustrate?

□   What kind of paper does the introduction make you expect, and why? (What is the tone of the introduction?)

□   What kind of reader do you think would make a good audience for the writer?

1.
Dangerous Books

Any list of the books most frequently banned in American schools is sure to strike a chord in the reader's mind. One title I recently saw listed took me back to my junior year in high school. An English teacher who trusted me took me to the storage room to give me a brand-new copy of Kurt Vonnegut's *Slaughterhouse-Five*. There on the shelves were two hundred more brand-new copies that had never been given to students. The principal had decided these books were "unsuitable" for young minds. It seems that often the books that are censored are the ones students would be most likely to read on their own, as "unrequired" reading.

2.
Job Dissatisfaction

In this day and age, Americans feel that the benefits they receive from their occupation are not quite in accord with the efforts they expend. Why do Americans feel this way? The answer probably lies in the American culture. Job dissatisfaction is in part due to the way Americans live at the present time.

3.
Ordeal by Fire

Sooner or later, we may expect to see a candidate for the office of the President of the United States pitted against a bear. The engagement could take place in Madison Square Garden or any other arena convenient for the television cameras. Over the years, the presidential campaign has become an increasingly trying ordeal for the candidates and for the public. . . .

4.
Television Shows

Many of my friends watch the music shows that are popular on television. There are also exercise shows, the news, situation comedies, specials, children's shows. The list could go on and on. What I am trying to show is that there are different types of shows on television, and I will try to describe a few of them in the following pages.

5.
Freeze!

The average police officer fires a gun at a criminal perhaps once in a lifetime of service. In the typical crime show on television, there is hardly an episode without a climactic shootout, with police officers' guns blazing away. The net results of these programs is not to promote respect for the law but to make the viewer accept guns and gunplay as an ever-present fact of city life.

EXERCISE 4   *Evaluating Conclusions*

Study the following *conclusions*. Which seem like a strong summing up or wrapping up, and why? Which are weak, and why?

1. *From an article on trade barriers American businesses encounter in Japan:*

    . . . Americans as well as Japanese know the pleasures of pointing the finger at someone else. It is frustrating for us Americans to have to think about matters that are our own responsibility, such as balancing our federal accounts or adapting to changing foreign markets. It is much easier to point the finger at our trading partners and shout "foul."

2. *From a paper warning against excessive emphasis on careers in a college education:*

    . . . Students today have an almost hypnotic fascination with the subject of careers. They eat, drink, sleep, and, above all, sweat jobs. As a dean of students said at a Midwestern school, "I sometimes think that if I stopped one of these students on the street and asked, 'Who are you?' the answer would be 'I'm prelaw.' "

3. *From a paper on appeals used by American advertisers:*

    . . . Advertisers know how to exploit our love of gadgets and our desire for a more glamorous life. They exploit the customer's yearning to be attractive, upward mobile, and forever young. Moral lectures will not stop advertisers from using methods that work. If we object to being exploited, we as consumers must learn to take a good look at what we really want. We must decide whether we want trendiness and surface glamor or value for the dollar.

4. *From a paper on test-tube babies:*

    . . . Do doctors have a right to produce life in a laboratory? Nobody knows who is right or wrong on this issue, but what is important is that humanity still has the desire to learn more and to explore this field of unknowns, trying to find answers in our never-ending quest for knowledge.

5. *From a paper on the way television mirrors the American family:*

    . . . The image of the American family has changed from one extreme to the other. Viewers used to watch the happy lives of ideal families. Now they watch the trauma-filled lives of families that are unstable. One cannot help wonder what direction the image of the American family will take from here.

MIDDLES: COHERENCE AND TRANSITION Effective writing moves ahead purposefully, taking the reader along. It has **coherence;** it "hangs together." Reading a coherent paper, we move ahead with confidence, as on a well-planned hike: We trust the guide to know the best route, to take us to

the important intermediate stops (perhaps with some surprises along the way), and to furnish the directions we need.

Relevant Material

A coherent paper uses materials that are clearly related to the topic. It develops its ideas with examples, reasons, and arguments that are **relevant;** we can see how they fit in.

EXAMPLES With the experienced writer, it is a conditioned reflex to follow up a general idea with a "for instance." Effective writing pushes from the general to the specific; it sets up the alternating pattern of general idea and specific illustration that makes the reader say: "I see what you mean."

> GENERAL: The draft horse was America's workhorse through most of the nineteenth and twentieth centuries.
> SPECIFIC: The draft horse was America's workhorse through most of the nineteenth and twentieth centuries, *pulling streetcars, beer wagons, stagecoaches, ambulances, war cannons, circus wagons, Christmas sleighs, and millions upon millions of plows.* Patricia Westfall

EXPLANATION Effective writing stops to explain when the reader begins to ask: "What does this term stand for? How does this process work?" Part of the pattern of coherent writing is the kind of systematic follow-through that would explain a term like *upscale* (in a discussion of marketing), *entitlements* (in a discussion of the federal budget), or *fast breeder* (in a discussion of nuclear energy).

REASONS Well-developed writing goes on from the statement of an opinion to the reasons for, or the arguments behind, what the writer said. It does not leave the reader with an unsupported statement like "In some situations, horses are better than machines." We are ready to be told why: On small farms, horses are cheaper to buy and to maintain. They can get into and out of difficult terrain more safely than machines. For stop-and-go work, they consume less fuel.

STATISTICS Often we need to back up a statement by looking at relevant facts and figures. Test scores are going up in the city schools—what *are* the scores? What do they measure? How do they compare?

Networks of Related Terms

Often, the coherence of a paper shows in a network of closely related terms. **Synonyms**—words that mean almost the same— keep our attention focused on the same issue: *crime, lawlessness, transgression, felony.* Other related terms may reassure us that the writer is sticking to the subject: *violence, enforcement, gunplay.* Suppose you are reading an article on the psychological effects that *overcrowding* has on people in modern cities. In a well-focused article, other terms and phrases will echo the central term: "overpopulation," "penned up," "massive congestion," "great numbers," "rush-hour crush," "cramped quarters," and the like. Such synonyms or closely related terms show that the writer is never straying far from the central point.

In the following passage, study the network of terms that all relate to the idea of *good will*—of generosity, or "big-heartedness":

key term
follow-up

> Our *big-heartedness* is one of our proudest attributes. We like to think of the *New Deal* and the *Marshall Plan* as reflective of the American spirit. *Disaster relief* is among our most gratifying national pastimes. Nowhere else in the world has *philanthropy* become such big business. In our heart of hearts, we suspect that we are the most decent, *generous* people ever to grace the earth. Sure, we have shortcomings. Other nations, for instance, spend more on the arts and enjoy lower crime and infant mortality rates, but we ascribe such unpalatable facts either to our bigness or to our rugged individualism or to our *hospitality* to immigrants or to—anything, other than a shortage of *good intentions.* Carll Tucker, "The Back Door," *Saturday Review*

Patterns of Expectation A paper will seem all of one piece when the writer sets up expectations that the rest of the paper satisfies. Such patterns of expectation range from simple (and sometimes plodding) **enumeration** to sequences that are more like an escalator, carrying the audience smoothly and unobtrusively to the destination. To give a reader a clear overview of a confusing subject, we may simply number major areas or major possibilities and present them in order. In the article excerpted below, we know from the beginning there are four major choices:

Serfdom and Seat Belts

Automobile accidents kill more than 40,000 Americans every year. Actually, we have made great progress over the past decades. The number of fatalities is half what it was in 1965. . . . Still, 40,000 deaths is too many. *Debate about where to go next has swirled around four options.*

Option one is the 55 mile-per-hour speed limit. According to a government study, it has saved 2,000 to 4,000 lives a year. . . .

Option two is raising the drinking age to 21. . . .

Option three is mandatory seat belt laws. New York's, the first to go into effect, cut traffic fatalities by almost a third. . . .

Finally, there are "passive restraints," meaning air bags or automatic seat belts. . . . Adapted from "TRB from Washington," *The New Republic*

Usually, we keep the reader moving ahead with less obvious nudging and pointing. Much writing takes the reader gradually from the easy to the difficult or from the familiar to the unfamiliar. Similar strategies may take a reader from mild or amusing examples of a problem to severe and perturbing ones. The following rough outline for a paper on corruption in government takes the reader by easy stages from relatively innocent examples to outright rascality:

Corruption Made Easy

I.   Personal favors for friends and relatives
II. Favors and patronage in return for financial support
III. Outright kickbacks and bribes

Note that in such a paper the final position is the most **emphatic;** the paper builds up to what is most important or challenging.

Transition   Effective writing provides the links that help the reader follow. It provides effective **transitions** from one point to the next. Study the way an experienced writer makes the beginning of a new paragraph point back to what came before while at the same time moving the reader forward to what comes next:

> In any family, there is a network of antagonistic desires. A young girl might want to practice her violin, while her brother insists that the noise interferes with his studying. . . .
>
> *These situations must be solved or managed.* If one parent dictates without consideration of the others, the family will be run in an authoritarian manner. Women used to bend to the wishes of an authoritarian husband. . . .
>
> *If no authority figure guides and directs these daily decisions,* the individuals in the family must create some method of living together. . . .

Familiar **transitional expressions** signal to the reader what turn an argument is taking or where a paper is headed. Words like *similarly, moreover,* and *furthermore* signal that an additional example or a further reason is about to reinforce the same point. *Indeed* and *in fact* signal that an exceptionally telling example or clinching argument will follow. *Admittedly* and *granted* tell the reader that we are about to recognize a legitimate objection; we are ready to grant or concede a point. Links like *nevertheless* or *however* show that we are ready to take on or refute the objection.

Weak transitions, often using *also* or *another,* merely add without showing why. If you can, show the logical connection with what went before:

> WEAK LINK: *Another* misleading image created by television is that of the typical married male. . . .
>
> BETTER: *After marriage,* the carefree young male of televisionland turns into the stereotypical middle-aged television male worried about insurance. . . .

Here is a brief survey of familiar transitional expressions:

ILLUSTRATION:	for example, for instance, to illustrate
ADDITION:	similarly, furthermore, moreover, too, besides
EXPLANATION:	that is, in other words
REINFORCEMENT:	indeed, in fact, above all
LOGICAL RESULT:	so, therefore, thus, accordingly, consequently, as a result, hence
CONTRAST OR OBJECTION:	but, yet, however, nevertheless, on the other hand, conversely, on the contrary
CONCESSION:	granted, admittedly, to be sure, no doubt, it is true that
SUMMARY:	in short, in brief, to sum up
CONCLUSION:	finally, in conclusion, to conclude
CHRONOLOGY:	first, next, later, soon, meanwhile, in the end

Remember: Transitional words or phrases are effective when they are used strategically, at a point where they are needed. Overused, they can become too obtrusive—they stand out like the pipes that run across the ceiling and down the walls in a converted basement apartment. Effective writers know how to use other ways of showing what goes with what. For instance, when two sentences are **parallel** in structure—exceptionally similar in form—we sense that they may be related examples or applications of the same basic point:

The family is the seedbed of economic skills, money habits, attitudes toward work. . . . *The family is a stronger* agency *of* educational success *than the* school. *The family is a stronger* teacher *of* the religious imagination *than the* church.   Michael Novak

Questions for Discussion How much attention do you pay to the nuts and bolts of coherence when you read? Scan a sample page of a newsmagazine (and photocopy the page for the class if you can). How much evidence do you find of the writers' use of enumeration, related terms, transitional expressions, parallel structure?

The Final Outline

Formal outlines serve two different purposes. A writer may prepare a detailed final outline as an editorial aid, using it as a final check on coherence. But a detailed final outline may also serve as a guide to the reader; it is often part of the prescribed format for a report, research paper, or other major project. Your instructor may ask you to submit a final outline with a paper that presents a substantial argument or a substantial body of material. Two major forms are common:

□ *Use the topic outline to present, in logical order, the topics and subtopics that a paper covers.* Like other outlines, the **topic outline** often starts with a thesis sentence summarizing the central idea of the paper. Notice the use and placement of Roman numerals for the major categories, of capital letters for the subdivisions, and of Arabic numbers for the sub-subdivisions.

Generations in Conflict

THESIS: The traditional conflict between parents and their teenage children is still with us.

    I.   The traditional generation gap
       A. Authoritarian fathers and rebellious sons
       B. Conformist mothers and independent daughters
   II. Modern causes of conflict
       A. Freedom to be yourself
          1. Dress
          2. Hairstyle
       B. Unchaperoned outings
       C. Choice of part-time jobs
       D. Choice of friends and associates

□ *Use a sentence outline to sum up, in one complete sentence each, what you have to say on each topic and subtopic.* The **sentence outline** forces you to think your material through more thoroughly than the topic outline, which merely sketches out the ground to be covered. The following sentence outline systematically takes stock of the factors that have helped or hindered women in their struggle for equal pay:

Why Women Earn Less Than Men

THESIS: While some traditional causes of women's low earning power are becoming less important, current patterns of professional advancement will have to change before true progress can take place.

    I. Some traditional causes for the low earning power of women are becoming less important as a result of social change.
       A. Traditional prejudices about "men's work" and "women's work" are weakening.
       B. Large differences in educational opportunities for men and women have slowly disappeared.
       C. Traditional conceptions of women as short-term employees are changing as many women spend most of their adult lives in the labor force.
   II. Current patterns of economic success and professional advancement continue to work against women, nevertheless.
       A. In most occupations, the years between 25 and 35 are crucial to future success.

1. Blue-collar workers discover the job openings and training opportunities that lead to highly paid skills.
2. Corporations identify promising candidates for advancement in management.
3. Professionals finish advanced degrees and compete for promising jobs.

B. The years between ages 25 and 35 are the most likely years for many women to be absent from the labor force or to work part-time because of family responsibilities.

III. For women to achieve more nearly equal earning power, society must revise its patterns of promotion and advancement to provide greater opportunities for mature women reentering the labor force.

Use the following checklist to revise your outlines:

☐ *Make your headings serve your purpose.* Writing about campus social life, you might divide students into Greeks, dorm dwellers, rent sharers, and loners. Writing about students' academic lives, you might divide them into grinds, crammers, prevaricators, and ad-libbers (who make up answers to exam questions as they go along).

☐ *Avoid a confusing mixture of criteria.* What is the point of dividing students into graduates of local high schools, low-income students, and Catholics? Your readers can see the point of your categories if there is some common principle of selection, for example, geographic origin (local, rest of the state, out of state, foreign) or religious belief (Catholics, Protestants, Jews, Muslims, agnostics).

☐ *Scuttle single subdivisions.* Where there is a section A, you will need a section B; where there is a subdivision 1., you will need a subdivision 2. If in a paper on campus dress styles your section D ("Religious garb of the mysterious East") has only one subdivision ("Hare Krishna"), leave the section undivided.

☐ *Reconsider a too-long sequence of parallel entries.* If you have eight or nine divisions under a single heading, see if you can set up subdivisions with two or three entries each.

☐ *Use parallel wording to point up the relation between parallel ideas.* Your original wording might have been "I. Breaking the ice II. How to get acquainted III. A lasting relationship" and additional headings similarly mismatched. Try making each entry run along similar grammatical lines:

I. Breaking the ice
II. Getting acquainted
III. Cementing a relationship
IV. Cooling off
V. Drifting away

Remember: Outlines, like introductions, conclusions, transitions, and other paraphernalia of the writer's craft, are a means to an end. Try not to lose sight of the end—of what your writing is meant to do for you as a writer and for your audience. Writing becomes mechanical when the author is too intent on putting the pieces together according to a set formula. You can learn from studying and imitating the devices that have worked for other writers, but ultimately you have to use such means creatively and imaginatively for your own ends.

EXERCISE 5   *Checking Coherence*

Study the following exceptionally well-focused and coherent writing sample. Answer the following questions:

☐   Which of the familiar methods of *development* does the writer use— examples, explanation, reasons, quotations, statistics? Where and how?

☐   Can you find any network of *related terms*? Which phrases in the passage echo the central idea that certain American companies flour- ished or did well in Japan? (Which phrases relate to the opposite thread of failure?)

James Fallows
HOW TO SUCCEED IN JAPAN

Many American companies have become insiders and flourished in Japan. The Shaklee pharmaceutical firm, for example, perceived that vitamin pills, which in Japan had traditionally been sold at drugstores, were not legally classified as drugs, and could therefore be sold directly to the consumer, through the door-to-door approach the firm had relied on in America. The Japanese drug companies watched, seemingly paralyzed, as Shaklee cornered the vitamin market. They were reluctant to imitate its direct-sales approach, for fear of offending the distribution chains on which they still depended for sales of prescription drugs. Schick razors crushed their established Japanese competitors and, according to Kenichi Ohmae, in his book *Triad Power,* "succeeded in changing the shaving habits of the nation—from evening in *ofuro* (bath) to the morning with their spray foam." Japanese grocery stores now feature products from Del Monte, Nabisco, and Beatrice Companies. IBM has 15,000 of its own employees in Japan, and it recently moved its Pacific region headquarters, along with several hundred staff members, to Tokyo from the United States. Coca-Cola dominates the Japanese soft-drink market, and the proliferation of successful food chains—McDonald's, Kentucky Fried Chicken, Shakey's, Mister Donut, and 7-Eleven— has led some Japanese to argue that the United States is bent on debauching the Japanese palate through junk food. "If one looks at the unprecedented speed of change in dietary habit of a nation as big as 120 million in population, one might be led to believe in the 'American conspiracy' theory," Ohmae writes.

Nearly all the success stories involve companies that have taken the trouble to understand what the Japanese are like and what they want, instead of willing them to desire American-style goods in American styles and sizes. Ohmae says that American refrigerator companies initially ran into trouble because their standard models seemed gargantuan when placed in tiny Japanese kitchens and because the exhaust fans blew at floor level, where most Japanese preferred to sleep. American automakers have traditionally pushed left-hand drive cars in Japan, as if in hopes that the Japanese would abandon their folly of driving on the wrong side of the road. Mister Donut and McDonald's altered the sizes and formulas of their wares (gradually readjusting them toward the American ideal over the years). Barbie dolls took off only after their bustlines were reduced and their hair and eyes modified to look more plausibly Japanese.   *Atlantic*

EXERCISE 6   *Tracing Related Terms*

Study the following passage. Trace the network of terms or expressions that refer in some way to the sending or reception of signals.

The transmission of television and other signals by satellite has become a technological commonplace. Communications satellites now ring the globe. They have made possible improved navigation and flight control, worldwide high-speed data transmission, business teleconferencing, and increased telephone service. (The annoying little delay in most international and many domestic phone calls is the time it takes a microwave, traveling at the speed of light, to zip back and forth between Earth and a satellite.) They have also brought about the rapid expansion of cable television, the wild proliferation of new programming, and in the past four or five years a brand-new industry aimed at enabling people to receive satellite signals in their homes. Perhaps a million Americans own satellite antennas of varying shapes and sizes. They use them to receive as many as a hundred different television channels bearing everything from X-rated movies to unedited network news stories to Russian weather reports to talk shows whose hosts are nuns.

Ten years ago no regular American television programming was transmitted by satellite. Today almost every viewer, whether or not he owns a satellite antenna, watches shows that have spent at least part of their lives bouncing through outer space.   David Owen, "Satellite Television," *Atlantic*

EXERCISE 7   *Tracing Transitions*

Study the two following passages from a discussion of sexual stereotypes. Find all the transitional phrases. Explain how they are used, how they steer the attention of the reader.

When people respond to one of the many stereotypes of women, they are reacting to an idea rather than to the real person. Therefore, their impressions are often wrong, and their behavior is often inappropriate. For example, if people think a woman is a soft and delicate creature incapable of reason, they may defend, protect, and think for her. They may substitute their reality for hers and deny her own experience its validity.

But worse than having her individuality denied by others, is the way she herself may identify with the stereotypes, treating herself as less than a person. . . .

Women have traditionally had their roles and their worth defined for them by their usefulness in the family. The woman who pours great energy and talent into the task of rearing children and making a home for her family fulfills a role which is vital to society's survival. However, she is unlikely to be paid or given any positive public recognition. Instead, she is known as "just a housewife," a label which belittles all her dedication and effort as well as the vital role she performs.

Although traditional roles for women are undervalued, they may nevertheless be very attractive. For one reason, these roles are systematically taught. For another, they deal with women's potential ability to create and shape human life and are thus a symbol of creative power. As a result, the woman who becomes a wife and mother is often responded to on the symbolic level alone.   James Hall, Nancy J. Jones, and Janet R. Sutherland, *Women: Portraits*

7

WORD PROCESSING

A Brief Guide

The student should see the computer as a tool, not a super-efficient authority.   Lillian S. Bridwell

HARDWARE AND SOFTWARE The technology of writing has changed greatly since officials and traders in the Middle East first used wedge-shaped markings on clay tablets for messages and records. Many professional writers, including most journalists, today use word processors that allow them to draft and revise on a monitor screen, to store documents on disks for future reference, and to print out finished copy. Many students do most or all of their writing on a personal computer (PC) with word processing capability; others have access to work stations hooked up to large **mainframe** computers. Increasingly, colleges are making easily used PCs available on campus—in public clusters or in specially equipped classrooms.

Word processing is making it easier for writers to write and rewrite. It greatly eases the task of reworking a text and getting it into final shape. The writer can simply type over wrong words, shift whole sentences or paragraphs without retyping, and add or delete without the drudgery of recopying a whole document. Increasingly, the software that programs the word processor includes editorial aids that help the writer start a paper, explore the subject, revise a first draft, spot spelling errors, and the like. Increasingly, writers will be able to call up on their screens input or feedback from peers, instructors, and computerized sources.

In your own use of the word processor, you may at first think of it as a challenge or as a gadget or both. In due time, you will come to use it simply as a tool that helps you shorten the distance between the ideas fermenting in your mind and the written communication that you transmit to your readers.

119

The hardware, or physical equipment, for your word processor includes familiar parts:

☐ The *keyboard* resembles a typewriter keyboard but has additional function keys (or additional functions for the same keys). You use the keyboard not only to type your text but to give the commands that tell the computer to add, delete, and move; to italicize and boldface (print in bolder type); or to file and retrieve.

☐ The *monitor* looks like a small television screen. It displays the text you are working on, text you have called up from your files, the index of the texts you have stored, or the **menu** of possible instructions from which the computer asks you to choose (for instance, to store or to print). Your word processing program may allow you to use a split screen to look at two parts of the same paper, or at two different documents, at the same time.

☐ The *disk drives* accommodate the software (program disk) needed to program your word processor as well as the data disks that will store what you have written. Manufacturers are constantly expanding the **memory** of computers—their capacity for handling elaborate programs and bulky texts.

☐ The *printer* produces the final printout, or **hard copy.** First-generation printers often produced unconventional lettering and hard-to-read pale print. Current equipment produces impressive professional-looking copy, with capacity for using different shapes and sizes of print (or **fonts**).

Software tells the hardware what to do. Word processing software varies in ease of use and range of features. Ideally, a program has simple key strokes for tasks ranging from deleting a paragraph to italicizing a phrase; it has elegant, simplified commands that soon become second nature for the writer. Some programs take on chores like alphabetizing and formatting a list of sources for a research paper. If you are doing your writing in a computer lab, you may find yourself using software that came with the equipment. Whatever the strengths or limitations of the program you are using, any time you can spare to become thoroughly familiar with its features will be well spent.

EXERCISE 1 *Comparing Notes*

Prepare to share your knowledge or your questions about word processing with your classmates. What software, if any, do you know? How do you add/insert? How do you delete/erase? How do you move/transpose? What is the meaning of recurrent commands like *return* or *escape*? How do you set up a file, index it, save it, and retrieve it? How do you handle margins, indenting, double-spacing? How do you underline, italicize, or boldface? What are special features or limitations of a word processing program that you know?

WRITING WITH A WORD PROCESSOR
Writers vary in how completely they become married to the word processor. Some will scribble a scratch outline or cluster a key term on a piece of paper before they turn on the machine. Some like to print out a trial draft to annotate by hand before they revise. But many others will use the word processor at every stage of the writing process. Note that in word processing, even more than in other kinds of writing, the different stages overlap and blend. For instance, the gathering of material shades over into preparing a first draft, because the writer can easily transfer and incorporate into an early draft ready-made material from prewriting—from notes, brainstorming exercises, or preliminary outlines. Similarly, the writer can easily return to a source late in the revision stage to plug in additional data.

Word processing makes it easier for us to implement writing strategies that in ordinary writing we may be tempted to skimp or bypass as too laborious:

Prewriting
The word processor makes it easy to brainstorm, to list tentative ideas. You can add new ones as they come to mind, take out those that seem to lead you in the wrong direction, and start reshuffling the items as a tentative pattern starts to emerge. Professional writers early start filing possibly useful news clippings, quotations, or statistics, arranging them under tentative headings to make them easily accessible for future use.

Drafting
Many users find drafting on the word processor a more flexible, more fluid process than drafting by hand or on the typewriter. They can infinitely reshape and transform their trial version as they follow their tentative lines of thought and try out different ways of saying things. The electronic medium encourages and facilitates experimentation. It enables us to change the text almost as easily as we change our minds; it narrows the gap between the way we think and the way we write.

Revising
Ease of revision is the great selling point of word processors. No more whiteout or messy erasures: You can delete or sometimes simply type over unwanted passages. You can add or insert examples and expla-

nations, pushing back and reformatting the rest of the text. You can move or transpose whole passages or blocks of material as you rethink the organization of a paper or restructure an argument.

After you delete, add, or transpose, check your revised passages to be sure that your changes have not left sentences garbled or the flow of thought unclear. Look at the way the revision of the following paragraph *integrates* new material, filling in the right logical and grammatical links:

ORIGINAL:

> After the stark functional surfaces of the past, post—modern architecture signals a return to frivolity, to decoration for its own sake. At the top of tall buildings, we suddenly see sloping surfaces, curved gables, rosette windows, and curlicues. Some of them look like the playful shapes we might draw in an idle moment on a piece of paper.

REVISED:

> After the stark functional surfaces of the past, post—modern architecture signals a return to frivolity, to decoration <u>for the fun of it</u> and for its own sake. <u>In the heyday of modern (Bauhaus) architecture, architects built totally functional boxes of glass and steel that were all right angles. Today, we look up to</u> the top of tall <u>new</u> buildings <u>and</u> see sloping surfaces, curved gables, rosette windows, and curlicues. Some of them look like the playful shapes we might draw in an idle moment on a sheet of paper.

Editing In final editing of your work, you can correct many spelling errors and punctuation problems with the stroke of a key. You may also be able to instruct the computer to find and correct *all* occurrences of a mis-spelled word (like *mideval*) in your text. If a spelling check is part of your software, it will identify clear-cut misspellings like *identifed* and *should of* and query possible confusions (*to* or *too*? *there* or *their*?).

Formatting Your word processor will do much of the work of arranging words on a page:

- It will automatically begin *a new line* when you reach the set margin. You will usually be able to fill in a very uneven right margin by going back over a block of text and hyphenating some words and shifting others. (You can also usually **justify** the lines—have the computer adjust and stretch the lines for an even right margin, as we are used to seeing in a printed text.)

□ Your word processor will automatically start *a new page* and number each page.

□ Your word processor will usually help you *center* titles or lines of poetry.

Storing Your manual or user's guide will usually urge you to store your paper (or each major chunk of a bigger project), transferring it from the computer's memory to a storage disk to keep it from being accidentally erased. You may print out a tentative draft, wait till you have a more finished copy, or store a document for future reference or later revision. When you are preparing a letter or other document to be sent out to different readers, you can easily *adapt* the same basic document for different recipients, adding a personal touch and adding or removing information as needed.

Researchers are beginning to ask how the new technology will affect the writing habits of a new generation. Will the ease of composing on the screen make writers move on too fast, producing bland and unstructured prose? Will the ease of revision make writers tinker too much with individual words and phrases, slowing them down, making them lose sight of the whole? To benefit fully from the capabilities of your word processor, remember advice like the following:

□ *Let the word processor help you overcome writer's block.* Most students write more freely when they know they can instantly erase, retrace their steps, take a different tack, or start over again. Use the equipment to think out loud, to talk to yourself, until writing becomes as natural as driving a car.

□ *Use the word processor as an electronic note-taker.* Feed in data, statistics, lists, trial outlines, quotable quotes, summaries, tips on promising sources. Include with each item a key word or retrieval code that keys them to a writing assignment or to a subdivision of a project.

□ *Feel free to break out of the linear mode.* Putting one sentence after another is not the only way to draft a paper. Many professional writers first sketch out a rough skeleton of ideas, leaving blanks to be filled in later. Gradually they flesh out the first rough scheme, filling in material from notes, making adjustments to reflect second thoughts.

□ *Do not lose sight of the larger structure of your paper.* Do not limit your view to the portion of a paper that appears on your screen. Scroll backward or forward as necessary to check how the passage you are working on fits into the larger whole. Experiment with moving blocks of material around to strengthen logical connections and to improve the flow of ideas.

☐ *Store earlier drafts or trial versions.* Do not always simply let earlier materials go down the memory hole. At times, you may want to reconsider changes you have made or rethink the way a paper has developed.

☐ *Do not be fooled by the finished appearance of word-processed copy.* Your text will look deceptively finished and publishable both on the screen and when printed out. But actually the speed and ease of typing on an electronic keyboard multiply transposed letters (*wrtier*), run-together words (*taggedon*), random misspellings, and miscellaneous glitches. Whenever you can, *double*proof all text: Proofread it first when it is still on the screen, then again when you print out a trial copy.

Skeptics among writing teachers warn that word processing may tempt students to take less time to churn out more stuff. Writing will become easier but not necessarily better. It's up to you to prove the skeptics wrong.

EXERCISE 2   *Thinking Out Loud*

In recent years, a number of widely read books have raised the question of cultural literacy. How much do today's students know about their own history and the common traditions of their culture? The following is a typical anecdote told by writers who give a pessimistic answer to this kind of question. Enter the passage on your screen. Then go on typing, writing your reactions, comments, examples or counter-examples, arguments or counter-arguments.

A history instructor found that an increasing number of her students could not understand what Hitler had done wrong. One student described Hitler as "a kid with a dream" who enjoyed "a pretty good run at the top of the charts."

EXERCISE 3   *The Missing Links*

How are the sentences in the following paragraph related? Enter the paragraph on your screen. Then, at the beginning of as many sentences as you can, *insert* a missing link. Choose a transition like *also, for instance, similarly, finally, however, but, in fact, it is true that,* or *on the other hand.*

Our history textbooks have often pictured the Spaniards as a haughty and fanatical people. Every school child used to read about the cruelties of the Spanish Inquisition in hunting down the enemies of the true faith. Anglo historians have often blamed the Spanish conquistadores for wholesale massacres of the native populations of Mexico and Peru. Recently historians have asked us to revise this negative picture. Millions of Indians died in the fifty years after the Spanish conquest. Most of them died as victims of Old World diseases like smallpox, against which they had no immunity. Prominent leaders in the Spanish church argued that the Indians were not savages but had immortal souls and deserved our love as fellow human beings. More than other colonial nations, the Spaniards intermarried with the conquered peoples.

EXERCISE 4   Squeezing the Text

Assume that you are editing a feature called "A Glimpse of the Past" for a student publication or a company newsletter. You have sent the following story of about 100 words to the printer, but there is space for only 80 words. Enter the complete passage on your screen. Then delete enough words to make the story fit the available space; make other adjustments as needed to make the story read smoothly.

In 1956, a member of Congress stood before the House of Representatives to report an outrage. He had come to say that a lobbyist had offered to pay him $2,500 for his vote on a bill deregulating the price of natural gas. Today this would be considered a paltry sum, not enough to bribe a building inspector. However, the congressman trembled with indignation and denounced the "pestilent stench of foul corruption." After the resulting outcry, the President vetoed the legislation. Another bill to deregulate the price of natural gas did not come before the House for twenty-two years.

EXERCISE 5   Changing the Flow

Study the following passage and enter it on your screen. Assume that you are the author and that you have decided to make two major changes. Move the second sentence to the end as a clincher sentence. Rearrange the order of the examples so that there will be a better flow from the least to the most serious.

Professionals often face a familiar dilemma: whether to reveal to others dark secrets that their clients have told them in the strictest confidence. Often the choice is to tell and feel like a rat or to keep silent and become an accomplice. Should a psychiatrist warn an ex-spouse that a patient is planning to "get even"? Should a priest tell the authorities that a parishioner has committed murder? Should a journalist go to jail for contempt of court rather than reveal to a judge the source for information about organized crime? Should a teacher tell parents about teenagers planning to elope?

COMPUTER-AIDED WRITING Publishers of word processing software promote a variety of computer programs designed to help writers write. These programs play the role of an electronic tutor or coach. For instance, they may take you through a set of questions that will help you bring your topic into focus, think about your audience, explore different facets of your subject, and consider standard ways of organizing your material. Some of these programs talk to the user in a very businesslike (or machinelike) fashion; others use an unfailingly friendly and encouraging tone. You need to remember that the electronic brain-in-a-box does not really understand what you are saying. It is merely programed to nudge you into exploring and developing your topic; if the program is sophisticated enough, it will pick up certain key words and basic question patterns in your queries.

Prewriting Prewriting programs keep you thinking and writing through a set of prompts, asking you, for example, to spell out what you know about the background, expectations, values, expertise, and probable attitudes of your audience (**audience analysis**). Programers are developing ingenious kinds of electronic **brainstorming,** asking you, for example, to list first possibly useful ideas and details and then asking questions like "What is the connection between Item A and Item B?"

Often a program will map out a standard method for approaching different kinds of writing, such as autobiographical narrative, definition, or comparison and contrast. To help you develop an autobiographical paper, the program might ask:

```
Who is the most important character (other than you) in your
story?
```

The program might then follow up with a battery of questions: How does she look? What does her appearance tell us about her? What kinds of things does she say? How does she act? The computer can thus nudge you to flesh out the character—to make your readers see the character, to bring her to life.

To help you analyze a character in a short story or a play, a program might ask you a set of questions like the following:

What is your first impression of the character?

What do we learn about his physical appearance, manners, or unusual characteristics?

What are key quotations that tell us how he thinks and feels?

What are revealing actions—or failures to act?

What do other characters say about him? What do we learn about his reputation?

The computer thus nudges you to follow up questions that experienced writers learn to ask themselves. Typically, the questions are intended as thought starters: When you enter a term, the program might ask you what its opposite is, what its causes are, and what its results are. It may often simply prod you by repeatedly saying "Explain" or "I'm not sure I understand."

Organizing The systematic questions asked by a program will often help you impose a preliminary structure on your materials—to create a kind of tentative order. Furthermore, if you tell the computer that your purpose is to compare the Greek and Roman civilizations, it might sketch out and explain for you two or three major ways to organize a comparison and contrast. A set of questions like the following might help you structure an argument:

What is the issue or controversy?

What stand are you taking on the issue?

What are your major reasons for taking this stand? What are the arguments on your side? What is the evidence for each?

What are the major opposing arguments? What is wrong with them? How would you show them to be wrong?

What doubts or questions might your audience have about the claim you are making? How would you answer their questions and reassure your audience?

A writing tutorial is likely to offer you ways of strengthening organization when you revise. A program may enable you to pull out and line up first (or perhaps first and last) sentences of paragraphs so you can check transitions and the flow of ideas. Or you may be able to highlight and then pull out key sentences (topic sentences)—not always necessarily the first sentence of a paragraph.

Editing Much thought is going into the development of programs that would improve style—help you make your writing clearer and more direct. You may be using software that provides a jargon alert—counting such telltale features as abstract nouns ending in *-tion* or *-sion* (*utilization, implementation, extrapolation, diminution*). The same program may flag for you frequent use of forms of *be*, such as *is, was,* and *were*, which help produce passive rather than active verbs ("The new immigrants *were deemed* undesirable" rather than "My family *disliked* the new immigrants"). Remember that the computer is counting, not judging. It can tell you that you are using many long sentences but not whether they are right for your purpose.

A style check programed to detect sexist language may flag for you gender-specific terms like *landlady, chairman, stewardess,* and *bellboy.* The strength of the computer is that it can quickly scan pages of material to alert you to *potential* trouble spots, including especially words easily confused, such as *accept* and *except* or *there* and *their.* Increasingly, on such items, you will be able to call up brief pointed instructions that help you make an informed choice. You may be able to call up *backup* instructions or additional examples to help explain the explanations. Increasingly, you will be able to call up help from an on-line dictionary or on-line handbook, with pointers for revision displayed next to your own text on a split screen.

Regardless of what the advertising says, editing software is a long way from providing the automated error control that would make human editors and proofreaders obsolete. However, much fascinating work is going on in teaching computers the rudiments of human language and teaching the computer's artificial intelligence to make some of the decisions today made only by human beings.

COMPUTERS TODAY AND TOMORROW In our high-tech world of rapid change, today's tomorrow will soon be tomorrow's yesterday. Designers and programers everywhere are working on products that will make today's hardware and software obsolete. Here are some current developments that give us a glimpse of the shape of things to come:

Networking Increasingly, writers will be linked by electronic networks enabling them to trade comments, secure speedy feedback, or work as a team. Your personal computer or college workstation may already be part of a network that enables other students to see and to comment on or react to your writing at various stages. **Peer criticism** can thus help guide and shape your writing; **collaborative** writing projects of various kinds become possible.

Your instructor may already prefer to have you turn in papers or exams on a disk, so that comments and suggestions entered on the disk can take the place of handwritten comments. Or your writing may reach the instructor (and the instructor's comments reach you) through a network linking the word processors of teacher and students. Comments may be attached to a text as a whole or pinpointed (and coded) to a specific section of a paper.

Computerized Research Computerized information services and research tools are greatly simplifying and speeding up a writer's search for sources. A system like INFOTRAC provides an instant listing of relevant current newspaper and magazine articles from hundreds of publications. By typing in key words or retrieval codes, you can call up on the screen (and print out if you wish) a formidable range of sources on subjects like marriage, divorce, acid rain, recessions, or men's fashions. You can call up book reviews, articles by or about a person, or sources of printed information about a company or business. The WILSEARCH system provides access to periodical indexes including the *Reader's Guide to Periodical Literature, Biography Index, General Science Index, Social Sciences Index, Art Index,* and *Book Review Digest.* You can instruct the computer to search for background information published on your topic over many years.

The DIALOG information service provides access to many different databases—collections of information stored in large computers. The service allows you to tap into sources of information covering areas like government statistics, science, medicine, law, business, finance, or current news events. A printed index (or a librarian) can help you find the right **descriptors**—subject labels or key words that will help the computer search for material on your topic. If your home computer has a **modem,** or telephone hookup, you may be able to have a complete reprint of an article produced on your own printer.

Desktop Publishing Another current development affects the publication or dissemination (rather than the genesis) of your writing: Desktop publishing makes possible the speedy local preparation of publications of profes-

---

THE WRITING WORKSHOP

The Cutting Edge

Team up with a group to investigate state-of-the-art writing tutorial programs or editing software. Farm out to different members of the group such areas as starting a paper, audience analysis, brainstorming, developing a comparison, writing a narrative, analyzing the beginning of a story, or style analysis. Pool your findings in a group report.

---

sional quality. An editorial committee of your classmates may take in hand the assembling and production of a high-quality collection of the best student writing in your class, of a group research effort, of writing focused on a timely theme, or of the results of an essay contest. In desktop publishing, the capability of a word processor for formatting text and justifying lines and the capability of a quality printer for using different font (or lettering) styles and sizes make possible a printed product comparable to one produced by offset printing. Writing is meant to be read; desktop publishing of student writing provides the logical final stage of the writing process that is missing when your writing goes no further than the instructor's desk.

Part Two

FROM EXPERIENCE TO EXPOSITION

Each writing task is different. Trucks, cars, dirt bikes, and bicycles are all modes of transportation, but they differ in what powers them and how we use them. Similarly, kinds of writing are means of communication, but they differ in purpose and technique. As you take on different tasks, you become more aware of the range of writing—from the personal to the public, from the subjective to the objective, from writing that draws mainly on personal experience to writing that synthesizes material from printed sources. **Writing from experience** allows you to write with confidence about what you know best; you can discover how personal involvement transforms writing and makes it come to life. **Writing from observation** can teach you to do justice to what is "out there"; you discover how much of being a good writer is being an alert observer. **Writing to inform** requires you to lay out information and ideas for your reader; you learn how to impose a grid upon experience in order to help your readers find their bearings. **Writing from sources** can teach you how to use authoritative information, how to synthesize informed opinion on a subject. These tasks are not mutually exclusive; they overlap and combine in fascinating ways. But by focusing on them one at a time, you can make sure they become part of your education as a writer.

8

EXPERIENCE

The Story with a Point

I write of one life only: my own. If my story is true, I trust it will resonate with significance for other lives.   Richard Rodriguez

Writing is like a mirror. Whoever goes to the mirror risks a confrontation with the self.   Student paper

Day after day, week after week, I sat there sorting things out. . . . Writing became a way to make thoughts and feelings precise, make order out of disorder.   Barbara Gordon

THE STORY WITH A POINT When you write about your personal experience, you write about what you know best. You may focus on a turning point in your life or trace the common strand in a series of related events. You may write about the first taste of success or failure, the struggle to be accepted by a group, or the divided loyalties after a divorce. When writing on such autobiographical topics, you take stock of who you are, what has made you what you are.

Writing from Experience: Why Writing about personal experience can teach basic lessons about good writing:

□ *Writing from experience helps you discover motives that make writers write.* Writing has a special drive when you justify hard choices or express pent-up disappointment or indignation. You are likely to write with conviction when you tell your side of a quarrel, or air a long-standing grievance, or come to terms with something that has held you back. Some of the most eloquent writing you do will be on topics that touch you personally, issues that are close to home.

135

☐ *Writing from experience helps give your writing substance.* Your family, your memories good or bad, your successes and disappointments—these you know better than anyone else. When you draw on these resources, your writing does not simply echo what others have said. If you write about violence or prejudice, you can put your readers in situations where they see people act out patterns of violent or prejudiced behavior. The student who wrote the following passage made sure *prejudice* did not just remain a word:

WRITING SAMPLE: PERSONAL EXPERIENCE

Stopping for Gas

I remember several incidents that helped me see the truth about race relations. Once my family was traveling across the country to South Carolina to visit relatives. I recall our stopping at a small broken-down gas station. We waited and waited for service. My father even backed up the car and went forwards to the pump again to make the bell ring a second time. I remember the attendant, wearing a white T-shirt and open red-checkered flannel jacket, leaning back in his chair, looking out at us, and then continuing to read his *Field and Stream* magazine. I asked my father what the problem was, and he replied that it must be closing time. I suspiciously looked out of the back window as we pulled away. I saw another car pull up with a white driver, and the attendant, throwing down his magazine, jogged out to pump gas.

☐ *Writing from personal experience tests your ability to organize material.* Much day-to-day experience is miscellaneous; writing about it in a journal or diary, you may fall into an "and-then . . ." pattern. To make others listen to your story, you will have to make it a story with a point. You need to bring some central issue into focus, to work out the pattern that gives shape to what occurred. The following excerpts from a student paper show a classic pattern of growing up—of developing a broader outlook as the writer moves through several stages:

WRITING SAMPLE: PERSONAL EXPERIENCE

Sports, Anyone?

first stage
the outsider

As a child, I had a marked disdain for sports. This was probably the result of my being very bad at them. While my grade school peers played Pop Warner football and Little League baseball, I went to art and music camp. This was no real problem until junior high school. There, adolescents were socially made or broken in gym class. People who were good at sports were cool. People who had the misfortune of having a pair of hands like masonry were seriously not cool. . . .

second stage
sports for status

I cowered my way through seventh grade, my self-confidence plummeting as I was picked last for every sport. That summer I grew a few inches and wondered how I would survive. One way was to become a fan of sports. I took up basketball. I rooted hard, studied statistics daily, and learned about jump shots and layups. Eventually, my basketball prowess enabled teams to pick me second or first. The real status leap occurred in the ninth grade when I became a gym helper, assisting the gym teachers with the lowly seventh graders. . . .

third stage
sports for personal
satisfaction

Since, I have graduated from basketball, soccer, and stickball in high school to volleyball, bicycling, and jogging in college. Today I enjoy sports for the physical pleasure of doing something well with my body, of feeling healthy, of learning the limits of my physical capabilities. I have moved beyond the kind of jock mentality that knows sports only for winning, for dominating the other side.

□ *Writing about experience can help you discover your audience.* When your classmates react to a personal story, you may discover that you can get others to care about something that mattered to you. Donald Murray, a widely known writing teacher, said, "If I am specific and honest about my grandmother, other people will be interested." If the result is a "good, honest, specific piece of writing," its meaning "will echo and re-echo in the reader's mind." Some autobiographical writing may seem to aim at a special clientele: The story of a refugee from oppression who found sanctuary in this country may seem to aim at Americans with a similar past or family history. But in fact the story of escape from hostile or oppressive authority is likely to strike a chord in many other readers.

Questions for Discussion Do you remember reading an autobiographical account that moved you or fascinated you? What was the writer's story? Why did it have a special meaning for you as a reader?

Writing from Experience: How

When you write from personal experience, what special skills will help you with the task? What will help you to bring your papers to life—to make them authentic, dramatic, provocative?

NARRATION You will often trace one key event or a series of related events. Good storytellers know how to hook readers into a story. They focus on the *high points*—events essential to moving the story along, incidents that reveal someone's true thoughts or motives. They set up *conflicts* that produce dramatic action. They know how to create *suspense*—to lead the reader up to a climactic confrontation or revelation.

Often an effective storyteller lets the story speak for itself, without getting in its way. Study the following dramatic account of an event that changed the writer's life:

The three of us had arrived at the incinerator, unlocked the locks, opened the gate, and pulled the truck close to the burner. We knew that as soon as this task was over we were free for the rest of the day. There were six hours of burning to do, but we tried to do it in four. We stuffed the 1,000 pounds of discarded printouts into the incinerator, fluffing as much material as possible for easier burning. The driver suggested gasoline to help speed things up, and we agreed. We spread the highly combustible liquid evenly over the papers. I promptly locked the four locks on the eight-foot doors, leaving only the fire check door open. Leaning through the fire door, I lit a match to a piece of paper, luckily not lighting one soaked in gasoline. I had not stepped two steps backward when the bomb exploded in front of us. Red, orange, and blue flames with a cloud of black ashes burst through the doors. The blast had thrown me against the barbed wire fence, covering me with black ash. I heard a shout, "I can't see! I can't see!"

DIALOGUE   Effective writers use **dialogue** to make people's thoughts and feelings real for the reader. They have an ear for how people talk—what they are likely to say, or say back, in a situation. In much good narrative, we hear authentic voices that praise, question, nag, tease, encourage, insult, or complain. In the following passage, a master storyteller makes people real for us by letting us hear them talk:

> The waitress came and stood by Dad. "Can I get you something from the bar?" she said. Dad blushed a deep red. The question seemed to imply that he looked like a drinker.
>
> "No," he whispered, as if he were turning down her offer to take off her clothes and dance on the table.
>
> Then another waitress brought a tray of glasses to a table of four couples next to us. "Martini," she said, setting the drink down, "whiskey sour, whiskey sour, Manhattan, whiskey sour, gin and tonic, martini, whiskey sour."
>
> "Ma'am? Something from the bar?" Mother looked at her in disbelief.
>
> Suddenly the room changed for us. Our waitress looked hardened, rough, cheap . . . .
>
> "Ed," my mother said, rising.
>
> "We can't stay. I'm sorry," Dad told the waitress. We all got up and put on our coats. Everyone in the restaurant had a good long look at us. A bald little man in a filthy white shirt emerged from the kitchen, wiping his hands. "Folks? Something wrong?" he said.
>
> "We're in the wrong place," Mother told him. Mother always told the truth, or something close to it.   Garrison Keillor, *Lake Wobegon Days*

EXPRESSING FEELINGS   A good account of personal experience does justice to what people do and say but especially also to what they feel. Much of the point of what you write will be in how you and other people react or respond. To make your readers share in your feelings, anchor them to actual situations, relationships, or events. As far as possible, reenact the situations that brought the emotions into play. Much of the strong feeling in the following student-written passage is carried by gestures, actions, comparisons:

> Our parents were always fighting. They would rage at each other's faults for hours on end. My mother's bitterness at having chosen the wrong man to marry

THE WRITING WORKSHOP

A Class Publication

Working with other members of your class, set up an editorial committee that will make plans for a class publication including one paper from each member of the class. Have each member of the class plan to submit one paper based on personal experience, designed to tell the reader something about the background or personality of the author. You may want to set up small groups for exchange of ideas and discussions of preliminary plans for papers, as well as for editorial sessions devoted to suggestions for revision or final editing. You may want to ask each member of the class to submit a final draft that is "print-ready"— ready for photocopying or other informal publication. The resulting publication would serve as a group portrait in print of your class.

In one representative class, the papers in the final class publication included

- a report on a summer spent as a volunteer worker in a convalescent hospital;
- the story of being raised in a strict Catholic family and deciding to join a religious order;
- the story of being torn between a popular, outgoing mother and a withdrawn, antisocial father;
- an account of growing up with a parent fighting a losing battle with alcoholism;
- the story of being raised in Japan by a Japanese-American father.

eventually destroyed us as a family. My brother tried to intervene, but that merely diverted their rage towards him for a while. I knew that if I got involved I would have to face those bitter, narrowed eyes and the assault of epithets that stung like gravel thrown by bullies. So I went into my room, shut the door, sat cross-legged on my bed, elbows on my knees, hands clamped over my ears, and read books.

POINT OF VIEW When writing about personal experience, you will normally be writing frankly in the **first person:** "*I* had a marked disdain for sports . . ." or "*my* parents fought. . . ." This personal perspective is clearly appropriate in **expressive** writing—when the focus is on expressing your own memories, thoughts, and feelings.

Remember: When you move on to other kinds of writing, your writing should preserve some of the qualities that bring accounts of personal experience to life. When readers see an article on the "new poverty," they hope that for the author poverty is not merely an abstraction that lives in statistics and government reports. When they see an article about excellence in education, they hope to find that the author has actually been in classrooms, has talked and worked with teachers and students. When you write on an issue of public concern, your writing will be more credible and more persuasive if at the right time you can say: "I was a witness: This is what I experienced; this is what I felt."

EXERCISE 1   *The Personal Voice*

What kind of person wrote each of the following passages? How did the writer make the people and events come to life? How do you react as a reader? What kind of readers would be an ideal audience for each passage, and why?

1.   The most vivid image I have of my childhood is of my uncle reading stories to my brothers and sisters and me. He would call us into the living room, and we would trip over each other trying to get through the doorway. There he would be waiting, a big man, sitting high in a big chair. We would sit at his feet, looking up into his dark, slightly scary face. He would wait until we settled down; then he would break into a wide smile and pull a book out from behind his back. He read us most of Roald Dahl's books; our favorite was *Charlie and the Chocolate Factory,* in which a young boy named Charlie and his grandfather go to a mysterious chocolate factory. Willy Wonka, the strange little chocolate magnate; Veronica, the spoiled rich kid; the boy who dressed up as a cowboy; the gas bubble room; and the candy that flew over air waves—these were all part of the story. My uncle knew how to make us laugh by acting out the story with giggles, grunts, groans, and grins. He raised and lowered his voice and waved his arms about. He created magic with those words, taking me places I had always wanted to go.   Student paper

2.   Contrary to what they showed in the movies in those days, the South didn't mean bourbon and hoop skirts, it meant red dirt and poor people, of which we had a lot. We also had our share of Southern historical monuments. Not antebellum mansions or statues of Robert E. Lee on his horse, for you could drive from Fayetteville to El Dorado and then backtrack to Texarkana without ever seeing any such thing. What you would see, though, was shanties, tarpaper houses, tumbledown barns, and chickens scratching industriously for bugs in bald front yards. In those days, if a car passed yours on the road, you'd have to roll the windows up or even pull over in the ditch and wait until the dust storm died down.   Shirley Abbott, "Southern Women," *Harper's*

3.   I had forgotten, in the rage of my growing up, how proud my father had been of me when I was little. Apparently, I had a voice and my father had liked to show

me off before the members of the church. I had forgotten what he had looked like when he was pleased but now I remembered that he had always been grinning with pleasure when my solos ended. I even remembered certain expressions on his face when he teased my mother—had he loved her? I would never know. And when had it all begun to change? For now it seemed that he had not always been cruel. I remembered being taken for a haircut and scraping my knee on the footrest of the barber's chair and I remembered my father's face as he soothed my crying and applied the stinging iodine. Then I remembered our fights, fights which had been of the worst possible kind because my technique had been silence.   James Baldwin, *Notes of a Native Son*

EXERCISE 2   *Words and Feelings*

How does the following student-written paragraph bring to life a general label for an emotion? Write a paragraph of your own in which you give concrete substance to a similar general label by relating it to personal experience. Choose a label like shyness, awkwardness, arrogance, hostility, suspicion, callousness, generosity, or naiveté.

Fear

Having taken a night class last semester, I learned the meaning of fear. I was new to this campus and had already signed up for night classes before I started hearing the stories of how dangerous it was to be out at night alone on the campus. Horror stories about rapes and murders had me wanting to drop my class which, ironically, dealt with abnormal psychology. Not being able to find a parking space in a lighted area within a block did not help things. Police phones were available to me but I always had the fear that, with my luck, my escort would be a mass murderer in disguise. I bought a key chain with a whistle attached and thought about taking a few self-defense courses. I never bought mace because I always feared that it would go off in my purse. I made it through that semester without a single incident, but I'd never take another night class again.

EXERCISE 3   *Capsule Portraits*

Study the following student-written capsule portraits of real people. How did the writer bring the person to life? Write five similar *one-sentence* snapshots of real people. Pack each sentence with authentic detail.

1. Dressed in an old plaid suit, the short, balding old man stumbled through the dark theater, unable to find the exit.
2. The young woman bending over the starting block, holding firmly onto its sides with

a look of concentration on her face, and staring into the as yet calm, unrippled water, was waiting for the sound of the gun that would start the race.
3. A friendly, middle-aged woman, with a pair of bifocal glasses and a chain that droops from each side of them, rings up groceries at the neighborhood market.
4. A stubby man with a few nails between his lips and one large and one small screwdriver in his shirt pocket stood at our door.
5. A relic from the sixties, the middle-aged man with the too-long hair jauntily sits dispensing change and banter, barely suppressing his favorite phrase: "Far out, man!"

EXERCISE 4 *Images and Feelings*

When you want to express feelings or attitudes, you will often use **figurative** language—imaginative comparisons to help you convey something that might be hard to put into words. What is fresh or different about the way the following sentences express feelings or attitudes? Write five similar *one-sentence* statements to convey feelings or attitudes that you have experienced or observed.

1. He had a joyful personality, like someone taking a shower in a soap commercial—full of zest.
2. She knew he was angry; his words hissed through his teeth like steam from a tea kettle.
3. The harried secretary felt like a marionette, strings pulled by an overzealous puppeteer.
4. She would look for dark spots in his character and drill away at them as relentlessly as a dentist at a cavity.   Mary McCarthy
5. He was like a piece of delicate china which was always being saved from breaking and which finally fell.   Alice Walker

EXERCISE 5 *Writing Dialogue*

Write a passage of dialogue in which you reconstruct an actual or typical conversation between two people. Recreate a conversation that brought strong feelings into play or revealed people's attitudes or motives. For example, recreate a discussion of security on campus; an argument over a slight, real or imagined; a complaint and the reaction to the complaint.

GATHERING: MOBILIZING YOUR RESOURCES

Writing about your personal experience, you should draw on a rich backlog of remembered events, thoughts, and feelings. Start by generating the material—working up an ample fund of material that you can then sort out and get into shape.

A Promising Topic

Your first step is to identify a promising topic—an issue or challenge, a recurrent strand in your experience. Your tentative topic might be a person who brings back vivid memories, a responsibility that has weighed on your mind, a conflict that forced you to take sides, or a situation that offered opportunity or limited your choices. Often a **journal entry** will contain the germ of a promising idea for a personal experience paper. The following example might lead to a paper focused on the pros and cons of old-fashioned discipline vs. personal independence:

> PREWRITING: JOURNAL ENTRY

> I went to Catholic schools for my education. I don't know if the experience helped me or not. I attended a Catholic grade school for eight years (where discipline was administered by the "Sisters of Mercy"). Then I went to a parochial high school in the same town, with reasonably good grades. Going to college has been a new experience for me, because it is the first time that I have had so much freedom. Usually there were so many rules that I could hardly breathe without getting into some kind of trouble. Now I am free to wear anything I want to school without having to answer to anyone. I know I am supposed to enjoy my new freedom but at times I am just floundering.

Make sure that the topic you settle on has a strong personal meaning for you. In a preliminary **planning report,** one student explained her choice of a topic as follows:

> PREWRITING: PLANNING REPORT

> Fitness has become a way of life for me. The benefits have always been obvious to me—improved health and an improved sense of well-being. These in turn lead to a certain self-assurance in other, unrelated endeavors. I can bring much from my own experience to this essay. I have played competitive tennis. I've hiked up and down the Grand Canyon. I jog every morning at 5 A.M. My family has a poor health and fitness background. My mother, a non-athlete, was a chain smoker and heavy coffee drinker most of her life and died of a heart attack in her early fifties. My older brother, born with a host of medical problems, is a non-athlete and a heavy drinker. In my essay, I would explain these facts as the motivation for my lifetime commitment to physical fitness.

Mobilizing Your Memory Take time to work up a rich preliminary collection of material. Rack your brains; start the flow of material that might be useful. As you study the following sample notes for a paper, ask yourself: Which of these materials seem especially promising? What overall conclusion or general direction do these notes suggest?

PREWRITING: ROUGH NOTES

Mother and Daughter

"looking nice"
"don't carry the ice chest"
"get good grades in school"
dependence—having to go for rides in the car to get out of the house and my mother being angry and staring out the window, head on her hand and not saying a word the whole time—I always thought that was ridiculous.

My grandmother was an independent woman. In 1928, she sailed from Canada to Manila, by herself, so that my grandfather and she could get married on his next leave from the Navy.

My mother was always concerned with what the neighbors would say, about anything. When I was in high school and went on a protest march, my mother wasn't concerned with the cause, if it was right or wrong, but "what will the neighbors say?"

Independence wasn't on the agenda for my mother's childhood. My grandmother, a woman of the 1920's, used her independence as a way and means. With the War, Depression, alone a lot and moving from base to base, she was outspoken, unconventional and atypical of an officer's wife.

My mother in contrast seemed meek and shy, growing in the shadow of their only other child, a boy. He was the one destined to follow in my grandfather's footsteps (although he never did).

Growing up with uncertainty, my sister seemed to flourish. She set a goal and has stayed with that same goal for 15 years. My brother and I floundered under a dual message. My father was a lightpost. Always there, sturdy despite his appearance, methodical and self-satisfied with himself. When my mother got furious and started slamming the kitchen cabinets and doors, my father would calmly ride out the storm. Trying to do the best that we could was father's objective for his children.

Thanksgiving dinner was always the same at our house. The women cooked the meal, served the meal and cleaned up after the meal, while the men sat down to watch the football game. Most of the women enjoyed this whole set-up. It was a chance to talk "girl talk": where the best bargains were, who was seeing whom (in terms of marriage), and what was happening on the soaps.

After you have had a chance to study or discuss this preliminary collection of material, read the paper that resulted from it. While working up and then rewriting her first draft, the writer brought out strongly the central thought or overall point that for her represented the unifying strand in her experiences. She developed some key incidents that were only hinted at in her notes. As you read the paper, ask yourself:

- □ What is the author's purpose or underlying motive?
- □ What is the thesis that the writer used to unify her material?
- □ What overall plan did she work out?
- □ What do you think is strong or weak about the finished paper?

WRITING SAMPLE: FINAL DRAFT

Declaration of Independence

I had a very fuzzy concept of the woman's role in society when I was growing up. My mother was a very dependent woman, relying on my father for everything from basic necessities to entertainment. She had a firm picture in her mind of what women should be. But at the same time I saw the frustration this vision of hers caused her, and I developed opposite tendencies for my benefit.

My mother wanted to be the type of woman that appeared in the *Dick and Jane* readers I grew up with in elementary school. Dick's and Jane's mother was always wearing crisp linen dresses with her curly hairdo and hanging the laundry in her well-trimmed yard. Already nicely dressed and made up, she would prepare breakfast for the whole family, kiss her briefcase-carrying husband goodbye as he drove off to his job, and send her immaculately dressed children off on the school bus.

My mother mirrored this blissful picture. She always tried to keep her appearance up with weekly trips to the beauty salon, and she exhausted herself by doing the first fifteen minutes of the daily exercise show. She spent much of her time being concerned with how things looked from the neighbor's viewpoint. She was especially pleased if her daughters were considered popular and her son considered brilliant. When I decided to become involved in a protest march, she didn't ask whether my decision was right or wrong; she asked, "What will the neighbors say?"

I first became confused about my own values when I realized how dependent my mother was on my father. On weekends, my mother expected to be "taken out." This usually meant going for rides, with my father driving, my mother in the other front seat, and the children in the back. I sometimes liked these rides—the warm feeling of being sandwiched between my brother and sister, the familiar smell of our old car, the chance to look at different houses and farms. Often, however, these rides would get off to a bumpy start. My father would be too tired, wanting to relax on the weekend. My mother would get irritated. Getting out of the house on the weekend, she felt, was her reward for taking care of the household during the week. She would start slamming doors and kitchen drawers until my father would say, "All right, let's go for a ride." By this time she would be so angry that she would slump into the car and stare out of the window, head on hand, and we would drive along in silence.

Part of my mother's philosophy was the notion that physical capabilities correlated with a person's sex. When I was thirteen and excited by the idea of a family camping trip, my mother stopped me from carrying a heavy ice chest with my father and had my less-than-average-size brother carry it instead. "She shouldn't be carrying that—she is going to hurt herself!" The only thing that was hurt in the incident was my pride.

I early saw what I did not want for myself by observing my mother's dependence. I had to take responsibility for my own happiness and well-being. I can't blame someone else if my life is not as I expect it to be. It can be frustrating trying to fix a drain or build a shelf, but it is satisfying to discover my own proficiencies. I push myself to the limits—physically in scuba diving and other sports, mentally in going to school while working. Pushing myself to the limit, I am trying to accommodate my own independent nature.

Questions for Discussion What helps bring this paper to life for you? Do you believe the reader would have to be a woman to respond favorably to this paper?

Covering the Story Some writers can call up ample material for an experience paper by following a chain of association, letting one memory lead to the next. Other writers do well when they ask themselves a set of strategic questions that explore major dimensions of the topic. Questions under headings like the following can serve as a **discovery frame** helping you work up a preliminary collection of material for your story with a point.

SETTING *Where* did the events take place? What sights and sounds can you use to make the place real for the reader? How are you going to set the scene?

PEOPLE *Who* took part or played a leading role in the events? How did these people look, act, and talk?

SITUATION *Why* could things happen the way they did? What events or relationships in the past led up to the present situation? What explains the confrontation that is waiting to happen, or the crisis that is ready to come to a head?

EVENT *What* actually happened? What was the high point? How did things come to a head?

POINT *So what?* What was the meaning of the incident for you? Why is it important to you? What did it make you think and feel? What did you learn from the experience?

The following example of a student paper follows the "Where-Who-Why-What-So What" pattern. What does the material under each heading contribute to the paper as a whole?

The Sad Kid

setting   The day room at the Dependent Unit of the County Juvenile Hall was a product of the Age of Institutions. Its entire L-shaped expanse was covered in an anonymous pale, speckled linoleum, except for one corner, which was carpeted in a military-green swatch of pile rug about five foot square. Across the room was gathered an assortment of seats: a formerly overstuffed sofa, growing thin by a tuft of stuffing at a time coming through its threadbare corners and edges; high-backed wooden chairs of the old principal's office variety, and a few metal folding chairs. The focal point for this arrangement was the television; when turned on, it provided the room's only color.

people   Scores of children gathered in the day room during the months I was counselor at the hall. They were abandoned, neglected, abused. What impressed me was their strength. They wasted no time before forming friendships, identifying adversaries, learning the rules and how to get around them, finding each other's strengths and weaknesses. Freddy was different. He spoke to no one but just watched with his great wary and suspicious eyes. He usually sat alone, cross-legged with his arms tucked against his body, his hands folded.

situation   Chance had brought me to Juvenile Hall. I was looking for a summer job and found someone who knew someone who could get me the job. A more tragic chance had brought Freddy there. His mother was undergoing intense psychiatric treatment, and there was no one to care for him. In his mind, he had been abandoned, and he had chosen to withdraw from all contact rather than risk betrayal again.

event   Saturday morning was the time we changed the bedding. All the children who were old enough were expected to do their own. Freddy fell into that category. But when, on my first Saturday on the job, I announced bed-making time, he didn't budge. Another boy informed me that Freddy never made his bed, a fact which they had all accepted as a kind of eternal truth. I knew then that it was vital that he make his bed. I lifted him bodily off the floor and carried him to his room. I then proceeded to make the sheets, discussing the process in great detail, and whenever possible tucking a corner of a sheet into his hand so he would be "helping."

Every Saturday thereafter, Freddy and I repeated this routine. As he came to expect that he would never be delivered from my mad obsession, he began to relax, making monosyllabic replies to my cheerful natterings. I found out he liked to draw, and he began to bring me pictures, which I put on the bulletin board. About six weeks after our initial confrontation, he came to me and said he had something to show me. I went with him to his room. There was his bed: not a single smooth place on it anywhere; the stripes on the bedspread made it look like the flag in a high wind. But he had made his own bed.

point   My battle with Freddy was the beginning of a change in my thoughts about a career. I had always wanted to teach, and I had thought that teaching students to

THE WRITING WORKSHOP

The Story with a Point

Suppose you have been asked to write about a memorable event from your own experience. Perhaps you have witnessed a quarrel that taught you something about the causes of violence. Perhaps you have had an encounter with the law. Or perhaps you have had a first serious experience with success or failure. For a *preliminary collection of material,* write responses to the kinds of questions listed under each of the five key headings that follow:

1. *The Setting: Where* did the event take place? What was the setting? What were some of the sights and sounds that helped create the atmosphere of the place? Re-create the place and the time for the reader.
2. *The People: Who* took part? What kind of people were they? How would the reader recognize them? How did they look, act, or talk? Provide capsule portraits of the key individuals involved.
3. *The Situation: Why* did things happen the way they did? What relationships, or what events in the past, led up to the present situation? Fill your readers in on any background that is important for them to know.
4. *The Event: What* actually happened? How did matters come to a head? Give the high points of the action in vivid detail.
5. *The Point: So what?* What was the meaning of the incident for you? What did you learn from the experience? Why, when you look back, does it seem important? What did the experience seem to show or to prove? Explain the point of the story or the meaning of the incident to your reader.

Share your collection of material with members of a small group or with your class as a whole. What parts of your material become real to them and why? What questions do they have that your preliminary material leaves unanswered? How do they react to the general direction or overall point of your paper?

think logically would be my best contribution to their success as adults. This was before I worked with children who had shut themselves off by various methods to avoid pain. I have discovered that there is joyful success as well as devastating failure in helping young people deal with their feelings.

Questions for Discussion Is the author of this paper male or female? Did the paper get you involved in the story; did it make you care? Why or why not?

EXERCISE 6   *Taking Notes*

Work up a preliminary collection of material for a topic that represents a major strand in your experience. Focus on a familiar abstract label for ways people act or interact—a label that at first was just a word for you but that gradually, as the result of firsthand experience, acquired a special meaning. Choose a topic like hostility, ambition, loyalty, conflict, rebellion, jealousy, rivalry, stress, competition, networking, dependence.

Try to work up a rich fund of possible material for your topic. Include what is *possibly* relevant so you can later pick and choose. Type up your preliminary notes and be prepared to discuss with your peers or with your instructor the possible focus and strategy of a paper based on these notes.

SHAPING: ORGANIZING YOUR EXPERIENCE
When you write about personal experience, you try to give shape and meaning to events that were miscellaneous, that occurred one after the other. When you merely string together events as they happened in time, your story may seem disjointed and half-finished. (As one writer said, "Life is all first draft.") You need to focus on a unifying issue; you need to discover the common strand. You need to chart an overall pattern that the reader can follow. Study some of the patterns that give shape to much writing about personal experience and adapt them for your own purposes:

A Turning Point
You will often follow **chronological** order—the order of events in time. You may take the reader along from a simmering conflict to a dramatic confrontation. Or you may trace the common thread linking events that occurred years apart. Remember to go beyond *mere* chronology. Break out of a miscellaneous "and-then" pattern: Highlight key events, set off

major stages, focus on a turning point. Each paragraph in the following excerpted paper takes the reader one important step forward:

WRITING SAMPLE: A TURNING POINT

The Price of Popularity

a phase in the writer's life

When I was sixteen, I tried to behave in a manner approved by my peers. The first rule in my high school was that members of the elite group socialized only with other members of the elite. Dreaming of acceptance, I began to emulate the trendy new styles worn by the social upper crust. . . .

the price of popularity

After my outward transformation was complete, I realized that my old friends were not good enough to be around a popular person. At lunch, I began to sit with people who were accepted. . . .

a serious turn of events

My time of popularity soon shattered, like a bottle that has been left underfoot. For two years, my old friends took a back seat to my new acquaintances. My old friends never complained. I still accepted rides from them, although I usually asked to be dropped off outside of school. That winter the doctors discovered that one of them had a tumor and needed chemotherapy. . . .

a climactic incident

When my friend returned to school, she had not changed inwardly, but her outside appearance had changed radically. Her long hair had disappeared, and she refused to wear a wig. The day she returned I was with my new associates. As she walked by, the people around me started to joke about her baldness. When I looked at their jeering faces, I realized that they were not my friends. . . .

a lesson learned

I have not talked to any of the popular people since that day in the spring of my junior year. For two years, I had neglected the two people who should have been closest to me. I had acted like a fool just to please other people.

Note: You are not *tied* to chronological order. For instance, you may be describing several incidents that illustrate an important source of tension or frustration in your life. You may then want to employ a **flashback** to an almost forgotten childhood event that helps explain some of your current attitudes or concerns.

An Instructive Contrast

Contrast is a familiar organizing principle in much autobiographical narrative. We used to be one kind of person; we now find ourselves changed. Our allegiance is divided between one side of the family and the other, or one part of the country and another. Here is a sample journal entry that contains the germ of an idea for a paper focused on such a contrast:

PREWRITING: JOURNAL ENTRY

I like to talk about myself (in case you have not noticed). I often talk about my childhood days in Brooklyn. My parents were both fairly young. We lived in a small apartment in the Canarsy section of Brooklyn where my parents worked in a small store. My fondest childhood memories are of playing whiffle ball with my friend in his backyard. After I finished fifth grade, my family moved to San Diego, where a whole new way of life awaited me. Even now I can't decide whether I'm a New Yorker or a Californian.

Often a writer developing such a contrast will devote the first half of the paper to the past, the second to the present. But the student developing the New York–California contrast chose to take up, in turn, three major changes in his way of life, showing the contrast between *then* and *now* for each:

WRITING SAMPLE: THEN AND NOW

Surf Is Up

It is hard for me to imagine what it must be like for a child to be transplanted from Vietnam or Hongkong to Lubbock, Texas. For me, it was traumatic enough to move from the fast pace and "mean streets" of Brooklyn to within a few miles of the Mexican border. In and out of school, I often felt like an actor playing a part he had not really had the time to memorize. I felt awkward around a surfboard (and still do).

first contrast In New York, I had been programed from the beginning of school to think that education was one of the most important things in life. My parents and my teachers were constantly talking about tests and test results. When I came to California, I soon found that although teachers were in favor of education, my friends did not consider it cool to compete openly for grades. . . .

second contrast I soon came to appreciate the climate that explained why my new friends would much rather be outside with others than inside doing such a trivial thing as homework. In New York, my friends had to be creative, inventing games to play indoors in case the weather was bad. In my new home, there was hardly a day when I could not ride my bike or play ball or join my friends around a pool. . . .

third contrast In the summer, parents in New York who had gotten tired of seeing their kids in the house all winter sent them upstate or to New Jersey to camp. In my early years, going to camp was a big thing. In California, some of my high school friends went to summer school (possibly to catch up with East Coast students). But for most of us, for three months in the summer, life revolved around the beach. . . .

From Experience to Exposition Much writing with a strong personal dimension relates the author's experience to a larger picture. It goes from the private to the public, from a personal truth to a more general point. In the following student paper, where and how does the writer test her own experience against the experiences of others?

The Right Move

thesis

Mobility: The word has come to mean something that a hundred years ago was unimaginable. We no longer simply move from one house to another as the family needs more room. Today, moves from city to city, from state to state, or from coast to coast are common. Are we losing something as a result of this ability to pack our possessions into a truck, wave goodbye to our neighbors, and leave our "sweet home"? I don't think so. The wonderful thing about our modern ability to move is that we can search out and find that location where we fit in or where we can be content.

personal experience

I grew up in a small town in Michigan; the population was 1000 people. The only Americans I knew were white middle-class farmers. Because I had friends out West and jobs were scarce in Michigan, I decided to move to Los Angeles at age eighteen. I carried a jar of pickled watermelon rind and some homemade strawberry preserves in my suitcase. At the airport, as I hugged my parents goodbye, I smelled the sweet hay scent of my father's flannel shirt, and I had to force myself to believe that I had made the right decision. However, no amount of college could have taught me as well how diversified America is as my move across the country. In my hometown there was only one black family. I had never met Filipinos, Mexicans, or Japanese. Today I work and go to school with people from many different backgrounds.

general pattern

We no longer load our belongings, children, and pets into covered wagons to forge ahead to a new territory. But our options are numerous. We can strike out in search of better jobs, better schools, or a more suitable environment.

supporting examples

Several of my friends have gone through the experience of making the right move. When I was still in high school, an older friend's parents announced that they were moving to the East Coast. My friend was reluctant. She had planned to stay in her hometown, raise a family, and farm like everyone else. But she finally sold her horse, threw away her overalls, and headed east. She is now one of the few from our town with a college degree and a different career.

Finding contentment does not always mean moving away from the farm. Another friend of mine had grown up in Los Angeles but had always dreamed of fishing, hiking, and raising children in a quiet country atmosphere. He drove to the city college every day, listening to country music in his old truck, until he earned his degree. He then moved to a tiny town in Iowa where, as he puts it, "even the mayor is unemployed." He is doing carpentry jobs to help support his family and is happier than ever before.

quoted source

A recent survey in *Better Homes and Gardens* found that four out of five people who had moved from one state to another were originally reluctant when the decision was first made. Three months after those moves, though, nearly all of them had positive feelings about the move and thought it a change for the better. People from farming towns in Michigan, steel towns in Pennsylvania, and fishing towns in Maine are discovering that moving can be a revitalizing experience.

EXERCISE 7   *The Larger Pattern*

In many classic autobiographical essays, the author's experience follows an archetypal pattern—a pattern that has close parallels in the lives
of many other people. The essay deals with the private experience of one
individual, but it at the same time illuminates an issue or a theme of
general human significance. Read an essay like the following. What is
the pattern of the author's experience? What is its larger significance?

- Maxine Hong Kingston, "The Woman Warrior"
- Richard Rodriguez, "Aria: A Memoir of a Bilingual Childhood"
- E. B. White, "Once More to the Lake"
- Alice Walker, "In Search of Our Mother's Gardens"
- James Baldwin, "Notes of a Native Son"
- George Orwell, "Shooting an Elephant"
- Henry David Thoreau, "Where I Lived, and What I Lived For"

REVISING: SECOND THOUGHTS
Your revision of an early draft is your chance
to have second thoughts about some basic questions: What kind of person is speaking in your paper? What is the point of the experiences you
describe? Look for opportunities to strengthen your paper in areas like
the following.

The Right Tone
What is your attitude toward your subject and toward your audience?
Is your main purpose to amuse or impress your audience? Or is it to
make your audience look sympathetically at something that matters to
you? Fight the temptation to present everything that happened to you
as hilarious or thrilling. Avoid the strained facetiousness of the writer
trying to make events seem funnier than they really were.

The Personal Voice
Our experiences are often fresh, personal, and intensely felt. But we
may be tempted to channel them into tired interchangeable phrases already
much used by other people. To keep your reader from saying, "I have
heard all these words before," avoid ready-made phrases like the following:

I experienced a *unique sense of accomplishment*. . . . My experience proved
that it is *possible to do anything if you want it badly enough*. . . . I learned to *work
together* with people *as a team*. . . . The experience was an *opportunity for personal*

growth that helped me discover *my self-identity.* . . . I learned that above all *communication is essential in a relationship.* . . .

One way to make your personal voice heard is to express the misgivings or mixed emotions that are part of true personal feeling:

On the subject of welfare I run hot and cold. One day I want to feed all the hungry people in the world. The next day I realize who is going to pick up the tab for this generosity, and I say, "Let them find a job."

The Unifying Thread As memories crowd in, you may wander from one favorite episode to another. Use your revision as an opportunity to focus on what is most important or closest to your heart. Will your readers become aware of a central issue or unifying theme? To strengthen unity in your paper, try including the kind of *preview* that sums up your thesis and at the same time sketches out the program for the rest of the paper. The following preview statement is still very open. The revision answers the questions in the reader's mind: What are some of the "differences"? Which of them are important?

TOO VAGUE: Although I have grown up in this country and am used to American ways, I am often reminded of the Hispanic culture of my parents, who came from "south of the border." Many differences exist between these two cultures—in religion, manners, and customs within the family.

REVISED: Although I have grown up in this country and am used to American ways, I am often reminded of the Hispanic culture of my parents. . . . In their traditional way of life, many things are part of a set pattern. There is a *right way to act as a Catholic, as an obedient child, or as an unmarried daughter.*

Have you made sure that at major turning points in your paper clear **transitions** point the reader in the right direction? Check the beginning of paragraphs, and if necessary, rewrite the opening sentences so that they will give clear signals like the following to your readers:

Two Lives

On many occasions I have felt that I am leading two different lives. I am being divided between my day-to-day life with my mother and stepfather and my occasional life with my natural father and his parents—my grandparents. . . .

My father's is the Italian side of the family. . . .

My mother, I am sure, is still bitter over what happened sixteen years ago. . . .

My grandparents provide somewhat of a bridge between the two sides of the family. . . .

The Telling Detail Look for opportunities to move in for a closer look, to build up detail. Watch for passages that make a promise but do not deliver. Have you merely *told* the reader that the Italian side of your family loved big family occasions? Move in for an actual look at a big wedding with its large gathering of people, laughter, dancing, and piles of food—pans of lasagna, mounds of spaghetti and meatballs, stuffed manicotti, pastries for dessert.

The Finishing Touch As in revising other papers, look at your start and finish, introduction and conclusion. Have you used a vivid memory or striking example to bring your topic into focus for the reader? Consider adding a revealing **anecdote**—a brief story with a point—to set your paper in motion:

Standing Up

When I was fourteen, I was still terrified of my father. Every time he told me to do something, I would do it without question. He knew that I had always been afraid of spiders. Nevertheless, he would often ask me to pick up a spider he had killed and take it to the trashcan. I would use a paper to pick up the dead spider, afraid that it would come back to life and take revenge on me. I often told myself to stand up for myself, but in the end, my father always had his way.

Have you brought your paper to a close in such a way that a major point—or *the* major point—will linger in the reader's mind? Consider concluding with a quotation or reference that will relate your own experience to a larger pattern:

. . . later that year, I got into trouble with the authorities and spent a night in Juvenile Hall. It was the first time I ever saw my father weep. From that point on, something started to happen between us. Without saying a single word, we seemed to have come to terms with one another. Much of the old tension was gone.

There is a story in the Bible about a son who strikes out on his own and refuses to come home. He refuses to come home until his father realizes that he must meet the son halfway.

Remember: Revising a personal paper to make it more candid or less defensive is like a chance to reshoot a blurry photograph to get a better likeness of who you really are.

WRITING TOPICS 7 *Writing from Experience*

From the following topics, choose one that has a personal meaning for you. Remember the features that will make a paper on your personal experience real for your reader: vividly described setting or settings; real

THE WRITING WORKSHOP

Questions for Peer Revision

In a small group or with your class as a whole, study early drafts of personal experience papers written by your peers. Help prepare suggestions for revision, focusing on questions like the following:

- ☐ What is the writer trying to do? Does the paper have some central purpose or motivation?
- ☐ How has the writer used material from personal experience? How real do the setting, the people, and the events become for the reader?
- ☐ Does the paper have a strong central point or thesis? Where and how does it emerge from the paper?
- ☐ What is the author's general strategy or overall plan? Does the paper provide clear enough guidance for the reader?
- ☐ How candid or how guarded is the paper, and with what effect? How well do you come to know the author?
- ☐ Does the paper interest you, move you, or affect you in some lasting way? Why, or why not?
- ☐ How strong or how weak do you think the paper is overall?

people; dramatic events or incidents; candid personal feelings or reactions; a unifying point or overall meaning.

1. Write about a turning point in your life. Do you remember an event that had a lasting effect on you, a decision that made a difference, or an unexpected change for better or for worse? Make your reader see what the event or change meant for you.

2. What does the word *family* mean to you? How has your family situation or your family background influenced you? How has it shaped your outlook? Give a vivid account of people, situation, or events.

3. What kind of person are you? Focus on one major character trait that has helped shape your personality. Show it as a common thread in several related experiences. Show how this side of your personality has affected what you do, how you act, or how you relate to other people.

4. Much biography focuses on how people rise to a challenge. Has a major challenge, issue, or obstacle played a role in your own life? How did it affect you? How did you cope with it?

5. What was your first taste of success or failure? How did it affect your attitude toward competition? What did you learn from the experience?

6. At times something that was only hearsay becomes real. It becomes a vivid reality in our lives or in the lives of people close to us. Write about one such subject, and show how it became real for you through firsthand experience. For instance, you might write about violence, a lawsuit, being laid off, divorce, jail.

7. Have you ever felt pushed in different directions by contrasting influences in your life? Have you ever experienced divided loyalties or felt caught between conflicting sources of advice? Write, for instance, about the conflicting influence of home and school, home and church, or two people with very different standards.

8. Much autobiographical writing is about the way we change. It traces a change in the writer's outlook, ambitions, ideals, or beliefs. For instance, have you changed your attitude toward marriage, toward school, or toward the army? Have you ever slowly revised a misleading first impression or an attitude you were taught?

9. Have you experienced the meeting of two cultures? In your family or among your friends, have you seen the clash of different traditions? Write about your experience with the conflict or merging of different ways of life.

10. People play different roles. Have you ever played a role that required you to change your behavior or assume a different personality? For instance, write about playing the role of supervisor, camp counselor, scout, college athlete, poor relation, confidant, parent, or spouse.

9

DESCRIPTION

Writing from Observation

My attention veered inexorably back to the specific, to the tangible. . . . In short, my attention was always . . . on what I would see and taste and touch. Joan Didion

Often while reading a book one feels that the author would have preferred to paint rather than write; one can sense the pleasure he derives from describing a landscape or a person, as if he were painting what he is saying, because deep in his heart he would have preferred to use brushes and colors. Pablo Picasso

Language is a net in which we catch glimpses of reality. Paul Hermann

FROM OBSERVATION TO DESCRIPTION

Good writers are alert observers. They take in the sights and sounds of the world around them, and they know how to put their impressions into words. Writing that records firsthand observation is called **description.** As descriptive writers, we recreate for our readers objects, scenes, and people; we share with them what we have seen, heard, and felt.

Description with a Purpose

In some kinds of writing, description is central to the writer's purpose. Much technical writing requires accurate description of products, equipment, or hardware. Travel writers put us in the square before the great cathedral in Mexico City or on a crowded train through the Punjab to feed our curiosity about other places. Nature writers make us watch the courting of hawks or the epic journey of the salmon upstream to rekindle our love of the natural world, to make us cherish and protect it.

In much other writing, effective description adds the authority that results when a writer can say: "This is what I saw with my own eyes." Descriptive writing teaches writers to pay attention to what is "out there." It trains their eyes for the telling, revealing detail that conjures up scenes, sites, and sights. A passage like the following convinces us that the author is not writing about farming from an office on Madison Avenue; it takes us out into the fields:

> The nearest harvester draws steadily closer, moving in at about the speed of a slow amble, roaring as it comes. Up close, it looks like the aftermath of a collision between a grandstand and a San Francisco tram car. It's two stories high, rolls on wheels that don't seem large enough, astraddle a wide row of jumbled and unstaked tomato vines. It is not streamlined. Gangways, catwalks, gates, conveyors, roofs, and ladders are fastened all over the lumbering rig. As it closes in, its front end snuffles up whole tomato plants as surely as a hungry pig loose in a farmer's garden.   Mark Kramer, "The Ruination of the Tomato," *Atlantic*

How do we make a reader visualize a scene or imagine a setting? What does it take to make readers imagine themselves in the observer's place? When writing description, we become sensitive to the questions that arise in the reader's mind:

- "a wonderful place" (What makes it wonderful?)
- "a shady character" (What did the person look like?)
- "the hustle and bustle of city life" (What was hustling and bustling?)

Words like *wonderful* and *beautiful* are merely a promise to the reader. To deliver on your promises, do justice to major dimensions of descriptive writing:

An Eye for Detail Trust your eyes and ears. Get close to the texture and feel of experience—close to what you can see and hear and touch. The author of the following passage walked through a city with open eyes:

> Those people who live and work there see a peculiar Manhattan every day, a Manhattan made up of individual gray blocks of concrete, signs that flash "Don't Walk" in red lights, the inside of elevators, the advertisements in subway cars, the back of the man ahead in the coffee line at the delicatessen, the stickers against the milky bulletproof divider that say the cabdriver cannot change more than $5 and is allergic to cigarette smoke, and the blurry faces of hundreds of people trying not to make eye contact.   Anna Quindlen, "About New York," *The New York Times*

The Right Word Find the right words for concrete, sensory detail so that the reader will see what you saw, hear what you heard. **Concrete** words appeal directly to our senses; they vividly call to mind sights, sounds, smells, textures, and tastes.

SIGHTS Look at the way the following passage makes us see shapes, textures, colors:

> With a wingspread of up to six inches, the Polyphemus is one of the few huge American silk moths, much larger than, say, a giant or tiger swallowtail butterfly. The moth's enormous wings are velveted in a rich, warm brown, and edged in bands of blue and pink delicate as a watercolor wash. A startling "eyespot," immense, and deep blue melding to an almost translucent yellow, luxuriates in the center of each hind wing. The effect is one of a masculine splendor foreign to the butterflies, a fragility unfurled to strength. The Polyphemus moth in the picture looked like a mighty wraith, a beating essence of the hardwood forest, alien-skinned and brown, with spread, blind eyes. Annie Dillard, *Pilgrim at Tinker Creek*

Study the way descriptive writers make us visualize actions and movements. To make us see birds in flight, a writer will use words like *soar, swoop, wheel, float, dart, glide, flap, flutter,* and *dive.* To make us see a fistfight, a writer will use words like *duck, feint, jab, punch,* and *slug.*

SOUNDS An alert observer has a quick ear for sounds. An article about parrots is likely to need words like *screech, squawk, honk, chatter,* and *caw.* In the following passage, the author makes us hear sounds for which specific words are not readily available:

> The whales rise and breathe all around us, sometimes just ten or fifteen feet away, making us jump and gasp. They are so close we can see their twin blowholes, like high-set nostrils, and the individual patterns of parasitic barnacles on their backs. We can hear the inhalation phase of their blow, the breathy resonance of the great lungs a little like the compressed and magnified sound of your own breath in a snorkel, with sometimes a slight whistle. Annie Gottlieb

SMELLS A hiker said, "There are thousands upon thousands of eucalyptus trees with their distinct musty odor, which seems to stick to the hikers' clothing as they walk under them." The author of the following passage took in the odors of a spring day at a lake:

> A breeze off the lake brings a sweet air of mud and rotting wood, a slight fishy smell, the sweetness of old grease, a sharp whiff of gasoline, fresh tires, spring dust, and, from across the street, the faint essence of a tuna hot dish at the Chatterbox Cafe. Garrison Keillor

What do you see? **Describe this scene in such a way that it will become real for your reader.**

The Vivid Image Effective writers use **figurative language** to call up vivid images; fresh, striking comparisons help us imagine what the writer observed, experienced, or felt. We get a graphic picture of the birds' nests when a writer says, "Swallows built mud nests in the rafters for their homes, which looked *like little mud igloos turned over.*" At the same time, effective figurative language brings physical reactions and feelings into play:

Great green-and-yellow grasshoppers are everywhere in the tall grass, *popping up like corn to sting the flesh.*   N. Scott Momaday

To the southeast, *under a glowing skullcap of fouled sky,* lay St. Louis.   William Least Heat Moon

SIMILE When a writer signals an imaginative comparison by words such as *like* or *as if*, we call it a **simile.** To help us visualize huge flocks of starlings in the evening sky, Annie Dillard in *Pilgrim at Tinker Creek* uses striking similes: As the huge flocks of birds, circling in lengthening curves, came toward the author, they seemed "transparent and whirling, *like smoke.*" As flock followed flock, the flights extended "*like an unfurling banner.*"

METAPHOR When a writer presents a comparison as if one thing were actually another (leaving out the *like* or *as if*), we call it a **metaphor.** A writer who describes Hadrian's Wall as running across the *neck* of Britain, dipping and rising along a *rollercoaster* ridge is speaking metaphorically. In the following passage, the author uses several metaphors to convey his impressions upon entering a livestock tent at a state fair in Minnesota:

> Wriggling and butting my way out of the crowd, I found myself in the sudden blessed cool of a *vaulted cathedral* full of cows. They stood silently in their stalls with the *resigned eyes of long-term patients.* The straw with which the stadium was *carpeted* gave the whole place a ceremonious quiet.   Jonathan Raban

A third kind of imaginative comparison involves **personification,** giving human qualities to objects or ideas ("The sound of the passing cars was *a steady whisper out of the throat of the night*").

The Overall Impression

Readers tire of miscellaneous unsorted detail. Try to steer their attention toward a unifying **overall impression**—a keynote that is echoed in many of the details. Look at the many details that follow up the opening statement in the following passage:

keynote

details

> The "kid's room" which was my billet for the night had the air of a museum. The kid was a married man with children of his own now, fifteen hundred miles away in Florida, but his room looked as if he'd left it yesterday. His football pennants decorated the walls: I lay under Saints, Colts, Cardinals, Redskins, Oilers, Vikings, Patriots, Raiders, Eagles, Buccaneers, and Seahawks. His old singles lay in heaps on the floor, their scratched black vinyl leaking from dog-eared cardboard covers. I remembered them from . . . way back. Patience and Prudence singing "Tonight You Belong to Me"; "Chantilly Lace" by the Big Bopper; Smokey Robinson and "You Better Shop Around." A wooden chest spilled with sports equipment: ski boots, a baseball bat, a tennis racket left out of its press.   Jonathan Raban, *Old Glory*

Objective and Subjective

Descriptive writing ranges from the objective to the subjective—from the technical or practical to the personal and imaginative. When you try to be **objective,** you report observable, measurable facts, leaving out personal preference. The expert or specialist writing to inform will often keep personal feeling to a minimum. The following account identifies and informs. Although it is vividly written, personal feelings and judgments (except for the author's obvious interest in the subject) are kept out:

> From the dock on the western shore, the surface of Mono Lake gleams blindingly in the morning sun. Spread across that bright surface as far as the squinting eye can see are the dark silhouettes of floating birds. Close to shore, in a little cove among pale pumice boulders, small gray and white birds swim and wade in erratic circles. The little birds are phalaropes, on their way south from the Arctic or the prairies of western Canada, where they breed. Right now, they're filling up on brine flies, accumulating enough fat to fuel them to their next stopping place. The birds farther out are California gulls, which have come here to breed, and migratory grebes. When their heads plunge toward the water, they are after not flies but brine shrimp, which thrive in the salty water of the lake.

In more **subjective** writing, the personal reactions and judgments of the writer will color much of what is being described. The following is from an account of a visit to a festival of handicrafts sponsored by the government of El Salvador to promote native Indian culture. In this passage, the writer's feelings and commitments play a central role:

> I had begun before long to despise the day, the dirt, the blazing sun, the pervasive smell of rotting meat, the absence of even the most rudimentary skill in the handicrafts on exhibit (there were sewn items, for example, but they were sewn by machine of sleazy fabric, and the simplest seams were crooked), the brutalizing music from the sound truck, the tedium; had begun most of all to despise the fair itself, which seemed contrived, pernicious, a kind of official opiate, an attempt to recreate or perpetuate a way of life neither economically nor socially viable. There was no pleasure in this day. There was a great deal of joyless milling. There was some shade in the plaza, from trees plastered with ARENA posters, but nowhere to sit. There was a fountain painted bright blue inside, but the dirty water was surrounded by barbed wire, and the sign read: "SE PROHIBE SENTARSE AQUI," no sitting allowed.   Joan Didion, *Salvador*

Even in this personal account, the author's reactions are anchored to what she makes the reader see: the crooked seams, the posters, the barbed wire, the sign. This is the basic lesson to learn about writing from observation: Stay close to what you can see, hear, smell, and touch. When you can, move in for a closer look.

Questions for Discussion Do you remember a piece of nonfiction—travel writing, nature writing, or other—that made a setting or a sight exceptionally real for you? What were some striking or memorable details? Did the account leave a lasting overall impression?

EXERCISE 1 *An Eye for Detail*

The following are selected impressions from a writer's account of a hike along the beaches of Cape Cod. How does he make the sights he saw come to life for his readers? Point out and discuss examples of striking details, well-chosen specific or concrete words, and effective imaginative comparisons.

I arrived on the beach near Eastham at dawn, about two hours before high tide. The wind was blowing from the southeast. There was a drizzle pockmarking the sand. . . . Two surf-casters were walking back and forth along the shore, checking their rods, which they'd stuck upright in metal tubes jammed into the sand. . . . By the time I reached Marconi Beach, the sun was out for good. Where the water retreated, on the sand, it left a silvery luster like the sheen of a dead fish. Styrofoam egg cartons, plastic six-pack holders, and empty bleach bottles washed up with the waves. . . . Where the beach was deserted, gulls stood in crowds, each gazing over the heads of the others, like guests at a chic party on the lookout for celebrities. . . . North of Truro, a surfer in a black wet suit flopped in flippers down to the ocean. He looked like a great lizard that had learned to walk erect. . . . For a while, I was kept company by a woman riding a horse along the sand. She would trot beside me, then suddenly canter into the waves, which would splash up and make the horse toss its head. . . . Another dead shark, dried, gutted, and collapsed like a punctured inflatable toy, lay nearby. Beyond that I found the arm of a doll, a rubber snake, a toy horse, and a plastic dinosaur scattered over the sand, looking like the failed attempts of a bungling god to populate a dead planet.   David Black, "Walking the Cape," *Harper's*

EXERCISE 2 *Details First*

Inexperienced writers tend to be satisfied with a general label—without going on to the striking details that keep a person or a place from remaining colorless or interchangeable. Study the following examples of sentences that give the details first. They then funnel the details into a general label at the end. Write five similar details-first sentences based on firsthand observation.

1. Rows and rows of tables, the floor littered with trash and crumbs, people shuffling through sluggish lines, the stale smell of overcooked food, dirty dishes everywhere: this is the cafeteria.

2. The sterile white floors and walls; the people pushed in their wheelchairs; the sad, lonely faces of people once young and spirited, now forgotten and left alone: this is a nursing home.

3. The 10,000-watt speaker system, the masses of bodies surging forward, the overwhelming stench of smoke, the gradually mounting roar as the performers appear on the stage: this is a rock concert.

4. The banging of blocks, the gushing of tears, the blowing of noses, the sound of laughter on tiptoe: my job at the children's day-care center has begun.

5. Flashing steel, stamping feet, grunts of effort, muscles protesting, eyes blinking sweat— such is the stuff of a fencing bout.

EXERCISE 3 *Sensory Detail*

Which details in the following sentences make sights, sounds, smells, sensations, and feelings real for the reader? Write five similar sentences packed with sensory detail.

1. The inside of the empty UPS trailer was filled with dust that clouded up and crawled into my nose each time a package hit the floor.

2. The sales representative superglued his face into the smile position as he stood in the doorway, overpowering the customers as they entered the showroom by his aftershave smell and his insistence that they "Have a sunny weekend."

3. On entering the cannery, the worker is greeted by the clicking of metal, the hissing of steam, the hubbub of workers shouting directions, and the nauseating smell of cooked tomatoes.

4. An orange glow from the safelights on the ceiling joined with the heavy odor of developer, fixer, and other chemicals to make the crowded room feel ten degrees warmer than its already elevated temperature.

5. The rollercoaster starts moving with a deafening rumble from the tracks; it inches up the steep rise as you look straight into the sky; there is a plateau of silence; then the car flips into a 90-mile-per-hour nosedive with a sudden drop of all that your gut contains.

EXERCISE 4 *Using Figurative Language*

Study the use of figurative language in each of the following sentences. What does each imaginative comparison make you see or imagine? How fitting or effective is each comparison? What feelings or reactions is each figurative expression likely to produce in the reader? Write five sentences using figurative language to make readers see or imagine what you describe.

1. As he wrote, his pen moved with the rapid, jerky motions of the needle on a seismograph, charting the flow of his thoughts.

2. Among piles of cement blocks and huge pipes, a crane extends upward into the sky, like a giraffe reaching for green leaves on the small branches at the top of a tree.

3. The hang glider, with bright rainbow colors on its back, dove slowly down, looking like a piece of paper floating down from a two-story building.

4. The heron looked like the shadow of death as it carefully picked in the mud for worms.

5. As the car raced down the straight forest road, the sun flashed behind the tall pines, shining a strobe light into our eyes.

EXERCISE 5   *The Alert Observer*

What do the authors of the following passages do to make a scene come to life for the reader? What use do they make of exact labels, concrete words, and imaginative comparisons?

1. The tunnel disgorges three young men in bright suits carrying gloves, then two more, then six. "Play catch?" one says to another. They sort themselves by twos, throwing baseballs hard at each other without effort, drawing ruler-straight lines like chalk stripes between them. The soft pock of caught balls sounds in attentive ears. The bullpen squad consists of a coach, a catcher, two long men, and two or three short men; they amble with fabulous unconcern, chewing as slowly as prize Holsteins, down the foul lines toward their condominium in right field. The ninth inning's fastballing superstar ace-relief man is not among them but is back in the trainer's room lying flat on his back, reading *Swann's Way* or *Looney Tunes,* waiting to trot his urgent trot from dugout to bullpen at the start of the eighth, the game 1–1, the one-man cavalry alerted to the threat of ambush at the mountain pass.   Donald Hall, "Baseball and the Meaning of Life"

2. It was coming. There was no stopping it now. January or not. One end of the cocoon dampened and gradually frayed in a furious battle. The whole cocoon twisted and slapped around in the bottom of the jar. The teacher fades, the classmates fade, I fade: I don't remember anything but that thing's struggle to be a moth or die trying. It emerged at last, a sodden crumple. It was a male; his long antennae were thickly plumed, as wide as his fat abdomen. His body was very thick, over an inch long, and deeply furred. A gray, furlike plush covered his head; a long, tan furlike hair hung from his wide thorax over his brown-furred, segmented abdomen. His multi-jointed legs, pale and powerful, were shaggy as a bear's. He stood still, but he breathed.

He couldn't spread his wings. There was no room. The chemical that coated his wings like varnish, stiffening them permanently, dried, and hardened his wings as they were. He was a monster in a Mason jar. Those huge wings stuck on his back in a torture of random pleats and folds, wrinkled as a dirty tissue, rigid as leather. They made a single nightmare clump still wracked with useless, frantic convulsions.   Annie Dillard, *Pilgrim at Tinker Creek*

SHAPING: FOCUSING DESCRIPTIVE WRITING
Some of the best descriptive writing is found in journals, trip diaries, and travel notes, which record the observations of the author from day to day. Yet even in such materials, the passages we remember are likely to have the unified impact of more structured writing. In working on a descriptive paper, you need to push toward a unifying overall impression. You need to work toward a meaningful pattern so that your readers will not lose their way.

Often a trip or a journey provides the framework for descriptive writing. (We see the sites and marvels of the ancient Mediterranean world as we retrace the travels of Ulysses.) To make us see the robots at work in a modern automobile factory, an author may walk us past major waystations along the assembly line, till finally we see the finished car roll through the gate. Study familiar organizing strategies that you may adapt or combine in a piece of descriptive writing:

The Keynote
In much well-focused description, a thesis stated early in the paper or article gives clear direction to what follows. The thesis, or keynote, sums up the dominant impression that the paper is trying to convey. It serves as a program for what follows. The writer of the following passage traveled through the Midwest, exploring the old and the new, watching and talking to people, taking in the strange and the familiar. Look at the details he took in as he came upon a new downtown shopping area—a maze of walkways and shopping plazas set in midair, several stories above the ground. What key idea came to dominate his reaction? What details and comparisons follow it up?

Jonathan Raban
THE MALL

It was a completely synthetic urban space. Glassed-in "skyways" vaulted from block to block, and the shopping plazas had been quarried out of the middles of existing buildings like so many chambers, grottoes and tunnels in a mountain of rock.

Here, fountains trickled in carpeted parks. The conditioned air smelled of cologne and was thickened with a faint, colorless spray of Muzak. The stores were open-fronted, like the stalls of a covered Arab souk. . . .

Here people had left their local nature behind altogether. It was something nasty down below, and the skyways floated serenely over the top of it. "Nature" here was of the chic and expensive kind that comes only from the most superior of florists: ornamental palms and ferns, rooted not in soil but in coppery chips of synthetic petroleum extract.

Voices melted into the musical syrup of André Kostelanetz that trickled from hidden speakers in the palm fronds. Footsteps expired on the carpeted halls. At a mock-Parisian street café, the shoppers sat out at gingham tables, drinking Sanka with nonsaccharin sugar substitutes. Skyway-city turned one into an escapee. It was a place where everyone was on the run—from the brutish climate, from carcinogens, from muggers, rapists, automobile horns. Even one's own body was being discreetly disinfected and homogenized by the deodorant air. Up here, everything was *real nice:* we were nice people who smelled nice, looked nice and did nice things in nice places. *Old Glory*

Patterns in Time or Space

Much description traces a pattern in time or space. Description easily becomes too static. Try to put things in motion; give the reader a sense of purposeful forward movement. The following excerpted student paper observes chronological order, taking us through the night shift at an all-night restaurant. Note the **transitions** or signposts that mark off major stages.

WRITING SAMPLE: A PATTERN IN TIME

A Good Night's Work

It's ten o'clock on a typical Friday night at the Lake St. Clair, a 24-hour restaurant. In the carpeted main dining room, there is the buzz of conversation, the tinkle of muzak, and the clink and clatter of silverware. But in the kitchen, the back room, and the prep room downstairs, the mood is not relaxed. At ten, the all-night restaurant
thesis is gearing up for its rush hour. *Much well-meshed activity is needed to run a successful restaurant; and, like clockwork, much of it takes place behind the surface.*
getting ready While cooking the dinner orders that still straggle in, the cooks stock up the drawers with eight kinds of meat, pickles, quartered lemons, and sliced tomatoes. Downstairs, the prep cook mixes five gallons of pancake batter and seven of scrambled eggs. . . .
the lull At twelve midnight, the feeling among the employees is a bit more relaxed. This time is the proverbial lull before the hurricane. In one hour, the bars will close (by state law), and the rush will hit the restaurant. In the kitchen, which is twenty feet long but barely three feet wide, the cooks check the temperature settings of their gleaming grills, broilers, and fryers.
the rush At one o'clock, in twos and threes and fours, chattering and with the slightest sway in their walk, the bar crowd starts coming in. The regulation plastic booths are filling rapidly. The waiters and waitresses spike their orders to the cooks on a spindle on the counter. With orders coming in faster than the cooks can pull them off, the spindle turns into a Christmas tree of flapping green tickets waiting their turn. . . .

the rest　The one good thing about the rush is that it keeps everyone busy; no one can pay attention to the time. *Suddenly it's 4:30,* and the rush is over. There's still more work to do: broilers to be cleaned, counters to be wiped, floors to be mopped, garbage to be taken out. But for the moment, everyone gathers around the employee table for coffee while the manager asks, "Who's watching the store?"

EXERCISE 6　*A Model Paper*

Study the following student-written paper and answer these questions:

☐　What was the student's strategy for organizing the material?
☐　What is the keynote that unifies the paper? Where is it stated? How or where is it followed up or reinforced?
☐　What transitions serve as signposts or directional signals to the reader?
☐　What are striking details—memorable sights and sounds?
☐　How effective are the beginning and end?
☐　What is your overall reaction to the paper? Who would be the ideal reader for it?

A Day in the Life

Quickly walking through the unending maze of unblemished ivory-white hallways, I see the familiar rectangular black sign on the wall, "This elevator for employee use only." I press the plastic button, suddenly the bell sounds, and the down arrow above the elevator door turns a bright red. Slowly the elevator door disappears into the wall. Making sure I do not overturn my shoulder-high polished-aluminum food-tray cart, I watch that the small black plastic wheels of the cart do not get caught in the crack between the elevator and the spotless tiled floor. Already in the capacious elevator is an orderly dressed in blue from cap to booties, standing next to a gurney with an unwrinkled snow-white sheet over a patient. As the door opens to the first floor, I pull my cart in to the hallway. As I turn to hold the door open, I notice a green tag dangling from the big toe of the patient, and I hear the orderly's voice: "Thanks, but I'm getting off in the basement."

The depression I always felt as a dietary technician (actually a dishwasher and gatherer of dirty dishes) at the Valley Hospital was a result of the dejecting atmosphere. Every day's sights and sounds reinforced my feeling of helplessness when confronted with pain and misery.

At six-thirty on a Sunday morning, the gentle hum of the giant black floor polishers seems to be the only sound audible in the hospital. As I enter the Intensive Care Unit, I see the nurse on duty engrossed in a book with a deserted beach on the cover—she is escaping for a short time from the suffering and dying around her. The patients have light-green name bands around their wrists. One has a cropped head

THE WRITING WORKSHOP

The Camera Eye

With the help of a small group or the class as a whole, collect and organize material from close firsthand observation. Take your project through several stages: Spend some time taking a close look at a downtown section, a redevelopment site, a theme park, a fishing town, a track meet, or a similar scene. Be the camera eye—simply take in what is there, trying to keep out comment or editorializing on your part. Take written notes and write them up as a series of vignettes—brief snapshots of parts of the larger scene. Register your candid impressions, including rich authentic detail. Here are some sample vignettes:

An old lady stops to put her mantilla on before she drags herself and her grocery basket into St. Joseph's.

Massive white pillars, stained glass windows, and silver domes are what I notice first. When I look more closely, I see that the pillars are chipped and worn and the sidewalk and steps are spattered with bird droppings and chewing gum.

The empty and abandoned Budget Store brings back happy childhood memories: Riding the elevators up and down and having the 66-cent special at the basement fountain when the store bore a different name and was very popular.

On the corner, there was a condemned thrift shop with a painting on the wall that had a tree on it and some writing saying, "If you love me, feed my sheep."

Some local boys lean toward me and unconvincingly ask me for a cigarette, as though this was a programmed question that they ask any likely looking person. Several teenagers are hanging around the pawn shop with their black leather jackets contemplating the knives.

Share and discuss your vignettes with other members of your group, asking: Is there a common thread joining some or all of these impressions? Is any kind of unifying pattern beginning to emerge? How could it be strengthened? Write a paper using your observations to support a unifying point or develop a prevailing mood.

of hair (impossible to tell the sex) and is chained to the bed by the drips, drains, and leads connected to a kidney machine and respirators.

I pass a cheerful young volunteer pushing a wheelchair-bound old woman past the bold red sign that reads, "Keep clear at all times—Emergency Access Area." I pick up some dirty food trays from the emergency room and move on.

"Code ninety-nine CCU east"—a calm voice breaks into the piped-in dentist's-office music that fills every hall and waiting room. As I move through the Coronary Care Unit, I see a defenseless grey-haired old man with tiny white stubs on his chin, lying in a fully automatic, do-everything, criblike bed. A doctor, a stethoscope around her neck, takes a pancake-shaped instrument with small plastic handles and black coiled wires to place on the old man's lean chest.

"For the protection of the patients, no matches, lighters, belts, ties, or drugs of any kind beyond this point." This sign appears at eye level on the locked door to a closed ward, my last place to pick up food trays for the day. I pick up the nearby white telephone and state my name, title, and business. A buzzer sounds, and I walk into the community "kitchen"—nothing more than a green sink, a light green refrigerator, a green formica table, and white plastic chairs. Four expressionless people sit around the table, as if they were not on this planet. They look as if they had been awake for days without sleep. They do not utter a word as I walk by.

After working in this environment for a time, I became used and perhaps immune to the depressing sights I saw around me. I gradually began to see the invigorating parts of life in the hospital, such as the maternity ward and the miracle of a dying patient's fighting and conquering a fatal disease. But these positive impressions will never quite balance the feelings of depression and helplessness that I felt in the beginning.

REVISING: THE CLOSER LOOK
When writers first experiment with descriptive writing, they are likely to do too much labeling and listing, moving too fast from one item to another. Try to look at what you have written through the reader's eyes. If you mention a marvelous old Victorian house, your readers want to *see* it: the woodwork, the turrets, the cornices, the trim. If you talk about the harsh beauty of a desert scene, *take* your readers there; let them look at the tumbleweed, the cactus, the lizards, the snakes.

Consider guidelines like the following in revising your descriptive papers:

☐ *Avoid overworked labels and travel folder clichés.* Be wary of labels that are too interchangeable—they have been applied to sights quite different from the ones you are trying to describe: *beautiful, spectacular, magnificent, peaceful, grandeur, sublime.* (Try to do without *interesting, wonderful, great, exciting,* and *unique* altogether.) Take out ready-made phrases or **clichés:**

"majestic mountain," "mighty ocean," "picturesque village," and "island paradise," not to mention "blue sparkling water," "cool breeze," "dance of the leaves," and "blanket of snow."

> CLICHÉ: At work, there was the usual *hustle and bustle* of a busy construction site.
>
> FRESH: At the construction site, cranes lifted steel beams thirty stories. The wet concrete flowed into huge wooden frames as the laborers shouted and banged their shovels against the chutes.

☐ *Revise purple prose.* Do not strain to make scenes more vibrant, thrilling, or meaningful than they were. ("I *greedily* pick the ripe berries and eat them as they *explode* in my mouth with a taste of *total* refreshment.") Do not smother the genuine appeal of a scene under a layer of flowery words:

> OVERWRITTEN: *Invitingly lured from slumber* by the sound of the rhythmic waves *gently caressing* the black rocks *lying lonely* in their salty pools below, I *witness the dawn's early morning rays thrust* their way through the layer of thick *frigid* clouds *curtaining* this *uniquely beautiful* spot by the sea.
>
> REVISED: At low tide, the black rocks are exposed among the salt-water pools. In the narrow channels between the rocks, incoming waves fill the crevices with foaming spray. Sea snails and small crabs hide among the masses of seaweed. Only yards away, sandpipers trot in and out after receding and returning waves.

☐ *Move in for a closer look.* In a first draft, you are likely to pass over things too quickly. In revising a paper, look for strategic places where added specifics will make a place or a person real for the reader, where more details will individualize and dramatize what you describe:

> GENERAL: The saloon has the old-fashioned swinging doors familiar from Western movies.
>
> SPECIFIC: The saloon has old-fashioned swinging doors. When someone enters, one can hear the doors flop back and forth, hitting each other until they come to rest.
>
> GENERAL: I remember seeing one of the street people pushing her supermarket cart filled with cans for recycling down the street.
>
> SPECIFIC: On a hot August afternoon on First Street, I saw a gray-haired woman in a ragged woollen coat and black basketball shoes pushing a supermarket wire basket filled with crumpled cans, her head hung low.

☐ *Strengthen the overall impression.* Often, we have to prepare a first draft and then think about it before the main drift or the central focus of a paper becomes clear. Revision then is a chance to choose one main direction, and to spell it out clearly for the reader. The following might be the thesis of a descriptive paper before and after revision:

UNFOCUSED: A camper brings back many pleasant memories of being out in the fresh air and enjoying the beauties of nature.

REVISED: The beauty of nature is not just in spectacular sunsets or sweeping panoramas. *The best part of camping is to have time to notice the little things*—the insects buzzing around a lantern, the frogs in a pond.

☐ *Strengthen the overall pattern.* Have you clearly identified segments or stages that give the reader a sense of purposeful forward movement? In revising a paper about a hike into mountain country, you may decide to focus on the major stages of the day's climb:

The early morning sky is beginning to turn from black to deep blue. We begin to walk up slowly the trail *that disappears into the trees.* Moisture is dripping from the dark green spikes of pine and aspen branches. . . .

The sun is getting hot now. I put my sweater away, since I am beginning to sweat. *We have climbed past the timber line,* beyond which trees will not grow. All we see now is dry grass, the dry soil of the path, and little sparks of color where wildflowers grow. . . .

I hear whoops of exaltation from the people ahead. I take the last step and am met by a blast of wind. *We have made it to the top.* . . .

WRITING TOPICS 8 *Writing from Observation*

Among the following topics, choose one that allows you to draw on close observation or vivid memories. Or choose one that allows you to schedule a field trip for a closer look.

1. Describe an undervalued but marvelously useful piece of equipment, such as an umbrella, an old-fashioned typewriter, a bicycle, or a hiker's portable tent. Write for an imaginary visitor from a different civilization or from the distant past.

2. For a pen pal abroad, describe a type of building or façade that is a familiar sight to Americans: a state capitol, an imitation-Gothic building on campus, a modern (or postmodern) office building, an economy-rate motel.

3. Make a natural setting real for someone who seldom gets close to unspoiled nature. Write about a setting where you have been closest to nature

THE WRITING WORKSHOP

Peer Revision

Within a small group, trade descriptive papers for feedback from and evaluation by classmates. What suggestions for revision does the group have for each writer? What strengths could the revision build on? What weaknesses could be corrected? As a group, try to pay special attention to the need for telling detail, vivid language, a unifying overall impression, and a clear organizing strategy.

unspoiled by human hands. Take a close look at a cliff, a stretch of beach, a lake, a river, a mountain ridge, a patch of forest, or the like. Aim at a unifying overall impression.

4. Much has been written in recent years about the crowding, decay, and paranoia of our cities. What is *your* image of the city? Take a close look at a city scene. You may want to focus on a public square, major avenue, parking lot, main street, shopping mall, or the like. Aim at a unifying overall impression.

5. Are you a person who loves or who hates crowds? Take a close look at the crowd at a bus terminal, airport, rock concert, county fair, church picnic, accident scene, political rally, or the like. Aim at a unifying overall impression.

6. For an armchair traveler, describe a place that turned out differently from what you had come to expect: a scenic wonder, a national monument, a famous site, an often-visited city, a ghetto. Concentrate on recreating your own authentic firsthand impression.

7. For a reader of the future, write about a setting that represents a vanishing part of our way of life: a mom-and-pop store, a small family farm, a theater about to be torn down. Concentrate on characteristic sights and sounds; re-create the atmosphere of the place.

8. For readers with little knowledge of local history, write a "then-and-now" paper about a scene that you have seen change recently or over the years. Write about a downtown area before and after redevelopment, an old part of town before and after gentrification, a waterfront that has been either upgraded or allowed to deteriorate, or the like.

9. What would you show a foreign visitor who asks to see a typically American scene? Recreate the scene for a visitor whose knowledge of the country has come mainly from books, television programs, and movies.

10. Is it true that young people today tend to be wary of or hostile to institutions? Take your reader inside an institution you know well: a clinic, a court of law, a mental hospital, an army base, a soup kitchen, a Salvation Army shelter. (Your instructor may ask you to visit an institution for a close firsthand look.) Bring characteristic sights, sounds, and smells to life for your reader. Make sure your description reflects your attitude toward or feelings about the setting you describe.

10

EXPOSITION

Process, Comparison/Contrast, Classification

A good piece of writing closes the gap between you and the reader. Linda Flower

Facts do not speak for themselves, nor do figures add up on their own. Even the most vividly detailed report or computer printout requires someone to make sense of the information it contains. Nancy R. Comley

WRITING TO INFORM In much of the writing we do, we aim at readers likely to say, "Show me how" or "Explain to me why." Our agenda is to make them say, "Now I see" or "Now I understand." Writing whose chief goal is to explain or inform is expository writing, or **exposition**; it "sets forth" or displays what we know and think about a subject. Expository writing puts a premium on the central shaping or organizing stage of the writing process, testing our ability to bring material under control, to sort out data, to chart a course through accumulated facts. Our mission is to lay out our material in such a way that it will make sense to the reader.

The Many Uses of Exposition Exposition is a label that covers a multitude of tasks. We use the word as the umbrella heading for writing that explains, informs, reports, or instructs. Writers write exposition when they present a position, report an experiment, chart a trend, or expound a theory—in short, whenever they share information or clarify ideas. You write exposition when you show your fellow students how to convert to a vegetarian diet. A scientist writes exposition when explaining how the burning of fossil fuels produces a greenhouse effect. A psychologist writes exposition when tracing our response to serious illness through major stages: denial, anger, acceptance.

177

Major patterns of expository writing mirror the way our minds process information. They reflect the sorting out and lining up that makes sense of unedited, miscellaneous data. Here are the key questions that guide us when we employ major organizing strategies for expository writing:

Process: "How does it work?"

Comparison and Contrast: "How are two things similar? How do they differ?"

Classification: "What goes with what?"

Like other traditional categories, exposition is not in a watertight compartment; it often spills over into argument or persuasion. To show how a procedure works is often the first step toward persuading readers to adopt it as a workable solution to their problems. Two kinds of writing often used for expository purposes also play a major role in systematic argument: **Definition** clarifies key terms for the learner or the outsider, but it is also an essential first step in much logical argument—needed to keep murky terms from blocking our vision, like a fogged-over windshield. (See Chapter 12, "DEFINING: Drawing the Line.") Analysis of **cause and effect** helps us understand the workings of a process, but it also plays a major role in arguments designed to pin guilt, to prove unsuspected connections, or to project the consequences of current behavior. (See Chapter 13, "REASONING: Structuring an Argument.")

Guidelines for Exposition Remember the following guidelines as you work on expository papers:

☐ *Establish yourself as an authority on your subject.* How do you know? (And why do you care?) Whenever possible, provide evidence of personal involvement, firsthand investigation, or fresh observation. For instance, are you writing about athletes threatened with suspension, teachers faced with mandatory new tests, or federal employees subjected to drug testing? Draw on your firsthand knowledge of athletes, teachers, or tests. Draw on your reading: articles, surveys, letters to the editor. Make use of personal interviews—show that you have listened to the people concerned, sorted out their grievances, become aware of their point of view.

☐ *Synthesize expert opinion and authoritative information.* Pull together the testimony of insiders or the findings of researchers: What is the common strand? What explains different points of view? In the following passage, the writer bolstered his own conclusions by pulling together supporting quotations from people in a position to know:

In spite of occasional rumblings of dissent, there is not much doubt that a person who exercises will be healthier for it both physically and mentally. According to Hal Higdon, author of *Fitness After Forty*, physical fitness "allows you to work without undue fatigue, to retain enough energy to enjoy hobbies and activities, and to make optimal use of your body." Moreover, "exercise is one of the best means of relaxation since muscular fatigue is conducive to physical and mental rest, and sleep." Dorothy Greeley, like many other physicians, believes that "inactivity is one of the chief saboteurs of health. . . . We don't wear out; we rust out."

□ *Break down complex subjects into their component parts.* Expository writing will often test your powers of **analysis**—defined by one writing text as separating things that "people have previously mushed together." At first, your material for a paper on the automated office of the future might be a jumble of sales talk, employee grievances, and assorted scuttlebutt. As you analyze the subject, you might set up headings for its major relevant dimensions: equipment, efficiency, work habits, and employee morale.

□ *Pay patient attention to detail.* If you are helping a customer to assemble an exercise bike, what size screws go where and in what order? If you are writing about the last of the wild salmon battling their way up the rivers to spawn, what can you tell your readers about the when, where, why, and how?

□ *Remember the needs of the reader.* Ideally, you will be leading your readers into a subject about which you know more than they do. Part of your job is to translate **technical terms** into plain English. Look at the way experienced writers provide informative capsule definitions, like the following brief definition of a psychologist's term:

> People with *Type-A personalities*—those uptight, compulsive, competitive, aggressive, sometimes hostile, insecure, overachievers—can greatly reduce their chances for a heart attack by modifying their behavior.

Use graphic comparisons to give your readers a picture of what is new or unfamiliar. One writer described a welding robot used on automobile assembly lines by saying that it has "a long neck stretching from a squat body, and a welding head that appears to have a single flame-spitting tooth." Experiment with using an **analogy**, or exceptionally detailed tracing of close parallels, to make ideas clear and concrete for your readers. For instance, you might use the analogy of the education factory in writing about your objections to large impersonal, bureaucratic educational institutions. You might trace such parallels as standardized production procedures, concern with low cost and high volume, and the turning out of a homogenized product ready for marketing.

Questions for Discussion How good an audience are you for expository writing? For instance, in studying a textbook (including this one), are any of the following easy or difficult for you: technical terms, explanations, examples, connection of ideas, exceptions and confusing details?

THE WRITING WORKSHOP

Let Me Explain

How good are you at explaining something technical to a lay audience? Participate in a group experiment exploring the features that make expository writing informative or instructive. Help the group choose an area from the history of art or music that they would like to learn more about, such as:

- *classical music*: the symphony, belcanto, Wagnerian opera, electronic music
- *popular music*: dixieland, bebop, bluegrass, the blues, punk rock
- *fine arts*: impressionism, expressionism, cubism, abstract painting

Have the group start by brainstorming the key term—have the members pool and discuss what they know and remember. Then have each member investigate the group topic and prepare a brief introduction (300–400 words) for the outsider. Finally, have the group vote to rank the different entries: Which are the most instructive or informative, and why?

Do any of the following help: comparisons, analogies, everyday examples, numbered or highlighted key points, summaries?

Remember: Readers expect expository prose to be businesslike. However, while some kinds of reports call for a strictly impersonal, formal style, most expository writing has room for informal touches and occasional leavening humor. One writer started his discussion of the nature of human intelligence by asking: "What makes us human? Language? Culture? Opposable thumbs?" Another writer, a neurobiologist, started by asking: "Can the brain understand the brain?" Show that you have an ear for the provocative or amusing phrase; experiment with the occasional lighter touch.

EXERCISE 1   *Informing the Reader*

One essential skill of the expository writer is to make technical information or expert knowledge accessible to the outsider. How do the authors

of the following passages make key concepts or technical terms clear to
the reader?

1. Photographs of earth taken from outer space have lost their novelty, but, like psychoanalysis, they have irreversibly altered the view. An extraterrestrial picture taken as the sun appears over the rim of the earth reveals the earth as a dark, convex semicircle and, above it, space as a dark, concave one; in between is a shining sliver, a fingernail paring of light, which is the atmosphere. Seemingly huge and inexhaustible, it is in fact quite small.   Tracy Kidder, "Trouble in the Stratosphere," *Atlantic*

2. Researchers in artificial intelligence . . . began to develop the first expert systems. They would closet themselves with a professor in some other department—an analytical chemist, for instance—and ask him a series of questions about how he concluded whatever he did from the data he got from his laboratory tests. "How did you know this was salt?" they might ask. "The pH meter read seven," he might answer, "and that's about right for salt." "Is salt the only substance that gives that reading?" "Well, no, ethanol does—but of course that's a liquid." The programmers could then write a salt-identifying expert system: someone with a mysterious substance would state whether the substance was a solid or a liquid and whether its pH was seven, and the system would print out whatever verdict followed from these facts.   Fred Hapgood, "Experts to a Point," *Atlantic*

3. When we come to consider the origin of life, the time scales we must deal with make the whole span of human history seem but the blink of an eyelid. . . . The customary way to provide a convenient framework for one's thoughts is to compare the age of the universe with the length of a single earth day. Perhaps a better comparison, along the same lines, would be to equate the age of our earth with a single week. On such a scale, the age of the universe, since the Big Bang, would be about two or three weeks. The oldest macroscopic fossils (those from the start of the Cambrian) would have been alive just one day ago. Modern humans would have appeared in the last ten seconds and agriculture in the last one or two. Odysseus would have lived only half a second before the present time.   Francis Crick, *Life Itself*

4. The earth is made up of two sections of radically different compositions (like an egg which is made up of a central yolk and a surrounding white). The "yolk" of the earth is the nickel-iron core, with a high density roughly about 10 times that of water. Around it, the "white" of the earth is the silicate crust, with a low density about 3 times that of water.   Isaac Asimov, *Is Anybody There?*

TRACING A PROCESS To make a reader see how something works or how it came about, we trace a process. Processes—of growth, of learning, of manufacture—are all around us in our world. When we trace one of these, we organize our writing the natural way; we follow an order already built into our subject.

The Uses of Process Writing

If you have a practical bent, process writing will appeal to you because of its usefulness; it is often directly practical, informative, or instructive. You can use it to give directions—how to bake bread, how to assemble an exercise bike, how to use a word processor, or how to build a model airplane. The emphasis then is on showing readers what to do, on how to make the process work. You can use process writing to explain a scientific process—how plants utilize sunlight, how television transmits images, or how the body converts food into energy. Or you can use process writing to trace a historical chain of events—how the railroad transformed rural America, or how the automobile transformed city life. The emphasis then is on helping readers understand, making them take into account the way things work.

Tracing a process can train your eye for the essential. (What does it take to produce a loaf of bread that is not hard as a rock and flat as a board?) Process writing can train you to follow necessary steps in the right order. Finally, it requires you to be audience-conscious: Often you will be writing for the newcomer, the outsider, the learner.

Guidelines for Process Writing

The following advice should prove useful when you write a process paper:

☐ *Explain the why as well as the how.* You might start by explaining the purpose or the benefits of the process. Let your readers see that you are showing how to do something difficult well, or something dangerous safely. Make the readers see the challenge or the usefulness of acquiring a skill:

The Natural Way to Eat Bread

Much of the bread we see on supermarket shelves is filled with preservatives so that it can stay on the shelves longer without spoiling. Much of it has an unnatural bleached appearance. It often has the consistency and the taste of a sponge. *To reduce the amount of dubious chemicals in our diet, we can learn to bake our own bread from natural ingredients.* . . .

☐ *Pay patient attention to detail.* As needed, provide information about materials, tools, or equipment. Include the details needed to make things work. Look at the details a student included in the following passage to make sure the dough would be properly prepared for the making of homemade bread:

Yeast is composed of minute organisms that grow when exposed to moisture and heat. After the yeast has been dissolved in hot water and milk, mix it with the other ingredients of the dough. Turn the dough out on a lightly floured pastry cloth and knead it for about five minutes until it is smooth and elastic. The bread is now ready to rise, with the entire process taking about four or five hours. Place the dough in a lightly greased bowl, cover it with a damp cloth, and let it rise to about double its original bulk. Make sure the temperature is about 80 degrees: A higher temperature will produce a dry bread. If the room is too cold, put the dough in the oven with a pan of hot water under it. After the dough has risen to about double bulk, turn the dough out on a lightly floured cloth and knead it again for about five minutes. . . .

☐ *Divide the process into major stages.* If you keep saying "and next . . . and next," things will become blurred in your reader's mind. Clear division into steps or parts lets your readers follow the process with a sense of direction; it makes them feel at each stage that they know where they are. When you give instructions or directions, dividing a process clearly into steps will build your readers' confidence, assuring them that they will be able to master one step at a time. The following might be the major stages for the paper on how to bake bread:

　　I.　Assembling the ingredients
　　II.　Mixing the dough
　　III.　Letting the dough rise
　　IV.　Baking the bread

☐ *Make your reader see your overall plan.* The more technical or demanding the process, the more your readers will profit from a *preview* or overview that lets them see the broad outlines and provides a program for what follows. Early in your paper, you might want to focus on the essential operating principle that makes the process work. The opening of the following paper focuses on an essential principle and then previews the major stages of the process:

From Forest to Front Porch

Paper, or some form of thin material to write on, has been in use for at least five thousand years. Archeologists have found evidence that the Egyptians were making papyrus sheets, made from the pith of the reedlike plant, three thousand years before Christ. In China, just as animal hairs had been matted to form felt, plant fibers—flax, hemp—were matted to form paper.

preview　　*Today, papermaking is a highly mechanized process, going through several major steps: preparation of the stock or fiber; formation of the paper web by machine; removal of water by gravity, suction or heat; and the rolling of the finished paper product. . . .*

Where you can, make use of a pattern in time or space to help guide your reader. One writer, for example, wrote about a button factory that had three stories: *On the first floor,* liquid plastic was hardened into rubbery sheets, and blank buttons were punched out; *on the second floor,* holes were drilled, patterns carved, and the buttons polished; *on the third floor*, the buttons were sorted into cardboard boxes, ready to be shipped.

Note: With a more complex process, several separate lines of development, taking place concurrently, might converge to produce a final product. (The undercarriage, the engine, and the hull of a car might come together after traveling down separate assembly lines.) Make sure your reader has a clear picture of the separate feeder lines—and of how, like freeway on-ramps, they feed into the main stream of traffic in your paper.

□ *Suit your language to your audience.* For the nonspecialist, translate technical concepts into nontechnical language. Look at the use of everyday language and vivid imaginative comparisons in the following passages:

> To power lasers and other possible space weapons with solar energy would require several hundred acres of solar panels that would somehow have to be *collapsed, carted up* in a space shuttle, and then *opened like a huge umbrella* in space.

> Evolution is a *branching bush, not a ladder.* Ancestors survive after descendants *branch off.* Dogs evolved from wolves, but wolves (though threatened) are hanging tough. And a species of *Australopithecus* lived side by side with its descendant *Homo* for more than a million years in Africa.   Stephen Jay Gould

A Sample Process Paper

Each process paper has its own history. The paper reflects the author's particular expertise; it serves a particular need. For instance, a student may write about the process of implanting artificial skin in burn victims because a brother had suffered extensive burns and had undergone a series of only partially successful skin grafts. Many other process papers merely satisfy our natural curiosity about something that we usually take for granted in our everyday lives.

Study the following example of a process paper that appeals to the natural curiosity of the general reader. Here is a brief account of the paper's history:

PREWRITING: WORKING UP MATERIAL

Being a lover of ice cream, and having tried many specialty ice creams, I decided to investigate the making of ice cream. I found a brief informative overview in the 1982 edition of *Collier's Encyclopedia.* A slightly more detailed account appears in Paul Dickinson's *The Great American Ice Cream Book,* which I discovered in the library. However, most of my information for the paper came from an interview with the manager of the ice cream plant at a local creamery and from a tour of the plant.

How well does the finished paper live up to the requirements for a successful process paper?

37 Flavors

relating the topic to current concerns

Ice cream is not exactly a health food, for it is high in calories and rich in fat and sugar. For the most part, however, the general public is willing to overlook the health issue and the chemical additives. According to a recent estimate, every American eats about fifteen quarts of ice cream a year.

overview

major stages

Ice cream is basically a mixture of milk solids and sugar. Mechanized manufacturing processes add numerous other natural and artificial ingredients, such as flavoring, coloring, stabilizers (which bind water and retard the growth of ice crystals) and emulsifiers (which coat the fat globules of cream during manufacturing in order to provide a more stable foam).

setting

In an unassuming brown stucco building at six o'clock one morning, I witnessed vanilla ice cream being made at a local creamery. While most of us are asleep, a small group of people dressed in white shirts and trousers, yet bundled up in plaid jackets against the low temperature, makes ice cream from eleven at night till the next noon. The workers look like sailors dressed in service whites while working in what looks like an engine room, criss-crossed with stainless steel pipes and filled with circular vats and compressors. The floor is made of red tile, with a big brass drain cover as its centerpiece. The floor works like the bottom of a large kitchen sink, ready to swallow any liquids spilled from the vats.

storage

The first step in the making of ice cream is to pipe in the basic ingredients from storage. In a separate room, two large holding tanks with doors like those of bank vaults hold one thousand gallons each of condensed skim milk and cream, which provide the milk solids for the ice cream. Next to them, sucrose and corn syrup are stored in upright holding cylinders of stainless steel.

preparing the base mix

The milk solids and sugars are piped out of their storage tanks into a "batching vat" and there pre-stirred according to the particular recipe. The raw product or "base mix" is then filtered out of the batching vat and heated at 362 degrees for twenty minutes. This heat treatment of the milk solids and sugars, called pasteurization, eliminates potentially dangerous bacteria, such as those that cause tuberculosis. However, as a result of pasteurization small fatty cream globules appear in the milk. These have to be broken down into smaller particles and spread evenly throughout the mixture. This breaking down of fat globules is called homogenization.

finishing

At this point, the pasteurized, homogenized liquid "ice cream" is still without special color or taste. The time has come to add flavoring, coloring, and special additives for the desired texture. For this purpose, the base mix is piped into one of several 200-gallon stainless steel mixing tanks that look like large washing machines with a catwalk that makes them accessible to workers. Here the necessarry ingredients are mixed in by large blades beating the mix.

freezing and packaging

The final two steps of the process, freezing and packaging, go hand in hand. The still-liquid ice cream is transferred to freezers that are shaped like submarine torpedo tubes with an array of gauges and tubes. (Nuts and candies for the more exotic combinations are added at this stage.) The freezers whip the cream with a mixture of air, so that a semblance of body takes shape before the final and more intensive freezing. When the liquid is about 45 percent frozen, it is shot out through pipes leading directly to upright, folded-out cartons that move on an assembly line. The cartoned ice cream is then led out of the machinery room and into an ammonia freezer that is kept at minus fifty degrees. Several dozen cartons at a time are frozen for several minutes, until the ice cream is practically solid. Soon the hardened ice cream cartons are led down a conveyor belt and covered with plastic wrap, ready for transportation and distribution.

looking to the future   Like many products in our world of processed foods, ice cream is no longer always what it seems to be. Imitation ice cream has been in existence for over fifty years. Coconut oil is used as a substitute for butter fat in imitation ice cream. New kinds of ice cream are being marketed in health food stores and specialty shops. Made from bean curd or from rice, they promise "No sugar!" and "No cholesterol!" They also contain none of the dairy cream and eggs that made old-fashioned ice cream a sinfully delicious treat.

Questions for Discussion Did the major stages in the process become clear to you? Do you remember any striking authentic details? What were key technical terms, and how or how well did the writer explain them? Do you remember any striking imaginative comparisons?

Reminders for Revision Keep in mind some special pointers when revising a process paper:

☐ *Clarify technical terms.* In writing about navigation in space, have you taken for granted terms like *zero gravity, guidance system,* and *ecliptic plane*? Experienced writers routinely clarify terms that are either new and difficult or familiar but only half understood:

> Green or partly green oranges are put into chambers where, for as much as four days, ethylene gas is circulated among them. The gas helps eliminate the chlorophyll in the *flavedo, or outer skin,* which is, in a sense, tiled with cells that contain both orange and green pigments.   John McPhee

☐ *Fill in missing links in the process.* Check for places where you passed over an essential step too quickly:

> Cotton and linen rags, hemp, flax and fibers are made into pulp by either being ground physically or *being broken down chemically.* The paper from mechanically ground pulp is used mostly in throwaway items, such as paper towels, magazines, and newspapers. . . . ("Chemically broken down"—how? What chemicals? What chemical process?)

THE WRITING WORKSHOP

Science and the Concerned Citizen

Collaborate with classmates on a group report on a scientific process that has been the subject of much speculation and debate, such as nuclear winter, desertification, nuclear fusion, or deforestation. Prepare the report for the concerned citizen or voter.

Help the group deal with questions like the following: Why is the subject of urgent concern? What principle or principles underlie the process? What major stages should be identified? What are key technical terms, and how should they be explained to the outsider? How much factual information is needed to make the process clear? What comparisons or analogies can be used to help the reader?

□ *Strengthen the structural elements of your paper.* Bring out more clearly the basic rationale or the overall sequence. Revise weak "and then" or "next this . . . next that" transitions; use links that clearly signal and label the next major phase.

EXERCISE 2 *Summing Up a Process*

Study the following capsule summaries of processes, techniques, or procedures. What essentials did each writer include? What did each writer do to make the process vivid or real for the reader? Write a similar sentence for each category.

1. Definition of a technique or procedure:

   The "Heimlich maneuver" involves encircling the victim from behind so that the rescuer's grasped hands press hard into the abdomen, forcing the diaphragm upward and creating a rush of air that expels whatever may be stuck in the windpipe.

2. Summary of a natural process or cycle:

   The flower begins as a seed; it takes root; it grows; it blooms; it dies, leaving behind a seed that will begin the process again.

3. Summary of an industrial or agricultural process:

   Tomatoes are grown, irrigated, fed, sprayed, now taken, soon to be cooled, squashed, boiled, barreled, and held at the ready, then canned, shipped, sold, bought, and after being sold and bought a few more times, uncanned and dumped on pizza.   Mark Kramer

4.   Description of a job or task:

The tree trimmer clinks and clanks as he climbs up the tree; the chain saw roars as it comes to life; sawdust comes raining down on our heads till finally there is a loud crack as another huge limb comes down with an earth-shaking thud: this is the end of a favorite tree's seventy-year-old life.

EXERCISE 3   *Conveying Technical Information*

Study the following sample paragraph introducing the reader to essential technical terms for a manufacturing process. What does the writer do to make key terms intelligible to the newcomer or the outsider?

The first step in producing processed cheese is to sterilize the milk in a large metal vat, usually about the size of a Volkswagen bug. The milk is heated under pressure in order to destroy unwanted bacteria. It is then allowed to cool to about 70 to 78 degrees. The milk is now ready for the addition of the "starter" organism. The starter organism is a bacterial culture added to the sterilized milk to start the production of lactic acids—acids that form when milk sours. Like the starter used to produce sourdough bread, this culture is specifically nurtured to stimulate a spoiling of the milk that will not prove harmful to the health of the consumer. Once the desired acid level is attained, the solution is said to be "ripe." This is the time to add rennet, an enzyme that causes the milk to coagulate, forming curds. Curds are large clumps of solidified milk from which the cheese will be eventually made; whey is the watery part of the solution that is left behind.

EXERCISE 4   *Analyzing a Scientific Process*

Study the following analysis of a process. What does the writer do to make a scientific process intelligible to the general reader? Where and how does the author explain key principles or technical terms? How clear are the major stages in the process? What are some key details or essential facts? What use does the writer make of graphic language or imaginative comparisons?

Tracy Kidder
THE GREENHOUSE EFFECT

The standard diagram of the carbon-oxygen cycle, the one that every schoolchild studies, shows a person and a tree and a couple of arrows connecting them. One arrow leads from tree to person, indicating that plants release oxygen and that people and animals inhale it. The other arrow goes the other way, from person to tree, signifying the fact that people and animals exhale carbon dioxide, which plants in turn photosynthesize. That's the general outline of the grand, circular dance. Within its circumference, and tangential to it, other dances proceed. A significant number of plants, including many algae, don't return the carbon in them to the air when they die. Instead that carbon is buried—deep in marine sediments below the ocean floor, for instance. The circle closes eventually, perhaps 100 million years later, when the buried carbon is uplifted in a new mountain range or, as one scientist put it, "processed through a volcano." Then the carbon that those plants inhaled, as it were, finally returns to the atmosphere as carbon dioxide.

Civilization has accelerated this slow but continuous portion of the carbon cycle by replacing forests with farms and cities, and especially by mining and burning buried carbon, which is fossil fuel. Civilization has been doing essentially what nature does, but doing it twenty times faster. Measurements taken since 1958 show that in only twenty-four years the amount of carbon dioxide in the atmosphere has increased by 6 percent, and there are estimates that it has risen by 20 percent since the Industrial Revolution. In the past 100 years, mankind has added to the atmosphere some 100 billion tons of carbon.

Some scientists began to feel concerned about the trend as long ago as 1938. Lately, many physicists, oceanographers, meteorologists, biologists, and chemists have turned their attention to a couple of difficult questions. They wonder how long it will take for carbon dioxide to double in the atmosphere. Estimates range from about fifty to several hundred years. They also want to know what a doubling would mean to the planet. The theoretical answer, the one with widest currency, holds that a doubling would intensify the so-called "greenhouse effect."

The analogy is old and apt. Like the glass in a greenhouse, carbon dioxide lets solar radiation pass but inhibits the passage of infrared radiation, which is heat. Carbon dioxide in the air lets the sun heat the earth but it keeps some of that heat from traveling away from the earth and into space. It makes a sort of thermal blanket around the globe, and as that blanket thickens—so most current theory holds—the average temperature of the earth will rise.

Some scientists reckon that the West Antarctic ice sheet will slide into the sea. In the event, water levels would rise, at least high enough to cover the world's coastal cities. Some have thought that the flood might come in as few as fifty years, but recent papers hold that it couldn't happen in less than 200 years. Almost everyone agrees, however, that climates would be affected. America's Corn Belt might need a new name, connoting infertility.

The carbon-dioxide theory conjures up visions of caravans evacuating the seacoasts, of farmers gazing sadly out over parched fields, of rain forest springing up where once was permafrost. Some nations might benefit, while others would decline.   "Trouble in the Stratosphere," *Atlantic*

WRITING TOPICS 9   *Tracing a Process*

Among the following topics, choose one that allows you to draw on close observation or detailed investigation.

1. We are often told that modern city dwellers have lost the traditional skills that used to make people self-sufficient. Help your readers recover such a lost art or skill: baking their own bread, growing their own vegetables, making their own clothes, doing their own woodwork or cabinet work, making their own pottery, making their own wine, making their own cheese, producing their own honey.

2. Much has been written about synthetic or substitute products that over the years have taken the place of natural, home-grown, or homemade ones. Investigate and explain the process that produces one such replacement, substitute, or "improvement." Possible topics: processed cheese, soybean burgers, imitation ice cream, reconstituted orange juice, the rubber tomato, imitation crabmeat, decaffeinated coffee. Write for alert consumers who like to know what they are eating or using.

3. Budget-conscious consumers look for do-it-yourself instructions that will help them do without highly paid skilled labor. Give detailed, helpful instructions for a task like the following: rebuilding an engine, renovating a house, doing cement work, installing wiring, arranging a do-it-yourself divorce.

4. High-tech technology is transforming many traditional procedures and manufacturing processes. Investigate and explain some new or advanced process or technology. Possible topics: an assembly line using robots, solar energy used to heat a house, using a computer to produce graphics, use of lasers in operations. Write for the uninitiated general reader; explain what is difficult to the newcomer or outsider.

5. Investigate and explain a complex natural cycle, such as the life cycle of the butterfly, the frog, the salmon. Choose a cycle that moves through several major stages. Write for readers who have become too far removed from the world of nature.

6. Are you a perfectionist? Do you believe that there is a right way to do a job that is often done too casually or imperfectly? Show your reader how to do an ordinary task right: how to brew a perfect cup of coffee, how to make the best pizza, how to pitch a tent right, how to make true old-style spaghetti.

7. A familiar type of science fiction describes the aftermath of a great catastrophe, with the survivors struggling to relearn the lost arts and skills of civilization. For such a contingency, prepare detailed instructions that would teach survivors how to make paper, sugar, steel, or some other staple product that is the result of a complex process.

COMPARING AND CONTRASTING

Comparison and contrast are basic strategies in the repertory of every writer. To inform or convince the reader, we often need to look at several related things and show how they are similar or how they differ. We may set out to show similarities between things that are superficially different or differences between procedures that seem alike at first glance. We may want to trace connections between customs or institutions widely separated in time or place.

Using Comparison and Contrast

Writing that compares and contrasts serves many purposes. Writers use it to

- make us see important *patterns*: How does a small college differ from a big university? How is the old-style family farm different from modern agribusiness?
- guide our *choices*: What are the advantages of a word processor over a typewriter? How does running compare with swimming as a boon to health?
- guide us in solving *problems*: What features set outstanding schools apart from poor ones? What do Japanese manufacturers know that Americans don't?

Writing to compare and contrast tests your ability to marshal facts and ideas. You will have to bring together things that are usually separate and show the connections between them. Often, there will be no built-in pattern or well-traveled road to follow. You will need to *work out* a strategy of organization that serves your purpose and makes your readers see what you want them to see.

Guidelines for Comparison and Contrast

Remember the following guidelines in working on papers that compare and contrast:

- *Discover your purpose.* Why are you setting up the comparison or contrast the way you do? What is the reader supposed to learn from it? Perhaps you are trying to guide readers in a current crisis by tracing parallels with a similar situation in the past. Perhaps you want to warn customers of an innovation that has serious disadvantages compared with what it replaced.

- *Systematically explore similarities and differences.* Brainstorm; take notes. Writing about the contrast between traditional and modern marriages, for instance, you might line up distinct features in two columns:

TRADITIONAL	MODERN
church wedding	live together first
till death do us part	high divorce rate
virgin bride	family planning
subservient wife	both work
husband works	backyard weddings
take the good with the bad	equal relationships
husband handles finances	supportive, caring male
housewife cleans and cooks	share chores
wait on the husband	mixed marriages
sex on demand	marriage contract
talk about sex is taboo	mutual sex
marry your own kind	discuss problems
feminine wife	

Working with this list, you can begin to sort things out. You can match the directly contrasting items (wife cleans and cooks—both share chores). You can set up tentative categories: religious or moral sanctions of marriage, the economic roles of the two partners, sex roles, the role of sex.

☐ *Consider tracing the comparison or contrast point by point.* A **point-by-point** comparison reminds your reader at every major step that your purpose is to make *connections:* You look at the safety record, say, or the maintenance needs of a domestic car to see how that record compares with that of its Japanese counterpart. You then go through your set of major criteria or major features, asking for each: *"On this point,* what is the record of Car A? What is the record of Car B?"

Study the point-by-point comparison in the following paper. Start with the planning report in which the student writer explains her agenda: her interest in the subject, her use of material from personal experience or contact, and her use of printed sources.

PREWRITING: PLANNING REPORT

Why Japan Is Number One

As a future business major, I have long listened with special interest to horror stories about companies being driven out of business by competition from the Far East. I have read a number of articles about the Japanese work ethic in publications like *Newsweek*. Recently I read a very detailed article about the Japanese system of education and especially the very rigorous system of examinations and the "cram schools" that prepare for them. A friend of mine works at one of the "joint venture" automobile factories run jointly by American and Japanese management, and it was interesting to compare his reactions with an interview in the campus newspaper with an economics major who spent a year in Japan.

Here is the finished paper:

WRITING SAMPLE: POINT BY POINT

Why Japan Is Number One

surface similarity

Travelers returning from Japan report that the stereotype of the invariably hard-working, well-disciplined, and polite Japanese no longer holds true. The Japanese are becoming more and more Americanized. The government tells them to work less and spend more. Divorce rates are up. Teenagers on bicycles taunt police officers and yell obscene phrases. Nevertheless, we can still learn much from the Japanese. In our scramble into the success-driven fast lane, we have lost something valuable the Japanese still have: good work ethics, bonding and loyalty to each other as co-workers and friends.

key differences

schooling

The contrast in cultural conditioning becomes evident early in the children's schooling. All through high school, I watched fellow students who had struck a bargain with the teachers: They would leave the teacher alone if the teacher left them alone in turn. It seemed as if the school allowed half of the students first to tune out and then to drop out.

By contrast, one of the most striking features of Japanese life is the general respect for the ideal of education. Literacy rates are among the highest in the world. In addition to their regular school hours, many students attend cram schools to prepare them for the frequent rigorous tests and examinations.

competition

As we go on to the world of work, we act according to the tradition of individualism. We look out for Number One. Worker distrusts supervisor, supervisor distrusts manager, as we jockey for advancement. We make sure management notices our good points—and the weak points of our rivals or competition.

Japanese workers *have a different attitude* toward their fellow workers. Returning from a visit to Japan, an economics major who has studied Japanese for a number of years was quoted as saying that "reciprocity" is the ideal for relations among fellow workers. Workers are encouraged to make suggestions for improved working procedures that will benefit them and their fellow employees equally.

labor relations

Not only workers among themselves, but also workers and employers in Japan are tied by strong bonds of mutual loyalty and common interest. In this country, labor unions have a tradition of bitter disputes with management.

In Japan, strikes are virtually unheard of. Company policies are not kept as jealously guarded secrets from employees. A friend who works at a plant run jointly by Toyota and General Motors was told early that employees should know what is going on.

No one claims that the Japanese way provides a perfect model for Americans to follow. Women are still by and large treated as second-class citizens. The schools stress cramming and rote learning. However, the Japanese have found ways to beat Americans at their own game in the pursuit of initiative, efficiency, and success.

Questions for Discussion How would you outline in your own words the way this writer has organized her thinking? How good is she at setting up expectations that she then goes on to satisfy, carrying the reader along from step to step?

☐ *Consider taking up two things separately—but covering the same points in the same order.* In comparing two poems, for instance, or two short stories, you may decide that you should not split up the discussion of each poem— your reader needs a feeling for each poem as a whole. Even though you discuss first one poem as a whole and then the other, the two parts of your paper will proceed in **parallel order**, taking up the same or similar features in turn. Study the use of parallel order for three major points in the following excerpted student paper:

WRITING SAMPLE: PARALLEL ORDER

It's Your Choice

Parents who send their children to day-care centers worry about everything from kidnapping to sexual abuse. But their most basic worry is that day care will do damage to the child's normal growth and development. The traditional method of "Mother-stays-home-with-the-child" is still widely considered best.

expert opinion Nevertheless, current research makes strong claims in favor of quality day care provided in group settings. In fact, recent studies claim that the language skills and social skills of day-care toddlers are more advanced than those of children who stay at home. In a recent *Newsweek* interview, a professor in the Graduate School of Education at UCLA claimed that children in day care "form friendships earlier and seem to be more cooperative."

preview In the light of these findings, working parents can perhaps suspend some of their feelings of guilt and instead concentrate on the hardest task: finding the right place for their children. *Three important qualities to look for in a day-care center are a stable staff, the right activities, and an active role for the parents.*

example A I have worked at two different centers. The first one I consider a bad example.
point 1 The staff changed every few months, mainly because we were paid minimum wage. The teachers who stayed did so because they did not feel qualified to work for a higher salary elsewhere. . . .

point 2 The children's day was as follows: TV—inside play—outside play—lunch— nap—outside play—TV— parents' pick up. The main goal was to make the children follow the rules and keep quiet. I remember one small girl particularly who was a very active child. . . .

point 3 Parents were not encouraged to participate; their role was to drop off the children and pick them up. . . .

example B
point 1

The second school I worked at was quite different. There was a very low turnover of staff. . . .

point 2

The children's schedule was as follows: Play—story time—work time—music—outside play—lunch—nap—independent work or play—story time—outside play—art—parents' pickup. . . .

point 3

Parents joined in all the outside activities and often stopped for lunch with the children. Parents should be wary of any school that does not allow drop-in visits. . . .

In a world of two-career or single-parent families, day care is going to be part of growing up for thousands of children. Instead of dropping a child off at the nearest center, parents must shop around to find a place designed to help children grow.

Questions for Discussion Can you show that there is a natural flow in the order of the three major points in this paper? What is the logic behind their arrangement?

☐ *Group similarities and differences together if that seems the best strategy.* In comparing the traditional Western with its modern offspring, you might first want to show the similarities: the setting, the familiar cast of two characters, the gunslingers intimidating the townspeople, the strong silent hero, the climactic shootout. Then you might go on to what makes a Clint Eastwood Western different.

A Sample Comparison-and-Contrast Paper Study the following comparison-and-contrast paper. What is the purpose? What is the plan? How do you react as the reader?

WRITING SAMPLE: COMPARISON AND CONTRAST

Your Personality May Be Harmful to Your Health

familiar stereotype

In a famous study, cardiologists Meyer Friedman and Ray Rosenman linked cardiovascular disease to what they called the Type A personality. David Jenkins, an expert on the subject, describes the Type A person as marked by "competitiveness, striving for achievement, aggressiveness, haste, impatience, restlessness, and feelings of being under the pressure of time and under the challenge of responsibility." The Type B person is everything Type A is not: relatively passive, relaxed, noncompetitive, more patient, and quick to find time for recreation. A barrage of studies by psy-

contrasting thesis

chologists and physicians has found connections between Type A behavior and ulcers, heart disease, headaches, asthma, and even cancer. *My own experience with Type B people, however, tends to show that they suffer from just as many and similar health problems as their Type A counterparts.*

point 1

One reason doctors find more wrong with Type A people may be that instead of going to a doctor a Type B person talks to a bartender. If a Type A person gets sick enough that her work is affected, she will take some money out of the bank and go to the doctor. A Type B person may want to see a doctor, but the chances are he has just spent his last hundred dollars on a triangular box kite or a pocket-size television set.

point 2   Type A people are known for pursuing money at the expense of their health, so it is not surprising that my mother, an upholsterer, has chronic back problems. My father, on the other hand, got his bad back and limp in a motorcycle accident. Type B personalities like my father tend to match in recreational injuries the damage Type A persons suffer from overexertion.

point 3   Many Type A problems are the result of substance abuse. The aspirin taken three at a time for tension headaches causes ulcers. The coffee that gets them through the day is hard on the digestive tract. They may drink to ease tension. But though these habits cause problems, they are at least kept in check by the need to perform. Type B people often have nothing to stop them from destroying their innards. The bar often is the focal point of what matters to them: conversation, friendship, laughter.

point 4   Type A ailments not shared by Type B people are balanced by unique Type B problems. Type A people at least tend to feed themselves and their families. Even during the hardest times there was always a gallon of milk, a loaf of bread, a block of cheese, and a sack of vegetables in my mother's refrigerator. While an upholsterer's wages usually keep her kitchen stocked like a bomb shelter, her ex-husband, my father, never has enough for groceries. His refrigerator is like half of a jigsaw puzzle. It holds hot sauce (no tortillas), pancake syrup (no flour or eggs), three bottles of imported mustard, the cardboard container from a sixpack, and a wedge of French cheese.

Reminders for Revision Comparison and contrast often prove instructive for the writer and may lead to unexpected discoveries. In a first draft, however, the writer's findings or conclusions may not yet come through clearly enough for the reader. Remember the following suggestions for revision:

☐ *Clarify the point of your comparison.* If necessary, provide a clearer overview to point directions early in your paper. If you have explored both similarities and differences in some detail, you may need a stronger conclusion that pulls together the different strands of your paper.

☐ *Check the plan of your paper against a formal outline.* Imagine yourself explaining the plan of your paper to a confused reader. Rearrange the sequence as necessary so that the inner logic of your plan becomes more evident. Try to make your final revised outline reflect a logical flow of major points, as does the following sample outline, which moves from familiar or predictable to less predictable and therefore thought-provoking:

The Fox and the Lion

THESIS: Odysseus and Achilles are both great warriors, but they differ in the other qualities that make an epic hero admirable.

THE WRITING WORKSHOP

Structuring a Comparison

Participate in a group-writing project devoted to working up and structuring material for comparison and contrast. Help the group choose a subject like the following:

- □ standard diet and health foods
- □ private transportation and public transit
- □ male-dominated sports and women's sports
- □ engineers and artists
- □ living together and marriage
- □ living together and living alone
- □ rural living and city living
- □ public school and parochial school
- □ army life and civilian life

Have each member of the group prepare preliminary notes for a comparison and contrast. Help pool the observations of the group, arranging their findings in two opposed columns. Discuss possible groupings and a possible outline for the material. Help the group decide whether to use the material in a group report or adapt it in individual papers.

I. Odysseus as epic hero
    A. Great warrior (unsurpassed in archery, etc.)
    B. Accomplished orator (successful in pleading his own cause)
    C. Shrewd counselor (carefully weighing facts and situations)
    D. Very human character (loves good food and wine)
II. Achilles as epic hero
    A. Great warrior (triumphs over Hector)
    B. Not a great speaker (tends to be haughty and insolent)
    C. Impulsive person (quick to yield to resentment)
    D. Half divine (indifferent to food)

□ *Strengthen the transitions from point to point.* As necessary, steer the reader toward similarities by using words and phrases such as *like, similarly, in parallel fashion, exact counterpart,* and *along similar lines.* Signal contrasts by words and phrases such as *whereas, however, by contrast, on the other hand, nearly opposite,* and *as a counterpoint.* Remember that comparison and contrast will test your ability to establish important connections and to make them clear to the reader.

EXERCISE 5   *Highlighting a Contrast*

Find a recent newspaper or magazine article focused on a difference or contrast of current interest. Summarize the contrast, pinpointing essential differences. Include key points, essential explanations, and selected examples. Choose a subject like the following:

- □ right brain and left brain
- □ Japanese and American work ethics
- □ word processor and typewriter
- □ agribusiness and family farm
- □ natural foods and imitation foods

EXERCISE 6   *Sample Outline*

Study the following sample outline of a *point-by-point comparison*. Does the outline suggest a clear purpose? Who do you think would make a good audience for this paper? Do the main points and their order make sense? What kind of material could you fill in under each heading? What does the conclusion suggest about the general strategy of the paper?

Marriage Is Back

THESIS: As marriage is coming back into style, the traditionally divided roles of breadwinner and homemaker are giving way to a new ideal of equal partners sharing responsibility.

   I. The effects of improved birth control
  II. Changing responsibilities
     A. Working wives
        1. Traditional marriage
        2. Modern marriage
     B. Household chores
        1. Traditional marriage
        2. Modern marriage
     C. Parenting
        1. Traditional marriage
        2. Modern marriage
     D. Financial independence
        1. Traditional marriage
        2. Modern marriage
 III. Benefits for husbands

WRITING TOPICS 10 *Comparison and Contrast*

As you write on one of the following topics, make sure your comparison or contrast serves a purpose and meets the needs of the intended reader.

1. With pairs like the following, we are sometimes told not to confuse the two things being compared—they are very different. At other times, we are told the two overlap—they are more alike than they seem. What do *you* think? Choose a pair like the following for a detailed comparison and contrast:

    ☐ city and suburb
    ☐ school and business
    ☐ drinking and drugs
    ☐ army life and civilian life
    ☐ married life and life after divorce
    ☐ employees and management
    ☐ commercial and public television

2. Pairs like the following present options or *alternatives* in many people's lives. Prepare a detailed comparison and contrast that could help guide the reader's choice. Draw on your observation, experience, and reading. Choose a pair like the following:

    ☐ a factory job and a service job
    ☐ immigrant tradition and the American way
    ☐ private school and public school
    ☐ marriage and the single life
    ☐ the business-oriented person versus the artist
    ☐ small company and big corporations
    ☐ small college and large university
    ☐ babysitters and day care

3. The following pairs represent *opposite poles* in arguments over public issues or public policy. Choose one for investigation and prepare a detailed comparison and contrast that could guide a voter's or an official's choices:

    ☐ private transportation and public transit
    ☐ "private affluence" and "public squalor"
    ☐ American and Japanese business practices or attitudes toward work
    ☐ downtown: pedestrian malls or street traffic
    ☐ wilderness areas or open parks

4. Many Americans believe in innovation and progress; many others look at them with a wary eye. Where do *you* stand? Prepare a detailed "then-

and-now" contrast that reflects your preferences. Choose a pair like the following:

- □ main street and shopping mall
- □ Victorian houses and modern architecture
- □ traditional and modern campus buildings
- □ corner grocery and supermarket
- □ the American car then and now
- □ a country inn and a Holiday Inn
- □ rerun versus current hit
- □ war movies then and now

SETTING UP A CLASSIFICATION

Classification is a basic organizing strategy that helps us chart our way. When we face a confusing array of data, we ask: "What goes with what?" We try to sort the material out into categories. Like a botanist, we set up a system of classification; we do the kind of sorting out and labeling that helps us find our bearings.

The Uses of Classification

Writing that classifies has many uses. Media watchers sort out television programs—sitcoms, prime time soaps, crime shows—to help their readers understand audience tastes. They take stock of the ploys of advertisers in order to make the audience more alert, to protect the customer against being an easy mark. Classification fills a special need when changing patterns make old guideposts misleading or when conventional labels no longer fit. A large receptive audience today is ready for writing that charts changing career opportunities, changing options in our personal lives, or changing roles for women in society.

Sometimes, ready-made categories are well established: urban—suburban—rural; gifted—average—retarded; married—single—divorced. But often the writer's task is to revise existing categories in order to make them more realistic or useful. For instance, the familiar division of social classes into upper class (aristocracy of status or wealth), middle class (bourgeoisie), and lower (or working) class has long served as a rough guide to differences in status, values, tastes, and manners. However, social scientists needed to revise or refine this scheme when large portions of the working class became homeowners preaching middle-class values (and voting Republican); at the same time, a new "underclass" was developing, made up of the chronically unemployed.

Guidelines for Classification Papers To put together an instructive classification paper, you have to do an honest job of investigating your subject and thinking the matter through. Keep in mind the following guidelines:

☐ *Start with established categories if appropriate, but modify or reject them as necessary.* A subject may divide along established lines. For instance, people who have come to this country from abroad differ in legal status:

The Stranger in Our Midst

  I. Temporary visitors (usually not allowed to work here and expected to return home)
 II. Illegal aliens (who live and work here but have no valid papers)
III. Resident aliens (allowed to work here and often planning to become citizens)
 IV. Naturalized U.S. citizens

This division is likely to prove useful in a debate on immigration policy, but a different set of categories may become relevant in an argument over bilingual education:

  I. Unassimilated (immigrants who live in foreign-speaking enclaves, where children hear little English)
 II. Bicultural (bilingual immigrants who want their children to be equally at ease in both languages)
III. Assimilated (fully Americanized immigrants whose children may know only snatches of the parents' first language)

☐ *In setting up your own categories, explore the full range of evidence.* If you choose your headings too hastily, you may exclude an important set of examples merely because they do not fit into a ready-made slot. Or you may set up a major category for something that turns out to be merely an exception or isolated instance. Start with a comprehensive survey of the territory to be charted. For instance, in sorting out the appeals used over and over by television advertisers, you may want to begin by compiling a **viewer's log** that looks in part like the following:

PREWRITING: VIEWER'S LOG

powerful truck drives over rugged country
the American dream family: doting parents, smiling kids, a dog
headache tablets are the "strongest" (wipe your headache away)
cars like panthers, mustangs, eagles
life insurance gives suit-and-tie young husband "peace of mind"
car with many electronic gadgets, control panel like a spaceship
magic oven cleaner makes grime disappear: "wipe it off"
smiling youngsters in swimsuits drink no-calorie drink
"nobody can be turned away" for insurance for veterans

macho beer drinkers work in rugged country with the boys, then drink with
admiring girls in bar
young woman with the right mouthwash cuddles with adoring young man
help buy food for the hungry in drought-stricken Africa

For a first rough sorting out, you may conclude that commercials
make promises of different kinds:

Appeals to basic needs and desires:
—promises of the magic touch (every chore made easy)
—promises of adventure
—daydreams of power
—daydreams of good looks and eternal youth
—daydreams of problem-free sex

A second major category might have two or three subcategories dealing with appeals to our anxieties and fears:

Appeals to basic fears:
—fear of rejection and loneliness
—fear of illness and death

You might use your introduction or conclusion to mention the public-
service messages that appeal to our better selves, to our need to think
of ourselves as generous and responsible people.

☐ *Set up a consistent principle of classification.* Are you applying the same
basic question as you set up each category? For instance, in classifying
the colorful variety of sports in contemporary life, you may ask, "What
is the nature of the *competition*?" This way, you would focus on the underlying motives of the participants, setting up a scheme like the following.
Notice that the thesis of the paper serves as a preview of the writer's
major categories:

PREWRITING: OUTLINE

Meeting the Competition

THESIS: Sports offer us a means of testing ourselves by facing and overcoming
opposition, whether human competitors, the forces of nature, animals, or
our own human limits.

    I. Competing with other human competitors
       A. football
       B. racquetball
       C. wrestling
   II. Competing against the forces of nature
       A. rock climbing

    B. skiing
    C. sailing
  III. Competing against animals
    A. rodeos
    B. bullfights
  IV. Competing with ourselves
    A. marathon running
    B. body building
    C. golf, bowling

If you asked a different question about sports, you would arrive at different categories. For instance, you might want to sort out sports by asking, "What is the *social status* of their followers?" A first tentative scheme might look like this:

    I. Upper-class sports: polo, yachting
   II. Middle-class sports: football, baseball
  III. Lower-class sports: professional wrestling, drag racing

Note: Often several closely related factors will *combine* to help us set up our categories. (For example, size, color, and taste may combine to guide a purchasing agent in classifying tomatoes as superior, average, or poor.) In a marketing study of the "youth market," age level, occupational status, and marital status might combine to set up groups that have distinct buying patterns:

    I. Late teens (still at home, with many of their needs provided there but spending money on hobbies and entertainment)
   II. College students (away from home and spending much money on snacks, sports equipment, traveling, long-distance calls)
  III. Working singles (rent, eating out, sports, cars are major budget items)
  IV. Young marrieds (conventional household expenses begin to play a major role)

☐ *Arrange your major categories in a meaningful sequence.* For instance, you might move from one extreme through intermediate stages to the opposite extreme. The following scheme for male stereotypes in popular entertainment starts with one extreme (the rugged macho type), then looks at in-between types (the authority figure, the well-intentioned father), and finally arrives at the opposite end of the scale:

    I. The outdoor macho type
   II. The male authority figure (doctor, professor, expert)
  III. The harassed, well-meaning father
  IV. The wimp

☐ *Develop each category with detailed, convincing examples.* Provide the kind of real-life details that will make your examples authentic and convincing.

A Sample Classification Paper Study the following example of a classification paper. Look for answers to the following questions:

☐ How did the writer set the paper in motion? What is the thesis? Is there a *preview* or overview?

☐ What are the major categories? Does the *order* in which they appear make sense to you as the reader?

☐ Which *examples* are most striking or convincing? Which least?

☐ How adequate or effective are the *transitions* from point to point?

WRITING SAMPLE: CLASSIFICATION

Meeting the Competition

Our word *athlete* is the Greek word for contestant. When we think of sports, we usually think of one contestant competing with another or others for a prize—an Olympic gold medal, a cherished trophy. On the surface, much of the world of sports presents human beings in contest with each other. When we go beyond the surface, however, we see that much of the time human contestants struggle against other kinds of opposition. Sports offer us a means of testing ourselves by facing and over-coming opposition, whether human competitors, natural forces, or animals. Often the adversary we are trying to overcome is our own human limits.

Obviously, many of the spectator sports that attract large crowds feature battles between teams of human competitors, with winners and losers, with victory cele-brations and the consequences of defeat. In football, opponents literally face each other, with one player shoving the other down the field. Wrestling is one of the oldest of these symbolic confrontations between human contenders, as one contestant con-tends with another, trying to pin the opponent's shoulders to the round.

On the other hand, some sports that seem to be a competition between human contestants really challenge athletes to test their own limits. For example, in marathon running the contest on the surface is between runners competing for first or second place. But many compete who have no chance to win and who are working toward a personal goal. Running the twenty-six miles is their challenge to themselves. An article in the *American Medical News* told the story of a twenty-three-year-old runner in the Triathlon World Championship in Hawaii:

> With only one hundred yards left between her and the finish, Moss fell to her knees. She then rose, ran a few more yards, and collapsed again. As TV cameras rolled, she lost control of her bodily functions. She got up again, ran, fell, and then started crawling. Passed by the second-place runner, she crawled across the finish line, stretched out her arm, and passed out.

This woman was in a race against herself, fighting the limitations of her own body. Other sports that seem competitive in the conventional sense also involve contestants who are basically testing their own limits. A golfer tries to get a lower score than in all previous games. A bowler tries to get a higher score than ever before.

In some sports, participants are pitting their own strength and skill against the forces of nature. In sailing, human beings struggle against the variables of wind and water. In the contest with nature, sports often cease to be play and become deadly serious instead: The mountain climber has to trust in a rope holding to break a fall; handholds and footholds in crevices or on ledges make the difference between life and death. Some three years ago, a brother of a friend of mine, in spite of warnings, went rock climbing alone and fell 150 feet to his death.

The grimly serious nature of the contest is strongest in sports that have their roots in prehistoric contests between human beings and animals. Modern rodeos entertain spectators by having riders try to control broncs and bulls, at danger to life and limb. In bullfighting, the matador kills the bull, and it appears that the animal is the inevitable loser. Yet according to Fodor's *Travel Guide to Spain* (1983),

> A bullfighter's chance of dying in the ring is one in ten. Chance of dying or being crippled is about one in four. They know, usually, what the horn ripping through the flesh feels like; no bullfighters finish their careers completely unscathed.

Wherever we look, the contest seems to be taking place on several levels. A race car driver is competing with other contestants for first place. At the same time, the driver is struggling to assert his or her mastery over a powerful, deadly machine. And the most basic contest is between pride, ambition, determination on the one hand and fear, fatigue, and human fallibility on the other.

Reminders for Revision As you rework the first draft of a classification paper, look for opportunities for improvement:

☐ *Strengthen the beginning of your paper.* Early in your paper, do you motivate and point directions for the reader? Should you do more to show why you are writing—to update outmoded categories, to alleviate confusion, or to chart current trends? Should you include a clearer or more inviting preview of the categories you have set up?

☐ *Push toward a unifying thesis.* For instance, you may have written a paper about three kinds of popular music that have had a strong hold on the imagination of young people: the blues, rock and roll, and punk rock. As you reread your first draft, you begin to see more clearly the common strand: Economic exploitation and substandard living conditions gave blacks many reasons to sing the blues. Young people of the fifties and sixties, though materially well off, used rock and roll as a means to express their rebellion against an uptight materialistic lifestyle. Punk rock expresses a violent anger and frustration. In your revision, you may want to bring out more strongly a unifying thesis:

THESIS: Several of the most influential forms of American popular music are rooted in a rebellion against established society.

☐ *Check to see if your categories are of roughly equal importance.* Are you slicing the pie into segments that are about equally significant? Should several of your categories be *sub*categories under one of your major headings?

THE WRITING WORKSHOP

Charting the Territory

Participate in a group project designed to chart developments in an area that is in a process of change. Help your group choose a subject like the following:

- □ jobs for young Americans
- □ dress styles of those dressing for success
- □ living arrangements for college students
- □ female stereotypes in advertising
- □ male stereotypes in advertising
- □ nontraditional students
- □ the new poor
- □ chances to start one's own business
- □ urban architecture

Have each member focus on one major category (one dress style, one job opportunity, one familiar stereotype), working up ample material from observation, reading, interviews, and the like. Then have the group work on pooling the materials, working toward a comprehensive system of classification. Have the group decide on a workable overall scheme and on the major categories that should be included. Help the group decide whether to use the results in a group report or adapt them in individual papers.

□ *Try to make the labels for your categories striking, informative, and attractive.* When you write about people's attitudes toward work, your readers will remember labels like the workaholic, the climber, the timeserver, the shirker. (But beware of stereotypes here.)

□ *Avoid unconvincing hypothetical examples.* Do not overdo imaginary examples that sound as if you made them up to fit your various headings.

As in other writing, one key example treated in convincing detail and supported by several briefer examples may provide the most effective mix as you treat each category. As in other writing, a mix of materials from personal experience, from firsthand investigation, and from related reading may prove best for making your system of classification seem sound to your reader.

Remember: Tracing a process, comparing and contrasting, and classifying are organizing strategies that we use over and over when we chart our course and set up signposts for those who come after. However, ready-made patterns and established think schemes are often like old maps or like organizational charts for institutions that have gone out of business. To organize a piece of writing, we need to map the route that will fit the territory, help our readers find their way, and take them to the desired destination.

EXERCISE 7   *Testing Established Categories*

From among the following, choose one set of familiar or established categories that seem useful or instructive. (Revise or modify the categories if necessary.) For each category in your chosen set, fill in related material that would help flesh it out: observations that give it meaning, associations that cluster around it, images that it brings to mind.

- urban—suburban—rural
- child—adolescent—adult
- authoritarian—permissive—firm but kind
- unskilled—semiskilled—skilled
- married—single—divorced
- exclusive neighborhood—middle-class neighborhood—low-income neighborhood
- science fiction—fantasy—horror
- honor student—average student—dropout

EXERCISE 8   *Checking Trial Outlines*

Study the following *capsule outlines* for classification papers. How promising is each outline? How sound or workable is the basic principle of classification? What is the order of the categories, and does it make sense? What examples or details could you provide for each category?

OUTLINE 1: KINDS OF JOBS
  I.   Glamor jobs
  II. Jobs for the ambitious
  III. Anonymous 9–5 jobs
  IV. Menial jobs

OUTLINE 2: COUPLES
  I.   Traditional marriage
  II. Modern marriage
  III. Living together

OUTLINE 3: CHANGING PATTERNS OF WOMEN'S WORK
   I.   Traditional homemaker
   II. Traditional pink-collar jobs
   III. Women in traditional male jobs (construction, police)
   IV. Middle management and professionals
   V.   Leadership roles

OUTLINE 4: SPORTS AND HUMAN DIGNITY
   I.   Grunt sports: boxing, wrestling
   II. Contact sports: football, hockey
   III. Skill sports: basketball, tennis
   IV. Inspirational sports: track, mountaineering

OUTLINE 5: FEMALE STEREOTYPES IN ADVERTISING
   I.   The sexy young single
   II. The successful career woman
   III. The harried housewife
   IV. The know-it-all mother-in-law

WRITING TOPICS 11   *Classification*

Choose a topic that will enable you to do something for the reader: clear up confusion, provide a new way of looking at something, or guide choices.

1.   No one wants to be a type; people resent glib labels that deny their individuality ("a typical jock"; "just like a woman"; "you know how Italians are"). Have you nevertheless been able to chart some major *personality types* that help you understand people you encounter? Write a paper in which you divide a group of people into three or four major categories. For instance, you might classify people who give advice to others as supporters, friendly critics, hostile critics, and nitpickers. Make sure that your principle of classification becomes clear to your readers.

2.   Set up a system of classification that could serve as a shopper's guide for a *concerned consumer*. (Your instructor may ask you to prepare a trial outline for class discussion.) Set up three or more major categories for one of the following:

   □   kinds of restaurants
   □   places to live (in your area or more generally)
   □   major options in buying a car
   □   kinds of parks
   □   types of television shows for children
   □   styles of tract homes

- kinds of exercise
- major choices in selecting a college

3. Set up a system of classification that would help a trend watcher understand *current trends*. (Your instructor may ask you to prepare a trial outline for class discussion.) Select an area like the following. Make sure your principle of classification becomes clear to your readers:

- male stereotypes in commercial television
- criminals in current crime shows
- sports as symbols of social status
- kinds of work open to women today
- barriers to women's advancement in careers
- how different types of men share in household duties
- kinds of marriages
- sports popular with young adults
- levels of sophistication in local entertainment offerings
- range of attitudes toward business among young Americans

11

READ/WRITE

Writing from Sources

We read often with as much talent as we write.
Ralph Waldo Emerson

Connection-making is at the heart of all analysis, whether it be among the parts of a single reading, between one reading and another, or between the text and something else you know or think. Patricia Chittenden

READING WITH THE WRITER'S EYE We do not write in a vacuum. We listen, view, and read. We take in a constant stream of images and messages, of information and ideas. As listeners and viewers, but especially as readers, we interact with materials that start up and fuel our writing.

The Uses of Reading Good writers are alert readers. When they take a break from working at the typewriter or word processor, they pick up a magazine or a book— to browse, to look something up, to take notes. They are print people— they read and talk about their reading.

As writers, we interact with our reading in a number of ways:

TRIGGERING We often write to answer a question raised by someone else. Much of our writing is triggered by our need to respond—to agree or disagree. We read an attack on something we value—baseball, rock lyrics, subsidies for the arts—and we rise to the defense. Writing is often part of a dialogue: We read what others say about vigilantism or censorship, and we are prodded into defining our own position, clarifying our own thinking. Much writing is *counter*statement: talking back, questioning someone else's facts or reasoning, setting the record straight. A writer who does not read is like a patient shut up in a plastic dome—deprived of much of the stimulus that triggers thoughts and actions.

211

EXPLORING Reading about a subject helps a writer map out the territory. When you write about prison reform, you cannot afford to sound like someone who stumbled onto the subject yesterday. You read what people close to the issue have said. You may want to check data compiled by advocates of penal reform, weigh the expert testimony of police chiefs and prison wardens, and read the inside story of ex-convicts. Exploratory reading makes your writing more informed and knowledgeable—less likely to be dismissed as one-sided or naïve.

BOLSTERING The most direct payoff for receptive readers comes when they draw on their reading for support in their own writing. Much effective writing uses a mix of firsthand observation and material from relevant reading. It draws on inside information, expert opinion, current news, eyewitness testimony, and eye-opening statistics. You do not want your ideas to be written off as one person's cranky opinion, so you turn to authorities, officials, witnesses, and alert observers to bolster your own conclusions. You clinch an argument by quoting testimony from someone widely admired.

Questions for Discussion On what current topic have you recently done much reading (and listening)? Computer crime? Fat substitutes? Covert operations? What key points and striking details do you remember?

The Active Reader Some people are good listeners; others seem to listen with only one ear. Similarly, some people are good readers. They early catch the author's drift. They read to learn: They are open to new ideas; they follow an author's train of thought. Other people read with a wandering, distracted eye, missing telling points and crucial distinctions. They bypass the main argument to pounce on a minor point. Active readers are good at taking in what an author has to offer; they do justice to the major dimensions of productive reading:

READING FOR STRUCTURE When we read a substantial piece of writing, we need to find our bearings. We ask, "What is this about? What is the issue? What is the point? What is the plan?" Remember the following guidelines when you look for answers to these questions:

- *Look for early clues to the author's intention and overall plan.* Be alert to key questions raised, key images presented, or striking examples used to dramatize the issue. In the following beginning of a column from *Newsweek*, the author sets up expectations that the rest of the column will satisfy:

Institution Is Not a Dirty Word

I watched Phil Donahue recently. He had on mothers of handicapped children who talked about the pain and blessing of having a "special" child. As the mother of a severely handicapped six-year-old boy who cannot sit, who cannot walk, who will be in diapers all of his days, I understand the pain. The blessing part continues to elude me—notwithstanding the kind and caring people we've met through this tragedy.

What really makes my jaws clench, though, is the use of the word "special." The idea that our damaged children are "special," and that we as parents were somehow picked for the role, is one of the myths that come with the territory. It's reinforced by the popular media, which present us with heartwarming images of retarded people who marry, of quadriplegics who fly airplanes, of those fortunate few who struggle out of comas to teach us about the meaning of courage and love. I like these stories myself. But, of course, inspirational tales are only one side of the story. . . .   Fern Kupfer

The author sets her essay in motion by making us share her reaction to a television program. The program dramatizes the issue: How do the parents of severely handicapped, "special" children cope—what attitudes are they expected to adopt, what role are they expected to play? The "heartwarming images" and inspirational stories dear to the media are "only one side of the story." By the end of this introduction, we are ready to hear the *other* side of the story, based on the author's experience as the parent of a severely handicapped six-year-old child.

☐ *Trace the development of key points.* Early in your reading, start identifying the key ideas that the writer is going to explain, illustrate, or defend. Identify a key idea, a key phrase, a focal point. Then trace the network of repeated or related terms that may echo the key idea. Follow the chain of supporting examples that bring it to life. The following passage touts the importance of running in sports other than running. This point was important enough for the writer to pile up four sets of supporting examples. Look at the repetition of the key term and study the examples in each set:

Though we no longer run for food and survival, the importance of this activity is still evident in the sports we most enjoy watching. *Football, basketball, baseball, and soccer,* it might be said, are complicated excuses for running. *Tennis and other racket, net, and wall games* involve a series of short, dancing sprints. *Pole vaulting, javelin throwing, high jumping, long jumping, and triple jumping* begin with and depend upon running. *Rugby, cricket, field hockey, team handball, hurdles, steeplechase, various forms of tag, hide-and-seek, and capture-the-flag*—all are running games.

At the very least, running can give you all the aerobic conditioning you need. . . . George Leonard, "Born to Run," *Esquire*

☐ *Trace the writer's chain of thought.* Look for the larger pattern that gives shape to an essay as a whole. In what order is the subject going to be covered? How is the argument going to take shape? What transitions signal turning points in the argument? In the following passage, the author sets up prominent signposts for his readers. He early strikes the keynote—the "fear of science"—and then shows this fear at work, lining up three causes in a clear "first-second-third" order. Here is how a reader might highlight and annotate the passage:

And what if the creationists win? They might, you know, for there are millions who, faced with the choice between science and their interpretation of the Bible, will choose the Bible and reject science, regardless of the evidence.

KEYNOTE: THE "FEAR OF SCIENCE"

This is not entirely because of a traditional and unthinking reverence for the literal works of the Bible; there is also a pervasive uneasiness—even an actual fear—of science that will drive even those who care little for Fundamentalism into the arms of the creationists. For one thing, science is uncertain. Theories are subject to revision; observations are open to a variety of interpretations, and scientists quarrel among themselves. This is disillusioning for those untrained in the scientific method, who thus turn to the rigid certainty of the Bible instead. . . .

① CHANGING SCIENTIFIC THEORIES

② "COLD" SCIENTIFIC UNIVERSE

Second, science is complex and chilling. The mathematical language of science is understood by very few. The vistas it presents are scary—an enormous universe ruled by chance and impersonal rules, empty and uncaring, ungraspable and vertiginous. How comfortable to turn instead to a small world, only a few thousand years old, and under God's personal and immediate care. . . .

③ DESTRUCTIVE POTENTIAL OF SCIENCE

Third, science is dangerous. There is no question but that poison gas, genetic engineering and nuclear weapons and power stations are terrifying. It may be that civilization is falling apart and the world we know is coming to an end. In that case, why not turn to religion and look forward to the Day of Judgment, in which you and your fellow believers will be uplifted into eternal bliss.   Isaac Asimov, "The 'Threat' of Creationism," *The New York Times*

Our task as readers is to follow the author's train of thought even when it traces a less straight line and when the logical links are not as clearly posted. Here are some familiar patterns that, alone or in combination, may give shape to an essay as a whole:

☐ Then and now: "This was the situation *then* . . . and this is the situation *now*—with both the advantages and the disadvantages that were the result of change."

☐ Causes and consequences: "This is the situation now, and these are its *causes*—and here are the *results* we can project if these causes continue to operate."

☐ Myth and reality: "This is widely believed . . . *however*, this is what we find when we take a closer look."

□   Pro and con: *"On the one hand,* there are strong arguments in favor of this proposal . . . *on the other hand,* there are also weighty arguments on the other side."

Develop your own system for highlighting or underlining key sentences; circle or otherwise mark key terms and phrases; use the margin to outline key points or to note your queries. Be an active reader: Get involved in what you read; work it through; make it your own.

READING FOR ATTITUDE   Not everything that steers our reactions to what we read is fully spelled out. We read between the lines. We react to belittling or admiring words; we note the choice of a shocking or a reassuring example.

Suppose you are reading an article discussing action by citizens who strike out at muggers, robbers, or intruders. Early in the article, you begin to notice a refrain of phrases that mobilize the reader's fear of violent crime:

□   "frightening realities of our streets"
□   "brutality on the subway"
□   "the fear and frustration of being a victim"
□   "the crime-oppressed average citizen"
□   "people living in a so-called free society who are in reality trapped in their homes by the fear of crime"

Soon, you begin to trace a parallel strand of sympathy and support for the beleaguered citizenry:

□   "decent citizens forced to fight back"
□   "threatened citizens striking out when forced to protect themselves"
□   "honest, wholesome, and hard-working citizens tired of being abused and victimized"

You conclude that even though stopping short of endorsing vigilante action outright, the author tacitly supports those who are frustrated by intolerable conditions and decide to take the law into their own hands.

READING IN CONTEXT   To do justice to an author's thinking, we try not to take words or sentences out of context. What role did a statement play in an essay as a whole? Was it a fully supported major point? Or was it a trial balloon, followed by debate of the pro and con? Note important qualifications or reservations signaled by a strategic *perhaps* or *most of the time.*

Questions for Discussion   How good a reader are you? Do you read quickly for the general idea? Do you read slowly, taking in details? Do you stop and go? (Why do you get bogged down? How do you start moving again?) What system do you have for highlighting and taking notes? Have you had any experience with speed-reading techniques or other reading helps?

Guidelines for Reading

To get the most from your reading, consider the following guidelines:

- *Read and reread.* On first reading, you may miss important connections; you may be puzzled by new concepts or involved explanations. As you go back to difficult passages or key points, things will fall into place.

- *Chart the author's thinking.* Try various kinds of informal outlining—in the margin, on scratch paper—to make sure you see the author's general strategy.

- *Look for passages that sum up the author's major points.* Pay special attention to introductions, conclusions, previews or overviews, thesis statements, and the like.

- *Look for definitions of key terms.* For instance, where does the author define "artificial intelligence"? Where does the author explain the workings of the artificial heart?

- *Be guided by emphasis and extent of coverage.* What are the questions or ideas that echo throughout a piece of writing? Which points does the author belabor, marshaling a formidable array of examples, evidence, or argument?

Remember: Authors vary in how much help they offer to the reader. Some make a special effort to aid the reader, furnishing the signs and on-ramps that make their material accessible. Others concentrate on doing justice to the material, getting things right even if the terrain might make rough going for the reader. Many other authors are in between; they neither underestimate nor overestimate the attention span and intelligence of the reader.

EXERCISE 1   *The Careful Reader*

Read the following sample of writing that traces causes and effects. Can you follow the author's thinking step by step? Answer the following questions:

- What kind of program does the first paragraph set up, and how and where does the author carry it out?
- What are the major causes of our modern insect problem? How does each of these causes operate? What are the major examples or appli-

THE WRITING WORKSHOP

Reading Between the Lines

Much of the time we do not read anonymous pieces of information or disembodied opinions. Rather, what we know about the author prepares us for a certain point of view, a certain line of argument. (Often what we know about the author made us turn to the source in the first place.) Working with a group, define the point of view, typical interests, and characteristic lines of argument of a major columnist, such as George Will, Ellen Goodman, Michael Royko, Jack Anderson, Meg Greenfield, William Safire, or Mary McGrory. With your group, study columns published over several weeks, or find columns on major events or issues during the last one or two years. What are typical concerns? What are recurrent themes? What is the author's characteristic slant on current events? Who would be this author's ideal readers?(Are you one of them?)

Help prepare a group report to be presented to your class and to be compared with similar reports on other opinion makers.

cations that the author traces for each? What key terms or key phrases help you follow the argument?

- □ What transitions provide major signposts for the reader?
- □ What parts of the passage provide clues to the author's attitude? Identify phrases that reveal the author's attitudes, preferences, or values.

Rachel Carson
OUR INSECT PROBLEM

Long before the age of man, insects inhabited the earth—a group of extraordinarily varied and adaptable beings. Over the course of time a small percentage of the more than half a million species of insects have come into conflict with human welfare in two principal ways: as competitors for the food supply and as carriers of human disease.

Disease-carrying insects become important where human beings are crowded together, especially under conditions where sanitation is poor, as in time of natural disaster or war or in situations of extreme poverty and deprivation. Then control of some sort becomes necessary. It is a sobering fact, however, that the method of massive chemical control has had only limited success, and also threatens to worsen the very conditions it is intended to curb.

Under primitive agricultural conditions the farmer had few insect problems. These arose with the intensification of agriculture—the devotion of immense acreages to a single crop. Such a system set the stage for explosive increases in specific insect populations. Single-crop farming does not take advantage of the principles by which nature works; it is agriculture as an engineer might conceive it to be. Nature has introduced great variety into the landscape, but man has displayed a passion for simplifying it. Thus we undo the built-in checks and balances by which nature holds the species within bounds. One important natural check is a limit on the amount of suitable habitat for each species. Obviously then, an insect that lives on wheat can build up its population to much higher levels on a farm devoted to wheat than on one in which wheat is intermingled with other crops to which the insect is not adapted.

The same thing happens in other situations. A generation or more ago, the towns of large areas of the United States lined their streets with the noble elm tree. Now the beauty they hopefully created is threatened with complete destruction as disease sweeps through the elms, carried by a beetle that would have only limited chance to build up large populations and to spread from tree to tree if the elms were only occasional trees in a richly diversified planting.

Another factor in the modern insect problem is one that must be viewed against a background of geologic and human history: the spreading of thousands of different kinds of organisms from their native homes to invade new territories. This worldwide migration has been studied and graphically described by the British ecologist Charles Elton in his book *The Ecology of Invasions*. During the Cretaceous Period, some hundred million years ago, flooding seas cut many land bridges between continents and living things found themselves confined in what Elton calls "colossal separate nature reserves." There, isolated from others of their kind, they developed many new species. When some of the land masses were joined again, about 15 million years ago, these species began to move out into new territories—a movement that is not only still in progress but is now receiving considerable assistance from man.

The importation of plants is the primary agent in the modern spread of species, for animals have almost invariably gone along with the plants, quarantine being a comparatively recent and not completely effective innovation. The United States Office of Plant Introduction alone has introduced almost 200,000 species and varieties of plants from all over the world. Nearly half of the 180 or so major insect enemies of plants in the United States are accidental imports from abroad, and most of them have come as hitchhikers on plants.

In new territory, out of reach of the restraining hand of the natural enemies that kept down its numbers in its native land, an invading plant or animal is able to become enormously abundant. Thus it is no accident that our most troublesome insects are introduced species.

These invasions, both the naturally occurring and those dependent on human assistance, are likely to continue indefinitely. Quarantine and massive chemical campaigns are only extremely expensive ways of buying time. We are faced, according to Dr. Elton, "with a life-and-death need not just to find new technological means of suppressing this plant or that animal"; instead we need the basic knowledge of animal populations and their relations to their surroundings that will "promote an even balance and damp down the explosive power of outbreaks and new invasions." *Silent Spring*

DRAWING ON YOUR READING

Effective writers know how to work material from their reading into the flow of a paper or article. They blend material from their sources smoothly into their own writing without a stop-and-go effect.

Adapting Material from Your Sources

Study and experiment with different ways of using material from your sources:

QUOTE/UNQUOTE Often, you will let the authors you draw on speak for themselves. You will use **direct quotation**—quoting something from your reading verbatim, word for word.

To use a direct quotation to advantage, introduce it effectively. In order to set the stage, let the reader know one or more of the following: Who said this and where? What is the writer's authority, or what are the author's credentials? In other words, why should we listen to this person? What is the point of the quotation? Why are you using it here? (See Chapter 18 for full identification of sources in a research paper.)

SOURCE:	Rachel Carson said in *Silent Spring* that "only within the moment of time represented by the present century" has one species—ours—acquired the power to alter the nature of the world.
CREDENTIALS:	Garrett Hardin, author of "The Tragedy of the Commons" and many other articles and books on "human ecology," has attacked "suicidal policies for sharing our resources through uncontrolled immigration and foreign aid."
POINT:	Garrett Hardin has used the lifeboat analogy to dramatize our limited capacity for helping the world's poor: "Our survival demands that we govern our actions by the ethics of a lifeboat, harsh though they may be."

Quote selectively, choosing and trimming your quotations in such a way that they will focus the reader's attention on what counts. Sometimes, you will quote a *single word or phrase* to highlight or dramatize an important idea:

QUOTED PHRASE: Koelsch and Jasany, like other advocates of artificial intelligence, tout the potential of expert systems, or "experts in a box."

Often you will use a **partial quotation**—part of a sentence that sums up an important point:

PARTIAL QUOTE: Historian Daniel J. Boorstin claims that vigilantism arose "not to circumvent courts, but to provide them; not because the machinery of government had become complicated, but because there was no machinery at all; not to neutralize institutions, but to fill a vacuum."

Often you will quote one or more *complete sentences,* introduced by a comma (or the more formal colon):

COMPLETE QUOTE: In the words of psychologist Hilda Ignes, "Neurosis is the condition where an individual's emotional elevators go to the top floor when least desired."

At strategic points, you may want to quote a whole passage. It may present a key example in striking detail, or it may express the heart of the author's argument. If the passage runs to more than four typed lines, set it off as a **block quotation**—indented ten spaces, *no* quotation marks. Look at the way the following excerpt from a student paper introduces and uses a block quotation:

Paycheck Equality

We flounder when we think that women worry a great deal about car door equality—whether the man should open a car door for the woman or whether she should now open it herself. What matters to the junior executive with her briefcase and umbrella or to the woman climbing up a telephone pole with tools strapped to her waist and working boots on her feet is economic equality. Historical changes have forced millions of women to find security in economic independence. Betty *author credentials* Friedan, the founder and first president of the National Organization for Women, *key phrase* writes that the women's movement was the result of "evolutionary necessity." In her *book title* book *The Second Stage,* she says about the economic roots of the movement:

block quotation (with Women could no longer live out an eighty-year life span as childbearers, wives, *one deletion)* and mothers alone. For function, identity, status in society, and their own economic support, women—for the first time in history . . . were forced by the longer span of their lives to take their own place, as individuals in society.

Note the many different ways you can weave quoted material into your own text. Study the whole range of introductory phrases, or **credit tags:**

> In the words of Mark Twain, "The very ink with which history is written is merely fluid prejudice."
> To quote Mark Twain, "The very ink . . ."
> As Mark Twain said, "The very ink . . ."
> According to Mark Twain, "The very ink . . ."

Note: Shift to **single quotation marks** when the quoted author in turn quotes someone else:

QUOTE IN QUOTE: In the words of Robert Wells, "Too many times I have sat in my office and heard the wrenching sorrows of couples who could not have children. I have listened to the pleas: 'Is there nothing you can do?' "

Use the **ellipsis**—three spaced periods—to show that you have deleted something in order to shorten a quotation. (If the omission occurs after the end of a sentence, use three spaced periods after the sentence period, for a total of four periods.)

OMISSION: In the words of Robert Wells, "Too many times I have . . . heard the wrenching sorrows of couples who could not have children."

Use **square brackets** to identify any clarification, correction, or comments that you have inserted in a quotation:

ADDITION: The *Tribune*'s restaurant critic calls it "the only place in town that serves decent snails, tripe, and boudin [French blood sausage] in old-country style."

PARAPHRASE When you **paraphrase** a passage, you put it in your own words. Although a paraphrase filters out the personal voice of the original author, it shows that you have fully digested what you have read. At the same time, in using your own words, you can translate difficult ideas into language your readers can understand. You can condense lengthy arguments or boil down complicated information to its essentials. Here is a sample passage that uses paraphrase—*in*direct quotation, *no* quotation marks:

Preschoolers who can speak two languages learn to read more quickly than their monolingual peers, reports Kenji Hakuta, psychology professor at Yale and author of *The Mirror of Language*. Hakuta says that reading involves the same skills as speaking two dialects. Learning that two sounds are symbols for the same object makes it easier for the child to understand that a printed word is also a symbol.

Practice in paraphrasing a whole passage provides training in close reading. Compare the following passage and the detailed paraphrase that follows it:

ORIGINAL: Running is one of the primal human acts, and the particular human form it takes, using a bipedal stride in a fully upright stance, has played an essential part in shaping our destiny. It was once believed that our hominid ancestors were rather pitiable creatures compared with the other animals of the jungles and savannas; lacking the fangs, claws, and specialized physical abilities of the predators, the hominids supposedly prevailed only because of their large brains and their ability to use tools. But there is now compelling evidence that our direct ancestors of some four million years ago had relatively small brains, only about a third the size of ours. What these hominids *did* have was a fully upright stance with the modern, doubly curved spine that enters the skull at the bottom rather than the back (as is the case with the apes). The upright stance increased the field of vision and freed the forelimbs for use in inspecting and manipulating objects, thus challenging the brain to increase its capacity through the process of natural selection.   John Leonard, *Born to Run*

In the following paraphrase, the ideas are attributed to the original author, but the *wording* is that of the writer who wrote the paraphrase:

PARAPHRASE: According to John Leonard in "Born to Run," running is a part of what makes us human, and the way we run—fully upright, striding on two feet—has helped determine what we are today. It was thought earlier that physically our near-human ancestors were pitifully weak creatures, who lacked the formidable teeth, claws, and physical strength of wild animals hunting for food in the jungles and open spaces and who prospered only because of their large brains and their invention of tools. But, according to Leonard, strong evidence proves that our forebears from four million years ago had comparatively small brains—about one-third of our own brain size. What these near-humans had was the ability to stand fully erect, with our modern *S*-curved spine entering the skull from below rather than from the back, as with the apes. Standing upright gave humans a wider range of sight and freed the arms for use in investigating and handling objects; it stimulated the brain to build up its potential through the evolutionary process of natural selection.

Part of the task of paraphrasing is to spell out the everyday meaning of technical or formal terms: *bipedal* stride/striding *on two feet*, hominid ancestors/*near-human* ancestors. But the larger part of the task is to show that you have made the original author's meaning your own, phrase by phrase: "Running is one of the primal human acts" becomes "Running is a part of what makes us human."

SUMMARY Often, you will use material from your reading in a much-abbreviated form. A familiar task for many writers is to summarize, abstract, or digest, bulky material. The following brief **summary** shrinks the "Born to Run" passage to its essentials:

BRIEF SUMMARY: According to John Leonard, early human beings, with relatively small brains, gained a competitive edge over other animals as the result of their fully upright bipedal stance, which increased their field of vision and freed the forelimbs for manipulating objects.

The following **digest,** while reducing the original passage by half, preserves some of the original author's train of thought:

DIGEST: According to John Leonard in "Born to Run," the way we run—fully upright, with bipedal stride—has shaped our human destiny. Our hominid ancestors were once thought pitiable compared with the fangs and strength of other predators, which, however, lacked large brains and tools. But evidently, four million years ago our ancestors had only one-third our brain size. They did have a full upright stance, with a larger field of vision, forelimbs free for manipulating objects, and gradually increasing brain capacity through natural selection. Their athletic ability assured survival, even without tools and high intelligence.

The writer has saved much of the original author's trend of thought as well as key details. Much of the original wording is still there: "bipedal stride," "hominid ancestors," "field of vision." But wherever possible, the writer has squeezed, shrunk, and combined sentences and phrases while trying to keep the essential ideas intact: "Has played an essential part in shaping our destiny" becomes "has shaped our destiny"; "there is now compelling evidence that" becomes "evidently." Note that when a condensation is clearly labeled a summary, a digest, or an abstract, it will often preserve some of the author's original wording without quotation marks. Such digests or abstracts are often used to guide readers to promising sources. *Be sure to use quotation marks for all directly quoted material when you incorporate it in your own text.* (See Chapter 18 on problems of **plagiarism.**)

Your writing of summaries will give you practice in close, attentive reading. Often you will be aiming at a summary about one third or one fourth the length of the original. Remember the following guidelines:

☐ *Make sure you grasp the main trend of thought.* Identify key sentences: the thesis that sums up the main point of an essay (or section of an essay), the topic sentence that is developed in the rest of a paragraph. Look out for major turning points—a strategic *however* or *on the other hand* that signals an important step in an argument.

☐ *Reduce explanations and examples to the essential minimum.* Leave out phrases that merely restate or reinforce a point already made. Condense lengthy explanations; keep only the most important details, examples, or statistics.

☐ *Use the most economical wording possible.* Write "negotiate" for "conduct negotiations"; "surprisingly" for "it came as a surprise to many observers that. . . ."

☐ *Beware of oversimplification.* Preserve an essential *if, but,* or *unless.* Keep distinctions between *is, will,* or *might.* Keep words like *only, almost,* or *on the whole.*

The following three versions of the same passage will help you reconstruct the process by which one writer produced a summary. Notice how in the second version the writer has crossed out everything that merely repeats or expands the main points:

ORIGINAL:

There are numerous cases of societies in which the armies of the night have ridden triumphantly over minorities in order to establish a powerful orthodoxy which dictates official thought. Invariably, the triumphant ride is toward long-range disaster.

Spain dominated Europe and the world in the 16th century, but in Spain orthodoxy came first, and all divergence of opinion was ruthlessly suppressed. The result was that Spain settled back into blankness and did not share in the scientific, technological and commercial ferment that bubbled up in other nations of Western Europe. Spain remained an intellectual backwater for centuries.

In the late 17th century, France in the name of orthodoxy revoked the Edict of Nantes and drove out many thousands of Huguenots, who added their intellectual vigor to lands of refuge such as Great Britain, the Netherlands and Prussia, while France was permanently weakened.

In more recent times, Germany hounded out the Jewish scientists of Europe. They arrived in the United States and contributed immeasurably to scientific advancement here, while Germany lost so heavily that there is no telling how long it will take it to regain its former scientific eminence. The Soviet Union, in its fascination with Lysenko, destroyed its geneticists, and set back its biological sciences for decades. China, during the Cultural Revolution, turned against Western science and is still laboring to overcome the devastation that resulted.   Isaac Asimov, "The 'Threat' of Creationism," *The New York Times*

WORKING VERSION:

~~There are~~ numerous ~~cases of~~ societies ~~in which the armies of the night~~ have ridden triumphantly over minorities in order to establish a powerful orthodoxy ~~which dictates official thought~~. Invariably, the ~~triumphant~~ ride is toward long-range disaster.

Spain dominated ~~Europe and the world~~ in the 16th century, but ~~in Spain orthodoxy came first, and~~ all divergence of opinion was ~~ruthlessly~~ suppressed. The result was that Spain ~~settled back into blankness and~~ did not share in the scientific, technological and commercial ferment ~~that bubbled up in other nations~~ of Western Europe. Spain remained an intellectual backwater ~~for centuries~~.

~~In the late~~ 17th century, France ~~in the name of orthodoxy revoked the Edict of Nantes and~~ drove out ~~many thousands of~~ Huguenots, who added their intellectual vigor to lands of refuge such as Great Britain, the Netherlands and Prussia, ~~while France was permanently weakened~~.

~~In more recent times,~~ Germany hounded out the Jewish scientists ~~of Europe~~. They arrived in the United States and contributed ~~immeasurably~~ to scientific advancement here, while Germany lost ~~so heavily that there is no telling how long it will take it to regain~~ its former scientific eminence. The Soviet Union, ~~in its fascination with Lysenko~~, destroyed its geneticists, and set back its biological sciences for decades. China, during the Cultural Revolution, turned against Western science and is still laboring to overcome the devastation ~~that resulted~~.

SUMMARY: Many societies have suppressed minorities to establish a powerful orthodoxy, with disastrous long-range results. Spain, a dominant power in the sixteenth century, suppressed all divergence of opinion; as a result, it did not share in the scientific, technological, and commercial progress of Western Europe. Seventeenth-century France lost the intellectual vigor of the Huguenots who took refuge in Great Britain, the Netherlands, and Prussia. Germany lost its scientific eminence when it drove out Jewish scientists who advanced science to the U.S. The destruction of the geneticists set back Soviet science; the revolution against Western science devastated science in China.

Combining Your Sources

Often your task as a writer is to bring together material from different sources. To assess progress on a community project, you compile information from various agencies and interested parties. To prove a point, you offer supporting testimony from several authorities. To challenge a mistaken opinion, you offer contrary evidence from a number of authoritative sources.

How do you splice together material from several different sources? How do you make it mesh? Study the way one student writer combined related material from her *reading notes* in one smoothly flowing paragraph:

PREWRITING: READING NOTES

("Man-Made Hearts: A Grim Prognosis," *U.S. News & World Report* 18 Aug. 1986, p. 8)

"Two winters ago, as William Schroeder sat in his hospital bed sipping a beer and declaring it 'the Coors cure,' the future looked good for permanent artificial hearts. Supporters said the devices might someday become as much of a long-term lifesaver as plastic valves and pacemakers. But by the time Schroeder died on August 6, that talk had all but vanished."

(Robert Bazell, "Hearts of Gold," *The New Republic* 18 Feb. 1985, p. 20)

"Exotic medical procedures certainly make compelling news stories, and for a time they can elevate relatively unknown medical institutions such as Loma Linda and Humana from obscurity. The trouble is that they are indeed experimental, and often they do not work. In the end they run the risk of attracting considerably more bad publicity than good. Despite hopes to the contrary, it takes more than one operation to make any medical establishment 'number one.'"

(Kathleen Deremy and Alan Hall, "Should Profit Drive Artificial Hearts?" *Business Week* 10 Dec. 1984, p. 39)

"Experts on medical ethics and health care costs are also questioning the wisdom of the current tests. If the use of artificial hearts becomes widespread it could add up to $3 billion a year to U.S. health care costs. And that will raise some onerous questions, says Henry Aaron, an economist at Brookings Institution. 'The funding mechanisms are open-ended. The dilemma is: Does everybody get it? If not, who does?'"

(Beth Vaughan-Cole and Helen Lee, "A Heart Decision," *American Journal of Nursing*, May 1985, p. 535)

"Finally, life-extending technology raises the 'right to die' issue. The committee drew the Clarks' attention to the clause in the consent form that stated that the subject could withdraw from the experiment at any time. If the recipient should be crippled physically or psychologically, the extension of life might be more of a curse than a blessing. Who could predict what the patient might want to do if he found himself in an inescapable position in which the activities that make life worthwhile might be impossible? The Clarks understood the alternative and could face that choice if necessary.

The moral issue of suicide arises, too: The artificial heart recipient has the key that turns off the machinery."

> In the finished paragraph, the student writer has used input from these notes to support the central point about the second thoughts and mixed feelings that replaced the initial euphoria about the artificial heart:

WRITING SAMPLE: FINISHED PARAGRAPH

key point

People have long had false teeth, artificial limbs, and pacemakers—why not an artificial heart? For a while, the future looked bright for another "breakthrough" or a "medical miracle." However, after the death of artificial-heart recipient William Shroeder, many observers had second thoughts about the outlook for the permanent artificial heart as "a long-term lifesaver." Doubts and reservations multiplied. As Robert Bazell said in *The New Republic*, "Exotic medical procedures make compelling news stories" but the "trouble is that they are indeed experimental, and often they do not work." The costs are horrendous: In an article in *Business Week*, Kathleen Deremy and Alan Hall estimated that the widespread use of artificial hearts could add up to $3 billion to the nation's health costs. And the procedure raises thorny questions of medical ethics: Who decides who gets the artificial heart and who is left out? What stand do we take on the "right-to-die" issue—does the patient have the right to suicide? (As Beth Vaughan-Cole and Helen Lee pointed out in *The American Journal of Nursing*, "the artificial heart recipient has the key that turns off the machinery.")

THE WRITING WORKSHOP

Quotes of the Week

Some publications feature a collection of "Words of the Week"—memorable or provocative or obtuse quotations from prominent people. Working with a group, help compile a collection of recent or current quotable quotes. Your group may want to focus on a selected category (inspirational, doublespeak, trivia) or a selected topic (the rise and fall of the stock market, a scandal). Check current newspapers, newsmagazines, magazines, or books for your own contribution to the group effort. Observe the following instructions concerning format:

- Introduce each quotation by including one or more of the following where they are useful and appropriate: source, credentials of author, occasion, point of quotation. *Vary* the way you introduce your quotations.
- Vary the length of your quotations—from snappy or memorable phrases to whole sentences. Include one or two block quotations.
- Include some examples of paraphrase and summary as well as direct quotation.

EXERCISE 2   *Quote/Unquote*

Study the following excerpt from a magazine article presenting a nonstereotyped view of life on America's farms. Look at the way the author throughout draws on authoritative sources to bolster his unidealized view of the farmer's life. Answer the following questions in particular:

- How does the author introduce each quotation?
- How does he establish the authority of his sources?
- How much is direct quotation, how much paraphrase?
- What are unusual features of some of the quotations?

Jeffrey L. Pasley
LIFE IS BETTER OFF THE FARM

How, then, did American family farmers become, in Harkin's words, "the most efficient and productive in the world"? Family farmers can keep labor costs very low because the family provides the bulk of the labor. Family farms operate under vastly different labor standards than the rest of American industry. "Child labor laws do not apply to family farms because family farms must have child labor to survive," wrote Minnesota politician and family farm alumnus Darrell McKigney. "Twenty or thirty years ago farm families commonly had ten or more children. [With automation] today five or six is a more common size." From a very early age, family farm children participate in every phase of the operation, from work with dangerous heavy equipment to close contact with carcinogenic chemicals and disease-carrying animals. In numerous farm areas, so many children are taken out of school at harvest time that the schools officially close until the harvest is finished. Practices that would be outrageous at a textile mill suddenly become all warm and cuddly when they appear on the family farm.

Family farmers also achieve efficiency through a draconian work schedule that no self-respecting union would allow. "The farm family does physically demanding and highly stressful work at least 14 hours a day (often at least 18 hours a day during harvest season), seven days a week, 365 days a year without a scheduled vacation or weekends off," wrote McKigney. "The farmer must endure all of this without the benefit of a health plan, safety regulations, a retirement plan, workmen's compensation, or any of the benefits that most U.S. labor unions demand." Psychologist Peter Keller, past president of the Association for Rural Mental Health, pointed out that many farmers are permanently tied to their farms. A dairy farmer, for instance, cannot just take off for a two-week vacation and not milk his cows. "Farmers lose perspective on the other things in life," said Keller. "The farm literally consumes them."

And the family farm physically consumes those who work on it, too. According to the National Safety Council, farming is the nation's most dangerous job—more dangerous even than working in a mine. In 1983 farming clocked in at 55 job-related deaths per 100,000 workers, or five times the rate for all major industries combined. In 1984 Tom Knudson of the *Des Moines Register* published a Pulitzer Prize-winning series that cataloged the myriad health and safety risks run by farmers. Farmers working with powerful farm machinery face death or maiming by crushing, chopping, asphyxiation, or electrocution. ("As he reached for a stalk of corn dangling from the corn picker, Vern Tigges of Dexter felt a jolt. In the next moments in a fierce and frantic struggle with the machine, three fingers were ripped from his hand.")

But what about the benefits of good-old-fashioned-lemonade values and the supportive friendliness of a rural community? Though hard data are difficult to come by, many small towns appear to suffer from teenage pregnancy, alcoholism, and other social maladies at rates that are higher than average. One New England study showed relatively high suicide rates among farmers during a period antedating the farm crisis. And rural communities haven't always stood by their financially troubled members. Sociologist Paul Lasley's Iowa Farm and Rural Life Poll reported that a majority of Iowa farmers felt they received little or no support from their churches, neighbors, schools, or local voluntary organizations. At a "town meeting" with Representative Tim Penny, Democrat of Minnesota, in New Market, Minnesota, I heard farmers ridicule the idea of slightly higher property taxes to improve the area's meager school system practically in the same breath that they demanded higher subsidies for themselves. These things never happened on "The Waltons."   *New Republic*

EXERCISE 3   *Working with Your Sources*

Read the following excerpt from a famous attack on television commercials. As you read, chart the author's train of thought. Study her use of key examples. Then do the following:

1. Write a *brief summary* running to three or four sentences.
2. Write a passage of 150–200 words in which you *quote extensively* from the excerpt. Give your reader the gist of the author's thinking, using quotations that range from brief striking phrases to several complete sentences. Include one or two block quotations.
3. Write a *paraphrase* of the last three paragraphs, translating the author's ideas into your own words.
4. Write an *extended summary*, or digest, of the whole passage, reducing it to about one third of its original length. Keep much of the author's wording, but condense wherever you can.

Mary Mannes
WHITER THAN WHITE

The producers of television commercials have created a loathsome gallery of men and women patterned, presumably, on a Mr. and Mrs. America. Women liberationists have a major target in the commercial image of woman flashed hourly and daily to the vast majority. There are, indeed, only four kinds of females in this relentless sales procession: the gorgeous teen-age swinger with bouncing locks; the young mother teaching her baby girl the right soap for skin care; the middle-aged housewife with a voice like a power saw; and the old lady with dentures and irregularity. All these women, to be sure, exist. But between the swinging sex object and the constipated granny there are millions of females rarely shown in commercials. These are—married or single—intelligent, sensitive women who bring charm to their homes, who work at jobs as well as lend grace to their marriage, who support themselves, who have talents or hobbies or commitments, or who are skilled at their professions.

We are left with the full-time housewife in all her whining glory: obsessed with whiter wash, moister cakes, shinier floors, cleaner children, softer diapers, and greaseless fried chicken. In the rare instances when these ladies are not in the kitchen, at the washing machine, or waiting on hubby, they are buying beauty shops (fantasy, see?) to take home so that their hair will have more body. Or out at the supermarket being choosy.

If they were attractive in their obsessions, they might be bearable. But they are not. They are pushy, loud-mouthed, stupid, and—of all things now—bereft of sexuality. Presumably, the argument in the tenets of advertising is that once a woman marries she changes overnight from plaything to floor-waxer.

To be fair, men make an equivalent transition in commercials. The swinging male with the mod hair and the beautiful chick turns inevitably into the paunchy slob who chokes on his wife's cake. You will notice, however, that the voice urging the viewer to buy the product is nearly always male: gentle, wise, helpful, seductive. And the visible presence telling the housewife how to get shinier floors and whiter wash and lovelier hair is almost invariably a man: the Svengali in modern dress, the Trilby (if only she were!), his willing object.

Woman, in short, is consumer first and human being fourth. A wife and mother who stays at home all day buys a lot more than a woman who lives alone or who—married or single—has a job. The young girl bent on marriage is the next most susceptible consumer. It is entirely understandable, then, that the potential buyers of detergents, foods, polishes, toothpastes, pills, and housewares are the housewives, and that the sex object spends most of *her* money on cosmetics, hair lotions, soaps, mouthwashes, and soft drinks.

Here we come, of course, to the youngest class of consumers, the swinging teenagers so beloved by advertisers keen on telling them (and us) that they've "got a lot to live, and Pepsi's got a lot to give." This affords a chance to show a squirming, leaping, jiggling group of beautiful kids having a very loud high on rock and—of all things—soda pop. One of commercial TV's most dubious achievements, in fact, is the reinforcement of the self-adulation characteristic of the young as a group.

As for the aging female citizen, the less shown of her the better. She is useful for ailments, but since she buys very little of anything, not having a husband or any children to feed or house to keep, nor—of course—sex appeal to burnish, society and commercials have little place for her. The same is true, to be sure, of older men, who are handy for Bosses with Bad Breath or Doctors with Remedies. Yet, on the whole, men hold up better than women at any age—in life or on television. Lines of their faces are marks of distinction, while on women they are signatures of decay. "Television: The Splitting Image"

EXERCISE 4   *Combining Material from Sources*

Assume that the following passages are part of your reading notes about the effect of television on young viewers. What general conclusion(s) do these passages support? Write a passage in which you use the material from these notes to support a conclusion. Identify your sources; use both direct quotation and paraphrase.

1. Two passages from *The Plug-In Drug: Television, Children and Family* by Marie Winn, author of many children's books:

"By its domination of the time families spend together, it destroys the special quality that distinguishes one family from another, a quality that depends to a great extent on what a family *does,* what special rituals, games, recurrent jokes, familiar songs, and shared activities it accumulates."

"The decreased opportunities for simple conversation between parents and children in the television-centered home may help explain an observation made by an emergency room nurse at a Boston hospital. She reports that parents just seem to sit there these days when they come in with a sick or seriously injured child, although talking to the child would distract and comfort him. 'They don't seem to know *how* to talk to their own children at any length,' the nurse observes."

2. A passage from a magazine article by Bruno Bettelheim, famous psychoanalyst and author of *The Uses of Enchantment,* a book about fairy tales:

"Children who have been taught, or conditioned, to listen passively most of the day to the warm verbal communications coming from the TV screen, to the deep emotional appeal of the so-called TV personality, are often unable to respond to real persons because they arouse so much less feeling than the skilled actor. Worse, they lose the ability to learn from reality because life experiences are much more complicated than the ones they see on the screen."

3. A selection from an interview with Jerzy Kosinski—Polish-born author of *Being There*—published in the periodical *Media and Methods:*

"Recently I heard of a college class in media communication which had been assigned to watch two hours of television and record the content of those two hours. They were asked to describe each element—including commercials—in as much detail as possible, classifying every incident and every character in terms of its relative importance to the story. All these students had been raised in front of TV sets and were accustomed to being bombarded by TV images; many of them hoped to be employed in the communications industry after graduation. Yet, not a single one could complete the assignment. They claimed that the rapidity and fragmentation of the TV experience made it impossible to isolate a narrative thought-line, or to contemplate and analyze what they had seen, in terms of relative significance."

WRITING ABOUT YOUR SOURCES Often we write to show what we make of our reading—what we have learned from it or how we react to it. We write to talk back—to take issue, to challenge basic assumptions, to quarrel with exaggerated claims. We write to endorse—to help circulate important information, to help advance the good cause. Or we write with a "yes, but" attitude, registering our qualified endorsement, venting our doubts and reservations.

Writing About a Single Source When you write about a single article or book, you take on several related tasks. Your major purpose may be to *report* or describe. What is the piece about? What was the writer's agenda? How did the writer go about the job? Your report will help the reader who wonders, "Is this of interest to me? Would it be worth my time?"

This first purpose easily shades over into the second: to *respond*, to react. Where does the author get you involved? Where do you agree or disagree, and why? Why does the piece anger you, please you, or provoke you?

The third possible purpose we tend to entrust to the professional critic or reviewer: to judge, to *evaluate*. How well has the author done the job? How does the piece rank next to other works on the same subject? Is it worth singling out from the flood of currently published work?

Suppose you have been asked to do a **reading report** whose main purpose is to inform. Here is a *checklist* of possible questions that you should try to answer:

- What is the subject? (What is this all about?)
- What is the writer's agenda? (What is the author trying to accomplish? Does the author have an axe to grind?)
- What is the writer's thesis or main point? (What central claim does the piece advance and support?)
- What is the writer's overall strategy? (How does the author raise the issue? What is the master plan or the grand design? What are major steps in the argument?)
- Where has the writer turned for support? (What are the writer's sources? What use does the writer make of experience, firsthand investigation, reading, viewing?)
- Who is the intended audience? (Who would make an ideal reader? Who would make a problem reader, and why?)

Study the following example of a reading report on a magazine article. Which of the above questions does the student writer answer, and where?

WRITING SAMPLE: READING REPORT

New Origins of Life

facts of publication "The New Origins of Life," an article written by Claudia Wallis for *Time* magazine, deals with the controversy regarding artificial new methods for creating human life. Her eight-page article, which appeared in the September 10, 1984, issue (pp. *overview* 16–53), explains in detail the techniques used for laboratory conception and the legal and ethical issues that have arisen from these techniques. The article focuses on *focusing on the problem* the problems of infertility that are faced by millions of couples and shows how new techniques might help these couples achieve their goal of having a child. Wallis starts

key quotation

definition of key technical term

key controversy

author's motive and intended audience

her article with some impressive, eye-opening statistics showing that the incidence of infertility among married women aged 20 to 24 jumped 177% between 1965 and 1982. Ironically, at the same time there has been a drastic reduction in the number of adoptable children because of more easily available abortions and because more single mothers decide to keep their babies. In the words of a counselor, "infertility rips at the core of the couple's relationship; it affects sexuality, self-image, and self-esteem." The couple usually goes through years of pain and the indignity of medical tests and treatments with no results. In-vitro fertilization is usually the last chance for the childless couple. Wallis explains what IVF or in-vitro fertilization is in easy-to-understand terms ("the mating of egg and sperm in a laboratory dish"). She gives statistics on the rate of success and also the cost of the procedure. She then eases into the subject that is in the spotlight of a much-publicized heated controversy: the surrogate mother. When a woman is not capable of carrying a child, the surrogate mother can be implanted with an embryo conceived by the couple. As one gyne-cologist says, "It is difficult to differentiate between payment for a child and payment for carrying the child." The audience Wallis aims at is the childless couple but also readers who are disturbed by the ethical issues surrounding the new techniques. She wants the reader to see this problem through the eyes of the couple faced with infertility. For many, IVF is a last resort.

Often you will go on from "This is where the author stands" to "This is where *I* stand on this issue." Read the following sample instructions asking for both a close reading of *and* a personal response to a passage. Then study the reading selection and one student writer's response. Note especially how the writer handles both parts of the task: (a) to do justice to the letter and the spirit of the reading selection, and (b) to go on record with personal opinions.

WRITING ASSIGNMENT: INSTRUCTIONS AND PASSAGE

INSTRUCTIONS: Read the following passage carefully, highlighting key points or taking notes. Then write an essay in which you answer the following questions:

1. What are the purpose and the main point of the passage?
2. In what order does the author present her ideas and examples?
3. Do you agree or disagree with the author, and why? (Which of her points are most convincing, which least? Which of her examples are most convincing, which least?)

Through recent unpleasant experiences we have learned to expect ambition, greed, or corruption to reveal itself behind every public act, but as we have just seen, it is not invariably so. Human beings do possess better impulses, and occasionally act upon them, even in the twentieth century. Occupied Denmark, during World War II, outraged by Nazi orders for deportation of its Jewish fellow citizens, summoned the courage of defiance and transformed itself into a united underground railway to smuggle virtually all eight thousand Danish Jews out to Sweden, and

Sweden gave them shelter. Far away and unconnected, a village in southern France, Le Chambon-sur-Lignon, devoted itself to rescuing Jews and other victims of the Nazis at the risk of the inhabitants' own lives and freedom. "Saving lives became a hobby of the people of Le Chambon," said one of them. The larger record of the time was admittedly collaboration, passive or active. We cannot reckon on the better impulses predominating in the world, only that they will always appear.

The strongest of these in history, summoner of the best in us, has been zeal for liberty. Time after time, in some spot somewhere on the globe, people have risen in what Swinburne called the "divine right of insurrection"—to overthrow despots, repel alien conquerors, achieve independence—and so it will be until the day power ceases to corrupt, which, I think, is not a near expectation.

The ancient Jews rose three times against alien rulers, beginning with the revolt of the Maccabees against the effort of Antiochus to outlaw observance of the Jewish faith. Mattathias the priest and his five sons, assembling loyal believers in the mountains, opened a guerrilla war which, after the father's death, was to find a leader of military genius in his son Judah, called Maccabee or the Hammer. Later honored in the Middle Ages as one of the Nine Worthies of the world, he defeated his enemies, rededicated the temple, and re-established the independence of Judea. In the next century the uprising of the Zealots against Roman rule was fanatically and hopelessly pursued through famines, sieges, and fall of Jerusalem and destruction of the temple until a last stand of fewer than a thousand on the rock of Masada ended in group suicide in preference to surrender. After sixty years as an occupied province, Judea rose yet again under Simon Bar Kochba, who regained Jerusalem for a brief moment of Jewish control but could not withstand the arms of Hadrian. The rebellion was crushed, but the zeal for selfhood, smoldering in exile through eighteen centuries, was to revive and regain its home in our time. . . .

I have always cherished the spirited rejoinder of one of the great colonial landowners of New York who, on being advised not to risk his property by signing the Declaration of Independence, replied, "Damn the property; give me the pen!" On seeking confirmation for purposes of this essay, I am deeply chagrined to report that the saying appears to be apocryphal. Yet not its spirit, for the signers well knew they were risking their property, not to mention their heads, by putting their names to the Declaration.

Is anything to be learned from my survey? I raise the question only because most people want history to teach them lessons, which I believe it can do, although I am less sure we can use them when needed. I gathered these examples not to teach but merely to remind people in a despondent era that the good in humanity operates even if the bad secures more attention. I am aware that selecting out the better moments does not result in a realistic picture. Turn them over and there is likely to be a darker side, as when Project Apollo, our journey to the moon, was authorized because its glamour could obtain subsidies for rocket and missile development that otherwise might not have been forthcoming. That is the way things are.   Barbara Tuchman, from "Humanity's Better Moments"

WRITING SAMPLE: A READER'S RESPONSE

Our Better Impulses

the main point

At a time when our world often seems a terrible place and our self-esteem as a species often seems to be at an all-time low, Barbara Tuchman, in "Humanity's Better Moments," writes to remind us that "the good in humanity operates even if the bad secures more attention." She wants to impress upon the reader that our "better impulses" still exist even if they are not always visible and that they will surface sooner or later.

the plan

Tuchman deals with three important or notable areas of human endeavor: the heroic actions of people trying to save the Jews from the Nazis during World War II; the zeal of groups and nations for liberty; and the drive toward the conquest of outer space.

the follow up
first area

Many individuals united in the task of saving Jewish lives. Occupied Denmark managed to smuggle all eight thousand Danish Jews to Sweden. Tuchman writes about a village in southern France, quoting one of the inhabitants who said: "Saving lives became a hobby of the people of Le Chambon."

second area

One of Tuchman's strongest examples of the strength of the human spirit is her discussion of Jewish history. The Jews repeatedly fought for independence, invoking the "divine right of insurrection" against cruel alien rulers. The people of Masada were willing to die rather than to be captured, choosing suicide over surrender to the Romans.

third area

Tuchman sees the darker side of some of humanity's heroic or inspirational moments. The use of Project Apollo on the journey to the moon to help obtain funds for rocket and missile development proves the mixed state of affairs.

the reader's reaction
area of agreement

I agree with Tuchman's basic point about the pessimistic self-image of human beings. Born in the sixties, I have witnessed racial conflict, disagreement over nuclear policy, and numerous wars, both hot and cold. Today, many claim that racism is again on the rise, as vigilantism directed at blacks and prejudice against Asian immigrants build up in our cities. At the same time, we do see humanity's better impulses at work. Events such as the famine in Ethiopia cause an outpouring of humanitarian appeals. Vigorous campaigns collect donations for the cure of diseases. Causes such as the hospice movement or the animal rights movement attract dedicated volunteers.

area of disagreement

However, I am not sure that Tuchman's argument will ultimately change the pessimistic outlook of many readers. Some of her own examples of the good in humanity remind us strongly of the human capacity for cruelty and violence. The "right to insurrection" brings out great bravery and heroic deeds, but it also reminds us of an age-old record of oppression. People would not have to rise against oppression "time after time" if oppression and exploitation were not everywhere part of human history.

Questions for Discussion Does this writer do justice to Tuchman's main points? Do you agree with the writer's reaction?

Comparing Two Sources Comparing and contrasting two sources can help you move beyond a one-sided view of an issue. You may be comparing the two to map out areas of agreement, to find a common thread. When two sources champion strongly opposing views, you may be moved to take sides. Or you may weigh the pros and cons, trying to find a compromise solution. In the following student paper, the writer tries to do justice to two opposing views and finally sides with one of them, telling us why.

WRITING SAMPLE: COMPARING TWO SOURCES

Sticks and Stones

overview

Are we willing to do something about pornography and the violence it promotes? Among American women today, opinion is sharply divided between those who feel that drastic action is long overdue and those who feel that we must not let our disapproval of pornography lead us to abridge freedom of speech, our constitutional right to communicate. Gloria Steinem, in her essay "Erotica and Pornography," writes that "the number of pornographic murders, tortures, and woman-hating images is on the increase in both popular culture and real life." She believes that by lumping all types of "nonprocreative sex" together, we let pornography off the hook. She distinguishes between erotica and pornography. Erotica deals with sex in a way that is compatible with love and respect, and with "the yearning for a particular person." Pornography is based on domination over women. Erotica appeals to both sexes, whereas the root word of pornography points to prostitutes or "female captives."

first major source

key terms defined

key quotations

Erotica celebrates "a mutually pleasurable, sexual expression between people who have enough power to be there by positive choice." On the other hand, pornography is abusive; its message is "violence, dominance, and conquest." It portrays an attitude of "conqueror and victim." Although Steinem does not state outright that she would use the law to restrict pornographic publications, she alerts us to their "lethal confusion of sex with violence."

second major source

Susan Jacoby, a widely read writer and feminist like Steinem, takes a quite different stand in her essay, "Pornography and the First Amendment." A journalist, she is a hands-on, self-described "First Amendment junkie." She believes that feminists have inflated the threat pornography actually poses. She refuses to believe that "porn books, magazines, and movies pose a greater threat to women than similarly repulsive exercises of free speech pose to other offended groups"—such as Jewish groups who object to the circulation of neo-Nazi propaganda.

first key argument

When it comes to the most offensive kind of pornography, "kiddie porn," Jacoby believes that we have obscured the issue. Kiddie porn is not a First Amendment issue, but rather an issue of the "abuse of power." She believes that the irresponsible parents of the children involved should be rounded up and put in jail.

second key argument

Her classic argument, however, is that feminists cannot agree among themselves on what is "good taste" and what is "harmful pornography." Are all pictures of nude women obscene? Where do we draw the line between the artistic nude and obscenity? Jacoby believes in the democratic process: "We should not shift the responsibility from individuals to institutions." She would have us wait until men decide "they have better uses for $1.95 each month than to spend it on a copy of *Hustler*."

personal response   However, it seems to me that democracy requires exactly the kind of soul-searching decision-making that Jacoby feels we are incapable of in the area of pornography. It is true that the courts have often refused to put publishers of pornography or actors in pornographic movies in jail. But as recent court decisions indicate, we are willing to search our souls and draw the line somewhere. As the connections become clear, will we start to hold people and groups accountable for the violence they propagate?

I agree with Steinem. We are not safe as long as our liberal-mindedness condones what should not be condoned. We should not just remain "offended" and yet afraid to take a stand.

Questions for Discussion Does this writer do justice to both sides of the argument? Do you agree with her?

Combining Several Sources When you deal with a difficult issue, you need to reassure the reader who is suspicious of snap judgments and personal bias. You "read up" on the subject; you explore its history, pool relevant information, and weigh conflicting views. The following paper is the result of purposeful background reading. It uses three major sources to stake out the territory and to marshal support for the writer's own view.

> WRITING SAMPLE: COMBINING SEVERAL SOURCES

An Eye for an Eye

dramatizing the issue   Ten years ago, blonde-haired, green-eyed Lucy and Beatrice D. were taken to a remote desert spot outside their town in Arizona and strangled with a telephone cord by Lucy's boyfriend. Lucy, 17, had read his diary and knew information that he did not want anyone else to know. Thirteen-year-old Beatrice's only mistake was being with her sister when the boyfriend decided to kill her. The friends and the family spent four agonizing weeks worrying about the missing pair, speculating with police about their possible whereabouts and the reasons for their disappearance, growing more desperate with each passing day. When police were led to the girls' bones, stripped bare by animals, a new nightmare began. It engulfed the entire town but was most painful for family and friends. Lucy was my sister's best friend, and Beatrice was mine.

thesis   Because of this experience, the issue of capital punishment is more than theoretical for me. Also because of it, even I am surprised that I do not support it.

It would be easy for me to argue that death is the only punishment severe enough for the man who took the life of those sisters. Our society believes that life is precious.

first source identified
key quotation   It is so precious that the murderer deserves to die himself. As Ed Koch, the mayor of New York City, says in his article on "Death and Justice," capital punishment "affirms life" (*The New Republic*, 15 April 1985).

first set of statistics

I could point out, as Koch does, that the murder rate in America rose 122% during a seventeen-year period. During the same time, the murder rate in New York City rose almost 400%. We should therefore be ready to take drastic action to change these statistics. I could further, like Koch, point to statistics showing that murderers

second set of statistics

will kill again. As Koch reports, in one two-year period, 85 persons arrested for homicide in New York City had a previous arrest record for murder. I could further argue that in reality "life sentences" are no such thing. According to Koch, during

third set of statistics

the seventies, the average time served in the United States for first-degree murder was ten years. (One study showed the median time served in Massachusetts for homicide was less than 2-1/2 years.)

turning point

On the other hand, two wrongs do not make one right. How can we tell ourselves that it is wrong for people to kill but that if they do kill, we will kill them to punish them for their crimes? Powerful arguments speak against the death penalty. Arguing

second source identified

against the "fallacy of capital punishment," Eugene B. Block, in *Why Men Play God*, cites statistics showing that the death penalty has not been proven to be a deterrent to violent crime. An FBI Uniform Crime Report published by the U.S. Department

key statistics

of Justice showed that, for a single year, the abolitionist state of Wisconsin reported half the murder rate compared with Indiana, which retained the death penalty.

A major argument against the death penalty is consistent evidence of discrimination. Many are convicted of murder each year. But the few who are actually

third source identified

executed for their crimes are predictably poor or black or both. In 1981, David Baldus, a law professor at the University of Iowa, directed an extensive and expensive research project that studied discrimination affecting death sentences in the state of

findings presented

Georgia. Baldus' results show that a defendant convicted of killing a white person is nine times more likely to be given the death sentence than one convicted of killing a black person. At the same time, the study confirmed that a convicted defendant who is black is more likely to receive the death penalty than one who is white.

I do believe murderers should be punished. But it is not up to us as fallible human beings with our fallible systems to decide when someone should die. We need to create a system of education and rehabilitation for those who merit it and can profit from it. For others, we must have a system where a life sentence "without

circling back to beginning

the possibility of parole" means what it says. I want the murderer of my friends to be truly punished, but I cannot endorse killing him in turn.

Questions for Discussion Are you tired of the topic of capital punishment? Why or why not? Did this paper make you change your mind or rethink the issue?

Reminders for Revision When you write a paper drawing on sources, you have your hands full choosing the right material, trimming and adapting it for use, and feeding it into your draft at the right points. When you revise your first draft, you can look at what you have done from the point of view of the reader. You can make sure the reader will not feel bogged down in

miscellaneous quoted material. You can anticipate predictable questions: "What is the plan? Why is this in here? What does it prove?" Do the following as necessary:

☐ *Strengthen a colorless, open-ended overview.* Do not just sketch out a "let's-see-what-we-find" program. Focus the readers' attention and arouse their interest by a more definite preview. Pinpoint the issue; sum up key findings; summarize the pro and con.

> TOO OPEN: Surrogate motherhood is an area filled with successes and problems. Some people believe in the surrogate program and others condemn the practice. Here we will explore some of the seemingly good and bad aspects of the program.
>
> FOCUSED: Conflicting voices on the use of animal experiments in medical research leave us unsure of which side to take. Our hearts tell us to listen to often-inflated news reports of cruelty and abuse. Our brains tell us that if it weren't for research involving other living creatures, many of the lifesaving techniques that are common today would not exist.

☐ *Avoid the "dumped" quotation.* Do not just spring a quotation on the reader. Prepare the ground for it, summing up who says what and why.

> DUMPED: Susan Jacoby is a "First Amendment junkie."
>
> REVISED: Susan Jacoby, who has written widely on women's issues, disagrees with the feminists on the issue of pornography. She is first and foremost a journalist who believes in free speech and the protection of the First Amendment. She is unequivocally a "First Amendment junkie."

☐ *Bundle related quotations effectively.* Add a lead sentence that shows what a set of quotations is supposed to prove. Look at the lead sentence that was added in a revision of the following paragraph:

> REVISED: *Infertility, now affecting one in five couples, has many causes.* J. H. Guenero, writing in *Science News*, identifies familiar medical problems: failure to ovulate, inflammatory disorders, blockage of the fallopian tubes. Hilary Rose, a professor of Social Policy at Bradford University, points to modern birth control methods as a more recent culprit. The prolonged use of the pill, damage due to badly fitted coils, and poorly performed abortions all help explain the rising incidence of infertility.

☐ *Strengthen weak links.* Look for lame transitions using *also* or *another*. Revise to help the reader who wonders, "Why is this in here at this point?"

> WEAK: Another expert on the dinosaur puzzle is Janice Rotha, who writes in the *American Scientist.* . . .

REVISED: An expert who disagrees strongly with the sudden-extinction theory is Janice Rotha. She writes in the *American Scientist*. . . .

☐ *Correct obvious imbalance in your use of sources.* When quoting authorities on a much-debated issue, give both sides a fair hearing. Suppose you have quoted several authorities who argue eloquently that in child custody cases, custody should preferably be awarded to the mother. You will seem to be stacking the deck if you quote only one weak voice speaking up for the rights of fathers.

Note: When you turn to expert opinion, to insiders and authorities, you do not abdicate your right of private judgment. Test what others say by comparing it with your own experience and firsthand observation. Dramatize an issue by showing where it has touched your own life. Apply theories to real-life situations; provide the test cases and personal examples that show you have made what you read your own.

WRITING TOPICS 12   *Writing About Your Reading*

1. Find a recent article on one of the following topics. Write a *reading report* that will help a reader decide if the article might be worth reading. Make your report instructive and informative.

   ☐ dressing for success
   ☐ current trends in child custody cases
   ☐ saving an endangered species
   ☐ how to be successful in a job interview
   ☐ dangers in diet fads
   ☐ dealing with divorce
   ☐ how to make a marriage work
   ☐ promising careers for today's students
   ☐ the adoption racket
   ☐ warnings for American travelers abroad
   ☐ reducing the risk of crime
   ☐ working for a Japanese company

2. Find an article in which the author takes a stand on a current issue. Write a paper that both reports on and reacts to the article. Do justice to the author's position or argument; explain and support your own stand on the issue. Some possible topics:

   ☐ raising the minimum wage
   ☐ drug testing
   ☐ beauty contests

    □   cheating on tests
    □   teenage curfews
    □   drugs on high school campuses
    □   recruiting scandals
    □   the drinking age

3. Find two articles that present similar or opposing views on a current issue. Write a paper in which you compare and contrast the two authors' positions. Go on to your own opinion on the issue and provide support for it. Some possible topics:

    □   stiffer penalties for drunken driving
    □   using lotteries to help finance education
    □   the press and a candidate's privacy
    □   rape prevention
    □   shelters for the homeless
    □   banning pornographic magazines
    □   coeducational varsity sports
    □   movie ratings

4. Find three articles that represent a range of opinion on the same subject. Write a paper in which you draw on these sources to give your readers a sense of some of the major dimensions and ramifications of the subject. Some possible topics:

    □   assimilating the new immigrants
    □   compulsory retirement
    □   protecting endangered industries
    □   mainstreaming the disabled
    □   taxing the rich

Part Three

WRITING AND THINKING

Writing is a way of thinking out loud, revealing not only what we think but how we think. In several kinds of writing, the reasoning processes that shape our writing are even more central than usual. When we write to define, we clarify our thinking by stabilizing the shifting boundaries between words. **Definition** is a vital first step toward sound argument: When we argue the merits of rehabilitation or comparable pay, we need to agree with our readers on what the words mean. In a systematic **argument**, we ask our readers to *re*think an issue; we take them from convincing evidence or shared assumptions to logical conclusions. The central question is: How did we arrive at our destination; what led us to believe as we do? Honest argument testifies to our faith in the intelligence of the reader; it assumes that reasonable people, using good judgment, can reach similar conclusions. Effective **persuasion**, however, goes a step further. To be persuasive, to change the readers' minds and ways, it may not be enough to lay out our own thinking in a clear, logical fashion. We may have to know what our readers think; we have to reckon with how *they* think and feel. Persuasive writers are audience-conscious: They know what obstacles they have to clear; they know what works for them and against them with their readers. Effective persuasion often combines logical argument with an appeal to the readers' emotions and to shared values.

12

DEFINING

Drawing the Line

Writers who handle abstract ideas fluently, and the more fluently because they never feel them as anything but abstract ideas, can do only a limited amount of good and may, in many circumstances, do harm.   John Wain

A definition is the enclosing of a wilderness of ideas within a wall of words.   Samuel Butler

THE NEED FOR DEFINITION Part of every writer's task is to define key terms. A common question in the reader's mind—next to "Who says?" and "How do you know?"—is "What do you mean?" When we define an important term, we mark off its boundaries; we map out the territory it covers. When we see a term like *equal opportunity*, we need to know: Where does it take us? When people agree in principle on equal opportunity, how far will they go in assuring job opportunities for people previously excluded: active recruiting? special training? preferential quotas? exceptions to normal standards for hiring and promotion? Such terms cry out for definition because they leave much room for interpretation.

Definition has many uses. In writing that explains or informs, we often need to translate insider's terms into plain English. Much material in textbooks serves to define key terms—*populism, abolitionist, realpolitik*—for the student. Most importantly, definition serves as a step toward sound argument. Arguments stall when the same word means different things to different people. (What kinds of admission standards, course content, and teaching styles are *élitist*?) When argument shades over into persuasion, a definition often implies an agenda; it charts a course of action. A writer defining the "right to privacy" may be enlisting the reader's support for the cause. A writer defining *pornography* may be mobilizing opposition.

245

Experienced writers seem to have a built-in signal light that flashes on to say "Stop to explain." Here are some categories of words that make a writer stop to define:

Key Terms

Every writer needs to clarify words that may be difficult or new for the reader. Writing as insiders, we demystify **technical** or specialized terms for the newcomer or the outsider. Sometimes, we simply give a plain-English synonym, or substitute, for a specialized term. ("*Recidivists*—repeaters—make up a large part of the prison population.") Often we fill in the meaning of key technical terms in passing:

> Medicine and *neurology*—the teasing, endless puzzle of how the brain controls our every thought and activity—has captivated me to this day. Roger Bannister

Questions for Discussion How good are you at taking in and explaining to others new buzzwords for current trends? How would you define for the uninitiated one or more of the following: *media event, quality time, disinformation, flextime, mainstream, upscale, high tech*?

Vague or Ambiguous Terms

Vague and ambiguous terms frustrate us because they do not tell us enough. They are often large **abstractions**—general terms too far removed from concrete reality. Sweeping terms like "social justice" or "contemporary community standards" badly need definition; they leave too much room for subjective interpretation or personal preference.

> VAGUE: Military academies do more than public schools to build a student's *character*. (What character traits do the academies develop? What makes such traits preferable to those fostered in public schools?)

Ambiguous terms have a possible double meaning; they cause misunderstandings because they allow people to use the same words while talking about different things. A term like *liberal* has a confusing history; people with different agendas use it as a term of praise or condemnation:

> POSITIVE: Liberals are convinced that without liberty life is not worth living. Thus, they have always striven for an individual's freedom from unjust restraints imposed by governments, institutions, and traditions. Free choice of occupation, free expression of opinions, and free movement from place to place are goals of the liberal.

> NEGATIVE: The modern liberal has become a believer in government control and in federal agencies. Liberals want the government to provide everything free to the citizens of the country. College educations should be free. Welfare programs should provide

for the people, whether they are needy or not. Private enterprise should be viewed with suspicion and regulated at every step.

Relative and Overlapping Terms

Often the key question a definition answers is "Where do you draw the line?" Many words are **relative**; to give them specific meaning, we need to fix a point on a scale. When we write about the

A Matter of Definition
Is it art? Why or why not?

"new poor" or about our "permissive" society, we deal with relative terms: Where do government agencies draw the poverty line, and why? When do rigid moral standards become permissive? We often need to draw the line when confronted with **overlapping** terms. Courts of law require juries to distinguish between ordinary carelessness and gross negligence or between misrepresentation and malicious libel. Labels like *gifted, average,* and *retarded* are a matter of definition; the scores and other criteria used to set up these categories depend on school policy.

Note: Frequently, a writer will redefine a weighty term to bring it up to date, to make it fit changing standards or values. For example, a writer may set out to show how a responsible modern patriotism differs from "my country right or wrong." Or a writer may want to distinguish a forward-looking neoconservatism from the backward-looking conservatism of earlier days.

EXERCISE 1   *Defining Specialized Terms*

In each of the following sentences, a writer clarifies a technical or specialized term. What makes each of these capsule definitions informative or helpful? What do you learn that you didn't know before? Write five similar capsule definitions, choosing technical or specialized terms from a range of different fields.

1.   Brief definition of a psychologist's or sociologist's term:

People with Type A personalities—those uptight, compulsive, competitive, aggressive, sometimes hostile, insecure overachievers—can greatly reduce their chances for a heart attack by modifying their behavior.

2.   Capsule definition of a current issue or problem:

One of the most stubborn environmental problems continues to be acid rain—the chemical-laden precipitation that has already browned or defoliated vast stretches of forest in the eastern United States and Europe and is spreading throughout the industrialized world.

3.   Summary of a scientific theory or prediction:

The theory of nuclear winter—the deadly world-wide blockage of the sun's rays that would follow an atomic conflict—was first presented to a conference in October 1983.

4.   Brief explanation of a metaphor or imaginative comparison:

The lifeboat analogy makes us imagine the rich nations as passengers in a lifeboat with ample provisions and the poor nations as swimmers struggling in the water, clamoring to be allowed in and likely to swamp the boat.

EXERCISE 2   *A Matter of Definition*

In each of the following passages, how or why does the need for definition arise? What does the author do to clarify the key term? How would *you* go about defining the term?

1. I met and heard black writers such as Alice Walker, Toni Morrison and Ntozake Shange in those days. Each of them talked about a term I had not heard before: *role models*. A role model is someone we could relate to, "one of us," someone who demonstrated, either through writing or through his or her life, the possibility of greatness.   Ronald D. White

2. *Terrorism* and *guerilla warfare* are clearly distinguishable on the basis of the actions involved. Terrorism strikes at civilians directly and intentionally. Guerilla warfare against an occupying army or repressive regime, on the other hand, is a legitimate recourse of oppressed peoples deprived of democratic expression.

3. The artist who tosses a pot of paint at a wall, or hangs a wrecked car from the ceiling, or holds the microphone up to record his gargling and then tells us to look and to "experience" is doing no more than the merchant who displays before us an assortment of textiles, threads, buttons, and braid, and suggests we choose what we like and make ourselves a dress. If *we* select the materials, and if *we* plan and execute the dress, the experience may be salutary for us, but do we call the merchant a couturier? Is his randomly heaped assortment of materials "art"? My criticism of these experiments in the random, then, is not that they may not produce interesting, beautiful, or moving things, but that they are simply not *art*. They may produce excitement, gaiety, tedium, or a headache, but so can a day on the beach. If there is no focusing, organizing intelligence behind it, there is no art in any meaningful sense of the word.   Sylvia Angus, "It's Pretty, But Is It Art?" *Saturday Review*

EXERCISE 3   *Drawing the Line*

The two italicized words in each of the following passages are *overlapping terms*. For each passage, write a sentence or two to show the difference between the two terms. Where do you draw the line that divides the two?

1. Some talk about *discipline* and mean self-discipline; others talk about discipline but really mean *regimentation*.   Olga Conolly

2. The young people today are much closer in their views on civil rights to the abolitionists of a century ago than they are to yesterday's liberals. The oppression of black people is to them a *sin* rather than a *wrong*.

3. "Yes," a student said to me, "I want to be *intelligent*, but I don't want to be a detached, emotionless *intellectual*."

4. Many people today hold strong religious *beliefs* while rejecting *dogma*.

5. The author said that her father was not an *educated* person in the conventional sense but nevertheless a deeply *learned* one.

THE STRATEGIES OF DEFINITION

Sometimes, we can sharpen the meaning of an important term in a single sentence. More often, we need an **extended definition** to chart the uses of a term and to head off misunderstandings and confusion. In writing an extended definition, a writer is likely to choose from a range of available strategies: tracing the history of the term up to its current meaning, looking at varied uses of the term for a common denominator, exploring important distinctions, linking the term to similar or contrasting terms.

Dictionary Definitions

You may want to start by citing a dictionary definition—*if* it raises a key issue or sums up important points. A dictionary definition like the following goes to the heart of the matter:

genocide   "the deliberate and systematic destruction of a racial, political, or cultural group" *Webster's Ninth New Collegiate Dictionary*

However, often the side trip to the dictionary tells readers only what they already know. Trying to define "social justice," you will gain little by quoting a definition of *justice* as the "quality of being just, impartial, or fair." When you quote a dictionary definition, make good use of it; explain how it relates to your own discussion of the term.

Formal Definitions

A **formal definition** first places a term in a larger class and then spells out distinctive features. It presents two kinds of information: First, we sum up what makes the term to be defined part of a larger group, or **class**. Then we spell out distinctive features that set off, or differentiate, the term from other members of the same class.

TERM	CLASS	FEATURES
Oligarchy	is a form of government	in which power lies in the hands of a few.
A martyr	suffers persecution	for refusing to renounce his or her faith.

Such capsule definitions prove useful for several reasons. They focus on essentials and yet can be packed with relevant information:

TERM	CLASS	FEATURES
A faun	is a Roman wood god	who is half man and half goat.

They make us spell out important nuances:

TERM	CLASS	FEATURES
To double-cross	is to betray someone	whom we have deliberately impressed with our trustworthiness or loyalty.

To make a formal definition informative, you may have to take precautions. If the general class is too shapeless, it will not start focusing your reader's attention. (Classifying an epic as "a type of literature" is less helpful than classifying it as "a long narrative poem.") The specific qualities you list may not be specific enough. (A patriot is "a person who promotes the best interests of the country," but we more specifically apply the term to those who do so *unselfishly*—not for gain or personal glory.) Finally, your definition may not make allowance for important exceptions. (A senator is "an elected representative of a state"—but some senators are not elected but appointed to fill a vacant seat.)

Extended Definitions A formal definition is designed to sum up rather than to explain or convince. To drive home a definition, you have to answer questions like the following: What does this term mean in practice? Where and how is it used? How did it get its meaning? How does it differ from similar or related terms?

THE COMMON DENOMINATOR Often our basic assignment is to push toward the common denominator that underlies different meanings or uses of the same word— to trace the common thread that links different uses of the word. The first step is to get down to cases: Where do we encounter the word to be defined? The student who wrote the following passage took the essential first step by relating his key term to his own experience:

> Segregation is not a word from the distant past. My father told me stories of his Air Force days in the South where he saw segregated water fountains, bathrooms, and restaurants. I was bussed to a black school in order to help desegregate the public schools of our city. My aunt, who lives in Alabama, told me that after desegregation laws were passed many people ignored them or merely showed their feelings in more subtle ways. A restaurant would not display a sign "Only Whites Allowed," but blacks knew they were not welcome because of the cloud of antipathy that pervaded the restaurant.

The second step is to identify and formulate the common element. The following rough scheme for a paper takes us through a series of test cases, each raising an issue of "fair play":

FIRST TEST CASE:	The honor code states that it is not "fair" to cheat.
SECOND TEST CASE:	A tennis player considers it "fair" to let her opponent regain her footing after she slipped.
THIRD TEST CASE:	Students consider it "unfair" to penalize a sick student for his failure to take a test.
COMMON DENOMINATOR:	Fair play makes us impose limits on competition in order to assure greater equality of opportunity. It shows our desire to "give everybody a chance."

In organizing the results of such an investigation, you have a choice of two different plans. You may decide to make your definition of the term the thesis that the rest of your paper will support. Early in your paper, you sum up your answer to the question that may be uppermost in your reader's mind: "What is the clue? What is the secret? What is the common thread?" Then you present and examine the case histories, test cases, and examples that illustrate the common element. Or you may decide to make your reader participate in the search. You proceed **inductively**—your readers share in the discovery of the common element as you examine test cases of fair play, or equal opportunity, or segregation. You sum up your definition in a strong conclusion that pulls together the different threads. An inductive plan may work best with a reluctant or skeptical audience, inclined to reject a new or different definition out of hand.

ANALYZING KEY ELEMENTS   Sometimes, a single criterion or requirement furnishes the clue to the meaning of an important term. More often, several key requirements combine to help us stake out its meaning. The following excerpts are from a magazine article written to explain a swing to the right that baffled liberal observers of the political scene. Look at how the writer fills in the major attitudes that make up the conservative temperament.

Susannah Lessard
THE TRUE CONSERVATISM

revealing introductory
anecdote

One autumn Saturday afternoon I was listening to the radio when the station switched to the Dartmouth-Harvard game. The game had not begun, and the announcer was rambling on about the nip in the air, the autumn colors, past games, this year's players, their names and hometowns. . . . Autumn, a new crop of players, New England: The world was *on a steady keel* after all. I could not remember having felt that *quiet sense of cycle*, of ongoing life and *the past* floating so serenely to the surface, in a long time.

key term

That morning, anyway, I felt like a conservative. . . .

first key attitude

Two elementary attitudes underlie the conservative tradition. *The first* is a passionate sense of the need to conserve—the land, the culture, the institutions, codes of behavior—and to revere and protect those elements that constitute "civilization." The conservative looks to the enduring values of the past. . . .

second key attitude

The second attitude is a cautious view of raw democracy, or direct representational government. The conservative believes firmly in the rights of minorities and those institutions that protect minorities from the whims of the majority, such as the Supreme Court—an elite, appointed body—and the Constitution, particularly the First Amendment. . . . These institutions that restrain the mass will are precious in the conservative view, not just because they protect the few from being trampled by the many, but also because they protect the majority from its own mistakes. . . .

further implication

An outgrowth of these attitudes—and one with particular value—is the humor that the skeptical turn of the conservative mind can bring to bear on confused, disaster-prone but unreservedly grand schemes for the betterment of mankind. . . .   "Civility, Community, Humor: The Conservatism We Need," *The Washington Monthly*

Questions for Discussion Does the writer's approach to her topic change your mind about the meaning of the word *conservative*? What parts of her definition are predictable or familiar; which seem different or new?

THE HISTORY OF A TERM Often, the best way to explain the current uses of a term is to trace its history. The following outline shows three major stages in the development of our concept of democracy:

We the People

THESIS: Over the centuries, the term *democracy* has moved away from its original Greek meaning of direct rule by the people.

I.   Ideally, democracy gives people a direct voice and vote in the common business of the community.

A. The Greek beginnings

B. Early town meetings

II. In practice, participation in the political process is often indirect and ineffectual.

A. Parliamentary democracy

B. Checks and balances

III. In modern "popular democracies," an authoritarian leadership claims to exercise power in the name of the people.

CONTRASTING OR RELATED TERMS We can often clarify an important term by marking it off from related terms that cover similar ground. We often introduce a new concept by contrasting it with a related familiar term. In the following excerpt, the student writer defines a controversial new term by contrasting it with a more familiar idea:

WRITING SAMPLE: CONTRASTING TERMS

Calibrating the Wage Scales

raising the issue   Single women know how difficult it is to make ends meet on the salaries offered to women holding predominantly female jobs. When women suggest that comparable pay for jobs of equal value should supplant the current system of pay equity for the same job, they shake the foundations of the male establishment in this country. . . .

established term   Pay equity, the system under which employment law currently functions, guarantees equal pay for equal work, and it is protected by existing antitrust and civil rights legislation. As long as female and male cashiers or truck drivers or supervisors are paid the same, employers have obeyed the law. . . .

new term   Comparable worth, on the other hand, would require equal pay for work of equal value. In the words of Jane Bryant Quinn, writing in *Newsweek*, it would require "equal pay for jobs that, although different from those held by men, call for a comparable amount of knowledge, skill, effort, and responsibility." Every study indicates that the more an occupation, no matter how valuable or important to society, is dominated by women, the less it tends to pay. . . .

legal difficulties   Legally, pay equity is much more clear-cut than comparable worth. What is the relative value of brains and brawn, education and experience, indoor work and outdoor work? How do we compare the value of a secretary's work with that of a garbage collector? . . .

Nevertheless, women need ways to advance economically without taking on "men's work." Like many others, I have tried taking on "different" jobs with unpromising results. For five months during the rainy season, I lifted fifty-pound bundles of newspapers and threw the Sunday edition. . . .

male opposition   Why is comparable worth so upsetting to businessmen? M. S. Forbes, Jr., of *Forbes* magazine called it "a pernicious, destructive idea." The chairman of the Civil Rights Commission called it "the looniest idea since Looney Tunes hit the screen."

THE WRITING WORKSHOP

Getting to Specifics

The first step toward successful definition is to go from the general to the specific—to move in on the concrete incidents, specific details, or particular traits to which the general label applies. Study the following passages as models for writing that translates a general idea into concrete reality. For group discussion, prepare a similar passage in which you give concrete substance to one of the following terms: *suburbia, ghetto, vigilantism, privacy, discrimination, sexism, small-town mentality, sophisticate, sensationalism*.

1. The urban society means crowded neighborhoods, poor housing, sometimes shacks on the fringes of the city inhabited by the fringes of humanity, more often fine old houses, tottering with age, wrinkled and cross-veined with partition. . . . Urban means poverty, hunger, disease, rats; it means unemployment, placement below skills, welfare and dependence perpetuated now to the third generation. . . . Urban means the decay of the central city, the moving out of business, the proliferation of "For Rent" signs, the boarding up of windows, the transformation of pride to embarrassment. . . . What once was city is now largely deteriorating buildings, empty stores, buildings about to empty themselves, and open spaces where buildings once stood.

2. He is self-confident. He believes in being in shape and completes an exercise program every morning. He believes appearances are important and pays careful attention to his clothes. He has always had a more expensive apartment or house than he could really afford, because he knew he would be moving up to the point at which he could afford it. He spends a lot of time "networking"; that is, he talks to people, has drinks with them, writes them notes—even when he does not have an immediate relationship with them. He works very hard—twelve-hour days are common—because that is what it takes to get ahead. He has an M.B.A. from Harvard, but he downplays it, knowing that many people who did not go to Harvard are put off by the name. He talks about loyalty and teamwork, but he has switched jobs whenever a better opportunity came along. His real loyalty is to himself—and to the bottom line. He knows the value of *things*: brand names, wines, antiques. He is a sophisticated consumer. Though he is in his early thirties, he is well on the way to running his own company.

That little summary is a profile of the prototypical hero of our age, the yuppie.   Adam Smith, "Yesterday's Yuppies," *Esquire*

Business people have traditionally believed that the free market fairly regulates wages through the free play of supply and demand. . . .

historical parallel   Historically, pay equity was itself in its time a radical idea. For some people, it was revolutionary to pay male and female sales representatives, or black and white coworkers, the same basic wage. It is no more revolutionary to give women a chance to support themselves and their children without climbing telephone poles.

Questions for Discussion Does the paper successfully explain the difference between pay equity and comparable pay for you? How would you sum up the distinction in a capsule definition?

EXERCISE 4   *Formal Definitions*

Which of the following student-written sentences are good examples of formal definitions? What makes them accurate, informative, or useful? Which of the definitions fall short, and why?

1.   Privacy is the privilege of having one's personal belongings, space, and thoughts free from intrusion.
2.   Islam is the religion of the Muslims and is widely practiced in the Near East.
3.   A referendum is a method of giving the public a voice in political decisions.
4.   A sorority is a private association that provides separate dormitory facilities with a distinct Greek letter name for selected female college students.
5.   Conformity is the adjustment from a unique individual state of being to a more socially acceptable, clonelike existence.
6.   Ecology is the study of the closely webbed interrelationships between organisms and their environment.
7.   Initiative is a personal quality that makes people attempt new and difficult things.
8.   Pacifism is the belief that disputes between nations can and should be settled without war.
9.   Jazz is a form of strongly rhythmic music played by black musicians.
10.   Due process is a traditional set of legal procedures that protect us against swift and arbitrary punishment.

EXERCISE 5   *Writing Formal Definitions*

Write formal one-sentence definitions for five of the following terms

censorship	human rights	expediency	primaries
dictatorship	avant-garde	jury trial	pollution
soap opera	Peace Corps	Puritanism	bigotry
evolution			

EXERCISE 6   *The Strategies of Definition*

> Study the following paragraph-length definitions. Why did each writer feel the need to define the central term (or pair of terms)? What was the writer's strategy for defining a key term? What kind of reader would make a good audience for each passage?

1.   *Planned obsolescence* as an ethic is one of the worst trends of our society. Aimed at maximizing profits, with little regard for environmental implications, the system makes it more expensive to fix an item than to buy a replacement. If manufacturers were sincerely dedicated to servicing worn or broken items, service jobs would be created to replace those lost in manufacturing. Because small items are cheap and disposable, we are conditioned to neglect simple repairs of items we own. And worse: many gadgets are designed to be nonrepairable, thus assuring more turnover and more waste. When will we realize that it is insane to throw away tons of nonbiodegradable plastic annually? How long will we remain slaves to the perpetual debt incurred by purchasing products (clothes, cars, appliances) designed to fall apart within a few years?

2.   The *action film* is a terrible vehicle in which to try to probe anything political, because it has to deliver shocks on schedule. And it colors anything political by its own brand of action politics. The viewer gets the feeling that the world is irredeemably violent: in a Clint Eastwood film, Eastwood can't go into a diner and ask for a glass of water without someone's picking a fight with him. Action movies say that the world is always threatening your manhood every minute of the day. In the forties, action directors used the anti-Nazi theme for hollow and sadistic violence; in the late sixties and early seventies, they used the anti-Vietnam War theme the same way (and we became the Nazis). In recent years, action directors have been using "survival." In other eras, the wilderness was sentimentalized as innocent. Now even nature is malevolent. . . . The idea that a man is defined in action (essentially by how good a fighter he is) comes out of a boys'-book world divided into the brave and the cowardly. It's an aesthetic and moral standard that had a romantic charm in the days when Gary Cooper was young.   Pauline Kael, "The Swamp," *The New Yorker*

EXERCISE 7   *Drawing the Line*

> Write a *two-paragraph paper* in which you draw the line between two overlapping terms. Devote one paragraph to each term. Choose a pair like the following:

□   privacy and secrecy
□   dissent and disobedience
□   justified force and violence

- ☐ authoritarian and totalitarian
- ☐ justice and getting even
- ☐ love and infatuation

THE PROCESS OF DEFINITION

When you write a definition paper, you will go through familiar steps in the writing process. Ideally, your writing will be triggered by a personal interest or commitment: Perhaps you have in turn been amused, annoyed, and angered by the media image of the "born-again" Christian. Or perhaps you have recently found yourself explaining why you are or are not a pacifist. Once you focus on your key term, you go on to the second stage: You take time for gathering, working up a rich body of relevant material. You look back over your personal experience; you investigate; you read and talk about your subject. Soon you will be involved in the third stage: sorting things out, thinking the matter through, getting your paper into shape. You will write a rough first draft, which revision and editing will turn into your finished paper.

The Process of Discovery

Suppose that you have become interested in some of the stereotypes and contradictory associations that cluster around the term *feminism*. To mobilize what you already know, you do some **brainstorming** on the subject:

PREWRITING: BRAINSTORMING

women in carpenter's boots; rough tough women opening their own doors; the "liberated woman"—tired of being second-class citizens, "one half of the human race"

marching, demonstrations, bra burnings: women in old dresses carrying flags, marching for the right to vote or for equal pay, rebelling against women being barred from colleges or the priesthood, synagogues

Sojourner Truth, Adrienne Rich; the black woman who helped slaves escape (name?); Friedan, *The Feminine Mystique*; abortion rights

women's groups; shelters for battered women; Chicana Alliance

"the feminization of poverty"; *Ms.* magazine; women in business; "dress for success"

no more face lifts or nose jobs, no makeup; women around a table reading women's poetry, discussing women's diaries

a black woman teacher said to me: "Every woman should be a feminist because she is a woman"

the stereotypes continue: movie in which woman is a lawyer but becomes emotionally involved with client (the eternal Eve)

In a group discussion, you may have an opportunity to compare your brainstorming notes with material collected by others. Your group may decide to set up a **discovery frame** covering the range of questions that seem particularly productive for this topic. Look at the sample materials that students in one group contributed under each heading. (What kind of material could *you* provide under each heading?)

PREWRITING: DISCOVERY FRAME

Feminism

1. *Surface Meaning*: What popular associations cluster around this term? What stereotypes does it bring to mind?

    When people hear the term *feminism*, the stereotypical women's libber image may flash through their minds. They may picture tough-looking, loud, boisterous man-haters, with unshaven legs and no makeup. Men (and some women) may still think of feminists as bra-burning radicals.

2. *Historical Background*: What do you know about the history of the movement? What are some famous names and events associated with it? Who are some outstanding women who symbolize feminist ideals?

    — women's suffrage movement: campaigning for women's right to vote (Susan B. Anthony, Elizabeth Cady Stanton)
    — tie-in with abolitionist movement: Sojourner Truth at the Women's Rights Convention in 1851
    — symbolic figures: Amelia Earhart was the first woman to pilot a plane across the Atlantic. Outstanding athletes: Florence Chadwick (swam the English Channel), Wilma Rudolph (runner)

3. *Media Coverage*: How do the media reflect changing attitudes? What images of women are projected by current movies, TV shows, advertising?

    Increasingly, in order to cash in on the large female market, the media cater to the image of the confident woman who is in control of her life. However, the images they project are often *ambiguous* (or dishonest?): The Maidenform woman is now a doctor—but she poses in her underwear among her fully dressed male colleagues. The female pilot has the hair and smile of a Clairol model and advertises deodorant.

4. *Personal Experience*: Where have the issues raised by the feminist movement played a role in your own life? How can you relate the term to your own experience?

    — I grew up with many girls whose parents were leading them down the road to housewifery, motherhood, or menial jobs by not urging them on to excel the way they did their sons. When the brother went out for varsity sports, the sister became a cheerleader. I remember being the only girl in my trigonometry class.

— I recently had a chance to observe a traditional sexist at work, so to speak. He enjoys dating women, but never for more than four or five weeks. He shows little interest in their lives and thoughts; he seems to enjoy them the way one might enjoy beautiful scenery. He once suggested to a friend of mine that she hem a pair of pants.

5.   *Related or Contrasting Terms*: What similar terms or near-synonyms come up in discussions of feminism? What opposite terms—or antonyms—can help clarify the term?

— similar or related terms: women's rights, women's liberation, the women's movement; emancipation—setting free from slavery or restraints
— suffragist—someone campaigning to have the right to vote extended to the disenfranchised, especially to women
— contrasting terms: sexism, chauvinism; patriarchy—a society or way of life where the male "father figure" rules

6.   *The Common Denominator*: What is the core meaning of the term?

A feminist need not be female but could be anyone—male or female—who believes in equal rights for both sexes. Feminism as a movement is designed to help women discover their own powers and their own self-worth. Its aim is to help women achieve equality in all areas of life—private, artistic, social, economic, and political.

The following might be the overall *plan* or *strategy* you decide to follow for using these materials in writing your actual paper:

PREWRITING: STRATEGY

☐   Start with misleading popular stereotypes that give contradictory signals to young women trying to define their self-image.
☐   Lead into "common-denominator" definition as the thesis of your paper, using some of your contrasting or related terms to clarify the central concept.
☐   Establish historical background, *quoting* one or two of the precursors to help convey the authentic spirit of the movement.
☐   Go on to your own personal experience to show how events in their own lives convert young women to the cause.
☐   Conclude by looking at current media coverage to help the reader judge how far the attitudes of society have changed.

The Finished Paper   Look at the following sample paper. How successfully does it implement the above strategy? Where and how does it use the materials from the student's preliminary investigation?

We Have Come a Long Way

We often hear women say, "I am not a feminist, but . . . ." When people hear the term *feminism*, the stereotypical women's libber image may flash through their minds. They may picture tough, loud, boisterous man-haters, with unshaven legs and no makeup. In many people's minds, the very term "women's liberation" acquired a negative connotation.

To overcome these negative stereotypes, we should start from the realization that feminism is first of all a state of awareness rather than a political movement. Feminism exists because women recognize that society does not serve their special needs. Through the women's movement, women strive to achieve equality in all areas of life. Through feminism, women are discovering their own powers and their own self-worth.

The growing awareness promoted by today's feminist movement has strong historical roots. The first major stage of feminism lasted from 1850 to 1920 and ended when women won the right to vote with the Nineteenth Amendment. The foremost women's group at the time was the National Woman Suffrage Association, headed by Susan B. Anthony, its best organizer, and Elizabeth Cady Stanton, its best philosopher and program writer. Sojourner Truth, a freed slave, fought equally hard for abolition and women's rights. At the Women's Rights Convention in Akron, Ohio, in 1851, a clergyman ridiculed suffrage for women, calling them weak and helpless. The women hesitated to argue with him until Sojourner Truth rose and said:

> The man over there says women need to be helped into carriages and lifted over ditches, and to have the best place everywhere. Nobody ever helps me into carriages or over puddles, or gives me the best place—and ain't I a woman? Look at my arms! I have ploughed and planted and gathered into barns, and no man could head me—and ain't I a woman? I could work as much and eat as much as a man—when I could get it—and bear the lash as well!

My own belief in independence and equality goes back to early childhood. Since no boys were born into my family, my sister and I were taught to be aggressive and goal-minded. I grew up with many girls whose parents were leading them down the road to housewivery, motherhood, or menial jobs by not pushing them to excel in subjects that would secure their financial and educational future. I can remember being the only girl in my trigonometry class. My friends couldn't understand why I was taking an unrequired and difficult course. Today, these same friends are either pushing baby carriages or cash register keys under the golden arches of McDonald's.

When women look around to see how far feminist awareness has spread in our society, they receive contradictory signals. The media are slowly changing their treatment of women. Commercials have a long history of portraying women as happy homemakers who are interested only in cleaning the house, doing the children's laundry, and brewing better coffee for their husbands. Advertisers have long used the scantily clad sex kitten to sell goods. Today, in order to cash in on the enormous female market, the media are catering to the image of the confident woman who is in control of her life. However, we must remember that this new image often remains ambiguous. The Maidenform woman turned into a doctor but still modeled her underwear among her fully dressed colleagues. The female pilot has the hair and smile of a Clairol model and advertises deodorant.

Although women today are constantly bombarded by the media with visions of their presumed great strides toward equality, there is much more to be accomplished. Feminism will fight on as long as women are denied freedom and equality in their economic, social, political, and private lives.

Questions for Discussion Has this paper clarified your own thinking about the subject? How do you react to the paper? Is it balanced? informative? too political? too mild? Do you expect a female and a male audience to react differently?

Reminders for Revision In revising a definition paper, look for predictable problems and possible solutions:

- □ *Revise circular definitions.* **Circular definitions** circle back to the original term; they merely repeat it in a somewhat different guise. Reading that "Puritanism is the religion of the Puritans" gives us no help with recognizing or understanding Puritans.

- □ *Resist the one-meaning fallacy.* When you advertise your definition as the one true meaning of freedom or democracy, you will seem to ignore other legitimate or historical uses of the term. You can make allowance for other points of view by injecting qualifiers like "as I see it" or "for my generation." Sometimes a writer will clearly label a definition as a **stipulated definition**: "*democracy* as used here." If necessary, use a distinctive label to clear up the ambiguities of a term. (In the seventies, critics of established "representative democracy" used the term "participatory democracy" to identify their own ideal.)

- □ *Pay attention not only to what something is but also to how it works.* Scientists, engineers, business people, and politicians are used to **operational definitions** that show something in action, that show how they can make it work. In defining the "new poverty," you may need to focus on the mechanisms that bring it about.

- □ *Reckon with the feelings and attitudes a word brings into play.* A definition of a word like *pornography* or *censorship* is going to mislead if it does not take into account the powerful feelings of hostility or disapproval that the

THE WRITING WORKSHOP

Using a Discovery Frame

Working with a group or with your class as a whole, prepare a preliminary collection of material for an extended definition of a term important to an understanding of contemporary American life. Your group may decide to choose a term like *permissiveness, pluralism, multiethnic, neoconservatism, assimilation, the work ethic, prejudice, fundamentalism,* or *women's rights.* Have the members of the group pool their answers to the questions in the following discovery frame. Use the resulting material as background for a possible definition paper.

1. *Surface Meaning:* What common associations cluster around the term? What images does it bring to mind? What popular misconceptions or stereotypes does it bring into play?
2. *History:* What are the historical roots of the term? What is the derivation of the word? When and how was it first used? What stages did it go through?
3. *Media Coverage:* When and where do you see the term in print? Has it recently been in news coverage? Does it appear as a theme in current movies or television entertainment? Does it play a role in a current controversy?
4. *Personal Experience:* What has been your own firsthand experience with permissiveness, or the work ethic, or prejudice? What incidents have you witnessed, and what have you learned from them?
5. *Related Terms:* What related terms cover similar ground? How does the word differ from its synonyms? What opposed terms, or antonyms, help bring the term into focus?
6. *Major Applications:* Does the word have several major different meanings or uses? Are they related?
7. *Common Denominator:* Is there a common strand in the different uses and applications of the term? What is the clue to its central meaning?

word may arouse. Such words have powerful **connotations**—they are emotionally charged; they have strong negative (or in other cases positive) associations.

Remember: Definition is often the first step toward clear thinking and sound argument. Readers become frustrated and arguments are derailed when key terms seem to shift their meaning in the middle of a discussion. Clear definition of important terms may not make your readers agree with you, but at least they will know what they agree with if they do.

WRITING TOPICS 13 *Writing to Define*

Which of the following topics remind you of a clear need for definition? Choose a topic that allows you to draw on observation, experience, and reading.

1. Which of the following is for you more than just a cliché? Write an extended definition that shows your readers why the term is important. Aim at the common element that underlies different uses of the term, or at its most important different or related meanings.

consumerism   assimilation   pluralism   permissiveness
the work ethic   born-again Christians   equal opportunity
law and order   bureaucracy   computer literacy   sibling rivalry
teacher burnout   privacy   bigotry   police brutality

2. Choose one of the following pairs of overlapping terms. Where do you draw the line? Write an extended definition comparing and contrasting the two terms. Write for a newspaper reader who has often seen or heard the terms but who is vague on the dividing line between the two.

   □ professional and amateur
   □ terrorism and guerilla warfare
   □ erotica and pornography
   □ authoritarian and totalitarian
   □ culture and popular culture
   □ art and kitsch
   □ love and a relationship
   □ soap opera and serious drama

3. Choose a key term from an area about which you can write as an insider. Write an extended definition that would initiate the newcomer or outsider. Choose a term like the following: *high tech, aerobics, human rights, environmentalism, vegetarian, modern dance, punk.*

4. Labels like the following are judgmental terms that we sometimes apply too quickly or thoughtlessly to what we dislike: *sentimentality, sensationalism, cynicism, expediency, corruption, nepotism, exploitation, sexism.* Choose one and write an extended definition to show what would be justified uses of the term.

5. Some words have a long history and are rich in contradictory meanings and associations. Choose one of the following: *liberal, conservative, radical, romantic love, feminism, Puritanism, anarchist, evolution*. Write an extended definition to help other students understand major uses and associations of the word. Aim at a common denominator or common center.

6. Write a paper that defines an ideal or a goal for the future. For instance, what is your vision of the ideal woman or man of the future? What is your vision of an ideal marriage? Try to make your ideal real for young people today.

13

REASONING

Structuring an Argument

The standardized shape of the essay cannot be superimposed like a grid into which the writer's thoughts are placed. On the contrary, the thoughts, the reaching for ideas, the searching for words, often suggest the shape of the essay.
Gabriele Rico

We think in generalities, but we live in detail.
Alfred North Whitehead

WHY AND HOW WE ARGUE Writing is the art of getting down on paper what we are thinking. The more serious we are about convincing our readers, the more we need to have them follow our train of thought—the more we try to make them see the logic behind the stands we take. In a logical argument, we show our readers not only what we think but *how* we think. We show how we arrived at our conclusions, enabling them to retrace our steps and reach (we hope) the same destination.

Writing that argues with the reader has a special drive; it pushes forward to the *therefore* or *consequently* that is the writer's goal. We are not talking here about arguments that are really quarrels—where in the heat of the argument we say things that we may regret on second thought. In a logical argument, we try to think clearly from the start, keeping our emotions from clouding the issue. We adopt a stance that implies: "If you look at the evidence, you as a reasonable reader will reach the same conclusions I have reached."

The Point of the Argument The purpose of a well-structured argument is to change the reader's mind. Writers with an argumentative bent will take on others who misunderstand or misrepresent and try to make them see the truth of the matter. Much argument attempts to set the record straight, to make the truth as we see it prevail. Often something more is at stake: We want to help people not only understand but take appropriate steps. We want readers to understand the nature of their problems and find sensible solutions. We wish to warn them of the consequences of ill-considered actions. Much argumentative writing in effect tells the reader: "This is what explains the current situation, and this is how you can cope with it. If you do so and so, then such and such will follow."

The Way We Think

Experts on artificial intelligence know that the human mind is a marvelously complex instrument, whose operations are difficult to analyze and simulate. It may at times work in linear one–two–three fashion, but it also works at least in part by intuitive leaps and imaginative bounds. Nevertheless, we can chart some recurrent thought patterns that help shape much of our thinking and writing. Some kinds of thinking we can see again and again when people process information or try to make sense of experience. In a thought-provoking argument, we can see the writer's mind at work, forging connections, exploring and rejecting alternatives. A simplified overview of thought patterns mirrored in systematic argument should include at least the following:

INDUCTION   A writer may look for a common strand, a common pattern, in related examples. For instance, you may study reports of violence at soccer matches, riots after a football game, tantrums on the tennis court, fist-fights in bars, and shootouts over a parking space. You may point to a common element, a central clue: the constant nervous irritability, the short fuse, that results from the pressures of modern living. This bundling of related evidence is one of the basic reasoning patterns we use to sort out information and make sense of multifarious data. This kind of thinking goes from the specific to the general, from isolated observations to a common clue. We call this generalizing kind of reasoning inductive reasoning, or **induction**.

Inductive reasoning helps us funnel related observations into a generalization that sums up a common pattern. It also helps us construct a hypothesis that correlates and explains puzzling data. A classic example from Monroe C. Beardsley's *Thinking Straight* looks as follows:

Fact 1:	The house across the street has shown no signs of life in some days.
Fact 2:	Some rolled-up, rain-soaked newspapers lie on the front steps.
Fact 3:	The grass needs cutting badly.
Fact 4:	Visitors who ring the doorbell get no answer.
HYPOTHESIS:	*The people across the street are away on a trip.*

All clues in the example point in the same direction: Papers are not picked up when the owner is away. The grass is not cut when the owner is away. No one answers the doorbell when the owner is away. (Other possible hypotheses: The people across the street have been the victims of foul play. Or the people across the street are in the basement, hiding from creditors.) In much of the writing we do, thinking the matter through means working out careful generalizations while taking apparent exceptions into account; it means constructing careful hypotheses to account for a state of affairs while not ruling out alternative explanations.

DEDUCTION Often we go from the general to the specific. We spell out assumptions about appropriate behavior and then show how they should govern behavior in specific situations. We argue from principle, applying a general principle in order to decide individual cases. (The principle we invoke is sometimes called the **warrant** in modern discussions of argument.) For example, after asking when we should withhold life support from the terminally ill, a writer might formulate a rough contemporary consensus on what constitutes a meaningful life. She may then provide guidance for doctors and relatives by applying this concept to test cases of terminally ill patients. When we apply general principles to specific cases, we argue deductively. We employ deductive reasoning, or **deduction**.

In much of our reasoning, we work with what we already know, bringing previous knowledge to bear on current problems, applying general rules to specific instances, invoking a prior law to judge a current crime. We move from shared assumptions, or shared **premises**, through logical steps to valid conclusions. An informal version of this deductive process guides us in everyday decisions:

GENERAL PREMISE: All the design engineers I know look well-groomed.
SPECIFIC FACT: While in college, I have let my hair grow frizzy, and I tie it up with a bandana.
CONCLUSION: Before I apply for a job as a design engineer, I should do something about my hair.

But similar reasoning determines the verdict on many matters of greater weight:

FIRST PREMISE: Only native-born Americans are eligible to run for President.
SECOND PREMISE: Dr. X is a naturalized citizen.
CONCLUSION: Dr. X is not eligible to run for President.

PRO AND CON A third kind of reasoning is not always stressed in introductions to logic, but it is one of the basic ways we make up our minds. In many situations, we need to weigh the pro and con before making the right decision. The issue may be whether to live at home or away from home while in college; it may be whether to boycott a company that uses non-union labor. Typically in such situations, we have to balance conflicting advice, opposing views. The kind of reasoning that goes from *on the one hand* to *on the other hand* and on to a balanced conclusion is the process of **dialectic**.

A paper exploring the dialectic of contrasting views will often lead up to a turning point: a strategic *however*, *nevertheless*, or *on the other hand* signaling that the writer will now look at the other side. Writing a paper on the role of ceremony in our lives, you may want to start with familiar objections: Audiences fidget at commencement speeches; formulas recited by rote at weddings do not express sincere feelings; hard-earned money is spent to rent ill-fitting tuxedos. On the other hand, as you point out in the second half of your paper, special occasions make us feel that we matter; they give others a chance to show that they care; they renew bonds of friendship and kinship. On balance, although ceremonies can be lifeless and boring, they can also be occasions for affirmation and renewal.

Advocates of a dialectic perspective recommend it as the antidote to either-or, right-or-wrong thinking. Do students need discipline and firm guidance? Or should they learn to make their own decisions and chart their own course? A dialectic perspective would make us answer yes to both questions and encourage us to work out the right balance between guidance and initiative.

Question for Discussion Can you give examples of inductive, deductive, or pro-and-con thinking from everyday life, from your current reading, or from current controversy?

Making a Case To give your paper an argumentative edge, you have to keep your goal clearly in mind and pursue it in a determined manner. When trying to make a strong case, remember advice like the following:

☐ *Pinpoint the issue*. Focus the reader's attention on the point at issue, on the question before the house. The issue should be an *open* issue—on which reasonable people have honest differences of opinion. The following passage effectively rekindles a current controversy:

The Right to Die

Does society have the legal right to force-feed aged or severely handicapped patients who are trying to end their pain-ridden lives? Should courts have the right to order life-prolonging surgery for infants doomed to a life of pain and severe retardation? Doctors have greatly extended their power to stave off death, but should there be limits on the use of this power? Should life be sustained by "heroic measures" and at any cost?

□ *Take a stand*. What are you trying to prove? A strong argument needs a clear, well-supported thesis. The writer makes a definite claim or argues a definite **proposition**. (Remember that some arguments *lead up* to a strong final thesis.)

THESIS: Maintaining the legal drinking age at 21 will save thousands of young lives every year.

THESIS: Women have to ask for more than equal pay for equal work; they need to ask for comparable pay for work of comparable value.

□ *Work out a clear logical plan*. Your readers will expect you to take them systematically from one logical step to the next. Make sure you can outline the overall course of your argument—make sure you can chart the major links in a chain of cause and effect, or a sequence of examples that prepare the reader for the inductive leap. Signal clearly the major turns in your argument.

□ *Mobilize the necessary evidence and support*. Buttress your argument with detailed examples, telling statistics, and expert testimony. Keep after your reader with facts, figures, and quotations:

The main reason for the wretched conditions existing in our prisons is over-crowding. When the two bloodiest prison riots in this country's history took place at Attica State Prison in New York and at Santa Fe prison in New Mexico, the population of these two prisons was at fifty percent over normal capacity. An official at the California Department of Correction said in April 1986, "Each day the population of the state's prisons shatters a record. The unprecedented numbers have caused a crisis that threatens to plunge an already violence-plagued system to new depths." The American Civil Liberties Union, in a study of prison conditions, found that "six inmates were sometimes housed in a 4 by 8 cell, with no beds, no lights, no running water, and a hole in the ground for a toilet." The effect of such conditions on the inmates was summed up by a chaplain at Riker's Island: "If you put a violent person in prison for a number of years, he will come out more violent than before."

□ *Take possible objections seriously*. What counterarguments is the opposing side likely to offer? Can you refute them, showing their weaknesses, defusing potentially damaging charges? Suppose you are arguing that divorced fathers cut off from their children should more often be granted extended visiting rights or divided custody. Are you prepared for counterclaims that shuffling a child between homes has harmful effects? It would strengthen your case to anticipate this objection and cite authorities claiming that shared parenting arrangements can demonstrate that both parents are devoted to their children.

Questions for Discussion How open-minded are you? How receptive are you to objections, questions, or arguments on the other side? Can you give some examples of objections or counterarguments to which you have given serious thought?

Argument and the Audience Successful argument presupposes an unwritten agreement between writer and audience: Both writer and reader will look at the subject calmly and rationally, following the argument to its logical conclusion. In practice, of course, staying calm may be equally hard for either party. We face a familiar dilemma: The more we care about a subject, the harder it is for us to argue dispassionately. A committed environmentalist may see in the coyote a symbol of endangered wildlife, everywhere driven to the brink by predatory human beings. Sheep ranchers may see the coyote as a wily, rapacious enemy that should be hunted down and its skin nailed to the wall. How are we going to keep an argument about the coyote from turning into a shouting match?

Modern discussions of argument offer advice on how to lower the emotional thermostat by downplaying disagreement and playing up shared values. **Rogerian argument**, named after the American psychologist Carl Rogers, avoids aggressive traditional modes of argument in order to adopt a more conciliatory, nonthreatening style. The traditional assertive style of argument encouraged writers to take a strong stand, to lay out points in a clear one-two-three order, and to drive them home. However, an assertive style can easily become overbearing, putting readers on the defensive, making them feel cornered. We may then try to change from a "No, you are wrong" to a "Yes, but" style of argument. The "Yes, but" style reckons with the readers' need for self-esteem; it respects their commitments and loyalties.

Advocates of a Rogerian style of argument give advice like the following:

- Try to keep the channels of communication open. Try to continue the dialogue. (Your paper will not convince anybody if the infuriated reader slams it down half-read.)
- Show that you know and respect the arguments on the other side. (Give opponents credit for good intentions; recognize legitimate interests of the other side.)
- Avoid a strong judgmental tone—either in condemning the views of others, or in identifying your own as those of all right-thinking Americans or truly responsible individuals.
- Try not to polarize opinion on a subject.

Argument and Persuasion Argument and persuasion are often treated together; they are indeed part of the same spectrum and shade over into each other. However, they differ in what the writer expects of (or wants from) the

THE WRITING WORKSHOP

The Final Argument

In public debate, the time available to each speaker is often strictly limited. In such a situation, you may have to select from your arsenal the single most telling argument. Suppose you were offered a chance to have the last word in a public discussion of one of the following issues, but time is severely limited. Team up with other members of a group; have each prepare a "closing statement" that would present his or her most important single argument on the issue. Have your group or your class as a whole discuss and evaluate the final arguments prepared by the group. Which seem forceful and why? Which seem weak and why? Have your group prepare arguments

- for or against school prayer
- for or against ROTC
- for or against the theory of evolution
- for or against marriage
- for or against fraternities and sororities
- for or against capital punishment
- for or against abolishing freshman English
- for or against keeping *Playboy* out of the campus bookstore
- for or against public financing of day-care centers
- for or against requiring students to have personal computers

reader. At one end of the spectrum, we may expect nothing of the reader except an open mind, a willingness to look at the evidence and follow an argument to its logical conclusions. Although we may be aiming at a practical result—a vote, a change in policy—we respect our readers' right to make up their own minds.

At the other end of the spectrum, the result—a sale, a vote, a promotion, or a client's freedom—has become the true test of a writer's effectiveness. When this happens, our attention inevitably shifts from the merits of the issue or the logic of the situation to the psychology of the audience. What goes on in the minds of the customers, the voters, or the jurors? How far are we going to go to humor their prejudices, appeal to their hopes and fears, and activate their hidden motives? As these questions become central, the emphasis tilts from logical argument toward emotional appeals. In advertising and political propaganda, the temptation is to bypass logical argument altogether and instead play on the emotions of the audience.

To argue effectively, we must believe that we do not have to choose between dry logic and emotional appeals. Effective argument often appeals to both the head and the heart. But the more faith we have in the readers' intelligence, the more we will appeal to their judgment, trusting in their ability to think for themselves.

EXERCISE 1   *Thought Starters*

Which of the following passages makes you say, "I would like to argue this point"? Select several of these and prepare to argue for or against the point made in each passage. What would be your main argument or arguments? Where would you turn for support?

1. Many people realize that journalism is a business like any other. A television station structures its news programs to attract high ratings and well-paying sponsors. A newspaper packages its news so that it will attract buyers for the paper. The network or newspaper executive's job is the same as that of the corner grocer: to attract paying customers.

2. Negative views sit well with the public in the wake of two Presidents in a row—Carter and Reagan—who have campaigned "against Washington." Americans are by nature skeptical of authority and inclined to believe the worst about government. This makes an anti-Washington or anti-Big-Government campaign the easiest to sell to the voters.

3. On the subject of male nurses: If a man wants to be a nurse, let him find a job in a veterans' hospital. Men should confine their nursing to men only (or they should stay in man's work altogether). Women are by nature caretakers. We take care of family members when they are sick. In the end, we women take care of elderly patients. Men are too self-absorbed to provide care for others; a fair percentage of them are child molesters, wife beaters, serial murderers, and general all-around louses.

4. In America, all ethnic groups watch the same TV shows, live in boxes of similar design and decor, wear about the same clothing, and eat the same convenience foods. . . . The nationality-based social club and athletic team, the foreign language newspaper, the church, the Kosher butcher, and the ethnic political organization are all in steep decline.   Martin Mayer

5. The TV manipulators of reality have discovered that Americans will trust anyone who is good-looking.

6. State-run lotteries exact a type of regressive tax that saps those who can least afford to lose the money. Perhaps it is true that the percentage of underprivileged people playing lotteries is no larger than the percentage in the general population. However, the poor spend a larger *share* of their disposable income on lotteries than high-income groups do. But the main objection is a moral one: Should the state be hyping gambling in front of children watching TV? Constant playing up of the bonanza that awaits the lucky winner creates the cruel illusion that people will be able to escape the reality of daily poverty.

EXERCISE 2   *Identifying the Issue*

College students are often accused of apathy on the social and political issues of the day. Identify and rank in order of importance three issues that matter to you. For each issue, prepare a paragraph in which you (1) spell out the issue, (2) explain why you care or how you got involved, and (3) explain what shaped your thinking on the issue.

EXERCISE 3   *Listening to the Other Side*

Choose a subject on which you hold strong opinions. Write a paragraph in which you describe as fully and as fairly as you can a point of view different from or opposed to yours. Sum up key arguments of the other side on a topic like registration of firearms, equal funding for women's sports, bilingual ballots, rent control, required courses outside your major, comparable pay, or resettlement of refugees in your community.

STRUCTURING AN ARGUMENT
How do we structure an argument? A live argument shows thought in action; it mirrors the reasoning processes that give direction to our thinking. We may search for the answer to a puzzling question, arriving at an answer different from what our readers might expect. We may lead them step by step to a culminating conclusion ("Therefore we must conclude . . .") or to a dramatic turning point ("However, we must point out . . ."). A live argument does not merely present packaged ideas, chopped and canned like cat food. It gets the reader involved in the drama of ideas, the "life of the mind."

Several strategies for structuring an argument are especially effective in bringing ideas to life. They carry the reader along; their built-in logic gives a paper an argumentative drive. Experiment with organizing strategies like the following:

Looking at the Facts

When an issue has generated more heat than enlightenment, we may want our readers to suspend judgment while checking out the facts. We invite them to join us in the search; we ask them to generalize cautiously on the basis of what we know.

This generalizing, **inductive** kind of reasoning underlies much of the writing we do. For instance, you may want to argue with fellow students who claim that young people today are more politically aware and responsible than their parents. You have been struck by the small turnouts for controversial speakers invited to your campus. You have studied the dismal statistics on recent elections for student government. You have seen reports on debates that fizzled. Your campus newspaper seems obsessed with the parking situation or the Ugliest-Man-on-Campus award. After reporting these and similar observations in vivid detail, you reach a general conclusion: A pervasive apathy toward political and social issues has overtaken your fellow students.

Normally, you would present this general conclusion first, as your unifying thesis, and then lay out the various striking examples you have collected. However, you have decided to involve the reader directly in the inductive process, in the *search* for a common pattern. If your readers follow you in your thinking step by step, the result may be more lasting conviction. When you start your paper with a strong initial claim, the skeptical reader's response may be: "Is that so?" When you make your whole paper lead up to a well-earned generalization, your readers may feel: "Yes, I have already reached the same conclusion."

Arguing from Principle

When we reason **deductively**, we apply general principles to specific cases. We spell out basic assumptions or beliefs and show how they apply to a given situation. For instance, we may first spell out at what point pranks cease to express youthful exuberance and instead infringe on other people's rights. We then show how this principle applies to recent examples of Animal House-type behavior on campus.

Much argument on public issues applies legal or moral principles to specific questions of policy. Suppose you have become concerned by the current drive to revive the death penalty. In spite of strong arguments in its favor, capital punishment goes counter to some of your basic convictions. Writing a paper on the subject gives you a chance to sort out your thinking. You may decide to structure your argument as follows:

PREWRITING: STRUCTURING THE ARGUMENT

Thou Shalt Not

thesis   In spite of strong current arguments in favor of the death penalty, capital punishment violates several basic principles underlying the American system of justice.

first principle   *Most basic to our legal system is our belief in even-handed justice.* We believe that equal crimes should receive equal punishment. However, the death penalty has always been notorious for its "freakish unfairness." In the words of one study, "judicial safeguards for preventing the arbitrary administration of capital punishment are not working." Judges and juries apply widely differing standards. In one celebrated case, two partners in crime were convicted of the same capital crime on identical charges. One was executed; the other is in prison and will soon be eligible for parole.

second principle   *We believe that all citizens are equal before the law.* Justice should be "blind" to wealth, race, ethnic origin. However, poor defendants are many times more likely to receive the death penalty than wealthy ones, protected by highly paid teams of lawyers whose maneuvers stymie the prosecution and baffle the jury. Minority defendants convicted of capital crimes have a much higher statistical chance of being executed than white defendants.

third principle   *Fairness demands that the judicial system make provision for correcting its own errors.* If someone has been unjustly convicted, there should be a mechanism for reversing the verdict and setting the person free. However, in the case of the death penalty, such a correction of error is aborted. We are left with futile regrets, like the prosecutor who said, "Horrible as it is to contemplate, we may have executed the wrong man."

Questions for Discussion How well-established are the principles evoked in this argument? (What would you do to impress readers with their importance or validity?) How relevant are they, or how well do they apply, to this issue?

The Pro-and-Con Paper

A **pro-and-con** paper lines up the arguments on two sides of an issue and then reaches a balanced conclusion. We may first discuss the advantages of a proposal or a program, and then the disadvantages. We first present arguments in support of a new method or approach; then we look at possible objections. Ideally, as the strengths and weaknesses of the opposing arguments become apparent, a balanced conclusion will emerge that reasonable people can accept.

The pro-and-con paper treats an issue as an open question, worth thinking about. Instead of driving stubbornly toward a foregone conclusion, we invite the reader to reconsider a matter of common concern. Here is how you might line up arguments for and against in a paper that moves from *on the one hand* to *on the other hand* on an emotion-charged issue:

PREWRITING: CHARTING THE PRO AND CON

The Right to Live, the Right to Die

THE ISSUE: Physicians, hospitals, and families of patients increasingly confront a cruel dilemma: Should patients with no hope for return to a meaningful life be allowed to die with dignity? Should doctors withdraw life-supporting equipment and feeding tubes keeping alive terminally ill or comatose patients?

PRO

(1) Death in America is too often controlled by machines rather than nature. An estimated 80 percent of Americans now die in hospitals or nursing homes, often surrounded by a thicket of tubes and life-extending apparatus. . . .

(2) Public opinion polls show that most Americans oppose the use of "heroic measures" to keep patients alive when there is no hope of recovery. A Louis Harris poll found that 82 percent supported the idea of withdrawing feeding tubes if it was the patient's wish. . . .

(3) Too many terminally ill patients in severe pain have their suffering prolonged by the indiscriminate use of technology. . . .

(4) About 10,000 Americans linger in a hopeless twilight zone known as a "permanent vegetative state." For their families, they are a constant source of anguish, and there is a tremendous financial burden (as much as $100,000 a year). . . .

(5) In many cases, the medical staff and the family agree that the comatose patient derives "no comfort, no improvement, and no hope of improvement" from further medical treatment. . . .

CON

(1) Some critics object bitterly to "selective starvation." Dehydration can be a gruesome way to die. . . .

(2) Many people warn us about the "slippery slope" toward wholesale euthanasia: "We start by dispatching the terminally ill and the hopelessly comatose, but then perhaps our guidelines will be extended to the severely senile, the very old and decrepit, and maybe even severely retarded children." . . .

(3) In the current political climate, decisions to withdraw life-support equipment may bemotivated by the pressure to cut medical costs rather than by concern for the patient's "dignity." Anne Bannon, president of Doctors for Life, says, "That's what this is all about, to get rid of people who are a burden to their families and the state." . . .

(4) The training and ethical sense of many physicians predispose them to save lives at all costs. . . .

CONCLUSION: Moral qualms and the fear of legal consequences often keep doctors from making decisions that would be in the best interest of the patients or of their families. Patients should as early and as clearly as possible make their own wishes known. Many states now recognize a "Living Will" that requests doctors not to prolong life by extraordinary measures. . . .

Note that in writing a pro-and-con paper you may anticipate the outcome by stating your conclusion as your thesis early in the paper. This strategy takes away the suspense but shows that you know your destination. Or you may leave the issue open, involving your reader in the dialectic of conflicting claims, leading up to a balanced conclusion at the end.

Questions for Discussion Which of the arguments in the "Right to Die" paper appeal to you most? Which least? Are there important arguments pro or con that the writer has overlooked? Would you yourself come down on the pro side or con side, or would you be ready for an in-between solution?

Tracing Cause and Effect

In analyzing a problem, we often try to identify the causes that helped create it. We ask: "What brought this on? What caused the present situation?" Once we sort out the major causes (or identify the main cause), our readers might be ready to listen to a possible solution. The following might be preliminary notes for a **cause-and-effect** paper that goes beyond surface symptoms to underlying causes and then suggests possible remedies:

PREWRITING: WORKING NOTES

Hotheads and Short Fuses

Symptoms

A professor drives his car back to campus in the evening to pick up papers at his office. He is unable to avoid hitting a jaywalker who suddenly appears in front of his car. The incensed jaywalker drags the driver out of the car while the car careens wildly across the street and smashes into the shop window of a boutique.

After a narrow victory over a traditional rival in a championship football game, the celebrating fans rock and overturn cars driven by supporters of the visiting team; one car is set afire; dozens of people are hurt.

At a local school, vandals spray paint library books and walls and scatter records, causing $50,000 worth of damage.

Causes

According to zoologists, primates mark their territories by scent or visual display; humans similarly "leave their mark" on territory they are otherwise unable to control.

Gangs that vandalize schools or public property as a group effort reinforce their sense of mutual loyalty, producing a stronger degree of "social bonding."

Much "unprovoked" individual violence is caused by people striking back at a threatening or frustrating environment. An oppressive or frustrating environment produces pent-up anger. Anger causes people to lash out, often at the wrong target. People who feel thwarted or hemmed in strike back at others who they rightly or wrongly feel are invading their turf.

Cures
Traditional Response: Nebuchadnezzar tried to counteract vandalism by issuing edicts against the defacement of temples in Babylon. We try to discourage misbehavior by public outcry, threats of punishment—with dubious results.

Modern Behavior Modification: Psychologists ask us to think about the underlying psychological mechanisms that precipitate (or prevent) violent and destructive behavior. One landscape architect in Seattle wraps newly planted trees in gauze. The gauze bandage, suggesting something wounded or vulnerable, is designed to produce a caring rather than a destructive response.

Questions for Discussion Do the symptoms listed in these working notes seem isolated instances or are they representative examples? Do the causes and suggested cures seem convincing or farfetched?

Eliminating Alternatives

An argument may lead to the right conclusion by a process of elimination. (A diner looking at a limited menu might reject the roast beef and the pork chop because of their high cholesterol and by a process of elimination opt for the sole.) Margaret Mead once wrote about how to fight sexual harassment on the job—belittling, condescension, unwanted familiarities. She started by taking a look at two familiar current remedies: (1) rules and regulations—guidelines, ordinances, and the like; (2) litigation—lawsuits against employers or fellow employees. Finding both of these wanting, she opted for a more lasting solution: (3) education—ways to change the attitudes and expectations of the next generation.

The "Yes, but" Paper

Much argument is devoted to countering objections, to refuting opposing arguments. Often we have no chance to make our views prevail unless we counter strongly held opposing views first. One strategy for dealing with opposing views is the "Yes, but" style of argument—we acknowledge opposing arguments and meet the opposition part of the way. We concede what is true and reasonable in the opposing view—before we show what is really wrong with it. Study the way the student writer implemented the "Yes, but" approach in the following paper:

The Law of the Gun

basic problem

When a famous person is assassinated—President Kennedy, Martin Luther King, John Lennon—lawmakers for a time seem ready to make guns less accessible and more easily tracked. But soon we forget, and the powerful National Rifle Association is able to weaken or defeat laws aimed at more effective gun control.

dramatizing the issue:
eloquent testimony

One person who has been unable to forget is Sarah Brady, whose husband Jim suffered permanent brain damage when he was shot during an assassination attempt on President Reagan. As an outspoken member of Handgun Control, Inc., she has pointed out that John Hinckley, the would-be assassin, purchased his gun in a Dallas pawnshop with no difficulty. "Had there been a waiting period or background check," she says, "Hinckley would not have been able to get that gun."

YES
BUT

It seems to be evident enough that, as the NRA claims, "guns don't kill people; people kill people." But because of the easy availability of guns, it is very easy for people to kill people with guns. In high school, a new boy enrolled one day, and within a week, everyone had heard that the reason he was so quiet was that a year earlier he had accidentally killed his brother with a gun. A week ago, we woke up to the news that a paroled murderer had held several people hostage in a downtown apartment and had shot and killed his girlfriend during the siege. Ten years ago, the same man had gunned down his wife in the parking lot of a hospital.

personal memory

media example

YES

I am well aware that there are many people in this country who use guns and are not cold-blooded murderers. My brother learned to hunt from my grandfather. He respects not only his guns but the land on which he hunts and the animals that he stalks. He lives a simple life, subsisting on the vegetables he grows and the game he hunts. Laws intended to keep guns out of the hands of people like John Hinckley will not interfere with his lifestyle.

BUT

close-up observation

But, to hear the NRA tell it, anyone who wants to make the purchasing of a gun at least as serious a proposition as buying a car or applying for a credit card is intent on taking away my brother's means of survival. One gun enthusiast I knew had NRA magazines piled up next to his bed alongside his chemistry textbooks. He used to study the ads for mail-order guns the way house-bound gardeners study seed catalogues in January. Playing on the analogy of guns as a symbol of freedom, the NRA has perpetuated a scenario of a Communist takeover easily accomplished because the conquerors obtain the lists that tell them about everyone who has had to register a gun. Many gun enthusiasts truly believe that they are keeping America free for democracy and that to register their guns is to endanger our freedom.

YES

Closer to home, many people feel that they have to have guns to protect their businesses or their families against armed intruders. It is true that every so often we read about an outraged citizen shooting down a burglar who brandished a gun. But police officers will tell you that most of the guns used by criminals were stolen by burglars in the homes of citizens who believe in the "right to bear arms."

BUT
quoted authority

Questions for Discussion How do you react to this argument? Do you think it would sway a member of the NRA? Why or why not?

Refuting Opposing Arguments
Sometimes, we need to meet opposing arguments head-on. We demolish the opposition; we systematically refute the arguments that stand in our way. The author of the following excerpted paper expressed a view that she expected to be unpopular with an audience of fellow students. She decided to present her arguments in an aggressive, assertive style, so that at the least her views would register and make her readers think.

WRITING SAMPLE: REFUTING OPPOSED ARGUMENTS

An Unpopular View

raising the issue   During the typical first-day "introduce yourself" routine in my speech class, a young woman announced proudly that she had served a two-year enlistment in the armed forces and that "every kid should have to do it." Most of the classmates balked at her suggestion, but for some reason I found myself seriously considering her idea. . . .

first objection examined   Many students feel that enlistment would interfere with their plans for a college education. However, many high school students take a year off before entering college. Six more months would not make a great difference. The armed forces provide financial incentives that can make the difference between a junior college and a university, or a Bachelor's and a Master's degree. . . .

second objection examined   Other students feel that enlistment would sidetrack them from their careers by removing them from the "real world." However, high school and college classroom "wombs" may do less than military service to prepare them for the real world of specific skills and responsibilities. . . .

third objection examined   Still others are apprehensive of the use of women in combat. However, there are dozens of options available to women other than combat or clerical work. When I took the Armed Services Vocational Aptitude test, at least forty percent of those taking the test were women. Their interests ranged from nursing to flight control or working on a Coast Guard cutter. . . .

Question for Discussion How do you react to this argument?

Reminders for Revision
When revising an early draft, pay special attention to points where your argument might slip a cog, where its forward movement might slow down. Advice like the following may prove helpful:

- *Dramatize the issue.* Consider starting with a striking example, a provocative incident.

THE WRITING WORKSHOP

Exploring the Pro and Con

Working with a group or your class as a whole, explore the pros and cons of a heated current controversy. Have one team explore in depth and then present the arguments on the one side. Have a second team explore and present the arguments on the other side. Use the results as material for a group report or as background for your individual pro and con paper. Choose a topic like the following:

- Is compulsory drug testing compatible with American traditions of privacy?
- Are AIDS victims entitled to protection of their privacy? Should they be obligated to tell employers (or insurance companies) of the state of their health? Are doctors and journalists justified in revealing the cause of death of prominent AIDS victims?
- Are the institutions of American democracy incompatible with secret intelligence activities, or "covert operations"? Do Americans have faith in or are they distrustful of agencies like the CIA? Do they condone or condemn the secrecy and deceit of intelligence work?

- *Revise sweeping charges and exaggerated claims.* Try to limit your claims to what you can support. For instance, modify or retract blanket charges. ("The average criminal is a brutal individual who deserves what he got.") Shelve cure-all remedies, or panaceas. ("To rid our streets of violent crime, we should lock up habitual criminals and throw the key away.")

- *Streamline your plan.* Try to smooth out bends and kinks; deal with backtrackings, overlappings, and detours that get in the way of the argument. Make sure you can chart the course of your argument clearly in your own mind.

- *Avoid the brush-off effect.* Revise passages where you might seem to be dismissing opposing views out of hand. ("This is another ridiculous proposal by our statehouse politicians." "Everyone knows that prison reform is a dead issue.")

- *Strengthen the logical links between steps in the argument.* Strengthen the network of links like *but, however, therefore, hence, nevertheless, consequently, similarly, in fact,* and *on the other hand* that holds an argument together.

Remember: A structured argument is different from a first brainstorming of ideas. Allow time for working out and strengthening your strategy. Try out your strong points on your friends and take their reactions into account. Take time to investigate and reconsider; take time to think.

EXERCISE 4   *Drawing Conclusions*

Assume that you and your classmates are studying a report that an American educator has prepared on the Japanese educational system. Key sections of the report follow below: a set of comparative statistics on Japanese and American schools, and a summary of conditions that provide the setting for Japanese education. Be prepared to discuss with your classmates the central question raised by the report: What can American schools and American teachers learn from these findings? What justified conclusions can we draw from them? What *un*justified conclusions should we avoid?

Statistics

Students graduating from twelfth grade:	Japan	90%
	United States	77%
Average daily hours of homework during high school:	Japan	2.0
	United States	.5
Daily absentee rate:	Japan	very low
	United States	9%
Years required of high school mathematics:	Japan	3
	United States (typical)	1
Years required of foreign language (grades 7–12):	Japan	6
	United States	0–2
Engineering majors in undergraduate population:	Japan	20%
	United States	5%

The Setting

The country has few immigrants and minorities. The divorce and unemployment rates are low. Drug problems are minimal, and juvenile delinquency is not a serious problem. The national Ministry of Education sets standards and prescribes curriculum for the whole country. University entrance exams are extremely competitive; newsmagazines carry pages and pages of stories and statistics about the examinations.

EXERCISE 5   *Cause and Effect*

> Chart the author's thinking in the following excerpt from a longer article. In your own words, what is the author's thesis? (What words and phrases echo the central idea later in the passage? Trace the network of *related* terms that help give the passage its coherence.) Chart the causes and effects outlined by the author. How does he *support* key points in his argument? How does he deal with possible *objections* or differing views?

James Fallows
THE JAPANESE ARE DIFFERENT

That the Japanese have a distinct culture seems to me an open-and-shut case. Some economists here have given me little speeches about the primacy of economic forces in determining people's behavior. Do the Japanese save more, stick with their companies longer, and pay more attention to quality? The explanations are all to be found in tax incentives, the "lifetime-employment" policy at big firms, and other identifiable economic causes. I'm sure there is something to this outlook, but I am also impressed by what it leaves out. We do not find it remarkable that the past 250 years of American history, which include revolution, settling the frontier, subjugating Indians, creating and then abolishing slavery, and absorbing immigrant groups, have given the United States a distinctive set of values. Is it so implausible that 2,500 years of isolation on a few small islands might have given the Japanese some singular traits?

Japan is different from certain "old" Western cultures because it has been left to itself so much. In the same 2,500 years the British Isles were invaded by Romans, Angles, Saxons, and Normans—and after that the British themselves went invading and exploring. Blood was mixed, and culture was opened up. During all that time the Japanese sat at home, uninvaded and disinclined to sail off to see what the rest of the world might hold. The effect of this long isolation was a distinctive culture *and* the isolation of a "pure" racial group, which tempted people to think that race and culture were the same.

I'm sure that someone could prove that the Japanese are not really mono-racial, or not clearly separate from the Koreans or the Chinese. The significant point is that as far as the Japanese are concerned, they *are* inherently different from other people, and are all bound together by birth and blood. The standard Japanese explanation for their horror of litigation and their esteem for consensus is that they are a homogeneous people, who understand one another's needs. When I've asked police officials and sociologists why there is so little crime, their explanations have all begun, "We are a homogeneous race . . ." Most people I have interviewed have used the phrase "We Japanese . . ." I have rarely heard an American say "We Americans . . ." "The Japanese Are Different from You and Me," *Atlantic*

EXERCISE 6   *Problem to Solution*

The following are rough notes showing a student paper in progress. To judge from these notes, what is going to be the overall strategy of the writer? How logical or how plausible is the overall pattern that is taking shape? What materials or details could you provide for some of the headings or topics that are sketched in only very briefly here? If you were writing on this topic, would you adapt a similar plan? How would you change it and why?

Starting the Clean-Up

Personal experience: A few weeks go, I was running on the canal road by my house with the sun just coming over the hills when I looked ahead and for a moment thought I was hallucinating: A large white truck was about a quarter of a mile ahead and a being in an oversize white suit with a hood to match was standing by the truck holding on to an enormous hose which was spraying a white liquid into the air; another white-hooded apparition was flashing a large white light up and down in an apparent warning gesture. . . . Recently, when I climbed out of the pool after a workout with my swim team, an attendant was putting up a "Danger: High Chlorine" sign (someone had left a switch open all night and 85 pounds of chlorine was pumped into the pool).

Main reason for our apathy about the polluting of our living space: We accept it as if it were an act of God or a natural catastrophe. This is especially true when the exact causes are hard to pin down. Example: acid rain.

However, in many cases the actual agents can be identified and pinpointed. Examples: strip mining and toxic waste dumped in rivers or imperfectly buried in inadequate sites.

The basic solution is a long educational campaign to promote *awareness*—create the feeling that something *can* be done. Start with symbolic acts—carry your own refuse back out of a wilderness area. Participate in tree-planting campaigns.

Next step: Organize, agitate, lobby to help fight the intermediate battles. Support recycling laws. Smog checks on cars.

Long-range objectives: Prepare public for the big battles—offshore drilling, slowing down nuclear industry.

EXERCISE 7   *Sample Paper: Eliminating Alternatives*

Study the following student paper and prepare an *outline* for it. Ask yourself questions like the following:

◻ What is the problem to which the alternatives examined in this paper are the solutions?

◻ Which alternatives are found wanting, and why?

◻ Which alternatives does the writer endorse, and why?

◻ What transitional sentences or phrases help us see the overall pattern of the argument?

◻ Where has the author turned for material?

◻ Which parts of this paper are for you most striking and effective? Which least?

The Dilemma of Prison Reform

In earlier times, serious crimes were often dealt with by physical punishments such as branding or mutilation. The ultimate punishment was dispensed in very harsh forms, including burning, beheading, hanging, and crucifixion. Compared to these older forms of punishment, our present system of imprisonment appears much more humane. However, the cruel realities of detention in today's dehumanized prisons are almost as harsh and inhumane as the older forms of dealing with lawbreakers.

Few people on the outside can imagine what it is like to be locked up for 24 hours day after day, and what a person in that situation goes through both mentally and physically. The smells are by far the worst. The fetid air with its odor of sweat, vomit, and urine seems to press in on the visitor. Couple that with the ever present undercurrent of violence and the terrible noise of a large cellblock and the result is a slow torture that is equal to anything that our ancestors inflicted.

What are the alternatives? Most of the literature written on penal reform agrees on one basic point: The system fails to rehabilitate most of the convicts, and an ex-convict is very likely to return to prison. The most common complaint about rehabilitation programs in today's prisons is that the trades or skills taught are often unrealistic or outdated. In one case, a prison in New York state provided prisoners with a course in driving diesel trucks. The course was very popular and received support from local charity organizations. The irony of the situation was that, once released, the ex-convicts found that the law barred them from acquiring a Class 1 driver's license for more than five years in most cases.

Other countries have tried different approaches to rehabilitation. In the province of Saskatchewan, in Canada, offenders have been allowed to work off their fines. Another alternative to serving time is a system that has been tried in Ottawa. This system is called diversion. In cases eligible for diversion, court proceedings may be halted if offender and victim agree on a settlement, as they do in the great majority of such cases. The offender pays his debt, in cash or work, to the individual victim or the community. The problem with such alternatives to incarceration is that public opinion in this country today pushes judges and parole boards in the opposite direction: The cry is for "getting tough" with criminals, for more prison sentences rather than fewer.

A system tried in Israel promises a solution to the problem of violence in prisons and fights among prisoners and to the sense of futility and lack of motivation that defeats many attempts at re-education and rehabilitation. The system divides the prison population into three groups, each with separate housing and differing privileges. The best-behaved prisoners are in the first group. Their privileges include longer visiting hours, the use of regular rooms to receive visitors, and unlimited movement within the prison. The second group has fewer privileges; the third group, the most violent, has the least.

The prisoners under this system are governed by the use of immediate rewards for good behavior according to a point system, and a prisoner can move from one group to another based on the accumulation of points. The system has caused violence to decrease as the result of the segregation of inmates and of the privileged prisoners' fear of losing their privileges.

Obviously prison reform is not a simple matter. What disturbs me is that in spite of the reports of numerous commissions and panels, few true reforms have been implemented in our overcrowded jails. Our record of failure makes me wonder whether our government is capable of dealing with more than the two or three popular issues that splash across the headlines during an election year.

THE HABIT OF STRAIGHT THINKING

How much does a writer need to know about logic? Traditionally, guides to straight thinking have been filled with advice on how *not* to think. Their authors castigate the human tendency to leap to conclusions, to find scapegoats for what goes wrong, or to mount elaborate investigations that conclude what the author believed in the first place. These guides to applied logic catalogue the most common **logical fallacies**, common kinds of defective thinking that skew our reasoning and make our readers distrust our ability to reach sound conclusions.

As a writer, you need not be able to spear every fallacy (or to call it by its Latin name). More important is developing the mental habits that protect you from common kinds of shortcut thinking.

Fact and Inference

The first step toward straight thinking is to realize that our ideas *are* the product of someone's thinking—preferably our own. We need to distinguish between observable facts (which can be verified by others) and the conclusions—right or wrong—we draw from them. We can see a car in the ditch; we can measure skid marks; we can take an injured passenger's pulse. The more factual a police report, the more it will stress exact time and location, the exact damage done to the car, or the observable condition of the victim. When we conclude that there has been an accident, we take a large step from fact to **inference**. We infer something we have not actually observed. Someone else might interpret the facts differently; they are subject to interpretation. An insurance adjuster, for instance, might investigate the chance that the accident was staged to defraud the insurance company. Moving farther away from the facts, we would arrive at inferences that need to be corroborated by further evidence:

- The type of car involved in the accident is unsafe.
- People in the driver's age group are careless drivers.
- Speed limits are too high.
- The driver was probably drunk.

To conduct a successful argument, you need to narrow the gap between fact and inference and to account for how you got from one to the other.

Limiting Your Generalizations

To argue convincingly, you need to develop the habit of limiting your generalizations. In a well-argued piece of writing, you work out cautious generalizations and support them well. After hearing case after case of neighbors' and friends' not bothering to report burglaries to the police, you infer that many citizens have lost faith in the ability of the police to protect them against theft. After learning that two more major downtown department stores are closing in order to move to suburban malls, you conclude that the city's efforts to revitalize the downtown business district are a failure. Such generalizations are useful and instructive when they take both supporting and contrary evidence into account.

However, when reasoning inductively, we tend to move ahead too fast, announcing the beginning of summer after the arrival of one swallow. Avoid **hasty generalization**; limit your generalizations to what you can support by an array of convincing examples. Make it a habit to scale down sweeping generalizations like the following:

> SWEEPING: Americans are the most generous people on earth.
> LIMITED: Although Americans are often accused of ulterior motives, other countries routinely turn to them for help in times of famine, earthquake, or economic collapse.

Consider advice like the following:

- *Aim at a representative sample.* What are the economic fortunes of professional athletes? We should not base our answer on headlines about football stars signed to million-dollar contracts. We need to investigate the salaries of the rank and file, of second-stringers; we need to check into the fate of players whose careers are cut short by injuries or by the changing policies of a team.

- *Be wary of inclusive terms and labels.* Reconsider sentences that begin with *every, all, anybody,* or the like. Use labels like *typical, normal,* or *average* with care. Occasionally, insert a cautious "frequently," "in most cases," "in ordinary circumstances," or "at least some of the time."

☐ *Lower the abstraction count.* Abstractions "draw away" from the messy detail of everyday reality toward general labels. Any paragraph carrying several abstractions like *freedom, responsibility, integrity, personal initiative,* and *civic duty* may already be in trouble. Tying one of these firmly to concrete reality is already a formidable task.

Question for Discussion Have you ever had to revise a hasty generalization—about teachers, police, a type of student, or a nationality?

Drawing Valid Conclusions

Just as we tend to move too fast from an isolated example to a general conclusion, so we tend to move too fast when applying a general principle to specific instances. Much deductive reasoning, taking us from accepted premises to justified conclusions, can be charted as a three-step argument, called a **syllogism**:

FIRST PREMISE:	All executives of the company are nephews of the founder.
SECOND PREMISE:	Biff Malone is an executive of the company.
CONCLUSION:	He must be a nephew of the founder.

FIRST PREMISE:	This fraternity admits no roundheaded Irishmen.
SECOND PREMISE:	I am a roundheaded Irishman.
CONCLUSION:	I am not eligible for this fraternity.

If the premises are true and the deduction logical, the conclusion is **valid**. In all of the above examples, the conclusion necessarily follows because the first premise applies to *all* members of a group—it includes or rules out all members of a group. Arguments that use *some* or *many* in the first premise are much less airtight. They are not true syllogisms; at best, they lead to a *probable* conclusion:

FIRST PREMISE:	*Most* members of the Achievement Club are business majors.
SECOND PREMISE:	Linda is a member of the Achievement Club.
CONCLUSION:	Linda is *probably* a business major.

Even when a premise uses a term like *all, no,* or *only,* we can easily draw unjustified conclusions. The word *all* includes all members of a group, but it does not *exclude* members of other groups; it often means "all these—and maybe others." When we overlook this nonexclusive nature of the word, we may be headed for a familiar kind of shortcut reasoning:

FIRST PREMISE:	All Marxists read the works of Karl Marx.
SECOND PREMISE:	My political science professor constantly quotes Marx.
CONCLUSION:	She must be a Marxist.

A rough chart of possible readers of Karl Marx will help us avoid this kind of **false syllogism**:

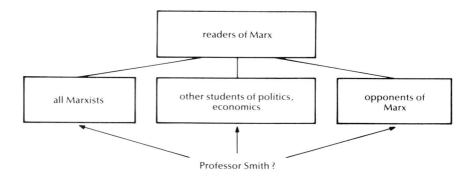

When you go from a general principle to a specific **instance**, make it a habit to think twice before you leap:

☐ *Examine your assumptions.* An argument may be technically valid; it may proceed according to the rules. But if it starts from unreliable assumptions, the results will still be untrue. When you present an argument like the following, your readers may want to challenge your **initial premise** rather than your conclusion:

Students learn best in a relaxed, permissive atmosphere.
The present system of exams induces tensions and anxieties.
Therefore, exams work against true learning.

(But is it *true* that a relaxed atmosphere is best for learning? Do not at least some people perform better under pressure?)

☐ *Spell out hidden premises.* Bringing unstated assumptions, or **hidden premises**, into the open gives you a chance to reexamine them. It also gives your readers a chance to see what underlying assumptions they are expected to accept.

PREMISE: Professor Metcalf is from a middle-class background.
CONCLUSION: She cannot be expected to sympathize with the poor.
HIDDEN PREMISE: (People cannot sympathize with someone from a different class?)

☐ *Avoid circular arguments.* Some arguments merely circle back to the initial assumptions. **Circular arguments** *seem* to move from premise to conclusion, but in fact they tread water:

CIRCULAR: True ability will always assert itself.
People of true ability see to it that their talents are recognized.
Therefore, true ability will not want for recognition.

Avoiding Logical Fallacies

Guides to logical thinking post frequent "Beware of the fallacy" signs to help us avoid familiar shortcuts, predictable detours, or blind alleys. To think productively, we have to resist reasoning that leads us down the slope to the too-easy answer or to what we want to believe. (See Chapter 14 for persuasive techniques—*ad hominem*, slanting—often included in inventories of logical fallacies.)

FOREGONE CONCLUSIONS   It is human nature to bypass contradictory evidence and to favor instead the evidence that reinforces a foregone conclusion. If you share a widespread prejudice against bureaucrats, you are likely to pounce gleefully on all evidence of bureaucratic bungling. You are likely to ignore or overlook useful bureaucratic activities, such as blocking the sale of a drug with disastrous side effects.

OVERSIMPLIFICATION   We are partial to the quick fix; we welcome the quick and simple answer to a complicated problem. Why is public transportation in such a sorry state? Why so many complaints about stalled commuter trains, late buses, or abandoned routes? One answer may well be the economic interests of car makers and oil companies. But we **oversimplify** if we ignore other factors. For instance, many people stubbornly use their own cars, braving congestion and pollution.

FALSE DILEMMA   A true dilemma puts us in a tight spot and leaves us only two ways out—both bad. A true dilemma faces medical researchers conducting animal experiments. Should they heed advocates of animal rights and abandon experiments that torture laboratory animals? Or should they continue experiments that promise to benefit suffering human beings? A **false dilemma** sets up a bad situation with only two ways out—while the author tries to block our view of a third. A false dilemma is often set up by people who want to push us toward an either-or choice. A developer might argue that the only alternative to further deterioration of a downtown area is to raze the area and rebuild. A third way out, tried successfully elsewhere, might be restoration and selective renovation. Many an "either-or" choice presented to us turns out to be a false dilemma.

POST HOC FALLACY   We tend to look for immediate, easily observable causes. We read about empty beer cans in the backseat of a car that smashed into a tree; these become a satisfying clue to why the accident occurred. *Post hoc ergo propter hoc*—Latin for "It happened *after* this; therefore, it happened *because* of this." Often, the *post hoc* fallacy makes us overlook more distant causes, or combined causes that work together to produce a result. Perhaps the beer cans had been in the car for some time, and the driver had a stroke. Someone gets married after the future spouse is left a trust fund—cause and effect? An office worker develops headaches after the company installs

THE WRITING WORKSHOP

Testing a Generalization

Researchers in the social sciences have developed elaborate safeguards against hasty generalizations and premature conclusions. Working with a group, test one debatable generalization about a current trend. Help plan and farm out different parts of the investigation: pooling personal experience of members of the group, arranging for firsthand observation, interviewing people in a position to know, or searching for published material. Help prepare a report that synthesizes the findings of the group. Test the generalization summed up in the following passage or a similar claim from an authoritative source.

Do women make better managers than men? According to a study by Marylee Bomboy of Cornell University, women are more effective in dealing with human relations and human interaction than men are. Female managers are likely to approach problem solving by considering the people and relationships involved, whereas men tend to approach the problem in terms of rules. Female supervisors are more likely to be rated "democratic" by employees; they are more aware than men of the need for creating a happy work environment.

a new computer—cause and effect? Remember that political, economic, or medical conditions are often the result of combined causes, perhaps with roots in the distant past.

FALSE ANALOGY A writer may compare the federal budget to a family budget in order to warn us against excessive debts or to promote the idea of a balanced budget. This analogy will sooner or later break down: A family cannot print money. It cannot raise taxes or implement policies that affect supply and demand. To make an analogy convincing, we have to trace the comparison through various related key features. Is the current world banking crisis similar to the situation that produced a crash in the thirties? If we were to answer yes, we would have to show several strong parallels.

RATIONALIZATION When we rationalize, we find comforting explanations for things that are unwelcome or unflattering. We find an explanation that will put us, or people close to us, in a better light: "I did poorly in algebra because the teacher did not like people from the South." (Therefore my possible lack of ability or effort is no longer the issue.) "Ambitious foreign-aid projects are often wasted when local populations are too backward to work with modern technology." (By blaming the locals, we absolve ourselves of charges of poor planning.)

Question for Discussion For which of the logical fallacies listed here can you give an example from your own observation, experience, or reading?

Remember: The best protection against shortcut reasoning is the willingness to reconsider. A reasonable person is willing to look at new evidence, to look at factors that might have been overlooked. We seldom approach any issue with a totally open mind, but at least we have to be open-minded enough to investigate further, to entertain doubts. We have to be willing to admit that our first impression (or a long-standing prejudice) might have been wrong.

EXERCISE 8 *Challenging Generalizations*

Study the generalizations in the following passages. On what level of generalization does the writer move? Which of the generalizations could you *support* with evidence of your own? Which would you *challenge*, and on what grounds? How would you scale down generalizations that are too sweeping?

1. Everywhere we see evidence of the new sobriety. Former martini drinkers drink white wine; former wine drinkers drink carrot juice; fraternities give parties without beer.

2. The turned-off, rebellious student questioning the educational establishment is an extinct species. Students today do not waste time arguing with a professor; they are eager to do what they are told.

3. We are all in favor of removing the traces of past discrimination. But the government has gone overboard in forcing the preferential hiring of minorities.

4. For the typical woman, divorce means financial insecurity and a lower standard of living.

5. Every week we read newspaper reports of college professors being challenged for teaching Marxist views. We are turning our colleges into centers of indoctrination in the Marxist view of economics and history.

6. Over and over we see movies that appeal to the vigilante mentality: First, we see a Charles Bronson type aroused by watching some ghastly unspeakable crime go unpunished; then we see him systematically hunt the criminals down.

7. The physical ideal for a woman in America today, I realized, was a man's body. The very curves and softness I had been trying to diet away were the natural qualities of a woman's body.   Kim Chernin

8. People like killers.   Ionesco

9. The mistakes of teachers are buried on the welfare rolls.

10. Never have as many people in our country lived openly in poverty and degradation.   Herb Caen

---

EXERCISE 9   *Sound Logic and Fallacies*

How sound is the logic in each of the following arguments? How sound are the premises? (Are there unstated premises?) What kind of logic is at work? How would you argue in *support* of the writer? On what grounds would you *challenge* the writer?

1. The main argument used by those, like myself, who believe in the existence of extraterrestrial civilizations is statistical. There are billions of suns. Some of these suns must have planets. As for these planets, the statistical chances are that some of them are habitable.

2. Public colleges are financed through taxes. They should therefore provide the kind of education that a majority of the taxpayers want them to provide.

3. Alcoholism is a terrible disease; therefore, beer should not be sold on college campuses.

4. The catalog makes it clear that this scholarship is reserved for business majors. As a music major, I need not apply.

5. Philip disappeared from the city a few days after the police started a crackdown on drug pushers. Philip must have been involved in the narcotics trade.

6. Where there is smoke, there is fire. If a public official comes under attack for misappropriating public funds, it is a good sign that some kind of wrongdoing has been committed. Officials accused of dishonesty should be removed before they can do further harm.

7. After the President ordered an air strike in retaliation for terrorist attacks on Americans, no further attacks took place during the following months. This shows that terrorists understand and respect the language of force.

8. A law has to be approved by the majority of the people before it becomes the law; therefore, everyone should obey the laws.

9. Students study because of the expectation of reward or the fear of punishment. Therefore, when there is no tough grading system to offer reward or punishment, students have no incentive to do their best.

10. There are cases on record of someone else confessing a murder after another person had already been found guilty of the crime "beyond a reasonable doubt." This proves that if we return to the death penalty, innocent people are bound to be executed, with no hope of a later correction of the jury's "mistake."

WRITING TOPICS 14 *Arguing a Point*

In writing on one or more of the following topics, aim at a reader who is wary of hasty generalizations and sweeping claims. Show that you respect the intelligence of your audience—rely on convincing evidence and sound argument to influence your readers.

1. Take a stand on an issue of current interest to students on your campus. Argue your position and support it with appropriate evidence, ranging from personal experience and firsthand observation to authoritative sources. Choose an issue like the following:

   □ Should students be forced to pay fees that support intercollegiate athletics—in particular, college football?

   □ Should college bookstores be required to remove *Playboy* and *Penthouse* from their shelves?

   □ Should colleges be required to offer equal support for men's and women's sports?

   □ Does official recognition or support for fraternities and sororities constitute discrimination against students not affiliated with Greek organizations?

2. A well-known critic of American society said some years ago, "there get to be fewer jobs that are necessary or unquestionably useful; that require energy and draw on some of one's best capacities; and that can be done keeping one's honor and dignity." Test these generalizations against what you know and can find out.

3. Write a pro-and-con paper about an issue on which there is something to be said on both sides. Do justice to arguments for and against. Aim at a balanced conclusion that will persuade a reasonable, well-informed reader. (You may want to state your conclusion as your thesis early in your paper, or you may want to lead up to it at the end.) Choose a topic like the following:

   □ Should citizens have the right to use arms in defending themselves against attackers or intruders?

   □ Should a major aim of instruction in the public schools be to promote one common national language?

   □ Should expressways and freeways have special lanes reserved for buses and cars carrying several passengers?

   □ Should government agencies be barred from damming the last remaining wild rivers?

   □ Should government agencies be barred from helping finance abortions for the poor?

      □   Should local governments be allowed to bar the homeless from their communities?

      □   Should drug testing be compulsory for people holding sensitive jobs?

4.   Write a paper in which you analyze major causes (or one single major cause) for one of the following. (Make a list of possible or alleged causes for preliminary class discussion.)

      □   unsafe city streets
      □   athletic success
      □   long-lasting marriages
      □   depression among young people
      □   charges of sexual harassment
      □   sexual discrimination
      □   high divorce rates
      □   the success of recent blockbuster movies
      □   popularity of television personalities

5.   Write a paper in which you critically examine alternatives in order to lead up to the one you consider most desirable or satisfactory. Choose one of the following topics:

      □   relieving traffic congestion
      □   combating sexual harassment
      □   promoting equal employment opportunities for minorities
      □   reducing vandalism at public schools or crime on campus
      □   securing better pay for women
      □   replacing the traditional family
      □   reducing drug abuse among young people
      □   countering violent or extremely rude behavior

6.   Do you hold any unpopular views? On an issue on which you have a strong opinion, are you aware of powerful objections or strong opposing arguments? Take on the opposition, using either a "Yes, but" or a "head-on" approach. Concentrate on refuting opposing arguments.

14

PERSUADING

The Strategies of Persuasion

*I have wondered whether we might legitimately try to intro-
duce . . . some new test for the exclusion of the inessential.
Suppose, for example, that we were permitted only to say
something that we could grow eloquent about.*
Kenneth Burke

*Raw emotion cannot win the day against opponents who
demand factual evidence, yet the dull recitation of statistical
facts may be meaningless unless you motivate readers and
get them involved.*   James D. Lester

THE WHY AND HOW OF PERSUASION Persuasion is the art of changing the
reader's mind—and the reader's ways. It aims at results: a product sold
or a bond issue passed; a change of policy or a change of heart. Most
other writing (except private notes and diaries) also aims at the reader:
We write to share information, to make our opinions known, to show
the logic underlying our arguments. Often we write for a double purpose: to clarify things in our own minds and to make our readers see
things our way. But in persuasive writing, swaying the reader, winning
the reader over, becomes the overriding aim.

The End and the Means We judge persuasive writing by how effectively it influences the
reader. Persuasive writers know how to motivate their audience. They
know how to overcome apathy and get their readers involved; they know
how to break down resistance. To produce these results, logical argument alone is often not enough. To make our readers care, we often have
to do more than argue logically and present the facts. To move people
to action, we need to stir their emotions; we appeal to their values. We

299

YOU CAN REALLY GO
PLACES WITH CRACK.

NEWSDAY

THE POWER OF WORDS How effective are these
messages? What gives them impact? How do they
affect you?

COCAINE.
THE
BIG
LIE.
CALL
1-800-662-HELP.

Ad Council · A Public Service of the National Institute on Drug Abuse
Department of Health and Human Services

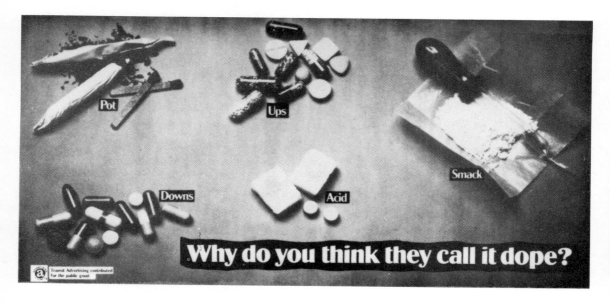

Pot

Ups

Smack

Downs

Acid

Why do you think they call it dope?

Transit Advertising contributed
for the public good.

try to arouse their compassion or their generous enthusiasm for a cause. Statistics about the slaughter of baby seals may remain dry and abstract. But a graphic account of the clubbing, of skinned carcasses and bloodied pelts, is likely to stir outrage. Successful persuasion is often the right blend of convincing logical argument, striking factual evidence, and effective emotional appeals.

The Uses of Persuasion Persuasion attempts to change attitudes or behavior. It often aims at a tangible result: a vote, a contribution, a subscription, or a sale. It often solicits support for a cause: to save a historical building or the wolves in Alaska. Addressing your fellow students, you might ask them

- to lend more effective support to the arts
- to help fight vandalism in living areas around the campus
- to protest (or to support) U.S. policy in Central America

Writing a letter to the editor of a local newspaper, you might ask people in your community

- to support (or stop) a new freeway project
- to provide more jobs for the disabled
- to build shelters for the homeless

Writing for the general reader, you might ask them to support (or challenge) stiffer no-smoking laws or stiffer sentences for drunk driving. Effective persuasion reminds us of the power of words: Words may not move mountains but they help move cars, shampoos, and deodorants; they create heroes, wreck careers, and derail political movements. The pen may not be mightier than the sword, but pamphlets have been known to be as explosive as grenades.

Questions for Discussion Where have you recently seen evidence of the power of words—to build or damage reputations, to make people care about an issue, to stir up protest, to arouse people to action? What techniques or strategies of persuasion were at work?

Targeting the Audience The first rule of persuasive writing is: Know your reader. Size up the audience. With a like-minded, receptive audience, we can build a strong sense of solidarity by voicing shared grievances. We can hiss familiar villains and champion the goals shared by the group. A newsletter for owners of small businesses and business executives is likely to find its audience receptive to proposals designed to "keep the taxpayers' money from going down the drain." This audience is likely to cheer at

THE WRITING WORKSHOP

Preparing an Audience Profile

Working with a group or with your class as a whole, prepare a set of **audience profiles** that would help an advertiser, promoter, or fund-raiser reach different target audiences. Help chart strategy and set up procedures. What groups should be targeted? What information should be included about the background, preferences, prejudices, interests, loyalties, or values of a typical member of each group? (Can you steer clear of stereotypes and oversimplification?) Possible target audiences for investigation:

- □ different types of students at your college, considered as potential customers (or as potential voters)
- □ minority students at your college (blacks, Hispanics, Asians, foreign students)
- □ public employees (police officers, social workers, office workers)
- □ women on campus considered as potential customers for a woman's magazine
- □ low-income, medium-income, and high-income voters in your community
- □ single, married, and divorced voters voting on school bonds

phrases like "derail the gravy train . . . slash the fat from government waste . . . crack down on inefficiency . . . blow the whistle on free-spending bureaucrats." The same newsletter, however, is likely to have a different effect on a *hostile* audience. For instance, for an audience of mail carriers, teachers, or social workers, cut-the-budget rhetoric will seem to promise belt-tightening, layoffs, speed-ups, and tinkering with pension rights. With a hostile audience, we may have to go out of our way to show our concern for interests different from ours.

Much persuasive writing aims at an audience between the two extremes—a fair-minded audience, open to persuasion. Fair-minded readers expect us to respect their intelligence. They tend to be wary of shrill language, cheap shots, and exaggerated claims. When we try to stir their sympathy or indignation, they want to be sure that we feel these emotions ourselves. They expect us to know the *limits* of persuasion. A fine line separates effective persuasion from propaganda, from hype and the hard sell.

EXERCISE 1   *Persuasion at Work*

Prepare a **critique** of an exceptionally effective (or ineffective) example of persuasion. For instance, choose a full-page advertisement, a newspaper editorial, a striking commercial, a fund-raising letter, or a promotional flyer for a candidate or a cause. (If you can, provide a photocopy, tape, or transcript of the original.) Explain what makes your choice effective or ineffective persuasion. What assumptions does it reflect about the target audience? What appeals or strategies does it employ? Does it have any features that are questionable or objectionable? What can a persuasive writer learn from this example?

THE TOOLS OF PERSUASION
What does it take to sway a reluctant reader? Some classic techniques, alone or in combination, occur over and over in writing designed to persuade. They are tools of the trade for preachers, promoters, social critics, or simply concerned citizens who make it their business to change people's minds or ways.

Establishing Your Authority
The persuasiveness of an argument often depends on the credibility of the speaker or writer. If you are to persuade skeptical readers, you may have to show that you are writing from inside knowledge, genuine commitment, or long-standing concern. Notice how the author of the following paper established his credentials. We gather early that this writer is writing as an insider, as someone who "was there."

WRITING SAMPLE: ESTABLISHING AUTHORITY

Too Drunk to Drive

We have all read blood-curdling reports on drinking-related accidents. Several people from my high school contributed to the drunken-driving statistics. In one case, a group of my friends left a beach party in a station wagon; the car was found a short time later wrapped around a tree. Of the five people in the car, four were seriously injured; two of them will be permanently impaired.

Nevertheless, I believe that in most of these cases raising the drinking age for young drivers won't help. Ideally, tougher laws should keep minors from drinking alcohol, but in practice they barely intimidate most. No matter what the legal drinking age may be, an underage party-goer can always obtain liquor. A major effect of raising the legal drinking age is increasing the number of false identifications. Some people cunningly doctor the date of birth on their drivers' licenses to show an earlier date. Others borrow someone else's I.D. I've been carrying a copy of my brother's license since I was sixteen and still use it as proof of my "official" age. In my home state, when the drinking age was raised, many students used various subterfuges to report their licenses missing and to obtain a new license with an adjusted age. Raising the drinking age does little more than to promote dishonesty and forgery; it is just another law to break—quite easily.

By the age of eighteen, a young person takes on a number of responsibilities. Eighteen-year-old citizens are allowed to vote for public officials and thus assume responsibility for the future welfare of the country. An eighteen-year-old criminal is tried as an adult, facing stricter penalties and a hard prison life. Part of an adult's responsibility is to face the dangers of drunk driving and act accordingly.

Raising the drinking age is an example of good intentions producing unintended adverse results. We should direct our efforts toward educating teens about drunken driving rather than toward more legislation. When a drunken driver hits your car head-on, the driver's age is not the issue. Drivers, young or old, have to learn to stay sober at the wheel.

Questions for Discussion Do you find this paper persuasive? Why or why not?

Dramatizing the Issue

The first assignment of the persuasive writer is to break through the crust of apathy—to get the reader's attention, to arouse concern. Accident statistics may make us shudder, but they do not jolt us as witnessing an actual accident does. When exhortations about violence in our cities fall on deaf ears, a single horrible event, involving someone widely loved or admired, can dramatize the issue.

Much effective persuasive writing starts with a "grabber"—a dramatic account of an incident that arouses indignation or compassion. The following beginning of a student paper dramatizes an issue by starting close to home:

WRITING SAMPLE: THE DRAMATIC LEAD

The Firing Line

I remember being awakened at about four o'clock in the morning. My parents told me they were leaving for the hospital—my brother-in-law, Art, had been shot. He had been at a small all-night store late that night buying some milk. A quarrel started in the store. As he stepped outside to avoid the whole scene, a car pulled up with three men inside. One of the men in the car shot at him, putting a bullet through his head. Art is now partially paralyzed in his left leg and arm, and he has restricted speech and vision.

Because there is little or no restriction on the purchase and use of guns, many innocent people are killed and injured every day. Looking through the local newspaper, I was amazed to find two or three articles a day dealing with gun-related deaths and injuries. One headline read, "Disturbed Composer Shoots Friend, Then

Kills Himself." An emotionally disturbed composer wounded a family friend who suggested he seek psychiatric help. After he shot his friend, the composer killed himself. A person in need of help was killed and a person trying to help was almost killed because a disturbed man with easy access to a gun pulled the trigger in a rage of frustration and despair.

Questions for Discussion Have you become apathetic about this issue? Why or why not? Does this writer's approach succeed in getting your attention? Why or why not?

Making a Plea Persuasive writers know when and how to speak out. True, sometimes we have to tiptoe around a subject in order not to alienate the reader. To defuse a controversial subject, we may have to be diplomatic. But ultimately, the reader wants answers to basic questions: "What do you want me to believe? What do you want me to do?"

Persuasive writers know how to give key ideas the proper **emphasis**—how to make key points stand out. They know how to sum up an idea bluntly, so that it will sink in:

Official war propaganda, with its disgusting hypocrisy and self-righteousness, makes thinking people sympathize with the enemy. George Orwell

Of all the drug problems afflicting the world, heroin is the most deadly and the one that most seriously affects American young people. Once addicted, the user needs cash to maintain the habit. The males steal and rob. The women become shoplifters and prostitutes. Horace Sutton

The author of the following passage knows how to speak out, how to make sure her message reaches the reader. Look especially at passages (italicized here) that *reiterate*—repeat and drive home—the central point:

Joan Ryan
GREASE, GASOLINE, AND DEATH

The sport that wears the undisputed crown of vapidity is auto racing. *Nowhere else in the realm of muscular activity is there such carefully constructed waste of time, money, and life.*

This weekend the city of Indianapolis is hosting approximately 500,000 people to create a two-day saturnalia out of the annual celebration of grease, gasoline, and death. To be sure, many look upon the trek to the Indy 500 as a sort of Midwest Ft. Lauderdale for celebrating the end of school. Thousands of college kids in camper vans descend on the city to drink, play, and toast complexions paled by too many hours in the library. They are the harmless infield spectators.

But the stands inside the Indy Speedway will be filled on Monday with hundreds of thousands of real racing fans. I can't help but think of them as sports vultures who come to watch the 500-mile race on the highway of death to nowhere, hoping that the monotony of watching cars flick by at speeds in excess of 190 mph will be relieved by mechanical—and human—catastrophe.

The beltway around Indianapolis is staked with grim white crosses, mute reminders to travelers of the fatal consequence of a too-heavy foot on the accelerator.

In 1966 there was a 16-car crash on the first lap, but—as auto racing fans triumphantly point out—no fatalities. It is a sport like Russian roulette—like rolling for snake eyes with your life on the line. Watching the race from the Indy grandstand is a little like watching hyperactive hamsters tread a cage wheel. The cars fly by like brightly painted berserk vacuum cleaners sucking the ground.

A sport that exists on the alluring promise of blood and death is no sport. It is a morbid vigil for human destruction.   Washington Post

Questions for Discussion   What would your attitude ordinarily be on this topic? Does the writer change your mind? Why or why not?

A persuasive writer knows how to keep after the reader. To achieve results, we have to insist, to persist. To build a strong case, a persuasive writer will lay down a barrage of striking examples, precedents, eloquent testimony, strategically selected statistics, dramatic case histories, or revealing inside information.

Appealing to Shared Values   Persuasive writers know how to motivate their readers. Sometimes, they can appeal directly to the readers' self-interest, touting the benefits of a product for the consumer or of a change of policy for the voter. Often, however, persuasive writers will try to appeal to the readers' standards, to mobilize their loyalties, to appeal to their better (and sometimes their worse) selves. Look at the following excerpts from an attack on huge damage awards for negligence assessed against businesses and individuals. How does the writer bring widely shared attitudes, feelings, and standards into play?

WRITING SAMPLE: THE COMMON BASE

Are You Insured?

appeal to our sense of fairness (extreme absurd example)

Courts are going out of their way to do away with traditional standards of fairness and shared responsibility. Increasingly, courts are disallowing the traditional defense of contributory negligence. One case involved a man who strapped a refrigerator on his back and ran a stunt footrace. One of the straps failed, and he collected $1 million from the strap manufacturer. . . .

appeal to our sympathy for the underdog

Little attention is paid to the limited financial resources of small businesses or of individuals. The costs of litigation and the enormous damage awards are driving small companies to the wall. . . .

appeal to our concern for
the public welfare
The effects on the pharmaceutical industry are especially harmful. Liability for rare side effects is driving many manufacturers out of the vaccine market, even in cases where medical opinion agrees that the good the vaccines do far outweighs the possible harm. Vaccines (such as those for diphtheria and tetanus) for children are steadily climbing in price. . . .

attack on selfish motives
Who benefits from the inflation of damage awards? The big winners (in case you had any doubts) are the lawyers. A Rand study found that a typical court case costs $380,000, of which $125,000 went to the defense lawyers, $114,000 to the plaintiff's lawyers, and $141,000 in net compensation to the plaintiff.

Using Persuasive Language

Persuasive writers know the power of words. They know how to use words that arouse and steer the readers' emotions, that channel their responses in the right direction. In the following passage, look at the words likely to sour us on "commercial civilization." Then look at the words that make us feel good about nature and individuals:

> Dams that *throttle* the Colorado River, tourism in Telluride and suburban *sprawl* *blurring* Phoenix into Tucson, bounty hunters and government coyote-*poisoners*, automobiles that *defile* the wilderness while they *slacken* the human body and spirit, all the *tacky trash* of commercial "civilization"—these are the targets of the author's irritable humor. . . . Against them he poses the *mysterious magnificence* of desert and mountain and the *saving vitality* of "human bodies and human wit . . . *united* in purpose, *independent* in action."   Annie Gottlieb, "Putting Down Roots," *Quest*

The italicized words in this passage are not neutral or value-free; they carry with them built-in reactions. They are meant to trigger responses, favorable or unfavorable, on the part of the reader. Some of the words—*tacky, trash, defile*—denounce or condemn. Some of the words are terms of praise: *magnificence, vitality, united*. But many words that are less obviously judgmental carry overtones of praise or blame; they help a writer influence our response. In the context of this passage, to *throttle*, to *sprawl*, to *blur*, and to *slacken* are clearly activities we should view with dismay. These words have negative **connotations**—they suggest unfavorable feelings or attitudes. Words like *united* and *independent* have positive connotations—they suggest desirable qualities; they put what they describe in a favorable light.

Note: While emotionally charged language can help us sway the reader, it can also set off wrong reactions. It easily becomes too pat: When we approve of people, we use labels like *entrepreneur, public servant, labor leader,* or *Washington representative*. When we disapprove of people, we use labels like *speculator, politician, union boss,* and *lobbyist*. **Catch phrases** like "tax and spend," "strong national defense," or "runaway arms race" lose their power to influence the reader; they become mere signals to the faithful, showing what side we are on. When writers let their emotions get the better of them, emotional language easily turns into personal insult, or **invective**. Terms like *redneck, gun nut, fem-libber, peacenik, eco-freak,* and *Uncle Tom* alienate fair-minded bystanders and bring out the worst in the opposition.

Aids to Persuasion
Experienced persuasive writers draw on devices designed to make their side look good and to weaken the case for the opposition.

SLOGANS Persuasive writers know how to sum up an idea or a program for action in a catchy phrase. **Slogans** like the following for a time (until they wear out) rally people to a common cause: *pluralism, computer literacy, affirmative action, comparable worth, right to life.* An imaginative analogy or striking metaphor—*spaceship earth, lifeboat ethics*—can help crystallize ideas and make them persuasive.

STRATEGIC COMPARISONS Comparisons can change our perspective; they can help us magnify or belittle a problem. Look at how the following passage puts an issue "in perspective":

> Japanese children are testing higher than any other children in the world. American children lag far behind, ranking with children in some Third World countries. The reasons for this astounding difference are obvious. Japan devotes 8.6 percent of its gross national product to education, the United States only 6.8 percent. To match the Japanese effort, we would need to spend about $1,000 more per student every year. Teacher pay in Japan is comparable with the wage levels in business, industry, and the professions.

THE BANDWAGON EFFECT When everybody seems to be moving in the same direction, the lone dissenter can be made to feel out of step. On subjects ranging from arms control to maternity leave, we can be made to feel odd to be going counter to what the rest of the civilized world believes.

EXPOSING CONTRADICTIONS Our sense of **irony** makes us smile at revealing contradictions in the position of people who disagree with us. Probing for weaknesses, we will often focus on such chinks in the opponents' armor. The author of the following passage looked with wry amusement at the spectacle of carnivorous Americans trying to stop Eskimos from hunting the whales on which they depend for food:

> Scientists, noting that whales exhibit more rapid growth than other mammals, have speculated that we may one day be forced to cultivate our great cetaceans to meet a world food crisis. When you consider that during a year's captivity at Sea World a young gray whale gained 10,000 pounds and grew 9 feet, this is a comforting

thought. Unfortunately these concepts are offensive to our well-fed society, although folks seem to feel no guilt at all about enjoying a "Big Mac" or buying beefsteak in plastic-wrapped packages. The stockyard scene, the plight of hothouse-raised, hormone-stuffed chickens and force-fed geese seldom concern us for long. Yet we pride ourselves on our compassion for sea mammals. Some of my Eskimo friends suggest that perhaps the best way to bring their point home would be to have every American personally kill and butcher one animal for his own consumption annually. Lael Morgan, "Let the Eskimos Hunt," *Newsweek*

Revision: The Limits of Persuasion
In writing and especially in revising a persuasive paper, watch for techniques that backfire with a thoughtful reader.

SUPERLATIVES Advertisements, editorials, and political speeches are full of **superlatives** or exaggerated claims. Most consumers tune out voices that promise "the best," "the whitest," or a "once-in-a-lifetime opportunity." Most voters have learned to discount inflated political rhetoric: "fatal to our most cherished institutions," "unparalleled in recorded history."

AD HOMINEM **Ad hominem** attacks, directed "at the person," shift attention from the issues to the personal lives of their advocates. Slurs aimed at a person's ethnic origin, marital history, sexual preference, or psychiatric record boomerang with a responsible audience. (Sometimes, of course, the person's honesty or personal competence *is* the issue.)

INNUENDO When we pledge to support welfare payments to the "truly needy," we imply, or insinuate, that others who claim to be needy are not truly so. When we claim that a candidate has been known to associate with kingpins of organized crime, we insinuate that their lack of ethics has rubbed off. Fair-minded readers resist **innuendo**; they expect us not to hint and whisper but to make charges openly and support them as best we can.

CHEAPENED IDEALS People cheapen shared ideals when they make a great show of patriotism or religion in order to sell insurance. Do not represent minor annoyances as threats to cherished American values. Let those who died at Lexington, at the Alamo, or at Pearl Harbor rest in peace. Many (says e.e. cummings) "unflinchingly applaud all/songs containing the words country home and/mother." But many also object to the use of such words to place a halo over the passing causes of the day.

SLANTING We slant material if we always (and too obviously) select only the evidence that supports our own cause.

THE WRITING WORKSHOP

A Letter-Writing Campaign

Working with a group or your class as a whole, help orchestrate a letter-writing campaign designed to influence decisions on a current local issue. Help the group identify an issue of urgent common concern. Help identify the audience to be targeted: officials, newspaper editors, local radio or TV stations, civic organizations, and the like. Assist in planning strategy and in the development of model letters. Arrange for a final evaluation of the effectiveness of the group effort. Some possible issues:

- ☐ saving a historical landmark
- ☐ saving trees threatened by progress
- ☐ permitting campus vendors or street performers to pursue their livelihood
- ☐ changing the route of a proposed freeway
- ☐ expanding public parks
- ☐ fighting or promoting a no-growth ordinance
- ☐ securing affordable housing for the elderly or for minorities
- ☐ constructing new jails

Questions for Discussion Have you observed a recent controversy where you thought personal attacks overstepped the limits—or where you thought they were justified? Do you ever object to the cheapening of shared values?

Remember: To avoid the pitfalls of persuasive writing, keep in mind the limits of persuasion. Readers with minds of their own do not like to be bullied or threatened. They do not like to feel manipulated or pushed.

EXERCISE 2   *Language in Action*

Examine the following examples of persuasive writing. What makes them effective or ineffective persuasion? Ask about each:

- ☐ What are the writer's aims?
- ☐ What are the writer's assumptions about the intended audience?
- ☐ What methods or techniques of persuasion does the writer employ?

- □ To what standards or values does the writer appeal?
- □ What use does the writer make of persuasive language?
- □ What are possible limitations of the writer's approach?

1. Consider this question from a standardized group IQ test. "No garden is without its ————." The desired answer is one of these five: "sun-rain-tool-work-weeds." A child who happens to know the expression will recognize the missing word (weeds) and complete the sentence "correctly." If he doesn't have that piece of information, he'll have to figure out the answer. He might explain to a tester, "It isn't 'tools' because I once planted a garden with my hands." But there is no tester to tell. He might continue, "I don't know how to choose between sun and rain, so I won't use either one." Again there's no tester to hear his reasoning. "So it's either 'work' or 'weeds.'" Another pause. "Well, if a gardener worked hard, maybe he wouldn't have any weeds—but, if he doesn't work at all, he won't have any garden!" Triumphantly, the clever, logical, analytical young mind has selected—the wrong answer!

    When a computer grades that test, "work" will simply be marked wrong, and no one will be there to explain the thought process to the computer. Nor will anyone point out the differences between the child who has personal experience with gardens and the child whose closest contact may be the city park, ten blocks away from his fire escape.   Arlene Silberman, "The Tests That Cheat Our Children," *McCall's*

2. We are encroaching on nature, in the U.S. and around the world, at an unprecedented rate. A large proportion of the chemicals in use in our present-day civilization were "invented" by nature, not by the chemist in the laboratory. An estimated 40% of all drug prescriptions in the U.S. contain as their chief ingredients compounds derived from plants. There is no end to the potential for discovery in nature, because we have only begun the chemical exploration of nature. Tragically, we are burning our library of priceless genetic treasures with our reckless destruction of species.

3. Day   1: I was conceived today. My sex, the color of my eyes, my physical features, and my special talents and gifts are already determined in my genes.

    Day   28: My heart started beating today. I think I will be strong and healthy.

    Day   49: All my vital organs are present. I have tiny fingers, feet, and toes. I can move my body, arms, and legs for the first time. My mother also could tell that I'm going to be a little girl if she wanted to. I have buds for little milk teeth, and you can record my brain waves.

    Day   56: I can grasp objects and even make a fist.

    Day   70: I have fingerprints and footprints, and I can suck my thumbs, fingers, or toes.

    Day   84: I am very sensitive to touch, heat, sound, discomfort, and pain. I have vocal cords, and sometimes I go through the motion of crying. I am also starting to look like my parents; I think I have my father's nose, and my mother's eyes.

    Day 112: I have fingernails, eyebrows, and eyelashes. I kick my feet and curl my toes. I think I'm going to be good-looking when I grow up.

    Day 114: Today my life was terminated. (Four months, two days)

EXERCISE 3 *Steering the Reader*

Study the two descriptions of the same place prepared by a student writer. How does she steer the readers' reactions in opposite directions? How much of the difference is due to the selection of detail? How much to the choice of language? How susceptible are you as a reader to the kind of influence these passages exert? (Your instructor may ask you to prepare two similar contrasting descriptions of a person, place, or situation.)

A. It is three o'clock on a Friday afternoon. A steady stream of students are busily moving their way through the ornate wooden door of the Airliner Bar on Clinton Street. Once inside, a mass of smiling and laughing people file up and down the aisles, drinks in hand and munching on the free popcorn. The yellow booths, besides the wear and tear over the years, support groups of talkative girls and boys happily discussing the latest in college gossip. The jukebox, playing the new Top 40 hit, spreads the "boogie" throughout the room: feet tapping with the beat below on the floor, fingers keeping time on the table tops, and those assorted others who "jive" up and down the aisles, meeting and greeting their friends. One walking on the sidewalk past the Airliner finds many a smiling person seated at the front window enjoying a pitcher of beer.

B. It is three o'clock on a Friday afternoon. A slow, steady stream of students are shuffling through the heavy, dark brown, splintering wooden door of the Airliner Bar on Clinton Street. Once inside, bodies are herded through the narrow, dimly lit aisles, grasping glasses of luke-warm beer and gorging themselves on burnt, greasy, over-salted popcorn. The floors are slick with unpopped kernels and assorted spilled alcoholic beverages. The yellow booths are scarred with various pen markings, cigarette burns, and slits in the vinyl patched with silver duct tape. The room itself is full of squealing girls, boisterous boys, and the jukebox blasting the latest Top 40 hit by the Rolling Stones. Those sitting at the window gawk at others walking by on the sidewalk, often making rude comments about those passersby who are physically undesirable.   Nancy Roberts, "Two Descriptions," *What Makes Writing Good*

EXERCISE 4 *Dear Editor*

Letters to the editor, ranging from eloquent to inane, are a favorite means of influencing the course of debate on current issues. Find a striking current example and photocopy it for discussion in class. Explore questions like the following:

□   What is the writer's aim?
□   Who is her intended audience?

     □   What methods or techniques of persuasion does she employ?
     □   How does she use persuasive language?
     □   What are special strengths of the letter?
     □   What are weaknesses of the letter or limitations of the writer's approach?

EXERCISE 5   *Taking a Stand*

Write a letter to the editor of a campus daily, local newspaper, or national magazine. Take a stand on a matter of current debate and try to sway the opinions of the reader. Try to make your letter persuasive for a reluctant or undecided audience.

THE STRATEGIES OF PERSUASION

In persuasive writing, your overall strategy, your game plan, is especially important. How do you make your point sink in, or how do you lead up to your point? You may start with a dramatic incident or example and then lead into your central plea or claim. You then marshal an impressive array of examples, evidence, inside information, striking statistics, and expert testimony in support. At other times, you may decide that you need a less direct, less head-on approach to put a reluctant or jaded reader in a receptive mood. Or you may decide to use a single test case, developed in painstaking detail, to drive home your point.

Cumulative Order

A persuasive writer will often start in a low-key or nonthreatening manner to reassure a wary reader. Then slowly the argument will pick up in intensity and build up to a **climax**. This kind of cumulative order can put the reader in an assenting, receptive mood. Once your readers have started to say "Yes, that's true" or "Yes, that's reasonable," they may be ready to say "Maybe this is also true" when you go on to a difficult or controversial point.

The following passages are excerpts from an article that starts in a low key, poking fun at "trendy young professionals" and "hip lawyers." The casual, amused, ironic tone assures us that the writer is not a fanatic who is always shouting at the top of his voice. But soon the tone gets more serious and insistent (*ruthlessness, gangsters, thugs*). Later the emphasis shifts from people close to drug traffic ("who might only be getting what they deserve") to innocent bystanders. We are well prepared for the writer's climactic charge in the final paragraph.

David Owen
BOYCOTT COCAINE

Among trendy young professionals in our major cities, there is no stigma attached to using cocaine. In particular, the hip lawyers, doctors, movie stars, and so on who use the drug are not deterred, or even bothered much, by the mere fact that it happens to be illegal. But perhaps they will be receptive to a more fashionable approach. After all, many cocaine consumers are the same sort of people who will boycott lettuce or grapes because farm workers are underpaid, or a cosmetic because the company tortures rabbits, or tuna to protest the killing of dolphins. . . .

Most of the coke sold in America originates in two South American countries whose preeminence in the drug trade is due mainly to the ruthlessness of their native practitioners. Several winters ago, rival gangsters broke into the New York home of an expatriate who was making a fortune importing coke from his native land. The thugs stole $15,000 in cash, abducted a ten-year-old son and a seventeen-year-old baby-sitter, and hanged the five-year-old daughter with a length of nylon Christmas wrapping. . . .

Murder is as much a part of cocaine culture as tiny silver spoons and rolled-up hundred-dollar bills. There is seldom a major coke bust that doesn't also turn up an arsenal of automatic weapons. In a recent year in Miami, the cocaine capital of the Northern Hemisphere, a quarter of the city's 614 murders were committed with machine guns. There was so much drug-inspired bloodshed in southern Florida that the Dade County medical examiner was forced to rent a refrigerated truck trailer to store corpses he couldn't squeeze into the morgue. . . .

The victims are not all businessmen, who might only be getting what they deserve. Cocaine hit men tend to be casual in their aim. "Children have been killed in cross fires, and so have innocent adults," says Brent Eaton, a special agent in the Miami division of the Drug Enforcement Administration. "We've had machine-gun fights as people were driving down expressways here in town. We've had people riddled with machine-gun bullets as they were waiting for traffic lights."

At the very least, cocaine has rent the social and economic fabric of two South American countries and fueled the decay of considerable sections of the United States. To buy cocaine is to subsidize a network of death and despair. Snorting cocaine is at least as bad for the planet as wearing a coat made from an endangered species. Join the cause. Boycott cocaine.   *Harper's*

Questions for Discussion How do you respond to this article? Does the writer come on too strong? Does he belabor the obvious? Are you the right kind of audience for this article? Why or why not?

The Test Case Sometimes, the most eloquent way to make a point is to document a test case in painstaking detail. One striking case, dramatizing the issue, may be worth many lesser examples. When we swim against the tide of fashionable opinion, we may decide to build our case around one single dramatic example in which the reader can get involved and that to a large extent speaks for itself.

In the paper that follows, the writer goes counter to fashionable popular opinion about the potential of the disabled. The germ for the paper was contained in a *journal entry* written earlier:

PREWRITING: JOURNAL ENTRY

I have spent much time around people with special needs. Several part-time jobs I have held served either the needs of the handicapped or the needs of hungry people. I worked as a dishwasher and gardener for a community kitchen that fed the poor. I drove a bus and participated in a recreation program for disabled children. Several years ago, while working on a construction job, a close member of my family fell thirty feet, breaking his neck. He sustained a spinal injury which left him paralyzed below the waist.

Look at the way the author uses a single test case to make the readers rethink their assumptions and expectations:

WRITING SAMPLE: THE TEST CASE

False Hopes

At an art gallery, there is an ink painting with detail so fine that it looks like a photograph. It was done by a brush held between the teeth of a totally paralyzed quadriplegic woman. In the newspaper, there is a picture of five men wheeling their *misleading media image* chairs down a muddy path. They have just completed a twenty-five mile backpack trip in wheelchairs. After winning a legal battle to win custody of her baby, an armless woman allowed the Red Cross to make a film of her performing her duties of mother and homemaker. She uses her feet to do everything, from driving her car to choosing tomatoes at the market.

The film was made in order to focus public attention on the capabilities of the physically disabled. The mainstreaming effort is causing these people to emerge from obscurity. They are encouraged to get an education, to work, to live independently, to marry and raise children—even to engage in athletic competition.

Many films have been made featuring disabled people who are overcoming their limitations. People like to see the underdog as hero, triumphing over odds. These success stories are inspiring, but when the media focus on these extraordinary individuals, the public perception of handicapped individuals begins to change. A grand illusion is being created in the public eye—that the disabled are capable of marvelous feats now that they are liberated from artificial restraints.

thesis Disabled people should not be expected to achieve standards set by the accomplishments of a small minority. At some point, every disabled person has to accept the limits a handicap sets for that person's life. These people have to learn to live with their disability and to work around it. They have to give up their right to many physical activities. When you are moved by the determination of a wheelchair-bound person, remember that these people are in the news because they are the exception to the rule. Let the visible handicapped people who strive to reach beyond their limits remind you of those who just can't.

case in point

The man I will call Jim suffered from paralysis caused by a spinal injury. No muscles worked below his shoulder line. One's first reaction to his condition usually was: "What a shame he can't walk." Looking into his condition a little further, one would learn that he also could not balance himself to sit upright in his wheelchair. He had only a fraction of his lung capacity to breathe with because the intercostal muscles surrounding his ribs were also paralyzed. Since all muscles were paralyzed, even those surrounding the blood vessels and capillaries were unable to hold their tone to keep his blood pressure or body temperature stable. Faintness, chills, and overheating were the result.

Yet Jim was made to feel that it was his responsibility to fight these insurmountable odds. His parents fell victim to the superquad image. On one visit, his mother brought along an article on a quadriplegic pushing his chair uphill, an exercise he undertook every day to stay in shape. The author attributed this feat to "hard work and determination." Jim's parents, hoping that their son could recuperate through hard work and determination, implored him to exercise.

Jim never allowed himself to dream of dunking a basketball; he was pleased to lift his own potato chip. In hopes of restoring some self-reliance, he once requested that we tie a string to his favorite TV dinners. That way he could pull one from the freezer; with one finger hooked in the loop he drove his electric chair backward, hoping the package would land on his lap and not on the floor. Then he tore open the box with his teeth. Of course, we had to upgrade the microwave oven and buy an expensive touch-controlled model so he could heat the thing. If he burned his hand taking the heated tray out, he didn't know it, for sensation in his paralyzed limbs was also lost.

We should support medical research to help amputees and spine-injured or brain-damaged people. We should give money to help find cures for crippling diseases, not to fund Special Olympics. This kind of support and your understanding are what disabled people need most.

Questions for Discussion What has shaped your own expectations concerning the ability of disabled people to "overcome their limitations"? Has this paper changed your thinking?

The Cause Célèbre A persuasive writer will often build a case by reexamining an incident already famous or well-known. An article may explore a famous court case or a much-publicized example of vigilante justice for the lesson we can learn from it. An opponent of nuclear power may retell in painstaking detail the story of Three Mile Island or of Chernobyl in order to convert us to the cause. To stir up readers who have become jaded about the

threat of environmental pollution, a writer may decide to retell in unrelenting detail the story of a much ballyhooed case in point, or *cause célèbre*.

Remember: Persuasion is effective when the reader revises an attitude, agrees to a policy, supports a cause, or makes the right decision. To produce these results, the persuasive writer needs a sense of where the readers are in their thinking (and, often, in their prejudices, mental habits, and loyalties). The assignment then is to move readers from where they are to where the writer wants them to be. Sometimes the best strategy is to confront the reader head-on, to state a message forcefully and to hammer it home. At other times, the best strategy is to take the reader to the destination by easy steps. The important thing is to *have* a strategy—to work out a plan that will use the writer's energy and resources to advantage.

EXERCISE 6   *A Review of Persuasive Writing*

Study the following newspaper column as an example of persuasive writing. Answer the following questions:

- □   What is the writer's aim?
- □   How does she size up the intended audience?
- □   What is the plan or overall strategy?
- □   What methods or tools of persuasion does the writer employ?
- □   What use does she make of persuasive language?
- □   How effective or persuasive is her approach?

Joan Beck
EQUALITY APPROACHES

The death or at least the dilution of the women's movement is still being freely predicted—not only by conservatives but also by a spate of sober sociobiologists and psychologists. Like it or not, the updated argument getting increasing attention in academic circles goes like this:

No evidence exists that there has ever been a human society where males were not dominant. Therefore some innate biological differences must cause and reinforce social patterns of male dominance. And even though we can remove educational, political, and economic barriers and change cultural expectations, women will never gain full equality.

What this old male supremacy argument in new sociobiological clothes overlooks is that now, for the first decade in all the eons of human history, women are not prisoners of their reproductive system. Only in this last eyeblink of historical time have pregnancy and motherhood not been the lifetime lot of women.

Because women are pregnant and mothering the young for only a fraction of their lifespan now, they have much less need to depend on males for provisions and protection—and much less incentive to play the old you-Tarzan-me-Jane games to attract dominant males.

At the same time, the risks of depending on men are increasing for women. Marriage is no longer an assurance of economic safety. Almost half of all married women are eventually divorced or deserted; most of those who aren't can expect to be widowed. In increasing numbers, women are coming to rely directly on themselves. And they are demanding equal opportunity to do so.

Today, the world no longer needs women to spend all of their adulthood bearing and caring for children. Mothering a two-child family is not enough to occupy a woman for five adult decades. Women need something else to do besides the dishes.

What the world does need women for, increasingly, is the same kind of work men do. As the burdens of inflation and taxation grow, it is increasingly necessary for women to take paying jobs if their families are to stay even. It now takes two incomes for many families to make middle-class; owning a home is impossible now for many families without a second salary.

Differences in physical strength between male and female are almost irrelevant today. Differences in mental abilities between the sexes are not evident through 12, 16, even 20 years of schooling; those apparent in later years are obviously due to differences in opportunities to continue to learn and develop. Women who have competed successfully with men until age 22, who know their college grades and scholastic aptitude test scores are just as good, are now much less content to settle for lesser jobs thereafter.

We are experiencing a long-term, major shift in relationships between the sexes. Like it or not, the historic reasons for male domination are dissolving. Whether there is any innate, biological basis for it won't be evident for decades, until the pervasive cultural overlay disappears—as it will.

We can do much to ease this transition: Strengthen marriage as a valuable joy for equals. Help resolve problems of child care. And change the world of work to accommodate the changing working force. But the pull of love, marriage, and children, and the joy of one sex in the other won't be lost.   *Chicago Tribune*

WRITING TOPICS 15   *Writing to Persuade*

As you write on one or more of the following topics, keep in mind three questions that are basic to success in persuasive writing: Who is my intended audience? What am I trying to achieve? What is my overall strategy?

1. Write a paper in which you persuade other students to opt for or against a law or regulation designed to promote the public welfare:

- □ a maximum speed limit
- □ a higher (or lower) driving age
- □ a higher (or lower) drinking age
- □ a smoking ban in public places or in the workplace
- □ special reserved lanes for buses and car pools
- □ mandatory use of helmets for cyclists or bicycle riders
- □ compulsory use of seat belts
- □ compulsory use of air bags
- □ warning labels for records with objectionable lyrics

2. Addressing yourself to the general public, write a paper "In Defense of . . ." an organization or institution whose critics claim its time has passed: the Boy Scouts, the fraternity system, ROTC, the D.A.R., the Democratic party, labor unions, college football, the nuclear family, the family farm. Or write to persuade supporters of the institution that the time has come for serious change.

3. Take on a reluctant or hostile audience and persuade them to change their attitudes or their ways. Know your readers: Read, investigate, interview to develop a good sense of what you are up against. For instance, try to do one of the following:

- □ persuade confirmed smokers to give up smoking
- □ persuade members of the National Rifle Association (or unaffiliated gun enthusiasts) to support some form of gun control
- □ persuade firm believers in the separation of church and state to allow recognition of religious holidays by schools or public agencies
- □ change the minds of people with strong views about the legalizing of marijuana
- □ change the minds of feminists (or civil libertarians) about the "war against pornography"
- □ change the minds of an audience with strong pro-abortion or anti-abortion views
- □ change the minds of tradition-bound males about the need for changing gender roles
- □ persuade fans of horror movies to support efforts to reduce violence in movie and television fare for young Americans

4. Do you feel that people have become too jaded about an issue that has received much media exposure? Write a paper in which you try to counteract public apathy about a familiar issue like environmental pollution, racial prejudice, sexual harassment, nuclear safety, neglect of the mentally ill, a rising divorce rate, or urban crime.

5. Write a promotional letter in which you champion a cause dear to your heart, such as community support for the arts, better employment

opportunities for the disabled, Little League baseball, exchange programs for foreign students, or the like. Try to make your letter persuasive for readers wary of huckstering or promotional hype. Try to find fresh and effective ways to enlist support for your cause.

6. Write a guest editorial or guest column for a student newspaper in order to help improve the public image of a group to which you have personal ties or in which you have a special interest. Try to change your readers' minds about a group that you think has received undeserved negative publicity: politicians, rock musicians, welfare recipients, illegal immigrants, producers of television commercials, yuppies, police officers, participants in beauty contests.

Part Four

THE WRITER'S TOOLS

How can you build up your confidence and extend your range in using words, sentences, and paragraphs—the basic tools of a writer? To use **words** effectively, you have to be a word watcher—alert to their meanings and overtones, to their manifold uses and unintended side effects. Writers who are good at "putting it into words" use more of language than routine conversation. To write better **sentences**, you need to develop your ear for the patterns and rhythms of the English sentence. You need to broaden your repertory, practicing sentences that focus clearly on the topic, highlight the point, and work in all needed details. To write more effective **paragraphs**, you can profit from the example of writers who know how to make a point and follow through. Inexperienced writers tend to underdevelop; experienced writers dwell on a key idea, supporting it, tracing its ramifications, until the reader is ready to say: "I see what you mean." When you study words, sentences, and paragraphs, remember to see them as parts of the whole. Judge them in context; try to see how they serve the writer's purpose. Whatever limbering-up exercises you do—work study, sentence building, paragraph practice—try to make sure that the results carry over into your actual writing.

15

THE WORD

Words Right for the Purpose

Via eye and ear, words beyond numbering zip into the mind and flash a dizzy variety of meaning into the mysterious circuits of knowing. Frank Tippett

Our language should be specific and concrete, eloquent where possible, playful where possible, and personal so we don't all sound alike. Edwin Newman

An honest writer makes every word pull its weight.
Ken Macrorie

THE RIGHT WORD In effective writing, we use *more* of language than we ordinarily do. We choose the words we need from a range of related words. The vocabulary of a good writer is like a memory bank that stores not only the single word *glad* but also many **synonyms**, or words with similar meaning (*delighted, gratified, pleased, lighthearted, happy*), as well as **antonyms**, or words with nearly opposite meaning (*sad, blue, dejected, downcast, heavyhearted, depressed*).

Which is the right word? From the rich inventory filed in the language centers of the brain, you need to retrieve the word that best serves your purpose. When you label an action a *crime*, you take it very seriously; you want the reader to think of it as a serious punishable breach of the law. When you call the same action an *offense*, you seem to judge it less severely. When you call it a *sin*, you identify it as a violation of a higher moral or religious law, whether the law of the courts recognizes it as an offense or not. When you call it a *vice*, you class it as a habitual, well-established pattern of behavior that degrades or corrupts the person involved.

In much technical and practical writing, the best word is the most literal, objective one. When writing to give accurate information about equipment, you will be using terms like *modem, digital,* or *analog* (remembering that such terms may have to be explained to the outsider). However, when writing about people, when dealing with ideas and emotions, you will be looking for words that can flash vivid images before the mind's eye or that can stir the reader's emotions. (One writer called prisons "vertical cemeteries.") A passage like the following helps the reader see, feel, and imagine:

> The historic function of the American school, and especially of the high school, has been to serve as a social and economic *ladder*—though today's school personnel, referring to a more passive clientele, sometimes thinks of it as an *escalator.*   Edgar Z. Friedenberg

The right word makes your readers see and feel what you want them to see and feel. The word that is right for one audience may be wrong for another. A campus group using words like *buddies, blast,* and *laid-back* in an informal party invitation is not likely to use those words in a letter apologizing to the dean after the party got out of hand. Part of the search for the right word is avoiding words that might have unintentional side effects, misleading or alienating the reader.

Accurate Words

You learn new words by watching them in action but also by studying them in dictionaries and other word books. The purpose of such vocabulary building is not to impress a reader with words like *quintessential* but to develop a diversified vocabulary for a wider range of information and ideas. In serious writing, we use much of the common stock of language, but we also use words that tell our readers more than a more familiar, all-purpose word might: To be *autonomous* is to be independent—but completely independent and self-ruled, not directed by any other authority. *Coercion* is force—but it is crude, resented force that compels people against their will.

A diversified vocabulary enables you to do the fine-tuning that makes words bring in exactly the right meanings and associations:

WORD	GENERAL MEANING	SPECIAL ASSOCIATIONS
incongruous	out of place	sticking out in a weird or ridiculous fashion
lucid	clear	making something *exceptionally* clear that might otherwise have been muddy or obscure
precarious	risky	already tottering on the brink
spurious	false	claiming to be authentic but actually completely fake

Specific Words When we write about the concrete examples or situations that bring ideas to life, we need specific words that bring the reader close to first-hand experience. Words that remain too general keep people and events colorless and anonymous:

GENERAL: An unidentified individual relieved the passer-by of his valuables.

SPECIFIC: The mugger made the dazed tourist hand over his digital watch, airplane tickets, and crammed wallet.

GENERAL: Rodeo artists lived a strenuous life, eating poorly, always exposed to injury.

SPECIFIC: Rodeo artists lived off hot dogs at county fairs and ruptured their intestines while twisting the necks of steers.

A first step toward bringing color and life into pale sentences is to call things by their names. Instead of lumping something in a general category, use names that call up shapes, textures, and colors. "Small animal" is colorless; *gopher, chipmunk, squirrel,* and *raccoon* call up contours, movements, habits.

GENERAL	SPECIFIC
tree	birch, elm, pine, fir, eucalyptus, poplar, cypress
weeds	dandelion, crabgrass, tumbleweed, thistle

As a second step, extend your range of **concrete** words—words that appeal to our five senses. They bring us close to what we can see, hear, and feel; they seem to conjure up sights, sounds, smells, textures, and motions. The concrete words in the following passage from a *New Yorker* article make us feel what it is like to be pitched about the deck of a lurching boat:

As the boat *lurches*, pails and shovels go *flying* from one side of the deck to the other; foul-weather gear hanging on a clothesline by the port bulkhead *swings out* until it is nearly horizontal, *slaps back* against the wall, and *swings out* again. A pot *skitters* past me across the engine housing, *smacks* the bulkhead, and *falls open* on the deck. Fried chicken—an enormous amount of fried chicken—*tumbles* out.   James Stevenson

Technical Terms We use **technical terms** where they are clearly useful or functional, making sure they are clear to the newcomer or outsider. A mechanic cannot operate efficiently without terms like *carburetor, alternator,* or *differential*. Science, engineering, medicine, and many other fields rely on precise, impersonal technical language to convey reliable specialized information:

TECHNICAL: High-yield airbursts will chemically burn the nitrogen in the upper air; converting it into *oxides of nitrogen*; these, in turn, combine with and destroy the protective *ozone* in the Earth's *stratosphere*.   Carl Sagan on nuclear winter

TECHNICAL: The *primates* are our nearest biological relatives; they have the same *neurochemical* pathways that mediate *affective states* like anxiety and apprehension—emotions once thought to belong only to humans.

Like the best technical writing, these sample passages use vigorous plain English (*airbursts, burn, destroy, pathways*) along with the necessary technical terms. Make sure technical language does not confuse or befuddle the outsider: Explain and illustrate new or difficult terms. In a paper on a mountain-climbing trip, you may need to define terms like the following:

bivouac: a temporary encampment in the open, with only tents of an improvised shelter

traverse: to move sideways across a mountain slope, making a slanting path

Denotation and Connotation

Words carry attitudes and emotions as well as information. They do not just report; they praise and condemn, warn and reassure, poison and heal. *Demagogue, politician, mercenary, speculator, crony,* or *bureaucrat* do not simply point to people. They point the finger; they reveal the likes and dislikes of the speaker. We call the added freight of attitudes, feelings, or value judgments the **connotations** of a word. Many words denote—that is, point out or refer to—roughly the same objects or qualities. But they connote—that is, suggest or imply—different attitudes, ranging from approval or admiration to disapproval or disgust. A *demagogue* was once literally a "leader of the people," but now the word vents our resentment at being led by the nose.

Connotative words most commonly mirror our likes and dislikes. When we like the bright colors of a shirt, we call it *colorful*; when we dislike it, we call it *loud*. But connotations often activate feelings more complicated than simple approval or disapproval. For example, the term *parenting* implies an enlightened or earnest view of the task; *biological father* sounds cold and uncaring; *stepmother* carries the burden of a centuries-old negative stereotype.

Words with the right connotations are a basic tool of persuasion. A discussion of the Japanese educational system will steer our reactions one way if it uses terms like *respect for authority, memorization,* and *discipline;* it will steer us another way if it uses terms like *submissiveness, rote learning,* and *regimentation.* You have to remember, however, that words carrying an emotional charge may set off the *wrong* reaction on the part of the reader. Some words are too negative (or too favorable) for what you are trying to say:

JARRING: She sings music that pleases listeners of all races and *emits* a feeling of love and warmth. (The word *emit* is too cold; we expect something to "emit" radiation or shrill sounds of warning.)

REVISED: She sings music that pleases listeners of all races and *creates* a feeling of love and warmth.

Questions for Discussion Why do some organizations representing the disabled prefer *disabled* to *handicapped?* What difference does it make? Is *hearing-impaired* better than *deaf?* Why or why not?

EXERCISE 1   *The Right Word*

Ernest Hemingway was known as a stickler for the right word—the word that accurately carried information or created the right picture in the reader's mind. Look at the general, colorless word at the beginning of each of the following sentences. Then compare it with the more concrete word that Hemingway used in one of his short stories. What does the concrete word add to the more general meaning?

1. (throw) The handler had *pitched* the bundle out of the door of the railroad car.
2. (move) The river *swirled* against the logs of the bridge.
3. (rock) There were big *boulders* at the bottom of the stream.
4. (flow) A mist of sand gravel was raised in *spurts* by the current.
5. (reflection) Looking for the river, Nick caught *glints* of the water in the sun.
6. (turn) These were not big grasshoppers with wings *whirring* out from their sheathing.
7. (eat) He saw the grasshopper *nibble* at the wool of his sock.
8. (shiny) The jointed belly of the grasshopper was black, *iridescent.*
9. (branch) Nick broke off some *sprigs* of the heathery fern.
10. (piece) With the ax he slit off a large *slab* of pine.
11. (stand) Around the *grove* of trees was a bare space.
12. (burn) When he tucked the chips under the grill, the fire *flared* up.
13. (fill) Nick *dipped* the coffeepot half full of water.
14. (noise) The mosquito made a satisfactory *hiss* in the flame.
15. (fog) He saw a *mist* rising in the swamp across the river.

EXERCISE 2   *Using Concrete Language*

Using language that is as specific and concrete as possible, write a paragraph that describes a scene or event. For instance, help the reader imagine the setting, the sights and sounds, the movements, colors, and textures of a rally, a subway commute, an episode from a wrestling match, a revival meeting. Rely on fresh observation; avoid stereotyped description.

EXERCISE 3   *Making the Abstract Concrete*

Write five two-part sentences that first state a general idea and then make it concrete by means of a striking example. Use specific language to make the abstract concrete.

EXAMPLE 1:   The phrase "mass culture" conveys emotional overtones of passivity; it suggests someone eating peanuts at a baseball game.   Northrop Frye

EXAMPLE 2:   We are more interested in success than in failure; we are more interested in the exploits of upwardly mobile young entrepreneurs than in the stories of people who spend their nights sleeping on heating grates.

EXAMPLE 3:   Many young people today are always in a hurry; they are on the go so much that their answering machines answer the phone more often than they do.

EXERCISE 4   *Reading for Connotations*

What is the shared meaning, or shared denotation, for the words in the following sets? How do they differ in connotations—in the attitudes or feelings they bring into play, in the associations they bring to mind?

1.   *loving* parents—*doting* parents
2.   a *complex* task—*complicated* instructions—*elaborate* preparations
3.   an *average* performance—a *mediocre* play
4.   a *break* with tradition—a *departure* from customary procedure—a *deviation* from established practice
5.   *workers* in Detroit factories—wages for *laborers*—company *employees*
6.   a current *movie*—a new *film*—a current *flick*
7.   the governor was *mistaken*—the President was *misinformed*— the senator was *wrong*

8. the *smell* of the perfume—a new *scent*—a delicate *fragrance*
9. a *bold* move—a *rash* decision—a *courageous* step
10. a belated *compromise*—an *accord* was reached—the hostage *deal*
11. an *intelligent* reply—an *intellectual* pursuit—a *cerebral* approach
12. a *frivolous* question—a *lighthearted* reply—a *silly* gesture
13. *ruined* the crops—*devastated* the city—*ravaged* the countryside
14. a *mysterious* event—an *enigmatic* response—a *mystical* experience
15. *acquitted* after a long trial—*cleared* of the charges—*vindicated*

EXERCISE 5   *Steering the Reader's Reactions*

Write three pairs of sentences, with each sentence in the pair describing the same situation, people, or event. Each time, use words with different connotations to suggest different attitudes or a different perspective toward what you describe.

> EXAMPLE: Each year, more derelicts loiter in downtown parks, panhandling for quarters from passers-by, and waiting for handouts from local do-gooders.
>
> Each year, more homeless people wander about the downtown parks, reduced to begging for a living and depending on donations from local charities.

Figurative Language Figurative language brings color into the black and white of literal speech. Effectively used, it can light up a whole sentence or paragraph. Figurative language employs imaginative comparisons, or **figures of speech**, to exploit the similarities that will translate ideas into striking images, that will set static concepts in motion. A brief comparison signaled by *as* or *like* is called a **simile**: "In much modern fiction, happiness is found only briefly and in unexpected places, *like a flower growing in the crack of a sidewalk*." An implied comparison that presents one thing as if it actually were the other is called a **metaphor**: "For many beginning poets, the traditional rhymed four-line stanza is *a jug into which the syrup of verse is poured*." An **allusion** is a brief mention that brings to mind a familiar story or set of facts; it makes us transfer the appropriate ideas or attitudes from the original to a parallel situation: "We are all *Custer*."

Figurative language accounts for much of the color and life of ordinary language: *whistleblower, hiring freeze, insurance crunch, deep pockets, brain drain, population explosion, green revolution, fast breeder*. Effective writers use fresh, well-chosen figurative expressions to catch our attention and to make us see the point:

> In this movie, "understanding" is sprinkled onto both sides of the conflict *like meat tenderizer.*   Peter Rainer

> Getting complete sentences out of him was like trying to put together *Homo sapiens* from a *few bones in a cave.*   Anita Strickland

Some figurative expressions, though already familiar, still have some mileage on them; to change the metaphor, they still serve as a convenient shorthand for ideas:

> Corporate law practice has always been *the Rolls-Royce* of legal careers.   Fred Graham

> A graduate student looking *for the fast track* at a university tends to avoid controversy.

But the most effective uses of imaginative language are those that make us take a fresh look, that make us take pleasure in an apt parallel that we had not thought of:

> The great economists of the last generation communicated their theories to a broad audience but *left few spores* within the profession.

> People who keep a journal turn experience into words before the sun sets twice; sometimes, *like dry cleaners, they give same-day service.*

Observe cautions like the following:

☐ *Figurative expressions should be apt.* The implied analogy has to fit, (and fit well):

> APT: In many of the author's stories, language is *like signals from vessels in distress, telling us of desperate needs.*
> (Distress signals are a particularly urgent kind of language.)

> INEPT: *Lacking the ignition* of advertising, our economic engine would run at a slower pace.
> (An engine without ignition would not run at a slower pace; it would just be dead.)

Reaching for a striking image, we can easily strain our metaphor. Imaginative comparisons should create a graphic image in the reader's mind, but sometimes the image becomes *too* graphic:

> DISTRACTING: Helplessly, Fred watched from his desk while his stomach tied itself into knots.
> REVISED: As Fred watched the event helplessly from his desk, he experienced a sick, tense feeling in the pit of his stomach.

THE WRITING WORKSHOP

A Way with Words

Good writing is where we find it. Good writers in any field use vivid, concrete language that conveys exact shades of meaning. A psychologist writing about our memories of special events might write in a dry, flat style like the following:

> We forget most things that happen to us, or they become confused with similar events. But a few memories stand out from among the sequence of forgotten events of which they were a part. . . .

Contrast this version with a passage on the same topic written by a psychologist with a gift for vivid, concrete, imaginative language. Working with a small group, or with your class as a whole, look in the following passage for wording that zeroes in on specifics, that gives us glimpses of concrete experience, and that uses figurative language—familiar or new—to create images, things that we can see and imagine. Then find a similar passage using exact, concrete, vivid language from a field of special interest to you. Photocopy the passage for examination and discussion by members of your group.

> We forget most things that happen to us, or they blur into similar events. . . . But a handful of memories shine out as vividly as a string of lights in the series of forgotten events tying them together. We don't have to deduce them or reconstruct them; nor does our recollection of them depend upon being in a mood similar to the one in which they originally took place. Flashbulb memories, as they have been labeled, are rather special. They are simply *there*, ready to appear in stunning detail at the merest hint. It's as if our nervous system took a multimedia snapshot of the sounds, sights, smells, weather, emotional climate, even the body postures we experience at certain moments.
>
> We remember the exact look, sound, and feel of a traffic accident; the midnight phone call bringing word of a loved one's death; the voice, manner, and surroundings of the doctors who broke the news of a serious illness; the fleeting twinge of pain that appears on a President's face as he is hit by an assassin's bullet and just before he is pushed to the floor of the limousine by a bodyguard.   Beryl Lieff Benderly, "Flashbulb Memory," *Psychology Today*

□ *Figurative expressions should be consistent.* If several figurative expressions appear together, they should mix well; they should blend into a harmonious whole:

> Everyone who is born holds *dual citizenship*, in *the kingdom* of the well and in *the kingdom* of the sick. Although we all prefer to use only *the good passport*, sooner or later each of us is obliged, at least for a spell, to identify ourselves with the citizens of that other place.   Susan Sontag

Avoid the **mixed metaphor,** which at first sails smoothly along and then suddenly jumps the tracks (hard to do on the trackless sea). Mixed metaphors create the impression that you are not listening to what you are saying:

CONSISTENT: If the new industrial robots have become the *arms and eyes* of our factories, computers have become their *brains.*

MIXED: America's colleges are the *key* to national survival, and the future of the country lies in their *hands.*   (Keys do not have hands.)

Remember: A writer with an impoverished vocabulary can give us only a highly generalized, blurry view of the world. If language is a net in which we catch glimpses of reality, a net that is not meshed finely enough will let much of reality slip through.

EXERCISE 6   *Figurative Language in Action*

Find and discuss figurative expressions in the following passage. What images or associations do they bring to mind? Which of these figurative expressions are familiar? Which are fresh or provocative? (Which are familiar but used or adapted in new ways?) Are any of them sustained or extended metaphors—carried through into several related details?

A great many words bring along not only their meanings but some extra freight— a load of judgment or bias that plays upon the emotions instead of lighting up the understanding. These words deserve careful handling—and minding. They are loaded. Such words babble up in all corners of society, wherever anybody is ax-grinding, arm-twisting, back-scratching, sweet-talking. Political blather leans sharply to words (*peace, prosperity*) whose moving powers outweigh exact meanings. Merchandising depends on adjectives (*new, improved*) that must be continually recharged with notions that entice people to buy. In casual conversation, emotional stuffing is lent to words by inflection and gesture: The innocent phrase, "Thanks a lot," is frequently a vehicle for heaping servings of irritation. Traffic in opinion-heavy language is universal simply because most people, as C.S. Lewis puts it, are "more anxious to express their approval and disapproval of things than to describe them."

The trouble with loaded words is that they tend to short-circuit thought. While they may describe something, they simultaneously try to seduce the mind into accepting a prefabricated opinion about the something described.   Frank Tippett, "Watching Out for Loaded Words," *Time*

EXERCISE 7   *Responding to Imaginative Language*

Point out uses of metaphorical and other figurative language in the following examples. Which are sustained or extended metaphors? Which are allusions? What images does each figure of speech call up? What emotions or attitudes does it activate? What associations does it bring into play?

1. If life is in some sense a status race, my parents never noticed the flag drop.   Aristides
2. It seems to me that any number of people have been through earthquakes in their private lives that haven't even made a crack in the walls of their philosophy.   Ellen Goodman
3. Each generation must get on the same old merry-go-round, only disguised in a new coat of paint.   Katherine Anne Porter
4. The last of the cyclical postwar recessions was ending, and a quarter century of burgeoning prosperity was on the launch pad.   Laurence Shames
5. The 1950s built for women in the United States a world of too-narrow walls, too-early marriage, too-little productivity.   Margaret Mead
6. Intelligence is a very real kind of armor, and like any armor it inhibits its owner's ability to float with the prevailing currents.   Peter S. Prescott
7. It is frightening to step off onto the treacherous footbridge leading to the second half of life.   Gail Sheehy
8. When books pass in review like the procession of animals in a shooting gallery, the critic has only one second in which to load and aim and shoot and may well be pardoned if he mistakes rabbits for tigers, eagles for barnyard fowls, or misses altogether and wastes his shot upon some peaceful cow grazing in a further field.   Virginia Woolf
9. At a time when the other social sciences—sociology, psychology, political science—are letting many flowers bloom and many schools contend, only economics has a fear of dissension.
10. The advice that most Southern mothers pass on is that men are the enemy: a pack of Yankees.   Shirley Abbott

---

EXERCISE 8   *Evaluating Figurative Language*

Evaluate the figurative expressions in the following sentences. Which work well to help the author make a point? Which are mixed or overdone? Rewrite any unsatisfactory sentences, using more apt figurative language.

1. The original educator is the family, which plants the seeds that teachers later build upon.
2. Immigrants bring new blood into our country to help us recharge our batteries.
3. Students often became used to high grades in high school; when they see their first college grades, they often feel like one of the lesser plankton in the food chain.
4. The Indianapolis 500 is the narrow end of the funnel for competitors who refuse to give up.
5. Family ties going back several generations have become deeply entrenched in many rural areas.
6. Many times a creative person is thrown into the limelight because she has created something totally new.
7. Frustration and depression will take over our minds the way bacteria do our bodies if we do not harness them.
8. The new law is a carefully tossed salad of penalties and incentives.
9. The subject of handguns triggers a deep-rooted and sensitive nerve in the minds of many Americans.
10. It is common for people to be unaware of the more difficult gut issues that are propelling them forward.

THE APPROPRIATE WORD

Good English is not a simple matter of right and wrong. A word may be right for one occasion and wrong for another. The right word is the appropriate word—fit for the situation, right for the audience. The right kind of English for most of your college writing will be **edited written English**—more formal than casual everyday talk, serious enough for the discussion of issues and ideas.

In most of your writing, the right tone will be near the midpoint between extremely formal and extremely informal language. One extreme is the weighty, very formal language of scholarship and law, of impersonal official documents. Closer to the center is the moderately formal English we use for the discussion of issues and ideas—serious but not solemn, formal with an occasional informal touch. Next on the spectrum is the relaxed informality of much writing that at the same time informs and entertains. Approaching the other extreme, we encounter the jazzy and often disrespectful informality of slang.

VERY FORMAL: There is a heavy legal presumption against prior restraint of adult journalists, and student journalists need similar protection.

MODERATELY FORMAL: The Freedom of Information Act is now under attack, on the grounds that it is interfering with the administration's defense of the Republic.   James Reston

INFORMAL: Democracy is a gabby business. There is no way to shut people up.   James Reston

SLANG: Publishers of language books have crowned me the great Poo-Bah of Plugsville because I happily blurb for books on how to write.   William Safire

Formal and Informal

Much of the best modern prose is **moderately formal**—serious without being solemn, formal with an occasional lighter touch. It never strays too far from the rhythms of living language; we hear in it echoes of the human voice:

Youth is a kind of genius in itself and knows it.   May Sarton

After she was married, there was a brief flurry of invitations, as if she had suddenly been declared alive after a long misunderstanding.   Anne Tyler

Where the more straitlaced traditional rules banned all personal reference, much first-rate modern prose uses the personal *I* ("*I* think," "in *my* opinion") or the personal *we*. The following example of current science writing uses vigorous plain English, with no more use of technical terms (*procession, gravitational*) than is necessary, and with a personal touch ("*our* ancestors," "*we* call them planets . . ."):

MODERATELY FORMAL: Our ancestors, watching the stars, soon noticed five of them that did more than rise and set in stolid procession among the so-called "fixed" stars; these five also slowly wandered with respect to the other stars. Today we call them planets, which is the Greek word for wanderers. We know now that the planets are not stars but are rather other worlds, gravitationally bound to the Sun and, like our own world, reflecting its light back to space. Sharing the odd apparent motion of the planets were the Sun and Moon, making seven wandering bodies in all.   Carl Sagan, "A Mission to an Unknown World," *Parade*

Much popular journalism, designed to instruct and entertain, tilts over to a distinctly **informal** style. It freely uses the folksy conversational phrase, occasionally drawing on slang—usually in tongue-in-cheek fashion. Its range of reference and allusion is likely to be that of patio, playing field, and movie theater rather than that of library or study. Its sentence structure may suggest the pauses, ramblings, asides and afterthoughts of speech. Here is a distinctly informal passage:

INFORMAL: Advertising is relatively a Johnny-come-lately. It did not exist in the mass-market form that we know much before World War I, and did not exist in any form at all before the late nineteenth century. But before advertising, there were newspapers and magazines. They were very much as we know them today, except of course that the pages were filled with news instead of paid hustle. Since they had almost no other source of revenue, the publications of that time lived or died by the reader's penny spent, and charged an honest price; if a publication cost five cents to produce, you can bet a publisher charged at least five cents for it, and hoped like hell that what the paper had to say was interesting enough to get enough people to pony up their nickels. It is no coincidence that the great muckraking magazines of American legend flourished under these game conditions; who pays the piper calls the tune, and the only paymaster was their readers, who apparently liked what the muckrakers were playing.   Warren Hinckle, "The Adman Who Hated Advertising," *Atlantic*

This author writes in a distinctly informal style, half serious and half amused. There are folksy conversational expressions ("Johnny-come-lately," "who pays the piper"). There is some outright slang (*hustle, pony up,* "hope like hell"). The sentences move on like those of a fast talker, with frequent uses of *and* to string ideas together. Pronouns are personal and familiar ("*we* know," "*you* can bet").

Revising Informal English

Your task in writing serious English is to avoid a breezy, chatty style—without lapsing into hyperformal language that would make your writing stiff and pretentious. Excessively informal English becomes a problem when a writer fails to shift gears as needed to move away from casual speech. The following guidelines should help you avoid excessive informality:

□   *Sift out the catchall words that punctuate everyday talk.* Avoid the routine use of words like *nice, neat, cute, terrific, great, wonderful, awful, terrible.*

□   *Limit words with a distinctly folksy or casual touch to informal personal writing.* Words like the following suggest casual talk:

INFORMAL	FORMAL	INFORMAL	FORMAL
boss	superior	kid	child
brainy	intelligent	skimpy	meager
bug	germ	sloppy	untidy
faze	disconcert	snoop	pry
flunk	fail	snooze	nap
folks	relatives	splurge	spend lavishly
hunch	premonition	stump	baffle

As needed, replace informal combined verbs like the following:

INFORMAL	FORMAL	INFORMAL	FORMAL
chip in	contribute	come up with	find
get across	communicate	cut out	stop
check up on	investigate	get on with	make progress

☐ *Edit out informal tags and abbreviations.* Avoid informal tags like *kind of, sort of, a lot, lots.* Revise clipped forms that have a "too-much-in-a-hurry" effect: *bike, prof, doc, fan mag, exec, econ.* But note that other shortened forms, like *phone, ad,* and *exam,* are now commonly used in serious writing.

☐ *Improve on tired informal expressions.* Avoid the familiar overused figurative expressions of informal speech. (See a later section of this chapter for more on trite language, or **clichés.**)

TRITE:	have a ball	polish the apple	jump the gun
	butter up	shoot the breeze	play ball
	hit the road	jump on the bandwagon	small potatoes

A Note on Slang

No one can fix the exact point at which informal language shades over into slang. Generally, slang is more drastic in its disregard for what makes language formal and dignified. Dictionaries may disagree, but for most readers, words like *zilch, crock, the fuzz, far out, yoyo, ballsy,* and *mooning* will have the true slung-about quality of slang.

> SLANG: The *crazies* will have poured in, already *blotto* on beer.
> Peter Fussell

Slang often has a zing missing in more pedestrian diction; it often, as it were, hits the spot: *blowhard, drunk tank, downer, pep pill, squeal rule, fat farm, junkie, clip joint, whirlybird.* New slang is often colorful or pointed (*spaced out, ripoff*), but much of it wears out from repetition. At any rate, much slang is too crude or disrespectful for most writing: *pig out, chew the fat, blow one's top, lay an egg.*

> TOO SLANGY: What *folks* have *dumped on marriage* in the way of expectations, selfish interests, and *kinky kicks* needs prompt removal if the institution is to survive.

Questions for Discussion How do you vary your language when talking to friends, professors, police officers, family? Can you give some specific examples?

Avoiding Sexist Language In many situations, avoiding the wrong word is as important as choosing the right one. Fair-minded readers are turned off by language that in crude or subtle ways mirrors prejudice. They will have no patience with outright racial or ethnic slurs: *limey, frog, greaser*, and others too numerous and ugly to mention. But they will also object to expressions that, intentionally or unintentionally, slight people because of race, sex, age, national origin, sexual orientation, or physical handicap. Many government agencies and many publications now require authors to observe guidelines on how to avoid offensive or prejudiced language.

In particular, readers are increasingly sensitive to language that belittles women. Doing without sexist language is not just a matter of avoiding obviously insulting or condescending terms, such as *chick, doll, gal,* or *old maid.* Many readers increasingly object to terms once considered neutral and used freely by both men and women writers. For instance, *man* as a **generic** term for the human species (*early man, the history of mankind*) was said to include both men and women, but it made people picture primarily the male of the species nevertheless. Current textbooks therefore use terms like *humanity, humankind, human beings,* or just plain *people* instead. The following guidelines should help you steer clear of sexist language:

□ *Replace biased labels for occupations.* Unisex labels for occupations or careers include *doctor, lawyer, carpenter, artist, teacher, mayor,* and *senator.* Replace labels that seem to reserve some occupations for men while shunting women off into others. Look especially for occupational labels ending in *-man* or *-ess*:

STEREOTYPED	UNBIASED
fireman	firefighter
policeman	police officer
mailman	mail carrier
weatherman	meteorologist
salesman	sales representative
Congressman	Representative
stewardess	flight attendant

Some balanced pairs, like *actor/actress,* are still acceptable to many people, but avoid the condescending *poetess* (use *poet*). Some terms, although recommended in official guidelines, still sound artificial to many writers, causing them to try alternatives:

STEREOTYPED	UNBIASED	ALTERNATIVES
chairman	chairperson	chair, head
spokesman	spokesperson	voice, representative, speaker
businessmen	businessperson	business people, executives, the business community

Questions for Discussion Will *waitperson* replace *waiter* and *waitress*? Should it? Where have you observed sexist language and attempts to overcome it?

☐ *Replace gender-biased pronouns.* Beware of stereotyping occupations by using *he* or *she* selectively when talking about typical representatives. Avoid loaded pairs like "the doctor—*he*, the nurse—*she*" or "the manager—*he*, the secretary—*she*." Use the double pronoun *he or she* (or *his or her*) to refer to a typical doctor, nurse, teacher, secretary, or executive. You can often sidestep the pronoun problem by talking about typical doctors, teachers, or secretaries in the plural:

STEREOTYPED:	A successful manager keeps a certain distance from *his* employees.
DOUBLE PRONOUN:	A successful manager keeps a certain distance from *his or her* employees.
PLURAL:	Successful *managers* keep a certain distance from *their* employees.

The plural usually works best when several *he-or-she, his-or-her*, and *himself-or-herself* combinations in a row would make a sentence awkward.

Note: Use the double pronoun *he or she* also to replace the **generic** *he* in reference to the generalized expressions like *everyone, somebody, anybody, anyone, nobody*, or *one* (**indefinite pronouns**). Everyday speech uses the plural *they* or *their* after these: "*No one* should be required to inform on *their* own family." Grammarians used to require the singular *he* or *him* (or *himself*): "*Everyone* has the right to make *his* own mistakes." In your own writing, use the unbiased *he or she* or change the generalized pronouns to a plural:

UNBIASED:	*Everyone* has the right to make *his or her* own mistakes.
PLURAL:	*We all* have the right to make *our* own mistakes.

Some writers alternate *he* and *she* in pointing back to pronouns like *somebody* and *everyone* or in talking about a typical student, a typical writer, a representative citizen.

□ *Revise expressions that imply there is something odd about men or women in a given situation or line of work.* Avoid the condescending *lady doctor* or *lady lawyer*; do not make a big point about a *female* pilot or a *male* secretary. You can often fill the reader in simply by using the right pronoun: "The new secretary handled *his* workload well."

□ *Mention sex, marital status, or family evenhandedly.* Provide such information equally for people of either sex, or omit it when it is irrelevant. Use courtesy titles impartially, and use first names, first-names-only, or nicknames only when you do so evenhandedly for either sex. (*Ms.*, like *Mr.*, allows people to keep their marital status their own business, although women who prefer the traditional *Mrs.* or *Miss* may so indicate by using them in signing their correspondence.)

> NO: Mr. John Greuber, local builder, and Mrs. Vitell, mother of three, were elected to the board.
>
> YES: John Greuber and Ann Vitell, both long active in community affairs, were elected to the board.
>
> NO: Dreiser and Edith Wharton are little read by today's students.
>
> YES: Dreiser and Wharton are little read by today's students.
>
> NO: Mr. Pfitzer and Jane will show you around the plant.
>
> YES: Mr. Pfitzer and Ms. Garner will show you around the plant.

Remember: Like the clothes we wear, our choice of language "makes a statement." It shows how serious or flippant, how respectful or condescending we intend to be. If we are unaware of the signals our choice of words sends to the reader, our writing may have unintended side effects.

EXERCISE 9 *The Range of Formality*

How good is your ear for formal and informal language? Rank the expressions in each of the following sets from the most formal to the most informal. Be prepared to compare your rankings with those of your classmates and to defend your decisions.

1. sales talk—presentation—spiel
2. hook up the equipment—hooked on drugs—got her off the hook
3. no sweat—sweat out a decision—sweat shirt
4. tear into someone—tear up a bill—that tears it
5. arrested—busted—taken into custody
6. go all out—go for it—have a go at it
7. live it up—live it down—live up to expectations

8. crack down on crime—his voice cracked—crack a book
9. go broke—go bankrupt—go belly-up
10. lush—alcoholic—problem drinker

EXERCISE 10   *Formal and Informal Writing*

Which of the following passages are written in formal English? Which in informal English? Is any one of these passages formal with an informal touch? Describe each author's purpose and attitude toward the subject or the audience. Identify specific words and expressions that make for a serious formal style. Point out words and expressions that make for a breezy or jazzy informal style. How do you react to each passage as a reader?

1. From an article in a newsmagazine:

The National Institute of Health is, in the words of Author-Physician Lewis Thomas, "one of the nation's great treasures." In the past few decades, the letters NIH have become almost as familiar to Americans as FBI or IRS. The federal research center has been a leading force in the U.S. and around the world for the study of cancer and heart disease, the development of vaccines and treatments for infectious illness (most recently AIDS) and the investigation of mental illness. Its scientists are at the forefront of probes into such fundamental mysteries as gene regulation, the workings of the immune system and the structure of complex organic molecules. Says Historian Stephen Strickland, author of two books on the NIH: "There is no other biomedical institution that has its scope." The NIH has underwritten the training of one-third of the nation's biomedical researchers; it has sponsored the work of two-thirds of those U.S. scientists who have won Nobel Prizes for Physiology or Medicine since 1945. It is clearly a major factor in America's primacy in medical research.   Claudia Wallis, *Time*

2. From a book review:

Life After Doomsday is a thoroughly readable book that tells you everything you need to know about nuclear war. If you want to chart fallout, find out how close you are to target areas, or build a shelter, this manual makes it all look easy. Even if the Soviets hit all primary targets, there are still many parts of the nation which have less than a two percent chance of receiving fallout. So what's the hysteria? Move to southern Oregon and avoid the rush later. Think of it: no more nine-to-five, no more relationships, and when the blast comes, you'll still be alive, and a much more important person than you are now. Not nearly so up is *Nuclear War: The Facts on Our Survival*. Taking as hypothetical targets San Francisco and New York's Kennedy Airport, the author constructs the full scenario of what would happen if either locale were nuked.

3. From a review of Shirley Abbott's *Womenfolks*:

The South that Abbott's maternal ancestors knew is far removed from the antebellum world of great plantations and a slave economy. It's a South without recorded historical tradition, a South of red-dirt farms and poor white folk of Scotch-Irish descent, the hillbillies who never owned a slave and very likely never saw one. Driven from Ulster in the 18th century by their English landlords, they arrived in Charleston only to find themselves among the English gentry again. Immediately they decamped for the back country, setting up lean-tos in the woods. These people were not, Abbott insists, merely benighted, but fiercely independent, even anarchistic: specialists in survival, they preferred to do without schools and churches than to submit to institutions and taxation. For them, the Civil War, to which they were obliged to surrender their men and their goods, was no glorious cause; it was the cause of endless desolation.   Peter S. Prescott, *Newsweek*

EXERCISE 11   *Editing for Excess Informality*

The following excerpts are mostly from articles written in a breezy, informal, personal style. For each italicized word or expression, write down a substitute that would be appropriate in more serious formal writing.

1. Many supporters of free expression *waffle* when free speech is said to endanger national security.
2. Ambitious young lawyers spend a few years as Justice Department *hotshots* before going into private practice.
3. Many law students aim at a career in one of the *well-heeled* law factories that service large corporations.
4. Teachers are *put off* by the prime starting salaries paid to engineering graduates.
5. With their financial *savvy*, new M.B.A.s could soon afford their BMWs and VCRs.
6. By the early 80s, new M.B.A.'s had become a *hot item, mediawise*.
7. Their style of dress showed that the *eager-beaver* ethos had *socked in*.
8. Overnight, yuppies became role models for everyone who did not *hate their guts*.
9. When two communication satellites suffered identical failures, insurers *shelled out* millions and began raising their premiums *sky high*.
10. At rock concerts, managers *pack in the kids*, and people who complain are *kicked out*.

EXERCISE 12   *Updating Your Dictionary*

Dictionaries published ten years ago may not yet include words like the following or do justice to their current uses: *wimp, nerd, klutz, guru, jock, hacker, punk*. Write a paragraph about one of these, explaining and illustrating its meaning and uses.

EXERCISE 13   *Revising Sexist Language*

Rewrite the following sentences to eliminate sexist language. Discuss the merits of different revisions with your classmates.

1. Thoreau, the Concord sage, and Emily Dickinson, the Amherst poetess, take us on fascinating explorations of inner space.
2. Risking his life for unconcerned or unappreciative citizens is part of a policeman's or a fireman's job.
3. Evolutionists are rewriting the history of mankind to show that early man branched off the evolutionary tree before the chimpanzee.
4. A doctor can walk away from his patients after a brief consultation; the nurse spends most of her day dealing with their pain and fear.
5. Everybody takes American history at least three or four times in his career as a student.
6. Justice Marshall and Sandra O'Connor, the first lady judge appointed to the Court, voted with the majority.

REVISION: WORDING AND REWORDING

Ideally, we would all write vigorous, plain English that carries our message without static. In practice, however, words may get in the way, confusing, distracting, or misleading the reader. Professional writers invest much of the time available for final editing in rewording passages that missed the mark, in rephrasing phrases that do not ring true.

Inaccurate Words

Some words are just plain wrong. One way to go wrong is to confuse words close in sound or meaning:

> CONFUSED: The work was sheer *trudgery* (should be *drudgery*).
> Similar choices *affront* every student (should be *confront*).
> Self-control is an *envious* asset (should be *enviable*).

Some words are only half right. Your revision of a first draft is your opportunity to replace a near-miss, approximate word with the word that is exactly right:

> BLURRED: Many parents today do not have time to *adhere to* the needs of their children.

(We *adhere to*—or stick to—an agreement. We *attend to*, or *satisfy*, someone's needs.)

ACCURATE: Many parents today do not have time to *attend to* the needs of their children.

Some words carry the right idea but are used the wrong way:

GARBLED: Most American teenagers do what they want without *consenting* their parents.

REVISED: Most American teenagers do what they want without *consulting* their parents (or without *obtaining* their consent).

GARBLED: Many young people have *lost their appeal* for fraternities.

REVISED: Fraternities have *lost their appeal* for many young people.

Unidiomatic Language

Some passages read as if they had been translated from a foreign language: We recognize the words, but they have been put together in an unusual or awkward way. Customary expressions or ways of saying something are called **idioms**; unidiomatic language mixes familiar expressions or turns them upside down:

UNIDIOMATIC: Older people are worried about the ardent *devotion* that young people *pay* to new religious cults.

(We *show* devotion; we *pay* attention.)

REVISED: Older people are worried about the ardent *devotion* that young people *show* to new religious cults.

UNIDIOMATIC: He served in the Peace Corps, but the ideal *did not live up to* the reality.

(The *reality* fails to live up to or measure up to ideal standards.)

REVISED: He served in the Peace Corps, but reality *fell short of* his ideals.

One test of idiomatic language is the use of the right preposition in expressions like *confide in, prevent from,* and *superior to.* Here is a checklist of idiomatic prepositions:

abide *by* (a decision)
abstain *from* (voting)
accuse *of* (a crime)
agree *with* (a person), *to* (a proposal), *on* (a course of action)
alarmed *at* (the news)
avail oneself *of* (an opportunity)
capable *of* (an action)
charge *with* (an offense)

compatible *with* (recognized standards)
comply *with* (a request)
concur *with* (someone), *in* (a decision)
confide *in* or *to* (someone)
conform *to* (specifications)
deficient *in* (strength)
delight *in* (mischief)

deprive *of* (a privilege)
die *of* or *from* (a disease)
disappointed *in* (someone's performance)
dissent *from* (a majority opinion)
dissuade *from* (doing something foolish)
identical *with* (something looked for)
inconsistent *with* (sound procedure)
independent *of* (outside help)
indifferent *to* (praise or blame)
inferior *to* (a rival product)
insist *on* (accuracy)
interfere *with* (a performance), *in* (someone else's affairs)
jealous *of* (others)

long *for* (recognition)
object *to* (a proposal)
oblivious *of* or *to* (warnings)
part *with* (possessions)
partial *to* (flattery)
participate *in* (activities)
persevere *in* (a task)
pertain *to* (a subject)
prevail *on* (someone to do something)
prevent someone *from* (an action)
refrain *from* (wrongdoing)
resolve *on* (a course of action)
succeed *in* (an attempt)
superior *to* (an alternative)
threaten *with* (legal action)
wait *for* (developments), *on* (a guest)

Wordiness Brevity may not always be the soul of wit, but certainly longwindedness is its enemy. Readers tire of wading through a stream of verbiage in search of a few nuggets of sense. Outright **redundancy** duplicates words that say exactly the same. In each of the following, one of the two ways of sending the message should be omitted:

REDUNDANT: *As a rule*, summers in Chicago are *usually* unbearably hot.
Prisoners were awakened *in the morning* at six *a.m.*
The President knew more about the events than *seemed apparent.*
This common *mis*conception is completely *wrong.*

Much inflated language is caused by familiar wordy tags:

WORDY	BRIEF
at the present time	now
due to the fact that	because
under the prevailing circumstances	as things are
in this time and age	today
at a period of time when	when
the question whether	whether

Often a simple logical link like *for example, however,* or *therefore* can take the place of a lengthy preamble like *Taking these factors into consideration, we must conclude that.*

WORDY: *In considering the situation, we must also take into account the fact that* the current residents often do not share our enthusiasm for redevelopment.

BRIEF: The current residents, *however,* often do not share our enthusiasm for redevelopment.

Vague all-purpose words like *element, factor, aspect, situation,* or *angle* are often mere padding:

PADDED: Another *aspect* that needs to be considered is the customer relations *angle.*

REVISED: We should also consider consumer relations.

EXERCISE 14 *The Wrong Word*

Write down a more accurate word or expression for each word or phrase italicized in the following sentences.

1. My parents have always *placed a high standard on* a good education.
2. Having high-spirited parents has given me a *jest* for life.
3. Diane soon discovered some of the problems *coherent* in managing a large department.
4. Her parents were idealists and tried to raise healthy, *opinionated* children.
5. Berlin became the decadent postwar capital where all kinds of sexual *deprivations* were practiced.
6. *Immortal* books should be removed from the library.
7. In my *analogy* of this essay, I hope to show its strengths and weaknesses.
8. The woman *braved* her life to save her fellow passengers.
9. The authoritarian father gave the orders, with no *lip service* in return.
10. Her press agent *contributed* the low attendance to poor publicity.

EXERCISE 15 *Revising Unidiomatic Prepositions*

Where did each writer use an unidiomatic preposition? Write a more idiomatic preposition after the number of each unsatisfactory sentence.

1. To seek a good grade at someone else's expense would be a violation to our standards of conduct.

2. During the past fifty years, deaths caused by highway accidents have been more numerous than those incurred from two world wars and the war in Korea.
3. Plans for cost reduction have been put to action by different agencies of the federal government.
4. Several families volunteered to take care for the children of flood victims.
5. Only the prompt help of the neighbors prevented the fire of becoming a major disaster.
6. During the first years of marriage, we had to deprive ourselves from many things that other people take for granted.
7. The arrival of the ship to its destination caused general rejoicing.
8. Though I support Mr. Finchley's candidacy, I take exception with some of his statements.
9. We will not hesitate to expose businesses that deprive their employees from these benefits.
10. As an instrument of the popular will, the Senate suffers from defects inherent to its constitution.

EXERCISE 16   *Pruning Wordy Sentences*

What makes each of the following sentences wordy? Rewrite each sentence to eliminate wordiness.

EXAMPLE: The reason that married students have high grades academi-
cally is that they have definite goals in the future to come.

REVISED: Married students have high grades because they have definite goals.

1. We are planning to move because in terms of employment there are few jobs in this area at the present time.
2. Mormons fleeing persecution founded the beginning of our community.
3. In due time, a new fad will eventually replace this current craze.
4. Many plants are closing due to the fact that a flood of cheap products is inundating the market.
5. In my opinion, I have always felt that a popular entertainer should be a happy, smiling type of person.
6. The central nucleus of the tribe was based around the institution of the family.
7. The weather bureau announced that at times there would be occasional rain.
8. At a period of time when schools face skyrocketing insurance costs, the aspect of insurance pools deserves consideration.
9. The setting of the play took place in a rustic part of rural Virginia.
10. In the modern world of this day and age, computer projections are among the basic fundamentals of business planning.

Clichés **Clichés** are ready-made phrases, worn out from overuse. Like phrases stored in the memory of an electronic typewriter, they practically type themselves: "few and . . . *far between*," "easier said . . . *than done*," "last but . . . *not least*." Many folksy clichés have outlived a rural past (*put the shoulder to the wheel, put the cart before the horse*). Other trite phrases survive from old-fashioned, flowery oratory (*intestinal fortitude, dire necessity, the bitter end*). Still others sound like part of a sales talk that has been replayed too many times (*let's look at the facts, look at the big picture, look at the bottom line*). To *say the least*, for *all intents and purposes*, the *bloom is off* such expressions, and *in the final analysis*, they *do more harm than good*.

Clichés make the reader feel that nothing new is being said; the writer has not bothered to take a fresh look. ("For a while it seemed as if things were falling apart, but when our backs were to the wall and the chips were down, everyone in the group seemed to come through and did a great job.") When you first encounter a cliché, it may seem vivid or imaginative ("this is only *the tip of the iceberg*"), but you have to remember that everyone has used it before you. Resist the pull of the cliché; phrase your ideas freshly, in your own words:

TRITE: He was always *wrapped up* in his own thoughts and feelings.

FRESH: Only the *cocoon* of his own thoughts and feelings existed for him.

TRITE: The dean let us have it, *straight from the shoulder*.

FRESH: The dean spoke to us directly and urgently, *like a scout just returned from the enemy camp*.

Avoid clichés like the following:

believe it or not
better late than never
beyond the shadow of a doubt
bolt out of the blue
burn the midnight oil
fine and dandy
the finer things
in one fell swoop
it goes without saying
the last straw
let's face it

malice aforethought
Mother Nature
off the beaten track
pride and joy
proud owner
rear its ugly head
rude awakening
a shot in the arm
sink or swim
a snare and a delusion
sneaking suspicion
straight and narrow

Questions for Discussion What are some current clichés in advertising, politics, educationese? What do they stand for? What seems to be their appeal? Can anything be said in their defense?

Jargon Familiar problems of diction result when a writer tries to impress the reader. **Jargon** is pretentious, pseudoscientific language that results when a writer uses two highbrow words where one lowbrow word would do. Jargon tries to make the trivial sound important: "Mandatory verification of your attendance record is required of all personnel exiting the work area." (Punch your time card when you leave.) Jargon creates a pseudoscientific air by using indirect, impersonal constructions and technical-sounding Latin and Greek terms:

JARGON:	He was *instrumental in the founding of* an Irish national theater.
PLAIN ENGLISH:	He helped found an Irish national theater.

JARGON:	*Procedures were instituted with a view toward the implementation* of the conclusions reached. (Note the impersonal passive.)
PLAIN ENGLISH:	We started to put our ideas into practice.

In much technical, scientific, or scholarly writing, technical and impersonal language is necessary. Jargon is the *un*necessary use of technical-sounding terms in order to borrow the prestige of science and scholarship. Remember advice like the following:

☐ *Deflate inflated substitutes for straightforward words.* In each of the following pairs avoid the big word if the simple word will do:

BIG WORD	SIMPLE WORD	BIG WORD	SIMPLE WORD
ameliorate	improve	residence	home
magnitude	size	maximize	develop fully
interrelationship	relation	insightful	intelligent
methodology	methods	preadolescence	childhood
prioritize	rank	correlate	match

☐ *Lower the abstraction count.* Watch for such symptoms as the piling up of too many words ending in -*ion*: *verification, utilization, implementation, modification, conceptualization.* Avoid using terms like the following to wrap personal opinions in a pseudo-objective aura: *factors, phases, aspects, elements, criteria, facets, phenomena, strata.*

JARGON: *An element of society that is most prevalent* in advertising is the desire for a carefree existence.

PLAIN ENGLISH: Advertising mirrors the yearning for a carefree life that is strong in our society.

☐ *Avoid impersonal tags.* Even in formal research reports, overuse of phrases like the following produces a stilted effect. Avoid them in ordinary prose:

STILTED	PLAIN
reference was made	I mentioned
the hypothesis suggests itself	we can tentatively conclude
careful consideration is imperative	we should study carefully
a realization of desired outcomes	producing the desired results

☐ *Avoid using or overusing buzzwords.* **Buzzwords** are currently fashionable terms that people use to make themselves sound like insiders. They are words that most people have already heard once too often: *parameters, bottom line, user-friendly, interface, cost-effective, upscale.*

Euphemisms

Euphemisms are "beautiful words"—words more beautiful than what they stand for: *memorial park* for *cemetery, waste management* for *garbage disposal, correctional facility* for *jail.* Some euphemisms are merely polite: *intoxicated* for *drunk, stout* for *fat.* But many stem from a desire to upgrade ordinary realities, leaving us inundated with fuzzy, vaguely complimentary terms: *human performance* (physical education), *sanitary engineer* (plumber), *research consultant* (file clerk), *language facilitator* (translator). Many become **weasel words**, covering up unpleasant facts that the reader is entitled to know: *negative economic growth* (recession), *straitened financial circumstances* (bankruptcy). An effective writer has to know when to be diplomatic but also when to be blunt and direct:

EUPHEMISMS	BLUNT
immoderate use of intoxicants	heavy drinking
lack of proper health habits	dirt
deteriorating residential section	slum
below the poverty line	poor

Flowery Language

Flowery language attempts to give a poetic varnish to prose. Resist the temptation to weave a flowery garland of fancy words around simple everyday events:

FLOWERY:	The respite from study was devoted to a sojourn at the ancestral mansion.
PLAIN ENGLISH:	I spent my vacation at the house of my grandparents.
FLOWERY:	The visitor proved a harbinger of glad tidings.
PLAIN ENGLISH:	The visitor brought good news.

Remember: Revision should not just make your writing safer and less striking (and more forgettable). One test of your success as a writer is whether your readers will remember something you said—a striking phrase, a fresh figure of speech, a playful adaptation of a cliché:

Harvard (across the river in Cambridge) and Boston are two ends of one mustache.   Elizabeth Hardwick

Optimists are people who cannot see the desert for the mirage.

I started to take riding lessons and got on—and off—about as well as anyone else.

In any but the most solemn kind of writing, there is room for touches of **word play** or verbal humor, for a striking current phrase, and the occasional pun (as when a columnist called a congested bridge the "car-strangled spanner"). Revision is partly trimming and pruning but at the same time also an opportunity to draw on a wider range of choices.

EXERCISE 17   *Watching Out for Clichés*

Which expressions in the following sentences are clichés? Rewrite each sentence to get rid of trite language, substituting language fresh enough to revive the reader's attention.

| EXAMPLE: | You will never rise to the top of the heap if every setback makes you throw in the sponge. |
| REVISED: | You will never make it to the top if every setback makes you think of defeat as inevitable, like the rain. |

1. We try to give foreign competition a run for their money, but in many areas, cheap foreign labor has forced American management to throw in the towel.
2. In a very real sense, politicians dealing with tax legislation often cannot see the forest for the trees.
3. Catching the street-corner pusher has become small potatoes. The major effort now is international, and it is a pathway strewn with political pitfalls.
4. Our new educational division has become an integral part of our marketing effort and will play a vital role in the challenging days ahead.
5. In the final analysis, party platforms never get down to brass tacks.
6. The meetings scheduled with the candidate will give people from every walk of life a chance to stand up and be counted.

THE WRITING WORKSHOP

Using and Abusing Language

Working with a group, participate in investigating the language of a field of general interest: national defense, foreign policy, education, the prison system, juvenile justice, planned parenthood, or other. How do people working or writing in the field use language? Is there evidence of features likely to interfere with informative, straightforward communication: clichés, self-important jargon, euphemistic upgrading of the unpleasant or the ordinary, doublespeak used as a verbal smokescreen? Help the group chart its strategy; contribute to a group report analyzing the characteristic lingo of the field and making suggestions for improvement. (Your group may decide to circulate its report to interested parties.)

7. When we try to give our neighborhoods a shot in the arm, appealing to self-interest is our best bet.
8. The opposing candidate was a Johnny-come-lately picked because he could be counted on to play ball with the real estate interests in the legislature.
9. Constantly testing students who don't know how to learn is putting the cart before the horse.
10. After all is said and done, its rabid fans are not going to turn their backs on boxing in the foreseeable future.

EXERCISE 18   *Jargon and Plain English*

Translate the following examples of jargon into plain English.

1. I sincerely believe that the government should divulge more on the subject of socialism and its cohorts, because its impetus has reached a frightening momentum.
2. In camp, cooking is done over open fires, with the main dietary intake consisting of black beans and rice.
3. To be frank about it, today an inadequacy can bring about the ruination of a person in later life when it happens in education.
4. Being in social situations in Washington subjected me to some embarrassing instances due to my deficiency in etiquette, which was superfluous at home because of its nonexistence.

5. The English language and its use have become very important factors in correlation with communication to large audiences.

6. In these two books, there are basic differences in character representation that are accountable only in terms of the individual authors involved.

7. Further insight into the article discovered that the writing insinuated a connection between the conviction of the accused and his working-class background.

8. Advertisements similar to those of Certs and Ultra-Brite are creating a fallacy in the real cause of a person's sex appeal.

9. The fact that we are products of our environmental frame of reference ensures that each of us has deeply ingrained within the fiber of our being preconceived ideas that influence our thoughts, actions, and reactions.

10. We say we believe in democracy while denying the partaking of its first fruits, justice and equality, to diverse members of our society. This is true in many aspects of our lives, but especially so in the context of racial prejudice.

EXERCISE 19   *Euphemisms and Flowery Language*

Cut through the euphemisms and the flowery language in the following examples and rewrite them in plain English.

1. Ready to leave the parental nest, I decided to pursue my education at an institution of higher learning.

2. After a most rewarding bout with a social research paper, something stirred my intellect and I possessed a burning desire to stay in school for another three-week session.

3. Offenders who have paid their debt to society at a correctional institution should be given a chance to become productive participants in community life.

4. All personnel assisting in preparation of food should observe proper hygiene after using the sanitary facilities.

5. After the annual respite from their secretarial toil, office workers resume their labors with renewed vigor.

DICTIONARIES AND THE WRITER

Some users turn to the dictionary only to check a spelling (*develop* or *develope?*) or an unusual word (*phlegmatic, serendipity*). Others appeal to the dictionary in order to settle an argument (to prove themselves right and someone else wrong). But many practicing writers think of the dictionary not as a final authority but as a guide; they turn to it regularly for information, advice, and inspiration. A good dictionary serves as an inexhaustible resource for people who love words. They trust it as a guide charting manifold meanings; tracing the geology of a word like *hand* or *mind* through layers and layers of significance; chronicling the history of a word, detailing its uses, and warning of possible limitations.

A Choice of Dictionaries

Like mass-volume cars, college dictionaries are becoming more alike. They compete in including new words: *sitcom, skyjacker, unisex, upscale, hot tub, pro-life, interface, preppie, survivalist, petrodollars.* They vie with each other in covering the language of science and technology, from *entropy* and *laser* to *microfiche* and *quark*. They provide **usage notes**, debating the pros and cons of *disinterested, hopefully, prioritize,* and *impact* used as a verb. Increasingly, they put names of famous people and places in separate biographical and geographical appendixes at the end. Nevertheless, the most widely recommended dictionaries differ in how they present information, in how they envision their intended audience, and in how successfully they reach it.

☐ *Webster's Ninth New Collegiate Dictionary* is published by Merriam-Webster, Inc., whose collection of several million citation slips has been called the "national archives of the language." The *Collegiate* is based on *Webster's Third New International Dictionary,* the most authoritative unabridged dictionary of American English. Historical information about a word comes first, followed by meanings in the order they developed. The current *Ninth New Collegiate* includes the year of the first recorded appearance of a word. The editors do not use the label *informal* (too arbitrary or subjective); they rarely use the label *slang.* Sample entry*:

> **fem·i·nism** \\'fem-ə-,niz-əm\\ *n* (1895) **1** : the theory of the political, economic, and social equality of the sexes **2** : organized activity on behalf of women's rights and interests — **fem·i·nist** \\-nəst\\ *n or adj* — **fem·i·nis·tic** \\,fem-ə-'nis-tik\\ *adj*

☐ *Webster's New World Dictionary* stands out because of its clear and helpful definitions. Historical information comes first; lists of idioms provide an excellent guide to the manifold uses of a word. The editors have a good ear for informal English and slang; they pay special attention to Americanisms—expressions first found in the U.S.A. Sample entry†:

> **Goth·am** (gäth′əm, gō′thəm; *for 1, Brit.* gät′-) **1.** a village near Nottingham, England, whose inhabitants, the "wise men of Gotham," were, according to legend, very foolish **2.** *nickname for* NEW YORK CITY —**Goth′am·ite′** (-īt′) *n.*

---

* By permission from *Webster's Ninth New Collegiate Dictionary* © 1988 by Merriam-Webster, Inc., publisher of the Merriam-Webster® dictionaries.

† *Webster's New World Dictionary,* Second College Edition. Copyright © 1984 by Simon & Schuster, Inc. Reprinted by permission of Simon & Schuster, Inc.

□ *The Random House College Dictionary,* Revised Edition (based, like *Webster's Ninth New Collegiate,* on a larger unabridged dictionary), caters to a conservative clientele. The most frequently used meanings come first; historical information is last. Both informal English and slang are marked; usage notes recognize many traditional restrictions. Sample entry[‡]:

> **cal·i·ber** (kal′ə bər), *n.* **1.** the diameter of something of circular section, esp. that of the inside of a tube. **2.** *Ordn.* the diameter of the bore of a gun taken as a unit of measurement. **3.** degree of competence, merit, or importance: *a mathematician of high caliber; the high moral caliber of the era.* Also, *esp. Brit.,* **cal′i·bre.** [var. of *calibre* < MF < early It *calibro,* ? alter. of Ar *qālib* mold. last. < Gk *kalópous* shoemaker's last = *kâlo(n)* wood + *poûs* foot] —**cal′i·bered;** *esp. Brit.,* **cal′i·bred,** *adj.*

□ *The American Heritage Dictionary, Second College Edition,* is intended as a sensible (moderately conservative) guide, less forbidding than traditional dictionaries. Definitions branch out from a central meaning that may not be historically the earliest sense of the word. Sample entry[§]:

> **im·promp·tu** (ĭm-prŏmp′tōō, -tyōō) *adj.* Performed or conceived without rehearsal or preparation: *an impromptu speech.* —*adv.* Spontaneously. —*n.* **1.** Something made or done impromptu, as a speech. **2.** *Mus.* A short lyrical composition esp. for the piano. [Fr. < Lat. *in promptu,* at hand : *in,* in + *promptus,* ready. —see PROMPT.]

Questions for Discussion Can you cite five or six words that have recently stretched your vocabulary? Where did you encounter them? Why were they important? Did you turn to your dictionary for help?

Dictionary Definitions

Dictionaries furnish several kinds of useful information before they explain the meaning of a word: spelling and division into syllables (in·aus·pi·cious), pronunciation, and grammatical label. *Annoy,* for instance, is labeled *v.t.* for transitive verb: It normally goes on to an object or target; we usually annoy somebody—we do not just annoy. However, the heart of a lexicographer's (or dictionary maker's) job is the writing of definitions that tell us what a word means and how it is used. To make the most of a dictionary definition, remember advice like the following:

□ *Take in exact information and shades of meaning.* For technical and historical terms, for example, dictionaries provide exact information in a very short space. Learn to take in key points and essential details:

[‡] Reprinted by permission from *The Random House College Dictionary,* Revised Edition. Copyright © 1988 by Random House, Inc.

[§] Copyright © 1985 by Houghton Mifflin Company. Reprinted by permission from *The American Heritage Dictionary,* Second College Edition.

TECHNICAL: A *laser* is a device that amplifies light rays (including rays with the frequencies of ultraviolet and infrared) and concentrates them in extremely narrow, intense, powerful beams that are used, for instance, in surgery, communications, and various industrial processes.

HISTORICAL: *Populism* was a late nineteenth-century political movement that championed the interests of the common people (and especially farmers) against the rich and powerful, in particular the large monopolies (like the railroads); today, a populist champions the rights and aspirations of ordinary people against self-appointed political and cultural elites.

Look beyond the general idea for the specifics that make language flexible and discriminating. For example, *terse* does not just mean *brief*; *mannerism* adds a special twist to *manner*:

terse: intentionally brief and pointed; deliberately avoiding the superfluous, devoid of idle chatter

mannerism: a habitual, noticeable manner, especially a recurrent quirky or eccentric feature of behavior

□ *Choose the right meaning from among multiple meanings*. Often you will have to work your way down a numbered list of meanings, like the meanings listed for the word *cell* in the following entry[||]:

> **cell** \'sel\ *n* [ME, fr. OE, religious house and OF *celle* hermit's cell, fr. L *cella* small room; akin to L *celare* to conceal — more at HELL] (bef. 12c) **1** : a small religious house dependent on a monastery or convent **2 a** : a one-room dwelling occupied by a solitary person (as a hermit) **b** : a single room (as in a convent or prison) usu. for one person **3** : a small compartment, cavity, or bounded space: as **a** : one of the compartments of a honeycomb **b** : a membranous area bounded by veins in the wing of an insect **4** : a small usu. microscopic mass of protoplasm bounded externally by a semipermeable membrane, usu. including one or more nuclei and various nonliving products, capable alone or interacting with other cells of performing all the fundamental functions of life, and forming the least structural unit of living matter capable of functioning independently **5 a** (1) : a receptacle (as a cup or jar) containing electrodes and an electrolyte either for generating electricity by chemical action or for use in electrolysis (2) : FUEL CELL **b** : a single unit in a device for converting radiant energy into electrical energy or for varying the intensity of an electrical current in accordance with radiation **6** : a unit in a statistical array comprising a group of individuals and formed by the intersection of a column and a row **7** : the basic and usu. smallest unit of an organization or movement; *esp* : the primary unit of a Communist organization **8** : a portion of the atmosphere that behaves as a unit

From its root meaning—"a small enclosed place"—the word *cell* has branched out into various historical and technical uses. Starting with its first use in English sometime before the twelfth century, we can sketch a rough history of this useful term as follows:

[||] By permission from *Webster's Ninth New Collegiate Dictionary* © 1988 by Merriam-Webster, Inc., publisher of the Merriam-Webster® dictionaries.

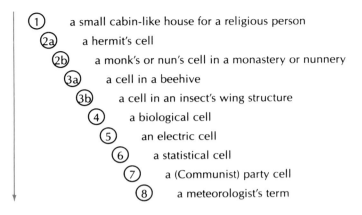

1. a small cabin-like house for a religious person
2a. a hermit's cell
2b. a monk's or nun's cell in a monastery or nunnery
3a. a cell in a beehive
3b. a cell in an insect's wing structure
4. a biological cell
5. an electric cell
6. a statistical cell
7. a (Communist) party cell
8. a meteorologist's term

☐ *Let your dictionary help you choose the meaning that fits the context.* The **context** of a word may be another word (*square* meal), a whole sentence or paragraph ("*Square* your theories with your practice"), a whole publication (a treatment of *square* roots in an algebra text), or a situation (a tourist asking for directions to a *square*). Depending on the context, a *program* may be the list of offerings for a concert, a scheduled radio or television broadcast, or the coded instructions for the operation of a computer. Dictionaries show how context determines meaning by showing a word used in a phrase or sentence and by specifying an area like economics or geometry*:

> **pro·duce** (prə dōōs′, -dyōōs′; *for n.*, präd′ōōs, -yōōs; prō′dōōs, -dyōōs) *vt.* **-duced′, -duc′ing** [L. *producere* < *pro-*, forward + *ducere*, to lead, draw: see PRO-² & DUCT] **1.** to bring to view; offer for inspection [to *produce* identification] **2.** to bring forth; bear; yield [a well that *produces* oil] **3.** *a)* to make or manufacture [to *produce* steel] *b)* to bring into being; create [to *produce* a work of art] **4.** to cause; give rise to [war *produces* devastation] **5.** to get (a play, motion picture, etc.) ready for presentation to the public **6.** *Econ.* to create (anything having exchange value) **7.** *Geom.* to extend (a line or plane) —*vi.* to bear, yield, create, manufacture, etc. something —*n.* something that is produced; yield; esp., fresh fruits and vegetables —**pro·duc′i·bil′i·ty** *n.* —**pro·duc′i·ble** *adj.*

Synonyms and Antonyms The quickest way to show the meaning of a word is to give a double, or **synonym** (*systematic* for *methodical*). We often get further help from its opposite, or **antonym** (*legitimate* for *illicit*). Synonyms usually mean *nearly* the same; they are not simply interchangeable. *Arrogant, insolent,* and *haughty* all go a step further than *proud.* "Synonymies" like the following help the writer who wants to make accurate distinctions*:

---

* *Webster's New World Dictionary*, Second College Edition. Copyright © 1984 by Simon & Schuster, Inc. Reprinted by permission of Simon & Schuster, Inc.

SYN.—**alien** is applied to a resident who bears political allegiance to another country; **foreigner,** to a visitor or resident from another country, esp. one with a different language, cultural pattern, etc.; **stranger,** to a person from another region who is unacquainted with local people, customs, etc.; **immigrant,** to a person who comes to another country to settle; **émigré,** to one who has left his country to take political refuge elsewhere See also EXTRINSIC—

Often synonymies alert us to differences in **connotation**—to the variable attitudes and feelings different words activate toward the same thing. To make a scheme sound impressive, we call it a *project*; to belittle a project, we call it a *scheme***:

SYN.—**plan** refers to any detailed method, formulated beforehand, for doing or making something [vacation *plans*]; **design** stresses the final outcome of a plan and implies the use of skill or craft, sometimes in an unfavorable sense, in executing or arranging this [it was his *design* to separate us]; **project** implies the use of enterprise or imagination in formulating an ambitious or extensive plan [a housing *project*]; **scheme,** a less definite term than the preceding, often connotes either an impractical, visionary plan or an underhanded intrigue [a *scheme* to embezzle the funds]

Idiomatic Phrases

A basic test for our mastery of a language is our command of its **idioms**—set expressions that follow no general rule and that we have to learn one at a time. To write idiomatic English, we have to know that we *do* a certain kind of work, *hold* a job, *follow* a trade, *pursue* an occupation, and *engage in* business. The following is a list of idiomatic phrases using the word *mind***:

watch out **4.** *a*) to care; feel concern *b*) to object —**bear** (or **keep**) **in mind** to remember —**be in one's right mind** to be mentally well; be sane —**be of one mind** to have the same opinion or desire —**be of two minds** to be undecided or irresolute —☆**blow one's mind** [Slang] to undergo the hallucinations, etc. caused by, or as by, psychedelic drugs —**call to mind** **1.** to remember **2.** to be a reminder of —**change one's mind** **1.** to change one's opinion **2.** to change one's intention, purpose, or wish —**give (someone) a piece of one's mind** to criticize or rebuke (someone) sharply —**have a (good or great) mind to** to feel (strongly) inclined to —**have half a mind to** to be somewhat inclined to —**have in mind** **1.** to remember **2.** to think of **3.** to intend; purpose —**know one's own mind** to know one's own real thoughts, desires, etc. —**make up one's mind** to form a definite opinion or decision —**meeting of (the) minds** an agreement —**never mind** don't be concerned; it doesn't matter —**on one's mind** **1.** occupying one's thoughts **2.** worrying one —**out of one's mind** **1.** mentally ill; insane **2.** frantic (with worry, grief, etc.) —**put in mind** to remind —**set one's mind on** to be determined on or determinedly desirous of —**take one's mind off** to stop one from thinking about; turn one's attention from —**to one's mind** in one's opinion

Usage Labels

Usage labels vary from dictionary to dictionary. Most dictionaries have dropped labels like *substandard* and *illiterate* as derogatory or insulting. Some dictionaries no longer label words *informal*, so that you may

---

** *Webster's New World Dictionary,* Second College Edition. Copyright © 1984 by Simon & Schuster, Inc. Reprinted by permission of Simon & Schuster, Inc.

have to decide for yourself that *umptieth, no-no,* and *party pooper* would sound very unbuttoned in serious writing. Even when a dictionary still uses the term *slang,* the label often, in the words of one reviewer, "flickers on and off like a loose light bulb." Nevertheless, the more traditional dictionaries apply restrictive labels to three varieties of English (or **levels of usage**):

NONSTANDARD **Nonstandard** English is for many Americans the workaday speech of street, neighborhood, or construction site; it differs from the **standard** English of the media, of school and office. Nonstandard expressions like *"don't* pay it *no* mind" and "brought it on *hisself"* stand out in writing because we usually associate them with the folk speech of people with limited formal education and with little occasion to write. *Anywheres, nohow,* and *irregardless* are likely to be labeled nonstandard in your dictionary.

INFORMAL Informal language is the variety of standard English we use in casual conversation; it is the chatty kind of language we use when at ease or with our friends. Some dictionaries label it **colloquial**—"conversational, right for informal talk." *Mom-and-pop store, booze, panhandler,* and *skedaddle* are likely to be labeled informal in your dictionary.

SLANG Slang is extremely informal language, usually too freewheeling and disrespectful (not to mention crude) for use in serious discussion. *Klutz, knock it off, blah,* and *humongous* are likely to be labeled slang in your dictionary.

In addition, dictionary makers use regional or dialect labels to show that words are not in common use throughout the country or the English-speaking world. Before the mass media helped homogenize a national language, different regions developed local varieties or **dialects** that often drifted far apart. The people who first sang "Auld Lang Syne" were speaking Scots rather than standard British English. (Other familiar words from Scotland or Northern England: *kirk, loch.*) In this country, the constant intermingling of settlers and the influence of newspapers, radio, and television have prevented the emergence of clearly distinct dialects, though periodically a wag will publish a "Texas dictionary" to explain words like *hunker down.* Words likely to carry a dialect label in your dictionary include *dogie, poke* (a pig in a poke), *reckon* (I reckon you're right), *tote,* and *you all.* Dictionaries show differences between American and British English; they increasingly identify words (or special uses of words) from Canadian, Australian, or South African English:

BRITISH: lorry, lift (elevator), torch (flashlight), wireless, fortnight, bonnet (hood of a car), chemist (druggist)

THE WRITING WORKSHOP

What's New in Dictionaries?

Take part in a group project designed to assist lexicographers of the future. Help research and write a glossary, or set of definitions, for one area of special interest to dictionary makers. Draw on current dictionaries, other printed sources, and interviews with users of the terms you want to define. Choose a project like the following:

1. Investigate words that have come into general use fairly recently and that may not yet be covered in dictionaries. Work with (and add to) the following list, which you may want to sort out according to major areas of interest:

acid rain	Chicano	residuals
aerobics	cosmonaut	schlock
aerospace	fast breeder	sexism
airbag	hospice	skydiving
bleep	hydrofoil	skyjacker
bluegrass	interface	tokenism
body stocking	kibbutz	transplant
brain death	no-show	unisex
buzzword	payload	upscale
CAT scan	replay	voiceover

2. Have your group work on the specialized vocabulary of an area of interest to members of the group. Members of the group may want to work on the vocabulary of jazz (dixieland to modern jazz), sports currently popular with students (surfing, diving, skiing), computers, modern art, or ethnic cuisine.

3. Have your group work on a guide of special regional or historical interest, such as a Texas dictionary, a Sooner dictionary, a 49er dictionary, or a dictionary of Pennsylvania Dutch.

CANADIAN: province, governor general, Grey Cup, permanent force, Calgary Stampede

SOUTH AFRICAN: apartheid, veldt, trek

Note: **Obsolete** words, or meanings of words, have gone out of use altogether. *Nice* in the sense of trivial and *coy* in the sense of quiet are obsolete. **Archaic** words are no longer in common use but survive in special contexts, such as the English of the Bible: *thou* and *thine, brethren, kine* (cattle).

EXERCISE 20   *Looking Up Words*

Which of the italicized words in the following sentences would you have to look up in your dictionary? What does your dictionary tell you about the meaning or uses of each new or difficult word?

1. The Japanese are a *homogeneous* people with a horror of *litigation* and an esteem for *consensus*.
2. China lost its *prominence* to Japan while ruled by a *decadent dynasty* or *feudal* warlords.
3. The reformers have taken care to avoid the mass rallies, *tirades*, and media *fanfare* of past campaigns.
4. The *staunchly* loyal upper ranks of the army had become a *stagnant gerontocracy*.
5. The new leaders have stretched the *procrustean* bed of *Maoism* to fit new needs.

EXERCISE 21   *Knowing Your Dictionary*

Familiarize yourself with your dictionary by investigating the following:

1. Read the definitions of *high tech, cliché, graffiti, gobbledygook, kitsch*. What do they say? Are they clear and informative?
2. Chart some of the major meanings of a word like *hard, hand, foot, head,* or *mind*. Study the order in which the meanings are arranged.
3. How clear and helpful are the definitions of technical terms like *laser, DNA, dialysis, ozone, microwave*?
4. Are there synonym studies for words like *alien, dogmatic, emotion, expedient*? How helpful are they? Find one set of synonyms that you find particularly helpful or instructive.
5. Are there usage labels or usage notes for any of the following: *go-go,* (being) *hip, persnickety, hopefully, bloke, boffo, starkers, funky, hit it off*?
6. What and where are you told about Sappho, Albert Einstein, Theodore Roosevelt, Stalingrad, Peoria, Susan B. Anthony?

EXERCISE 22   *Studying Synonyms*

Study the synonyms in the following sets. What meaning do the three words share? How do they differ? Which differences are differences in connotation?

1. stride—shuffle—slink
2. settlement—compromise—deal
3. obedient—docile—obsequious
4. intelligent—clever—shrewd
5. juvenile—youngster—adolescent
6. childish—childlike—infantile
7. paternal—patriarchal—paternalistic
8. revolt—revolution—mutiny
9. treason—betrayal—treachery
10. expedient—pragmatic—opportunistic

EXERCISE 23   *Checking Usage Labels*

Which of the following words carry usage labels in your dictionary? Which are labeled informal or slang? Which have regional or dialect uses? Which are archaic or obsolete?

bonkers	cove	habitant	prexy
boodle	Franglais	hangup	Sooner
boot	gig	one-liner	sweetie
bower	goober	one shot	tube
complected	goodman	petrol	wonted

Word History   Often we understand a word better and use it with more confidence when we know its history—when we can see how it developed its current meanings and associations. If we know the common root in words like im*pel*, com*pel*, com*pul*sive, and re*pul*sive, we can still sense the force of the Latin word for *push*—pushing us on, or ahead, or away. If we know that the root *eco-* goes back to the Greek word for household, we get a vivid sense of the interrelatedness and interdependence (as of the elements in a household) emphasized in words like *ecology, ecosystem,* and *ecosphere.*

College dictionaries often give a quick rundown of a word's **etymology**, or history, using abbreviations like OE and ME (for Old and Middle English), ON (for Old Norse or early Scandinavian), or IE (for Indo-European, the hypothetical common parent language of most European languages). Here is a capsule history of a word that came into English from Latin by way of Italian and French[††]:

pop·u·lace \'päp-yə-ləs\ *n* [MF, fr. It *popolaccio* rabble, pejorative of *popolo* the people, fr. L *populus*] (1572) **1** : the common people : MASSES **2** : POPULATION

The basic vocabulary of English goes back to the language the Anglo-Saxon tribes brought to England after A.D. 450 from what is now Denmark and Germany: *father, mother, hand, house, bread, water, sun, moon.* But roughly three-fourths of the words in your dictionary came into English from other sources. Throughout its history, English has borrowed heavily from Latin, which Christian missionaries first brought to England as the language of the Roman Catholic church. For centuries, to be educated meant to know Latin and often also Greek, the language of ancient Greek literature, science, and philosophy. Our language of politics, scholarship, science, and technology draws heavily on Latin and Greek roots.

LATIN: history, index, individual, intellect, legal, mechanical, rational
GREEK: anonymous, atmosphere, catastrophe, chaos, crisis, skeleton

When the French-speaking Normans conquered England after A.D. 1066, French became for a time the language of law, administration, and literature. Over the next two centuries, thousands of words from the French of the Norman overlords were absorbed into Middle English: *castle, court, glory, mansion, noble, prison, privilege, servant, treason, war.* Since the beginning of Modern English (about 1500), French has supplied many words for fashions, the arts, and military organization. Italian furnished words to help us talk about opera and music; from Spanish or Portuguese, English took over words derived from New World sources.

FRENCH: ballet, battalion, cadet, corps, façade, infantry, negligee, patrol
ITALIAN: concert, falsetto, sonata, solo, soprano, violin
SPANISH: alligator, banana, cannibal, cocoa, mosquito, tobacco, tomato

Today, words continue to come into English from other languages. We have seen French restaurants reduce portions and raise prices as they switch to *nouvelle cuisine.* Reporters use the Arab word *jihad* for a holy war against the enemies of Islam. We are getting used to encountering words from Russian or Japanese:

RUSSIAN: troika, apparatchik, sputnik, gulag, nomenklatura, glasnost
JAPANESE: samurai, shogun, kamikaze, hibachi, karate, haiku

[††] By permission from *Webster's Ninth New Collegiate Dictionary* © 1988 by Merriam-Webster, Inc., publisher of the Merriam-Webster® dictionaries.

When such words are not yet fully naturalized, your dictionary may put a special symbol in front of them or label them French, Chinese, or whatever is appropriate.

FOREIGN WORDS: uhuru (Swahili), mensch (Yiddish)

Latin and Greek Roots

Writers trying to fortify their vocabularies profit from the way dictionaries highlight Latin and Greek roots, especially if these are still active in the formation of new words. Knowing the Latin root *mal-* for "bad" helps us understand *malpractice, malfunction, malnutrition, malformation,* and *malfeasance.* Knowing that the Greek root *bio-* means "life" helps us with *biopsy, biochemistry, biomass, biofeedback,* and *bionics.* Here is a brief list of common Latin and Greek roots:

ROOT	MEANING	EXAMPLES
arch-	*rule*	monarchy, anarchy, matriarch
auto-	*self*	autocratic, autonomy, automation
capit-	*head*	capital, per capita, decapitate
chron-	*time*	chronological, synchronize, anachronism
doc-	*teach*	docile, doctrine, indoctrinate
graph-	*write*	autograph, graphic, seismograph
hydr-	*water*	dehydrate, hydraulic, hydrogen
phon-	*sound*	euphony, phonograph, symphony
port-	*carry*	portable, exports, deportation
terr-	*land*	inter, terrestrial, subterranean
urb-	*city*	suburb, urban, urbane
verb-	*word*	verbal, verbiage, verbose
vit-	*life*	vitality, vitamin, revitalize
vol-	*will*	volition, involuntary, volunteer

Prefixes and **suffixes** are exchangeable attachments at the beginning or end of a word: *pre*war, *post*war, *anti*war; organ*ize*, organ*ic*, organ*ism*. Knowing that the Latin prefix *sub-* means "under" helps explain *subconscious, submarine, subterranean,* and *subzero.* The Latin suffix *-cide* means "killing"—helping us understand not only *homicide* and *suicide* but also *fratricide* (killing of a brother) and *parricide* (killing of a parent). Here is a brief list of common Latin and Greek prefixes:

PREFIXES	MEANING	EXAMPLES
bene-	*good*	benefactor, benefit, benevolent
bi-	*two*	bicycle, bilateral, bisect
contra-	*against*	contraband, contradict, contravene
dis-	*away, apart*	disperse, disorganize, discourage
ex-	*out*	exclude, exhale, expel
extra-	*outside*	extraordinary, extravagant, extrovert
mono-	*one*	monarch, monopoly, monolithic
multi-	*many*	multilateral, multinational, multiethnic
omni-	*all*	omnipotent, omnipresent, omniscient
per-	*through*	percolate, perforate, permeate
pre-	*before*	preamble, precedent, prefix
poly-	*many*	polygamy, polysyllabic, polytheistic
post-	*after*	postpone, postwar, postscript
re-	*back*	recall, recede, revoke, retract
tele-	*distant*	telegraph, telepathy, telephone
trans-	*across, beyond*	transatlantic, transmit, transcend

New Words Our language is always creating new words for new needs. Lexicographers, who at one time frowned on new words, now compete in their coverage of **neologisms**, or newly coined expressions. Technology, space exploration, genetics, medicine, and computers create a constant demand for new words, as do the drug culture and changes in lifestyle (a fashionable new word). Many new words fill an obvious need and are rapidly accepted: *astronaut, fallout, data base, flextime, space shuttle, aerobics, high tech*. Other new words at first sound clever or imaginative but soon become simply convenient shorthand for what they stand for: *palimony, petrodollars, no-show, baby boomer, floppy disk, joystick, boat people, laugh track*. Still other coinages, however, sound cute, awkward, or far-fetched and alienate conservative readers. Avoid coinages that smack of media hype, advertising prose, or bureaucratic jargon:

MEDIA HYPE:	megabuck, docudrama, infomercial, sexploitation
ADVERTISING WORDS:	jumboize, paperamics, outdoorsman, moisturize, usership
BUREAUCRATIC:	escapee, definitize, prioritize, socioeconomic

Remember: A modern dictionary is not intended as an arbiter of right and wrong but as a guide to the marvelously rich resources of our language. Do not consult it only the way you would a telephone book—to find a quick answer to a limited question. Browse: follow up cross references; let one word lead to another. Become fascinated by the way words allow us to register our observations, crystallize our experience, systematize our knowledge, and formulate our thinking.

EXERCISE 24   *Words and Their History*

What does your dictionary tell you about the history of the following words? Select ten, and report briefly on the history of each. What language did it come from? How did it acquire its current meaning?

algebra	hogan	paradise	pundit
crusade	immigrant	pogrom	Sabbath
disaster	laissez faire	police	slalom
ecology	millennium	primadonna	virtuoso
gospel	nirvana	propaganda	xenophobia

EXERCISE 25   *Going to the Roots*

What is the meaning of the common element in each of the following sets? How does the shared root or suffix help explain each word in the set?

1. anesthetic—anemic—amoral
2. antibiotic—biography—biology
3. audiovisual—audition—inaudible
4. cosmic—cosmopolitan—microcosm
5. disunity—discord—dissent
6. eugenics—eulogy—euphonious
7. heterogeneous—heterosexual—heterodox
8. magnify—magnificent—magnitude
9. monarchy—oligarchy—anarchy
10. synchronize—symphony—sympathy

EXERCISE 26   *Studying Prefixes*

Explain the basic meaning of each *Latin and Greek prefix* used in the following words: *ambivalent, antedate, antipathy, circumvent, concord, hyper-*

sensitive, international, introvert, multimillionaire, neofascist, pseudoscientific, retroactive, semitropical, ultramodern, unilateral.

EXERCISE 27 *Words Foreign and Domestic*

What does each of the following expressions mean? What language did it come from? Which of them does your dictionary still consider foreign rather than English?

ad hoc	El Dorado	paparazzo
aficionado	fait accompli	quod erat demonstrandum
blitz	habeas corpus	reich
Bushido	karma	samurai
de jure	kung fu	shiksa

16

THE SENTENCE

Building Better Sentences

> *By an almost miraculous process, we eventually learn to expand the minimal sentence "Birds sing" into a sentence like "The huddling gray birds sing forlornly in the bare branches of the tree."*   Edward P. J. Corbett

> *Just imagine a sentence-producing computer capable of printing out sentences day after day, year after year, without ever producing the same sentence twice. The language area of your brain is like that.*   Martha Kolln

> *Language is the medium through which we see the world.*   Paul Roberts

A RATIONALE FOR SENTENCE WORK The writer's most basic tool is the sentence. Sentences come in all shapes and sizes. Some are brief. They come right to the point:

Time flies. Money talks. Speed kills.

Most are longer, specifying which one and what kind, telling us when, where, or how:

Mickey Mouse, the ratty character of *Steamboat Willie*, evolved into the cute and inoffensive host of the Magic Kingdom.

A fully developed sentence does not merely string together pieces of information the way computers print out strings of data. It does not merely record what we know; it shows how we think. We are not likely to write: "The Beatles were playing in obscure clubs. Record company executives discouraged them. They went on to become the idols of a generation." Instead we are likely to write:

The Beatles were playing in obscure clubs, *and* record company executives discouraged them, *but* they went on to become the idols of a generation.

Similarly, we are not likely to write: "The space shuttle had several successful flights. The last flight of the *Challenger* turned into a disaster. It had been touted as a special event." We are more likely to write:

Although the space shuttle had had several successful flights, the last flight of the *Challenger, which* had been touted as a special event, turned into a disaster.

Each time, the combined sentence shows the connection between ideas; it makes each separate statement a link in a chain of thought.

How do you learn to write better sentences? The answer is study and practice—watching the experts, setting up a schedule of workouts, starting with simple moves but pushing on to exercises that might have daunted a beginner. Several kinds of productive sentence work combine in a program designed to improve your confidence and extend your range as a writer.

Sentence Recognition

Effective writers have a lively sense of how good sentences are put together. They recognize major sentence-building techniques that help us develop, expand, or combine sentences:

BASIC PATTERN:	Americans love sports.
MODIFIERS:	*Many* Americans love the *traditional spectator* sports.
COMPOUNDING:	Many Americans love *football, baseball, and basketball.*
COORDINATION:	Many younger Americans love the traditional spectator sports, *but* they also practice every kind of exercise.
SUBORDINATION:	The older generation drinks beer at football games *while* the younger generation jogs or works out.

Sentence Combining

Sentence-combining exercises take you systematically from simple building blocks to more elaborate structures. A typical exercise will furnish brief source sentences and show you how to combine them in a larger sentence. A longer sentence is not always better than a short one, but an effective writer knows how to put together a long detailed sentence when it is needed. Here are some examples of simple source sentences feeding into a larger combined sentence:

FIRST SOURCE:	Some people despise yuppies.
SECOND SOURCE:	Even these people admit something.
THIRD SOURCE:	Yuppies work hard.

COMBINED:	*Even* people *who despise yuppies* admit *that they work hard.* Peter Baida
FIRST SOURCE:	We sat together.
SECOND SOURCE:	We were holding our lunch buckets on our knees.
THIRD SOURCE:	We were looking out at the trees beside the road.
COMBINED:	We sat together, *holding our lunch buckets on our knees, looking out at the trees beside the road.* Lois Phillips Hudson

Sentence Imitation

Often the best way to learn is by imitation, by modeling your own performance on that of the outstanding practitioner. When doing sentence imitation exercises, you take in the pattern of a model sentence and then write a sentence of your own that follows closely the pattern of the original. Sentence imitation provides the bridge between sentence practice and your own writing. Although you pattern your sentence on a model sentence, you draw on your own observation; you bring your own imagination (and sense of humor) into play. Study the following models and student-written imitations:

MODEL:	Economy is the art of making the most of life. G. B. Shaw
IMITATION:	Cooking is the art of making the most of food.
MODEL:	Corporations have discovered that buying computer software is cheaper than hiring consultants.
IMITATION:	Students have discovered that using cheap calculators is better than making mistakes.

Sentence Revision

Sentence building of all kinds helps you use the full range of your sentence resources. Even so, in writing and revising, you will often need to improve sentences that say what you mean in an awkward, roundabout way. To clarify a confused sentence, you may have to ask yourself questions like "Who does what? What goes with what?"

MIXED:	In today's world, almost anything anyone does wrong is being taken to court to get some money out of it. (*Who* is taken to court? *Who* wants to get money out of it?)
REVISED:	Today, *anyone* who does something wrong is likely to be taken to court by *someone* who wants to profit from the mistake.

Remember: In a good sentence, the shape seems a natural fit for the content; the medium serves the message. Well-written short sentences highlight a key point or a key event. They give the reader something to remember and to think about. Well-written long sentences carry a rich array of details, showing the full ramifications of a situation or an idea, helping us take in the main points and keep the lesser points in perspective.

THE WRITING WORKSHOP

Fabulous Realities

Every so often, a sentence stands out because the writer had a quick eye for the "fabulous realities" (Ken Macrocrie) or astonishing facts that lurk in the world around us or on a newspaper page. Study the following examples of sentences packed with striking, revealing, or unusual detail. Participate in a group-writing project: Have each member of the group submit sentences for possible inclusion in a collection of fabulous realities; have the group (or your class as a whole) vote on or rank the best entries. Sample sentences:

1. Every night, 20 million bats flap up from Bracken Cave, Texas, in a chirping brown tornado and gulp down enough bugs to fill six tanker trucks.

2. On a trashy and treeless street, there is a huge billboard of a woman in a slinky dress looking back over her shoulder, saying, "I assume you drink Martell."   Joel Achenbach

3. Surrounded by a black cast-iron cage, the spindly tree makes its way toward the sky, a smattering of green leaves spreading out to catch the occasional ray of sunlight poking through the maze of highrises.

4. A tense young figure in a starched white cotton coat gingerly enters a long silver suture needle into a laceration above a staring blue eye which alone is visible in a masked and shrouded face.

5. The old theater has a huge screen, a musty smell, torn seats, and a sticky floor that grabs the spectator's feet and won't let go.

EXERCISE 1   *The Short Sentence*

Proverbs and other memorable sayings often use a minimum of grammatical machinery. We remember them because they are short and to the point. For the following sayings, write an updated modern saying that stays close to the sentence structure of the original.

MODEL SENTENCE: Brevity is the soul of wit.
SAMPLE IMITATION: The laugh track is the bane of situation comedy.

1. A little rebellion is a good thing.   Thomas Jefferson
2. A young doctor requires a big cemetery.   Dutch proverb

3. An empty pocket goes quickly through the market.   Scotch proverb
4. Loneliness is the poverty of the self.   May Sarton
5. Birds of a feather flock together.
6. A day of battle is a day of harvest for the devil.
7. One must never turn his back on life.   Eleanor Roosevelt
8. One man's meat is another man's poison.
9. Death devours all lovely things.   Edna St. Vincent Millay
10. The ox never says "thank you" to the pasture.   Creole proverb

EXERCISE 2   *The Long Sentence*

Lead sentences in newspapers or newsmagazines often sum up the essentials of a story in a single sentence. Such sentences are often weighty and informative; they carry considerable freight. Study the following examples of long, weighty sentences. Then write five similar packed sentences of your own, each summing up important details of a current or recent news story. (You need not follow the sentence structure of the originals.)

1. On July 16, 1969, the tall slender rocket, like an inverted torch, lifted off the launch pad in a billow of white steam to carry three men to the moon.
2. In August of 1976, a tornado swept through the streets of Henry County, Georgia, slurping everything in its path and leaving behind it numerous towns destroyed beyond repair.
3. In a move that shocked farmers, the Interior Department yesterday decided that it will close the polluted Kesterton wildlife refuge and shut off irrigation water to cropland that drains toxic waste into the sanctuary.
4. The Defense Department has allowed construction companies to pocket millions of dollars for shoddy work in recent years while letting them act as inspectors of their own projects and rarely forcing them to repair their mistakes.
5. In the largest shipment ever of animals from one continent to another, one thousand rhinos, giraffes, zebras, and birds are being moved in twenty-two trips from Grand Prairie's International Wildlife Park in Texas to the new Taipei City Zoo in Taiwan.

A WRITER'S GRAMMAR

In the beginning, the grammarian created nouns and verbs. (And they brought forth abundantly the adjectives and adverbs, the phrases and clauses, the participles and gerunds, each after their own kind.) How much grammar does a writer need? The **grammar** of a language is the system that regulates how words work together in a sentence. To talk about how sentences work (and how they break down), we need to recognize their basic building blocks and the way these combine to form familiar patterns.

Grammarians have traditionally furnished a thorough inventory of such basic sentence parts and the functions they serve. However, like history or mathematics, grammar has experienced revisionist movements, causing grammarians to rearrange some of their mental furniture. By and large, modern grammar has moved in a direction beneficial to the writer who asks: "What does this help me *do*?" In a *writer's grammar*, we look for less emphasis on taking sentences apart and more on how to put them together—less sentence analysis and more sentence construction. We put less emphasis on how sentences go wrong and more on how to make them go right.

Basic Sentence Parts

You may have studied more than once the kinds of words (or **parts of speech**) that we employ in building sentences: nouns, pronouns, verbs, adjectives, adverbs, prepositions, and conjunctions. Make sure you understand the *uses* we make of them—how we arrange them in patterns that carry our message, how we make them work for us in a sentence. Stripped to its essentials, the English sentence has only two basic parts: the subject and the predicate. Somebody acts, or something happens, or something exists:

> The driver brakes. Volcanoes erupt. God exists.

SUBJECT

The **subject** of a sentence brings something to our attention, so that the predicate can make a statement about it. The core of the subject is most commonly a **noun**—a word we use to name or label things, people, animals, places, and ideas: *driver, volcano, bicycle, horse, prairie, freedom.* The names of products listed in a mail-order catalog are all nouns (*flashlight, exercycle, kayak*); so are the labels that show people's occupations (*chiropractor, violinist, technician*).

Familiar clues help us spot nouns in a sentence. Most stand for things we can count; they add the *-s* ending to change from singular to plural: one *swallow*, several *swallows*; one *family*, several *families*; one *ticket*, several *tickets*. (A few do not use the *-s*; irregular plurals include *people, children, women.*) Nouns often follow a noun marker, a word signaling that a noun is about to follow: *the* Constitution, *a* surprise, *an* agronomist (**articles**); *this* land, *these* grievances, *that* treaty (**demonstrative pronouns**); *my* fault, *your* choice, *our* duty (**possessive pronouns**). Typical noun endings can also help us recognize nouns: child*hood*, Christen*dom*, forgive*ness*.

Some pronouns, instead of preparing us for nouns, take the place of one; they serve as shorthand for something whose identity is already clear: *She* brakes. *They* erupt. *He* exists (**personal pronouns**).

PREDICATE The **predicate** of a sentence makes a statement about the subject. (Sometimes it asks a question about the subject.) The core of the predicate is the verb: *preaches, assemble, complained, has left, may return, was indicted, has been driving, could have been avoided.* Verbs report actions, events, or conditions. They help us set things in motion; they often stand for something we can do: *leave* the key; let's *celebrate; pass* the butter.

Familiar clues help us recognize verbs in a sentence. Verbs can show a change in time (or **tense**) by a change in the word itself: *asks* (now), *asked* (then); *steals* (in the present), *stole* (in the past). Verbs are often not single words; to form the complete verb, we often put one or more **auxiliaries** (helping verbs) before the main verb: *will* arrive, *may* happen, *is* raining, *has* expired, *should be* notified, *was* reported, *could have* forgotten, *might have been* dreaming. (Note that an auxiliary like *will, can,* or *may* comes before the auxiliaries *have* and *be.*) Some verbs have typical verb endings like *-fy, -en,* or *-ize*: magni*fy*, weak*en*, saniti*ze*.

MODIFIERS In practice, we seldom use the simple noun-and-verb sentence (Birds fly). Usually, we already include **modifiers** that develop, expand, or narrow the meaning of the basic sentence parts:

> *Most American songbirds fly south in the winter.*

Some of these modifiers are single words. **Adjectives** modify nouns, answering questions like "Which one?" or "What kind?" They typically appear immediately before the noun (often between the noun marker and the noun): a *cheap* shot, a *tall* order, the *right* answer, *high* hopes, *terrible* news. Number adjectives tell us how many or which of several: *three* blind mice, the *first* date, *last* chance. Unlike nouns and verbs, many adjectives fit in after words that show differences in degree: very *cold*, fairly *new*, extremely *dangerous*, absolutely *spectacular.* Such adjectives have special forms for use in comparisons: small—*smaller*—*smallest*; good—*better*—*best*; harmful—*more* harmful—*most* harmful. Another clue that can help you recognize adjectives is the use of typical adjective endings, such as *-able, -ic, -ish, -ive, -ous,* and *-ful*: dispos*able*, gener*ic*, thirty*ish*, abus*ive*, raven*ous*, bounti*ful.*

As adjectives typically cluster around nouns, so **adverbs** cluster around verbs. They modify verbs by answering questions like how, when, where, or how often:

HOW?	cautiously, timidly, arrogantly,
WHEN?	now, tomorrow, immediately,
WHERE?	here, upstairs, downtown,
HOW OFTEN?	twice, frequently, rarely.

Many adverbs have the *-ly* ending (*rapidly, basically, eventually*), but so do some exceptional adjectives (a *friendly* conversation, a *leisurely* drive).

Like adjectives, many adverbs fit in after words that show degree: very *cheaply*, more *relevantly*, most *certainly*. A special feature of adverbs is greater freedom of movement in a sentence:

> The fire started *suddenly.*
> I *suddenly* remembered her warning.
> *Suddenly* we had a new principal.

Nouns, pronouns, verbs, adjectives, and adverbs are five word classes that we use over and over in putting together short sentences. Two additional parts of speech become important as links between other sentence parts:

- **Prepositions** are words like *at, of, with, in, for, to, with,* or *without*; we use them to tie a prepositional phrase to the rest of the sentence: Thousands *of* cars were stalled *on* the approaches *to* the bridge. (A **phrase** is a group of words that work together, but it does not have its own subject and verb.)

- **Conjunctions** are words like *and, but, if, because,* and *whereas.* They become important when we start combining several clauses in a larger, more elaborate sentence: *Before* we left, we called the agency, *but* a machine answered. (A **clause** is a group of words that has its own subject and verb.)

Sentence Patterns

The subject-verb pattern is only one of the basic sentence models that provide the skeleton for more fully developed sentences. As there are two-wheel vehicles, three-wheel vehicles, and four-wheel vehicles, so there are sentence models with two, three, or four basic parts. In the subject-verb pattern (S–V), we need not go on after the verb; the verb alone can tell the whole story: Seals *bark.* Radioactivity *lingers.* We call such verbs **intransitive** verbs: They need nothing further to make a complete statement; they "are not going anywhere."

Many other verbs require a third basic sentence part to make the sentence complete; they require a completer, or **complement**:

> Angelica repaired _____ (what?).
> Dudley is making _____ (what?).
> The mayor announced _____ (what?).

We call the missing target or result the **object** of the sentence: Angelica repaired *watches.* Dudley is making *sandals.* The mayor announced *her resignation* (S–V–O). Note that the object adds a second noun to the sentence. (Verbs that carry the action across to an object are **transitive** verbs.)

Sometimes a fourth sentence part becomes part of the basic structure. Before we go on to the product or result, we can specify the intended destination. We call the added part the **indirect** object: The panhandler gave *the tourists* directions. The sixth grade wrote *Gorbachev* a letter. Mario sends *his ex-wives* Valentines (S–V–IO–O). Verbs that work in this pattern include *give, lend, sell, promise, ask,* and *tell*. Compare these first three basic patterns:

S–V:	Seals bark.
S–V–O:	Sharks attack seals.
S–V–IO–O:	The keeper was feeding the seals fish.

A second set of sentence patterns uses a special kind of verb. Instead of an action verb aimed at a target or result, we use a **linking verb**, which pins a label on the subject: The ape was *a gorilla*. The warden is *my friend*. The audition had been *a disaster* (S–LV–N). Note that here the second noun is not the target or product of an action; it merely puts a new label on the first. The two nouns refer to the same thing or person. ("Susan loved a biker" involves two people; "Susan was a biker" only one.) Often the linking verb is a form of the verb *be: am, is, was, will be, has been, might have been*. Other words used as linking verbs are *become, remain, stay,* and *seem*: Reagan became *President*. Kennedy remained *a senator*. In a similar pattern, an adjective replaces the noun as the third basic part of the sentence: Carrots are *nutritious*. The stores remained *open*. His face turned *blue*. Compare the two patterns using linking verbs:

S–LV–N:	The cook was *a vegetarian*.
S–LV–ADJ:	The donor remained *anonymous*.

Two additional sentence models combine features of the first and second set. The verb first carries the action across to an object and then pins a label on the object. Verbs used in these patterns include *name, make, call, elect,* and *appoint*. The additional completer that follows the object may be a second noun: The mayor called his accuser *a liar*. Presidents have made their supporters *ambassadors* (S–V–O–N). Or the second completer may be an adjective: The critic called the movie *deplorable*. Exams made my life *miserable* (S–V–O–ADJ). An overview of the seven basic patterns would look like this:

S–V:	Bees buzz.
S–V–O:	Ranchers hate coyotes.
S–V–IO–O:	Lemonade gave Filbert the hiccups.
S–LV–N:	Whales are mammals.
S–LV–ADJ:	Patricia was ambidextrous.
S–V–O–N:	Our manager considered the tour a success.
S–V–O–ADJ:	Beer made Milwaukee famous.

The basic patterns give us the stripped-down models that in most actual sentences come equipped with extras. However, remember that not all sentences are statements; many are questions or requests. To turn a statement into a question, we can often simply move all or part of the verb in front of the subject:

Is Patricia your friend?
Has her story been checked?
Will your guests consider pizza low-class?

To turn a statement into a request or command, we can often simply delete or omit the subject (the *you* being addressed is understood):

Honor labor.   *Remember* the Alamo.   *Praise* the Lord.

Modern grammarians call the reshufflings or adaptations that turn statements into questions or requests **transformations**. A third important transformation turns active sentences into **passive** ones, which start not with the active element (the doer or agent) but with the target, result, or product of the action. "*Edison* invented the light bulb" becomes "*The light bulb* was invented by Edison." In a passive sentence, the original object has moved out in front and become the new subject. The original subject appears after *by* or has disappeared altogether: Vegetables should be steamed (*by the cook*). The suspect has been questioned (*by the police*).

Remember: To understand how sentences work and to use them more effectively, you need to grasp the basic structures from which real-life sentences have evolved. A limited number of basic patterns provide the underpinnings for most of the infinitely varied sentences you will encounter.

EXERCISE 3   *Using the Patterns*

In the following sentences, adjectives and adverbs have been used to round out some of the basic patterns. (What is the basic pattern underlying each sentence?) For each sentence, write a sentence of your own that follows the structure of the original as closely as possible.

1. Little strokes fell great oaks.
   SAMPLE IMITATION: New ideas disturb little minds.
2. The used key is always bright.
3. Misery loves company.
4. You cannot teach an old dog new tricks.
5. A cheerful look makes a dish a feast.
6. Debt makes another person your master.

THE WRITING WORKSHOP

Following the Rules

We can demonstrate how grammatical rules operate by showing them at work in sentences that are perfectly grammatical even if they do not make perfect sense. Working with a group, prepare and help select a collection of sentences that follow the basic rules for sentence building in English while at the same time they sound as if they had been written by someone with a wild imagination. Help weed out sentences that are ungrammatical. Here are student-written examples of real English sentences with fantastic content:

1. Alleyways filled up with chop suey.
2. Running down a tree, the garbageman slid into a chocolate pie.
3. Backward staples flew off the page and into the bathtub.
4. Downtown buildings waltzed down the boulevard.
5. Gangsters joined the swift pigeons for an early dinner.
6. Concerned orioles laid their quotas of eggs.
7. Fern enthusiasts eat daintily.
8. The skinheads called the squirtgun a miracle.
9. Herds of lambchops spoke ingratiatingly.
10. Nerfballs slithered along the ignorant plains.

7. Time flies.
8. Laziness makes all things difficult.
9. A small leak will sink a great ship.
10. Time is money.

EXERCISE 4   *Sentence Recognition: Basic Patterns*

In each of the following sets, two sentences are very similar in their basic structure. Even though they may have been expanded somewhat, they illustrate the same basic sentence patterns, or they illustrate the same transformation or variation of a basic pattern (question, request, or passive). The remaining sentence in each set is different; it is put together in a different way. Write the number of the set, followed by the letter of the different sentence.

EXAMPLE: 4.   (a)   Our country offered the refugees asylum. (S–V–IO–O)

                        (b)   Exams gave Timothy a headache. (S–V–IO–O)

                        (c)   Her teacher had called the idea brilliant. (S–V–O–ADJ)

ANSWER: 4.   c

1. (a) Her grandparents had been Lithuanian immigrants.
   (b) The newcomers became American citizens.
   (c) The judge asked the candidates simple questions.

2. (a) The city will host the convention.
   (b) Our computer has made a mistake.
   (c) The signature was illegible.

3. (a) Lenders were charging customers exorbitant interest.
   (b) The angry customer called the charges a scandal.
   (c) The governor had labeled deregulation a disaster.

4. (a) The school board banned our humor magazine.
   (b) Malnutrition had become a national menace.
   (c) Bromo-Seltzer will cure that headache.

5. (a) The country reluctantly entered the war.
   (b) China had been invaded by the Japanese.
   (c) The documents were copied by a German spy.

6. (a) The authorities had denied her husband a passport.
   (b) The parents gave the happy pair their blessing.
   (c) Her decision will keep the voters happy.

7. (a) Leonard foolishly lent strangers money.
   (b) The voters had elected an actor governor.
   (c) The couple named their first child Miranda.

8. (a) Reports from the combat zone arrived daily.
   (b) Report all violations immediately.
   (c) Record your complaints carefully.

9. (a) Corruption was common in high places.
   (b) The apartment was searched by the police.
   (c) Her uncle looked different without a wig.

10. (a) Charitable people give generously to charities.
    (b) Please contribute freely to the heart fund.
    (c) Members contributed heavily to the war chest.

SENTENCE BUILDING: MODIFICATION AND COMPOUNDING

Sentences stripped to their basic patterns give us only a minimum of information: "The woman stood." "The man started his pitch." A fully developed sentence fills in details, answering the questions that arise in the reader's mind: What did she do? What kind of man? What kind of pitch?

SIMPLE: The woman stood.
EXPANDED: *The* short, wrinkled old *woman* with bifocals *stood* behind the counter reading a fishing magazine.

SIMPLE: The man started his pitch.
EXPANDED: *The* middle-aged *man* wearing black-rimmed glasses, a dark blue suit, and a white shirt opened his worn-out briefcase and *started his* sales *pitch* to sell encyclopedias.

We use two kinds of material to build up bare-minimum sentences. First, **modifiers** develop or narrow the meaning of the basic sentence parts. A modifier may be a single word: The burglar *cautiously* opened the *heavy* door. But often a modifier is a **phrase**—a group of related words working together in a sentence:

They crossed the river *in a small rubber raft.*
The rhinoceros, *an animal built like a tank,* faces extinction.
Pursued by reporters, the President hurried on.

Second, we develop simple sentences by **compounding**—using more than one of the basic sentence parts or a set of similar modifiers. Notice the doubling (or tripling) of sentence parts in the following examples:

The walrus and the carpenter were walking close at hand.
Early in the movie, a robot *is struck* by lightning, *runs* amok, and *achieves* true human consciousness.
A French designer has designed made-to-order shoes for *Elizabeth Taylor, Rudolph Nureyev,* and *the Rolling Stones.*

Adjectives and Adverbs

Adjectives are modifiers that cluster around nouns. Mark Twain once called someone a *long, slim, bony, smooth-shaven, horse-faced, ignorant, stingy, malicious* tyrant. (Sometimes other words are used in the place of an adjective, such as the first nouns in combinations like *police* dog, *sales* tax, or *labor* union.) **Adverbs** are modifiers that cluster around verbs: The mail carrier *frequently* rings *twice.* (Adverbs also modify other modifiers: The *extremely* hungry guests ate *incredibly* fast.) We can use strings of related adjectives or adverbs to pack in information or to bring a sentence to life:

ADJECTIVES: An *appetizing round ripe homegrown juicy navel* orange is worth a sackful of *greenish dry tasteless supermarket* fruit.

ADVERBS: They *solemnly* promised *never* to play *outside alone again.*

Prepositional Phrases

Prepositions are words like *of, at, in, to, for, into, as, by, before, after, during, from, since, until, through, under, with,* and *without* (as well as combinations like *out of, because of, in spite of,* and *as to*). They link a noun (or equivalent) to other sentence parts, combining with it to form a **prepositional phrase**. Often several prepositional phrases build up information in the same sentence: *To my surprise,* the portrait *of her predecessor* hung *behind her desk.* Singles nights *at museums* have become popular *in several cities.* Several prepositions may serve as links in a chain of prepositional phrases (notice that prepositional phrases often include additional material):

A Maine couple sued their neighbors *for* painting their garage *with* a large red face *with* its tongue sticking out.

Caution: When modifiers are split off from the sentences to which they belong, they cause **sentence fragments** that mirror the afterthoughts and asides of stop-and-go conversation:

FRAGMENT: The rescue party found the climbers. *Exhausted but alive.*

COMPLETE: The rescue party found the climbers exhausted but alive.

FRAGMENT: The earth moves around the sun. *In an elliptical orbit.*

COMPLETE: The earth moves around the sun in an elliptical orbit.

EXERCISE 5 *Sentence Building: Modifiers*

Build up the following simple sentences by adding adjectives, adverbs, and prepositional phrases. Use at least one of each kind of modifier in your expanded sentence.

EXAMPLE: The cowboy rode the horse.

ANSWER: The *handsome screen* cowboy *slowly* rode the *magnificent* horse *into the sunset.*

1. The comic strip showed characters.
2. The detective questioned the suspect.
3. Reporters trailed the candidate.
4. The tourist asked the guide questions.
5. The conquerors destroyed civilizations.
6. The woman approached the gate.

7. Athletes are tested.
8. The victims had been attacked.
9. Movies feature aliens.
10. The judge admonished the lawyer.

EXERCISE 6   *Sentence Imitation: Modifiers*

Study the use of adjectives, adverbs, and prepositional phrases in the following model sentences. For each model, write a similar sentence of your own, following the sentence structure of the original as closely as you can. (You need not follow it in all details.)

1. As a basketball player, I am fast, quick, patient, smooth, sharp, sensible, magnificent, great, unbeatable, outstanding, outgoing, fantastic, marvelous, and humble. Jesse F. Kingsberry

   SAMPLE IMITATION: As a driver, I am experienced, calm, casual, prepared, courteous, patient, efficient, trustworthy, and uninsured.
2. At the head of the gulch, they found the deuce of clubs pinned to the bark with a bowie knife.   Bret Harte
3. Imported motorcycles—flashy, reliable, durable, and less expensive—drove the Harley-Davidsons off the market.
4. A place without birds is like food without seasoning.
5. Three golden eye-catching poisonous barbed lizards basked in the warm dry lazy afternoon sun.
6. The dream of every manager is to find employees who will work hard, cheaply, reliably, silently, and fast.

Using Appositives

When your sentences sound too flat and predictable, you can vary their rhythm or improve their texture by using appositives. An **appositive** is a second noun that (usually) follows and modifies another noun: my son, *the doctor*; my enemy, *the dean.* The appositive is often in turn modified by other material: Margaret Mead, *the famous anthropologist*; my aunt, *a vigorous woman of fifty-five.* More than one appositive may inject explanations into a sentence:

In *My Antonia, her best-known book,* Willa Cather writes about her favorite region, *the prairie country of south-central Nebraska.*

Look at the way we can lift an appositive from an additional statement and insert it into a sentence pocket in the original sentence:

SEPARATE: The Siberian tiger _____ may soon survive only in zoos. It is an endangered species.

COMBINED:	The Siberian tiger, *an endangered species,* may soon survive only in zoos.
SEPARATE:	The story dealt with telepathy _____. It is a kind of mind reading often found in science fiction.
COMBINED:	The story dealt with telepathy, *a kind of mind reading often found in science fiction.*

Using Verbals

Verbals are the most versatile of the elements we use to bring color and life into anemic sentences. Verbals are parts of verbs or special forms that can no longer serve as the complete verb in a sentence. (*He writing* or *the letter written* is not a complete sentence.) Instead, verbals serve many needs, such as greatly broadening our range of modifiers. Forms like *writing, burning, eroding,* or *tantalizing* (present participles) and forms like *written, hidden, burnt, betrayed,* and *anesthetized* (past participles) can take the place of adjectives: a *burning* issue, a *tantalizing* prospect; *hidden* inflation, the *anesthetized* patient. Often the verbal brings additional material with it into the original simpler sentence:

SEPARATE:	He heard the officers.
	He had hidden in the cellar.
	They were searching the house.
COMBINED:	*Hidden in the cellar,* he heard the officers *searching the house.*

Study the full range of possible positions for such added verbal phrases:

Swiss researchers *studying joggers* have found lacerations from bird attacks.
I lay on the couch in the kitchen, *reading* The Last Days of Pompeii and *wishing I were there.*   Alice Munro
Manuel, *leaning against the barrera, watching the bull,* waved his hand and the gypsy ran out, *trailing his cape.*   Ernest Hemingway

A second kind of verbal is also used as a modifier—the *to-*form, or **infinitive**: *to love, to sympathize, to have served, to be arrested.* Like other verbals, infinitives often carry other material with them:

His friends would drive five hundred miles *to hear the Grateful Dead.*
It seemed a good time *to strike out on her own.*
To evaluate future employees, the company fed a psychological profile into the computer.

Some verbals bring along their own subjects (as if they were still used as verbs). Such **absolute constructions** allow us to blend a second statement into the original simpler sentence:

SEPARATE:	The picture showed the champion.
	Her hands were raised in victory.
COMBINED:	The picture showed the champion, *her hands raised in victory.*

The verbal may be missing from an absolute construction if the complete verb in the original separate sentences would have been a form like *is* or *was*:

SEPARATE: A reporter from the campus paper was on hand.
Her notepad was open.
Her camera was around her neck.

COMBINED: A reporter from the campus paper was on hand, *her notepad open, her camera around her neck.*

Study the variety in sentence rhythm that writers achieve by working absolute constructions into a sentence:

The truck, *its radiator steaming,* came to a rumbling halt.
My head bursting with stories and schemes, I stumbled in next door.   Frank O'Connor
Another car, traveling slowly by, hesitated opposite, *its red dome light blinking.*   Hortense Calisher

Caution: Like other modifiers, appositives and verbals cause fragments when split off from the rest of the sentence:

FRAGMENT: We were reading "I Stand Here Ironing." *A short story by Tillie Olsen.*

COMPLETE: We were reading "I Stand Here Ironing," a short story by Tillie Olsen.

FRAGMENT: *Dallas* is about the rich and the would-be rich. *Driven by lust and greed.*

COMPLETE: *Dallas* is about the rich and the would-be rich, driven by lust and greed.

EXERCISE 7   *Sentence Combining: Appositives*

Combine each of the following statements in a single sentence. Work the material from the second statement into the first as an appositive, using a comma (or commas) to set the appositive from the rest of the sentence. Where should the appositive go in the sentence?

EXAMPLE: Bible scholars study Hebrew.
It is the language of the Old Testament.

ANSWER: Bible scholars study Hebrew, *the language of the Old Testament.*

1.   Many successful writers share a hobby.
It is the study of foreign languages.

2.   Chaucer translated poems from the French.
He was the best-known English poet of the Middle Ages.

3. John Milton had written poems in Italian.
   He was the author of *Paradise Lost*.
4. The author of "The Ancient Mariner" had studied German poetry.
   It is a poem known to every student.
5. George Eliot (Marian Evans) translated *The Life of Christ*.
   It was a controversial book by a German author.
6. Ezra Pound translated from the Chinese.
   It is a language rarely studied in this country.
7. Margaret Mead studied the native language of New Guinea.
   She was the famous American anthropologist.
8. Polish-born Joseph Conrad wrote his novel *Lord Jim* in English.
   It was his second (or third) language.

EXERCISE 8   *Filling in Appositives*

For each blank in the following sentences, fill in an appositive (a second noun and any additional material) that would provide a brief capsule description. Write the completed sentence.

EXAMPLE: King Kong, _____, has been the subject of several Hollywood movies.

ANSWER: King Kong, *the big ape with a heart*, has been the subject of several Hollywood movies.

1. Penicillin, _____, was discovered accidentally.
2. Sitting Bull, _____, defeated General Custer at the battle of Little Bighorn.
3. Iran, _____, suddenly became the center of media attention.
4. Cities began to convert downtown streets into malls, _____.
5. Columbus, _____, landed at San Salvador, _____.
6. Sigmund Freud, _____, changed the modern view of the mind.
7. Amelia Earhart, _____, disappeared over the Pacific during a flight around the world.
8. Tarzan, _____, travels through the forest with Cheetah, _____.
9. The new coin was to commemorate Susan Anthony, _____.
10. Marilyn Monroe, _____, experienced both success and failure in Hollywood, _____.

EXERCISE 9   *Sentence Combining: Verbals*

Combine each of the following statements in a single sentence, working the material from the second statement into the first as a verbal or verbal phrase. Make sure the verbal points clearly to what it modifies. (Where should the verbal go in the sentence?)

EXAMPLE: Oliver asked for more.
             He was still feeling hungry.
ANSWER: *Still feeling hungry, Oliver asked for more.*

1. Many people have laughed and cried over the novels of Charles Dickens.
   They are living in all parts of the world.

2. His books have sold millions of copies.
   They have been translated into many languages.

3. His stories usually have a strong moral message.
   They were written in Victorian England.

4. Dickens reforms the old miser Scrooge.
   He turns him into a warm-hearted, generous employer.

5. In *David Copperfield*, the hero does well.
   He leads an upright moral life.

6. Steerforth perishes in a shipwreck.
   He had strayed from the right path.

7. Dickens had a flair for melodrama.
   He often put extreme unselfishness next to grotesque evil.

8. The heroine of *Hard Times* is Rachel.
   She bears misfortune with saintly patience.

9. *A Tale of Two Cities* shows us bloodthirsty revolutionaries.
   They are driven by the spirit of revenge.

10. Dickens found a huge audience around the world.
    He was called sentimental by his critics.

EXERCISE 10   *Sentence Imitation: Verbals*

Study the way the following model sentences use verbals and absolute constructions. For each model sentence, write a sentence of your own that comes very close to the structure of the original.

1. Gazing up into the darkness, I saw myself as a creature driven by vanity.   James Joyce
   SAMPLE IMITATION: Looking at my wet clothes, I saw myself as a person saved by sheer luck.

2. Jules was driving a truck filled with flowers around the unflowery street of Detroit.   Joyce Carol Oates

3. The band came marching down the street, the trumpets blaring, the banners flying.

4. Eyes shining, mouths open, we watched the magician perform.

5. The bull was hooking wildly, jumping like a trout, all four feet off the ground.
   Ernest Hemingway

6.   I imagined myself saving people from sinking ships, cutting away masts in a hurricane, or swimming through the surf with a line.

7.   The classroom was an impersonal place, its block walls painted "Institution Yellow" and its gray tile floor covered with plastic chairs connected to graffiti-covered desks.

EXERCISE 11   *Sentence Combining: Modifiers*

Combine the separate statements in the following sets, keeping the first statement as the main clause or main part of the sentence. Use the information in the additional statements as modifiers—adjectives and adverbs, prepositional phrases, appositives, verbals.

EXAMPLE: The lizard watched me.
It was basking in the sun.
It had beady eyes.

ANSWER: The lizard basking in the sun watched me with beady eyes.

1.   Scientists are studying dolphins.
Dolphins are warm-blooded, intelligent mammals.
They are able to communicate by a set of complex signals.

2.   The *Amsterdam News* condemned the violence.
It is one of the nation's largest newspapers.
The violence was senseless.

3.   Thousands of migrants were coming into California.
They were often called "Okies."
They came from Midwestern farms.
The farms had been ruined by drought.

4.   John Delmas stopped the car.
He was a rookie police officer.
He was from Buffalo.
The car was a black limousine.
It had drawn curtains.

5.   The relatives watched the ship leave.
They were standing on the pier.
Tears were streaming down their faces.

Compounding   **Compounding** is a doubling (and sometimes tripling or quadrupling) of sentence parts that allows us to pack a sentence with closely related details. Compound structures are sets of several sentence parts of the same kind, often tied together by *and* or *or*. Three or more parts of the

---

THE WRITING WORKSHOP

Expanding the Simple Sentence

Effective writers use *more* of language than ordinary people do. Working with a group, help put together a collection of passages (fiction or nonfiction) that each illustrate exceptionally full or versatile use of *one* of the elements that help us expand a simple sentence: adjectives and adverbs, prepositional phrases, appositives, verbals, compounding. List all examples of the modifier illustrated or of compound structures in each sample passage. Study the following passage as an example of the exceptionally full use of adjectives (list all examples):

In time this commerce . . . gave employment to hordes of rough and hardy men; rude, uneducated, brave . . . heavy drinkers, coarse frolickers, heavy fighters, reckless fellows . . . elephantinely jolly, foul-witted, profane, prodigal of their money, bankrupt at the end of the trip, fond of barbaric finery, prodigious braggarts; yet, in the main, honest, trustworthy, faithful to promises and duty, and often picturesquely magnanimous. Mark Twain, *Life on the Mississippi*

Study the following passage as an example of the exceptionally full use of prepositional phrases (list all examples):

Canton-flannel gulls flew near and far. Sometimes they sat down on the sea, near patches of brown seaweed that rolled on the waves with a movement like carpets on a line in a gale. The birds sat comfortably in groups, and they were envied by some in the dinghy, for the wrath of the sea was no more to them than it was to a covey of prairie chickens a thousand miles inland. Often they came very close and stared at the men with black beadlike eyes.   Stephen Crane, "The Open Boat"

---

same kind are called a **series**. (Note the commas that separate items in a series.)

DOUBLING: *Fission and Fusion* are very different ways of producing nuclear energy.
The hooves *slipped and struggled* on the steep mountain path.
Korea started to build *cheap and reliable* cars.

SERIES: The dissenting journalist plays a fundamental role as *monitor, critic, and rival* of the politician.

Compounding is an open-ended process; there is no theoretical limit to how much material we can pack into a sentence through compounding. By combining a rich buildup of modifiers with the compounding of similar sentence parts, we can move far beyond the simple "Birds fly" sentences with which we started:

In Jacksonville, Florida, recently, *a sinkhole opened*, swallowing a motorcycle, a family sedan, two trucks, a garage, and several palm trees.

People tested for male and female stereotypes *rated* male speech *patterns* as dominant, competitive, aggressive, forceful, hostile, and loud.

EXERCISE 12   *Sentence Building: Compounding*

In each of the following model sentences, compound structures appear. These are *sets* of several sentence parts of the same kind (often tied together by *and*). Find the compound structure in each sentence. Then write a similar sentence of your own. Use (or adapt) the sentence frame that follows the model sentence.

1. Europeans used to think of the United States as the most wealthy, advanced, disinterested, organized, and invincible country of all time.
   Americans used to think of _____

2. In westerns or war movies, Americans always appeared bigger than life, decent, plucky, brave, ruthless, successful, and ready to defend the underdog and hang horse thieves.
   In TV shows and movies, _____

3. The ideas of foreign visitors about America were usually based on insufficient and distorted information, myths, wishful thinking, cheap novels, and the cinema.
   The ideas Americans have about _____

4. The American model dominates the world today in large and small matters, even in fads and fashions, newly invented sports, and gadgets of all kinds.
   The _____ model _____

5. People of other countries imitate our pursuit of affluence, our efficiency, our scientific discoveries, and our technological improvements.
   People _____ imitate _____

6. Americans sometimes seem a loose mixture of people of different races, origins, cultures, religions, and values.
   (Americans) (The Japanese) (other) sometimes seem _____

7. America's symbols often preserve an eighteenth-century style: federal monuments and architecture, the eagle engraved on official stationery, the striped and starred flag.
   _____ symbols often _____

8. Europeans have fought many insane wars, started many ruinous revolutions, believed many myths, and followed blindly many fanatical leaders.
(Americans) (Southerners) (other) have _____

9. The murders of President Kennedy and Martin Luther King, the defeat in Vietnam, and Watergate changed the attitude of many Americans toward their country.
The _____ changed _____

10. Until recently, Americans freely, artlessly, proudly, and naively advertised their belief in America as a shining example to the world.
Until recently, _____

EXERCISE 13 *Sentence Imitation: Compounding*

Study the role of compounding in each of the following model sentences. For each model, write a similar sentence of your own, following the sentence structure of the original as closely as you can. (You need not follow it in all details.)

1. Noise—hums, hisses, rumbles, pops, clicks, and the like—has ruined many a recording.
SAMPLE IMITATION: Canned laughter—giggles, titters, chuckles, guffaws, and the like—punctuates the sound track of situation comedies.

2. The child of immigrant parents goes off to school and comes home knowing more about British kings than about his grandfather's travail.   Richard Rodriguez

3. The people know the salt of the sea and the strength of the wind.   Carl Sandburg

4. On the floor of the Capitol is a pattern made from six flags—the flags of Spain, Mexico, France, the United States, the Confederacy, and Texas.

5. Using their dreams alone, creative people have produced fiction, inventions, scientific discoveries, and solutions to complex problems.   Jean Houston

---

SENTENCE COMBINING: COORDINATION AND SUBORDINATION

Most English sentences combine several shorter, simpler sentences. We start with two or more short statements, each with its own subject and verb. We then put them together in a combined sentence that shows how they are related—as stages in a process, as choices, or as links in a chain of cause and effect. When a short sentence, with its own subject and verb, becomes part of a larger whole we call it a **clause**. Most real-life sentences are made up of several clauses, strung together like simpler molecules in a larger molecular chain.

Coordination When we coordinate two things, we make them work together. When a link like *and, but,* or *however* coordinates two statements, the ideas in both are about equally important:

Matthew was subeditor on a large London newspaper, *and* Susan worked in an advertising firm.   Doris Lessing

When we coordinate two clauses, we link them the way we assemble the components of modular furniture: We piece them together intact, and we could easily disassemble them again. Clauses that could easily separate again and function alone are **independent** clauses.

INDEPENDENT: The climber behind me slipped; *however,* the rope held.
SEPARATE: The climber behind me slipped. *However,* the rope held.

□ The simplest way to coordinate independent clauses is to use a coordinator. **Coordinating conjunctions** (or **coordinators** for short) are easy to remember: *and, but, for, so, yet, or,* and *nor.* The typical punctuation is a comma between the two clauses, before the *and* or *but* that ties them together:

Legislators should make the laws, *and* judges should interpret them.
Many are called, *but* few respond to telephone solicitations.
The tombs contained food, *for* the dead needed nourishment on the final journey.
Conditions changed, *so* the dinosaurs became extinct.
We are drowning in information, *yet* we are thirsting for knowledge.
Communities must support local artists, *or* the arts will wither.
The new law did not lower taxes, *nor* did it simplify them.

□ A second way to coordinate two or more independent clauses is common in serious explanation and argument. We often use more formal links called **conjunctive adverbs** (or adverbial conjunctions). These include *however, therefore, moreover, nevertheless, consequently, besides, accordingly,* and *indeed,* as well as combinations like *in fact, on the other hand,* and *as a result.* Whereas coordinators stay locked in place, conjunctive adverbs are mobile (like other adverbs); they can shift to a position later in the second clause. The typical punctuation is the semicolon, which stays at the juncture between the two clauses even if the adverb shifts its position. (Note the optional commas that set off the adverb from the rest of the second clause in relatively formal prose.)

Prisons are overcrowded; *however,* few communities want a new jail.
Cars clog our roads and bridges; new modes of transportation, *therefore,* should be our highest priority.
Lung cancer and emphysema befall smokers; many continue to smoke *nevertheless.*

□ A third way to coordinate independent clauses is simply to join them without a connective, using a semicolon instead of a period. In pairs like the following, we see the connection without a link like *and* or *however:*

People scurried aimlessly through the streets; an atmosphere of panic reigned.

Throughout Latin America, stadiums serve as sports arenas in peacetime; they turn into prison camps in times of war.

The early twentieth century was the brass age of the American comic strip; impudence and lunacy were the order of the day.

Note that in a fully developed sentence more than two independent clauses may be joined by coordination. Traditionally, sentences combining two or more independent clauses are called **compound** sentences. Sentences like the following coordinate three clauses, each with its own subject and verb:

Farmers work long hours, and their families may be working for free, but their profit margin may still remain razor-thin.

Ads urge us to "buy American," and unions warn of mass unemployment; the consumer buys Japanese nevertheless.

EXERCISE 14   *Sentence Combining: Coordination*

In the following sets, join each pair of short statements in a larger combined sentence. Of the connecting words given as choices, use the one that seems to fit best. (Be prepared to explain or defend your choices.)

EXAMPLE: American steel mills used to dominate the market.
Steel from Korea now floods the country.

ANSWER: American steel mills used to dominate the market, but steel from Korea now floods the country.

(Choose one: *and, but, so, for, yet, or.* Use a comma.)

1.   Students have lost interest in political issues.
Attendance at political rallies is low.

2.   Students studied hard.
Competition for grades was keen.

3.   Some critics protest against our overreliance on tests.
Students take more tests every year.

4.   American products often cannot compete abroad.
Workers are asked to accept pay cuts.

5.   Engineering graduates may go into industry to take well-paying jobs.
They may stay in school to earn graduate degrees.

(Choose one: *therefore, however, moreover, nevertheless, besides, indeed, in fact.* Use a semicolon.)

6.   Roads and freeways were deteriorating.
The state budget included little money for maintenance.

7. The university was a huge, impersonal institution.
   New students often felt isolated.

8. People no longer want to be like everyone else.
   Many Americans are rediscovering their ethnic roots.

9. Many American newspapers used to be family-owned.
   One large chain now controls over ninety papers.

10. After a terrorist attack, travelers cancel their reservations.
    Usually, the tourist trade is back to normal a few weeks later.

EXERCISE 15 *Sentence Imitation: Coordination*

Study coordination in the following model sentences. For each model, write a similar sentence of your own, following the sentence structure of the original as closely as you can. (You need not follow it in all details.)

1. Governments declare war on drugs, and politicians denounce pushers, but the drug trade continues to thrive.
   SAMPLE IMITATION: Governments try to stamp out guerillas, and bishops denounce violence, but guerilla warfare continues to flourish.

2. The movie lot is open to the public; three times a day stunt actors act out Western scenes.

3. Everything important has already been said, but nobody ever listens; therefore, we always have to start all over again.   André Gide

4. The morning wind forever blows, the poem of creation is uninterrupted, but few are the ears that hear it.   Henry David Thoreau

5. Words are cheap; most people, therefore, judge us by our actions.

Subordination Subordination makes an added clause dependent on a main clause, welding them together more permanently than coordination does. Dependent clauses can*not* stand by themselves; like a two-wheel trailer, they depend on something else. If we split off a dependent clause from the main clause, the result is not a sentence but a sentence fragment:

DEPENDENT: The manager will notify you *if a position opens.*
FRAGMENT: The manager will notify you. *If a position opens.*

When we use subordination, the main clause typically makes the main point, while the dependent clause fills in the where, when, why, or what kind:

PLACE: The edge of the cape was wet with blood *where it had swept along the bull's back.*   Ernest Hemingway

TIME: El Salvador had always been a frontier, *even before the Spaniards arrived.*   Joan Didion

REASON: We need to demand more, not less of women . . . *because historically women have always had to be better than men to do half as well.*   Adrienne Rich

KIND: The evil *that men do* lives after them.   *Julius Caesar*

Note: Sometimes the dependent clause is only technically subordinate; it actually carries the main point of the sentence: "The honor society was looking for students *who had a 4.0 average.*"

☐ The most common way to subordinate an added statement to the main clause is to use a **subordinating conjunction** (or **subordinator**, for short). Subordinators include *if, unless, because, when, before, after, until, since, though, although,* and *whereas,* as well as combinations like *so that, as if,* and *no matter how.* We call the clauses they add **adverbial clauses,** since they give the same kind of information as many adverbs, specifying time, place or conditions. Punctuation depends on how essential the added clause is to the meaning of the whole sentence. There is no comma when the added clause spells out an essential *if* or *when* that narrows or restricts the possibilities:

RESTRICTIVE: Illegal aliens can become citizens *if they meet the criteria.* (only if)
Defendants go to jail *unless they pay the fine.*
Vince became vague *when he was asked about marriage.*
No flights will depart *until the fog lifts.*

We use a comma when the main clause is true *regardless* of what is added; the dependent clause does not change or restrict the original point:

NONRESTRICTIVE: Myrna travels widely, *although she hates planes.*
Sharks are fish, *whereas whales are mammals.*

When a subordinator introduces the added clause, we can reverse the order of the two clauses. A comma then shows where the main clause starts:

Unless they pay the fine, defendants go to jail.
If you don't register, you can't vote.

☐ The second way to subordinate an added clause is to use a **relative pronoun**: *who (whom, whose), which,* or *that.* The clause that the relative pronoun starts is called a **relative clause.** When we combine two statements by turning one of them into a relative clause, the *who, which,* or *that* takes the place of a noun (or pronoun) in the original pair:

FIRST STATEMENT: A Chicago dating service costs $1250 a year.

SECOND STATEMENT:	*The service* helps clients with their image.
COMBINED:	A Chicago dating service *that helps clients with their image costs $1250 a year.*

Relative clauses modify a word in the main clause (*the pause* that refreshes; *people* who care). They need to appear close to what they modify and may therefore interrupt rather than follow the main clause. Punctuation again depends: *No comma* when we need the added clause to narrow choices, to specify which one or what kind, to single out one among several:

RESTRICTIVE:	The candidate *who plagiarized his speeches* is no longer running. We righted the boat *that had capsized during the storm.*

When the added clause does not identify one of several, when it merely adds optional details, we use a comma:

NONRESTRICTIVE:	President Johnson, *who had been majority leader,* knew the workings of the Senate.

Note: The relative pronouns *whom* and *that* are often left out. The brackets in the following examples enclose the missing links:

The witnesses [whom] *he had threatened* refused to testify.
Several inmates were writing books about the crimes [that] *they had committed.*

□ A third and more complicated way of subordinating a statement is to turn it into a **noun clause**. The whole added clause then takes the place of a noun in the main clause:

NOUN:	The contractor denied *the charge.*
NOUN CLAUSE:	The contractor denied *that the parts were defective.*
NOUN:	*Their fate* remains a mystery.
NOUN CLAUSE:	*What happened to the crew* remains a mystery.

Noun clauses often start with *that* but also with question words like *what, why, who, where,* or *how.* Noun clauses blend into the larger combined sentence without punctuation:

The ad campaign told teenagers *that spray-painting the subways with graffiti was not cool.*
The article explained *how people without talent become celebrities.*

Note that words like *who, what,* and *that* all have uses other than joining two clauses in a larger combined sentence. So do words like *for, before, after,* and *since:*

THE WRITING WORKSHOP

Writing the Capsule Plot

Each of the following capsule plots sums up the story of a film or television program in a single sentence. Study the way each example combines several clauses in a larger sentence. As part of a group project, write similar capsule plots of your own, making full use of coordination and subordination. Your group may decide to collect capsule plots for a guide to current hits, famous movies, science fiction classics, or the like. (You need not imitate the structure of the sample plots.)

1. Poker Flat, which practices vigilante justice, exiles a gambler and other shady characters, and most of them perish in a storm.
2. After he is badly burned in an accident at a nuclear reactor, an army colonel grows at the rate of ten feet a day.
3. After the Germans overrun most of France, a tough-talking American who lives in Casablanca helps the French Resistance movement.
4. Although he is plagued by memories of earlier disasters, a veteran flier takes over a plane whose pilot and copilot have become ill.
5. A sheriff who really died years ago saves a frontier town when it is terrorized by thugs.

COORDINATOR:	We had no choice, *for* the lease had expired.
PREPOSITION:	He needed a license *for* his pretzel stand.
SUBORDINATOR:	We left *before* the movie reached its gory ending.
PREPOSITION:	We left *before* the end of the movie.

Remember: When a sentence is developed to its full potential, two or more dependent clauses may cluster around a main clause, and often coordination and subordination go hand in hand (as they do in the sentence you are reading):

When the short days of winter came, dusk fell *before we had well eaten our dinners.*   James Joyce

Although he had tried to rebel against the oppressive government, Winston Smith, like all others *who had tried,* is finally converted by Big Brother.

A Florida plumber was showering *when a rifle butt smashed in his bathroom window and a man from the local SWAT team, which had staked out the wrong home, climbed in.*

Traditionally, we call a sentence that coordinates two or more independent clauses a **compound** sentence. A sentence that subordinates one
or more dependent clauses is a **complex** sentence. A combined sentence
using both coordination and subordination is **compound-complex**.

EXERCISE 16   *Sentence Combining: Subordination*

In the following sets, join each pair of short sentences in a larger
combined sentence. Of the connecting words given as choices, use the
one that seems to fit best. (Be prepared to explain or defend your choices.)

    EXAMPLES: The rich get richer
                   The poor get poorer.
    ANSWER: The rich get richer while the poor get poorer.

(Choose one: *when, where, before, after, until, while, as, if, unless, because.*
Use no comma.)

1. Unions complain.
   Imported goods take over the market.
2. The accused will go to jail.
   A higher court overturns the conviction.
3. Hi-tech companies move manufacturing plants to Korea or Taiwan.
   Labor costs are low.
4. Companies prefer to relocate.
   Local taxes are low there.
5. Americans of the future will order their groceries by computer.
   Current predictions come true.

(Choose one: *though, although, whereas, no matter how, no matter what.* Use
a comma. Put the dependent clause first when it seems appropriate.)

6. The Japanese pay teachers like engineers.
   Americans pay teachers less than truck drivers.
7. Many large cities have only one newspaper.
   Americans believe in free competition.
8. Violent crime was rising.
   Politicians were preaching law and order.
9. The last big wave of immigrants came from Eastern Europe.
   Today's immigrants come across the Pacific and the Mexican border.
10. American-built airplanes dominate the sky.
    Some airlines are flying European-built midsize planes.

(Choose one: *who, whom, whose, which,* or *that.* Use a comma, or commas, for the first three examples. Use no comma for the remaining two.)

11. The Reuben sandwich was invented by Reuben Kay.
    He was a wholesale grocer in Omaha.
12. The Earl of Sandwich wanted to snack without using fork and knife.
    His creation was named after him.
13. During a lifetime, the average American eats 2900 pounds of beef.
    This is equal to six head of cattle.
14. The barbecue sandwich is made up of shredded pork in sauce on a bun.
    People eat it in North Carolina.
15. The hero sandwich was originally eaten by Italian construction workers.
    They had a strong appetite.

EXERCISE 17   *Sentence Imitation: Subordination*

Study the way the following model sentences use subordination. For each model, write a similar sentence of your own, following the sentence structure of the original as closely as possible. (You need not follow it in all details.)

1. Fools rush in where angels fear to tread.   Alexander Pope
   SAMPLE IMITATION: Panic sets in when ratings begin to drop.
2. If you save one person from hunger, you work a miracle.
3. She was not happy with those masterful women, but she would not go back East where she came from.   Dorothy M. Johnson
4. On registration day, some confident souls know exactly where they are going, whereas others wander aimlessly around the campus.
5. Energy is the power that drives every human being.   Germaine Greer
6. The person who jumps to conclusions often lands on unfirm ground.
7. Corporations have discovered that buying computer software is cheaper than hiring consultants.
8. The man with a new idea is a crank until the new idea succeeds.   Mark Twain
9. An interview need not be an ambush to be good, but it should set up a situation in which the subject can be surprised by what he or she says.
10. Those who expect to reap the blessings of freedom must undergo the fatigue of supporting it.   Thomas Paine

---

EXERCISE 18   *Sentence Combining: Sentences in a Paragraph*

In the following set of sentences, the information from a paragraph has been laid out in bite-sized statements. Reassemble the paragraph, using the resources of modification, coordination, and subordination. Try to fill in the logical links that show the writer's train of thought.

An Italian scientist had turned priest.
He was named Lazzaro Spallanzani.
Back in 1765 he heated up meat extracts and other foods.
They were in sealed glass flasks.
He found out something.
They would last several weeks without going bad.
Other scientists repeated his experiments.
Neither they nor Spallanzani understood.
How did the sealing and heating process preserve food?
We now know the reason.
Bacteria inhabit all raw and unsterilized food.
They feed and multiply.
They break the food down.
They turn it rancid and inedible.
Bacteria can be killed by heat.
An airtight seal will prevent something.
Airborne microorganisms cannot reenter and recontaminate the food.

SENTENCE STYLE: EFFECTIVE SENTENCES

Why is one sentence merely adequate while another makes its point with telling effect? What makes us remember and quote a sentence that stands out? Good sentences have **style**—they use language with special skill, with a flair that makes them a pleasure to read. They have qualities that plodding sentences lack: emphasis, variety, balance.

Sentence Emphasis

A good sentence puts the emphasis on what matters; it highlights essentials and plays down minor details. It focuses attention on the main point.

EMPHATIC POSITION

The beginning of a sentence can pull a key idea out for special attention:

Enormous amounts of time, money, and talent go into commercials. *Technically,* they are often brilliant and innovative, the product not only of new skills and devices but of imaginative minds.   Marya Mannes

More often, however, the most emphatic position in the sentence *is the end*. If we allow a sentence to build up to the main point, the payload comes last. The key idea stays imprinted on the reader's mind:

Earth dwellers now have the choice of making their world into a *neighborhood or a crematorium.*   Norman Cousins

What my sons have is a world that is small enough to be readily understood, where those responsible *wear a human face.*   Carolyn Lewis

The choice of the emphatic final position channels the reader's attention in the following pair:

Although he died bankrupt, Rembrandt had been a *successful painter who commanded high fees.*   (emphasis on success)
Although Mozart had played at the royal courts of Europe, he was *buried in a pauper's grave.*   (emphasis on failure)

EMPHATIC REPETITION   Intentional, deliberate repetition can help emphasize important points—reinforce them, drive them home. While overzealous repetition, like beer commercials during a football game, can alienate the audience, repetition at strategic points shows that an idea matters, that we mean to insist. Look at the way a key term echoes in passages like the following:

In the meantime, the oiler *rowed*, and then the correspondent *rowed*, and then the oiler *rowed.*   Stephen Crane

I cannot remember when I was not surrounded by *sports*, when talk of *sports* was not in the air, when I did not care passionately about *sports.*   Joseph Epstein

Less dramatic and more common than the actual repetition of words or phrases is the insistent repetition of the same idea in different words:

If we are constantly presented with what we are not or cannot have, the *dislocation deepens, contentment vanishes*, and *frustration reigns.*   Marya Mannes

EMPHATIC PREDICATION   In many effective sentences, the subject and predicate, technically the mainstay of the sentence, also carry a major share of the meaning. Many simple sentences are built on the "Who does what?" model. They first focus our attention on something that serves as the subject and then set the subject in motion:

Our pets eat better than our poor.
Death devours all lovely things.   Edna St. Vincent Millay
American business must learn to hold its own against the international competition.

In sentences built on this model, the subject focuses on a possible agent or cause; then the verb (with the rest of the predicate) specifies the action, event, or effect. When a sentence seems blurry, bringing it closer to the "Who does what?" model can put the spotlight on whoever took action or whatever was the cause. Try to make the subject name the doer or agent; then let the verb and the rest of the predicate make the point:

UNFOCUSED: *An example* of the trend toward vigilantism *is* the father who shot the suspect accused of kidnapping his son.
FOCUSED: *An outraged father illustrated the trend* toward vigilantism by shooting the suspect accused of kidnapping his son.

UNFOCUSED:	*One crucial factor* in the current revolution in our social structure *is* the relationship between the white police officer and the black community.
FOCUSED:	*The white policeman* standing on a Harlem street corner *finds himself at the very center* of the revolution now occurring in the world. James Baldwin
	(The "crucial factor"—the white police officer—is now the subject of the sentence.)

In rewriting sentences on the "Who does what?" model, you may have to shift the action from static nouns to active verbs. When a noun ending in *-ion*, *-ment*, *-ism*, or *-ing* serves as the subject of a sentence, it may blur our view of who does what. When such nouns label actions, events, or activities, try specifying the agent or doer while shifting the action to a verb. Verbs make things happen; they help us dramatize key points:

UNFOCUSED:	Violent *arguments took place* in front of the children.
FOCUSED:	*Our parents* often *argued* violently in front of us.
UNFOCUSED:	*Confusion marked* the opening speech.
FOCUSED:	*The opening speaker confused and lost* the audience.
UNFOCUSED:	*A criticism* often found in modern poetry *is* that we have cut ourselves off from our natural roots.
FOCUSED:	*Modern poets* often *charge* that we have cut ourselves off from our roots in nature.

COORDINATION OR SUBORDINATION We sometimes string ideas together loosely as they come to mind. To tighten relationships in revision, we may opt for effective subordination instead, using it to mirror the relative importance of ideas in a sentence. *Coordination*, using a link like *and* or *but*, is most appropriate when two ideas are about equally important:

EFFECTIVE:	Radioactivity is a threat to workers at nuclear plants, *and* [equally important] radioactive wastes are a threat to the environment.

A special use of "add-on" coordination is the reporter's *and*, which merely registers events without editorializing about cause and effect:

There was a shock, *and* he felt himself go up in the air. He pushed on the sword as he went up and over, *and* it flew out of his hand. He hit the ground *and* the bull was on him.   Ernest Hemingway

To correct *excessive* coordination, remember that *and* merely says "more of same." In the revisions of the following sentences, modifiers and compounding helped the writer tighten the relationship between ideas:

LOOSE:	Salmon return to the same spot upstream where they were hatched, *and* they have to go against the stream to get there, *and* that takes much strength and determination.

TIGHTER: Salmon return to the same spot upstream where they were hatched, *struggling against the current to get there*, *showing tremendous strength and determination*.

LOOSE: Fingerlings hatch a few days after the female salmon has laid the eggs, *and* they learn to swim on their own, *and* they head for the ocean.

TIGHTER: A few days after the female salmon has laid the eggs, the fingerlings *hatch*, *learn* to swim on their own, *and head* for the ocean.

Often *subordination* helps us integrate sentences too loosely strung together. Feeding several related statements into a larger combined sentence, the writer of the following passage reserved the main clause for the idea that deserves special emphasis:

SEPARATE: The term *democracy* originated in ancient Greece. Different people have used it to describe quite different political systems. Often, the person who uses the word thinks it has only one meaning.

COMBINED: *Democracy*, a term that originated in ancient Greece, *has been used to describe quite different political systems*, though the person who uses it usually thinks it has only one meaning.

Note: Avoid upside-down subordination. "*I was four* when men landed on the moon" focuses our attention on your age. "When I was four, *men landed on the moon*" focuses our attention on the moon. Upside-down subordination results when the wrong item seems to stand out—when it catches the reader unaware, with an unintended ironic effect:

IRONIC: The wage was considered average by local standards, *though it was not enough to live on*.

STRAIGHT: *Although it was considered average by local standards*, the wage was not enough to live on.

CUMULATIVE OR PERIODIC Sentences differ in how tightly they subordinate related material to a main point. The **cumulative** sentence (also called **loose** sentence) gives us the main point early and then gradually elaborates, leading to further details, proceeding to further comments and ramifications. The resulting sentence is an expandable sentence; it reads as if it had been built in stages:

CUMULATIVE: She liked a simple life and simple people,
  and would have been happier, I think, if she had
  stayed in the backlands of Alabama
    riding wild on the horses she so often talked about,
      not so lifelong lonely for the black men and
      women who had taught her the only religion
      she ever knew.　Lillian Hellman

A **periodic** sentence, though also using considerable detail, does not fully state the central point until the end. An essential part of the main statement is held in suspense; the sentence ends when the main statement ends. Everything else is worked into the sentence along the way. A periodic sentence is often appropriate for a tightly organized summary or definition:

> PERIODIC: *Comedy*, though often showing us cranks or eccentrics, nevertheless *aims its ridicule*, as many critics have said, *at common failings of human nature.*

You can sometimes improve a sentence that is too loosely structured by shifting the main point toward the end, especially if a final modifier sounds too much like a belated concession or lame afterthought:

> WEAK: Richard Wagner became one of the most successful composers of all time *in spite of the jeers of his contemporaries.* (This version may make your readers remember the jeers rather than the composer's success.)
>
> IMPROVED: Richard Wagner, *though jeered at by his contemporaries*, became one of the most successful composers of all time.

EXERCISE 19 *Emphatic Endings*

Study the way the following model sentences save the key point till the end. For each, write a similar sentence of your own, following the structure of the original as closely as you can. (You need not follow it in all details.)

1. One of the troubles of colorful language, slang or other, is that its color rubs off. Paul Roberts
2. Slang terms for money, like *lettuce* and *grand*, first had their highest frequency in those districts where police officers would prefer to go in pairs.
3. College professors had to learn that the expression "dig that crazy course," coming from their students, was not a criticism but high praise.
4. What sounds cute and clever to the young often sounds merely banal to older ears.
5. Among my friends, *louse* had the plural *lice* when it referred to insects but *louses* when it referred to people.

EXERCISE 20 *Emphatic Predication*

Rewrite the following sentences for more *effective predication*. If possible, make the subject and the predicate tell the reader who does what.

1. Vigorous discussion of current political events often took place among the patrons.
2. It is very probable that intimidation of witnesses will result from such threatening remarks by the defendant.
3. A recent development is the encouragement of new technology for extracting oil by the Canadian government.
4. There has been vigorous support among the voters for rent control measures of different kinds.
5. As the result of unruly demonstrations, repeated interruptions of the committee's deliberations took place.
6. The conclusion is inevitable that considerable impairment of our country's military strength has come about as the result of these cuts.
7. A plan for safe driving is of no use if the cooperation of the individual driver is not present.
8. The contribution of the alumni to the growth of the college will be in proportion to their information about its educational needs.

EXERCISE 21   *Coordination or Subordination*

Rewrite the following passages to correct *excessive coordination*. Tighten relationships by replacing coordinators with subordinators (such as *if, when, because, although*) or relative pronouns (*who, which, that*).

1. Gun owners were fighting back against the new restrictions, and the city council passed a new ordinance, and it omitted the requirement for a 14-day records search.
2. My father came from a wealthy family, and my mother came from a very poor home, and it was strange that she held the purse strings in the family.
3. Many high school teachers follow a textbook word for word, and they go over each page until everyone understands it. In college, many teachers just tell the student to read the textbook, and then they start giving lectures on the material covered in the text, but they don't follow it word for word.

Sentence Variety

Linguists assure us that no two sentences we write need ever be the same. An effective writer, like an effective speaker, avoids monotony by exploiting the infinite variety of English sentences.

VARIED SENTENCE LENGTH Some sentences are short. Other sentences are more elaborate, embarking on a full explanation, marshaling a range of supporting details, noting reservations and spelling out implications, wending their way through multiple modifiers and assorted clauses until the reader is ready to say "Enough!" Vary the length of your own sentences to bring plodding passages to life. Use a short sentence to set off a key idea, to give pointed advice. The following short sentences are emphatic and to the point; they are easy to quote and to remember:

POINTED: Punctuality is the thief of time.   Oscar Wilde
           You should write, first of all, to please yourself.   Doris Lessing
           To conquer fear is the beginning of wisdom.   Bertrand Russell

Use a longer sentence for detailed description, explanation, and argument. Sentences like the following can provide the details and examples needed to answer the questions that might arise in the reader's mind:

DETAILED: Opening the trap, he dropped the noose over the big snake's head and tightened the thong.   John Steinbeck

           Few themes have gripped the imagination of Americans so intensely as the discovery of talent in unexpected places—the slum child who shows scientific genius, the frail youngster who develops athletic ability, the poor child who becomes a captain of industry.   John Gardner

Remember the following advice about sentence length:

☐ *Avoid choppy sentences in explanation and argument.* In description and narrative, we sometimes use a series of short sentences to create a bare-fact, one-at-a-time effect:

I arrive at my office. I work, taking frequent breaks. I visit the water cooler. I gossip with friends on the phone.

But in explanation and argument, a series of short sentences, unless intended for special emphasis, is likely to seem disjointed and juvenile:

CHOPPY: We listened to AM radio most of the day. The format never seemed to change. There was one advertising jingle after the other. The fast-talking DJ would give a number to call. You name the song and you win a prize. You could call an agency for tickets to this concert or that. The DJ would play oldies but goodies and then the current number-one song, the big hit.

REVISED: We spent most of the day listening to AM radio, whose format never seemed to change. Punctuating the advertising jingles, the DJ would give a number to call so listeners could name the song to win a prize or order tickets to this concert or that. The DJ would play oldies but goodies and then the current number-one song, the big hit.

☐ *Use short sentences for preview or summary, following them up with longer sentences that elaborate or explain.* The shift from short to long often mirrors the shift from general to specific that shapes the basic pattern of many paragraphs:

Most of Wyoming has a "lean-to" look. Instead of big, roomy barns and Victorian houses, there are dugouts, low sheds, log cabins, sheep camps, and fence lines that look like driftwood blown haphazardly into place.   Gretel Ehrlich

Newspapers give a distorted view of life. They overemphasize the unusual, such as a mother's giving birth to quintuplets, the development of a Christmas tree that grows its own decorative cones, the minting of two pennies which were only half engraved, gang fights, teenage drinking, or riots.

Sometimes we reverse this pattern and use a short sentence to set off an important conclusion or key observation at the end:

With the great growth in leisure-time activities, millions of Americans are turning to water sports: fishing, swimming, water skiing, and skin diving. *Clean water exhilarates and relaxes.*   Vance Packard

Games are supposed to bring out the highest standards of sportmanship in people. *They often bring out the worst.*   Glenn Dickey

VARIED WORD ORDER   Sentences become monotonous when they march down the page in a simple subject-verb pattern. Break up the monotony by experimenting with variations in word order. To perk up a sentence, pull another sentence part out in front of the subject. For instance, use one or more **introductory modifiers**:

Wandering among the shoppers, standing on O'Connell Bridge, walking the quays, I turned the past and the present over and over in my mind.   Elizabeth Cullinan

The Trans World Terminal stems from the work of contemporary architects like Corbusier of France and Nervi of Italy, masters of the curve in concrete. *Like a true eagle,* this building is all curves and muscle, no right angles. *Built of reinforced concrete,* the whole structure swoops and turns and rises.   Ken Macrorie

Sometimes a writer will move an object or other completer from its usual position after the verb and pull it to the beginning of the sentence for special emphasis. This turning around of the more common pattern we call **inversion**. (The more common word order for the preceding sentence would be: "*We call this turning around . . .* inversion.") Other examples:

Ma's Café catered to locals and tourists. *The tourists* she charged extra.

Gone are the days when gas stations had eager attendants and clean restrooms.

The committee asked him to betray his friends. *That* he refused to do.

What else can you do to bring variety into a group of plodding sentences? At strategic points, you may decide to turn to the reader with a key question:

Where do the terms of businessese come from? Most, of course, are hand-me-downs from former generations of business people, but many are the fruit of crossfertilization with other jargons.   William H. Whyte

VARIED STRUCTURE   Variety results naturally from the variations and substitutions that are part of our normal sentence resources. For instance, the *to* form, or **infinitive**, may replace the subject or also a noun later in the sentence: *To err* is human. *To know me* is *to love me*. Like other verbals, such infinitives often carry along other material. To experiment with such infinitive phrases is a step toward greater sentence variety:

To live day by day is *not to live at all.*

To do good is noble: *to teach others to do good* is nobler, and no trouble.   Mark Twain

To envision a human being without technology is *to envision a dead naked ape*, not a happy noble savage.   Ben Bova

Another verbal we can substitute for a noun is the *-ing* form, then called a **gerund**, or verbal noun: *Seeing* is *believing*. *Speeding* causes accidents. Again the verbal may carry other material with it to form a verbal phrase: *Speeding on curving roads at night* causes accidents. Using such verbal phrases at different points in a sentence can help a writer counteract monotony:

Stealing has always been a means of *redistributing the wealth.*   John Conyers

Helping the country look more like Harvard won't necessarily make it more humane.   Ralph Keyes

A major departure from the normal pattern of a sentence is the substitution of a noun clause as the subject. What would normally be a noun is then a clause with its own subject and verb:

How migrating birds navigate remains a mystery.

What is now proved was once only imagined.   William Blake

EXERCISE 22   *Writing the Pointed Sentence*

Study the following examples of short, pointed statements as model sentences. For five of these, write a sentence of your own that follows the structure of the original as closely as possible. (You need not follow the model in all details.)

1. Love is as necessary to human beings as food and shelter.   Aldous Huxley
   SAMPLE IMITATION: Attention is as essential to children as are clothes and shoes.
2. Curiosity, like all other desires, produces pain as well as pleasure.   Samuel Johnson
3. Perversity is the muse of modern literature.   Susan Sontag
4. Everyone is a moon and has a dark side which he never shows to anybody.
   Mark Twain
5. Real old age begins when one looks backward rather than forward.   May Sarton
6. Better be a nettle in the side of your friend than an echo.   Ralph Waldo Emerson
7. I've been too busy living lately to know what is happening.   May Sarton
8. Those who cut their own wood are twice warmed.
9. Work expands so as to fill the time available for its completion.   C. Northcote
   Parkinson
10. A nail that sticks out will be hammered down.   Japanese saying

---

EXERCISE 23   *Writing the Elaborate Sentence*

     Study the following examples of long, elaborate sentences that carry along many details. For each write a similar sentence of your own that carries nearly as much freight as the original. (You need not follow the structure of the original except in its large outlines.)

1. The name Bell Labs usually conjures up images of white-coated physicians sequestered in cubicles, equipped with super computers, and subjecting ions to megawatt laser blasts in an effort to "improve communications."

2. Sir Thomas More, a man of high position, enjoying the respect of his peers and the friendship of his king, is brought to ruin by his inability to betray his conscience.

3. Whereas most science-fiction writers spend their time predicting, say, the discovery of planets ruled by angry, invisible dogs, Clarke has largely confined himself to predicting things that actually come to pass.   David Owen

4. I felt I'd just waked from some long, pillowy dream and taken a look at where I was: still friendless, sallow, peculiar, living alone with my mother, surrounded by monstrous potted plants taller and older than I was.   Anne Tyler

5. In most housewife commercials, the housewife is portrayed as little more than a simpering, brainless jelly, almost pathologically obsessed with the world of kitchen floors or laundry, or of the celebrated "bathroom bowl."   Michael J. Arlen

---

EXERCISE 24   *The Long and the Short*

     In the following examples, study how a short summarizing sentence and a long elaborating sentence can work together. Then write three similar pairs of your own.

1. *Training is everything.* The peach was once a bitter almond; cauliflower is nothing but cabbage with a college education.   Mark Twain

   SAMPLE IMITATION: *Confidence helps.* The self-assured young woman smiled inwardly when the interviewer announced that the job was hers.

2. *Good families are hospitable.* Knowing that hosts need guests as much as guests need hosts, they are generous with honorary memberships for friends, whom they urge to come early and often and to stay late.   Jane Howard

3. Although the automotive industry moved to Detroit early in this century, Indianapolis is still a motor city, swarming with car washes and auto-parts stores, and the sign on the road into town from the airport, WELCOME TO INDIANAPOLIS: CROSSROADS OF AMERICA, seems to imply that you're entering a place best reached by car. *Here, nobody walks.*   Paul Fussell

---

EXERCISE 25   *Combining Choppy Sentences*

Combine the separate sentences in each of the following sets. Make use of *effective subordination*. In each new combined sentence, use at least one dependent clause, starting with a subordinator (*if, when, because, where, although, whereas,* or the like) or with a relative pronoun (*who, which,* or *that*).

1. Campus elections are ridiculous.
   Nobody qualified runs.
   I refuse to have anything to do with them.

2. Piloting a boat is easy.
   It is like driving a car.
   The controls are about the same.

3. Monkeys are of low intelligence.
   They are imitative.
   They can be trained to perform simple tasks.

4. Primates are our close cousins biologically.
   They are ideally suited for experiments.
   These cannot be performed on human beings.

5. Automated factories are promoted in the name of progress.
   The average worker is suspicious of them.
   They mean fewer jobs for the rank and file.

EXERCISE 26   *Varied Word Order*

Each of the following sentences starts with a variation from the usual subject-verb or noun-verb-noun order. Choose five of these as model sentences. For each, write a similar sentence of your own.

1. Stronger than the mighty sea is almighty God.
    SAMPLE IMITATION: Bleaker than a misspent youth is life without experience.
2. On a huge hill, cragged and steep, truth stands.   John Donne
3. To err is human; to forgive, divine.   Alexander Pope
4. To describe with precision even the simplest object is extremely difficult.
    Aldous Huxley
5. In this country, at least in theory, no one denies the right of any person to differ with the government, or the right to express that difference in speech, in the press, by petition, or in an assembly.   Charles E. Wyzanski
6. Having chosen what she wants to become, a woman must be prepared to commit herself over a long period of time to reach her goal.   Margaret Mead
7. What makes democratic politics different from most other professions is that, occasionally, the politician has a duty to risk his job by performing it conscientiously.   George F. Will
8. Building a beautiful cabinet is a labor of days; destroying it with an ax takes only a minute.
9. To create a little flower is a labor of the ages.   William Blake
10. What I call my self-respect is more important to me than anything else.
    Dorothy Lessing

Parallel Structure

Good sentences have a satisfying rhythm. They fall into a pattern, balancing off similar or opposed ideas, fitting related ideas into a neat frame ("Better active today than radioactive tomorrow"). Sentences like the following make full use of our sentence resources, using **parallel structure** to line up parallel ideas, fitting much related detail into a satisfying whole:

Commercials try to sell us cars that attract women, scents that attract men, seasonings that enhance the flavor of food, and mouthwash that will kill the odor later.   Student paper

When financial reverses prompt a young person to quit school and go to work, when marriage does not happen at the hoped-for time, when a child is born unusually early or late, when people simply can't seem to find themselves and their occupational achievement is delayed—these are what we might call untimely events.
Gail Sheehy

When we make parts of a sentence parallel, we put related ideas in similar grammatical form. We thus channel the reader's attention, laying out related material in a satisfying pattern, setting up the rhythm that makes a well-balanced sentence a pleasure to read:

Studies serve *for delight, for ornament,* and *for ability.*   Sir Francis Bacon

Cars serve *for transportation, for recreation,* and *for ostentation.*   Student imitation

THE WRITING WORKSHOP

Studying Sentence Style

Find a passage that makes especially effective, varied, or imaginative use of our sentence resources. Photocopy it for discussion in a small group or with your class as a whole. Study the following passage as an example. What features in the passage make for an effective sentence style? Look for features like varied sentence length, emphasis, parallel structure.

There was a photo on the front page of *The New York Times*, a midair shot of an Indy racer all blown to shrapnel, the driver battered unconscious, his limp arms helplessly flung upward by the centrifugal forces contained in the whirling asteroid of junk that only a millisecond before had been a $180,000 automobile. The TV cameras were late to the scene. They give no clue to what happened. From a great distance you see an orange fireball as the March hits the inner retaining wall. Only pieces emerge from the glow, nothing bigger than your easy chair, some of them still spewing flame, all of them bounding, caroming, cartwheeling through the air, spraying turf as they recoil again and again from the infield grass, still paying dividends of racing speed, a gust of fragments moving forward to litter the entire north end of the Speedway.   Patrick Bedard, "The Anatomy of a Crack-Up," *Esquire*

Chart the **parallel structure** that makes each of the following sentences a well-balanced whole:

It is about time we realize that many women make
   better teachers than mothers,
   better actresses than wives,
   better diplomats than cooks.   Marya Mannes

The attempt to suppress the use of drugs
   is as futile as
the wish to teach cooking to an ape.   Lewis H. Lapham

The only advice one person can give another about reading is
   to take no advice,
   to follow your own instincts,
   to use your own reason,
   to come to your own conclusions.   Virginia Woolf

In experimenting with parallel structure, keep the following points in mind:

☐ *Parallel structure can help you line up related ideas.* The reader sees that several points are part of the same picture or of the same story:

To succeed as a writer, you must have *the perseverance* of Sisyphus, *the patience of a saint,* and *the hide of an armadillo,* as well as *ambition, energy,* and *thorough mastery of your craft.*   Student paper

☐ *Parallel structure can help you juxtapose opposite ideas for a striking contrast.* When two opposing ideas are neatly polarized, we call the resulting balance of opposites an **antithesis**: "To err is human; to forgive, divine." Sentences like the following owe their pointed, quotable quality to their antithetical style:

Propaganda is a monologue which seeks *not a response but an echo.*   W. H. Auden

The idols of every campus generation have always been *against everything* and *for nothing.*   Peter F. Drucker

☐ *Parallel structure is often cumulative.* It frequently builds up to the most emphatic or climactic item in a series:

The choice made, she could surrender her will to *the strange, the exhilarating, the gigantic* event.   Graham Greene

☐ *Parallel structure disorients the reader when it breaks down.* **Faulty parallelism** results when your sentence seems to set up a parallel sequence, only to have one or more items snap out of the expected pattern. Revise for a more consistent pattern when part of a series has jumped the tracks:

FAULTY: The prosecution kept coming back to *the fibers* found at the scene, *the bloodstains* on the defendant's clothing, and *where he was* on the night of the crime.

PARALLEL: The prosecution kept coming back to *the fibers* found at the scene, *the bloodstains* on the defendant's clothing, and *his whereabouts* on the night of the crime.

Remember that sentence style is not a matter of isolated sentences. Sentences stand out or blend in as part of a larger passage. The repetition of an identical pattern gives the following passage its urgency and eloquence:

We need more patterns of desire. *We need* models of women—and men—who expect everything, and set out to get it. *We need* people in novels as well as in life to show us how to have the courage to walk out.   Gail Godwin

Remember: Effective writers have an ear for the rhythm, the characteristic pattern of a sentence. They write sentences that focus clearly on who does what, on what is happening, on what counts. Subordinating minor details, they highlight what matters; they emphasize key ideas. They bring color and life into their sentences by varying familiar patterns. They use repetition and parallelism to channel our attention, to underline connections, to lead up to a high point.

EXERCISE 27   *Playing Off Opposites*

Study the way the following well-balanced sentences play off opposites. For each, write a similar balanced or antithetical sentence of your own, following the structure of the original as closely as you can.

1. Cunning is the art of concealing our own defects and discovering other people's weaknesses.
    SAMPLE IMITATION: Politics is the art of making one's own record look good and making the other person's look bad.
2. We must begin the journey to tomorrow from the point where we are today.
    Garrett Hardin
3. We vow to teach our young the virtues of resistance as well as those of allegiance; we vow to teach them a love of conscience stronger than their love of the state.
    Peter Marin
4. We have exchanged being known in small communities for being anonymous in huge populations.   Ellen Goodman
5. Democracy substitutes selection by the incompetent many for appointment by the corrupt few.   George Bernard Shaw

---

EXERCISE 28   *Parallel Structure*

Study the use of *parallelism* in the following passages. For each, write a passage of your own on a subject of your own choice, following the structure of the original as closely as you can.

1. Studies serve for delight, for ornament, and for ability.   Sir Francis Bacon
2. The press as an institution has evolved through alternating chapters of disgrace and honor, of prostitution and martyrdom, of somnolence and vigilance, gradually assuming the role of public protector.   Jack Anderson
3. To assign unanswered letters their proper weight, to free us from expectations of others, to give us back to ourselves—there lies the great, the singular power of self-respect.   Joan Didion
4. Women feel just as men feel; they need exercise for their faculties and a field for their efforts as much as their brothers do; they suffer from too rigid a restraint, too absolute a stagnation, precisely as men would suffer.   Charlotte Brontë

5.   It is about time we realize that many women make better teachers than mothers, better actresses than wives, better diplomats than cooks.   Marya Mannes

REVISING AWKWARD SENTENCES Writers vary greatly in how finished their sentences are when they first write them down. Some linger over each sentence, trying to get it right the first time. Others push ahead, content to polish rough sentences while writing a second or third draft. Whatever your own practice, be prepared to deal with familiar sentence problems when you write or rewrite.

Revising for Economy Effective writers avoid padding; they know how to write sentences in which every word counts. In an economical sentence, each word carries its share of the load:

O'Keeffe tramped across the New Mexico landscape, and her camera found beauty in the bleached skulls of long-dead animals.

Revise sentences where too many words are unnecessary props or mere filling. Remember to cross out **redundant** words, which merely duplicate a meaning: Write *October* instead of *the month of October, consensus* instead of *consensus of opinion, combine* instead of *combine together*. Edit out circumlocutions—talky constructions that "take the long way around." Instead of "it is unfortunate that," write *unfortunately*; instead of "it is possible that we will," write "we may."

INFLATED	BRIEF
because of the fact that	that
during the time that	while
a large number of	many
at an early date	soon
in the event that	if
at the present point in time	now

Remove unneeded props: Instead of "*those of* adolescent *age*," write *adolescents*. Trim superfluous *there are*'s and *who were*'s, especially if several pad the same sentence:

AWKWARD: *There are* many farmers in the area *who are* planning to attend the protest meeting *which is* scheduled for Memorial Day.

REVISED: Many farmers in the area plan to attend the protest meeting scheduled for Memorial Day.

Many editors (as well as much editing software) flag weak, routine use of the linking word *be* (*is, are, was, were,* and so on). Sentences like the following become less flabby when an unneeded *is* or *are* has been trimmed:

FLABBY: Navratilova *is a tough competitor* and bounced back after her defeat at Wimbledon.

TRIM: *A tough competitor,* Navratilova bounced back after her defeat at Wimbledon.

Revising Awkward Repetition

Unintentional repetition can grate on the reader's ears. Revise for awkward repetition like the following:

AWKWARD: Close examina*tion* of the results of the investig*ation* led to a re*organization* of the *organization*.

REVISED: Close study of the results of the inquiry led to a reorganization of the company.

Use pronouns to avoid awkward repetition of words and labels:

AWKWARD: A child of preschool age often shows a desire to read, but *the child's* parents often ignore this *desire*.

REVISED: A child not yet in school often shows a desire to read—*which* the parents ignore.

Revising the Awkward Passive

Avoid the unneeded **passive**, which makes sentences roundabout and impersonal. An active sentence goes from the doer or agent through the action to the target or result ("NASA aborted the mission"). A passive sentence turns this perspective around and puts the target first, converting the original object to the subject of the new sentence ("The mission *was* aborted *by* NASA"). The passive thus highlights the target or result; it works well when the doer or performer is secondary, hard to identify, or beside the point:

LEGITIMATE: *The dusky,* a subspecies of the seaside sparrow, *has never been found* anywhere except on Merritt Island and along the St. John's River.

Marcia's parents were killed in a car accident when she was very young.

When the source of an action is known and important, the passive makes us look at what happens from an awkward angle. Many verbs work best in active sentences telling us who does what:

AWKWARD: Monumental traffic jams *are endured by* many motorists on the way to work.

ACTIVE: Many motorists *endure* monumental traffic jams on the way to work.

AWKWARD: After each simplification of the tax laws, longer and more impenetrable instructions *must be puzzled out by* the taxpayer.

ACTIVE: After each simplification of the tax laws, the taxpayer *must puzzle out* longer and more impenetrable instructions.

Avoid the pretentious passive that is often part of a self-important impersonal jargon:

JARGON: Today the *effort* of the average person seems *to be* largely *placed* in trying to ignore commercials and advertisements.

REVISED: The average *consumer* seems *to make* a constant effort to ignore commercials and advertisements.

Revising Indirect Constructions

Sometimes an introductory *It is* or *There are* sets up the main point of a sentence for needed emphasis:

It is *the result* that matters—not good intentions.

There are *a thousand* hacking at the branches of evil to one who is striking at the root.   Henry David Thoreau

More often, the *it is* or *there is* merely postpones the main point and causes an awkward reshuffling later in the sentence:

AWKWARD: In 1986, *there was* a protest march to the state capitol participated in by 15,000 people.

REVISED: In 1986, 15,000 protesters marched to the state capitol.

Equally expendable is the impersonal *one* when it serves as a mere prop in a sentence:

ROUNDABOUT: *If one is a citizen of a democracy, she* should exercise her voting rights.

DIRECT: *A citizen of a democracy* should vote.

Revising Sentence Overloads

In a well-written sentence, several dependent clauses may specify time, place, or conditions, bringing in material that dovetails neatly into the sentence:

If all the world hated you and believed you wicked, *while* your conscience approved you and absolved you from guilt, you would not be without friends.   Charlotte Brontë

However, several dependent clauses may begin to jostle each other, creating a logjam of confusing provisos and specifications. For instance, interlocking *that-if*, *if-because*, or *which-when* constructions are often awkward:

AWKWARD: I think *that if* an actor with moderate acting ability can earn over fifty million in one year something is wrong with our system of incentives and rewards.

REVISED: In my opinion, *if* an actor with moderate acting ability can earn over fifty million in one year, something is wrong with our system of incentives and rewards.

In "house-that-Jack-built" sentences, several dependent clauses of the same kind follow each other, causing the sentence to trail off into a confusing succession of explanations:

AWKWARD: Nitric oxides have an overfertilizing effect on deciduous trees, *which* are trees *that* lose their leaves during the winter, *that* has the effect of encouraging them to keep their leaves far into the winter, *which* makes them sensitive to frost.

REVISED: Nitric oxides have an overfertilizing effect on deciduous trees— trees *that* lose their leaves during the winter. The excess fertilizer encourages them to keep their leaves too far into the winter and thus makes them vulnerable to frost.

Seesaw sentences start with what seems like an important reason or condition but later end with a reason or condition that seems to ignore or overrule the first:

AWKWARD: *Because* many students change their majors, they take more than four years to graduate, *because* most majors are loaded with requirements.

REVISED: Most majors are loaded with requirements. As a result, students who change their majors often take more than four years to graduate.

Note: Even a brief modifier may throw a sentence off balance if it is awkwardly placed. For example, revise sentences weakened by a lame afterthought like the following:

LAME: An epidemic can be prevented if the authorities take firm action from the start, *usually*.

REVISED: *Usually*, an epidemic can be prevented if the authorities take firm action from the start.

Remember: An awkward sentence, like a fogged-over windshield, keeps us from getting a clear view of where we are headed. Revise awkward and confused sentences to give your readers a clearer view of who does what, what is truly important, and how parts fit into a larger whole.

EXERCISE 29   *Revising Padding and Impersonal Constructions*

Revise the following sentences, pruning deadwood and eliminating impersonal constructions.

1. As a skier, it is essential to stay in good physical shape.
2. When one owns a farm, there is a constant stream of forms and questionnaires to fill out.
3. There are many ways in which a student who is interested in meeting a foreign student may come to know one.
4. My friend badly needed a government loan, but the income level of this friend's parents made her ineligible for the loan.
5. This year has been a discouraging one for those who are committed to the cause of better public health services.

EXERCISE 30   *Revising the Awkward Passive*

Rewrite the following sentences to convert awkward or unnecessary passives back to active statements. Who does what? Who should do what?

EXAMPLE: When writing about actions being performed, the awkward passive should be avoided.

REVISED: When writing about what people do, writers should avoid the awkward passive.

1. Our food was carried in sturdy backpacks, and many a simple but nourishing meal was enjoyed along the trail.
2. All instructions should be read carefully and all blank spaces filled in before this form is signed by the applicant.
3. If any experimenting endangering human lives is to be done by the government, the voters should be consulted first.
4. When information about summer school is received, the necessary deadlines may have already passed.
5. Various ways of living are being tested today and experimented with by youth whose dominant characteristic is the desire for flexibility.

EXERCISE 31   *Revising Awkward Sentences*

Rewrite the following awkward, overburdened, or confusing sentences.

1. We watched the officer who questioned the suspects who had been apprehended.
2. There was an antinuclear demonstration participated in by over 20,000 people.

3. There will be an investigation by the mayor's office of the unauthorized distribution of this information.

4. From small incidents, like receiving too much change and pocketing it, to larger issues, like cheating on a test, a lifelong pattern may be established.

5. When people are constantly under supervision when at work and asked immediately where they are going when they leave their station, a feeling of harassment is experienced.

6. Saturday mornings used to be my best time for studying, because I knew nothing was due the next morning (which was Sunday), until I started working.

7. Motorists are quickly informed of the whereabouts of restaurants, motels, and, of course, speed traps set by the police, by other CB operators.

8. The dreary weather, mainly rain, that never seemed to stop, and my problems with my parents, which were serious, upset me.

9. A child's first impressions of people and places shape the course of her future life, frequently.

10. The government continued its disregard of the wishes of the inhabitants of the region.

17

THE PARAGRAPH

Compositions in Miniature

Most beginning writers underdevelop, underestimating the reader's hunger for information. Donald Murray

Paragraphs . . . punctuate (i.e., point up) the whole structure of the essay. Marie Ponsot and Rosemary Deen

THE PARTS AND THE WHOLE Paragraphs enable us to cover a subject one step at a time. The paragraph is to writing what the verse is to the song, what the inning is to the game. It marks off a part of a larger whole, enabling us to focus on one idea at a time, on one link in a chain of thought. A well-planned sequence of paragraphs, like a well-planned itinerary, makes us feel that we are making progress, with strategically placed rest stops reached when we have accomplished a significant part of the task. Each well-written paragraph is a group of sentences that focus on one part of the subject and do it justice.

Although paragraphs differ widely in shape and purpose, the kind of paragraph that does most of the work for you as a writer answers basic questions in the reader's mind. The prototype paragraph will focus on one limited point or issue. (What are you talking about?) It will present a central idea or overall conclusion. (What is the point?) It will back up the main point with examples or other supporting material. (What makes you think so?)

It is true that in some kinds of writing a paragraph merely gives us a convenient break. In much *newspaper writing*, paragraphs are very short. There may by a paragraph break after every two or three sentences.

In *dialogue*, we use a paragraph break to signal a change from one speaker to another. If this textbook were written in the form of a dialogue, the next few lines might look like this:

"Why does the average length of paragraphs vary for different kinds of writing?"

"It varies because the authors make different assumptions about the attention span of their readers."

Nevertheless, in writing that explains, informs, editorializes, or argues with the reader, the basic unit is the solidly developed paragraph that is a composition in miniature. It is written for readers who are likely to say: "Tell me what is on your mind. Show me what it means. Give me examples. Move in for the closer look." A paragraph like the following focuses clearly on a limited part of a larger subject (how we dress), makes a strong point (about how uniforms transform people), provides detailed explanation (how it works), fills in striking and varied examples (where to look for evidence), and spells out the unfortunate results:

The extreme form of conventional dress is the costume totally determined by others: the uniform. No matter what sort of uniform it is—military, civil, or religious; the outfit of a general, a nun, a butler, a football player, or a waitress—to put on such livery is to give up one's right to act as an individual—in terms of speech, to be partially or wholly censored. What one does, as well as what one wears, will be determined by external authorities—to a greater or lesser degree, depending upon whether one is, for example, a Trappist monk or a boy scout. The uniform acts as a sign that we should not or need not treat someone as a human being, and that they need not and should not treat us as one. It is no accident that people in uniform, rather than speaking to us honestly and straightforwardly, often repeat mechanical lies. "It was a pleasure having you on board," they say; "I cannot give you that information"; or "The doctor will see you shortly."   Alison Lurie, *The Language of Clothes*

In your finished paper, your paragraphs are the major structural elements that determine the shape of the piece as a whole. As a characteristic string of atoms determines the identity of a molecule, so the way your paragraphs are strung together shapes the basic architecture of your paper. In a well-developed paper, each major paragraph moves the presentation or the argument ahead one important step. It makes its point, explains it, illustrates it, supports it. Then the next paragraph goes on to the next point, often with a transition that spells out the logical connection.

The sequence of paragraphs in an article on television coverage of political conventions might in part proceed as follows:

Smile—You're on Camera

first point   *Television continues to change the look of political conventions.* Speeches are fewer and shorter. Sweaty orators, bellowing and waving their arms for an hour or more, have yielded almost completely to TelePrompTer readers, younger and brisker, some of them very slick and many of them no fun. Both parties have shortened sign-waving, chanting demonstrations. . . .

transition to second point   *While many of the changes may be for the best, there is something synthetic about this new kind of convention.* There is a lack of spontaneity, a sense of stuffy self-consciousness. There is something unreal about seeing a well-known newscaster starting across the floor to interview a delegate and getting stopped for an autograph. . . .

transition to third point   *Nevertheless, television coverage of conventions manages to get across to us a great deal about the way our political system works.* We are still a nation of different parts. The conventions are the occasions that bring various coalitions together every four years to pull and haul at one another; to test old power centers and form new ones; to compromise and, yes, to raise a little hell together in a carnival atmosphere. . . .

SHAPING THE PARAGRAPH

How does a successful paragraph take shape? The basic paragraph-writing skill is to funnel related observations or details into a paragraph with a point. This pulling together of related material in a paragraph is a crucial step in the process that takes us from the initial brainstorming or loosely organized reading and interview notes to a finished paper.

Bundling Related Data

The raw material for a paragraph is a group of related data or observations. As we focus on one limited area of a subject, we bring together different details that seem to be part of the same general picture. Suppose an education writer is visiting a campus that has recently been much in the news. Repeatedly during the visit, he sees evidence that garnering maximum media coverage seems to be official university policy. The following might be the structure of a paragraph that would bring together his observations and funnel them into a general point:

MAIN POINT: "Getting covered" is a Brown University policy.

The *Brown Daily Herald* prints rundowns of how much "good copy" Brown rates, and *Issues*, a student monthly, leads off a big issue on Brown's future with speculation about what the school's "image-makers" will do now, after years of "exorbitant media coverage."

A recent appeal to alums to come take classes included photos of staff with captions such as: "Giles Milhaven, Professor of Religious Studies, guest on 'CBS Sunday Morning.'"

Every quarter the administration publishes a tabloid called *Brown in the News*, packed with the latest, including stories about student stars Amy Carter, Vanessa Vadim, and Cosima von Bulow.

A recent cover highlighted the visit by the "Today" show. There was a picture of President Howard R. Swearer getting comfy with Jane Pauley in front of space heaters on the green. It was hard to tell which one was the TV personality.   Peter Weiss, "Good Times vs. Great Books," *New Republic*

A similar bundling of related data to make paragraphs operates in many different kinds of writing. Suppose a science writer is focusing on the role leaves play in the lives of plants. Repeatedly, she is struck by the fact that even parts of plants that do not look like leaves were originally leaves. The following might form the basic structure of a passage that channels these related observations into a paragraph with a point:

MAIN POINT: As their functions become specialized, leaves take forms that are scarcely recognizable as leaves.

— The spines of cactuses are actually vestigial leaves.

— The bulb of an onion is a cluster of specialized leaves.

— Thorns of spiny plants and tendrils of climbing plants are often modified leaves, as are the needles of pine trees. . . .

— The hard, woody sheathing of palm trees is a modified leaf, so large in one Amazonian plant that local tribes use it as a makeshift canoe. Dian M. Bolz, "A World of Leaves," *Smithsonian*

Remember that in the printed paragraph, we see the finished product, the end result. To understand how a writer works, we need to reconstruct the process by which the paragraph was produced. Here is how we might bring together observations that all relate to the same basic topic: the food-tracking equipment of sharks. As we think about these observations, we channel them into a general conclusion:

first observation | Sharks can smell blood from a quarter of a mile away, and they follow the faint scent to their prey.

second observation | Sharks sense motion in the water with special sense organs. Something thrashing about in the water is for sharks a signal of food.

third observation | Sharks are sensitive to bright light. They are attracted to bright and shiny objects, and to contrast between light and dark.

conclusion | *Sharks are well equipped for identifying and tracking down food.*

In the finished paragraph, we usually put the general conclusion first. It appears early in the paragraph as the main idea that gives focus and direction to the details that back it up. We call the sentence that sums up the main idea the **topic sentence**:

topic sentence | *Sharks, known as voracious eaters, are well equipped for identifying and tracking down food.* As they prowl the water, they seem to sense the presence of unsuspecting prey from a considerable distance. There are several reasons why sharks are efficient at hunting down their prey. They can smell blood from a quarter of a mile away, and they follow the faint scent to a wounded creature. Sharks sense motion in the water with special sense organs; something thrashing about in the water is for them a signal of food. Finally, sharks are sensitive to bright light. Light reflected from something

---

THE WRITING WORKSHOP

The Parts and the Whole

Much editing software asks writers to check the flow of ideas in a paper by highlighting the key sentence or main idea of each paragraph. These key sentences are then printed out, giving the writer the logical structure of the paper at a glance. Print out or copy out such a sequence of key sentences from a paper you have recently completed or from a paper in progress. Share the results with a group of your classmates. Does the flow of ideas become clear to them? What can you learn from their comments or suggestions?

---

moving in the water alerts them, especially if it is the reflection from the shiny scaly surface of large fish.

Using a Topic Sentence The topic sentence sums up the main point or central idea of a paragraph. It tells our readers, "This is what I am trying to show. This is what I am trying to prove." Often the topic sentence is the very first sentence. Many paragraphs are constructed on this basic model: A topic sentence sums up the writer's claim, then the writer presents the evidence—the examples, details, statistics that back it up. Look at the way the author of the following paragraph backs up her claim about the role of slavery in ancient Greece:

topic sentence

evidence

Greeks enslaved foreigners and other Greeks. Anyone captured in war was dragged back as a slave, even if he was a Greek of a neighboring polis. In Athens slaves, especially women, were often domestic servants, but of 150,000 adult male slaves, 20,000 were set to work in the silver mines, in ten-hour shifts, in tunnels three feet high, shackled and lashed; the forehead of a retrieved runaway was branded with a hot iron. Aristotle called slaves "animate tools," forever indispensable, he thought, unless you were a utopian who believed in some future invention of automatic machinery. In Athens it was understood that the most efficient administrator of many slaves was someone who had himself been born into slavery and then freed; such a man would know, out of his own oppressive experience with severity, how to bear down hard.   Cynthia Ozick, "The Moral Necessity of Metaphor," *Harper's*

STATEMENT–EXPLANATION–ILLUSTRATION A topic sentence often carries its message most effectively if it is brief and to the point. However, it may call for some *explanation*: A second and perhaps a third sentence may restate the main idea, explaining a key term, spelling out how, when, or where. Then the paragraph may go on to *illustration*: The main point gets needed support from the examples or details that back it up:

statement   *I always wished to be famous.* As other people have an imagination for disaster,
explanation   I have had an imagination for fame. I can remember as a boy of nine or ten returning home alone from the playground in the early evening after dinner, dodging, cutting,
illustration   stiff-arming imaginary tacklers on my way to scoring imaginary touchdowns before enormous imaginary throngs who chanted my name. Practicing free throws alone in my backyard I would pretend that I was shooting them at a crucial moment in a big game at Madison Square Garden. Later, as a boy tennis player, before falling off to sleep, I imagined the Duchess of Kent presenting me with the winner's trophy on the center court at Wimbledon.   Aristides, "A Mere Journalist," *American Scholar*

After providing illustration, the writer may decide to remind us of the point in a **clincher sentence**:

statement   *The new trend toward vocationalism is particularly counterproductive in an uncertain economy, when jobs are both scarce and changeable.* It makes slim indeed
explanation   the chances of picking the right specialization years in advance of actual entry into the labor market. The writer of an article in the *New York Times Magazine* extrava-
illustration   gantly extolling the virtues of New York's Aviation High School appeared unaware of its own ultimate contradiction: only 6 members of that year's 515-member grad-uating class reported that they had found jobs in the aviation industry. *The primary
restatement   reason for youth unemployment is not lack of training but lack of jobs.*   Fred M. Hechinger, "Murder in Academe," *Saturday Review*

TOPIC SENTENCE LAST Sometimes we delay the topic sentence till the end of the paragraph. We take our readers along, making them look at our evidence or exam-ples, steering them toward a conclusion very similar to our own. To make such a paragraph work, we have to be especially careful that the details add up, so that the reader can follow our train of thought:

examples first   The shops of the border town are filled with many souvenirs, "pinatas," pottery, bullhorns, and "serapes," all made from cheap material and decorated in a gaudy manner that the tourist thinks represents true Mexican folk art. Tourists are every-where, haggling with the shopkeepers, eager to get something for nothing, carrying huge packages and boxes filled with the treasures bought at the many shops. Car horns blare at the people who are too entranced with the sights to watch where they are going. Raucous tunes pour from the nightclubs, open in broad daylight. Few children are seen in the town, but some boys swim in the Rio Grande and dive to retrieve the coins that tourists throw as they cross the bridge above. People come for
topic sentence last a cheap thrill or cheap liquor. *A border town is the tourist's Mexico, a gaudy caricature of the real country.*

Remember: A good topic sentence is your promise to your readers. It gives them a sense of what to expect. In each of the following examples, the topic sentence steers the paragraph in a different direction:

VERSION 1:   *The dormitory reminds me of a third-class hotel.* Each room has the same set of unimaginative furnishings: the same pale red chest of drawers, the same light brown desks. . . .

VERSION 2:   *The dormitory reminds me of a big office building.* People who half know each other pass in the hall with impersonal friendliness. . . .

VERSION 3:   *The dormitory reminds me of a prison.* The study room is enclosed by windows with lines on them, giving the student a penned-in feeling. . . .

Often a good topic sentence hints at how the paragraph is going to be organized. It gives the reader a preview of points to be covered; it hints at the procedure the writer is going to follow. Look at the program implied in each of the following topic sentences:

TOPIC SENTENCE: Just as traffic lights may be red, amber, or green, so job interviews may be classified according to their probable results as hopeless, undecided, or promising. (We now expect a description of the three kinds.)

TOPIC SENTENCE: During my high school years, I saw a major change in the way schools treated bilingual students. (We now expect an account of the situation first before and then after the change.)

Questions for Discussion How consciously do you aim at a strong topic sentence when you write a paragraph? As your paragraphs take shape, do you start with the topic sentence, or does it come into focus later?

Marshaling Examples

In a well-developed paragraph, the topic sentence is backed up by examples or details. Following through with specific examples or details is second nature for experienced writers; after making a point, they naturally go on to the "for example" or the "for instance."

MULTIPLE EXAMPLES Successful writers know how to pile on the examples that make the reader say, "Enough! I see what you mean." Notice how many different examples the writer has brought together in the following sample paragraph. Notice how directly they all relate to the author's central point:

topic sentence   *Latin American culture has been and is a dynamic element in the development of our own.* It has, *for example*, furnished more than 2000 place names to the United

multiple examples States postal directory. Its languages have influenced American English, as such simple examples as "rodeo" and "vamoose" indicate. Its customs are part of our "Westerns" on television. Its housing, its music, its dances, its scenery, its ruins, and its romance have been imitated and admired in the United States. One third of the continental area of this republic was for a long period, as modern history goes, under the governance of Spanish viceroys or of Mexico. The largest single Christian church in the United States is identical with the dominant church in Latin America.   Howard Mumford Jones, "Goals for Americans," *Saturday Evening Post*

If you chart the supporting material in this paragraph, you see a solid array of details that all point in the same direction: Much in our culture has roots or parallels in Latin American culture and history. Here is a rough chart:

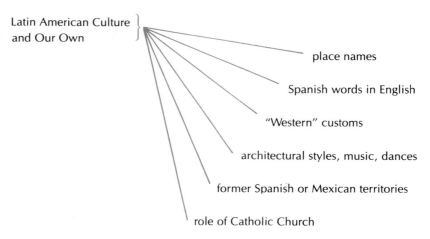

Latin American Culture and Our Own

place names

Spanish words in English

"Western" customs

architectural styles, music, dances

former Spanish or Mexican territories

role of Catholic Church

KEY EXAMPLE Sometimes we use one exceptionally detailed example to drive home a point. We decide that a key example or a striking case in point will be remembered where more routine examples might be forgotten:

topic sentence

key example

As more and more clerical workers use computers, they increasingly find that their work is monitored from afar. For example, computerization changed the working conditions in the accounting department of a large airline: The company hired a computer consultant to observe the work of clerks sifting through flight coupons and tabulating revenues. The consultant then devised a computerized system that enabled supervisors to keep exact count of how many tickets each clerk was processing each day. The system also identified periods during the day when productivity would dip while workers socialized or took breaks. The system enabled supervisors to set work quotas and to identify electronically those employees who fell short. Like the chickens on a computerized chicken farm, the workers were no longer allowed to waste the company's time.

DOWNSHIFTING Often we choose one of several examples for more detailed treatment. After giving more general examples, we push toward specifics; we move in for the closer look. In such a paragraph, we **downshift**—we move into a slower gear to allow the reader to take a closer look at one part of the scenery. An informative paragraph frequently moves through three levels: It starts with a fairly general statement or key idea (topic sentence). It then takes one step toward specifics by following through with several brief examples (intermediate level). Finally, it zeroes in on one or more examples for more detailed treatment (specific level):

1 topic sentence
(general point)

2 sample area
(intermediate)

3 close-up
example (specific)

Most commercials succeed by working on the viewer's need to be loved and most commercials appeal to hidden fears. For example, we have been schooled from early childhood (sociologist David Riesman calls the American child a "consumer trainee") that our bodies produce numerous odors which "offend." Those who advertise deodorants, toothpastes, mouthwashes, colognes, and soaps have laid out billions of dollars to convince us that natural odors are unnatural. In an attempt to appeal to the environmentally conscious younger generation, the makers of Gillette Right Guard once announced: "A new anti-perspirant as natural as your clothes and makeup."   David Burmester, "The Myths of Madison Avenue," *English Journal*

To help you visualize the downshifting that occurs in this kind of paragraph, imagine the paragraph laid out in a step pattern like the following:

1 general

2 intermediate

3 specific

We constantly expect more of computers. Our tests for the artificial intelligence we build into electronic computers are constantly becoming more demanding. ————————————→

When machines first performed simple calculations, people were amazed to see a collection of gears and levers add 2 and 2. Early computers amazed people by winning a game of tic-tac-toe. ————————————→

Current tests of computer intelligence ask a human subject to type questions and comments on a communication typewriter and then to judge which responses are being returned by another human being and which by a computer. For instance, a computer program called DOCTOR simulates the responses of a human therapist. According to a recent article on artificial intelligence, "some of the individuals interacting with DOCTOR thought they were getting typed responses from a real therapist."

USING STATISTICS In many well-developed paragraphs, facts and figures assure the reader that the main point is not just one person's superficial impression. In the next paragraph, the main point is sandwiched in between statistics designed to make the author sound like an insider or an authority on the subject:

statistics

topic sentence

statistics

Four of the ten hardcover bestsellers last year were fitness books. Americans spent more than a billion dollars on exercise devices, and many people have turned their homes into private gymnasiums. Nevertheless, *in spite of the fitness craze that has swept the nation, Americans are actually less physically fit than they were five years ago.* Between 80 and 90 percent of Americans still do not get enough exercise. (Exercise is defined as any activity that boosts heart and lung performance to 60 percent or more of its capacity for at least twenty minutes three times a week.) According to a study published by the Department of Health and Human Services, American children are fatter today than they were in the 1960s. Only 36 percent of our children today can pass minimum fitness standards set by the Amateur Athletic Union.

USING QUOTATIONS We often bolster a paragraph by the use of well-chosen quotations. We quote eyewitnesses, insiders, officials; we draw on authoritative printed sources. Look at the use of quotations in the following paragraph from a student editorial:

topic sentence

examples

quotations

For decades, Dali, the bizarre Spaniard with the erratic eyes and the antenna moustache, has been the uncontested leader of the art movement that expresses the unanalyzed subconscious. In their illogical and hallucinatory patterns, his paintings look like the record of extravagant dreams. These paintings bear such titles as "Rotting Mannequin in a Taxi" and "Debris of an Automobile Giving Birth to a Blind Horse Biting a Telephone." Images of ants, snails, melting watches, cauliflowers, lobsters, and women with chests of drawers in their abdomens appear throughout his work. When he first burst upon the art scene with an exhibition of surrealist paintings in Paris, one critic said, "We have here a direct, unmistakable assault on sanity and decency." A French poet called Dali "the great legislator of delirium." Dali has said of himself, "The only difference between me and a madman is that I am not mad."   Student editorial

Questions for Discussion How much supporting material in a paragraph is enough? Do any of the sample paragraphs in this section seem to have too many examples or not enough? How easy or how difficult is it for you to dredge up supporting examples for a paragraph?

Strengthening Coherence
Paragraphs, like people, have to be coherent if we are to make sense of what they say. When a paragraph has **coherence**, it "hangs together"; the material in it is relevant—it helps the writer make the

point. A good paragraph has built-in signals that help the reader follow, that steer the reader's attention in the right direction.

TRANSITIONS Transitional words or phrases ease the reader's way from here to there. *For instance, for example,* and *to illustrate* steer us from general point to specific example. *Similarly, furthermore, moreover* and *in addition* nudge us to continue the same line of thought. *But, however, on the other hand, on the contrary,* and *by contrast* signal a turning point—objections will follow; complications are about to set in. *It is true* or *admittedly* signals a concession—the writer is (reluctantly) granting a point. Trace the transitional expressions that guide the reader through the following paragraph:

topic sentence	Doctors have found that the way a drug is given can be important. The commonly
example	prescribed antibiotic tetracycline is *one example*. It is completely absorbed when injected in a vein or muscle and fairly well absorbed in pill form on an empty
caution	stomach. *But* because the presence of food in the stomach interferes with absorption, patients are advised to take tetracycline before meals. *Further*, drugs are not absorbed
additional point	equally after injection into different muscles. *Therefore*, doctors now pay more atten-
result	tion to the site at which drugs are injected. *For example*, in the case of a drug called lidocaine, which is used in the treatment of heart rhythm abnormalities, studies have
example	shown that it was absorbed faster following its injection into the deltoid muscle in the arm than into a muscle in the leg. Lawrence K. Altman, "Drugs—How Much Is Enough?" *New York Times*

RELATED TERMS In many paragraphs, a network of related terms makes for coherence and keeps the reader's attention focused on the point at issue. In a well-focused paragraph, the same central term, as well as various doubles or synonyms, may come up several times. Such **recurrent terms** form a semantic network—a network of words closely related in meaning. In the next paragraph, note the many words and phrases that echo the idea of purity: *naked—nude—pure—elemental—beyond corruption—natural—basic.*

	To the Greeks, who get the credit for inventing it, gymnastics was "the *naked* sport" (the word *gymnos* means "*nude*"), and the phrase manages to be both evoc-
topic sentence	ative and correct. There is something *pure* about gymnastics, something so *elemental* that the sport seems *beyond* either *corruption* or *adornment*. The athletes do not work against an opponent or against some arithmetical measure of time, distance, or weight. The gymnast works, instead, against the body's *natural* limits, with little protective clothing or equipment to help when courage or talent fails. The appara-tuses of gymnastics are *basic* and symbolic, nothing more than artificial tree limbs, level tumbling lawns, and imitation saddles. When the sport advances, it is (for the most part) because a single athlete is able to make his or her body do something that no one has ever done before. Geoffrey Norman, "The Naked Sport," *Esquire*

PARALLEL STRUCTURE   Often, similar or parallel sentence structure signals to the reader that several ideas or details are closely related. In the following paragraph, the repetition of similar sentence openings signals that the writer is continuing the same trend of thought. The sentences starting "They are . . . They are . . . They tend . . ." each pinpoint something that is part of the same basic attitude on the part of reviewers. Later, two sentences that are again similar in structure describe the contrasting attitude of ordinary readers:

> With a few splendid exceptions, professional reviewers do not really read books. *They are* in the book business. And that makes a big difference. *They are* so bored and so jaded with the sheer volume of books which pass through their hands that if they manage to respond freshly to one, it's nothing short of a miracle. *They tend* to regard all books as guilty until proven innocent. But readers are different. *They regard* each book with optimism. *They expect* their lives to be changed—and often write to tell me that they were.

In the following paragraph, similarity in sentence structure helps us take in the two parts of a comparison:

> Baseball does not pay its officials nearly as well as basketball does. *In basketball, an NBA official with ten years' experience* may make perhaps $600 per game, with over eighty games on the schedule. The official would make over $45,000 a season. *In baseball, an umpire with ten years in the majors* until recently made closer to $200 a game, with a schedule of about 160 games. . . .

Remember: The detail work of rounding out individual paragraphs tests your ability to make your writing live up to its promises—to give concrete substance to your opinions, to back up your claims. The prose of the amateur tends to move on too fast, like a sightseeing tour with no time for the tourists to descend from the bus and inspect the monuments. Learn from the prose of pros: If a question is worth raising, it is worth answering; if a point is worth making, it is worth following up.

EXERCISE 1   *The Missing Topic Sentence*

What should be the topic sentence missing from each of the following paragraphs? In each of the following passages, related material has been brought together for a paragraph. However, the general conclusion suggested by the material has been left out. For each passage, write a sentence that could be used as the topic sentence of the complete paragraph.

1.   _____. In some arid countries, per capita consumption of water has risen tenfold thanks to improved sanitation. Underdeveloped countries need huge

---

THE WRITING WORKSHOP

Paragraphs in Action

Regardless of the subject area, a basic tool of every writer is the expository paragraph that focuses on a limited point and supports it with detailed examples. Scan publications in an area of special interest to you for sample paragraphs. You might look at specialized magazines or textbooks, for instance. Share your choice of a statement-and-examples paragraph with a group of your classmates; have them discuss the sample paragraphs submitted and select those that best fit the type.

---

new water supplies for industrialization and irrigation. In the United States, many communities are facing water shortages. We have tapped most of the easily accessible sources of water in lakes, rivers, springs, and wells, and the fresh water that remains will often be prohibitively expensive to collect and distribute.

2. _____. People trying to protect whales have steered their small boats between the hunted whales and the sailors of catcher boats attempting to harpoon the animals. Other volunteers have harassed sealers on the harp seal breeding grounds on the ice of the Magdalen Islands. They have sprayed baby seals with organic dye that would make their pelts worthless for the hunters who club the defenseless cubs and then strip them of their fur. In one widely reported incident, an American released dolphins caught and penned up for slaughter by crews of Japanese fishing boats as threats to their catch.

3. _____. Many companies now employ private security guards to protect business property. The sales of burglar alarms and other security equipment for private homes have increased steadily over the years. Locksmiths do a booming business fitting entrance doors with multiple locks, dead bolts, and the like. Increasing numbers of private citizens buy handguns intended as last-ditch protection of their families and their property.

EXERCISE 2   *Following Through*

Study the following topic sentences. What is the author's point or intention? How might the author follow up the main point? What details, examples, statistics, or the like could you provide to help develop the rest of the paragraph?

1. It is becoming harder for the average high school graduate to get into and to stay in college.
2. The typical American car has many features that have nothing to do with providing cheap and efficient transportation.
3. Americans increasingly run into the ever-present computer during the business of an ordinary day.
4. A major industry can shape the quality of life of a whole town.
5. Violence in movies is getting more brutal.
6. Women in the judiciary are still the exception rather than the rule.
7. Many young people have negative attitudes toward the police.
8. Corporations ceaselessly develop marketing strategies designed to make what we already own obsolete.
9. At one time or another, most people's lives are touched or changed by divorce.
10. Terrorism, like auto accidents, has become a standard part of the news.

EXERCISE 3   *Downshifting*

How would you complete each of the following paragraphs? For each, downshift to one or more striking examples developed in detail. Modify or adapt the opening sentences if you wish.

1. *The fitness craze shows no signs of abating.* Sportswear stores carry twenty different kinds of running shoes, with the price of each pair representing three days' wages for the person working at MacDonald's or Burger King. . . .

2. *It is hard for young people to find heroes in the political arena.* Several recent Presidents have started in office with much popular support, only to be discredited or disgraced before they finished their duties. What Waterloo was to Napoleon, Watergate was to Richard Nixon, who resigned in disgrace when his White House "plumbers" were caught breaking and entering. . . .

3. *In our modern society, what cannot be counted does not count.* Numbers are the very models of modern facts. We expect to be served our customary diet of statistics— to be kept up to date with the latest swing in the unemployment rate, the consumer price index, or the President's standing in the polls. . . .

4. *Moviegoers and television viewers are fascinated by the possibility of extraterrestrial life.* Several years ago, the hit of the movie season was a spindly-fingered, child-size extraterrestrial who looked like an intelligent lizard. . . .

5. *Many outstanding athletes know that their careers may be brief or come to a premature end.* They know that their careers can be shortened with devastating swiftness

by an injury. After a few seasons, broadcasters begin to refer to a player as a "veteran" while the club is acquiring high draft choices to groom for the older player's position. . . .

EXERCISE 4   *The Well-Developed Paragraph*

Study the way a central idea or main point is developed in the following paragraphs. Answer the following questions about each:

- □ What is the main point? Is it stated in a topic sentence? Where in the paragraph?
- □ Is any part of the paragraph a restatement or explanation of the main idea?
- □ What is the nature of the supporting material—multiple examples, one key example, downshifting to a more detailed example, statistics, or a variation of these? (What is the source of the supporting material?)
- □ Does the material follow a pattern, such as from familiar to new, or from less important to more important?
- □ How do you react to the paragraph as a reader? What kind of reader would make a good audience for the paragraph?

1.   The influx of women into the corporate world has generated its own small industry of advice and inspiration. Magazines like *Savvy* and *Working Woman* offer tips on everything from sex to software, plus the occasional instructive tale about a woman who rises effortlessly from managing a boutique to being the CEO of a multinational corporation. Scores of books published since the mid-1970s have told the aspiring managerial woman what to wear, how to flatter superiors, and when necessary, fire subordinates. Even old-fashioned radicals like myself, for whom "CD" still means civil disobedience rather than an eight percent interest rate, can expect to receive a volume of second-class mail inviting them to join their corporate sisters at a "networking brunch" or to share the privileges available to the female frequent flier.   Barbara Ehrenreich, "Strategies of Corporate Women," *New Republic*

2.   When I was in grade school, I had many friends. They often invited me over to their houses. My parents would let me go if I asked politely. They sent me off with the usual warnings about not riding my bike in the middle of the street or being back in time for supper. One year my mother and I were looking at my class picture, and I pointed out a good friend of mine whose house I had often visited. Looking at his picture, my mother realized he was of a different race. I was never given permission to visit his family again. When I complained, I was told my friend was not a desirable influence. I believe that we are born with no natural instinct for prejudice but that we learn prejudices later in life from others.

3.   Commercial fishing around the world can barely keep up with the growing demand for scarce protein. In a recent year, the total catch amounted to 74 million tons, which works out to 16 kilograms per person for the world, or almost a quarter

of all animal protein consumed. More than a hundred species of finfish and shellfish are harvested commercially around the world, and 22 species provide 100,000 tons or more. However, per capita catches have been slowly dropping during the last decade. At least eleven major fisheries have been depleted to the point of collapse, ranging from the anchovy in Peru to the Alaska crab. In fact, only squid and the Antarctic krill are still underfished, since harvesters find it hard to make them palatable to new consumers.

4.   Outside the Arctic, which is my second home, I find little comprehension of the remarkable skill, work, and endurance it takes for Eskimos to live off the land and sea in one of the world's most inhospitable climes. The whale has traditionally been, and still is, a large and important part of the Eskimo diet. Even today, natives usually hunt it as their ancestors did—paddling up to the quarry in homemade driftwood-framed sealskin boats, then dispatching the giant with a hand-thrust harpoon or shoulder gun, the design of which was patented in the 1800's. As part of the hunt ritual, the Eskimos return the whale's skull to the sea to appease the spirit of the magnificent beast. Since bowheads are fairly wily, weigh a ton a foot, and sometimes grow to be 60 feet long, the crews require considerable courage. Their primitive method of hunting definitely limits the take, which, until 1978, was unrestricted by law.   Lael Morgan, "Let the Eskimos Hunt," *Newsweek*

EXERCISE 5   *The Coherent Paragraph*

Study the devices that make for coherence in the following paragraphs. Which of these paragraphs relies mainly on transitional expressions to guide the reader? In which of these paragraphs is there a strong network of related terms that echo or reinforce the key idea? Which of these paragraphs relies strongly on parallel sentence structure?

1.   All the evidence indicates that the population upsurge in the underdeveloped countries is not helping them to advance economically. On the contrary, it may well be interfering with their economic growth. A surplus of labor on the farms holds back the mechanization of agriculture. A rapid rise in the number of people to be maintained uses up income that might otherwise be utilized for long-term investment in education, equipment, and other capital needs. To put it in concrete terms, it is difficult to give a child the basic education it needs to become an engineer when it is one of eight children of an illiterate farmer who must support the family with the produce of two acres of ground.   Kingsley Davis, "Population," *Scientific American*

2.   Hate letters are a fact of life for anyone whose name appears in print or whose face is seen on television or whose voice is heard on radio. They are terribly disturbing—but after the first few, you begin to catch on to the fact that they have nothing whatever to do with you (or your book) but are sheer projections on the part of their writers. They are often unsigned. They often begin with sentences like: "My

mother was a lady who never used four-letter words and —s like you are what's rotting America and weakening our morale [sic] fiber. . . ." They are often misspelled and ungrammatical, and full of mixed metaphors and malapropisms.   Erica Jong, "The Writer as Guru," *New York*

3.   Most often the male role in advertising is that of the strong, silent outdoorsman, athlete, or adventurer. The archetypal male figure in advertising is, of course, the Marlboro Man. This famous mythic figure was the product of an intensive campaign which transformed a poorly selling cigarette, originally aimed at women smokers, into the biggest selling filter-tip on the market. At the same time, it promoted an attitude about male roles still being sold in almost every cigarette ad currently in print. Commercials for beer also push the take-charge male image, showing men, generally in groups, participating in active, physically demanding sports or jobs and being rewarded with a cool bottle of beer. Rarely are women seen in these commercials other than as silent companions to these he-men. The Marlboro Man and his descendants exemplify the self-sufficient, highly individualistic male who provides the complement to the sexy, empty-headed female of toiletry commercials.   David Burmester, "The Myths of Madison Avenue," *English Journal*

PARAGRAPH TOPICS 1   *The All-Purpose Paragraph*

1.   Write a paragraph that focuses on one strand in your growing up. Select an issue or important concern that will help your classmates know you better as a person. Show in vivid detail why it mattered to you. Study the following sample paragraph as a possible model:

> My personal Mexican-ness eventually produced serious problems for me. Upon entering grade school, I learned English rapidly and rather well, always ranking either first or second in my class; yet the hard core of me remained stubbornly Mexican. This chauvinism may have been a reaction to the constant racial prejudice we encountered on all sides. The neighborhood cops were always running us off the streets and calling us "dirty greasers," and most of our teachers frankly regarded us as totally inferior. I still remember the galling disdain of my sixth-grade teacher, whose constant mimicking of our heavily accented speech drove me to a desperate study of *Webster's Dictionary* in the hope of acquiring a vocabulary larger than hers. Sadly enough, I succeeded only too well, and for the next few years I spoke the most ridiculous high-flown rhetoric in the Denver public schools. One of my favorite words was "indubitably" and it must have driven everyone mad. I finally got rid of my accent by constantly reciting "Peter Piper picked a peck of pickled peppers" with little round pebbles in my mouth.   Enrique Hank Lopez, "Back to Bachimba," *Horizon*

2.   Write a paragraph that explains a characteristic attitude or emotion of the young (frustration, rebellion, ambition) to older people—or that explains

a characteristic attitude or emotion of the old to the young. Provide a detailed example or several striking examples that will bring your key term to life for your reader.

3. Write a details-first paragraph that creates a setting or a mood likely to be unfamiliar to your readers. First, fill in striking, characteristic details. Then, at the end, fill in the meaning the place or the mood has for you. Study the following sample paragraph as a possible model:

> It is Friday night at any of ten thousand watering holes of the small towns and crossroads hamlets of the South. The room is a cacophony of the pingpong-ding-dingding of the pinball machine, the pop-fizz of another round of Pabst, the refrain of "Red Necks, White Socks and Blue Ribbon Beer" on the juke box, the insolent roar of a souped-up engine outside and, above it all, the sound of easy laughter. The good ole boys have gathered for their fraternal ritual—the aimless diversion that they have elevated into a life-style.   Bonnie Angelo, "Those Good Ole Boys," *Time*

4. Write a multiple-example paragraph documenting a current trend for the readers of a small-town newspaper. Focus on a topic that has become the center of media attention, the object of marketing efforts, a favorite topic of pundits and politicians, or the preoccupation of other trend makers. Sum up the trend in a topic sentence and pile on many striking examples.

5. Write a paragraph devoted to the exception to the rule. Remind readers who tend to share the opinions of the majority that there are important exceptions to something that is often claimed or something "everybody says." Present exceptions in striking detail, or concentrate on one especially striking exception.

THE FUNCTIONS OF PARAGRAPHS

No two paragraphs are alike. The basic expository paragraph launches a main idea and then follows it up with examples or details. Many other paragraphs follow a somewhat different pattern. Their organization mirrors their function: to trace a step in a process, to compare two related things, or to choose one of several options.

Narration and Description

A paragraph narrating an event, describing a scene, or giving directions often follows a pattern built into the subject matter. We follow the order of events, or we trace necessary steps in the right order.

ORDER IN TIME Often a paragraph traces a pattern in time. It follows the order of events, presenting major stages or key developments in **chronological order**. The following paragraph tells the story of a playground from its opening to its gradual abandonment by the author and his friends. Note the transitional phrases that signal major stages. Notice also that in a narrative paragraph, the events may take shape without an introductory topic sentence:

beginnings

major event

turning point

intermediate stage

end result

The orphanage across the street is torn down, a city housing project *begins to rise* in its place, and on the marvelous vacant lot next to the old orphanage they are building a playground. Much excitement and anticipation as *Opening Day draws near.* Mayor LaGuardia himself comes to dedicate this great gesture of public benevolence. He speaks of neighborliness and borrowing cups of sugar, and of the playground he says that children of all races, colors, and creeds will learn to live together in harmony. *A week later,* some of us are swatting flies on the playground's inadequate little ball field. A gang of Negro kids, pretty much our own age, enter from the other side and order us out of the park. We refuse, proudly and indignantly, with superb masculine fervor. There is a fight, they win, and we retreat, half whimpering, half with bravado—my first nauseating experience of cowardice, and my first appalled realization that there are people in the world who do not seem to be afraid of anything, who act as though they have nothing to lose. *Thereafter,* the playground becomes a battleground, sometimes quiet, sometimes the scene of athletic competition between Them and Us. But rocks are thrown as often as baseballs. *Gradually* we abandon the place and use the streets instead. The streets are safer, though we do not admit this to ourselves. We are not, after all, sissies—that most dreaded epithet of an American boyhood.   Norman Podhoretz, *Doings and Undoings*

Many accounts of events, trends, or developments follow an approximate order in time even when they do not follow an exact time sequence step by step. The following *Time*-style paragraph about opening day at Disneyland takes us from the beginnings (the glut of cars on the freeway) to the morning-after newspaper report:

topic sentence

getting in
early snafus

high noon

morning after

Disneyland was capitalism with a human face—or a smiling rodent's—and its opening day was set for July 17, 1955. *Even the mastermind recalled it as "Black Sunday"; everything went wrong.* The glut of visitors turned the Santa Ana Freeway into a seven-mile parking lot. Refreshment stands ran out of food and drink for the nearly 30,000 invited guests and thousands more ticket counterfeiters who stormed the gates. Rides broke down almost immediately. A gas leak forced the shuttering of Fantasyland. The day's corrosive heat sent women's spiked heels sinking into the asphalt on Main Street. Nor was this debacle to be covered over with Tinker Bell dust: the whole sorry spectacle was broadcast on a live TV special co-hosted by Ronald Reagan. WALT'S DREAM A NIGHTMARE, proclaimed the Los Angeles *Tidings.   Time*

ORDER IN SPACE A paragraph describing a scene will often trace a pattern in space. In describing a scene, we try to lay out a pattern that the reader can follow with the mental eye. The following model paragraph makes the eye travel from what is close by (the house and its garden) to the far distance (the tropical forest):

topic sentence
this side of gorge

river at bottom

opposite bank

distant forest

> *The house stood in what was certainly the best position in Mamfe.* It was perched on top of a conical hill, one side of which formed part of the gorge through which the Cross River ran. From the edge of the garden, fringed with the hedge of the inevitable hibiscus bushes, I could *look down* four hundred feet into the gorge, to where a tangle of low growth and taller trees perched precariously on thirty-foot cliffs. Round gleaming white sandbanks and strange, ribbed slabs of rock, the river wound its way like a brown sinuous muscle. *On the opposite bank,* there were small patches of farmland along the edge of the river, and *after that* the forest reared up in a multitude of colors and textures, spreading endlessly back until it was turned into a dim, quivering, frothy green sea by distance and heat haze.   Gerald M. Durrell, *A Zoo in My Luggage*

Paragraphs in Exposition

In paragraphs that explain, we often try to make the reader see how something works or how two things compare. We try to show connections; we lead from causes to their effects or results.

PROCESS   To help us understand how something works (or how to make it work), a paragraph may trace a process step by step. The following paragraph traces the stages in a natural cycle. Notice the transitional expressions that take us a step forward in time:

topic sentence

initial cause

seasonal pattern

reason for change

end of cycle

> *Beavers often create forest ponds that for a time become the home of insects, reptiles, fish, otter, herons, and other animals.* Beavers can transform a pine forest into an entirely new habitat by damming a stream. The pond will flourish for a short time—perhaps a few decades. The pond's creatures adapt to seasonal changes. *In the winter,* the pace slows beneath the frozen surface. Frogs and turtles bury themselves in the mud. *But soon after the ice thaws,* the natural rhythms accelerate. Dragonflies breed, fish spawn, and soon all the energies begin to prepare for another winter. *But when the food supply is exhausted,* the beavers will leave. Without their hard work and constant maintenance, the dam falls into disrepair and the water runs out. The area reverts to a swamp, *then* a marsh, a meadow, and *finally* a forest once again in this never-ending natural cycle.

Much historical writing shows the chains of cause and effect that explain historical processes:

topic sentence
key cause

immediate result

current reminders

> *At the time of the migration to the North, the sharecroppers in Mississippi were moving off the land, because they were being replaced in the fields by machines.* Heavy tractors and cotton-picking machines became common equipment on farms in the fifties; by 1960 what was once the work of fifty field hands could be done by only three or four. Typically, the sharecroppers were simply dismissed; white farmers in Canton who had dozens of people living on their property have no idea where they are today. Deserted sharecropper cabins are a common sight in the country

outside Canton, falling down at the edges of open fields, some of them in rows, some half a mile from the nearest building or road. A few are still occupied, mostly by old people who sometimes still dress in homespun and use wood fires to warm themselves and cook.   Nicholas Lemann, "The Origin of the Underclass," *Atlantic*

COMPARISON/CONTRAST We often use a paragraph to line up two things for comparison or contrast. We help our readers grasp something difficult or new by comparing it with something familiar. We alert our readers to important differences or distinctive features in order to help them evaluate things or make a choice. The following paragraph illustrates a common pattern for combined comparison and contrast, showing first similarities and then differences. Note the *however* that signals the turning point:

topic sentence

similarities

differences

> *People riding a moped should remember that it is not really a motorcycle but only a bicycle with a small motor attached.* The moped may look like a lightweight motorcycle, and it can weave through stalled traffic and crowded places like a motorcycle. Like a motorcycle, it is cheaper and easier to maintain than the bulky, gas-guzzling family car. *However,* the moped creates a real safety problem for people who ride it in ordinary traffic. It has much less weight and power than a real motorcycle. The driver depends on a very small, underpowered engine. The wind caused by a passing truck or bus can make the lightweight moped impossible to control.

DEFINITION We often use a paragraph to define a key term: We explain an important technical term or pin down a word that has confusing or changing meanings. The following paragraph defines the term *conjunction* as used by astronomers and then illustrates its use:

explanation

key term

examples

> In addition to Venus, there are four other planets visible to the naked eye—Mercury, Mars, Jupiter, and Saturn. During their movements across the sky, two planets may sometimes appear to pass very close to one another—though in reality, of course, they are millions of miles apart. *Such occurrences are called conjunctions;* on occasion they may be so close that the planets cannot be separated by the naked eye. This happened for Mars and Venus on October 4, 1953, when for a short while the two planets appeared to be fused together to give a single star. Such a spectacle is rare enough to be very striking, and the great astronomer Johannes Kepler devoted much time to proving that the Star of Bethlehem was a special conjunction of Jupiter and Saturn.   Arthur C. Clarke, *Report on Planet Three*

ANALOGY An **analogy** is an exceptionally detailed comparison that traces a close parallel through several specifics. The two things being compared have to be alike in basic and instructive ways, not just similar in some superficial or isolated way. The following paragraph uses an analogy to make us think about an essential feature of growing up:

topic sentence

> *We are not unlike a particularly hardy crustacean.* The lobster grows by developing and shedding a series of hard, protective shells. Each time it expands from

within, the confining shell must be sloughed off. It is left exposed and vulnerable until, in time, a new covering grows to replace the old. With each passage from one stage of human growth to the next we, too, must shed a protective structure. We are left exposed and vulnerable—but also yeasty and embryonic again, capable of stretching in ways we hadn't known before. These sheddings may take several years or more. Coming out of each passage, though, we enter a longer and more stable period in which we can expect relative tranquillity and a sense of equilibrium regained.   Gail Sheehy, *Passages*

Paragraphs in Argument

In writing that argues with the reader, a well-developed paragraph presents an important step forward in the argument. Several kinds of paragraphs follow familiar logical patterns designed to take the reader along.

REASONS   A paragraph may support a point with convincing reasons. In the following paragraph, the student writer shows that her attitude toward convenience food is more than a personal dislike:

topic sentence   *I object to convenience foods because they do not serve the cause of good nutrition.* These expensive, elaborately packaged, highly processed products are

reasons   usually a combination of many ingredients, some of which have nothing to do with nutrition. Often the extra ingredients are there to provide long-term preservation and to improve coloring, texture, or taste. Refined sugar is one example of an often unnecessary ingredient. We eat too much sugar without realizing that much of the sugar we consume is hidden sugar. Almost every processed foodstuff contains sugar in some form: honey, molasses, sucrose, corn syrup, dextrose, and the like. Too much sugar plays a role as a cause of heart disease, diabetes, and high blood pressure. Salt is also abundantly used in processing beyond what is necessary for good health. The biggest argument against processed convenience foods is that during processing and packaging many of the original nutrients are lost and then artificially replaced by "enriching."

CAUSE AND EFFECT   We often try to change the reader's ways by showing the consequences of different courses of action. We take a look at causes and their effects so that our readers can take them into account. In the following paragraph, a crucial *therefore* takes us from cause to effect:

cause   Japan is a nation that, lacking natural resources, must live by its wits, by social discipline, and by plain hard work. It is not surprising, *therefore*, to discover that

effect   during the last twenty years Japan has quietly been establishing a new, higher set of educational standards for the world. On a whole raft of international tests of achievement in science and math, Japanese students outperform all others. Japan's newspaper readership level is the world's highest. A considerably larger percentage of Japanese (90 percent) than Americans (75 percent) or Europeans (mostly below 50 percent) finish the twelfth grade, and a greater proportion of males complete university B.A. degrees in Japan than in other countries. Japanese children attend school about fifty more days each year than American students, which means that, by high-school graduation, they have been in school somewhere between three and four more years than their American counterparts.   Thomas P. Rohlen, "Japanese Education—If They Can Do It, Should We?" *American Scholar*

PRO AND CON A well-focused paragraph may line up the pros and cons that we need to weigh when faced with a decision. The following paragraph lines up advantages and disadvantages in an exceptionally well-balanced way. Note the transitions that take us from the pro to the con in each set of examples:

topic sentence   *Like other modern inventions, computers have a capacity for use and abuse, a potential for good and bad.* Computers allow people to fly safely and quickly across continents, *but* they also make it possible to send missiles from one country to another. Computers can speed credit cards to us and help us use them with ease, *but* they can also be used to compile records that invade a citizen's privacy. Computers serve as electronic tutors; pocket-size electronic calculators can solve complicated problems with amazing speed. *However,* the students who start early to rely on calculators may see their own math abilities remain underdeveloped. The same computers that help administrators and accountants can ruin a student's class schedule or bill the wrong person for a thousand dollars' worth of merchandise.

WEIGHING ALTERNATIVES We sometimes start a paragraph by looking at one proposed solution and finding it wanting. We then go on to the more likely or more promising possibility. The following paragraph first looks at a desirable alternative but then goes on to the more likely prospect:

History shows that wars between cities, states, and geographic regions cease once the originally independent units have amalgamated under the leadership of a single government with the power of making and enforcing laws that are binding *first alternative rejected* upon individuals. *One might reason on this basis that* if all of the industrialized and semi-industrialized regions of the world were to federate under a common government, the probability of another war would be greatly decreased. It seems likely that this conclusion would be valid if the resultant federation were as complete as was the federation formed by the original thirteen colonies in America. *On the other* *second alternative* *hand,* it is extremely unlikely that such a highly centralized federation could come *supported* into existence at the present time; nationalistic feelings of individuals and groups, and conflicts of economic interests, are too strong to permit rapid transition. *Also,* those nations which have high per capita reserves of resources and high per capita production would be most reluctant to delegate their sovereignties to higher authority and to abandon the economic barriers that now exist.   Harrison Brown, *The Challenge of Man's Future*

Patterns in Combination   Obviously, paragraphs do not always follow a textbook pattern. You will often need to combine or adapt familiar patterns to accomplish your aims. For instance, you may trace causes and effects but at the same time present them in chronological order. The following paragraph combines a chronological pattern, contrast between then and now, and the tracing of important causes:

topic sentence	*In many American colleges, intercollegiate athletics has become a big business.*
contrast with past	How did these institutions become as deeply involved as they are? *A hundred years ago,* athletic events at American colleges were true amateur events, with free admis-
milestone event	sion. One of the first big stadiums was built *in 1903,* when the Harvard class of 1878, to celebrate its twenty-fifth anniversary, offered the university $100,000 to
major factors	build a stadium for track and football. As costs rose, spectators were *soon* charged for their seats. Institutions began to build bigger and bigger stadiums to outshine each other. Financial guarantees for visiting teams grew. The costs of scouting, recruiting,
end result	and traveling grew. *Today* a single large institution may employ forty coaches. The total athletic budget at a big football university may be between five and ten million dollars.

EXERCISE 6   *The Functions of Paragraphs*

Study the following *sample paragraphs*. Ask about each:

- ☐ What is the overall function of the paragraph?
- ☐ What is the main point, and where and how is it stated?
- ☐ What is the pattern of the paragraph—how is it organized?
- ☐ Does the paragraph serve a combination of purposes, or does it combine familiar patterns? Show how.
- ☐ What transitions help steer the reader?
- ☐ Who would make a good reader for the paragraph?

1.   Three fourths of the world's people receive very little attention from American reporters. They are the peasants, the three billion people who are still traditional subsistence cultivators of the land. There should be no doubt that these people are worth our attention: all the major contemporary revolutions—in Mexico, Russia, Cuba, Angola—have involved peasant societies. In almost every case, the revolution was preceded by cultural breakdown out in the villages, because the old peasant ways and views of life no longer worked. The 450 or so American foreign correspondents only rarely report on these billions, because the peasants live in the world's two million villages, while the governments, wealth, and power—as well as telephones, cable offices, files, and typewriters—are in the cities.   Richard Critchfield, *Columbia Journalism Review*

2.   The most disquieting aspect of the silicon chip is not that it distances us from nature; even before the Industrial Revolution, man was trying to do that. The more troubling fact is that electronic developments distance us from understanding. Any

THE WRITING WORKSHOP

Paragraphs in Tandem

In some kinds of writing, the function of each paragraph is exceptionally well defined. For instance, two related paragraphs may develop a contrast between then and now, or between the two stages of a process, or between two ways of accomplishing the same thing. Similarly, the first of two related paragraphs may present the surface advantages of a procedure or proposal, with the second paragraph pointing out the neglected other side—important disadvantages or unexpected side effects.

Study the following example of such a one-two paragraph sequence. Then write a two-paragraph paper of your own, with each paragraph serving a clearly defined function. Join with a group of your classmates to obtain reactions to your preliminary plans and feedback to your writing.

Peter Potterfield
AFTERMATH

Mount St. Helens changed the way Northwesterners think about the land on which they live. It happened on the morning of May 18, 1980. The mountain launched an eruption that sent a square mile of pulverized rock 14 miles into the atmosphere and completely tore apart the perfect cone of the volcano. At least 62 people, including loggers and campers, lost their lives. Mudflows created by melting glaciers buried river valleys. And with the eruption came fast-moving flows of superheated steam, ash, and gases that killed everything in their path. Hundreds of square miles of timber and other vegetation were laid waste. Wildlife was wiped out, the landscape rendered barren and unrecognizable. Cities like Yakima, 80 miles away, were blanketed by ash.

But in the years since, plant life has regained a foothold on some of the ashen hillsides. A few animals have been sighted. This has happened faster than most biologists believed possible. Even some of the mud-choked rivers now show signs of returning salmon. Much of the blown-down timber has been harvested, except for a section set aside as a permanent memorial to the power of the blast.   "God's Country U.S.A.," *Continental*

child of fifty years ago looking inside a household clock, with its escapement and weights or spring, could see in a few minutes how it worked. A child of today peering at a digital watch can learn nothing. Yesterday's children could appreciate that pushing a switch on a television set meant completing a circuit. Today's children, using remote control devices based on ultrasound or infrared radiation, can scarcely comprehend what they are doing. The real danger of the microelectronic era is posed by what was called, even in the days of macroelectronics, the black box mentality: passive acceptance of the idea that more and more areas of life will be taken over by little black boxes whose mysterious workings are beyond our comprehension.   Bernard Dixon, "Black Box Blues," *The Sciences*

3.   My mother once instructed me to say, "I am an American of Mexican descent." By the time I was nine or ten, I wanted to say, but dared not reply, "I am an American." Immigrants come to America and, against hostility or mere loneliness, they recreate a homeland in the parlor, tacking up postcards or calendars of some impossible blue—lake or sea or sky. Children of immigrant parents are supposed to perch on a hyphen between two countries. Relatives assume the achievement as much as anyone. Relatives are, in any case, surprised when the child begins losing old ways. One day at the family picnic the boy wanders away from their spiced food and faceless stories to watch other boys play baseball in the distance.   Richard Rodriguez, "Does America Exist?" *Harper's*

4.   When a beachcomber discovers a marooned marine mammal, center volunteers jump into their rescue truck to collect it. This can be a tricky business, because the arrival of humans is likely to excite the animal enough to stimulate his instinct to attack. The rescuers approach small seals and sea lions behind a "herding board" that protects the people and guides the animal into the rescue truck. They may briefly pop a blanket over the animal's head, says Schramm, "so they can't see where to bite." The uninitiated might be tempted to pet a young seal or sea lion with its invitingly thick coat and big cow eyes. But the animals are not as adorable as they look. Even the youngsters have very sharp teeth, and they're not afraid to use them. A larger elephant seal or sea lion is a bigger challenge and must be approached "with great caution," Schramm says. To collect the larger animals, rescuers use a "bull pull," a long pole with a rope on the end that is slipped over a large pinniped's neck to keep the biting end a safe distance from the people herding it into the truck.   Linda Currey Post, "Shelter from the Storm," *San Francisco Focus*

PARAGRAPH TOPICS 2   *Models for Paragraphs*

1.   Write a paragraph that traces a central theme through several stages or sections of a movie or book. Make your paragraph follow a rough chronological order. Study the following student-written paragraph as a possible model:

In a scene from *The Odd Angry Shot*, an antiwar film directed by Tom Jefferey, Bung, a young naive army draftee, pulls off his shoes and socks to find that a fungus is eating away his feet. Bung is in Vietnam as part of his country's "peace-keeping" force. Throughout his tour of duty, Bung is faced with the horrors, pains, and hopelessness of war. On his first night in the jungle, his camp is attacked by guerillas using rockets. One of the men that Bung is playing cards with has a hole blown through his back. He dies screaming. Later, on a mission to ambush guerillas, Bung and his patrol are caught by surprise, and another of his friends dies screaming in agony. Bung is obviously shaken as he says over and over, "Why can't he stop screaming?" To the bitter end, the viewer follows Bung and his patrol through a duty consisting of horrible living conditions, terrifying encounters, and painful deaths.

2. Write a "then-and-now" paragraph that traces a contrast between old and new customs or patterns of behavior. Study the following paragraph as a possible model:

> We have lost contact with many of our traditional rites of grieving. In rural America everybody had a role in the rites of death. Farm women dressed the body while the men built the casket. The body was buried on the family's land or in a nearby cemetery, by community members. Mourners wore black, or black armbands, for a long time—often a full year. The black would say, "I'm grieving; be gentle with me." Now, mourners are invisible. If a bank teller is short with me, there's no way to know that he is upset because his mother just died. For most of this society, grieving is set aside after a few days. Companies give three days bereavement leave for the death of an immediate family member, no time for the death of a friend. After three days, we are supposed to come back and perform as usual.

3. Write a definition paragraph that explains and illustrates a current buzzword, such as *lifestyle, quality time, the old boys' network, sexual harassment, primetime soap,* or *animal rights.* Study the following paragraph as a possible model:

> Examples of Doublespeak—the sometimes unwitting but more often deliberate misuse of words to cover up, rather than explain, reality—are easy to find almost everywhere. Government bureaus, for instance, have been instructed to eliminate the word poverty from official documents, replacing it with low-income, a term not nearly as alarming as poverty. For similar reasons, the unpleasantness of slums or ghettos has long given way to inner city. Instead of *prisons*, there are now only correctional facilities. U.S. State Department employees are not *fired* but *selected out*, a term that sounds like an award for excellence. Other government types tend to be terminated. In each instance, the aim is to make things appear better than they are or, in the case of correctional facilities, actually to seem what they decidedly are not. If all this were only a matter of semantics and style, there would be little cause for concern. Unfortunately, the truth is that the linguistic cosmetics are often used to create the impression that nasty problems have already been solved or were not really too nasty in the first place.   Fred M. Hechinger, "In the End Was the Euphemism," *Saturday Review/World*

PARAGRAPH TOPICS 3   *Paragraphs with a Purpose*

1. Write a paragraph that traces a clear pattern in space or time for the confused newcomer or outsider. Start with a topic sentence that sums up or previews what you describe. Choose a topic like the following:

    □   the layout of a baseball field
    □   building the foundation for a house
    □   disassembling the engine of a car
    □   the layout of your favorite park
    □   typing a letter on a word processor or computerized typewriter

2. Write a paragraph that develops a comparison or contrast to help guide the choices of an undecided reader. Start with a topic sentence that sums up the comparison. Choose a topic like the following:

    □   driving a car and riding a motorcycle
    □   organic and ordinary food
    □   downhill and cross-country skiing
    □   jogging and walking
    □   old-style and digital watches

3. Develop an analogy as a guide to the curious. Complete one of the following statements and use it as a topic sentence for a paragraph that fills in the details or examples needed to follow up the analogy. (Or develop an analogy of your own choice.)

    □   A college is like _____ .
    □   A big city is like _____ .
    □   A small town is like _____ .
    □   Love is like _____ .
    □   Failure is like _____ .
    □   The army is like _____ .
    □   Marriage is like _____ .

4. Write a paragraph in which you take a stand and then give reasons for the position you have taken. Keep in mind the unconverted or hostile reader. Start your paragraph with a statement like the following: "I believe in ____ because ____"; or "I object to ____ because ____." In the first blank in the sentence, fill in a topic like the following:

    □   large families
    □   stronger support for the U.S. military
    □   stricter speed limits
    □   rent control
    □   health foods

- □ financial aid to minority students
- □ more financial support for women's sports
- □ calculators in math classes

Use the rest of your paragraph to present your most important reason or reasons.

5. Write a paragraph whose purpose is to explain cause and effect, to examine pros and cons, or to weigh alternatives. Write to convince a reluctant or unconverted reader. Choose a topic like the following:

- □ diets
- □ early retirement
- □ protecting nonsmokers
- □ cheating on exams
- □ a national speed limit
- □ mandatory helmets for cyclists
- □ graffiti

REVISING THE PARAGRAPH In a first draft, paragraph development tends to be uneven. Some paragraphs, dealing with points close to the writer's heart, may already be fully fleshed out. But others are likely to look undernourished, in need of a strong transfusion of explanation and evidence. Use revision as an opportunity to make an underdeveloped paragraph live up to its promise. Remember the reader who is likely to say: "Tell me more—go into it more."

Guidelines like the following will help you strengthen weak paragraphs:

□ *Spell out a key idea that was only implied.* Look over your shoulder at the reader who wants to know: "What does this prove? What does this show? What is the point?" The following revision of a weak paragraph adds the topic sentence that spells out the point:

IMPLIED: The Lone Ranger—what a man! He doesn't need anybody. Fearless and brave, he rides in on his white horse, sending the bad guys running for cover. After rescuing the heroine and saving the town, he rides off into the sunset, alone. How about Tarzan, Lord of the Jungle, or Dirty Harry Callahan with his .44 Magnum ablazing? My favorite heroes were the mountain men—rugged solitary men fighting Indians, wrestling bears, and discovering the only safe route through the mountains. I read every book I could lay my hands on about such giants as Jedediah Smith and Joseph Walker.

SPELLED OUT: *When I was growing up, I was totally taken in by movies and books that glorified the rugged outdoors type. The Lone Ranger—there was a man!* Fearless and brave on his white horse, he sent the bad guys scrambling for cover. After rescuing the heroine and saving the town, he rode off into the sunset alone. Tarzan, Lord of the Jungle, another loner, single-handedly thwarted the evil designs of poachers or thieves of tribal treasure. My favorite reading was books about the mountain men—rugged solitary men fighting Indians, wrestling bears, and discovering the only safe route through the mountains, all in one day. I read every book I could find about such giants as Jedediah Smith and Joseph Walker. These men spent months, even years, in the mountains trapping beavers and living off the land, completely alone.

□ *Build up supporting material in weak paragraphs.* Look at the following paragraph before and after revision:

BEFORE: *Images of blacks in the media have certainly changed.* They now sell deodorant and toothpaste and light beer, just like other people. Bill Cosby's show, which became a top-rated program on television, presents a comfortable middle-class family and its everyday problems. The family happens to be black, and we hardly notice.

AFTER: *Blacks at one time were hardly visible in the media except as stereotypes (the field hand, the porter, the maid). That certainly has changed.* Blacks now sell deodorant and toothpaste and light beer. Bill Cosby's show, which became a top-rated program, shows a comfortable middle-class family and its everyday problems. Some black viewers have complained that Cosby's Dr. Huxtable doesn't represent the average black person. It is true that the average black family is not headed by a doctor father and a lawyer mother. On the other hand, neither is the average white family. But when Cosby identifies his son's room as "the room where clothes go to die," we don't think about whether this is a black family. We know it is a real family. And this seems to be the heart of the matter. When whites grow accustomed to the idea that blacks differ very little from them, it becomes more and more difficult to keep prejudice alive.

□ *Fit your supporting details into a pattern that the reader can follow.* For instance, in writing designed to inform or explain, the first draft of a paragraph will often present interesting bit facts, facts that remain too miscellaneous. To help the reader grasp and remember the information, work details into a pattern that the reader can take in. Notice how the following paragraph answers questions about comets in the order in which these questions might arise in the reader's mind:

topic sentence
where observed

how produced

Comets strew debris behind them in interplanetary space. Some of it is seen from the earth as the zodiacal light, which is visible as a glow in the eastern sky before sunrise and in the western sky after sunset. (It is brightest in the tropics.) Much of the zodiacal light near the plane of the earth's orbit is sunlight scattered by fine dust left behind by comets. Under ideal observing conditions, cometary dust also appears as the Gegenschein, or counterglow: a faint luminous patch in the night sky in a direction opposite that of the sun. Comets need to contribute about 10 tons of *how ended* dust per second to the inner solar system in order to maintain this level of illumination. Over a period of several thousand years, the particles are gradually broken down by collisions with other particles, or are blown away by solar radiation.   Fred L. Whipple, "The Nature of Comets," *Scientific American*

☐ *Strengthen the transitional signals that will guide your reader.* Set up clearer signposts for readers who might lose their way. Look at the way the signals in the following sample paragraph nudge the reader in the right direction:

then

now

emphatic reinforcement

     Some of us are old enough to recall when the stereotype of a "liberated woman" was a disheveled radical, notoriously braless, and usually hoarse from denouncing the twin evils of capitalism and patriarchy. *Today* the stereotype is more likely to be a tidy executive who carries an attaché case and is skilled in discussing market shares and leveraged buy-outs. *In fact,* thanks in no small part to the anger of the earlier, radical feminists, women have gained a real toehold in the corporate world: about 30 percent of managerial employees are women, as are 40 percent of the current MBA graduates. We have come a long way, as the expression goes, though clearly not in the same direction we set out.   Barbara Ehrenreich, "Strategies of Corporate Women," *New Republic*

     Remember: A series of short, two- or three-sentence paragraphs usually signals that you are skipping from one point to the next. (Sometimes a writer will use a one-sentence or two-sentence paragraph to make a key point stand out boldly from the rest.) A page or more without a paragraph break generally means that you are not laying your material out in the kind of step-by-step pattern that the reader can follow. Solid, well-developed paragraphs that average perhaps half a dozen sentences each show that you have brought your material under control and have followed up the key points you raise.

EXERCISE 7   *Rewriting Weak Paragraphs*

     What is needed to strengthen each of the following paragraphs? For each of these, do a rewrite that would strongly present and support a central point.

1.   Many parents think that once their children are at school anything they do is the responsibility of the school. Parents blame schools for not maintaining strict supervision on campus. However, although most schools have strong policies, these can also be broken. The staff cannot possibly watch all of the students all of the time. Parents should teach their children to have more respect for others.

2.   Let us look at the average worker in an average American factory. Henry, an assembly worker, punches in at eight in the morning. On the line, he does the same repetitive job all day. At five o'clock, he punches out and heads home.

3.   In many of my classes, teachers have asked me about my Irish heritage. Without my telling them that my father is Irish, they assume I am Irish from merely looking at my name. Many people admire the "fighting Irish" of the Notre Dame football team. On Irish holidays like St. Patrick's Day, many Americans share in the nostalgia for old customs and the old songs. Newspaper articles about the Irish often dwell fondly on their folklore and their love of song and story.

EXERCISE 8   *The Missing Links*

In the blank spaces in each of the following paragraphs, fill in the missing transitions that will steer the reader in the right direction.

1.   Often, creativity and practicality go hand in hand. _____, the creative person might use the creative, pattern-forming right side of the brain to design a stained-glass window. _____, the actual process of producing the window is painstakingly methodical, bringing into play the linear, systematic left side of the brain. The artist who creates a stained-glass window needs both imagination and highly developed technical skill. _____, the pacemaker—a device that artificially stimulates the heart when the heartbeat is too slow—was at first someone's creative concept, requiring an imaginative leap beyond the tried and true. _____, building a pacemaker is a practical process, requiring finely honed technical skill.

2.   The search for new sources of energy has often proved disappointing. _____, the extracting of oil from shale rock has proved less viable than its promoters had hoped. Companies looking for alternative sources of oil started to mine shale, heat it to 900 degrees F, and draw off the raw shale oil, to be refined and made into petroleum. One ton of rock can yield 35 gallons of oil. One project was designed to produce as much oil as a medium-size oil field in Oklahoma. _____, oil prices failed to rise as predicted, and development costs shot through the roof. _____, oil companies put their shale projects on hold.

EXERCISE 9   *Revision Practice*

Choose a weak paragraph from a paper you have recently written. Revise it with three major goals in mind:

- clearer statement and fuller explanation of the main point
- building up relevant examples and details
- helping the reader follow by strengthening the overall pattern or strengthening transitions

Part Five

SPECIAL ASSIGNMENTS

Writers often have to meet special expectations. They write to a set format; they satisfy special criteria; they follow a conventional style. For instance, **the research paper** assigned in many college courses requires you to meet exact specifications. A successful research paper emerges from a demanding ritual: It is based on a thorough study of the best current information and the best informed opinion on a subject. It leans heavily on a range of authoritative sources, quoting them at length, and it follows an exact format for full disclosure of those sources. Although not tied to a specific format, **writing about literature** similarly requires you to meet special expectations. A critical paper on a literary subject builds on but also goes beyond your first spontaneous response to a poem, story, or play. You write about what a work makes you think and feel, but you also ask *why*. You write about how a poem works, what patterns a story sets up, or what conflicts a play acts out and how they are resolved. You compare and contrast; you examine recurrent patterns and themes of imaginative literature viewed as a way of organizing human experience. Finally, **writing essay exams** tests your ability to write under pressure—to think on your feet, to assemble material quickly from memory and use it to advantage.

18

THE RESEARCH PAPER

From Search to Documentation

Research of any sort is an activity fundamental to education and, in fact, to all learning, whether it occurs inside or outside of school. Mary Trachsel

All forms of knowledge about human history are forms of engagement in it. Edward Said

TRIGGERING: STARTING YOUR SEARCH For many students, writing a research paper is like taking a crash course in how to become an authority on a subject. In some ways, you will do on a larger scale what you always do as a writer: You become involved in the subject; you size up your audience; you work up material; you pull it into shape. You write to make a point, to correct a misunderstanding, or to promote a cause. But the research paper will also take you two steps beyond ordinary writing projects. First, you will be synthesizing material from a wider range of sources; you will draw on the best available information or the best current thinking on your subject. Second, you will document your sources, identifying them fully, enabling your reader to trace them and verify the use you have made of them.

A Program for Research Your ideal subject for research is something that has intrigued or puzzled you in the past but that you have not had time to investigate in depth. By definition, research is an expedition into imperfectly known territory. At times, you will recognize landmarks described by earlier travelers, but you will often be revising older maps or filling in blank

459

spaces. Consider the following guidelines while choosing a promising topic and charting your course:

- □ *Work on a subject that will be worth the time and energy you invest.* If your topic is to catch fire, it should have a personal meaning for you or offer you some personal satisfaction as a writer. A topic may be right for you because it satisfies a latent curiosity: You might want to investigate space stations, solar energy, or nineteenth-century railroads. Or a topic may be right for you because it relates to a personal commitment, like Amnesty International or computers for the blind. Or a good topic may allow you to build on insider's information, enabling you to share your expertise about the juvenile court system or bilingual education.

- □ *Close in on a limited part of a general subject.* The threat to animal life on our planet is a vast general subject—a story that would take many installments to tell. To arrive at a workable topic, you may want to focus on changing attitudes toward predators like the wolf or the coyote or on the vanishing habitats for the big birds: the condor, the whooping crane, or the bald eagle. You may want to close in on a single endangered species: the return of the American buffalo or the prospects for saving the whales.

- □ *Make full use of your library.* Discover the full range of library resources and of more informal sources available to you. A good researcher needs the perseverance (and the optimism) of a prospector, always hunting down promising leads and managing not to be discouraged by those that don't work out.

- □ *Synthesize material from a wide range of sources.* Avoid subjects that would make you lean heavily on one main source, such as an entry in an encyclopedia or a survey article in a magazine. Your task is to assemble scattered facts, to weigh conflicting opinions, or to reconcile the testimony of different authorities. Your finished paper will have to show that you have examined the best current information or the most authoritative opinion and that you have funneled it into conclusions of your own.

- □ *Stay close to the evidence you present.* A research paper tests your ability to follow the evidence where it leads, your willingness to revise tentative conclusions. Your stance toward the audience should be: "This is the evidence. This is where I found it. You are welcome to check these sources and to verify these facts."

- □ *Document your sources.* Identify and describe the sources of all material you have used, borrowed, or adapted in your paper. Whenever you quote, make sure your reader knows who said what and where. Give credit for information, opinion, or ideas that you use as evidence. The running text of your paper will identify your sources briefly, usually including an exact page reference in parentheses. A final bibliography or alphabetical listing of "Works Cited" (which may include both print and nonprint sources) will give full publishing data, enabling the reader, for instance, to find the right article in a magazine, the right volume in a series, or the right edition of a book.

Note: By and large, you will want to stay away from highly technical subjects, which may require more knowledge of mathematics, physics, biochemistry, or the law than you can muster or than you can explain to the nonspecialist reader.

Avoiding Plagiarism

Careful documentation helps a writer avoid **plagiarism**. Writers who plagiarize lift material from their sources without acknowledgment. They reap where others have sown; they appropriate the fruits of someone else's research without giving credit where due. The penalties for plagiarism range from failing grades to ruined reputations and wrecked careers. To avoid charges of plagiarism, hold yourself accountable for whatever use you make of your sources. Whenever you draw on a source, anticipate questions like the following: Who said this? Who found this out? Who assembled this information? Who drew these conclusions? Granted, many facts and ideas are common knowledge. Major historical dates and events, key ideas of scientific or philosophical movements—these are, as it were, open to the public; they are easily found in reference books. However, identify your source whenever you use information recently discovered or collected, whenever you adopt someone's personal point of view.

Remember a few simple don'ts: Never copy all or part of a sentence without marking it as a quotation. Never cannibalize unidentified sources, including in your writing large badly digested lumps of material of uncertain origin. Never simply take over someone else's plan, procedure, or strategy without acknowledgment. As a practical precaution, make sure that a brief *source tag*—showing author, publication, and page number—always accompanies borrowed material in your notes and in successive drafts.

Subjects for Research

The following are some general areas for research. Carve out a topic from a general area like the following:

1. *Saving the animals*: the history of a major endangered species; the story of the disappearance of the buffalo or other nearly vanished animal; current conservationist efforts to protect endangered species of birds or other animals; the struggle to protect fur-bearing animals; in defense of the wolf or the coyote.

2. *The limits of technology*: Is manned space travel necessary? Are animal experiments necessary for medical research? Do heart transplants have a future? Was the green revolution a success?

3. *Running out of energy*: the future of solar energy; the story of coal; wind power through the ages; fission and fusion; damming the last wild rivers.

4. *The graying of America*: changing attitudes toward age and aging; the passing of the youth culture; traditional stereotypes about old age; the changing self-image of senior citizens.

5. *The price of progress*: the story of the supersonic passenger plane; natural versus synthetic foods; more about additives; the automobile and the environment; acid rain; toxic waste.

6. *Fighting words in American history*: the abolitionist movement; the American suffragette; the tradition of populism; the story of segregation; the roots of unionism; robber barons or captains of industry.

7. *Future shock*: talking computers; the future of space stations; life on other planets; robots.

8. *The story of censorship*: controversial authors and the schools (Kurt Vonnegut, J. D. Salinger, Joyce Carol Oates); creationism and evolution; the definition of obscenity; unwelcome books (*1984, Grapes of Wrath, Brave New World*).

9. *Bilingual Americans*: the pros and cons of bilingual education; Hispanic versus Anglo culture; the politics of a bilingual community; the new immigrants; English as the official language.

10. *Ethnic identity and the writer*: the search for roots (Alexander Haley, Maxine Hong Kingston); the search for black identity (Richard Wright, Ralph Ellison, Lorraine Hansberry, Alice Walker, Gwendolyn Brooks, Toni Morrison, Maya Angelou); the immigrant's America (Willa Cather, Upton Sinclair, William Saroyan); discovering Latin American literature (Jorge Luis Borges, Pablo Neruda, Octavio Paz, Gabriel García Márquez).

11. *The American Indian*: the story of a forgotten tribe; the Cherokee nation; the Pueblos of the Southwest; the last wars; assimilating the Native Americans.

12. *Nostalgia time*: the vanishing passenger train; a short history of the stage coach; the passing of the American streetcar; ocean liners and their day of glory.

Questions for Discussion Which of these topics sound interesting or intriguing and why? On which would you have a headstart because of relevant background or previous study? Which would you rule out and why?

Charting Your Course As you start your project, your first steps will be tentative. It is normal to be drawn first toward one subject, then another; to head first in one direction, then another. As you read, think, and explore, try to formulate preliminary plans under three familiar headings:

☐ TRIGGERING—*Why* are you interested in your topic? What previous experience or exposure will help you with your project? What do you hope to learn? What do you hope to prove? Who would make a good audience?

☐ GATHERING—*What* sources are likely to prove helpful? Who has written about this topic, and from what perspective? Who are the experts in this field? What axes do they have to grind? Will there be opportunities for firsthand investigation—field trips, interviews?

☐ SHAPING—*How* are you going to proceed? What is your tentative plan for laying out your subject? What might be a workable strategy for covering major parts of your topic?

Your instructor may ask you to prepare a **planning report** that can serve as a preview for your paper. Study the following example. How is the project shaping up? Does it have a purpose? What is the general strategy behind the outline?

PREWRITING: PLANNING REPORT

"Unnecessary Force": Police Brutality

why?   My main reason for choosing police brutality as a subject for research is a personal experience I had at age fifteen. While Christmas shopping with a friend, I witnessed a brutal chase by undercover police officers who were in pursuit of a teenage boy accused of shoplifting. The boy had fled from the store to the parking lot, where two huge men caught up with him. Watching them grab the suspect and throw him to the ground as blood dripped with every punch, I felt my stomach in my throat. That scene has always remained embedded in my mind, and I have often wondered how necessary it was for the police to manhandle the boy the way they did.

what?   Merely by entering the words *police brutality* into the computerized periodical index in the library, I have found numerous articles on the subject. In the last few years, publications like *Time*, *Newsweek*, and *The New York Times* show titles like "New York's 'Bad Apples,'" "13 Police Suspensions," "Police Suspend 2 After Complaint," or "Police Attacks Not Uncommon." Since the topic is of urgent concern in minority neighborhoods, it is not surprising to find many relevant articles in publications aimed at minority audiences: "The Blacks and the Blues: A Special Report on Police Brutality" (*Essence*) or "Excessive Force: A National Look at Police Brutality" (*Nuestro*). I am beginning to look for relevant material in back issues of the local newspaper, and I have already informally interviewed somebody who was an actual victim of police brutality. I plan to schedule interviews with police officers to hear the other side.

how?   I feel that trying to do justice to both sides is a necessity to make this paper work. I plan to establish first the timeliness and urgency of the topic by looking at a range of news reports and current articles. I will then look in detail at the concerns and problems of the person who is charged with a crime and feels he or she was mistreated during or after an arrest. An important facet is how such incidents are perceived by the community, especially in minority neighborhoods. I then will explore the motives or needs of the police officers involved, looking for explanations or justifications. Many young people feel the way I do about police brutality, and I am hoping to uncover some information in defense of the police and to make people see another side to this issue.

Keeping a Research Log

Professional writers researching an article or a book often accumulate shoe boxes full of clippings, folders bulging with tattered notes, or disks crammed with stored information—with a filing system that may range from computerized precision to near chaos. Writing a research paper is your chance to develop your own style of charting your investigation, scouting possible sources, storing promising material, and coding it for future use. Consider starting a **research log** or search diary. Use it to write notes to yourself about early leads and tentative plans. Enter lists of promising sources with brief reminders of why they sound useful. Record tentative conclusions and trial outlines as your project gets underway. You will soon be taking more formal notes (on note cards or as computer entries), quoting and summarizing material for future use. Use your research log as an informal record of your findings, plans and thoughts.

Here are some sample entries from a research log for a paper about changing attitudes toward aging:

☐ *Promising Leads*—sources the writer has seen mentioned; individuals and organizations that should be investigated; key terms that keep coming up.

> Gray Panthers (over 65 years old)
> geriatrics - treating the diseases of old age
> periodicals : *Gerontologist, 50 plus*
> National Institute on Aging
> AARP- American Assoc. of Retired Persons
> National Retired Teachers Assoc.
> National Council of Senior Citizens
>
> Check : Eliz. Kuebler-Ross, Margaret Mead,
> Maggie Kuhn, Simone de Beauvoir - book on aging ?

☐ *Scouting Sources*—lists of possible sources the writer has copied from reference guides such as *Sociological Abstracts* or *Social Sciences Index*; brief notes on especially promising materials:

> _Sociological Abstracts_ (1982)
> ✓ Ageds' status change M3697
> ✓ Aged, popular culture centers M2680
> ~~Aged, prestige decline M3699~~
> ✓ Aging news, no longer negative image M5180
> ~~Sociological perspective M6758~~
> ✓ Attitudes toward age S15182
> ✓ Alex Comfort M5513
>
> _Social Sciences Citation Index_ (1983)
> micro - Mehlinger, L.J., "Intergenerational
>   Programs – The Changing Faces of Aging,
> " _Gerontologist_ 23: 227
>
> Check: S. Seixas, "Fighting to Stay on the Job,"
> _Money_ 13 (Feb. 84): 113-14 (ousted 61-yr. old
> executive Ron Anderson)

☐ *Record of Observations*—the writer's notes on firsthand investigation, including interviews, conversations, viewing of news programs, and the like:

> CHANNEL 7 NEWS
> WHAT: Senior Swingers' softball – annual event for men and
>   women 60-80 yrs. old
> WHO: "Geritol Giants" and "Amazing A's"
> WHERE: St. Mary's in San Francisco
> WHY: "to have fun ... and win"
> HIGHLIGHTS: 1) changed rules to suit themselves (no
>   strikeouts, no walks, 7 pitches, all may bat);
>   2) cheerleaders; 3) newscaster's thought: "I
>   thought what you were supposed to do
>   when you got to be this age was to lie in a
>   hammock"

◻ *Trial outlines and tentative conclusions*—the writer's preliminary attempts to sort out and add up the results of her investigation:

> my thoughts:
> 1) people who years ago called for changing attitudes toward aging have helped to bring about much of what they called for: greater dignity, more self-assertion, and more independence on the part of older people
> 2) the baby boom generation is getting older – changing from glorification of youth to more sympathy with the feelings of older people

◻ *Agenda for Research*—the writer's notes on issues to be explored, facts to be checked, data to be updated:

> AARP had 9 million members – how many today?
> "fountain-of-youth" drugs – status of current research?
> new breed of older people in current TV drama?
> check current educational programs offered the elderly
> more recent study on retirement preferences?

Involving Your Audience

Much research is published by specialists for other specialists. Your own research paper will aim not at the specialist but at educated readers willing to learn more about your subject. Give them a reason to read—arouse their curiosity, involve them in your subject, activate their generous concern or indignation. Keep in mind that even a superficially dull subject can become fascinating when you move beyond the surface. The ideal subject will generate the excitement that will keep you moving ahead and that will prove contagious for your readers.

EXERCISE 1   *Brainstorming a Research Topic*

Choose a research topic in which you have a tentative interest: saving the whales, animal experiments, the birth dearth, or the like. Brainstorm the topic: Writing rapidly, put down any memories, images, associations, and details that the topic triggers in your mind. Bring in anything from your personal experience, observation, reading, or viewing that might be at all related to the topic. Leave any sifting, sorting, or censoring for later. Try to draw on any previous exposure to or involvement with the topic.

THE WRITING WORKSHOP

A Planning Report

Write a planning report for a paper on a research topic that you have tentatively selected. Include the why, what, and how. What previous interest or exposure can you build on? What do you hope to accomplish? What are possible sources or promising leads? What might be your overall plan or strategy? Are you aiming at a special audience or the general reader? Present your report for discussion by the class or a small group. Take notes on the queries, comments, or suggestions offered by the group. Consider them in refining or giving final shape to your plans.

EXERCISE 2   *A Reading Report*

On which of the tentative research topics that you are considering have you done some previous reading? Take stock of what you remember: authors, their agenda, key points, major arguments, material covered, nature of their sources or evidence, and the like. (Choose *one* tentative topic.)

GATHERING: GOING TO THE SOURCES
To be a successful researcher, you need to be both an idea person and a detail person. As an idea person, you chart the course of your investigation. You seize on connections between ideas; you quarry the right materials and build them into the grand design of your paper. As a detail person, you do the groundwork. You follow up leads, you accurately transcribe and identify quotations, you carefully record publishing data, and you place the commas and colons correctly in listing your sources. In a successful project, you attend to detail without losing sight of the larger purposes of your investigation.

Finding and Evaluating Sources
To conduct a successful search, you have to know how to tap the resources of your college library. Although your search strategy

will vary from subject to subject, you will normally explore three major kinds of materials:

- *reference works* (encyclopedias, specialized dictionaries, guides) that provide an overview or summary of your subject
- *magazine or newspaper articles* that deal with limited areas of your subject or with current developments
- *books* (or sections of books) that deal with your subject in some depth

Remember that your library is not the *only* source of information or inspiration: Your phone book has a special section listing government agencies where you might write for advice or enlightenment. Your college as well as local businesses and organizations will employ experts who might consent to be interviewed. On subjects touching on local history, relatives or neighbors might serve as resource persons for your project.

In a successful search, one find leads to another. For instance, when writing about the competitive edge enjoyed by Japanese industry, you may turn first to classic treatments of the subject—books often mentioned or quoted, such as William Ouchi's *Theory Z* or Ezra Vogel's *Japan as Number One*. Checking one familiar area of competition, you may look in a periodical index under "Automobiles—Export/Import" and find articles with titles like "We're a Colony Again, This Time of Japan." (This article turns out to be an interview with Lee Iacocca, published in *U.S. News & World Report*.) Looking up the broader topic "Balance of Trade," you may find articles like "Japan is Fanning Protectionist Fires on the Hill" (published in *Business Week*). One of these articles provides a helpful bibliography, listing articles with titles like "Meeting the Japanese Economic Challenge" (*Business Horizons*), "Why the Japanese Seem to Be Eight Feet Tall" (*Fortune*), and "Learning from the Japanese" (*Management Review*). In the meantime, you have found some insiders to interview— a worker in an American plant under Japanese management, a student who spent a year in Japan.

At the beginning, you may welcome almost anything in print on your subject, but soon you will turn selective. Your aim is to draw useful information and expert opinion from reliable sources. This means that you will have to distrust some of the more perishable kinds of publication: campaign biographies, chamber-of-commerce brochures, nonbooks improvised to exploit a current trend, sensational exposés written by instant experts. More generally, you will have to ask yourself: "Who is talking? How does this author know? What side is the writer on, or what is the hidden agenda?" When evaluating possible sources, keep in mind test questions like the following:

- *Is the writer an authority on the subject?* Experts are not infallible, but it's reassuring to know that an author has written and lectured widely on the subject and is frequently quoted or consulted. It's comforting to find that an author writing about agribusiness has been in the fields to talk with workers and supervisors, has studied government and corporate reports, and has read recent studies of relevant trends.

☐ *Is the work a thorough study of the subject?* Does it show a grasp of the historical background; does it seriously explore causes and effects? Does it take the opinions of others seriously, carefully weighing the pro and con on debated issues? Is it short on opinion and long on evidence?

☐ *Does the author draw on primary sources?* Reliable authorities do not simply accept secondhand accounts; they settle important questions by turning to **primary sources**—legal documents, diaries, letters, eyewitness reports, transcripts of speeches and interviews, reports on experiments, statistical surveys. They take us close to unedited firsthand facts.

☐ *Is the author biased?* The bailout of a large automobile manufacturer through government loans will be viewed one way in the autobiography of the company's chief executive; the story will be told differently by an aggressive critic of corporate politics. Whenever possible, try to look at both sides; try to find accounts by less directly interested parties to balance one-sided views.

☐ *Is the work up to date?* Has it profited from recent research or newly discovered facts? If it was first published ten or twenty years ago, is there a revised, more recent edition? Keep in mind that a writer may have been left behind by new findings and new thinking in a burgeoning field.

As you sift the input for your paper, think of the library as a resource center and service center. Learn how to retrieve material recorded in miniaturized form on **microfilm** or **microfiche**. Learn how to draw on **data banks** and other computerized sources of information. Use facilities for photocopying articles or pages from a book. When stymied, ask a librarian about reference works, indexes, library services, or research strategies.

Using Reference Works

Reference books were the memory banks of the print age. (Many are now being converted to the technology of the chip age.) Commonly available reference works range from weighty multivolume sets to handy manuals and guides. Often a well-established guide becomes the bible of music lovers, car mechanics, or electronics engineers. You will find specialized reference works in a guide like Eugene P. Sheehy's *Guide to Reference Books*, published by the American Library Association. Here is a brief sampling of reference works that are often consulted:

ENCYCLOPEDIAS An encyclopedia is sometimes a good place to start—but not to finish—an investigation.

□ The *Encyclopaedia Britannica* (an American publication) is the most authoritative of the general encyclopedias. It is brought up to date each year by the *Britannica Book of the Year*. A complete revision, called *The New Encyclopaedia Britannica*, was published in 1974 and has been updated since. It has two major sections: a ten-volume quick-reference index (the *Micropaedia*) and a nineteen-volume guide to more detailed information on many subjects (the *Macropaedia*).

□ The *Encyclopedia Americana* is sometimes recommended for science and biography. General subjects are broken up into short articles, arranged alphabetically. The annual supplement is the *Americana Annual*.

□ The one-volume *Columbia Encyclopedia* serves well for a quick check of people and places.

BIOGRAPHY In addition to biographical entries in encyclopedias, libraries usually have ample materials for a paper reassessing the role or reputation of a famous person.

□ *Who's Who in America*, a biographical dictionary of outstanding living men and women, provides capsule biographies of important contemporaries. (The original *Who's Who* is a British publication. Specialized offshoots of the same publication include *Who's Who of American Women*.)

□ The *Dictionary of American Biography (DAB)* gives a more detailed account of the lives of significant persons. (The British counterpart is the *Dictionary of National Biography*.)

□ The *Biography Index* is a guide to biographical material in books and magazines. It may lead you, for example, to material on the married life of George Washington or the evangelism of Billy Graham.

□ *Contemporary Authors* (a frequently updated multivolume work) gives information on authors of current books and includes biographical facts, excerpts from reviews, and comments by the authors.

LITERATURE A library project may deal with an author's schooling or early reading, recurrent themes in the books of a well-known novelist, or the contemporary reputation of a nineteenth-century poet.

□ The fifteen-volume *Cambridge History of English Literature* and the *Cambridge Bibliography of English Literature* take stock of English authors and literary movements.

□ The Spiller-Thorp-Johnson-Canby *Literary History of the United States*, with its supplementary bibliographies, lists as its contributors an impressive roster of American literary scholars.

□ *Harper's Dictionary of Classical Literature and Antiquities* is a comprehensive scholarly guide to Greek and Roman history and civilization. (Books like Michael Grant's *Myths of the Greeks and Romans* and Edith

Hamilton's *Mythology*, available as paperbacks, introduce the reader to famous names and stories.)

OTHER FIELDS OF INTEREST Every major field of interest has its own specialized reference guides: specialized encyclopedias, dictionaries of names or technical terms, or yearbooks reporting on current developments. For instance, a student majoring in business administration will come to know books like the *Dictionary of Economics, The Encyclopedia of Management, The Encyclopedia of Banking and Finance*, and the *Handbook of Modern Marketing*. Here is a sampling of specialized reference works frequently consulted:

- *American Universities and Colleges* and *American Junior Colleges* provide basic facts about educational institutions.
- The *McGraw-Hill Encyclopedia of Science and Technology* is kept up to date by the *McGraw-Hill Yearbook of Science and Technology*.
- The *Encyclopedia of Computer Science and Technology* is a multivolume guide to a rapidly growing field. (Harry Thomas' *Electronic Vest Pocket Reference Book* is a classic pocket guide to electronics.)
- The *Dictionary of American History* by J. T. Adams is a six-volume guide.
- Langer's *Encyclopedia of World History* is a long-established reference guide in one volume.
- The *International Encyclopedia of the Social Sciences* is a multivolume reference work.
- *Grove's Dictionary of Music and Musicians*, a multivolume reference guide for music lovers, covers biography, history, and technical terms.
- The *McGraw-Hill Encyclopedia of World Art* has fifteen volumes.
- The Funk and Wagnalls *Standard Dictionary of Folklore, Mythology and Legend* is one of several well-known guides to basic themes in folk culture and folk tradition.
- *Vital Speeches of the Day* can help you find recent speeches by government officials or business executives on topics like Third World debt, threats to free trade, or the impact of new technologies on employment.

BIBLIOGRAPHIES For many subjects of general interest, you will be able to find a printed **bibliography**—an inventory of important books and other sources of information. Writing about Emily Dickinson, John Steinbeck, or William Faulkner, you should be able to find a book-length bibliography of publications by and about the author. Shorter bibliographical listings often appear at the end of an entry in an encyclopedia or a chapter in a textbook.

Especially helpful are **annotated bibliographies** that provide a capsule description of each source. The following might be a sample entry:

> *Edsels, Luckies, & Frigidaires* by Robert Atwan, Donald McQuade, and John W. Wright (New York: Dell, 1972) is a

large-format paperback which resembles nothing so much as a 100-year scrapbook of American advertising. Over 250 full-page ads are organized under three main headings, "Advertising and Social Roles," "Advertising and Material Civilization," and "Advertising and the Strategies of Persuasion." Chronological arrangement of the ads reflects changes in the "good life" over the last century.

BOOK REVIEWS The *Book Review Digest* excerpts book reviews written shortly after publication of a book. Book review sections are a regular feature of many professional publications. The following is an example of a short book review from the *Library Journal*:

> **De Santis, Marie. Neptune's Apprentice: adventures of a commercial fisherwoman. Presidio Pr. Jun. 1984. c.256p. illus. by Patricia Walker. ISBN 0-89141-200-X. $15.95.**
>
> SOC SCI. PER NAR
>
> There are innumerable books about the lure of the sea but very are few by women. De Santis was a doctoral student in the late 1960s when she heard the siren call and, after brief apprenticeships on California commercial fishing boats, she determined to be her own captain. To describe the way the sea "shaped the spirit of its people" she tells of the people in the fleet for the eight years she fished: toil, fear, acceptance by the fishing fraternity, greed, fish and game bumbling—and always the search for the elusive fish. She left just before much of the fishing collapsed, but the sea remained with her. This is a fine testament to an individual's maturing and to the environment. Recommended, not just for libraries near the sea.—*Roland Person: Southern Illinois Univ. Lib., Carbondale*

Finding Articles in Periodicals

Periodicals, ranging from daily newspapers to monthly or quarterly magazines, supply the large need of a society addicted to a steady flow of commentary and information. Writing about the vanishing whooping crane, you might find useful articles in periodicals such as *National Geographic, National Wildlife, Audubon, Outdoor Life,* and *Smithsonian.* Writing about robots in automobile factories, you might find useful articles in periodicals such as *Car and Driver, Technology Review, Business Week, Omni,* and *Science Digest.*

Most libraries have a compact catalog for all periodicals to which the library subscribes. This catalog, separate from the general catalog of the library, will show the location of recent issues and back issues, as well as availability on microfilm or microfiche.

COMPUTERIZED INDEXES Many libraries now have a central computerized index that will call up for you a battery of current magazine articles on a given subject. Trying to find material on changing patterns of modern marriage, you might punch in the key word MARRIAGE. The following might be a partial printout of what would appear on the screen:

```
                                    InfoTrac Database
                                    1/1/90 at 12:28
MARRIAGE
 -ADDRESSES, ESSAYS, LECTURES

        Changing relationships between men and
    women; scope of the problem. (transcript) Vital
    Speeches—Oct 1 '84 p757(8)

MARRIAGE
 -ANALYSIS

        What is this state called marriage? by
    Elaine Brown Whitley il Essence Magazine—Feb
    '85 p54(5)
    #32D2299

MARRIAGE
 -CASE STUDIES

        First marriage after 40, by Lynn Normont il
    Ebony—Jan '83 p28(7)
    #15A2292

MARRIAGE
 -ECONOMIC ASPECTS

        The money side of marriage. il Changing
    Times—June '85 p32(6)
    #27K5219

        Equal pay for different work saved our
    marriage. (physician pays wife for domestic
    duties) by Daniel L. Brick, Medical Economics—
    Feb 4 '85 p95(3)

MARRIAGE
 -FORECASTS

        Changes in marriage and the family: looking
    back from the twenty-first century. il
    Futurist—April '85 p84(3)
    #23B2988
```

Database Printout

PRINTED PERIODICAL INDEXES To find magazine articles on your subject, you will often search the printed periodical indexes in your library. Published in monthly or semimonthly installments, these are later combined in huge volumes, each listing articles for a period of one or more years.

□ The *Readers' Guide to Periodical Literature* indexes magazines written for the general reader. These range from megacirculation newsmagazines like *Time, Newsweek,* and *U.S. News & World Report* to periodicals with more specialized audiences—*Working Woman, Science Digest, Technology Review,* or *The American Scholar.* Articles are listed twice—once under the author's name and once under a subject heading. At times, you will look up a much-quoted, much-interviewed authority—Isaac Asimov on robots, Betty Harragan on corporate gamesmanship for women. More often, you will scout for material under subject headings like "Engineering," split into categories like "Management," "Social Aspects," and "Study and Teaching" and followed by "Engineering and the Humanities," "Engineering Research," and "Engineering Students." Some subject headings in the *Readers' Guide* are the names of people—scientists, artists, politicians, celebrities—written up in an article.

Compare two entries for the same article as listed in the *Readers' Guide.* The first of these is the *author entry,* the second the *subject entry*:

AUTHOR ENTRY:	**HARRIS, Michael** Junk in outer space. il Progressive 42:16-19 N '78
SUBJECT ENTRY:	**SPACE pollution** Junk in outer space. M. Harris. il Progressive 42:16-19 N '78

The author entry begins with the full name of the author; the subject entry begins with the general subject: space pollution. The title of the article is "Junk in Outer Space." (The abbreviation *il* shows that the article is illustrated.) The name of the magazine comes next: *Progressive.* The *volume number* for the magazine is 42. *Page numbers* follow after the colon: 16 through 19. (Sometimes the symbol + appears after the last page number; it shows that the article spills over to a later section of the magazine.) The *date of publication* was November 1978.

Whether you use the *Readers' Guide* or a more specialized index, don't miss the introductory page: Study the list of abbreviations and the list of the periodicals indexed. Look at sample entries to study the listing of individual articles and the system of cross-references.

Other guides to periodicals intended for a general audience:

□ *Essay and General Literature Index* may help you when you are not satisfied with what you find in the *Readers' Guide.*
□ *Poole's Index to Periodical Literature,* covering the years from 1802–1907, is a guide to British and American magazines of the past. You might

consult it, for instance, when looking for contemporary reactions to Wagner's operas or Ibsen's plays.

☐ *Popular Periodicals Index*, published since 1973, will prove helpful to students of popular culture.

The following are guides to periodical literature in specialized subject areas:

☐ *Applied Science and Technology Index* (see the *Industrial Arts Index* for years before 1958)
☐ *Art Index*
☐ *Biological and Agricultural Index* (called *Agricultural Index* before 1964)
☐ *Business Periodicals Index*
☐ *Education Index*
☐ *Engineering Index*
☐ *General Science Index*
☐ *Humanities Index* (now a separate publication, combined with the *Social Sciences Index* during the years 1965–1973)
☐ *Social Sciences Index* (formerly *International Index*; lists articles in sociological and psychological journals)

Note: A number of special reference guides are useful for papers on a political subject or on current events:

☐ *Facts on File* is a weekly digest of world news, with an annual index. It gives a summary of news reports and comments, with excerpts from important documents and speeches.
☐ The *New York Times Index* (published since 1913) is a guide to news stories published in the *New York Times*. Look up an event or a controversy in this index to find the approximate dates for coverage in other newspapers and magazines.
☐ The annual index to the *Monthly Catalog of the United States Government Publications* lists reports and documents published by all branches of the federal government.

ABSTRACTS You can often identify useful articles by looking at **abstracts**—short summaries of articles in a field, usually collected and published several times a year. The following is an example from Volume 30 of *Sociological Abstracts*:

> 82M2679
> Fly, Jerry W., Reinhart, George R. & Hamby, Russell (Georgia Coll, Milledgeville 31061), **Leisure Activity and Adjustment in Retirement**, *Sociological Spectrum*, 1981, 1, 2, Apr-June, 135–144.
> ¶ A sample of retired persons (N = 134) in a southern metropolitan area responded to a questionnaire designed to investigate the interrelationship between level of leisure activity & adjustment in retirement. Adjustment was measured by two indices, life satisfaction & alienation. Results show that persons who have more leisure activities are more satis-

fied with their lives & are less alienated than those who have few leisure activities. 2 Tables. HA © 1982 Sociological Abstracts Inc., reprinted by special permission.

Finding Books Through the Library Catalog

A key event on your research itinerary is to go book hunting in the central catalog of your college library. The traditional catalog has been a card catalog with rows of drawers holding printed index cards in alphabetical order. Today, users increasingly view computerized catalog information on screens. However, the kind and arrangement of the information will be similar under the different systems.

In the typical library catalog, the same book is listed several times: by *author* (under the author's last name), by *title* (under the first word of the title, not counting *The*, *A*, or *An*), and by *subject*. At times, you will be tracking down a promising author or book, following up leads you already have. But often you will have to ferret out possibly useful books under the right subject headings.

AUTHOR CARDS   Author cards provide complete publishing information for each separate book by an author; cards for books by the same author are arranged in alphabetical order. (Such a set of several cards may be followed by catalog cards for books *about* the author.)

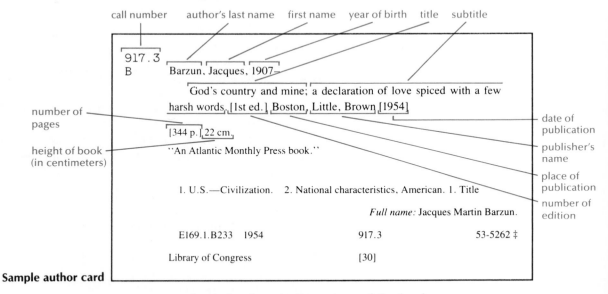

Sample author card

Look for clues to the nature of the book:

□ *The number or description of the edition.* If the catalog lists both the original edition and another marked "2nd ed." or "Rev. ed.," generally choose the one that is more up to date.

☐ *The name and location of the publisher*. For instance, a book published by a university press is likely to be a scholarly or specialized study. The *date of publication* is especially important for books on scientific, technological, or medical subjects, where information dates rapidly.

☐ *The number of pages* (with the number of introductory pages given as a lowercase Roman numeral). It shows whether the book is a short pamphlet or a full-scale treatment of the subject. If the book contains *illustrations* or a *bibliography*, the card will carry a notation to that effect.

Often, a card lists the several major *subject headings* under which the book can be found. For instance, a card for a sociological study of a Midwestern town may carry the following notation concerning various headings under which the study is listed:

1. U.S.—Social conditions.   2. Cities and Towns—U.S.
3. Cost and standard of living—U.S.   4. U.S.—Religion.
5. Social surveys.   6. Community life.

TITLE CARDS Title cards carry the same information as author cards. However, the title is repeated at the top for alphabetical listing. The following title card uses the style you are likely to see on a computer-generated card:

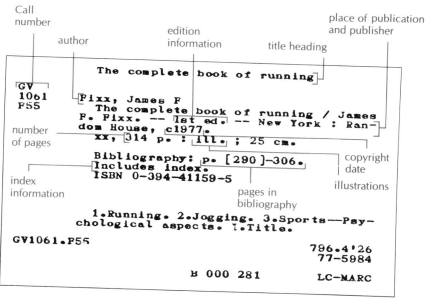

Sample title card

SUBJECT CARDS Subject cards will often be your best hope for finding usable books. Under what headings is material for your topic likely to surface? For instance, books on the American Civil War might appear under *U.S.—*

History—Civil War, under *U.S.—History—Military*, under *Slavery in the United States*, or under *Abolitionists*. Try to think of other key terms that might appear in the catalog: *Confederacy* or *Emancipation*. Pay special attention to the **cross-reference cards** that often appear at the beginning of a set of related subject cards:

FISHES, see also

    Aquariums

    Tropical fishes

       (also names of fishes, e.g., Salmon)

Here is an example of a typed subject card from the card catalog of a special division of a college library:

978   MORMONS AND MORMONISM - HISTORY
S

      Stegner, Wallace Earle, 1909-

      The gathering of Zion; the story of the Mormons, by Wallace Stegner. 1st ed. New York, McGraw-Hill, 1964

      331 p. illus. maps 23 cm (American Trails series)

      Bibliography: pp. 315-319

Sample subject card

Note: Librarians recommend that you consult the *Library of Congress Subject Headings* as a guide to finding material by subject in the card catalog.

CALL NUMBERS Once you decide that you should consult a book, copy its call number. The **call number** directs you, or the librarian, to the shelf where the book is located. Your library may use either the Library of Congress system or the Dewey decimal system.

    □ The **Library of Congress system** divides books into categories identified by letters of the alphabet. It then uses additional letters and numerals to subdivide each main category. For instance, the call number of a book on religion starts with a capital *B*. The call number of a book on education starts with a capital *L*.

□ The **Dewey decimal system** uses numerals to identify the main categories. For instance, 400–499 covers books on language; 800–899 covers books on literature. The 800 range is then further subdivided into American literature (810–819), English literature (820–829), and so on. Additional numerals and letters close in on individual authors and individual works by the same author.

Preparing a Working Bibliography

From the beginning, record complete data for all promising sources. Prepare **bibliography cards** or bibliography entries for each book, pamphlet, or article in a magazine. Some of the information is mainly for your own use in locating the book or article: the complete call number or a location in the library. But most of the information will be essential when you identify your sources in your finished paper. A bibliography card for a book may look like this:

```
HV
947
M58        Mitford, Jessica. Kind and Usual
1973       Punishment: The Prison Business.
           New York: Random, 1973.
```

Bibliography card—book

For accurate identification of a book, you will need to record the author's name, the title of the book, and complete publishing data. Start with the *full name of the author*—last name first to facilitate alphabetizing. Second, give the *full title* of the book, including any subtitle (separate it from the main title by a colon). Underline or italicize title and subtitle of a book, pamphlet, or other work that appeared as a separate publication.

(Underlining in a handwritten or typed manuscript converts to italics in print.)

The publishing data, or *facts of publication*, for a book may include the following:

- *editor's or translator's name* if the book has been put together or translated by someone other than the author(s): "Shakespeare, William. *The Complete Works*, ed. G. B. Harrison" or "Chekhov, Anton. *The Cherry Orchard*, trans. Tyrone Guthrie and Leonid Kipnis."
- *number or description of the edition* if the book has been revised or brought up to date: "3rd ed." or "Rev. ed."
- *number of volumes* if a work consists of several and all relate to your investigation: "2 vols."
- *place of publication* (usually the location of the main office of the publishing house, or of the first office listed if several are given).
- *name of the publisher*, leaving out such tags as "Inc." or "and Company": "Random"; "McGraw-Hill."
- *date of publication* (if no date is listed on the title page, use the latest copyright date listed on the reverse side of the title page).
- *number of the volume used* (if only one volume of a larger work seems relevant to your investigation): "Vol. 3."

For accurate identification of an article, you will need to record both the *title of the article* (in quotation marks) and the *title of the periodical* (underlined or italicized). The quotation marks show that an article, story, or poem was *part* of a larger publication. An annotated card, including brief reminders about the article, may look like this:

> Periodical Room   Schorer, Mark. "D. H. Lawrence: Then, During, Now," *Atlantic* March 1974: 84-88.
>
> The author, one of Lawrence's biographers, traces Lawrence's reputation as a writer from its low point at the time of his death to its present "position of primacy among great twentieth-century prose writers in English."

Annotated card—article

THE WRITING WORKSHOP

Knowing Your Library

Team up with several classmates to prepare a report on the resources of your library. You might farm out areas like the following to different members of the team:

1. What is the nature of the *central catalog*—card catalog or computerized system? How does it work? What system of classification does it use—Dewey decimal or Library of Congress? Spot check library holdings on a few selected topics, such as fly casting, World War I, body language, the history of English, or bilingual education.

2. How does the library guide you to its periodical holdings? Is there a central *periodical index*? What is the policy for access to current magazines? When are bound volumes available? (And how long does it take for magazines to get back from the bindery?) Spot check the library's subscription list for periodicals in selected areas, such as architecture, computer science, pharmacology, art, or poetry. Try out microfilm or microfiche services.

3. Are there *special collections* or special branches of the library? Are there special collections for rare books, ethnic studies materials, authors' memorabilia, or the like? How accessible are these materials to students? What are the materials like? Is there a special department for government publications?

4. What kind of *media services* does your library provide? Where and how do users obtain records, videotapes, art prints, films, and maps? Spot check the library's holdings in such selected areas as Shakespeare plays, Bach cantatas, and classic films.

5. What access does the library provide to *databases* such as those available from the DIALOG Information Retrieval Service? What are the procedures and the cost? If you can, obtain an example of a computer-generated bibliography on a subject like women in sports, the artificial heart, or English as the official language.

6. What are the special *strengths* or weaknesses of your college library? Interview librarians or instructors who are especially concerned about library resources in their fields.

Normally, your entry for a journal or newspaper article will not include the publisher's name or the place of publication, though the latter is sometimes needed to identify a small-town newspaper: *Daily Herald* [Ely, NV]. Record the *date* of the issue and complete *page numbers*: *Surfer's Companion* Sept. 1987: 13–18. *The Honolulu Enquirer* 10 Jan. 1988, 24–26. To point your readers to the right pages in back issues of a journal or newspaper, you may need additional data like the following:

▫ In many professional or technical journals, page numbers are consecutive through the issues of the same *volume*—usually all the issues published in one year. Record the number of the volume (in Arabic numerals), the year (in parentheses), and the page numbers of the article: *Modern Ornithology* 7 (1987): 234–38. When page numbers of different issues are *not* consecutive for the same volume, you may have to include the number of the issue: *Birdwatcher's Quarterly* 17.3 (1988): 17–20 (for volume 17, no. 3).

▫ The full-service modern newspaper often publishes more than one daily edition, with several sections whose pages are not numbered consecutively throughout the issue. Include the specifics needed to guide your reader: *Bogtown Gazette* 25 Oct. 1988, late ed.: C18. (Include *p.* or *pp.* for page or pages only if omitting them might cause confusion.)

Remember: Your record keeping at this point serves a double purpose. You register the results of your search for your own use, tagging your finds and setting up a file. But at the same time, you are storing information that you will need to retrieve later when you document your sources in your finished paper.

EXERCISE 3   *Studying Reference Tools*

Study *one* of the following often-mentioned reference tools. Prepare a brief report on its scope, usefulness, and format. Try to provide useful advice to prospective users; include some interesting sidelights.

1. *Books in Print*
2. *National Union Catalog (NUC)*
3. *Library of Congress Subject Headings*
4. *Sociological Abstracts*
5. *Contemporary Authors*
6. *Readers' Guide to Periodical Literature*
7. *Who's Who of American Women*
8. *Wall Street Journal Index*
9. *Historical Abstracts*

10. *Sheehy's Guide to Reference Books*
11. *Dictionary of Scientific Biography*
12. *Bartlett's Familiar Quotations*
13. *Comprehensive Dictionary of Psychological and Psychoanalytic Terms*
14. *McGraw-Hill Dictionary of Art*
15. *Concise Encyclopedia of Living Faiths*

EXERCISE 4   *Using the Readers' Guide*

Interpret and discuss the following sample entries from the *Readers' Guide.*

Ocean pollution *See* Marine pollution; Oil pollution
Ocean travel
    See also
   Cruising
   Voyages
   Voyages around the world
Oceanic
    See also
   Nuclear-free zones—Oceanic
Oceanic earthquakes *See* Earthquakes
Oceanographic submersibles
  Deep seeing. W. Sullivan. il *Oceans* 19:18-23 Ja/F '86
  Explorers of dark frontiers [Deep Rover] S. Brownlee. il
   Discover 7:60-7 F '86
  Finding the Titanic [images from the Argo] M. Spalding
   and B. Dawson. il *Byte* 11:96-100+ Mr '86
Oceanography
    See also
   Artificial satellites—Oceanographic use
   International Oceanographic Foundation
   Ocean-atmosphere interaction
   Ocean bottom
   Ocean Drilling Program
   Oceanographic submersibles
   Sea water
   Space flight—Oceanographic use
   United States. National Oceanic and Atmospheric
    Administration
Oceans (Periodical)
  Changing of the watch. C. du P. Roosevelt. *Oceans* 19:2
   Ja/F '86
  Defining Oceans. M. W. Robbins. *Oceans* 19:3 Ja/F '86
O'Connell, Brian F.
  Soviet Christians one year after Gorbachev. il *Christ Today*
   30:44-6 Mr 21 '86
O'Connell, Maurice R. (Maurice Rickard)
  Myths in Irish history. *America* 154:200-3 Mr 15 '86
O'Connell, Tom
  Less corn, more hell. il *Progressive* 50:15 Ja '86

O'Connell-Cahill, Catherine
   There's got to be a mourning after [with readers' comments] *U S Cathol* 51:14-19 Mr '86
O'Connell-Cahill, Michael
   Whiskey river please run dry: alcoholism in the Christian family. il *U S Cathol* 51:18-26 F '86
O'Connor, Colleen
   Who's afraid of the F.E.C.? *Wash Mon* 18:22 + Mr '86

EXERCISE 5   *Finding Magazine Articles*

In the *Readers' Guide, Social Sciences Index,* or *Humanities Index,* find an article on *one* of the subjects listed below. Write a brief report. Include the facts of publication, the purpose of the article, intended audience, main point or points, overall plan or strategy. Comment on level of difficulty, handling of technical terms or difficult material, and the like. Include one or two key quotations.

☐   talking computers
☐   the artificial heart
☐   sign language for apes
☐   schizophrenia
☐   reevaluations of the CIA or FBI
☐   competency tests for teachers
☐   women executives
☐   dissent in the Soviet Union
☐   drug testing for athletes
☐   basketball recruiting
☐   the homeless
☐   mainstreaming the disabled

EXERCISE 6   *Checking Out Books*

Through the card catalog of the library, find *one* of the following books. Study its preface or introduction, table of contents, and a key chapter or sample entries. Then prepare a brief *book review* that tells your reader about the purpose of the book, its intended audience, the scope of the book, and its overall plan. Include one or two characteristic or revealing quotations.

☐   Bruno Bettelheim, *The Uses of Enchantment*
☐   Leo Rosten, *The Joys of Yiddish*
☐   G. M. Trevelyan, *History of England*
☐   Barbara W. Tuchman, *A Distant Mirror*
☐   Kenneth Rexroth, *Classics Revisited*

- □ Norma Lorre Goodrich, *Ancient Myths*
- □ Margaret Mead, *Male and Female*
- □ Alden T. Vaughan, *New England Frontier: Puritans and Indians*
- □ Robert Coles, *Children of Crisis*
- □ Thomas Pyles, *The Origin and Development of the English Language*
- □ Mari Sandoz, *Cheyenne Autumn*
- □ Margaret M. Bryant, *Current American Usage*
- □ Desmond Morris, *The Naked Ape*
- □ Konrad Lorenz, *On Aggression*
- □ Joseph Campbell, *The Hero with a Thousand Faces*
- □ Simone de Beauvoir, *The Second Sex*
- □ Alice Walker, *In Search of Our Mothers' Gardens*
- □ Adrienne Rich, *On Lies, Secrets, and Silence*
- □ Maxine Hong Kingston, *Chinamen*
- □ Richard Rodriguez, *Hunger of Memory*

EXERCISE 7   *Preparing Bibliography Entries*

Prepare annotated bibliography cards or entries for three possible sources for a research report on changing public attitudes on a current issue. Choose *one* of the following:

- □ nuclear safety
- □ prison reform
- □ age and aging
- □ safe sex
- □ damage awards
- □ capital punishment
- □ mercy killings
- □ space flights

For your sources, choose one book indexed in the central card catalog, one article indexed in the *Readers' Guide*, and one current magazine article. Provide full bibliographical information; include call numbers when appropriate.

GATHERING: TAKING AND USING NOTES

As you check out possible sources, you will always be looking ahead. Like a chef shopping for vegetables at a produce market, you will be asking yourself: "What *use* will I make of this material? What will it contribute to the finished product?" What promising material does a source contain? How will the material fit in? What conclusions will it support?

When you are in doubt about the usefulness of material you are examining, apply criteria like the following:

☐ Am I *learning* something new here about my topic? Does this help answer a question that has come up in my earlier reading? Does this offer a different perspective on what I already know?

☐ Does this *reinforce* something that has come up earlier in my reading? Does it point toward a major common concern? Does it point toward a possible thesis for my paper?

☐ Does this suggest a way of *organizing* what I have so far? Does it point toward a major subdivision that should be part of my overall plan? Does it point toward a major stage in a process or major link in a chain of cause and effect?

☐ Does this suggest directions for *further investigation*? What questions does this passage raise and leave unanswered? What does this suggest I should look for in my later reading?

Taking Notes—Note Cards or Computer Entries Whether you write your notes by hand, type them, or feed them directly into your word processor, accurate and usable notes provide the essential supply line for your paper. For handwritten or typed notes, 3″ × 5″ or 4″ × 6″ note cards enable you to shuffle your information as the pattern of your paper takes shape. If you feed notes into your word processor, use a clear **retrieval code** (like WS for women in sports), followed by a specific identifier (like "track coach interview" or "women's Olympic marathon"). Refine your retrieval code later as subdivisions of your paper take shape (for instance WS–hst for "Women in Sports—history"). The following procedures will save you time and grief:

☐ Include a *heading*—first only a specific identifier, but later also the tentative subdivision of your paper—with each card or entry.

☐ Include the *author and title* of your source (in shortened form) at the end, along with exact page numbers. (It's frustrating to have to hunt through a book for a lost page reference.)

☐ Use each card or entry for *closely related information* or for quotations centered clearly on one limited point. (This way you will not have to disentangle material later for use at different points in your grand design.) Include the kind of specific detail that you will need to support generalizations: selected quotations, key examples, statistical figures, definitions of difficult terms.

☐ Be flexible—*adapt* the material to suit your purpose. Summarize background information; condense lengthy arguments. Paraphrase material, putting information and ideas into your own words, emphasizing what is most useful and cutting down what is less important. Use direct quotation for striking phrases, key points in an argument, revealing statements of the author's point of view. The following sample note combines paraphrase with a brief striking quote:

Indian Education

    Indian children were put in crowded boarding schools and fed at the cost of 11 cents a day (with their diet supplemented by food that could be grown on school farms). From the fifth grade up, children put in half a day's labor on the school farm. They were taught "vanishing trades of little or no economic importance."

Johnson, "Breaking Faith" 240

Mixed paraphrase and quote

    ☐ Use *extended direct quotation* for key passages. Record passages that sum up an argument or a trend; let authors speak in their own words on difficult or controversial points. The following is a meaty passage on the trend toward vegetarianism:

Vegetarianism

    "Welcome to Vegetarian Chic, the latest consuming consequence of healthier attitudes among Americans. While few people have totally forsworn meat, they're loading their plates high with veggies and fruits—11 percent more of the former and 7 percent more of the latter than five years ago. According to a 1985 Gallup poll, some 6.2 million Americans now call themselves vegetarians (although many eat the odd morsel of fish or chicken or even beef)."

Givens, "Going for the Greens" 79

Extended direct quotation

Using Quoted Material

As you start your first draft, you will have to work material from your notes smoothly into your own text. Study effective ways of integrating material from your notes in your paper. Avoid the temptations to plagiarize that might arise.

LONG QUOTATION (BLOCK QUOTATION) —to be used sparingly:

source and point of quotation

In her biography of President Johnson, Doris Kearns summed up the factors that weakened the role of the traditional political party:

block quotation

> The organization of unions, the development of the Civil Service, and the rise of the welfare state deprived the party of its capacity to provide jobs, foods, and services to loyal constituents, thus severing its connection with the daily lives and needs of the people. . . .

ellipsis—spaced periods—for omission

> Technology provided access to new forms of amusement and recreation, such as movies and television, which were more diverting than party-sponsored dances and made it unlikely that people would attend political meetings and speeches for their entertainment value. During the 1960's, more and more people declined to affiliate themselves with a party and identified themselves as independents. (162)

page number

COMMENT: In this example, the introductory sentence sums up the point of the quotation. (Readers easily become discouraged if they do not see the relevance and the point of numerous lengthy quotations.) Then the author's account of an important political change is quoted at some length. The excerpt is set off as a **block quotation**—indented ten spaces, *no quotation marks*. The introductory sentence gives credit to the original author; the full title of her book will appear after her name in the final listing of "Works Cited." The number in parentheses at the end of the quotation directs the reader to the exact page of the book. Remember to use such long quotations *sparingly*. Excerpt or break up bulky quotations to keep the reader from merely skimming them or passing them by.

Note: No additional paragraph indentation is used with block quotations unless the quotation runs to more than one paragraph. An additional *three* spaces then shows the beginning of each actual paragraph in the original source.

PLAGIARIZED VERSION —illegitimate, unacknowledged paraphrase:

> The political party no longer plays its traditional role. The growth of the unions and the welfare state deprived the party of its capacity to provide jobs, food, and services to people. New forms of amusement and recreation, such as movies and television, were more diverting than party-sponsored dances and made it unlikely that people would attend political meetings for their entertainment value. More and more people declined to affiliate themselves with a party and became independents instead.

COMMENT: Much **plagiarism** takes this form. The passage takes over someone else's words and ideas in a slightly shortened, less accurate form—*and without acknowledgment*. Even if the source were identified, this method of adapting the material would be unsatisfactory. Far too much of the original author's way of putting things has been kept—without the use of direct quotation. Much of the wording has been copied: "deprived the party of its capacity," "more diverting than party-sponsored dances."

LEGITIMATE PARAPHRASE —attributed to the original author:

> As Doris Kearns reminds us, major changes in our society weakened the traditional political party. The old-style party had provided jobs, favors, and even free food to the party faithful, but the unions, the Civil Service, or the welfare state took over many of these functions. People no longer depended on social events sponsored by the party or on rousing political speeches for entertainment; they had movies and television instead. During the 1960's, fewer and fewer people declared a party affiliation; many listed themselves as independents (162).

COMMENT: This paraphrase (followed by the page reference) keeps the essential meaning of the original. But the information is given to us in the adapter's own words, sometimes with added of touches that help make the point clear or vivid: "the party faithful," "rousing political speeches." The last sentence is parallel in structure to the original, but the other sentences are put together very differently. This is clearly an independent *interpretation* and adaptation of the original.

COMBINED PARAPHRASE AND QUOTATION —worked closely into the text:

> In her biography of President Johnson, Doris Kearns traces
> the changes that weakened the role of our political par-
> ties. The growing labor unions, the expanding Civil Ser-
> vice, and the welfare state began to provide the jobs, the
> favors, and the free food that the old-style party had
> provided for the party faithful. These changes cut off

quoted phrase

> the party's close "connection with the daily lives and
> needs of the people." Movies and television made the old-
> style party-sponsored dances and rousing political speeches
> obsolete as entertainment. During the 1960's, voters more

quoted part of sentence

> and more "declined to affiliate themselves with a party
> and identified themselves as independents" (162).

COMMENT: Here the adapter explains the main points but at the same time keeps some of the authentic flavor of the original. Direct quotation is limited to characteristic phrases and key points. By using this technique, you can show that you have paid faithful attention to the original material and yet have made it truly your own.

SUMMARY —for preview or overview:

> Doris Kearns shows how the unions, the Civil Service, the
> welfare state, and the mass media all helped weaken party
> affiliation. They provided the jobs, the favors, and the
> entertainment for which voters once turned to the
> traditional party organization (162).

COMMENT: This summary, getting at the gist of the passage, could serve as an overview or recapitulation—reinforcement of major points.

Combining Different Sources

Writing a research paper tests your ability to synthesize, to make things add up. During the early stages, your notes will be a rich accumulation of promising but unsorted material. Your job is to trace the connections—to group together material that points in the same direction, to correlate evidence that proves a point.

In a well-written research paper, a paragraph will often integrate material from several different sources. It may start with a conclusion suggested by the evidence that you have brought together. It will then present the evidence from the different sources. Study the following sample notes recording data that bear on the same point. Then look at the way this material has been integrated in a single paragraph.

PUNCTUATING QUOTATIONS: AN OVERVIEW

DIRECT QUOTATION—quotation marks, introduced by comma or (more formally) by colon:

According to the report, "Engineering, medicine, and law are no longer male bastions."

The author emphasized her conclusion: "Engineering, medicine, and law are no longer male bastions."

QUOTED WORDS OR PHRASES—*no* introductory comma or colon:

Like Horace Mann, Americans have long considered education the "great equalizer" in society.

QUOTE-WITHIN-QUOTE—single quotation marks when someone you quote is in turn quoting someone else:

The article concluded: "She is a hard worker and, in the words of a fellow judge, 'very much in charge of herself.'"

LINES OF POETRY—When more than one line of a poem is part of your running text, use a **slash**—with one space on each side—to show where a new line starts. (Normally, set off *two or more* lines of poetry as a block quotation centered on the page.)

As Juliet says, it is Romeo's name that is her enemy: "That which we call a rose / By any other name would smell as sweet."

EXCERPTED QUOTATION—Use an **ellipsis**—three spaced periods—to show that you have omitted material in order to shorten a quotation. (Use four periods, with *no* extra space before the first period, if the omission occurs after a complete sentence.)

The reviewer called the book a "searing indictment of the extent to which Americans . . . failed to respond to the plight of European Jews."

ADDITIONS—Use **square brackets** to show interpolations:

According to the report, "Powerful tribal antagonisms are a basic political fact of life in countries like Nigeria and Rhodesia [now Zimbabwe]."

PREWRITING: SAMPLE NOTES

Endangered Species--Counts   Card 1

    The bald eagle became the national symbol in 1782,
and there were nesting pairs in all the lower 48 states.
The current bald eagle population has been estimated at
5000 in the lower 48 states. As of 1975, only 627 nests
remained active, and they produced approximately 500
young.

Graham, "Will the Bald Eagle Survive?" 99

Endangered Species--Counts

    "In 1948, the wild whooping crane population was up
by just two from a decade earlier--to 31. The count sank
Card 2 to 21 in the winter or 1951-52, then rose gradually to
an encouraging 74 in 1978-79. Last spring there were
six yearlings to join the flight north. . . . The wild
whooping crane count now stands at 76, an improvement
deriving in large measure from protective practices at
Arkansas."

Wilson and Hayden, "Where Oil and Wildlife Mix" 37-38

Endangered Species--Counts

    "Whooping cranes, the largest cranes inhabiting
North America, are on the U.S. endangered species list.
Card 3 The big birds' population dwindled to 14 in the late
1930s but is now estimated at 95."

Freedman, "Whooping Cranes" 89

WRITING SAMPLE: SAMPLE PARAGRAPH

For years, nature lovers have been keeping an anxious count of such endangered species as the bald eagle and the whooping crane. When the bald eagle became the national symbol soon after Independence, there were nesting pairs everywhere in what is now the continental United States. Two hundred years later, Frank Graham, Jr., writing in Audubon magazine, reported a current estimate of 5000 bald eagles left in the lower forty-eight states. According to his figures, only 627 nests remained active, and they produced approximately 500 young (99). In 1981, Steven C. Wilson and Karen C. Hayden, writing in the National Geographic, reported a count of 76 for wild whooping cranes left in the United States, up from a dismal count of 21 thirty years earlier (37–38). Another estimate puts the current population at 95 (Freedman 89).

Remember: To convert your first rough jottings into a successful paper, you go through stages: First you work up a rich backlog of notes. Then you sort them out, working out a pattern that makes sense. Finally, you funnel your notes into a rough first draft. As always in the process of writing, these stages will overlap. When almost ready to start your draft, you may decide to hunt further for missing material; you may decide to reshuffle major sections of your paper. What counts is that in the early stages you feed in an ample supply of usable material that your finished paper will synthesize.

EXERCISE 8   *Taking Notes*

Select a magazine article or a chapter in a book on one of the topics listed below. Assume that you are extracting information or opinions for use in a larger research project. Prepare five note cards illustrating various techniques of *note taking*: Include examples of summary, paraphrase, mixed indirect and direct quotation, and extended direct quotation. Choose one:

▫ deregulation
▫ the history of advertising
▫ secret wartime codes and how to break them

THE WRITING WORKSHOP

Using Your Sources

Alice Walker, who later wrote the Pulitzer Prize–winning novel *The Color Purple*, wrote her first published essay in the winter of 1966–1967 on the topic "The Civil Rights Movement: What Good Was It?" (*The American Scholar*, Autumn 1967). Suppose that in a paper on Martin Luther King, Jr., you are making use of the following excerpt from Walker's essay. Prepare several different versions of a passage that would use material from this excerpt:

- ☐ a passage introducing an excerpted *block quotation* using part of the material
- ☐ a passage using an extended *paraphrase* of much of the material
- ☐ a passage combining paraphrase and *direct quotation*
- ☐ a passage using only a brief summary

In each version, identify author and source. Introduce the material in such a way that the reader can see the point or the significance of the material. Make photocopies of your material for discussion in class or in a small group.

The life of Dr. King, seeming bigger and more miraculous than the man himself, because of all he had done and suffered, offered a pattern of strength and sincerity I felt I could trust. He had suffered much because of his simple belief in nonviolence, love, and brotherhood. Perhaps the majority of men could not be reached through these beliefs, but because Dr. King kept trying to reach them in spite of danger to himself and his family, I saw in him the hero for whom I had waited so long.

What Dr. King promised was not a ranch-style house and an acre of manicured lawn for every black man, but jail and finally freedom. He did not promise two cars for every family, but the courage one day for all families everywhere to walk without shame and unafraid on their own feet. He did not say that one day it will be us chasing prospective buyers out of our prosperous well-kept neighborhoods, or in other ways exhibiting our snobbery and ignorance as all other ethnic groups before us have done; what he said was that we had a right to live anywhere in this country we chose, and a right to a meaningful well-paying job to provide us with the upkeep of our homes. He did not say we had to become carbon copies of the white American middle class; but he did say we had the right to become whatever we wanted to become.

  □   the history of photography
  □   the Long March
  □   Hollywood's early stars
  □   the Cherokee nation
  □   the suffragette (suffragist) movement
  □   space stations
  □   the war on drugs

EXERCISE 9   *Combining Different Sources*

Combine closely related material from different note cards in a finished *sample paragraph*. Prepare three note cards that all bear on the same limited point. Turn to sources that you have used for one of the previous exercises, or to sources related to your own current research paper project. Use the material on your cards in a sample paragraph that introduces the material clearly and helpfully to your reader. Hand in the note cards with your finished paragraph. (Include page references in parentheses.)

SHAPING: FIRST DRAFT AND REVISION In a successful research project, the gathering and sorting of material go hand in hand. Even while you are collecting material, you will be ordering and shaping it so that you can channel it into a first draft. How do you work out a tentative outline that will guide you in the writing of your first draft?

Developing an Outline With some research projects, you may truly be mapping uncharted territory. But often the nature of the subject or its history will suggest a tentative working plan. Writing about bilingual education, you are likely to operate tentatively with a rough pro-and-con sorting. On the con side, you may accumulate material from articles titled "Against a Confusion of Tongues," "In Defense of the Mother Tongue," "Avoiding Canada's Problem," or "Bilingual Classes? In U.S. But Few Other Nations." On the pro side, you may gather material from articles titled "Progress in Bilingual Education" or "Bilingualism: The Accent Is on Youth." Soon you may set up a third category for sources weighing advantages and disadvantages, from articles titled "Bilingualism: An Answer from Research" or the like.

As you proceed, you will be pushing from such tentative groupings toward a definite outline for your paper. One major function of your first draft will be to let you see how your outline works—and to let you adjust it or reorganize it if necessary. As you set up and refine your working outline, remember the following guidelines:

☐ *Set up groupings for related material*. Assign tentative common headings to notes that deal with the same limited question or the same part of a larger issue. For a paper on prison reform, you might decide early that your major groupings should include "Old-style penitentiaries," "Rehabilitation," "Experiments—U.S.," and "Experiments—Abroad." As you continue your reading, additional headings and subheadings may become necessary.

☐ *Working toward a unifying thesis*. Ask yourself, "What is this paper as a whole going to tell the reader?" Try to sum up in one sentence the overall conclusion that your research has led you to. Present this sentence as your thesis early in your paper—preferably at the end of an effective but short introduction:

The Isolated Americans

THESIS: The failure of Americans to learn foreign languages is producing a growing isolation of our country from the rest of the world.

☐ *Work out a clear overall plan for your paper*. Suppose you are writing about the threatened survival of the American bald eagle. You may decide early to group your note cards under major headings like the following:

> Population counts
> Dangers from pesticides
> Dangers from sheep ranchers
> Conservation measures

These headings suggest a plausible general strategy: You may want to start with a review of past history, go on to a discussion of current problems, and then conclude by discussing promising solutions. Here is a preliminary outline for a paper about the bald eagle as an endangered species:

PREWRITING: PRELIMINARY OUTLINE

Saving the Bald Eagle

THESIS: The bald eagle will become extinct unless we come to understand and respect the special needs of this endangered species.

   I. The history of the bald eagle
  II. Dangers to the bald eagle
      A. Pesticides used by farmers
      B. Poisoned bait, traps, and bullets used by ranchers
      C. Technological dangers

III. Steps toward improvement
   A. New eagle refuge
   B. Stricter control of poisons
   C. Better power line structures

☐ *Use your outline as a working outline.* As your overall plan takes shape, it serves as your agenda in the final stages of the paper. The more definite your plan becomes, the more clearly you will see which of your notes deal with unrelated materials and should be set aside. By the same token, you will see more clearly in which areas your notes should be supplemented by further reading.

Remember: Any outline is subject to revision. Adjust your plan as necessary. If necessary, shift important background information to an earlier part of your paper. Revise your strategy if you decide to leave the more controversial parts of a proposal till later in your discussion.

Writing the First Draft

Once you have settled on a working outline, you use it as a guide in organizing and shuffling your notes. When your notes are in the right order, you can start writing your first draft. As you push ahead, keep in mind the needs you have to meet:

☐ You will have to show that your conclusions are not just *one person's* opinion. Throughout, you need to satisfy the reader who asks, "Who said this? What is the source of this information? What do the experts say? Is there another side?" All the way through, you will be feeding into our draft information, testimony, and commentary from your sources.

☐ You need to *integrate* the material from your notes in your text. This means that you have to select, adapt, and splice together material from your sources in such a way that there will be a smooth, natural flow.

☐ You need *links* that make the reader see your plan and that guide the reader's attention in the right direction. You need to raise the issue or dramatize the topic; you need an early preview or early hints of your general strategy; you need to mark major turning points.

Study the texture of writing that integrates substantial material from sources, and use it as a model. In much of your draft, you will have to do the splicing together that produces a smooth blend of quotation, paraphrase, and interpretation:

ONE SOURCE: Phyllis Schlafly has long been one of the most prominent critics of the women's movement. For the founder of the conservative Eagle Forum, twenty years of NOW have added up to an "anti-family" crusade that has contributed to the deterioration of family life in America. "The first goal the feminist movement set for itself was divorce on demand—easy, no-fault divorce," Schlafly has said. "The result has been incredible social, financial, and emotional devastation for women." She charges that the ideology of the women's movement aims at a "gender-neutral" society in which we "are forbidden to make reasonable distinctions" (22–23).

Much of the time your task will be to confront your sources with each other—to correlate information, to compare similar testimony, to line up the pro and con. Study the way the following paragraph integrates material from several different sources:

SEVERAL SOURCES: Every month, it seems, produces a new spate of articles about the new career woman, telling us, for instance, that American companies "have discovered that selecting only male candidates means ignoring about half of the best talent available, and many are now actively recruiting women as managers" (Castro 64). For many young women, unfortunately, this media publicity creates a misleading picture of the actual job market. Even though 55 percent of all women are working today (Kitch 229), over half of them are either clerical or service workers (Smith 46–47), not highly paid executives as glossy magazine ads would lead us to believe. In her book 90 Highest-Paying Careers for the 80's, Anita Gates has a last chapter entitled "Careers That Didn't Make the List." This list of lower-paying careers includes all of the traditional female occupations (203–6). As Shirley Radl tells young women, "You haven't come a long way, and you're not a baby" (1).

The best advice during the first-draft stage is: Push on; polish and fine-tune later. You need to see the whole take shape; you need to see that your legwork is paying off. Even while you are typing, you will try to solve problems as they come up: You may have to fill in gaps or show connections. You may have to resolve apparent contradictions when on page 10 you find yourself saying something different from what you said on page 1.

Revising the First Draft The first draft of your research paper gives you the opportunity to check what you have and to see if it will work. After a day or two, you will be ready to look at your draft with the reader's eye. Will the reader see early what your agenda is? Have you spelled out what you really want to show? Can your reader follow in your footsteps as you marshal the facts or develop your argument? Consult the following checklist as a guide to revision:

☐ *Spell out fully what you have learned.* You may have to make explicit what you merely implied; what is obvious to you may not be obvious to your reader. Can you identify a sentence or a passage that sums up what you are trying to prove? Does a strong **thesis** appear in a strategic position—at the beginning or at the end?

☐ *Revise your paper to reflect second thoughts.* A first draft may end more optimistically or more pessimistically than it began. It may at first follow your initial plan but then veer off in a different direction. You may at first have stressed common misconceptions about mental illness—only to conclude later that many people are more enlightened on the subject than you thought. Check especially your opening pages to make sure that they are consistent with the rest of the paper.

☐ *Reorganize if necessary.* Check the flow of your paper and rechannel it as needed. Suppose you are writing your paper on the conflict between ideal and reality faced by many career women today. The central idea of your paper is that Madison Avenue has created a myth of the successful career woman that many women, faced by conflicting demands, find hard to live up to in the real world. In your first draft, you have followed this outline:

    I.   The media image of the New Woman
   II. Unresolved conflicts
        A.   The homemaker stereotype
        B.   "Femininity" versus being a professional
        C.   Career and motherhood
  III. The realities of the workplace
        A.   Predominantly female occupations
        B.   Disparity in pay
  IV. The price of progress
        A.   Health problems and stress
        B.   Difficult personal relationships

As you read your first draft, you may decide on some major reshuffling. On second thought, your Part II delves too early into material colored by personal grievances, so you decide to start with a "let's-look-at-the-cold-facts" approach. In your second draft, you reverse the order of Parts II and III. You also plug in some material from the history of women's work to add perspective. The outline you follow in your revised draft looks as follows:

 I. The media image of the New Woman
 II. The working woman then
 III. The working woman now
    A. Predominantly female occupations
    B. Disparity in pay
 IV. Unresolved conflicts
    A. The homemaker stereotype
    B. "Femininity" versus being a professional
    C. Career and motherhood
 V. The price of progress
    A. Health problems and stress
    B. Difficult personal relationships

□ *Strengthen support for key points.* For example, in reading your first draft on the subject of the "Graying of America," you may decide that your statistics on forced retirement are too skimpy and dated. Revision is your chance to bring in updated information or to use a recognized authority to bolster your point.

□ *Integrate quoted material better.* A poorly revised research paper often resembles the overloaded barge, ready to sink under the load of lengthy quotations. Should you do more to get your reader ready for a quotation, explaining the what and the why? Should there be a better mix of sentence-length quotations and brief quoted phrases, worked more organically into your text?

□ *Strengthen coherence.* Give your readers a reason to keep on reading as they move from point to point. Revise weak lines like the following:

WEAK LINK: *Another* point to consider is . . .
We might *also* look at . . .
Some observers feel that . . .

REVISED: A *similar, more recent* argument is that . . .
People *outside the profession* usually look at the problem from a *different* perspective . . .
A *younger generation of psychiatrists* seem to be departing from . . .

□ *Check for clear attribution.* Are the beginning *and* the end of each direct quotation clearly marked? Can the reader tell throughout where your

THE WRITING WORKSHOP

The Trial Outline

Prepare a trial outline for discussion in a small group or in class. Present it as an informal working outline, subject to refining and revision. Study the following example as a possible model: What kind of paper is it sketching out? What are likely to be the strong points of the paper? What are likely to be weak points or problems?

PURPOSE:

I feel very strongly about population control and putting into practice zero population growth if necessary. I want to show that having large families can have disastrous effects on the world's population and on the quality of life.

PLAN:

why population control is a vital health issue—introduction
pollution as a result of overpopulation
    environmental pollution
    noise pollution
population in history of world
    population stable 10,000 years ago
    how Agricultural Revolution created rapid growth
    how Industrial Revolution created rapid growth
problems facing family planning
effects of overcrowding in rats—used to show comparison with humans
    behavioral disturbances in males
    maternal problems in females
    high infant mortality rate
built-in population control in animals
culturally acceptable population control in humans prior to Agricultural Revolution
population problems in America
conclusion—Having large families is not a right. Basic rights are threatened unless a population control is enforced.

information came from, whose judgment you have trusted, or to whose opinions you have become converted? Remember that full documentation, like the listing of ingredients on a package of supermarket bread, means full disclosure of what went into the final product.

EXERCISE 10   *Writing a First Draft*

> Prepare a first draft of your paper. Your instructor may ask you to submit it for suggestions for revision or for peer review.

EXERCISE 11   *The Final Outline*

> Write a final outline that reflects your revision of your first draft. Observe the format of a formal outline.

DOCUMENTATION: IDENTIFYING YOUR SOURCES (MLA STYLE)

Documentation does for your research what an open-door policy does for government bodies: It enables people to check what goes on behind the scenes. Effective documentation enables your reader to search out an article or book you have used and turn to the right page. You are not keeping secrets from your readers; they are welcome to check where you found and how you selected your material.

Documentation: An Overview

The style of documentation shown in this section was recently developed by the Modern Language Association (MLA). It is similar to the style of documentation recommended by the American Psychological Association (APA) for research in the social sciences. Learning a style of documentation is similar to studying the instructions booklet when applying for a driver's license: At first the many regulations are bewildering, but gradually major principles come into focus, and in the end many minor details are found to serve a purpose.

The new MLA style frees writers of the need to construct an elaborate footnote or endnote when they first mention a source—allowing them in effect to organize their thinking first and document their sources later. Three principles underlie the provisos of the new style:

- ☐ Identify your sources briefly in your text.
- ☐ Give page references in your text, including the author's name and sometimes a shortened title as needed.
- ☐ Give a complete description of each source in a final alphabetical listing of "Works Cited."

Often your typed text will name the author and the work you are quoting: "Doris Lessing writes in *The Golden Notebook*, . . ." For such standard citations, include only the page reference in your text, putting it in parentheses (93). Your final list of "Works Cited" will give full information about the source:

Lessing, Doris. The Golden Notebook. New York: Simon, 1962.

If your text does not identify the author and the work, give the last name with the page reference: "One well-known chronicler of the space program kept referring to the astronauts as 'fighter jocks' " (Wolfe 413). Again, the list of "Works Cited" will give full information:

Wolfe, Tom. The Right Stuff. New York: Farrar, 1979.

You need to include a shortened form of the title with the page reference if you have drawn on more than one work by the same author: (Wolfe, *Right Stuff* 413).

Follow this current MLA style unless told otherwise by your instructor. In preparing research papers in other academic fields, you may be required to follow a different style. Widely followed guides to style for documentation include *The Chicago Manual of Style* and Kate L. Turabian's *Manual for Writers of Term Papers, Theses, and Dissertations*, both published by the University of Chicago Press.

Parenthetical Documentation Identify your source whether you quote directly, paraphrase, or summarize. In addition, show the source of all facts, figures, or ideas that are the result of someone else's effort or inspiration. You need *not* identify a specific source when you have merely repeated something that is widely known or believed:

NO SOURCE:	George Washington was elected to the Virginia assembly in 1758.
	(This is common knowledge, the kind of fact recorded in public documents and found in many history books.)
SOURCE SHOWN:	Samuel Eliot Morison describes Washington as "an eager and bold experimenter" in new agricultural methods (62).
	(This is a judgment the historian made on the basis of firsthand investigation. The text mentions his name; the number in parentheses directs us to the right page. We will find the exact title and the facts of publication in the list of "Works Cited" under "Morison.")

Study the following possibilities:

1. *Simple Page Reference*   Put page number (or page numbers) in parentheses after a closing quotation mark but before a final period:

    For Gwendolyn Brooks, the "biggest news" about the events
    in Little Rock was that the people there "are like people
    everywhere" (332).

2. *Identification by Author*   Include author's last name with the page reference if author and work do not appear in your text (and if you cite only *one* source by this author):

    The familiar arguments in favor of bilingual education
    have been challenged by an outstanding Hispanic author
    (Rodriguez 32, 37–39).

3. *Identification by Title*   Include a shortened form of the title if you are going to use *more than one* source by the same author. Underline (italicize) the title of a book or whole publication; enclose the title of an article or part of a publication in quotation marks:

    Alex Comfort has frequently told us that the blunting of
    abilities in the aged results at least in part from "put-
    downs, boredom, and exasperation" ("Old Age" 45); the
    changes we see in old people, according to him "are not
    biological effects of aging" (<u>Good Age</u> 11).

4. *Identification by Author and Title*   Include author's name and a short title if you use more than one source by an author you have not identified in the text:

    The traditional stories that the Arabs brought with them
    into medieval Spain were always fairly short (Grunebaum,
    <u>Medieval Islam</u> 294, 304–10).

5. *Reference Within a Sentence*   Put page reference and identification where needed for clarity part way through a sentence:

    As Mahoney (14) had predicted, recent surveys show that
    many who are forced to retire would prefer to continue
    working (Bensel 132).

PARENTHETICAL DOCUMENTATION: A SAMPLE PAGE

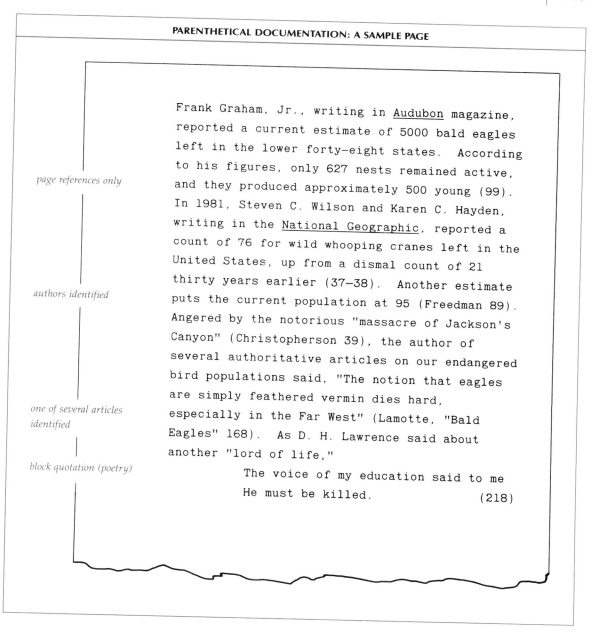

page references only

authors identified

*one of several articles
identified*

block quotation (poetry)

Frank Graham, Jr., writing in <u>Audubon</u> magazine, reported a current estimate of 5000 bald eagles left in the lower forty-eight states. According to his figures, only 627 nests remained active, and they produced approximately 500 young (99). In 1981, Steven C. Wilson and Karen C. Hayden, writing in the <u>National Geographic</u>, reported a count of 76 for wild whooping cranes left in the United States, up from a dismal count of 21 thirty years earlier (37-38). Another estimate puts the current population at 95 (Freedman 89). Angered by the notorious "massacre of Jackson's Canyon" (Christopherson 39), the author of several authoritative articles on our endangered bird populations said, "The notion that eagles are simply feathered vermin dies hard, especially in the Far West" (Lamotte, "Bald Eagles" 168). As D. H. Lawrence said about another "lord of life,"

> The voice of my education said to me
> He must be killed.   (218)

6. *Reference with Block Quotation* Although a parenthetical reference usually comes before a comma or a period, put it *after* final punctuation that concludes a block quotation:

alone. Few of them show signs of mental
deterioration or senility, and only a small
proportion become mentally ill. (114)

7. *Reference to One of Several Volumes* Use an Arabic numeral followed by a *colon* for one volume of a work published in several volumes:

According to Trevelyan, the isolationist movement in America and the pacifist movement in Britain between them "handed the world over to its fate" (3: 301).

8. *Reference to a Preface* Use lowercase Roman numerals if used in a book for the preface or other introductory material:

In his preface to <u>The Great Mother</u>, Erich Neumann refers to the "onesidedly patriarchal development of the male intellectual consciousness" (xliii).

9. *Reference to a Literary Classic* Use Arabic numerals separated by periods for act, scene, and line (*Hamlet* 3.2.73–76) or "books" and lines of epic poems (*Odyssey* 2.315–16). However, some authors prefer the more traditional use of capital and lowercase Roman numerals (*Hamlet* III.ii.73–76).

In Shakespeare's <u>Tempest</u>, Gonzalo, who would prefer to "die a dry death," fits this archetype (1.1.66)

10. *Reference to the Bible* Use Arabic numerals for chapter and verse (Luke 2.1), although some authors prefer to use a traditional style (Luke ii.1).

11. *Quotation at Second Hand* Show that you are quoting not from the original source but at second hand:

William Archer reported in a letter to his brother Charles that the actor playing Pastor Manders never really entered "into the skin of the character" (qtd. in Ibsen 135).

12. *References to Nonprint Materials* When you refer to an interview, a radio or television program, or a movie, make sure your text highlights the name of the interviewer, person being interviewed, director or producer, scriptwriter or whoever whose name appears in alphabetical order in your list of "Works Cited"—and whose name will direct your reader to a full description of the nonprint source. Sometimes you may name a production or movie in parentheses to direct your reader to the right entry:

In an interview in 1988, Silveira discussed the roots of

ABBREVIATIONS AND TECHNICAL TERMS FOUND IN SCHOLARLY WRITING

©	copyright (© 1981 by John W. Gardner)
c. or ca.	Latin *circa*, "approximately"; used for approximate dates and figures (c. 1952)
cf.	Latin *confer*, "compare"; often used for **cross-references** instead of "see"; "consult for further relevant material" (Cf. Ecclesiastes xii.12)
et al.	Latin *et alii*, "and others"; used in references to books by several authors (G. S. Harrison et al.)
f., ff.	"and the following page," "and the following pages" (See p. 16 ff.)
Ibid.	an abbreviation of Latin *ibidem*, "in the same place" (When used by itself, without a page reference, it means "in the last publication cited, on the same page." When used with a page reference, it means "in the last publication cited, on the page indicated.")
loc. cit.	Latin *loco citato*, "in the place cited"; used without page reference (Baugh, loc. cit.)
MS, MSS	Manuscript, manuscripts
n.d.	"no date," date of publication unknown
op. cit.	short for *opere citato*, "in the work already cited"
passim	Latin for "throughout"; "in various places in the work under discussion" (See pp. 54–56 et passim.)
rev.	"review" or "revised"
rpt.	"reprint"; a current reprinting of an older book
q.v.	Latin *quod vide*, "which you should consult"

---

his work in Aztec and Inca art.

The Caldwell production of La Traviata broke new ground without alienating traditional opera fans.

A news special by a local station fanned the long-smoldering controversy into bright flames (Poisoned Earth).

"Works Cited"—General Guidelines At the end of your research paper, you will furnish an alphabetical listing of your sources. This listing, titled "Works Cited," serves as a directory guiding the interested reader to the sources you have drawn on during your search. It will often be more than a bibliography (a "book list" or list of printed materials) and include non-print sources. Before you study a range of sample entries, learn the broad outlines of the style you will be required to follow. Think of implementing the format outlined here as a test of how accurately you can code information—making it readily available in compact form to its intended user.

Start your page with the centered heading "Works Cited." Then type your first entry, with the first line *not* indented, but with the second line and additional lines indented five spaces. Remember:

- *Put the last name of the author first.* This order applies only to the first author listed when a book has several authors. (The bibliography is an *alphabetical* listing.)

Brooks, Gwendolyn. The World of Gwendolyn Brooks. New
      York: Harper, 1971.
Himstreet, William C., and Wayne Murlin Baty. Business
      Communications: Principles and Methods. 7th ed.
      Boston: Kent, 1984.

If *no name of author or editor* is known to you, list the publication alphabetically by the first letter of the title, not counting *The, A,* or *An.*

- *Show major breaks by periods.* Separate the name of the author or editor from what follows by a period. Set off the facts of publication for a book from what precedes and what follows by periods. (Leave *two* spaces after periods separating blocks of information.)

Silverberg, Robert, ed. Science Fiction Hall of Fame. 2
      vols. London: Sphere Books, 1972.

- *Underline (italicize) the title of a complete publication; enclose the title of part of a publication in quotation marks.* Underlining (when your typewriter has no italics) tells the printer to use italicized print. Italicize titles of books, collections, newspapers, or magazines: *A Brief Guide to Lean Cuisine.* Put in quotation marks titles of articles, reports, stories, or poems that were part of a larger publication: "How to Deep-Freeze Bait." *Angler's Monthly.* Remember: quotation marks for the part, italics for the whole.

- *Include complete page numbers for an article.* Entries for books do *not* include page numbers, but give the inclusive page numbers for articles in periodicals or for parts of a collection. (If part of an article spills over onto later pages not consecutively numbered with the beginning of the selection, use a plus sign to show that there is more on later pages.)

```
Lane, Chuck.  "Open the Door: Why We Should Welcome the
     Immigrant."  The New Republic 1 Apr. 1985: 20-24.
Miller, JoAnn.  "The Sandwich Generation."  Working Mother
     Jan. 1987: 47-48.
Kaplan, Janice.  "Politics of Sports."  Vogue July 1984:
     219+.
```

When a periodical uses continuous page numbering through several issues of an annual volume, include the *volume number* as an Arabic numeral. Use a colon before the inclusive page numbers: *PMLA* 96 (1981): 351–62. When page numbering is not continuous from one issue to another, you may need the number of the specific *issue* as well as the volume number. The following would guide the reader to volume 2, issue 2: *Kentucky Review* 2.2 (1981): 3–22.

☐ *If you list several publications by the same author, do not repeat the author's name.* In the second and later entries, use a line made of three hyphens instead:

```
Comfort, Alex.  A Good Age.  New York: Simon, 1976.
---.  "Old Age: Facts and Fancies."  Saturday Evening Post
     Mar. 1977: 45.
---.  Practice of Geriatric Psychiatry.  New York:
     Elsevier, 1980.
```

Sample Entries
The following sample entries start with models for the entries most frequently found in a list of sources and then go on to more unusual situations. Pay special attention to kinds of information included, use of abbreviations, spacing, and punctuation. For exceptional situations not covered here, consult the *MLA Handbook for Writers of Research Papers,* Second Edition.

1. *Standard Entry for a Book* Include place of publication, name of publisher, date of publication:

```
Schell, Jonathan.  The Fate of the Earth.  New York:
     Knopf, 1982.
```

Note: In the current style, identification of publishers is often heavily abbreviated: *NAL* for New American Library, *Harcourt* for Harcourt Brace Jovanovich, Inc. Other examples:

(Oxford University Press)	New York: Oxford UP, 1988
(Prentice-Hall, Inc.)	Englewood Cliffs: Prentice, 1989
(Academy for Educational Development)	Washington: Acad. for Educ. Dev., 1983

2. *Newspaper or Magazine Article*   Give the date of issue, separated from page numbers by a colon. Include the abbreviations *p.* or *pp.* (for "page" or "pages") only if confusion would otherwise result. If necessary, specify the edition of a newspaper: (*Wall Street Journal* 10 May 1983, eastern ed.: 37).

Weinberg, Steven. "The Decay of the Proton." Scientific
    American June 1981: 64–75.

"Environmentalists See Threats to Rivers." New York Times
    15 July 1981, late ed., sec. 1: 8.

Note: Page numbers of a newspaper will often already include a letter indicating the section of the paper: A15, C32. Identify special features of newspapers and magazines, such as letters to the editor or reviews:

Franciosa, Maria. Letter. San Francisco Chronicle 14
    Jan. 1989: 54.

Bromwich, David. "Say It Again, Sam." Rev. of The Oxford
    Book of Aphorisms, ed. John Gross. The New Republic
    6 Feb. 1984: 36–38.

Harlan, Arvin C. Rev. of A Short Guide to German Humor,
    by Frederick Hagen. Oakland Tribune 12 Dec. 1988:
    89–90.

3. *Anonymous Article or Editorial*   If the author of an article or editorial remains unnamed, begin your entry with the title. (Note, however, that newsmagazines increasingly give the names of authors of major articles.)

"The Boundaries of Privacy." Time 30 Apr. 1984: 64.

"A Frown on the Interface." Editorial. Software News 3
    Sept. 1988: 3.

4. *Article with Volume Number*   Enclose the year or month in parentheses:

Weaver, Kenneth F. "The Promise and Peril of Nuclear
    Energy." National Geographic 155 (Apr. 1979): 458–93.

5. *Work with Subtitle* Have a colon separate title and subtitle unless the original has other punctuation. Underline the subtitle of a book; enclose both title and subtitle of an article in the same set of quotation marks:

> Rodriguez, Richard. Hunger of Memory: The Education of
> Richard Rodriguez. Boston: Godine, 1982.
> Schmidt, Sarah. "From Ghetto to University: The Jewish
> Experience in the Public School." American Educator
> Spring 1978: 23–25.

6. *Work with Several Authors* Give the full names of coauthors. If there are more than three, put *et al.* (Latin for "and others") after the name of the first author instead:

> Gilbert, Sandra M. and Susan Guber. The Madwoman in the
> Attic: The Woman Writer and the Nineteenth-Century
> Literary Imagination. New Haven: Yale UP, 1979.
> Gale, Noel H., and Zofia Stos-Gale. "Lead and Silver in
> the Ancient Aegean." Scientific American June 1981:
> 176–77.
> Stewart, Marie M., et al. Business English and
> Communication. 5th ed. New York: McGraw, 1978.

7. *Unspecified or Corporate Authorship* Reports prepared by an organization or agency and major reference books may list a group as the author or not specify authorship:

> Carnegie Council on Policy Studies in Higher Education.
> Giving Youth a Better Chance: Options for Education,
> Work, and Service. San Francisco: Jossey, 1980.
> Literary Market Place: The Directory of American Book
> Publishing. 1984 ed. New York: Bowker, 1983.

8. *Edited or Translated Work* Insert the editor's or translator's name after the title, using the abbreviation "Ed." or "Trans." The editor's name may come first if the author is unknown, if the editor has collected the work of different authors, if the editor has brought together an author's work from different sources, or if you are quoting *the editor* rather than the original author.

> Mencken, H. L. The Vintage Mencken. Ed. Alistair Cooke.
> New York: Vintage, 1956.

Griffin, Alice, ed. <u>Rebels and Lovers: Shakespeare's</u>
<u>Young Heroes and Heroines</u>. New York: New York UP,
1976.

Lorenz, Konrad. <u>On Aggression</u>. Trans. Marjorie Kerr
Wilson. New York: Harcourt, 1966.

Note: Identify two or more joint editors: *Dictionary of Proverbs*. Ed. Barbara Freed and Carl Wechsler. Use *eds.* for "editors" if you are putting the editors first:

Foster, Carol D., Nancy R. Jacobs, and Mark A. Siegel,
eds. <u>Capital Punishment: Cruel and Unusual</u>? 4th ed.
Plano: Instructional Aides, 1984.

9. *New Edition* Place the number of a revised edition before the facts of publication:

Friedan, Betty. <u>The Feminine Mystique</u>. 4th ed. New
York: Norton, 1983.

Note: If a work has been republished unchanged (perhaps as a paperback reprint), include the date of the original edition:

Ellison, Ralph. <u>Invisible Man</u>. 1952. New York: Vintage–
Random, 1972.

10. *Special Imprint* A line of paperback books, for instance, is often published and promoted separately by a publishing house. Put the name of the line of books first, joined by a hyphen to the publisher's name: *Laurel Leaf-Dell, Mentor-NAL*.

Hsu, Kai-yu, ed. and trans. <u>Twentieth–Century Chinese</u>
<u>Poetry</u>. Garden City: Anchor–Doubleday, 1964.

11. *Work Published in Several Volumes* Use an Arabic numeral to show the number of the volume you are quoting:

Woolf, Virginia. <u>The Diary of Virginia Woolf</u>. Ed. Anne
Olivier Bell. New York: Harcourt, 1977. Vol. 1.

Churchill, Winston S. <u>The Age of Revolution</u>. Vol. 3 of <u>A</u>
<u>History of the English–Speaking Peoples</u>. 4 vols.
New York: Dodd, 1957.

Note: Sometimes, you will want to list a complete multivolume work:

>Trevelyan, G. M. <u>History of England</u>. 3rd ed. 3 vols.
>   Garden City: Anchor-Doubleday, 1952.

12. *Article in a Collection* Identify fully both the article (or other short piece) and the collection of which it is a part. Give inclusive page numbers:

>Rogers, Carl R. "Two Divergent Trends." <u>Existential
>   Psychology</u>. Ed. Rollo May. New York: Random, 1969.
>   87–92.

>Oates, Joyce Carol. "Where Are You Going, Where Have You
>   Been?" <u>The American Tradition in Literature</u>. Ed.
>   Sculley Bradley et al. 4th ed. 2 vols. New York:
>   Norton, 1974. 2: 1916–30.

13. *Encyclopedia Entry* Page numbers and facts of publication may be unnecessary for entries appearing in alphabetical order in well-known encyclopedias or dictionaries. Date or number of the edition used, however, should be included because of the frequent revisions of major encyclopedias.

>Politis, M. J. "Greek Music." <u>Encyclopedia Americana</u>.
>   1956 ed.

>"Aging." <u>Encyclopaedia Britannica: Macropaedia</u>. 1983.

14. *Special Edition of Bible or Classic* You will have to specify the edition used if textual variations are important, as with different translations of the Bible or different editions of a Shakespeare play. (Put the name of the editor first if you are citing the editor's introduction or notes.)

>The Holy Bible. Revised Standard Version. 2nd ed.
>   Nashville: Nelson, 1971.

>Hubler, Edward, ed. <u>The Tragedy of Hamlet</u>. By William
>   Shakespeare. New York: NAL, 1963.

15. *Quotation at Second Hand* List only the work where the quotation appeared:

>Ibsen, Henrik. <u>Ghosts</u>. Ed. Kai Jurgensen and Robert
>   Schenkkan. New York: Avon, 1965.

16. *Pamphlet or Unpublished Material* Show the nature and source of the materials: mimeographed pamphlet, unpublished doctoral dissertation,

and the like. Use quotation marks to enclose unpublished titles—publications duplicated informally for limited use:

```
Calif. Dept. of Viticulture.  Grape Harvesting.
     Sacramento: State Printing Office, 1986.
Lopez, Fernando, ed.  "Tales of the Elders."  Albuquerque,
     mimeo., 1988.
Latesta, Philip.  "Rod McKuen and the Sense of Deja Vu."
     Diss. Columbia U, 1986.
```

17. *Nonprint Source* Give the information needed to identify interviews, lectures, recordings, television programs, filmstrips, videotapes, and the like:

```
Silveira, Gene.  Personal interview.  30 June 1988.
Massini, Ottavia.  "The Art of Picasso."  Valley Lecture
     Series.  Los Angeles, 12 Mar. 1985.
Holiday, Billie.  Essential Billie Holiday.  Verve, 68410,
     1961.
The Poisoned Earth.  Narr. Sylvia Garth.  Writ. and prod.
     Pat Fisher.  WXRV News Special.  23 Oct. 1983.
Creation vs. Evolution: "Battle of the Classroom."
     Videocassette.  Dir. Ryall Wilson.  PBS Video, 1982.
     58 min.
Caldwell, Sarah, dir. and cond.  La Traviata.  By Giuseppe
     Verdi.  With Beverly Sills.  Opera Co. of Boston.
     Orpheum Theatre, Boston.  4 Nov. 1972.
```

18. *Computer Software* Include writer of the program (if known), title of the program or material, and distributor or publisher. Further information may include the equipment (like Apple IIe) for which the software is designed and the form in which the program is recorded (disk, cassette, or the like).

```
Wordmaster.  Computer software.  Webtronics, 1985.
Mongus, Irene.  Write/Rewrite.  Computer Software.  IPCM,
     1984.  FSV-92, cartridge.
```

19. *Material from Services* If you have obtained documents or printed material through a computer service or centralized information service, identify the service and provide identifying number or access number:

Phillips, June K., ed. <u>Action for the '80s: A Political, Professional, and Public Program for Foreign Language Education</u>. Skokie: Natl. Textbook, 1981. ERIC ED 197 599.

Schomer, Howard. "South Africa: Beyond Fair Employment." <u>Harvard Business Review</u> May–June 1983: 145+. DIALOG file 122, item 119425 833160.

20. *Title Within a Title* Sometimes, a phrase or title that needs quotation marks becomes part of a title that already *has* quotation marks around it. Shift to single quotation marks for the title-within-a-title: "Sentimentality in 'The Outcasts of Poker Flat.' " Sometimes, an italicized (underlined) book title includes the name of another book. Shift back to roman (*not* underlined) for the title-within-a-title: *A Guide to James Joyce's* Ulysses.

Using Footnotes/Endnotes

In much traditional scholarly writing, footnotes (now usually **endnotes**) have been used to identify sources and add information. Such notes are usually numbered consecutively. A raised footnote number usually appears outside whatever punctuation goes with the sentence or paragraph, as in this example.[2] At the bottom of the page, or on a separate page at the end of a paper or article, the note itself appears. It starts with the raised number, is indented like a paragraph, and ends with a period or other end punctuation.

A traditional footnote identifying a source might look like this:

[2]Robin Northcroft, <u>A Short Guide to Fine British Cooking</u> (New York: Culinary Arts, 1989), p. 85.

Even when you use a system of documentation that does not identify sources in footnotes, you may want to use footnotes for the kind of backup or branching out that can help satisfy an interested reader. For instance, your text may have mentioned the recent outpouring of books with titles like *Aging: Continuity and Change* or *Aging and Society*. For the interested reader, you may decide to provide a more extended listing in a note:

[3]Books on aging from the publication list of a single publisher include <u>The Social Forces in Later Life</u>, <u>Social Problems of the Aging</u>, <u>Biology of Aging</u>, <u>Human Services for Older Adults</u>, <u>Families in Later Life</u>, <u>The Later Years</u>, <u>Working with the Elderly</u>, <u>Late</u>

THE WRITING WORKSHOP

Checking the MLA Format

The following are possible sources for a paper exploring the advice young women currently receive on how to be successful in a business career. Prepare an alphabetical list of "Works Cited," following the MLA style of documentation. Prepare photocopies for a meeting in which your class or small group will check and discuss format.

1. A book titled Women Like Us by Liz Roman Gallese, published by William Morrow in New York in 1985.

2. A book by Betty Legan Harragan called Games Your Mother Never Taught You: Corporate Gamesmanship for Women, published by Warner Books in New York in 1977.

3. Several articles by Betty Legan Harragan: How to Take Risks and Make More Money in Harper's Bazaar for August 78, starting on page 82 and continued later in the magazine; and Getting Ahead in Working Woman for December 1982, starting on page 44 and continued later.

4. A book called The Right Moves: Succeeding in a Man's World Without a Harvard MBA, written by Charlene Mitchell and Thomas Burdick, published by Macmillan in New York in 1985.

5. A book edited by Ralph E. Smith and titled The Subtle Revolution: Women at Work, published by the Urban Institute in Washington, D.C., in 1979.

6. The fourth edition of Betty Friedan's The Feminine Mystique, published by W. W. Norton in New York in 1983.

7. An article by Kay Mills in the Los Angeles Times for September 18, 1984, and titled Despite Gains, Job Future Still Uncertain for Women, to be found in Section I on page 1.

8. A book called Letitia Baldridge's Complete Guide to Executive Manners published by Rawson Associates in Toronto in 1985.

9. An article by Barbara Ehrenreich titled Strategies of Corporate Women, printed in The New Republic for January 27, 1986, to be found on pages 28 through 31.

10. An article by Mary Bralove, titled Corporate Politics: Equal Opportunities and printed in a periodical called Masters in Business Administration, to be found in volume 12 for Aug.–Sept. 1978, starting on page 26 and continued on page 30.

11. A personal interview about Harragan's Games Your Mother Never Taught You, conducted with a business school instructor named Kaye Schonholtz on March 17, 1987.

12. An unsigned article in the Oakland Tribune for February 14, 1987, titled Superwoman: Coping with Stress, appearing in a late edition in Section B on pages 7 and 8.

13. A book by Marilyn Loden called Feminine Leadership: Or How to Succeed in Business Without Being One of the Boys, published by Times Books in New York in 1985.

14. A photocopied brochure published by the Fresno Boosters Club, titled Preventing Executive Burnout and written by Jordan K. Pagodian and three coauthors, published in Fresno, California, in December 1986.

<u>Adulthood</u>, and <u>Aging: Politics and Policies</u>, among others.

Other common uses of such notes include the following:

- showing your familiarity with earlier research in the field
- dealing with objections likely to be raised by insiders
- clearing up possible confusions over technical terms
- providing additional context (or more of the exact wording) of a key quotation
- pointing to an interesting parallel or precedent

Writers sometimes use the first footnote or endnote for **acknowledgments**—thanking collaborators, mentors, resource persons, or well-wishers for their contributions. (Sometimes these expressions of indebtedness become parts of a separate acknowledgments page.)

THE MAKING OF A SAMPLE PAPER

Studying a sample research paper may teach you more than theoretical advice. You can see how the writer sets the paper in motion, gets the reader involved in the argument, and maintains its momentum. You can observe how the writer at strategic points integrates supporting material from authoritative sources and how the guidelines for documentation work out in practice.

Sample Research Paper: Genesis

As you study the sample paper that follows later in this section, you should try to reconstruct the process that produced the finished result. The following planning report shows that from the start the author wrote with a purpose. She had an agenda; her topic had a personal significance for her as a writer.

PREWRITING: PLANNING REPORT

I want to investigate the area of women in sports. It's a good topic for me because I love sports both as a spectator and as a participant. My thesis has not yet crystallized in my mind, but I want to focus on the *changes* that have occurred in the last 10–15 years with respect to opportunities for women in athletics. I may wish to go back farther for more historical perspective. I know women did not compete in the first Olympics, but they have been in Olympic competition for as long as I can personally remember. In my own experience, however, women who wanted to participate in the drama of competitive sports either had to become cheerleaders or join a small organization of girls rumored to wear combat boots, the GAA or Girls' Athletic Association. I realized last year how much things have changed when I watched a women's sectional volleyball game at the local high school. The local team won a victory that sent them to the state finals. The exciting part was that the entire boys' football team had turned out to cheer the girls on. When the final buzzer sounded, the fans exploded, absolutely jubilant, and total bedlam ensued. One thing was obvious: These women athletes were neither cheerleaders nor truckdriving types—they were a new breed, and they made me feel proud. This incident might make a good introduction.

A definite purpose—a point to prove, a cause to promote—helps keep the search for material going when the road turns steep. The following search record shows how the author of the women-in-sports paper capitalized on promising leads, useful pointers, and lucky finds.

PREWRITING: SEARCH RECORD

My plan was to start by scanning periodicals that seemed obvious sources for material on women athletes: *Sports Illustrated, Ms.* magazine, *Womensports, Women's Sports and Fitness.* I was also going to look for material on outstanding professional athletes such as Billie Jean King, Chris Evert, or Babe Zacharias. My older *personal resources* sister earlier in the year had received a brochure that was part of a fund-raising drive for scholarships to women athletes; I decided to try to track down a copy of the brochure. A promising source was the coach of the local volleyball team at the high school—very committed to women's volleyball and consistently coaching championship teams.

During the early informal reading, I found that many magazine articles about female athletes deal with current "sports celebrities" or with current fads, like female body-builders. I felt that I needed to find material that focused more directly on the issues faced by women in sports, on their changing self-image, and on future direc-*card catalog* tions. Through the card catalog, I found two key sources providing essential historical background: Janice Kaplan's *Women and Sports* and, in a collection called *Sports in Literature,* an article by Marie Hart ("Sport: Women Sit in the Back of the Bus"), *periodical index* reprinted from *Psychology Today.* The electronic periodical index at the college library had hardly any listings under WOMEN IN SPORTS but had much material under the umbrella heading WOMAN ATHLETES, with numerous subheadings such as "Achievements and Awards," "Competition," and "History."

Some of the most useful material I found was focused on two major topics. The first was Title IX, designed to promote greater equality of opportunity for women in collegiate athletics. Much has been written on the original legislation, its guidelines and applications, and later changes. The second topic was the 1984 Olympics, which for many observers was a turning point in the recognition awarded female athletes. *local angle* Lucky find: I found that an author who had written a book on sports sociology was a local resident, and I was able to arrange an interview. While I worked on the *media input* paper, I watched the newspaper for relevant news reports, such as a story on a woman who won a dogsled race in Alaska. I learned much by talking to people about my paper.

As they digest their material, most writers at first use a rough working outline. They then gradually refine it until they arrive at a trial outline to guide the writing of the first draft. To keep the effort on track, they push toward a tentative thesis, stated early in the first draft. (Often, they find that their tentative thesis needs sharpening as the rest of the paper takes shape.) Here is the trial outline that guided the writing of the first draft for "Women in Sports":

PREWRITING: TRIAL OUTLINE

Women in Sports

THESIS: The revolution in women's athletics is producing two kinds of fallout: It is leading us to reevaluate the nature of athletics, and it is refashioning the way women see themselves.

    I. The historical perspective
        A. 1890–1950: Conventional roles, some advances
        B. 1950s and 60s: Changes begin
        C. 1970s: Commercial money and Chapter IX
        D. The 1984 Olympics
    II. Reevaluating Athletics
        A. Challenging excessive competition
        B. Challenging excessive violence
   III. Refashioning women's self-image
        A. Physical fitness and emotional fitness
        B. Breaking physical barriers
        C. Increased self-esteem
        D. Carryover into other areas of life

Sometimes a trial outline works out well. Revision of a first draft can then focus on page-by-page detail: clarifying points, bolstering evidence, strengthening connections. But often some real rethinking and reshuffling seems advisable. Here is a note on how her view of her audience guided the author of "Women in Sports" in a major reshuffling of material:

REVISION: REFINING THE PLAN

I had a sense of the basic architecture of the paper early in the process, but the interior decorating happened as I went along. I early had a sense of three major sections of the paper: There would be a historical section on the traditional obstacles faced by women in sports and on their slow progress in overcoming them. There would be a section on how the increasing visibility of women in the world of sports has begun to change the spirit of sports, with less emphasis on violence and winner-takes-all competition. There would be a section on women's growth in self-esteem and self-confidence as the result of emphasis on physical fitness and increased participation in sports.

Originally I thought that the section on women and how they see themselves should be last since it contained much eloquent material. But the more I thought about it, the more it seemed that the more general section on changes in sports and our general attitude toward sports should come last. Ending with the section on women and their changing attitudes would have made this a paper primarily on women, aimed primarily at women as an audience. Ending the paper with the section on changing attitudes towards sports made this a paper on sports in general, aiming at both men and women as an audience.

Sample Research Paper: The Text

As you study the sample research paper, pay attention to both content and form. Make sure you see how the author tackles her subject, guides the reader, and maintains the reader's interest. Equally important, look at how the author has used and identified her sources. How does she introduce quoted material? What is the mix of short direct quotation, paraphrase, and longer block quotations? What is the range of her sources?

title page if required by instructor

Women in Sports:
Pushing the Limits
by
Barbara Meier Gatten

English 2A
Professor Lamont
April 9, 1988

A Note on Format: Your instructor may ask you to provide a separate title page and a formal outline with your paper. The first two pages of the sample paper provide models for both of these items. However, the first page of the actual text of the paper also shows the **author block** (author, instructor, course, date) used to identify the paper when a separate title page is not used. *Omit* this author block if you provide a title page.

Note the use of *double spacing* throughout the paper—including block quotations and the list of "Works Cited." (Exception: Quadruple spacing between title and text on first page of text.) Note also the **running heads**—author's name and initials followed by the page number at the top of each page.

outline if required by instructor

Outline

THESIS: The revolution in women's athletics has changed both what women expect of themselves and what we expect of athletics.

- I.   Today's highly visible women athletes
- II. Progress towards equality in sports
    - A.   Challenging traditional restrictions
    - B.   Making progress: The 50s and 60s
        - 1. The Sputnik effect
        - 2. The spirit of political activism
    - C.   Breakthroughs: The 70s
        - 1. Commercial sponsorship
        - 2. Title IX and its aftermath
    - D.   Turning point: The Los Angeles Olympics
- III. Sports and the changing self-image of women
    - A.   Fitness: body and mind
    - B.   Testing the limits
    - C.   Increased self-esteem
    - D.   Sports and life
- IV. Women's athletics and traditional sports
    - A.   Competition vs. participation
    - B.   Downplaying violence
- V.   A new concept of sport

Study the way the author introduces her subject and leads up to her thesis. She *dramatizes the issue* by turning to personal experience: She tells (briefly) the story of the volleyball playoff that helped crystallize her own thinking about the progress of women in sports. This account sets up the "then-and-now" contrast that provides the basic historical perspective for the paper. (Notice the rich array of examples of today's women athletes from tennis players and cyclists to fencers and soccer players.)

Note that the opening incident was mentioned in the author's planning report and helped trigger her investigation of her topic.

Barbara Meier Gatten

Professor Lamont

English 2A

April 9, 1988

author block (omit if there is a separate title page)

quadruple spacing

Women in Sports:

Pushing the Limits

The gym was packed. Each time the home team scored, there was a roar, followed by a deathly quiet that magnified the slap of a hand on the ball or the squeak of rubber on wood. When the final buzzer sounded, signaling victory for the home team and a *dramatizing the issue* trip to the state playoffs, the gym went wild. Classmates and friends rushed out onto the floor, lifting the players up in the air. A few years ago, this scene could have meant only one thing: the men's basketball playoffs. Tonight, it was the women's volleyball sectionals.

Twenty years ago, such a scene would have been unlikely. Then women who enjoyed sports had two *then-and-now contrast* choices: They could join the Girls' Athletic Association (GAA) and play intramurals, or they could participate vicariously as cheerleaders on the sidelines. Today, in addition to the highly publicized women tennis players, runners, ice skaters, and

After she has brought the issue into focus, the author states her thesis at the end of the second paragraph. The thesis sums up briefly and memorably the gist of the paper. At the same time, it provides a *preview* or program for the paper as a whole. It sets up expectations that are later fulfilled:

1. The author will provide a historical survey of the "revolution" in women's sports.
2. She will write about the changing self-image of women as the result of increased participation in sports.
3. She will write about what the increasing participation of women is doing to change what we expect of athletics.

running head

volleyball players, there are women cyclists, swimmers, squash players, rowing crews, mountain climbers, fencers, soccer players—and a rugby team called
thesis with preview of
key points
"The Gentle Women of Aspen." What has happened? The
revolution in women's athletics has changed both what
women expect of themselves and what we expect of
athletics.

For many years, progress toward equality of the
sexes in sports was slow. Women were free to participate in genteel games like tennis or golf as long as
paragraph integrating
several sources
they did not perspire too freely or appear too intent
on winning. From the beginning, women athletes had
to reckon with the traditional ideal of the ladylike
woman, who could not appear tough or assertive. Outstanding athletes like the swimmer Esther Williams or
the ice skater Sonja Henje were praised for their
beauty and grace rather than for their athletic
source quoted at second
hand
achievement. In 1936, the editor of Sportsman magazine wrote, "As swimmers and divers, girls are as
beautiful and adroit as they are ineffective and
unpleasing on the track" (qtd. in Hart 66). Janice
partial quotation—author
and book identified
Kaplan claims in her book Women and Sports that as
recently as the 60s practically the only sport at
which a woman could hope to make money was ice skat-
ing, since "ice shows were always looking for pretty
girls who could stand up on skates" (54). Writing in

B. M. Gatten 3

partial quotation—author and article identified

1971, Marie Hart, in an article titled "Sport: Women Sit in the Back of the Bus," concluded that "the emphasis in periodicals is still largely on women as attractive objects rather than as skilled and effective athletes" (66). It was not until the 80s that a swimmer who had just won her third Olympic gold medal could say: "Once the Marilyn Monroe look was really in. Now it's the lean, muscular, runner look" (qtd. in O'Reilly, "Out of the Tunnel" 73).

In the 1950s and 1960s, real opportunities for women in sports were slowly beginning to open up, partly as the result of political pressures. Phyllis Bailey, Assistant Director of Athletics at Ohio State University, described a kind of athletic "Sputnik effect":

block quotation for key development (no quotation marks—double indentation)

> The international scene of the 1950s and 60s had put pressure on the government to take women's college sports more seriously. The Olympics had become a political battlefield, and our men were getting medals, but our women weren't. We had to do something to protect our standing in the world and get American women on a par with others. (qtd. in Kaplan, Women in Sports 59)

B. M. Gatten 4

At the same time, the climate of political activism of the 60s and growing agitation for individual rights encouraged women to knock on doors previously closed. In 1967, Kathrine Switzer crashed the then male-only Boston Marathon. She filled out the entrant's application as K. Switzer and then "was nearly shouldered off the course by officials when they noticed she was, in fact, female." The attempted ouster and resulting controversy "infuriated Switzer and galvanized her into action to change the system," making her a major force in the movement that led to the inclusion of the first women's marathon in the 1984 Olympics (Ullyot 44, 50–51).

part paraphrase, part quotation in account of a key event

The major breakthroughs for women's sports occurred in the 70s. First, a few major companies gingerly invested in women's pro sports and soon realized that they had discovered a gold mine. Colgate-Palmolive became the controlling dollar behind women's golf, skiing, and tennis. The company decided to put its advertising money into the women's pro circuit instead of afternoon soap operas, and the gamble paid off. Another company to place a lucky bet was Phillip Morris, the tobacco company. The Virginia Slims tennis tour put women's tennis on the map. The effect of the Slims tour with its lucrative prize money was to establish for the

Look at how the author introduces quotations and other material from sources in the opening pages of the paper. Look at how she accomplishes one or more of the following purposes:

- identify the source
- establish the authority or the credentials of the source
- signal the point or the relevance of a quotation or other material

Study examples like the following:

> In 1936, the editor of <u>Sportsman</u> magazine wrote,...
>
> Janice Kaplan claims in her book <u>Women and Sports</u> that as recently as the 60s ...
>
> Phyllis Bailey, Assistant Director of Athletics at Ohio State University, described a kind of athletic "Sputnik effect":...
>
> In this area, according to George R. LaNoue, former head of the Task Force of Higher Education of the U.S. Equal Employment Opportunity Commission, "the treatment of women athletes ..."
>
> Linda Schreiber writes about how running helped to increase her energy and change her outlook, how she experienced the sharpened physical and mental edge of being in shape:...

B. M. Gatten 5

first time the role model of the well-paid, well-respected female athlete. By the early 1980s, Martina Navratilova, a top player on the Virginia Slims circuit, could win over two million dollars in tournament action in one year, not counting the income from endorsements (Sherman 194).

summary of factual information, credited to source

While women were gaining in the professional arena, a landmark event changed women's athletics in academia. In 1972, Congress passed the Education Amendments Act. Chapter IX of the Act barred an institution from receiving federal funds if it practiced any form of sex discrimination. The heated controversies about how to implement the law "focused on the relative facilities and funds available to male and female athletes." In this area, according to George R. LaNoue, former head of the Task Force of Higher Education of the U.S. Equal Employment Opportunity Commission, "the treatment of women athletes by universities was often shabby at best" (28).

credentials of authority

The net effect of the new law was to promote sudden growth in women's athletics. Headlines like "Big Ten Begins Women's Program" began to sprout in sports publications. According to Kaplan, before Title IX, colleges spent an estimated 2 percent of their athletic budgets on women's sports; by 1984, the figure was close to 20 percent. Before, there

summary of statistics (from second publication by same author)

As the paper unfolds, keep an eye on the writer's use of her sources:

□ What kind of sources does she turn to? Do they seem easily accessible or from out-of-the-way places?

□ Do the sources represent a *range* of authorities?

□ What are their *credentials?* Do they seem qualified, and do they merit attention?

□ Does the writer seem *biased* in selecting sources—is there a predictable point of view?

□ Which of the quoted sources seem most *relevant* or useful? Which least?

□ Do any of the *quotations* seem especially eloquent or memorable? Why?

□ Are any of the *facts and figures* surprising or startling? Why? Do any of them seem incomplete or bewildering? Why?

B. M. Gatten 6

were virtually no athletic scholarships for univer-
sity-bound women; by 1984, there were more than ten
thousand ("Politics" 219). Robert Sullivan, writing
in <u>Sports Illustrated</u>, said:

excerpted block quotation for statistical evidence

> There were 32,000 females participating in
> college athletics in 1972, the year the law
> was enacted; by 1983 the total had
> increased to 150,000....From 1974 to 1981
> the number of colleges granting athletic
> scholarships to women increased from 60 to
> 500, while expenditures on women's programs
> by NCAA schools soared from $4 million to
> $116 million. This greater commitment to
> women's athletics resulted in vastly
> improved performances by females not just
> in basketball, but also in track and field,
> swimming, and most other sports. (9)

In 1984, a Supreme Court ruling took some of the
teeth out of Chapter IX, stipulating that Title IX
should be regarded as "program specific." In other
words, it would ban sex discrimination only in a specific program (such as math or science) that was
receiving federal funds, not in the institution as a
whole. Since little federal aid goes directly into
sports programs, discriminatory athletic departments
no longer endangered federal aid for a college or

Study the three note cards with material on the 1984 Olympics. Then study the way material from these cards has been integrated into the finished paper. Study the mix of partial quotation, paraphrase, and block quotation in the finished passage.

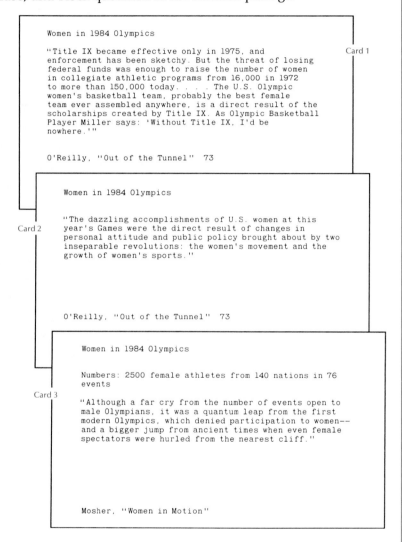

Women in 1984 Olympics

"Title IX became effective only in 1975, and
enforcement has been sketchy. But the threat of losing
federal funds was enough to raise the number of women
in collegiate athletic programs from 16,000 in 1972
to more than 150,000 today. . . . The U.S. Olympic
women's basketball team, probably the best female
team ever assembled anywhere, is a direct result of the
scholarships created by Title IX. As Olympic Basketball
Player Miller says: 'Without Title IX, I'd be
nowhere.'"

O'Reilly, "Out of the Tunnel" 73

Card 1

Women in 1984 Olympics

"The dazzling accomplishments of U.S. women at this
year's Games were the direct result of changes in
personal attitude and public policy brought about by two
inseparable revolutions: the women's movement and the
growth of women's sports."

O'Reilly, "Out of the Tunnel" 73

Card 2

Women in 1984 Olympics

Numbers: 2500 female athletes from 140 nations in 76
events

"Although a far cry from the number of events open to
male Olympians, it was a quantum leap from the first
modern Olympics, which denied participation to women--
and a bigger jump from ancient times when even female
spectators were hurled from the nearest cliff."

Mosher, "Women in Motion"

Card 3

B. M. Gatten 7

quoted key phrases

university as a whole. Nevertheless, according to
Sullivan, "having been forced to beef up women's programs by Title IX," most schools now claimed to be
"morally committed" to parity for women's athletics
(9). Pete Hamill, widely read columnist for The New
York Post and The New York Daily News, said that

*endnote will mention
dissenting view*

Title IX "gave women solid coaching and structured
competition" and that "there now is no going back"
(19).[1]

For many women, the twenty-third Olympic Games
in Los Angeles marked a turning point in the quest
for recognition for female athletes. During the 1984
Olympics, 2500 female athletes from 140 nations competed in 76 events. In the words of Cheryl Mosher,

*block quotation for
striking assessment of key
event*

> Although a far cry from the number of
> events open to male Olympians, it was a
> quantum leap from the first modern Olym-
> pics, which denied participation to women--
> and a bigger jump from ancient times when
> even female spectators were hurled from the
> nearest cliff. (82)

Like other observers, Jane O'Reilly, writing in
Time magazine, saw the "dazzling accomplishments" of
U.S. women at the 1984 Games as the result of the
advances triggered by Title IX. She said that the
U.S. Olympic women's basketball team, which she

B. M. Gatten 8

called "probably the best female team ever assembled
anywhere," was a "direct result" of the scholarships
and the support created by the law ("Out of the Tunnel" 73).

turning point: transition to second major part of the paper

What have the recent advances in women's sports
done for the self-image of women? When the doors to
free participation in sports swing open, so do other
doors, many of them psychological. The grass roots
movement towards greater fitness among women affects
both body and mind. In Marathon Mom, Linda Schreiber
writes about how running helped to increase her
energy and change her outlook, how she experienced
the sharpened physical and mental edge of being in
shape:

excerpted block quotation

> The more I ran, the easier hauling grocer-
> ies and carrying babies became. I found I
> had more pep, needed less sleep. Running
> also seemed to allow me to see things in a
> more mellow perspective....I didn't feel so
> narrow and confined, because my day had at
> least included a run. Somehow I didn't
> feel so "small" and events at home so
> petty. (8)

Beyond the joy of simple fitness, there is for
many the added dimension of testing limits, of having
the opportunity to "push back the envelope," in test

B. M. Gatten 9

pilot jargon. Looking back over the Los Angeles
Olympics, Jane O'Reilly said, "These women tested
their limits, and having a chance to do that is what
sports and feminism are all about" ("Out of the Tunnel" 73). Every athlete has the experience of pushing at the barrier of his or her own limitations, and
many experience the satisfaction felt when the barrier yields to persistent effort. A case in point is
long-distance running for women: Women runners were

extended account of case
in point

always assumed to lack endurance. The 1928 Olympics
were the first games where women were allowed to run
anything longer than a sprint. Eleven women that
year entered an 800-meter race. Officials predicted
disaster and were correct. Five women dropped out,
five collapsed at the finish line, and the strongest
collapsed in the dressing room afterwards. Kaplan
believes that these women failed because they were
expected to fail: "None of them had ever trained for
long distances, and they were psyched out by the
adumbrations of doom and the ambulance waiting at the
finish line" (37).

Ironically, today women are thought to exceed
men in their physical potential for endurance because

endnote will provide
further detail

of a superior ability to metabolize fat.[2] According
to an article in <u>Science Digest</u>, statistical projections based on available sports records show that

Although the author of this paper has mobilized an array of printed sources, she also draws on interviews and informal talks. This material helped her write with greater confidence and a better sense of direction. Here is a more extended selection from one of the interviews:

PREWRITING: INTERVIEW

QUESTION: How long have you been involved with horses?
ANSWER: All my life. My parents owned a small farm with a few horses.

QUESTION: What made you want to compete?
ANSWER: The thrill of showing off a beautiful horse at its best. I also had friends who were involved in showing.

QUESTION: What kind of financial support is available for top-level competing?
ANSWER: The cost depends on where you go for shows. At the lower levels, there is no organization to help pay the bills. The USET (United States Equestrian Team) generally helps pay costs for American riders to attend international competitions, but they can't pay the whole bill.

QUESTION: Do judges accept women riders?
ANSWER: Actually, many of the judges are women themselves and believe that women are better riders. Women can develop the strength needed, and they have the grace needed to ride well. Most men have the strength needed, but it is much more difficult for them to develop grace on horseback.

QUESTION: What explains the large number of women riders now competing at the top level?
ANSWER: Women riders overall are doing much better than in the past. Equestrian competition is one of the few events where men and women compete on an equal basis. Men used to dominate the sport because they were trained in the military and because of the common misconception that the sport was only for men. Now women are taking the top positions in every area. Maybe this will be the sport that proves that women are better than men.

B. M. Gatten 10

"women may equal men in certain events, most notably the marathon, in the next few decades" (Torrey 91).

The experience of overcoming physical and mental barriers in sports is giving many women increased confidence and self-esteem. Women athletes are talking about their efforts and achievements with a newfound pride. In a recent interview, a woman who trains young riders for competition in equestrian events said:

> Equestrian competition is one of the few events in which men and women compete on an equal basis. Men used to dominate the sport because they were trained in the military and because of a common misconception that the sport was only for men. Now women are taking top positions in every area. Maybe this will be one sport where women will prove better than men. (Costello)

This increased sense of self-worth is not limited to sports that require money and leisure and may seem the province of the privileged few. As the director of International Running Circuit, sponsored by Avon Cosmetics, marathon runner Kathrine Switzer has organized races for women from Japan, Brazil, Malaysia, and Thailand, disregarding warnings that

B. M. Gatten 11

women running in the streets would precipitate
chaos. In Sao Paulo, Brazil, 10,000 women ran a
race, 2000 with no shoes. Switzer said afterwards,
"Some had nothing else in their lives, but they took
part and were changed" (qtd. in O'Reilly, "The Year
of Getting Tough" 292).

second publication by same author

Much testimony from women athletes indicates
that self-confidence and determination carry over
from athletics into other areas of life. Sally Voss,
all-American golfer, said that the pressures she
encountered in her work as an anesthesiologist were
easier to deal with because of her experiences in
athletic competition: "Having been exposed to intense
athletic competition, I am better able to assess difficult situations and react in a rational and even
manner." Sally Ride, first American woman in space,
said, "Athletics teaches endurance and the value of
pursuing beyond one's perceived limits to achieve
higher levels of ability" ("A Winning Combination"
1-2).

quotations from a brochure with no author given

turning point: transition to third major part of the paper

The fact that women are participating in sports
in unprecedented numbers is obviously having a strong
impact on women. In turn, what impact, if any, is
this flood of female participants having on sports
themselves? Although the extent of actual change is
difficult to assess, women's athletics is challenging

B. M. Gatten 12

two features of traditional sports: excessive competition and violence. Many women would agree with
Betty Lehan Harragan, a management consultant, that
"women have to learn about competition and developing
a winning attitude" (qtd. in Kaplan, Women in Sports
112). But they would also agree that excessive
emphasis on competition is one of the main things
wrong with sports, leading to such abuses as "the
ridiculous salaries of the pros (and some college
players!), the rah-rah chauvinism, and the corruption

quoted from the preface of
a collection

of recruiting" (Chapin vii-viii).

   Women's sports have traditionally laid stress on
participation. Because athletic programs for women
tended to be recreational and low-budget, the "every-
one-can-play" ethic prevailed. Today, dazzled by the
rewards of increased money and prestige, women's athletics is in danger of losing sight of the ideal of
sport-for-all. Competition systematically narrows
the field of participants to only those who are good
enough to compete. When there are limited recreational facilities or team berths, some get to play
and others become spectators. If the only thing that
counts is being Number One, then only a select few
battle it out while the many watch. Recruiting and
training of top performers become the overriding
priorities.

In the revision of her first draft, the author faced a familiar problem for writers of research papers: In her first draft, she had used an excessive number of block quotations, giving the paper too much of a stitched-together effect. In her revision, she made a special effort to excerpt and integrate quoted material more. Read the third and last major part of the paper, and answer the following questions:

□ Which paragraphs excerpt and integrate material from *several sources*?

□ Where and how does the author use *partial quotations* and sentence-length quotations as part of her running text?

□ Where does she use *block quotations*, and why? Is the more extended quotation justified by an important point, by an eloquent personal statement, or by helpful authentic detail?

□ What is the proportion of quoted or paraphrased material and *interpretation* or discussion by the author?

□ How effective or adequate are the *transitions* that take the reader from paragraph to paragraph?

B. M. Gatten 13

From the beginning of the current expansion of women's sports, there have been voices warning against an imitation of the "male model." George R. LaNoue, in an article in <u>Change</u>, said in 1976:

> Among the leaders of women's athletics there is strong opposition to turning women's sports into an imitation of men's. They do not want to engage in widespread off-campus recruiting. They would prefer to remain teachers instead of becoming win-at-any-cost sports promoters. (30)

one of several related quotations supporting the same point

Sports sociologist Stephen Figler said in <u>Sport and Play in American Life</u> that funding mandated by Title IX was leading to hasty expansion, "fostering the development of the same faulty mechanism that drives men's school athletics" (289). Figler quoted Katherine Ley, a faculty member of the United States Sports Academy as saying, "as much of a boon as equal opportunity legislation has been," it "derailed the early attempts of women to devise an improved athletic model" (285).

Nevertheless, the search for the "improved model" continues, and the rallying cry of "Sport for all!" continues to be heard. Kaplan writes:

> The desire to have sports available to women does not have to translate into programs with the same questionable priorities

B. M. Gatten 14

as the men's, where millions are poured
into money-raising games that few can play
but many watch. It's time to raise a generation of participants, not another generation of fans. (<u>Women in Sports</u> 167)

She commends some of the smaller schools that have
opted for cuts in big-budget sports like football in
favor of more even distribution to sports like volleyball, basketball, and tennis. Figler has suggested the broadening of intercollegiate competition
by the creation of parallel, independent teams for
those not skilled enough to make varsity teams. As
he explained in a recent interview:

*material from telephone
interview*

The element that gives collegiate sport its
excitement is competition between schools--
that's why intramurals don't really fill
the need. A better idea would be a kind of
extramural program in which a team had a
budget, a schedule, and a coach, all funded
by either state money, tuition, student
fees, or some combination. Often P.E.
departments have good former coaches on
their staffs because they didn't like certain aspects of big collegiate sports--
these people would be ideal for a program
of this type.

B. M. Gatten 15

Excessive competition and glory-for-the-few is not the only idea being challenged by the women's sport movement. Another area of traditional athletics to come under attack is the notion that violence is an inescapable element of sport. Traditional male sports often seem motivated by "an inherent aggressiveness in man stemming from the Darwinian struggle for existence," with sports serving "as substitutes for actual fighting, mock struggles that satisfied the urge to conquer" (Nash 181). Some of the most popular men's sports—football, ice hockey, boxing— are extremely violent. Don Atyeo says in <u>Blood and Guts: Violence in Sports</u> about football: "Each year it kills on average twenty-eight players and maims thousands more. It leaves everyone who reaches its higher levels with some form of lasting injury." He quotes a former player for the Los Angeles Rams as saying that people who play for any length of time "carry the scars for the rest of their lives." These may not "be showing on the outside, but they'll have knees that are worn out, shoulders that don't work right, fingers that point in a different direction" (219-20). Part of the code of the male athlete has been that one must take the pain to prove his manliness. As Kathryn Lance says in <u>A Woman's Guide to Spectator Sports</u>, "The idea of playing with pain, of

B. M. Gatten 16

giving everything, including the integrity of one's
body, to the team/club/lodge is so extreme that players will enter a game anesthetized to the point where
they can bear the pain of possibly severe injuries"
(13).

The growth of women's sports, if not eliminating
violence in sport, is at least helping to temper it.
Women's sports are not burdened with the tradition of
violence linked to the idea of sport as a proving
ground for sexual identity. This is not to say that
the risk of pain and injury are not part of the challenge of sports for many women athletes. Ann Roiphe,
reminiscing about field hockey, her favorite game
when a young girl, says:

> I remember a girl named Karen with blood
> pouring down her face and onto a white
> middy blouse and a dark accusing hole where
> her front teeth had been. It is blurred in
> my mind whose stick was responsible, but I
> was close enough to feel guilt and fear and
> the excitement of both those emotions. It
> never occurred to me that a simple child's
> game, a ball playing, might not be worth a
> lifetime of false teeth. (14)

B. M. Gatten 17

Increasingly, women are competing in tests of endurance that were once male-only events. In 1985, Libby
Riddles became the first woman to win the Iditerod, a
1000 mile dogsled race from Anchorage to Nome,
Alaska. Riddles won by driving her dogs through a
howling blizzard that no other contestant would challenge. This race "pits the wits of a cold, sleep-
starved musher against the vagaries of weather,
author not previously   trail, and dogs. More than speed and experience, it
identified   takes audacity" (O'Hara 40).

While women are increasingly facing up to tests
of courage and endurance, at least some men in the
world of sports seem ready to turn away from the
image of the violent, aggressive man as the male
ideal. Former football heroes such as O. J. Simpson
and Al Cowlings are telling youngsters to play tennis
instead of football because tennis will benefit them
longer and because they will not have to spend their
lives suffering from football knees (Schmerler 8).

Women's sports are helping society move away
from the glorification of violence as media time is
increasingly devoted to women's sports like tennis
and golf. Both the airing of women's athletics and
increased participation in sports by women are creating a wider audience of female spectators, which in
turn creates greater demand on the networks for coverage of women's events.

Students often ask: Is there room for *personal opinion* in a research paper? The answer is that the personal conclusions the author draws need to be firmly anchored in the supporting evidence. Looking back over this paper, ask:

☐ What is the balance of personal opinion and supporting evidence in this paper?

☐ Does the writer ever seem to draw hasty conclusions? Does she ever seem opinionated?

☐ How do you react to her conclusions as a reader? To what extent do you agree? Where do you disagree and why?

☐ Who would be the ideal reader for this paper?

B. M. Gatten 18

In conclusion, the struggle for the acceptance
of women's sports is not a battle between men and
women. The real enemies of sport for women are the
same as they are for men: the lethargy of being a
mere passive spectator, the philosophy that winning
is the only thing, and finally the idea of violence

summing up of key points as a normal, inescapable part of sport. What is
needed is a new concept of sport for both men and
women, one that sees the purpose of sport as lifelong
enjoyment and pleasure, increased fitness for life
and its challenges, a feeling of health and well-
being and joy.

Much scholarly writing is loaded down with an impressive array of explanatory notes. However, in a short student-written research paper, the emphasis is on *integrating* essential material in the main body of the paper. Look at the notes on the opposite page. What is their function? Do they seem helpful to the reader?

Note the format: These endnotes are indented (*first* line only). Each note starts with a raised number, followed by a space.

B. M. Gatten 19

endnotes directing reader to additional sources for details or opposing view

Notes

[1] A sobering dissent, chronicling the negative impact of court decisions and institutional backsliding, is G. Ann Uhlir's article on "Athletics and the University: The Post—Woman's Era" in <u>Academe</u> for July—August 1987 (25–29).

[2] A more complete examination of this point can be found in Kaplan's chapter on "Physiology" in her book <u>Women and Sports</u>. Along with the documentation on fat metabolism, she uses medical research to explode a number of other myths about female physiology. <u>Science Digest</u> (Torrey 91) corroborates the research on fat metabolism and explains the use of sports records in making predictions regarding progress in sports.

This list of works cited puts in alphabetical order all sources used by the author. It includes not only books and articles but also such informal sources as personal interviews and a locally published promotional brochure.

Study the entries as *model entries* for your own list of "Works Cited." Note the following especially:

- Note variations from the standard entry for books: book listed under an editor's name, book with subtitle, book with more than one author.
- Note inclusive page numbers for articles in magazines and newspapers. (Note the plus sign for articles continued later in the same issue.)
- Note the treatment of an article in a collection, of the locally published brochure, and of the interviews.

Remember a few basic rules:

- First line of each entry is *not* indented; the remaining lines are.
- Last name of author comes first (only for the first one if there are several coauthors).
- Titles of *whole* publications are underlined (or italicized); titles of parts (articles, poems, short stories) are enclosed in quotation marks.

B. M. Gatten 20

Works Cited

book with subtitle   Atyeo, Don. <u>Blood and Guts: Violence in Sports</u>. New
York: Paddington, 1979.

unsigned article   "Big Ten Begins Women's Program." <u>Coaching Women's
Athletics</u> Oct. 1981: 20.

editor of collection   Chapin, Henry B., ed. <u>Sports in Literature</u>. New
York: David McKay, 1976.

interview   Costello, Arlene. Personal Interview. 6 Jan. 1988.

Figler, Stephen K. <u>Sport and Play in American Life</u>.
Philadelphia: Saunders, 1981.

telephone interview   ---. Telephone Interview. 8 Feb. 1988.

monthly periodical   Hamill, Pete. "Women Athletes: Faster, Higher, Better." <u>Cosmopolitan</u> Nov. 1985: 19+.

inclusive page numbers   Hart, Marie. "Sport: Women Sit in the Back of the
Bus." <u>Psychology Today</u> Oct. 1971: 64-66.

monthly periodical   Kaplan, Janice. "Politics of Sports." <u>Vogue</u> July
1984: 219+.

same author   ---. <u>Women and Sports</u>. New York: Viking, 1979.

standard entry for book   Lance, Kathryn. <u>A Woman's Guide to Spectator Sports</u>.
New York: A & W Publishers, 1980.

article with subtitle   LaNoue, George R. "Athletics and Equality: How to
Comply with Title IX Without Tearing Down the
Stadium." <u>Change</u> Nov. 1976: 27-30+.

Mosher, Cheryl. "Women in Motion." <u>Women's Sport
and Fitness</u> May 1985: 82.

B. M. Gatten 21

article in a collection Nash, Roderick. "Heroes." <u>American Oblique: Writing About the American Experience</u>. Ed. Joseph F. Trimmer and Robert R. Kettler. Boston: Houghton, 1976. 180–88.

newspaper article O'Hara, Doug. "Libby Riddles Beat a Blizzard to Become Top Musher." <u>Christian Science Monitor</u> 28 Mar. 1985: 1+.

weekly periodical O'Reilly, Jane. "Out of the Tunnel into History." <u>Time</u> 20 Aug. 1984: 73.

same author ---. "The Year of Getting Tough." <u>Vogue</u> Nov. 1984: 290–92.

two authors Roiphe, Ann. Interview <u>Ms.</u> June 1982: 14.

Schreiber, Linda and JoAnne Stang. <u>Marathon Mom</u>. Boston: Houghton 1980.

monthly periodicals Schmerler, Cindy. "Splitting Ends." <u>World Tennis</u> May 1985: 8.

Sherman, William. "The World of Tennis's Top Women." <u>Tennis News</u> May 1983: 194–97+.

weekly periodical Sullivan, Robert. "A Law That Needs New Muscle." <u>Sports Illustrated</u> 4 Mar. 1985: 9.

plus sign for nonconsecutive page Torrey, Lee. "How Science Creates Winners." <u>Science Digest</u> Aug. 1984: 33–37+.

Uhlir, G. Ann. "Athletics and the University: The Post-Woman's Era." <u>Academe</u> July–Aug. 1987: 25–29.

Ullyot, Joan. "Forcing the Pace." <u>Runner's World</u> Jan. 1986: 43–51.

B. M. Gatten 22

local publication   "A Winning Combination." Cardinal Club Brochure.
                Stanford CA: Stanford U Dept. of Athletics,
                1986.

THE WRITING WORKSHOP

The Reader's Turn

As with other kinds of writing, the test of a research paper ultimately is how it reads. Prepare copies of an intermediate draft or of your final paper to distribute to members of a small group. Have them provide a running commentary as they read—marginal glosses of the kind editors and reviewers often provide for professional writers. Ask your peers to use the margin for the queries, comments, endorsements, rebuttals, and words of praise (or exasperation) that run through a responsive reader's mind. In a group session, discuss what you have learned from your readers' reactions. Do your readers diverge widely in their responses? Is there substantial agreement on any points? Has the experience made you more conscious of your audience?

ALTERNATE STYLES: APA

Styles of documentation vary for different areas of the curriculum. Not only the nature of research but also the expected ways of reporting the results differ from one specialized field to another. Many publications in the social sciences follow the APA style of documentation, outlined in the publication manual of the American Psychological Association. You will encounter this style (with some variations) in periodicals in areas like psychology, linguistics, or education.

For identification of sources in the text of a paper, this style uses the **author-and-date** method. The date of publication appears with the parenthetical page reference: (Garcia, 1985, p. 103), or (1985, p. 103) if the author has been named in your text. Often, the APA style identifies an authority and the publication date of research *without* a page reference—with interested readers expected to familiarize themselves with the relevant research and consider its findings in context: (Garcia, 1985).

Parenthetical Identification

Study the following possibilities. Note use of commas, of *p.* or *pp.* for "page" or "pages," of the symbol *&* for *and*, and of similar distinctive features.

1. *Author and Date Only:*

   The term <u>anorexia nervosa</u> stands for a condition of emaciation resulting from self-inflicted starvation (Huebner, 1982).

2. *Date Only—* author's name in your own text:

   As defined by Huebner, <u>anorexia nervosa</u> is a condition of emaciation resulting from self-inflicted starvation (1982).

3. *Page Reference—* for direct quotation or specific reference:

   Anorexia nervosa is "not really true loss of appetite" but "a condition of emaciation resulting from self-inflicted starvation" (Huebner, 1982, p. 143).

4. *Work by Several Authors—*use *et al.* only in second or later reference: (Filmore et al., 1984).

   Much advertising leads young women to believe that weight control equals beauty and success (Filmore, Suarez, & Thomas, 1984, p. 128).

5. *Same Author—*for several publications in same year, use *a, b, c,* and so on, in order of publication:

   Gamarken has conducted several similar experiments (1978, 1981a, 1981b).

6. *Reference to Several Sources—*list in alphabetical order, divided by semicolons:

   Statistical estimates concerning the occurrence of the condition have varied widely (Gutierrez & Piso, 1982; Huffman, 1981).

7. *Unknown or Unlisted Author—*identify source by shortened title:

   The influence of the media is pervasive and more often than not harmful ("Cultural Expectations," 1985).

List of References   Use the heading "References" for your final alphabetical listing of works cited or consulted. The APA style provides essentially the same bibliographical information as the MLA style. However, note the author-and-date sequence at the beginning of the entry. Watch for differences in the use of capitals, quotation marks, parentheses, and the like. (The following entries are adapted from *Researching and Writing: An Interdisciplinary Approach*, by Christine A. Hult.)

1. *Book with Single Author*   Use initial instead of author's first name. Capitalize only the first word of title or subtitle (but capitalize proper names that are part of a title as you would in ordinary prose).

   Bruch, H. (1973). Eating disorders: Obesity, anorexia nervosa, and the person within. New York: Basic Books.

2. *Book with Two or More Authors*   Put last name first for each of several authors. Use the symbol & (ampersand) instead of the word *and*.

   Minuchin, S., Rosman, B., & Baker, L. (1978). Psychosomatic families: Anorexia nervosa in context. Mass: Harvard U. Press.

3. *Magazine or Newspaper Article*   Do not put titles of articles in quotation marks; do not use italics (or underlining). If there is no volume number, use *p.* or *pp.* for "page" or "pages." If an article is concluded later in the issue, use a semicolon between the two sets of page numbers.

   Miller, G. (1969, December). On turning psychology over to the unwashed. Psychology Today, pp. 53–54; 66–74.

4. *Article with Volume Number*   Underline (italicize) the volume number for a periodical, with inclusive page numbers following after a comma: *6, 152–69.* If the number of the issue is needed, put it in parentheses between the volume number and the page numbers: *6(3), 152–69.*

   Holmi, K. (1978). Anorexia nervosa: Recent investigations. Annual Review of Medicine, 29, 137–48.

   Steinhausen, H. & Glenville, K. (1983). Follow-up studies of anorexia nervosa: A review of research findings. Psychological Medicine: Abstracts in English, 13(2), 239–45.

5. *Unsigned Magazine or Newspaper Article* Alphabetize by the first word of the title, not counting *The, A,* or *An.*

> The blood business. (1972, September 11). <u>Time</u>, pp. 47–
> 48.

6. *Edited Book or New Edition* Put abbreviation for "editor" (*Ed.* or *Eds.*) or for number of edition in parentheses.

> Hartman, F. (Ed.). (1973). <u>World in crisis: Readings in</u>
> <u>international relations</u> (4th ed.). New York:
> Macmillan.

7. *Several Works by Same Author* Repeat the author's name with each title; put works in chronological order.

> Bruch, H. (1973). <u>Eating disorders: Obesity, anorexia</u>
> <u>nervosa, and the person within</u>. New York: Basic
> Books.
> Bruch, H. (1978). <u>The golden cage: The enigma of anorexia</u>
> <u>nervosa</u>. Mass: Harvard U. Press.

8. *Part of a Collection* Reverse initial and last name only for author or editor of the part, not of the collection.

> Cherns, A. (1982). Social research and its diffusion. In
> B. Appleby (Ed.), <u>Papers on social science</u>
> <u>utilisation</u>. Loughborough U. of Technology: Centre
> for Utilisation of Social Science Research.

9. *Encyclopedia Entry* If the author of an entry is identified, include the name.

> Anorexia nervosa. (1978). <u>Encyclopedia of Human Behavior</u>.

10. *Nonprint Media*

> Maas, J. B. (Producer), & Gluck, D. H. (Director). (1979).
> <u>Deeper into hypnosis</u> [Film]. Englewood Cliffs, NJ:
> Prentice–Hall.
> Clark, K. B. (Speaker). (1976). <u>Problems of freedom and</u>
> <u>behavior modification</u> (Cassette Recording No. 7612).
> Washington, DC: American Psychological Association.

Brewer, J. (1979, October). <u>Energy, information, and the control of heart rate</u>. Paper presented at the Society for Psychophysiological Research, Cincinnati, OH.

<u>Problems of Freedom</u>. (1982, May 21). New York: NBC-TV.

Hult, C. (1984, March). [Interview with Dr. Lauro Cavazos, President, Texas Tech University].

Remember: Part of your job as a newcomer in a field of study or a line of work is to learn to write to an established format and to the specifications that are part of the conventions of your chosen field. Often the people in the field will judge how serious you are about becoming one of theirs by your willingness to master exact details—the little things that count. Note the following example of a professional research paper in the social sciences.

8

<u>Society's Effect upon the Rise of Anorexia Victims</u>

A second direct cause of anorexia is the expectation society has regarding beauty. Over the years,
society's ideal of a beautiful body has changed. The
current look is angular and lean. Starved, emaciated
models portray this image in the media, and it is
promoted through diet pills, drinks, foods, weight-
first reference loss centers, and buldge-hiding clothes (Garfinkle,
lists all four authors Garner, Schwartz, & Thompson, 1980). Adolescents,
vulnerable to peer pressure, see these norms and
strive to conform. The male is exposed to ideal
beauty also, through such models as Miss America or
<u>Playboy</u> centerfolds appearing on television and in
magazines. These models tend to exaggerate parts of
the body (DeRosis, 1979). A number of researchers
have linked these sociocultural pressures to the
apparent increase of anorexia victims. Dieting is a
"sociocultural epidemic" and fashion's ideal may
indirectly affect adolescent women who eventually
believe that weight control is equal to self-control
second reference and will surely lead to beauty and success (Garfin-
uses et al. kle, et al., 1980).

<u>Survey</u>

In order to discover whether or not the family
and cultural pressures that lead to anorexia in young

19

THE CRITICAL PAPER

Writing About Literature

The poet, lacking the impediment of speech with which the rest of us are afflicted, gazes, records, diagnoses, and prophecies.   Richard Selzer

Great literature, if we read it well, opens us up to the world. It makes us more sensitive to it, as if we acquired eyes that could see through things and ears that could hear smaller sounds.   Donald Hall

A book is like a garden carried in the pocket.
Chinese proverb

WRITING AND THE IMAGINATION "This morning," the poet Javier Gálvez says, "the sun broke / my window / and came in laughing." Poets and storytellers often seem to write with a heightened sense of awareness, with a special intensity—"in a fine frenzy," in Shakespeare's words. They seem to take in more of life and respond to it more fully than others do. Samuel Taylor Coleridge, the English Romantic poet, said that imaginative literature brings "the whole soul" of the reader into activity. F. Scott Fitzgerald, the American novelist, said that authors mostly draw on two or three great moving experiences in their lives—"experiences so great and moving that it doesn't seem at the time that anyone else has been caught up and pounded and dazzled and astonished and beaten and broken and rescued and illuminated and rewarded and humbled in just that way ever before." In the mirror of imaginative literature, joy and grief, love and friendship, often seem to become more focused and intense than in real life, revealing to us their true meaning.

The Purpose of Critical Writing

When we write about imaginative literature, we try to explain to ourselves and to others why it moved us, how it transformed our perspective, or how it changed our thinking. Literature opens windows for us on new worlds of thought and feeling. Writing about it gives us a chance to relive the experience, to come to terms with it, and to compare our reactions with those of others. Three major purposes, alone or in combination, help give shape and direction to critical writing about literature:

APPRECIATION   Contrary to a common misunderstanding, the critic's basic motive is not to find fault but to help others respond to what an author has to offer. Often a good critic writes as an advocate, a missionary, trying to show how an imaginary ideal reader would respond to the poem, the story, or the play. You are likely to write with conviction when you write to share your enthusiasm for a writer not widely enough known or not always understood.

INTERPRETATION   The first motive of critical writing often shades over into the second. To make readers appreciate a work we admire, we find ourselves explaining how it works, what it says. What does Emily Dickinson mean when she says, "Oh Sacrament of summer days, / Oh Last Communion in the Haze"? What does the great white whale symbolize in Herman Melville's *Moby Dick*; what is the meaning of the fatal encounter between the whale and the obsessed Captain Ahab who is his pursuer? At the end of his story "The Open Boat," Stephen Crane says that the survivors of the harrowing encounter with the implacable sea could now be "interpreters." Good criticism will not reduce a story or a play to a simple moral for better living, but it will help us interpret the images and events the author has created for the mind's eye.

EVALUATION   A critic's generous enthusiasm for what is excellent is often matched by exasperation with what is shoddy or second-rate. We may criticize a work because it caters to prejudice, paints a distorted picture of reality, or provides a quick fix of false hopes. When we write to evaluate, we do not simply register personal likes and dislikes; we set up criteria (spelled out or implied) that the reader can ponder, question, or accept.

The Dimensions of Literature

As you respond to imaginative literature, you have to remember that a poem or a story is not just information to be stored and retrieved. It presents to us images, actions, events, and feelings. To do it justice, we have to respond to dimensions that make imaginative literature more than a statement of dry facts or an abstract summing up of ideas. Look at the following short poem as an example. As you read it, ask yourself, "What does it make me see? How does it take shape? What does it make me feel? What does it make me think?"

Jon Swan
THE OPENING

Seed said to flower:
   You are too rich and wide.
   You spend too soon and loosely
   That grave and spacious beauty
   I keep secret, inside.
   You will die of your pride.

Flower said to seed:
   Each opens, gladly
   Or in defeat. Clenched, close,
   You hold a hidden rose
   That will break you to be
   Free of your dark modesty.

What does such a poem do? What does it do that a short story, a play, or a novel does on a larger scale, and with somewhat different means? First, the poem makes us participate in experience: It makes us see and hear and feel. A miniature drama is acted out on the small stage set by the poem. We hear voices of warning and of threat ("You spend too soon and loosely"; ". . . a hidden rose that will break you"). There is a contest, a conflict. We are made to feel the apprehension that keeps us from opening up to life. But we are also made to feel the restrictions that hem us in.

Second, the poem imposes a pattern upon experience. The pendulum swings one way: "Seed said to flower . . ." Then it swings back the other way: "Flower said to seed . . ." A note is struck and then echoed: "rich—wide—spend—soon—loosely—spacious—free." And again: "secret—clenched—close—hidden—dark." It is as if a network of closely related terms held the poem together. We take pleasure in seeing things fall into place. The poem has **form**; it has structure.

Third, the poem has meaning. It is not really about flowers but about people. The protected seed and the open, lavish flower are **symbolic**. Two views of the world are in contention, and the poem seems weighted in direction of the second, which has the last word. We are made to fear what is stifling, and we are encouraged to break out.

Questions for Discussion What expectations do you bring to a poem? Did this poem live up to them? Why or why not?

Guidelines for Critical Writing How do you translate your response to a piece of literature into writing that will take your reader into a poem, story, or play? Consider the following guidelines:

☐ *Show evidence of close, careful reading.* Whether your readers agree with you or not, they should feel: "This person has read the text." No matter how you argue or classify, your paper should always come back to the actual poem or story. Talk in detail about images, characters, and events. Make ample use of striking, revealing quotations. The following excerpt from a student paper brings a character from a play to life by using numerous short quotations from the play itself:

Lady Macbeth

Lady Macbeth has long been recognized as the prime mover of her husband's actions. Without her prompting, Duncan might have enjoyed ripe old age. But in order to aid her husband, she must step out of the traditional feminine role that will not permit a woman the attributes necessary for such grisly deeds: fortitude, purposefulness, and a strong stomach. Therefore, she must metamorphosize into a male. She is hardly on stage when she beseeches the darker spirits to "unsex me here / And fill me . . . top full of direst cruelty . . . And take my milk for gall" (*Macbeth*, I.v.).

There are many passages illustrating the exchange of sex roles between this murderous couple. The recurrence of milk-and-babe imagery is quite striking: Macbeth is "too full o' the milk of human kindness" (I.v.) to murder for a throne. Pity "like a new-born babe" (I.vii.) would stay his hand. On the other hand, his wife, to underscore her resoluteness, vows she would have unhesitatingly snatched the "babe that milks me" (I.vii.) from her breast and "dash'd the brains out, had I sworn as you / Have done to this." She is astonishingly capable and stout-hearted. As her husband notes, "her undaunted mettle should compose / Nothing but males" (I.vii.).

☐ *Respond fully to the language of literature.* Poets and writers of fiction use the same language we all use, but they use more of it, and they use it in more meaningful, imaginative ways. The language of poets and other imaginative writers is rich in shades of meaning, in overtones and associations. It is often figurative rather than literal, using imaginative comparisons that are often bold and unexpected.

Sometimes, a poet will signal the comparison by a word such as *like* or *as*. We then call the comparison a **simile**: "My love is *like a red, red rose*." But more often a poet will use a **metaphor**—an *implied* comparison that treats something as if it actually were the thing to which it is compared: "A *hard tin bird* was my lover." Metaphors often call up a vivid, striking image in the mind's eye. They bring into play attitudes and emotions. Hamlet says, "What should such fellows as I do crawling between earth and heaven?" The word *crawling*, rather than make us imagine human beings who stride or walk proudly, makes us visualize a worm or an insect; it strongly projects a feeling of self-loathing and disgust. The meaning of the words themselves may be enhanced or modified by sound effects, such as the plodding repetition in a line like "Generations *have trod, have trod, have trod.*"

☐ *Respond to the overall pattern of a poem, a story, or a play.* Take in the way a piece of literature develops. A work of literature is not something static and finished that we take in all at one time. A poem, for instance, may move from point to counterpoint, from question to answer, or from a familiar comfortable cliché to a striking, original insight. In the following passage, a student traces a movement from point to counterpoint that helps organize a poem:

> In several of these poems, the poet shows the ironic contrast between illusion and reality, between an idealized view and the truth of the matter. In "Flight Handbook," the man sitting next to the poet on the bus "dreams of birdlike mannerisms"; he wants to fly through the air free from the everyday details that weigh us down. But the poet brings this dreaming back down to earth when he ignores the fellow passenger's thoughts and instead stares at "one of the largest thumbnails he has ever seen." Instead of being the graceful, perfect, soaring bird, this man is huge and clumsy and earthbound.

Instead of delivering a ready-made message, a play will often act out a central **conflict**. A strong lead character, or protagonist, is challenged by a formidable adversary, or antagonist. Familiar ideals or beliefs are challenged by powerful doubts. A major character is torn by divided loyalties or conflicting motives. In a truly dramatic play, the issue is in suspense; we live through what happens as the conflict moves toward its resolution.

Questions for Discussion Do you remember a play with a strong central conflict? Was it a conflict between two powerful personalities? opposed ideas? conflicting motives?

☐ *Go beyond a mere plot summary.* A weak critical paper may merely summarize the plot of a story, a play, or a novel. The writer may simply follow the action of a novel from chapter to chapter, or the action of a play from act to act and from scene to scene. The paper tells us what happens but not why it happened or what it means. We get the dry bones of a story.

It is true that sometimes you do well to sum up what actually takes place—to refresh the reader's memory or to acquaint readers with something they have not read. You may want to clarify the major outlines of the action if a plot moves through various twists and turns. However, to help your readers understand a work, you often have to depart from mere chronological order in order to develop one major strand or one major theme. For instance, to follow up a central issue in a play, you may

THE WRITING WORKSHOP

The Poem and Its Audience

When we look for guidance as readers of literature, we encounter at least two schools of thought. One school wants us to think of the poem or story as a finished artifact (like a painting or sculpture) that is basically the same for all competent readers. We should concentrate on not missing the clues provided by the author, on not missing what the poet has put into the poem. The second school wants us to recognize the strong personal element in our encounter with imaginative literature. Each reader brings to the poem his or her own expectations and makes sense of it in a highly personal way. The poem provides the stimulus for a personal experience conditioned in large part by the reader's own world of thought and feeling. This is why some poems that powerfully affect us may move others not at all.

Work with a group to organize an experiment in audience response. Have the group select a twentieth-century poem. Have all members of the group record their interpretation of and reaction to the poem. Pool and discuss the responses. What is the range of reactions? What agreement is there on how the poem works or what it says? Are there cases of important clues missed or plain misreading? What are strong personal elements in the readers' responses?

have to bring together what a key character says on the same subject in different scenes. To help us understand Shakespeare's *Macbeth*, you may want to bring together from different parts of the play quotations to show he is "too full of the milk of human kindness." You will then present the references that mirror the "doubts and fears" that make him a *reluctant* murderer, an assassin with a conscience: "Is this a dagger which I see before me?" "Will all great Neptune's ocean wash this blood / Clean from my hand?" ". . . these terrible dreams that shake us nightly . . ." "O full of scorpions is my mind."

☐ *Support your judgments.* Defend your likes and dislikes. Remember that our reaction to a work of literature is very personal. Something may disturb us profoundly but leave other people cold. Something may shock us but strike others as ordinary. To make a reader understand our reactions, we try to explain how we feel, and why. If we use terms like *sentimental* or *escapist*, we do not just use them as labels to paste on what we dislike. We try to explain and justify the standards we apply.

EXERCISE 1 *Reading a Poem*

A. Write about the following poem. What does it say? What does it mean? How do you react?

May Swenson
QUESTION

> Body my house
> my horse my hound
> What will I do
> When you are fallen
>
> Where will I sleep
> How will I ride
> What will I hunt
>
> Where can I go without my mount
> all eager and quick
> How will I know
> in thicket ahead
> is danger or treasure
> when Body my good
> bright dog is dead
>
> How will it be
> to lie in the sky
> without roof or door
> and wind for an eye
>
> with cloud for shift
> how will I hide?

B. How good a reader is the student who wrote the following response to Swenson's poem? Does she notice things you overlooked? Does she overlook things you noticed? How does her overall response compare with yours?

> In simple, almost childlike terms, the poem asks the age-old question: "What will happen to me when I die?" Swenson explores what the body represents to the soul of the individual. She skips over the arguments of whether people have souls that are separate from the body and deals instead with the dilemma of the separation of body and soul. The body's functions for the soul are seen as protective: the house with the roof to keep away the elements and a door to allow free movement in or out, the dog who warns of the thicket ahead, and the clothing (shift) which conceals flaws, provides warmth, and also wards off the weather. The body is also a "mount" that produces excitement for the soul, carrying it to places unimagined, to hunts with

unknown outcomes, to treasures undiscovered. Swenson poses the question of what the soul will do without the protection and excitement that the body now provides, though it will soon "fall." Swenson seems to address a very serious concern for all people in a very light way. The poem forces us as readers to acknowledge the question of death, but the light tone removes some of the fear and intense morbidity usually surrounding it.

EXERCISE 2   *Reading a Story*

The following is the opening of one of the best-known American short stories—Stephen Crane's "The Open Boat," first published in 1897. How does the story take shape for you as a reader? How does the author create the world of his story for you? Look at the following familiar dimensions of a story:

☐ *Setting*: Where are we? How does the author create the setting for us? What are striking details? What is the prevailing *mood*, and how does the author create it?

☐ *Character*: Who are the people in the story? What is our first impression of them, and how is it created? What are some striking or revealing details? How do the snatches of *dialogue* help shape our impression of the characters?

☐ *Point of View*: From what perspective or vantage point does the author write about the characters or the events of the story? How much of the passage is a reporting of the "facts"? How much is comment or discussion by the "intruding" narrator?

☐ *Symbol*: To judge from this passage, what might be the symbolic meaning of the sea, the boat, and the ship?

☐ *Tone and Style*: Are the words and sentences bookish or familiar, dignified or slangy? Is the story going to be sentimental, emotional, hard-boiled, low-key, melodramatic? How can you tell?

☐ *Plot*: There is little action in this opening passage of the story. What kind of action does this introduction make you expect—fantastic adventure? miraculous rescue? a grim ordeal? paranoia and cannibalism? On what do you base your guess?

None of them knew the color of the sky. Their eyes glanced level, and were fastened upon the waves that swept toward them. These waves were of the hue of slate, save for the tops, which were of foaming white, and all of the men knew the colors of the sea. The horizon narrowed and widened, and dipped and rose, and at all times its edge was jagged with waves that seemed thrust up in points like rocks.

Many a man ought to have a bathtub larger than the boat which here rode upon the sea. These waves were most wrongfully and barbarously abrupt and tall, and each froth-top was a problem in small-boat navigation.

The cook squatted in the bottom, and looked with both eyes at the six inches of gunwale which separated him from the ocean. His sleeves were rolled over his fat forearms, and the two flaps of his unbuttoned vest dangled as he bent to bail out the boat. Often he said, "Gawd! that was a narrow clip." As he remarked it he invariably gazed eastward over the broken sea.

The oiler, steering with one of the two oars in the boat, sometimes raised himself suddenly to keep clear of water that swirled in over the stern. It was a thin little oar, and it seemed often ready to snap.

The correspondent, pulling at the other oar, watched the waves and wondered why he was there.

The injured captain, lying in the bow, was at this time buried in that profound dejection and indifference which comes, temporarily at least, to even the bravest and most enduring when, willy-nilly, the firm fails, the army loses, the ship goes down. The mind of the master of a vessel is rooted deep in the timbers of her, though he command for a day or a decade; and this captain had on him the stern impression of a scene in the greys of dawn of seven turned faces, and later a stump of a topmast with a white ball on it, that slashed to and fro at the waves, went low and lower, and down. Thereafter, there was something strange in his voice. Although steady, it was deep with mourning, and of a quality beyond oration or tears.

"Keep 'er a little more south, Billie," said he.

"A little more south, sir," said the oiler in the stern.

EXERCISE 3   *Reading a Play*

A playwright often uses the opening scene or scenes to introduce the characters and create a dramatic situation—setting up the tensions or conflicts that will set the plot in motion. Read the opening scene or scenes of a play often included in literature anthologies for college students, such as Tennessee Williams' *The Glass Menagerie*, Henrik Ibsen's *A Doll's House*, Arthur Miller's *Death of a Salesman*, or Lorraine Hansberry's *Raisin in the Sun*. Write a passage in which you tell your readers everything you learned from this opening part of the play. What kind of people does the playwright present? What is their background; what seem to be major concerns or expectations? What possible tensions or conflicts is the playwright setting up?

FOCUSING A CRITICAL PAPER

Just as the drama of life does not neatly divide into acts and scenes, so literature does not neatly come apart into elements that we can analyze separately, forgetting their part in the larger organic whole. Nevertheless, we can sharpen our understanding of the whole by focusing our attention in turn on different dimensions of the reader's task, always remembering that the elephant's leg (which is very much like the trunk of a tree) and the elephant's trunk (which is very much like a snake) are both part of a larger living elephant. When we focus our discussion of a work on one of the familiar **elements of literature**—image, character, symbol, conflict, theme—we concentrate on one major question we can ask about what and how a work means.

Interpreting a Poem

In a short poem, the poet says "much in little." The poem has a richer texture than everyday language; to understand it, we have to listen for the full implications of a word, a phrase, or a figure of speech. We have to look for how a pattern takes shape—how different images or references reinforce each other, or how they are played off against each other. A good poem is often full of concentrated meaning; it deserves careful, patient reading of and between the lines.

The following student paper is based on a careful reading of two poems on the same subject. Study the **comparison and contrast** the writer has worked out, tracing the common theme and stressing one important difference.

| WRITING SAMPLE: INTERPRETING POETRY |

Today We Have Naming of Parts

overview   After the disillusioning experience of World War II, Henry Reed in "Naming of Parts" and Richard Eberhart in "The Fury of Aerial Bombardment" condemn and reject the horror of war. Both poems condemn our failure to see war as it is, attack our indifference, and reflect postwar anti-war feeling. We shall see that Eberhart's poem takes the attack on indifference one step further than Reed's poem does.

first poem   Henry Reed's "Naming of Parts" satirically attacks the callousness of the military. By using impersonal, neutral words and phrases ("Today we have naming of parts. / Yesterday we had daily cleaning"), the speaker satirizes how precise and impersonal these lessons are. The trainee learns a process, without being taught or made aware how terrible and ugly practicing that process is. References to "the lower sling swivel," "the upper sling swivel," and the "slings" describe machinery. Such references to mechanical parts evoke neutral or even positive feelings, since most machines are used for the good of humanity. This technical language conceals the horror of using this particular machinery. Saying that "you can do it quite easy / If you have any strength in your thumb" obscures the possibility that it might be difficult emotionally to gun down a fellow human being.

Reed uses a comparison to nature at the end of each stanza. Jumping from the mechanics of the gun to the beauty of the garden in consecutive sentences presents a contrast between the gun and the flower, the one a symbol of death and the other a symbol of life. The references in the first two stanzas stress the innocence of nature. The line "Japonica glistens like coral in all of the neighboring gardens" evokes an image of serenity and peace. The branches "with their silent and eloquent gestures" paint another image of bliss. The sterile descriptions of the gun and the beautiful descriptions of nature proceed in a point-counterpoint fashion.

second poem (similarities)   Richard Eberhart's "The Fury of Aerial Bombardment" shares the theme of "Naming of Parts" in that both poems attack indifference to violence and suffering. By saying that "History, even, does not know what is meant," the poet seems to lament that even painful experience does not teach us to prevent the senselessness of war. We are "no farther advanced," making the poet ask: "Was man made stupid?" Here again, as in Reed's poem, technical, impersonal references to the "belt feed lever" and the "belt holding pawl" imply a criticism of the callousness with which people handle the subject of war. A lesson about a belt feed lever might be more instructive if the part were named the genocide lever, for instance.

(difference)   However, "The Fury of Aerial Bombardment" contrasts with "Naming of Parts" because Eberhart goes beyond attacking human indifference by attacking divine indifference to the horror of war. The poet questions why God has not intervened to stop the aerial bombardment. The answer, that "the infinite spaces / Are still silent," is a criticism of God's looking passively upon "shock-pried faces." There are the faces of the people who have witnessed the horrors of the bombing but to whom God offers no respite. The poet seems to expect a thinking, feeling entity to intervene, but no such intervention takes place. Men still kill with "multitudinous will." In the third stanza, the poet asks: "Is God by definition indifferent, beyond us all?"

relevance for the modern reader   Both of these poems were written about forty years ago, yet their relevance remains undiminished today. In an age when we read daily of war and death, indifference is commonplace. The way in which a news reporter casually reads death tolls from Beirut is reminiscent of the cold, sterile wording of "Naming of Parts." The casual and callous projections of the cost in human lives of "winning" a nuclear war are another example of what is under attack in these poems. And people who ponder such atrocities as Auschwitz and Hiroshima have cause to question divine indifference, for the earth is long on suffering.

Questions for Discussion Does the student writer provide enough evidence from the poems to prove his points? Do you make a good audience for this paper? Why or why not?

Studying a Character

Often, a critical paper focuses on one major **character** in a story or in a play. The writer tries to find a clue to how the character thinks and acts, a pattern reflected in different actions and events. Or the writer may focus on the character's conflicting motives or divided loyalties. A paper of this kind makes you bring together from *different* parts of a story or play the evidence that helps you understand a fictional person. That evidence may be of different kinds. In the traditional novel of the type Charles Dickens and George Eliot wrote, the **omniscient**, or "all-knowing," author may tell us what the characters think as well as what they say and do. In later fiction, like that of Henry James or William Faulkner, we may see a character only through the eyes of an outside **reflector**. We may have to infer thoughts and motives on the basis of puzzling or contradictory behavior. In a Shakespeare play, we soon learn to listen not only to what a character says but also to what *other* people say about the character.

The following first impressions of the central character in a short story by Joyce Carol Oates could be developed into a more detailed paper:

PREWRITING: PORTRAIT OF A CHARACTER

Connie

Oates frequently seems to present the female protagonist in her short stories as a stereotypical female "victim." This victim inspires no real sympathy, and remains, like most of the Oates characters, somehow bloodless despite the suggested and overt violent experiences, the violations and self-degradation. Case in point is the story "Where Are You Going, Where Have You Been" with the protagonist, 15-year old Connie, filling all the stereotypical requirements: (1) the value placed on female physical appearance—the necessity for the female object to be "pretty," while little else is required, and (2) the necessity for this female object to have herself (imagined self) defined by the man as chosen "love object."

Connie, straining at her estrogen level, is "pretty," languid, passive, bored, and probably lazy. The mother is both suspicious of, and in awe of, her youth and beauty. The daughter's big time consists of wandering around the shopping plaza, hanging about at the local hangout, the drive-in, exhibiting herself, boy-watching, looking for half-admitted means to realize her fantasies. Connie, stylized all the way from her ballerina slippers (50s I think) to her two laughs ("cynical and drawling at home . . . but high-pitched and nervous anywhere else"), is "dazed by dreams" about the boys and "finding them dissolved into a single face that was not even a single face but an idea, a feeling, mixed up with the urgent, insistent pounding of the music."

Tracing the Central Symbol   A critical paper may trace the role of a **symbol** that is central to a work as a whole. Symbols are objects that have a meaning beyond themselves. Conventional symbols include the flag, the cross, the dove of peace, and the laurel wreath of fame. In a poem, a story, or a play, we become aware of symbolic meanings when an object appears at crucial turns of events or becomes part of a pattern.

Examining a central symbol makes us look at a poem, short story, or play as a whole. The last stanza of Robert Frost's "Stopping by Woods on a Snowy Evening" reads as follows:

> The woods are lovely, dark and deep.
> But I have promises to keep,
> And miles to go before I sleep,
> And miles to go before I sleep.

Are the dark, lovely woods a symbol of restful, peaceful death? Such a symbolic reading is supported by many details earlier in the poem. The woods are dark and filling up with snow—and both darkness and snow are hostile to ordinary purposeful activity, to ordinary life. The traveler has stopped, "without a farmhouse near," between "the woods and frozen lake"—far from a village or other center of human activity. His horse acts as if stopping there "is some mistake," since in ordinary life people are usually "getting somewhere." The traveler has to choose between "promises" that keep him going into the future and the "easy wind" and "downy flake" that suggest rest, sleep. Though the poet does not spell out the symbolic meaning of the dark woods, they appear throughout the poem as the opposite of life and of going on into the future.

Tracing the Theme   A critical paper may focus on the underlying theme that gives unity to a work as a whole. When we state the **theme** of a poem, short story, or play, we try to sum up a key idea that helps give it shape and direction. A true theme is not simply a "lesson for today." It may be nowhere directly stated but may gradually become clear as we think about the whole poem, story, or play.

The following paper makes us see how the images, the settings, the characters, and the events all relate to a unifying central issue:

WRITING SAMPLE: TRACING THE THEME

Hemingway and the World of Illusion

Much of Hemingway's work concerns our struggle to cope in a world that is painful when stripped of illusions. His short story, "In Another Country," drawing on the author's own experiences, centers on wounded soldiers in Italy in World War I. In the story, people use different devices or contrivances to give themselves the illusion of physical and psychological well-being. These illusions are created so that no one will have to face squarely the realities of deterioration and death. The author makes us see our human need for illusion by contrasts in images, settings, and characters.

thesis and *preview*

The opening paragraphs of the story present several such contrasts. The story takes place in Milan in Italy during World War I. It is fall, it is cold, and "dark comes

contrasted images

early." *War*, *fall*, *dark*, and *cold* are words that suggest death or the ceasing of activity. Contrasted with these images are electric lights that come on at dark to shed light on the streets and shops. Light is a life image. Electric lights resurrect the cold, dark, dead world, making it appear beautiful and pleasant. The artificial light softens the reality that without these human contrivances the world is a cold, dark place where people deteriorate and die.

We soon encounter another death image: Hanging outside the shops are various kinds of game. Even if the snow picturesquely powders the fur of the dead foxes and even if the wind stirs the feathers of the birds, the fact remains that the animals are dead. "The deer hung stiff and heavy and empty" is a terse, blunt description of death. However, in the next paragraph, the men choose to get to the hospital by walking over a bridge where a woman sells roasted chestnuts. She roasts them over a charcoal fire (another human invention) that sheds warmth and light amidst the cold and darkness of the surroundings. Since the chestnuts stay warm in the men's pockets, they have the feeling of well-being that warmth affords while they are walking the remainder of the way to the hospital.

contrasted settings

There is an old notion that people go to hospitals to die. The initial description of the hospital as "old and beautiful" lessens the natural terror one might feel of such an institution. However, the sentences that follow offer no such comfort but explain in matter-of-fact fashion that people usually walk in the front gate alive and are carried out dead, by way of a funeral procession starting in the courtyard of the "old and beautiful" hospital. The only obstacle to this natural progression of events seem to be the "machines" housed inside the new brick pavilions, to the side of the hospital, where the men go for physical therapy.

The doctor presiding over the pavilions perpetrates illusions of healing by making the patients believe that they will be completely cured. He offers hope, with his "healing machines" and glib talk, to those who will believe in the illusions. To those with doubts, the doctor shows photographs of cured wounds, pointing out how, by the miraculous powers of the machines, badly wounded bodies have been resurrected so that they function "better than ever."

contrasted characters

The central character of the story would like to believe these illusions. He is a young man, and it is devastating to him to have to face the reality of being badly deformed for the rest of his life. He wants to believe that he will be cured but notices contradictions between what the doctor professes and the realities of the situation. The doctor tells him he will "play football again like a champion" in spite of the fact that he has no calf and a knee that refuses to bend after months of manipulation by the machines. He also observes that the photograph of a "cured" hand is only slightly larger than that of the withered hand of the major, another patient.

The major, who takes treatment next to the young man, provides the counterpoint to the young man's need for illusions. The major is an older man who knows that no one has control over death and infirmity. His young wife has unexpectedly died after only a few days of illness. No manufactured machine or medicine could help her while she was ill, and nothing can resurrect her after her death. The young wife's death has taken from him the last tiny shred of belief in illusions.

summing up of central conflict

The major's point of view offers a startling contrast to that of the doctor. Throughout the story, the young man is caught between those who believe in illusions and those who discard illusion and attempt to live with blunt reality. He recognizes the foolishness and untruth of the doctor's illusions, but he also notices the bitterness and resignation of the major who has discarded all illusion. After his wife's death, the major returns to the hospital resigned to the fact that nothing we can do will delay, for long, death. He just sits on his therapy machine and stares out of the window. He seems to be marking time. He does not believe in the machines, yet he comes each day to use them.

restatement of central theme

Through the major's example and the many contrasts presented in "In Another Country," Hemingway makes us see that, although life based on illusion is dishonest, most of us cannot live as functioning human beings without some illusions. The blunt reality of death and infirmity is too painful and frightening for most human beings to face. Our capacity for illusion provides the minimum of hope we need to go on living.

Questions for Discussion Does the student writer get you into the spirit of Hemingway's short story? How does she succeed, or why does she fail? Do you think you would respond to the story the same way she did?

Tracing a Dramatic Conflict

True drama results from the conflict between opposing forces. In a truly dramatic confrontation, powerful opposites clash, with the issue in doubt. In Sophocles' *Antigone*, one of the most famous of the ancient Greek plays, Antigone is a strong-willed young woman (the daughter of Oedipus) who makes a fateful decision that sets the events of the play in motion. Her brother, who died fighting against his own native city, has been left unburied, dishonored as a traitor, his corpse a prey to birds and dogs. Antigone decides to obey her conscience and the command of the gods in burying her brother's body. She becomes the **protagonist**, or main character, of the play, who champions what she considers a just cause.

Opposing her is her uncle Creon, the new ruler of Thebes, who has decreed that anyone burying the traitor's body will be put to death. He is the **antagonist**, a strong second character who provides the counterpoint in the play. He represents the authority of the state. The other characters in the play—Antigone's sister, her fiancé Haemon (the king's son), and the citizens of Thebes—are forced to take sides, to choose between loyalty to country and obedience to the gods. As the conflict moves toward its final **resolution**, Antigone dies (committing suicide in the tomb in which she has been walled up alive), but Creon's son decides to join her in death. Creon realizes too late that in his stubborn pride he has made a terrible mistake: "The greater your arrogance, the heavier the gods' revenge."

The central conflict in a play (and also in a short story or novel) may be an **internal conflict**: Shakespeare's *Macbeth* has the "vaulting ambition" that leads him to murder King Duncan and make himself king of Scotland. But he also has a conscience that makes him hesitate. As Lady Macbeth says, he has too much of "the milk of human kindness." He tries to abort the planned assassination at the last minute; he has fearful visions of a bloody dagger and of the ghost of one of his later victims; he is shaken in his sleep by terrible dreams. Macbeth is a reluctant murderer, an assassin with a conscience, who listens to conflicting voices.

Testing a Critical Term A critical paper may apply an important critical term to a key example. Critical terms help us find our way. They guide our expectations. They help us put into words important differences and similarities. We would find it hard to talk about drama if we did not have terms like *tragedy, comedy, farce, theater of the absurd, protagonist, subplot,* or *dénouement.*

When you apply a term like *tragedy* to a single major play, you sharpen your sense of the term; you put it to the test. The following excerpts are from a paper that works out its answer to the question asked in its title:

WRITING SAMPLE: DEFINING A CRITICAL TERM

Death of a Salesman—a Tragedy?

raising the question

Ever since Willy Loman trudged into his living room and set down his heavy sample satchel in the first stage production of *Death of a Salesman*, critics have been arguing whether or not Arthur Miller's creation is a tragedy. . . .

definition
first criterion

We recognize great tragedies in part by the effect they work on their audiences. The Greeks used the words *pity, fear, catharsis* to classify this effect. Tragedy fills its audience with pity for the tragic hero. This pity is not patronizing but implies equality, a sharing of grief. The word *fear* is not restricted to fright or terror but includes anxious concern, awe, reverence, and apprehension. . . .

second criterion

Though the point has been overly emphasized, it is necessary that the tragic hero have some *tragic flaw* which shapes his actions and helps bring about his eventual downfall. We assume that the hero has free will; and we look in his or her character for a flaw that begins the chain of events leading to ruin. . . .

third criterion

In the agony, humiliation, and suffering of defeat, the hero invariably reaches a point of *increased self-awareness.* The hero or heroine is able to look back and see the steps leading to disaster. . . .

application
first criterion
second criterion

Is Miller's play a modern tragedy?

Miller certainly achieves the effects of *pity* and *fear.* . . .

Certainly, Willy Loman possesses a *tragic flaw,* if not several. But this flaw is not a personal characteristic coming from his own nature, but rather it is a burden given

THE WRITING WORKSHOP

A Critical Vocabulary

Some literary terms are part of the everyday equipment of critics and reviewers; others are in vogue for a time. Help organize a group project that will produce a short glossary of critical terms with definitions designed to be useful or instructive for students. Farm out terms like those listed below to individual researchers or teams. Ask contributors to check each term in at least one handbook of literature or guide to literary terms and in one collection or anthology that both explains a term and illustrates its use. Your finished glossary should contain a useful definition and a helpful example for terms like the following:

persona	personification	didactic
point of view	theme	allegory
allusion	free verse	irony
image	plot	parody
metaphor	tragedy	satire
symbol	tragic flaw	stream of consciousness
meter	hubris	sentimentality
stanza		

to him by society. Willy believed in the American Dream because he was brought up to do so. . . .

third criterion   Willy, however, never enters into the period of *self-realization* characteristic of true tragedy. If the play were tragic, Willy would realize in the last act that "he had all the wrong dreams." But this conception remained beyond him. He died considering himself a great man, worth more dead than he was alive.

Organizing the Critical Paper Several familiar strategies for organizing material are likely to be especially useful in writing a critical paper:

☐ *Thesis and Supporting Examples*: Often, you will present a carefully worked out generalization—about a character, a central theme, or a prevailing mood—as the thesis of a critical paper. Your paper will then provide a rich array of supporting examples from the text.

☐ *Comparison and Contrast*: Pointed comparison or contrast will frequently help you alert your readers to significant features of a poem, story, or play. Especially when you are dealing with literary conventions—well-established traditional ways of dealing with a subject—a careful point-by-point comparison can reveal to your readers the patterns that shape a work.

☐ *Lining Up Opposites*: In tracing a central conflict, you will often line up opposites in a statement-counterstatement fashion.

☐ *Definition and Application*: Often you will start by defining a key term—*sentimentality, irony, alienation*. You will then test your definition by showing key features illustrated in a poem, story, or play.

EXERCISE 4   *The Poet's Language*

In one paragraph, explain in as much detail as you can the *implications and associations* that contribute to the full meaning of one of the following passages from Shakespeare's sonnets and plays:

1.   O, how shall summer's honey breath hold out
     Against the wreckful siege of battering days,
     When rocks impregnable are not so stout,
     Nor gates of steel so strong, but Time decays?
                                          (Sonnet 65)

2.   That time of year thou mayest in me behold
     When yellow leaves, or none, or few, do hang
     Upon those boughs which shake against the cold,
     Bare ruined choirs, where late the sweet birds sang.
                                          (Sonnet 73)

3.   Love's not Time's fool, though rosy lips and cheeks
     Within his bending sickle's compass come;
     Love alters not with his brief hours and weeks,
     But bears it out even to the edge of doom.
                                          (Sonnet 116)

4.   O, she doth teach the torches to burn bright!
     It seems she hangs upon the cheek of night
     Like a rich jewel in an Ethiop's ear—
     Beauty too rich for use, for earth too dear!
                                          (*Romeo and Juliet*, I.v)

EXERCISE 5   *Love and the Modern Reader*

Find a twentieth-century love poem or poem that deals in some way with love. Photocopy it for reading and discussion in class. How does the poem do or fail to do what you expect from a poem about love? How do you and your classmates react to the poem, and why? (Your class may want to look at poems like e. e. cummings' "all in green went my love riding," Richard Brautigan's "Love Poem," John Nims' "Love Poem," Edna St. Vincent Millay's "Love Is Not All," or Ted Hughes' "Love Song.")

EXERCISE 6   *A Lifelike Character*

We all understand that the characters in a short story, novel, or play are shaped by the author's imagination. Nevertheless, we at least sometimes start to identify with or react to such a character as if we were reacting to a real-life person. Describe and discuss one such literary character that became exceptionally real for you. How did you relate to the character? What do you think was the secret of the character's appeal or fascination for you?

EXERCISE 7   *A Central Symbol*

Find a twentieth-century poem in which a central symbol, or several related symbols, play a key role. Discuss the role, the associations, and the implications of the symbol as fully as you can. You might choose a poem like "Stopping by Woods on a Snowy Evening," "Fire and Ice," or "The Silken Tent" by Robert Frost, or a poem like "The Water Rat" or "Frog Autumn" by Sylvia Plath.

EXERCISE 8   *Reexamining a Central Theme*

Choose a much-anthologized poem that has often been read (and quoted) for its central theme. What message does the poem have for a reader of your generation? How do you respond or react? Choose a poem like Thomas Hardy's "Convergence of the Twain" or "The Darkling Thrush," Emily Dickinson's "Because I Could Not Stop for Death," Theodore Roethke's "My Papa's Waltz," Walt Whitman's "When I Heard the Learned Astronomer," or Gwendolyn Brooks' "Little Rock."

WRITING A SAMPLE PAPER When you write about literature, you need to allow time for your reactions to come into focus: Why did a mother-and-daughter poem have a special hold on you? Why did a modern short story confuse or anger you? Develop a system for making the text of a story or play your own: Highlight or underline key passages; write queries or notes in the margin; do some rough charting of plot developments or stages in a character's growth. Prepare reading notes that include quotable quotes. Make sure you stay *close to the text* as you work on your first draft.

Laying the Groundwork Suppose you have become interested in the unsentimental quality of many modern short stories as contrasted with the sentimentality of much nineteenth-century fiction. You decide to choose as your test case a widely anthologized nineteenth-century American short story: Bret Harte's "The Outcasts of Poker Flat." It is the story of several shady characters—two prostitutes, a gambler, a drunk—who are driven from a small Western town by the moral majority and who perish when a snowstorm traps them in the mountains. Early in your project, you may decide to brainstorm the key term that you are going to test:

PREWRITING: BRAINSTORMING

Sentimentality: The word brings to mind true love and romance, life lovingly and beautifully portrayed, with death only a momentary transition to a better place. Every cloud has a silver lining. Life may be harsh and cruel, but redemption and salvation are the eventual outcome. Everything is loaded with sympathy, empathy, compassion, caring. There is some good in everyone. "Life is real; life is earnest." Life is invigorating, challenging.

Death is softened, described almost tenderly. Mother holds the hand of darling child dying of tuberculosis. Dying soldier props himself up on elbow to remember his loved ones. The gentle easing from sleep to death. Nothing gory, bloody, sickening.

Hearts, flowers, sunsets, baby shoes. Make the reader feel good. Life may be cruel, but there is justice and beauty. Hallmark greeting cards.

Sometimes, you will find it useful to prepare a **plot summary** to fix the major outlines of a story or play clearly in your mind. Here is a student-written plot summary of the Bret Harte story:

PREWRITING: PLOT SUMMARY

On November 23, 1850, the citizens of Poker Flat fulfill a decision (brought on by a sudden burst of crime in the area) to "rid the town of all improper persons." Mr. John Oakhurst, a gambler, accepts the town verdict calmly and, along with "The Duchess" (a prostitute), "Mother Shipton" (a madam), and "Uncle Billy" ("a suspected sluice robber and confirmed drunkard"), is escorted to the edge of town. The group is exiled under punishment of death.

The group's destination is Sandy Bar. The town is a hard day's travel on a narrow trail over the Sierras. At noon the Duchess tires, forcing the group to stop and make camp, against Oakhurst's wishes. Soon all the party save Oakhurst is drunk. Oakhurst recognizes a horseman on the trail, Tom Simson ("The Innocent") of Sandy Bar. The youth has run away with his fifteen-year old sweetheart, Piney Woods. They intend to be married in Poker Flat. They decide to set up camp with the exiles, again, against Oakhurst's wishes. Uncle Billy, scorning the amicable group, concocts an evil plan.

The women go to sleep in a ruined cabin, and the men sleep outside. Oakhurst is awakened towards morning by snow falling, and he discovers that Uncle Billy has gone and taken the mules with him. It is determined that the snowed-in group can last ten days on their provisions. The cheerfulness of the youths keeps up the spirits of the rest of the group, and the members of the group are brought closer together.

After a week, the group is still snowed in with twenty feet of snow. Mother Shipton starves herself to death to give her rations to Piney. Oakhurst has a plan for Tom to reach Poker Flat for help on a pair of makeshift snowshoes. Oakhurst intends to accompany Tom as far as the canyon and return to watch the women. However, Oakhurst does not return. By the time a rescue party reaches the camp, Piney and the Duchess are dead. Oakhurst is found under a pine tree at the head of the gulch; he is covered with snow, dead from his own bullet through the heart. He has written his epitaph on a playing card tacked to the tree.

Note that this plot outline does not comment, interpret, or judge. The following *reading notes* go considerably beyond a plot summary. The focus on Harte's sentimentality guides the reader's search for striking examples and revealing quotations:

PREWRITING: READING NOTES

appeal to our sympathy: the heartless, self-righteous townspeople turn out the band of sinners in the dead of winter

(Holman and Harmon on *sentimentality* in *A Handbook of Literature*: "an optimistic overemphasis on the goodness of humanity") finding goodness in unexpected places: Oakhurst, the gambler, gives up his horse to the Duchess, trading for her "sorry mule"; later, Oakhurst decides to stay with his "weaker and more pitiable companions"

the naive young "innocents": "they unaffectedly exchanged a kiss, so honest and sincere that it might have been heard above the swaying pines"; note: the naive purity of the innocents softens the hardened sinners

Mother Shipton, notorious for her coarse language and violent oaths, becomes the hooker with the heart of gold who starves herself so that the virginal Piney may eat an additional portion of the rations and so have a chance to live

final good deed: Oakhurst piles firewood by the cabin before he dies with a flourish, "handing in his checks"

softening of death: the Duchess and Piney (sin and innocence) die "wrapped in each other's arms," with the "younger and purer pillowing the head of her soiled sister upon her virgin breast"; they "fall asleep"; the fatal blizzard becomes a flurry of soft flakes—"feathery drifts of snow" cover the dead
saving touches of grim realism: Uncle Billy is a true rascal and hard-bitten cynic (and he survives when the others die); the hypocritical citizens of Poker Flat are satirized for their self-righteousness

The Finished Paper

A successful critical paper takes shape as you read, take notes, reread, and discuss your reactions with others. As you work on the Bret Harte story, your reactions may begin to fall into a "Yes, but" pattern. Yes, Harte's story illustrates many key features of sentimental fiction: We feel pity for the unfortunate; sinners are redeemed; we find good in unexpected places; the harsh realities of death are glossed over.

But there are also bracing touches of realism, and, above all, Harte has a redeeming sense of humor. We have a chance to laugh at hypocrisy, pretense, and naiveté. The following finished paper weighs the role of sentimentality and humor in the story:

WRITING SAMPLE: THE CRITICAL PAPER

The Sentimental Sinners of Poker Flat

definition

Driven out of town by the moral majority, "The Outcasts of Poker Flat" perish (with one exception) in an early snowstorm that traps them in the mountains. Two prostitutes, a gambler, and a drunk—these, along with two innocents, are the main characters of Bret Harte's sentimental tale. In sentimental writing, the tender emotions, such as love and pity, are superabundant, and evil exists mainly to stimulate our pity for the victims and our moral indignation. We feel tender pity for the innocent victims, and we feel a warm glow of emotion when evildoers repent or show an unexpected noble side.

thesis

Bret Harte's characters do indeed form the basis for a story that has most of the elements of nineteenth-century sentimentality. Nevertheless, somehow the story does not leave us with that sickeningly sweet, cloying sensation that a truly sentimental narrative often produces. Harte's skillful use of humor rescues "The Outcasts" from complete mawkishness.

the sentimental side

The story is indeed sentimental. A group of characters who are extremely unlikely candidates for sainthood nevertheless exhibit heroic virtue and selflessness. Their ordeal, rather than demonstrating the baseness of human nature, shows humanity's basic goodness.

The only appearance of anything less than virtuous is in Uncle Billy, the drunk. He steals away in the night with the mules, stranding the others in the snowstorm. The rest of the group are inspired to attain a saintly goodness. There is no fighting over food or shelter; each individual is concerned only for the others. The "Duchess," the younger prostitute, decorates the ramshackle cabin, while Tom Simson, the "Innocent," patches its roof. Piney, his bride-to-be, plays her accordion, while all join in a rousing gospel song around the campfire. To fill the void left by the lack of food, Simson tells the story of *Iliad* to an enthralled audience. The real heroics, though, come from the greatest "sinners," in true sentimental fashion. The gambler, Oakhurst, although he is known to be "a coolly desperate man," never "thought of deserting his weaker and more pitiable companions." Mother Shipton, the legendary prostitute with a heart of gold, starves herself to save the young virgin.

the humorous side

However, Harte's story as a whole is more successful and more enjoyable than this description would suggest. Humor is the key to Harte's success. Harte's humor— a Western, often ironic brand—runs throughout the story, setting it apart from other sentimental writing and allowing a modern reader to appreciate it.

The beginning of the story sets the moral tone with wry humor. The community of Poker Flat, having lately suffered the loss of "several thousand dollars, two valuable horses," and (almost as an afterthought) "a prominent citizen," is experiencing "a spasm of virtuous reaction." Harte adds that this reaction is "quite as lawless and ungovernable as any of the acts that provoked it."

The real reason the townspeople are after Oakhurst is not simply that he is a gambler but that he is a better one than they are—and they want their money back. Oakhurst himself is presented as a worldly-wise character who looks at life with dry ironic humor: "With him life at best was an uncertain game, and he recognized the usual percentage in favor of the dealer."

Harte's attitude toward the innocents of the story, Tom Simson and Piney, is not in the vein of most sentimentality either. Their naiveté is seen not as an ideal but as a charming ignorance that has its funny side. When Tom refers to the Duchess as Mrs. Oakhurst, only a swift kick from the gambler keeps Uncle Billy from bursting out laughing. One of the funniest scenes in the story is the recital of the *Iliad* in Western jargon, with the Innocent persisting in calling the great Achilles "Ash-heels." Because we see the humor in this naiveté, we tend to identify with the sinners, not the innocents, a different state of affairs from most sentimentality.

conclusion echoes initial thesis

The ending of the story is the closest approach to cloying sentimentality. The virgin and the prostitute huddle together in the snow and freeze to death in each other's arms. However, the story does not end there but with a final touch of humor. Oakhurst has left his own epitaph, scribbled on the deuce of clubs and pinned to a tree with a knife. In keeping with his character, it reads: "Beneath this tree lies the body of John Oakhurst, who struck a streak of bad luck . . . and handed in his checks on the 7th of December 1850."

Questions for Discussion Do you share the negative modern attitude toward sentimentality? Why or not? Does this paper make you want to read (or reread) Harte's story? Why or why not?

Reminders for Revision In writing a critical paper, you need to take your readers along as you respond to what you have read. In revising an early draft, anticipate familiar ways of losing the reader:

☐ *Beware of overinterpretation.* We are sometimes tempted to make too much of a single quote, a single image. If something has a major thematic or symbolic significance, we should be able to show how the author has led up to it, alerted us to it, or highlighted it. We can show how a key idea or major theme is echoed or followed up. In Shakespeare's *Romeo and Juliet*, the comparison of passionate young love to a brilliant flash of light that for a short time lights up the universe is not just mentioned once in passing. Light imagery pervades many of the scenes; we can quote many lines to show how central the contrast between light and darkness is to the atmosphere of the play.

☐ *Break up unexamined chunk quotations.* Literary and especially poetic language is rich in meaning, in overtones and associations. Instead of putting before the reader lengthy unexamined quotations, excerpt, explain, interpret.

☐ *Guard against uncritical use of the critics.* When perplexed, we often turn to a critic, reviewer, or scholar who can serve as a guide. A critic may fill in helpful background, explain conventions, alert us to key themes or issues, or clear up difficult passages. But ultimately we have to test a critic's explanations against our own reading. We have to test a critic's judgments against our own response. When you quote a critic, show that you have tested what the critic says against your own reading.

☐ *Correct a stitched-together effect.* For instance, a comparison of Bret Harte's sentimental story with a decidedly *un*sentimental modern short story might seem to break apart into two separate minicompositions. You will need to integrate the material on the two stories—by a strong preview or overview at the beginning, by a strong transition, by pointing back repeatedly during your discussion of the second story to similar or contrasting features in the first.

Remember: You are trying to share your reactions to a poem, a story, or play with a reader. Even when you assume your readers know *Hamlet* or remember a well-known poem, you will have to refresh their memory; you will have to bring the play or the poem to life for them. It is possible to err on the side of too much cool judgment, too much analysis. Whatever else you do in writing about literature, you need to show that you care about what you have read. Who would want to read a dry factual analysis of an exuberant poem or of a story of heartbreak and despair?

THE WRITING WORKSHOP

A Group Critique

Prepare for a group critique of a paper you are writing about poetry or short fiction. Provide copies both of your draft and of the poem(s) or story (stories) you are discussing. Ask your readers to discuss questions like the following:

- ☐ Can they see what your purpose is in writing your paper?
- ☐ How carefully have you read the literature? Have you missed major clues? Have you exaggerated or played down major elements?
- ☐ Do they agree with your interpretation? If not, what explains differences?
- ☐ Does your paper have a clear plan or effective strategy?
- ☐ Is your personal reaction to what you have read or your personal involvement in the literature weak or missing, making your paper sound impersonal and perfunctory? Or is your personal reaction too subjective, coloring your perceptions?
- ☐ Do your readers agree on suggestions for revision? Why or why not?

WRITING TOPICS 16 *Writing About Literature*

In writing about topics like the following, aim at bringing the literature you have read to life for your reader.

1. Write about a poem that uses an animal as the central symbol. Possible examples are Emily Dickinson's "A Bird Came Down the Walk," D. H. Lawrence's "The Snake," Howard Nemerov's "The Great Gull," or May Swenson's "The Centaur" (about a mythical animal). What did the animal mean to the poet? What ideas, associations, or emotions does the symbol bring into play?

2. Compare and contrast a traditional love sonnet with a modern poem about love. Or compare and contrast a World War I poem by a poet like Wilfred Owen or Siegfried Sassoon with a later poem on the subject of war.

3. Write a character study of a central character in a play as seen through the eyes of a minor player. For instance, look at Romeo or Juliet through

the eyes of Friar Lawrence, at Macbeth through the eyes of Lady Macbeth, or at Hamlet through the eyes of Polonius. Use ample detail from the play.

4. Write a paper in which you help your readers understand the central character in a story focused on that character. For instance, write about Herman Melville's "Bartleby the Scrivener," Willa Cather's "Paul's Case," Nathaniel Hawthorne's "Young Goodman Brown," Kate Chopin's "A Pair of Silk Stockings," Eudora Welty's "A Visit of Charity," or Joyce Carol Oates' "Stalking."

5. Find a story of childhood or adolescence that deals with the theme of growing up—the "rite of passage" from childhood to adulthood, the initiation into a man's or woman's world. How does the author deal with the theme? How do you react as a reader? (Your instructor may ask you to check out such classics of adolescent literature as Alice Munro's "Boys and Girls," Jean McCord's "My Teacher the Hawk," John Knowles' "A Turn with the Sun," or Farley Mowat's "Two Who Were One.")

6. Write about the role of the central symbol in a story like John Steinbeck's "The Chrysanthemums," William Stafford's "The Osage Orange Tree," Franz Kafka's "The Metamorphosis," Flannery O'Connor's "Enoch and the Gorilla." What role does the symbol play in the story? What clues does the author provide to its meaning?

7. Write about a play in which the conflict between the generations plays a major role. For instance, study a play like Henrik Ibsen's *The Wild Duck*, Arthur Miller's *All My Sons*, Lorraine Hansberry's *Raisin in the Sun*, or Tennessee Williams' *The Glass Menagerie*. What is the nature of the conflict? What is its resolution?

8. In recent years, critics have begun to reread familiar classics from a woman's perspective. Look at a familiar literary heroine from this point of view. Choose a character like Charlotte Brontë's Jane Eyre, Bertolt Brecht's Mother Courage, Henrik Ibsen's Nora (in *A Doll's House*), Lady Macbeth, or Juliet. How is a current reader's perception of the character likely to be different from that of earlier audiences?

9. Addressing an Anglo audience, discuss one book that can give readers a fuller sense of the country's cultural pluralism. Discuss a major theme or major themes in a book like Maxine Hong Kingston's *The Warrior Woman* or *Chinamen*, Richard Rodriguez's *Hunger of Memory*, or Alice Walker's *The Color Purple*.

20

TESTS

Writing the Essay Exam

Don't let the test situation panic you or control you. Be calm, or you'll probably forget even the few facts that you think you do know. Elizabeth Cowan Neeld

TAKING WRITTEN TESTS One of your survival skills as a student is writing essay exams—writing under pressure, keeping cool, showing to advantage what you have learned. Written exams force you to abbreviate the process of writing, with little time for exploration and second thoughts. The premium is on *recall*—assembling quickly what is relevant to the topic; on *planning*—moving expeditiously to work out a general strategy; on *execution*—pushing ahead to flesh out your rough outline in what is usually the first and (after quick proofreading) the final draft.

Format and instructor's expectations vary from exam to exam, but the following advice is worth keeping in mind:

□ *Know what you are expected to do.* Start by getting an overview of the exam, especially if it comes in several parts. Then take in specific instructions: Are you being asked to *summarize* information? *compare* two procedures or historical events? *explain* a point of view and show why you agree or disagree? *define* and illustrate a key term? Be sure to respond to the last part of a three-part or four-part question (the last part may be the most important one in the instructor's mind).

□ *Budget your time.* Allow time at the beginning for rough written or mental notes—collecting your thoughts, organizing your thinking. Allot the right share of time for different parts or different tasks. Save some time for last-minute proofreading.

□ *Work from a rough outline.* If you can, have a clear three-point or four-point program in mind as you write. Do not just plunge in—a well-

589

worked out plan will minimize backtrackings, afterthoughts, and lame repetition.

☐ *Make strategic use of detail.* Select a key example to illustrate a concept or to support a point. Include an apt quotation or a striking statistic to show your familiarity with the subject.

☐ *Remember your reader.* Keep in mind that the reader is likely to be reading against the clock, seeing passage after passage on the same subject, trying to form a quick judgment of what you know or of how convincingly you can deal with your topic. Dispense with long roundabout introductions; avoid a tedious restatement of the exam questions. Make your main points stand out. To set your exam off from the rest, use striking supporting detail or a fresh personal example; quote an instructor's favorite phrase or allude to class discussion.

ANALYZING A PASSAGE

A test in a subject like composition, literature, history, or political science will often ask you to read and react to a passage. Often you will have to do justice to two separate questions: "What does it say? How do I react, and why?" Suppose you are asked to explain a passage that the American poet Walt Whitman wrote about capital punishment. You are then asked whether you agree or disagree with the writer, and to show why. To help you focus your reading and organize your response, remember guidelines like the following:

☐ *Sum up the author's central message.* Early in your response, give an overview or preview that summarizes the main idea, including important distinctions or reservations:

main idea In this passage, Whitman does not say outright that he is for or against the death penalty. Instead, he attacks the system that *implements* the punishment—a system riddled by indecision and contradiction. Whitman feels that society should make a definite choice, for or against the death penalty, and then act firmly on that resolve.

☐ *Organize your answer around major points.* Try to mark off major steps in the argument, major segments in the author's train of thought:

first reason Whitman touches on at least three reasons why the contemporary practice concerning capital punishment is unsatisfactory. First, the application of the law is fitful and *inconsistent*. The law seems undecided whether to inflict capital punishment for murder, and the authorities often find ways to spare or pardon the offender. . . .

second reason Second, the application of the law often seems patently *unfair*. When an execution does take place, as often as not the condemned prisoner belongs to a racial minority. . . .

third reason
Third, and above all, the authorities *procrastinate*. Any minor technicality can delay a case indefinitely. . . .

☐ *Respond to the author's style.* Respond to hints and implications that help you read between the lines. Respond to what makes the writing eloquent, witty, harsh, conciliatory, or different. Quote striking or revealing phrases:

revealing quotes
Although Whitman does not state his own position on the justification of capital punishment outright, we can infer that he personally favors it from several remarks he makes in the passage. With a sarcastic tone, he refers to "soft-hearted (and soft-headed) prison philanthropists" who sympathize with convicted criminals. He refers to "penny-a-liner journalists" who write melodramatically about the plight of convicted murderers. He criticizes judges and lawyers who bend the law to give "the condemned every chance of evading punishment."

☐ *Take a stand.* State your own position clearly and forcefully. Use precedent, parallels, or revealing contrast to clarify and bolster your own point of view:

personal response
There are times when our anger makes us clamor for the death of an offender. But in our more thoughtful moments, we are likely to think differently. In Tolkien's *Lord of the Rings*, there is a passage that goes roughly as follows: "There are many who live who deserve to die. There are many who die who deserve to live. Can you give life? If not, do not be so quick to take it."

☐ *Back up the stand you take.* Fortify your position with reasons or examples:

support
My main reason for opposing capital punishment is that it is too arbitrary and unpredictable. Too much hinges on the cleverness of lawyers and on the prejudices of juries. One recent study found that good-looking, personable defendants are more likely to be acquitted than those who look threatening, gloomy, or disturbed. To judge from this study, juries may well send a man to his death because he *looks* like a villain; they thus make a mistake that can never be made good.

EXERCISE 1 *A Sample Test*

Instructions: In the following passage from *Progress and Privilege*, William Tucker joins in the debate between advocates of progress and advocates of conservation. Where does he take his stand? What is his argument in this excerpt? Is it in any way new or different; does it shed new light on the issue? Where do you stand on the issue raised in this excerpt, and why?

The fact is that, from a human perspective, nature, for all its diversity, is still not very stable. For most of nature, the laws of survival still mean matching the ever-present possibilities for catastrophe against the inborn capabilities of organisms to reproduce fantastic numbers of offspring to continue the genetic line. Let me give an example. In 1963, scientists doing an oceanographic survey in the Indian Ocean came across a 4,000-square-mile area covered with dead fish. The number equaled about one quarter of the world's catch at the time. The fish had not died from human activity but were the victims of the inevitable nutrient cycles that govern most of the ocean environment. . . .

The unpleasant truth is that natural cycles, for all their diversity, are still enormously unstable. Genetic diversity can protect diversified forests from diseases, for example, but fires can still destroy whole forests. It is this uncertainty that evokes the widely used strategy of fantastic procreative abilities among plants and invertebrates.

As mammals, we have tried to overcome these unpredictabilities through a different strategy—by internalizing our environment and building self-correcting controls. That is why we do not need the heat of the sun, as reptiles do, to warm our blood and give us energy at the start of the day. Nor are we as devastated by dryness or changes in the weather. (Some insect populations have been shown to go through population explosions and crashes from temperature changes of only a few degrees.) By building internal controls, we have been able to stabilize the relationship between our internal and external environments.

The business of human progress, then, has been a *continuation* of this evolutionary line of development. Human progress has not been "growthmania" or "growth for growth's sake," as environmentalists often charge. It has been a deliberate effort to extend our control over the external environment so that we are not subject to the instabilities and unpredictabilities of nature's cycles.

Thus, we do not guarantee ourselves any kind of stability in human affairs by foregoing the effort to humanize the environment, and letting nature take its course. That only returns us to nature's unpredictabilities. What we *can* do is be very cautious about disrupting natural systems any more than is necessary, and conserve wildlife wherever possible. This does not have to be strict preservation, but only a matter of taking concern for wild systems where they still exist.

TESTS ON PREVIOUS READING Many tests, whether open-book or written without books or notes, ask you to show how well you know the material you have studied. To do well on such tests (and to reduce test anxiety), you need to study with a sense of purpose; you need to come to the examination prepared for what lies ahead. Keep in mind guidelines like the following:

□ *Prepare for a writing test.* Obviously you want to immerse yourself in the material as much as you can. But much of your preparation for your bout with the testmaker is to chart and to outline, to identify key points—to *prestructure* the material that you might use in a paragraph or short essay.

Identify key terms that could provide the focal point for explanation or discussion; chart the main steps in a procedure or the key parts of an argument: *Photosynthesis*—what are the essential processes that make it work? *Alienation*—what does a character in short story say and do to show his alienated condition? *Agrarianism*—where, when, and why did it originate?

☐ *Memorize key supporting details.* Imprint on your memory for strategic use some pointed definitions, striking examples, and telling statistics. By all means memorize some key phrases and short pointed quotations. Nothing establishes your credentials as a well-prepared student more reliably than sentences like the following:

> Modern civilization, what D. H. Lawrence calls "my accursed human education," has alienated us from our roots in the natural world.

> According to Barbara Tuchman, dates are fundamental to the historian because they show order in time and thus make possible "an understanding of cause and effect."

☐ *Check the exact wording of instructions.* Assume the question in a history exam is "What do you consider the most important difference between the fall of Greece and the fall of Rome?" Do not simply put down everything you can remember about the fall of Greece and the fall of Rome. Focus on the key word in the instructions: *difference.* What *is* the difference? How can you line up material that will bring out this difference as clearly and convincingly as possible?

☐ *Structure your answer.* No matter what the pressure of time, do not simply spill out what you remember. Especially in a paragraph-length response, try to come straight to the point—make your first sentence sum up your answer or your stand on the issue. Proceed to cover major parts of the problem or key reasons in a clear order, for instance, from simple to difficult or from unlikely to probable. (Avoid lame transitions like *also* or *another.*)

Study the following instructions for an essay exam on a literary subject and a student response that a teacher selected as a model:

INSTRUCTIONS: *A common type of character in much contemporary literature is the individual who is trapped by a trick of fate, by the environment, or by his or her own nature. Choose such a character from a short story you have recently read. Define the trap in which the character is caught. Describe any struggle on the part of the character to become free.*

ANSWER: Katherine Mansfield's Miss Brill finds herself trapped by her spinsterhood and the advancement of age. She is old, as the story tells us; she's as old as her out-of-date fox fur. She is alone, with no friends, relatives, or close neighbors. This is her

THE WRITING WORKSHOP

A Practice Run for Test Takers

Work with a group that shares an interest in one of the topics listed below. Find and study background material in a textbook or encyclopedia. Help set up a timed essay test on the topic chosen by your group. In writing your own short essay on the topic, start with a preview or overview. Trace clearly the major steps, arguments, or dimensions of the topic. Include some striking details or examples. After the test, share in a group critique of the results. Possible topics:

- □   evidence for the theory of evolution
- □   Marx's critique of laissez-faire capitalism
- □   the Ptolemaic and the Copernican view of the solar system
- □   Luther's criticism of the Roman Catholic church
- □   diet and heart disease
- □   the abolitionist movement
- □   the Mayan civilization
- □   causes of the Great Depression

trap. Like a bird that will create its own prison in its own territory, Miss Brill makes hers. She does not socialize, nor does she try to make something useful out of her life but rather preys like a parasite on other people's more interesting, colorful lives. In her own way, Miss Brill struggles to escape her prison. She daydreams. The world that she lives in is a fantasy world where all people are friendly and related. She "belongs" in this world, whereas in the other world, the real world, she actually belongs to no one.

Quite successfully, Miss Brill loses the real world for a time, but she cannot escape the real world entirely. The real world sticks its head in, in the form of a boy who says "Ah, go on with you now." So she goes home, more aware than ever of her prison's boundaries and helpless (by her own nature) to do anything else. She can only fly on home to the security and solitude of her cold, dark nest.

Note the following points about this answer:

- □   It responds directly to the *key term* or *key idea* in the assignment. The assignment asks about a character who is *trapped*. This word and its synonyms keep echoing throughout the student's answer: *trapped, prison, boundaries*.

☐   The first sentence sums up the answer as a whole. It gives the brief, clear definition of the "trap" that the question asks for.

☐   The point about the character's trying to escape through daydreaming responds to the *second* part of the question. But note that this point is worked organically into the first paragraph. The student has planned this answer; there are no afterthoughts, no "Oh-I-forgot" effect.

Grammar and Usage

USING THE HANDBOOK

1 FRAGMENT AND COMMA SPLICE

a Sentence Fragments
b Fused Sentences
c Comma Splices

2 GRAMMAR AND USAGE

a Standard English
b Formal and Informal

3 VERB FORMS

a Regular Verbs
b Irregular Verbs
c Subjunctive

4 AGREEMENT

a Singular or Plural
b Compound Subjects
c Blind Agreement
d Logical Agreement

5 PRONOUN REFERENCE

a Vague or Ambiguous Pronoun
b Agreement of Pronoun

6 PRONOUN CASE

a Subject and Object
b *Who* and *Whom*

7 MODIFIERS

a Adjectives and Adverbs
b Misplaced Modifiers

8 CONFUSED SENTENCES

a Omission and Duplication
b Mixed Construction
c Faulty Predication
d Faulty Appositives

9 INCOMPLETE CONSTRUCTIONS

a Incomplete Comparison
b Incomplete Coordination

10 CONSISTENCY

a Shifts in Tense
b Shifts in Reference
c Shifts to the Passive
d Faulty Parallelism

Sentence Punctuation

11 END PUNCTUATION

12 LINKING PUNCTUATION

a Semicolon Only
b Coordinators
c Conjunctive Adverbs
d Subordinators
e Relative Clauses
f Noun Clauses

USING THE HANDBOOK

Ideally, writing teachers would help each student by explaining problems and offering detailed suggestions for improvement. However, in practice they code problems that come up again and *again*. They use correction symbols or guide numbers directing you to help in two areas: (1) **usage**—differences between the language of casual talk and edited written English; and (2) **mechanics**—conventions for putting words on a page, including correct spelling and appropriate punctuation.

Suppose you are carrying over to the written page the sentence fragments of stop-and-go conversation. (Fragments like this one.) The abbreviation *frag* or the guide number 1a will guide you to the section of this handbook that describes fragments and offers guidelines for revising them. Here is a list of other symbols frequently used:

SYMBOL	GUIDE NUMBER	EXAMPLE
agr agreement	4c	The typical diet article in newspapers and magazines *treat* food as if it were a foreign agent. (agreement between subject and verb requires "The article . . . *treats*")
ap apostrophe	19b	Stations use enticing "newsbriefs" to catch the *viewers* attention. (apostrophe is needed to mark the possessive: *whose* attention? the *viewer's* attention)
ca case	6b	Children may not know *who* to trust. (pronoun case requires the right form for the object of the verb: *whom to trust*)
cap capitals	20a	Alice Walker's *The Color Purple* won the Pulitzer Prize and was read by millions of *americans.* (names of nationalities and languages are capitalized: *Americans*)
CS comma splice	1c	Blue jeans recognize no *classes, they* are merely American. (comma between paired statements should be replaced by semicolon: *classes; they*)
DM dangling modifier	7b	*Sitting on top of an animal filled with furious energy,* the gate opens and the bronco dashes frantically for the other side of the stadium. (where is the rider?)
FP or // faulty parallelism	10d	We went to the apartment to pick up the bills, financial statements, and *finally clean out the refrigerator.* (after the *and*, the reader expects a third item to be picked up)

SYMBOL	GUIDE NUMBER	EXAMPLE
gl glossary	24	*A* anchorwoman on a local TV station felt harassed because of her looks and age. (see glossary for *an* before a vowel: *an* ape, *an* error)
hy hyphen	21c	Vietnamese immigrants slowly transformed our *low rent* district. (hyphenate the group modifier: *low-rent district*)
inf informal	2b	*Well,* my senior year started out *with a bang*. I had *tons* of friends and was *doing great* in school. (language is too informal or colloquial)
mx mixed construction	8b	The *main objective* of the article *compared* the use of glittering generalities by the two candidates. ("*the article* compared" or "*the objective* of the article *was* to compare")
p punctuation	13b	Our retina, which has maybe 125 million rods and cones performs the equivalent of 10 billion calculations per second. (second comma needed after *cones*)
ref pronoun reference	5b	Although the study of techniques is helpful to an artist, *they* do not need a degree to paint. (*they* could refer to *artists* but not to *an artist*)
sf shift	10b	From *my* window, *you* could see most of San Diego. (who is looking out of the window—"I" or "you"?)
sp spelling	18	Changes in our laws have not *detered* people from *commiting* crimes. (doubled final consonant needed in *deterred* and *committing*)
vb verb	3b	According to the inspector, someone else *could have wrote* the suicide note. (the standard form is *could have written*)

Additional symbols identify writing problems discussed earlier in this book:

awk	awkward sentence
coh	coherence lacking or connection not obvious
d	inaccurate or inappropriate diction, or word choice
dev	more development or support needed
id	unidiomatic English
sl	slang
trans	stronger transition needed
w	wordiness

The following is a sample page of a student paper with correction symbols and instructor's comments:

#98869

wrong form?

As a consequence of our (strive) for better technology and efficiency Americans are becoming severely disatisfied with their job environment and organization. This businesslike drive for profit and speed causes three serious problems in the American worker: lack of loyalty, lack of praise, and lack of knowing youre needed.

sp

in or for?

ap

clarify what you mean?

Lack of loyalty is caused primarily by the very impersonal interaction that goes on between employee and boss. I started a job at a company where I was referred to as only "98869." I stayed for only a short while and quit. I felt no loss at leaving anybody behind, because they were just faces with numbers written on them. No one ever bothered you. It was more efficient that way!

good revealing detail — but give additional evidence?

sf (10b) (shift from I to you?)

Another major problem that causes dissatisfaction is the lack of praise for a job well done. After I quit my first job, I got a job as an assistant legal secretary. Each day I had to prepare wills, depositions, and basically run the office. Little by little I became more annoyed by my constant lack of any kind of praise. Then one day it hit me all at once. The lawyer called me from a phone in the city courtroom. He needed me to prepare some things and bring them to him in court. He gave me half an hour. He proceeded to tell me all the things he needed. I had one hand on the typewriter, one on the copier, and one in my briefcase looking for my car keys! When I got downtown with one minute to spare, he said: "I wish I could have looked this over before I got in there. Was there a lot of traffic or

w

choppy sentences? combine? FP (10d)

nice exaggeration (this whole paragraph is better developed)

600

1   FRAGMENT AND COMMA SPLICE

What is the most basic test of literate English? Most teachers and editors would specify the writer's ability to write a complete sentence. Whatever else you attend to in final editing, check for sentence fragments—incomplete sentences split off from the larger statement of which they should be a part. You may also need to check for the opposite problem: fused sentences—two complete sentences blurred without a visible dividing line. You will need to check for comma splices—two complete sentences spliced together loosely without a logical link, connected only by a comma. (See Chapter 16 for a review of sentence structure and grammatical terms.)

frag   1a   ## SENTENCE FRAGMENTS

Use periods to mark off complete sentences.

Except for requests and commands, a sentence needs a subject and a complete verb: *My friends* (S) *vote* (V) for losers. *The team* (S) *was studying* (V) insects. When a period marks off a group of words without a subject and complete verb, the result is a **sentence fragment.** Most sentence fragments transfer to the written page the afterthoughts and asides of stop-and-go conversation:

FRAGMENT: My friends vote for losers. *Most of the time.*
            The team was studying insects. *Roaches, as a matter of fact.*

As a first step toward dealing with fragments, learn to identify two major kinds:

☐ Most sentence fragments are **phrases**—groups of words that work together but that do not stand up as separate statements. They lack a subject, or they lack all or part of the verb:

ADJECTIVES: The grizzly is a magnificent creature. *Magnificent but deadly.*
PREP. PHRASE: Sarah was studying Hebrew. *In Israel.*
APPOSITIVE: The graduating class invited Sandra O'Connor. *The Supreme Court Justice.*
VERBAL: Each day he spent hours on the road. *Fighting the traffic.*
            Kevin had quit the band. *To start a dry-cleaning business.*

☐ Many other fragments are **clauses**—dependent clauses that do have their own subject and verb. However, they start with a word meant as a link but not used here for a hookup with the main sentence. The unused link may be a subordinating conjunction (subordinator, for short): *if, because, unless, when, before, after, while,* and especially also *whereas* or *although.* Or the unused link may be a relative pronoun: *who, which,* or *that.* Splitting the dependent clause off from the main clause causes a fragment:

SUBORDINATORS:	We will refund the money. *If you return the part.*
	Lawrence is in Kansas. *Whereas Kansas City is in Missouri.*
RELATIVE PRONOUNS:	The birds were storks. *Which are common in Egypt.*
	Our neighbor was an ex-convict. *Who was still on parole.*

Some fragments are a combination of the two kinds: a phrase and a dependent clause. ("My roommate was a foreign student. *An Iranian whose father had served the Shah.*") To revise a sentence fragment, do one of the following:

(1) Reconnect the fragment to the main sentence without a break. Most prepositional phrases and infinitives (*to* forms) should blend into the sentence without punctuation to show the seam:

| REVISED: | Sarah was studying Hebrew *in Israel.* |
| | Kevin had quit the band *to start a dry-cleaning business.* |

(2) Reconnect the fragment, using a comma. Use the comma when an appositive or a verbal adds **nonrestrictive** material—nonessential information (or "extras") not used to eliminate possibilities or limit the main point. (See **13b.**)

| REVISED: | The graduating class invited Sandra O'Connor, *the Supreme Court Justice.* |
| | Each day he spent hours on the road, *fighting the traffic.* |

(3) Use a colon to introduce a list or an explanation. The colon then says "as follows"; note that it comes after a complete statement:

| FRAGMENT: | Jerry devoted his weekends to his two great loves. *Football and beer.* |
| REVISED: | Jerry devoted his weekends to his two great loves: *football and beer.* |

(4) Use a comma when an explanation or example follows a transitional expression. Use a comma before (but not after) *especially* and *such as:*

| COMMA: | The school attracted many foreign students, *especially* Arabs. |
| | Our laws protect religious minorities, *such as* Mormons or Quakers. |

Add a second comma after *for example, for instance,* and *namely.* (The second comma, however, is optional and often left out in informal or journalistic writing.)

| TWO COMMAS: | We learned to like strange food, *for example,* raw fish. |

(5) Join a dependent clause to the main clause. Use no punctuation if the added clause is **restrictive**—if it spells out an essential condition or limits our choices:

NO COMMA: We will refund the money *if you return the part.*   (only then)
He befriended people *who had money.*   (only those)

Use a comma if the added clause is **nonrestrictive**—if the first statement is true regardless or if what it maps out will not be narrowed down. (See **12d** and **12e**.)

COMMA: Lawrence is in Kansas, *whereas Kansas City is in Missouri.*   (both true)
The birds were storks, *which are common in Egypt.*   (true of all storks)

(6) Turn the fragment into a complete separate sentence. If all else fails, convert the fragment to a complete sentence with its own subject and verb:

FRAGMENT: I appealed to the officer's sense of humor. *Being a futile effort.*
REVISED: I appealed to the officer's sense of humor. *The effort was futile.*

Note: Experienced writers occasionally use **permissible fragments** for a thinking-out-loud effect:

DESCRIPTION: On the left, a bank of elevators. *Straight ahead, a long burnished corridor, spooky as a lit tunnel. And empty, all empty.*   Cynthia Ozick
NARRATION: There he is: the brother. *Image of him. Haunting face.*   James Joyce

---

ℱℐ   **1b** | FUSED SENTENCES

Separate two sentences that have been run together.

The opposite of the fragment is the complete sentence that has become the Siamese twin of another sentence—linked without punctuation or a connecting word like *and, but, if,* or *because.* Use a period to separate the two parts of such a **fused sentence**—or a semicolon to show that the two parts are closely related:

FUSED: Matthew no longer lives there *he moved to Katmandu.*
PERIOD: Matthew no longer lives there. *He moved to Katmandu.*

FUSED: She took the exam over *this was her last chance.*
SEMICOLON: She took the exam over; *this was her last chance.*

603

CS   1c   **COMMA SPLICES**

Use the semicolon to correct comma splices.

We often pair two closely related statements. They form part of the same picture; they are part of the same story. Use a semicolon (as in the pair you just read) to show the close tie between the paired sentences. Note that there is no connecting word or logical link like *and, but, or, if, unless, although,* or *whereas.* Correct **comma splices,** which use a comma instead of the semicolon and result in a pair of complete statements (independent clauses) too loosely spliced together:

COMMA SPLICE: Paula loved London, it was a wonderful city.
REVISED: Paula loved London; it was a wonderful city.

COMMA SPLICE: Some doctors inform their patients, others keep them in the dark.
REVISED: Some doctors inform their patients; others keep them in the dark.

(1) Use the semicolon also with conjunctive adverbs. A word like *therefore* or *however* may link the two paired sentences. These and similar words are **conjunctive adverbs**—adverbs used as connectives: *therefore, however, nevertheless, consequently, moreover, accordingly, besides, indeed,* and *in fact.* Again, a comma used instead of the semicolon would splice the pair together too loosely and result in a comma splice. (Often a comma is used as *additional* punctuation to set the conjunctive adverb off from the second statement—see **12c.**)

COMMA SPLICE: The weather turned ugly, *therefore* the launch was postponed.
REVISED: The weather turned ugly; *therefore*, the launch was postponed.

(2) Use commas in a set of three parallel clauses. In a set of three or more, commas instead of semicolons are all right. ("I came, I saw, I conquered.")

COMMAS: Students in India demonstrate against the use of English, African nationalists protest against the use of French, young Israelis have no use for the languages once spoken by their parents.

Note: Some writers use the comma with two **parallel** clauses—statements where the logical connection or the similarity in structure is especially strong. However, many teachers and editors frown on this practice; to be safe, avoid it in your own writing.

EXERCISE 1   Some headlines are *complete sentences*—with a subject and complete verb. Others are incomplete, lacking a possible subject, or all or part of a verb.

The following were selected by the managing editor of the *New York Times* as the ten most important headlines of the twentieth century. Mark each *C* (complete) or *I* (incomplete).

1. Man's First Flight in a Heavier-than-Air Machine
2. The Great Powers Go to War in Europe (1914)
3. The Bolshevik Revolution in Russia
4. Lindbergh Flies the Atlantic Alone
5. Hitler Becomes Chancellor of Germany
6. Roosevelt Is Inaugurated as President
7. Scientists Split the Atom, Releasing Incredible Power
8. The Nightmare Again—War in Europe
9. Surprise Japanese Bombing of Pearl Harbor
10. Men Land on the Moon

EXERCISE 2 Find the *sentence fragments* in the following passages. If the second part of a pair is a fragment, write *frag* after the number of the sentence. If the second part is a complete sentence, write *C* for complete.

1. Many communities no longer want rapid growth. Free of all controls.
2. The story begins like a typical short story. A story about a small town having a drawing once a year.
3. The "good woman" in Victorian literature is the angelic wife and mother. Her opposite is the "fallen woman."
4. She left the convent after two years. To take over her father's business.
5. Many minority students went out for sports. Because it gave them their only real chance.
6. People used to grow up in larger families. For example, parents, grand-parents, Uncle Salvatore, and three or four children.
7. The place was called the loft. It was a big room at the top of the building.
8. The veterinarian told us the animal had died of a heart attack. While he was preparing to operate.
9. A regulation target resembles an upside-down saucer. Measuring five inches in diameter.
10. She simply could not satisfy anybody's standards. Not those of her superiors and not those of her co-workers.

EXERCISE 3 Revise *sentence fragments* and *fused sentences* in the following examples. Write the italicized part of each example, adding or changing punctuation as necessary. Use a period followed by a capital letter to separate two complete sentences.

605

1. We were studying pre-Columbian *architecture. Such as Aztec pyramids and Mayan temples.*

2. Outside Mexico City, construction workers found priceless *murals. In buried buildings.*

3. Jobs were plentiful *in the area rents were reasonable.*

4. The lone survivor had hiked *down into the valley. To get help.*

5. One woman was *a jockey the other woman interviewed was a commercial pilot.*

6. Tom Peters co-authored *In Search of Excellence. The best-selling business book in history.*

7. The men of the tribe had *clearly defined roles. Hunting and fishing.*

8. The new management promoted a highly touted *sales technique. With meager results.*

9. Science fiction takes us to the brink *of the impossible. For example, robots with human emotions.*

10. Americans neglect the languages *of the Third World. Especially Arabic and Chinese.*

EXERCISE 4   In each of the following pairs, use a semicolon to join two independent clauses. (A comma would cause a *comma splice*.) Write the last word of the first clause and the first word of the second, joined by a semicolon.

EXAMPLE: His hair was very neat every strand was in place.
ANSWER: neat; every

1. I enjoy running it becomes an almost unconscious act.

2. Everyone did calisthenics executives joined the workers and super-visors.

3. The class was inventing imaginary new products one of them was a stringless yo-yo.

4. Cost overruns were horrendous therefore, the project was abandoned.

5. People were shouting commands everyone with a flashlight was direct-ing traffic.

6. The suspect had stepped out of the lobby he was walking down the street.

7. Zoos used to be dismal places however, modern zoos provide more nat-ural habitats.

8. The sloth is genuinely lethargic its metabolism runs at half the normal rate for animals of its size.

9. Factories in Japan maintain a minimal inventory supplies are used right away.

10. A pawnshop is on the ground floor above it is a fleabag hotel.

GRAMMAR AND USAGE

In writing and revising, you shift gear from the language of casual talk to the written English that readers expect when asked for their serious attention. You write "can hardly afford" where you might say *"can't hardly afford"*; you write "this kind of request" where you might say *"these kind* of requests." You need to make the right choices when faced with differences in **usage**—between words (*failure* or *flop*?), forms of words (*who* or *whom*?), and ways of constructing a sentence (*reason is that* or *reason is because*?).

NS   **2a** ## STANDARD ENGLISH

Use standard English in all your written work.

Standard English is our common currency of communication—the language of schools, business, government, and the media. It is used by teachers, lawyers, office workers, and others who daily deal with books, records, memos, notes, and other forms of the written word. However, for many Americans some form of **nonstandard** English is the natural speech at home, in their neighborhood, or on the job. They need to be able to shift to standard English in order to succeed in school and office. In any dealings with city hall, insurance agents, loan officers, car dealers, or social workers, the person limited to nonstandard English is already at a disadvantage.

See the "Glossary of Usage" for nonstandard expressions like *a error* (instead of *an*), *being as, hadn't ought to, irregardless, learn* instead of *teach, off of,* and *used to could.* Watch out especially for the following:

(1) Revise nonstandard forms of verbs. Avoid forms like *knowed, you was, had wrote, might have went.* (See **3** for more on verbs.)

NONSTANDARD: The earthquake struck while we *was* loading the car.
STANDARD: The earthquake struck while we *were* loading the car.

NONSTANDARD: Her co-workers had already *went* home.
STANDARD: Her co-workers had already *gone* home.

(2) Revise nonstandard pronoun forms. Use *himself* and *themselves* instead of *hisself, theirself, theirselves,* and *themself.* Write "We tried out *those* new machines" instead of "We tried out *them* new machines."

607

(3) Revise double negatives. Double negatives say no twice (could*n't never* get him to agree); triple negatives tell us no three times (*never* did *nobody no* harm).

NONSTANDARD: They *never* told *nobody* the family secret.
STANDARD: They never told *anybody* the family secret.

---

inf   **2b**   FORMAL AND INFORMAL

Use English that is right for your purpose.

People who use standard English vary it for different occasions. They use **informal** English in casual conversation but also in personal letters and in writing with a folksy or humorous touch. They use a more **formal** kind of English in writing on serious subjects but also in formal speeches, lectures, or discussions. The advice given in this handbook will help you write moderately formal English—serious enough for all but the most solemn or official occasions, but close enough to vigorous everyday speech not to sound stilted or affected.

Here are some features of informal English that are usually edited out of serious writing: between you and *I, like* I said, *real* strange, it was *them*, wish it *was* true. When your writing is criticized as too informal, check the following especially:

(1) Check for conversational tags and contractions. Do without the folksy introductory *"Well,* I am not sure" or *"Why,* they never replied." Avoid the overuse of shortened forms like *can't, won't, isn't, I'm, you're,* and *there's.*

(2) Recognize the informal pronouns used everywhere in casual speech. These range from *it's him* to a *you* or *they* disconnected from any specific reference:

INFORMAL: The only time *you* see anybody in California in a tuxedo is when *they're* burying him.   Joan Rivers

(3) Recognize expressions widely considered too informal for serious writing. See the "Glossary of Usage" for the following:

between/among	*like I said*
can and *may*	*most everybody*
cannot help but	*reason is because*
couple of	split infinitives
due to	*these kind*

it's me
less/fewer

used to/didn't use to
you with indefinite reference

EXERCISE 5　Suppose an editor had flagged for you the following sentences as containing *nonstandard or informal expressions*. Where is the problem? For each sentence, write down a word or phrase that should replace the inappropriate part of the sentence.

EXAMPLE:　He acted like we had insulted him.
ANSWER:　as if

1. The new management wanted results irregardless of the cost.
2. We have never had no doubts about her good intentions.
3. The ejected patron had wrote an angry letter to the mayor.
4. The shipment arrived early, like he had promised.
5. The new owner disapproves of these kinds of books.
6. The priceless vase had fallen off of the desk.
7. They had always been real kind to those "less fortunate."
8. Denied admission, he created a ugly scene.
9. I had heard of the McGregors; it was them who first settled the valley.
10. My cousins always took good care of theirself.

3　VERB FORMS

High on the list of items that frequently need revision are forms of verbs. Verb forms differ noticeably in standard and nonstandard English. And verbs are a familiar stumbling block for students speaking English as a second language.

ub　3a　## REGULAR VERBS

Use the standard forms of regular verbs.

The **tenses** of a verb show the relationship of events in time. We *worry* in the present; we *worried* in the past; and we *will worry* again in the future. We *have worried* before this (perfect tense); others *had worried* about similar matters before us (past perfect tense); and a few years from now we *will have worried* about matters of which we are still unaware (future perfect tense). Note that we need only two basic forms of this verb (*worry* and *worried*) to make up these different tenses. Most English

TENSES OF ACTIVE VERBS		
	NORMAL	PROGRESSIVE
Present	I ask, he (she) asks	I am asking
Past	I asked	I was asking
Future	I shall (will) ask	I shall be asking
Perfect	I have asked	I have been asking
Past Perfect	I had asked	I had been asking
Future Perfect	I shall (will) have	I shall have been asking
TENSES OF PASSIVE VERBS		
Present	I am asked	I am being asked
Past	I was asked	I was being asked
Future	I shall (will) be asked	———
Perfect	I have been asked	———
Past Perfect	I had been asked	———
Future Perfect	I shall (will) have been asked	———

verbs, the **regular** verbs, make do with two basic forms, drawing on a third—he was always *worrying*—when dealing with action in progress. (See chart, "Tenses of Verbs.")

(1) Use *-ed* or *-d* for the past. We use the plain form for the **present** tense—something happening now, or done regularly, or about to happen: we *travel* often, I *consent*, they *exercise* regularly, they *depart* tomorrow. We add *-ed* or *-d* for the **past** tense: we *traveled* often, I *consented*, they *exercised*, they *departed* yesterday.

PAST: Many pioneer families *perished* in the desert.
The witness *invoked* the Fifth Amendment.

(2) In the present tense, use *-s* for the third person singular. Use the special *-s* ending when talking about one single person or thing, with action now: he *travels*, she *consents*, it *departs*. The **first person** is speaking (*I* or *we*): the **second person** is spoken to (*you*). The **third person** is a third party (or object or idea) that we are talking about: *he, she,* or *it* for the singular; *they* for the plural. Use the *-s* ending for the third person singular:

THIRD PERSON: Brian *works* as a shoplifter.   (*He* works.)
Marcia *collects* beer mugs.   (*She* collects.)
Inflation *continues*.   (*It* continues.)

(3) **Use -ed and -d after have and be.** With regular verbs, the *-ed* form does double duty as a verbal (called the past participle) that combines with *have (has, had)* to form the perfect tenses. The **present perfect** has police. He *has supported* us loyally. The **past perfect** had already happened prior to *other* events in the past: They *had asked* me ahead of time. Often additional auxiliaries come before *have*. The **future perfect** will have happened before some time in the future: The dust *will have settled*.

PERFECT:	The police *has consulted* a psychic.
PAST PERFECT:	They *had* already *encased* the reactor in cement.
FUTURE PERFECT:	The country *will have depleted* its oil reserves.

The verbal ending in *-ed* or *-d* is also used in all forms of the **passive voice**—forms showing that the subject of the sentence is acted upon rather than acting:

PASSIVE:	Many elephants *are slaughtered* by poachers.
	A protest *was filed* by the Animal Rights Committee.
	The passages *had been lifted* verbatim.

(See Chapter 16 on "Revising the Awkward Passive.")

(4) **Use -ing for the progressive construction.** The verbal ending in *-ing* (present participle) serves in forms showing an action or event in progress, taking place:

PROGRESSIVE:	The agency *is processing* your application.
	The architect *was redesigning* the entranceway.

---

ub   3b | IRREGULAR VERBS

Use the standard forms of irregular verbs.

Irregular verbs often have three basic forms, with the past different from perfect: I *write* now. She *wrote* last week. He *has written* regularly. The second and third forms are more unpredictable than those of regular verbs: *begin—began—begun, blow—blew—blown, go—went—gone.* (See chart, "Standard Forms of Verbs.") Remember:

(1) **Use the standard past tense.** Revise nonstandard forms like *knowed, blowed, catched, brung,* and *drug*.

STANDARD:	Ancient Greek scientists *knew* that the earth was round.
	We cruised all day but *caught* few fish.
	Telegrams seldom *brought* encouraging news.

(2) Use the right form after *have* and *be*. Know the third basic form for use in the perfect tenses:

STANDARD: Our pious neighbors *had gone* to church.
The python *has* already *eaten* the rabbit.
You *should have taken* the blue pills instead.
Overeager reporter *had* already *written* his obituary.

Use the right third form in all passive verbs after *be* (*am, is, was, were, has been,* and so on):

STANDARD: The mammoth *had been frozen* and preserved in the Arctic ice.
The potato salad and pickles *were stolen* during the night.

(3) Know the difference between *lie* and *lay*. We *lie* in the sun (and we let sleeping dogs *lie*), but we *lay* mines, bricks, tiles, and similar objects of a verb. We *lie*, and *lie down*, without an object (we just *lie* there). For *lie*, the past tense is *lay*, and the third basic form is *lain*:

LIE, LAY, LAIN: Let's *lie* in the shade. We whistled, but he just *lay* there. The statue *had lain* on the ocean floor. You *should lie* down. Coins *were lying* on the ground.

We lay *something*, with *laid* as the past tense (*laid* an egg) and as the form used after *have* (*had laid* the rumors to rest).

LAY, LAID, LAID: Bricklayers *lay* bricks. Our forefathers *laid* the foundation. She *had laid* a wreath at the tomb. He was always *laying* odds.

(4) Know the difference between *sit* and *set*. To *sit* (*sit—sat—sat*) is to be seated. *Sit down* follows the same scheme:

They *sit* in the pew in which their parents *sat* and their grandparents *had sat* before them. (S–V)

Set (*set—set—set*), one of the few verbs with only one basic form, means *place* or *put*. You yourself *sit*, or *sit down*; you *set*, or *set down*, something else:

When you *have set* the timer, *set* the device down gingerly behind the screen we *set* up. (S–V–0)

Note: Sometimes we have a choice of two acceptable forms. Both are right: *lighted* or *lit*, *dived* or *dove*, *waked* or *woke*, *thrived* or *throve*, *dreamed* or *dreamt*.

STANDARD FORMS OF VERBS			
	PRESENT	PAST	PERFECT
Group 1	begin	began	have begun
	bend	bent	have bent
	blow	blew	have blown
	break	broke	have broken
	bring	brought	have brought
	burst	burst	have burst
	buy	bought	have bought
	catch	caught	have caught
	choose	chose	have chosen
	come	came	have come
Group 2	dig	dug	have dug
	do	did	have done
	drag	dragged	have dragged
	draw	drew	have drawn
	drink	drank	have drunk
	drive	drove	have driven
	drown	drowned	have drowned
	eat	ate	have eaten
	fall	fell	have fallen
	fly	flew	have flown
Group 3	freeze	froze	have frozen
	get	got	have gotten (got)
	go	went	have gone
	grow	grew	have grown
	know	knew	have known
	prove	proved	have proved (proven)
	ride	rode	have ridden
	run	ran	have run
	say	said	have said
	see	saw	have seen
Group 4	sing	sang	have sung
	speak	spoke	have spoken
	steal	stole	have stolen
	swim	swam	have swum
	swing	swung	have swung
	take	took	have taken
	tear	tore	have torn
	throw	threw	have thrown
	wear	wore	have worn
	write	wrote	have written

subj   3c | SUBJUNCTIVE |

Use subjunctive forms in special situations.

Many languages have one set of verb forms for straight facts and another set for maybes, wishes, and hypotheses. The factual form is the **indicative** (I know it *was*); the hypothetical form is the **subjunctive** (I wish it *were*). In English, only a few uses of the subjunctive mode (or **mood**) survive:

(1) Choose the hypothetical *were* or the factual *was* after *if, as if, as though*. Use *were* if a possibility is contrary to fact or highly improbable— a remote chance:

SUBJUNCTIVE: For a moment, the statue looked as if it *were* alive.   (It wasn't really.)
I f I *were* you, I would ask for a refund.
The new manager acted as if asking questions *were* a crime.

Use the hypothetical *were* also to show a mere wish:

SUBJUNCTIVE: I wish she *were* more assertive.
Napoleon wished it *were* spring in Paris rather than winter in Moscow.

Use the factual *is* or *was* when pondering a genuine possibility:

FACTUAL: If the courier *was* ill, he should have declined the assignment.
(Maybe he really was.)
It looks as if the statue *was* thrown overboard in a storm.

(2) Use a subjunctive after verbs asking that something be done. After words like *ask, order, insist, demand, recommend, require,* and *suggest,* use a plain or unmarked form (*be, have, go*) instead of the *-s* ending (*is, has, goes*).

SUBJUNCTIVE: Her supervisor insists that she *spend* more time in the office.
I move that this question *be* referred to a committee.

EXERCISE 6   What form of the verb in parentheses is missing from the sample sentence? (Fill in a single word each time.)

1. (steal)   Radioactive material had been _____ from the plant.
2. (throw)   We spotted the swimmer and _____ her a lifeline.
3. (go)   The witnesses should have _____ to the police.
4. (examine)   Before they filed the report, they _____ every shred of evidence.
5. (choose)   Last year, we _____ a blind student as class president.

6. (know) Without the call, we would not have _____ about her disappearance.
7. (drive) The car had been _____ on next-to-impossible roads.
8. (grow) Everything had _____ well after the heavy rains.
9. (develop) In its early years, the company _____ educational software.
10. (write) He might have _____ you a lukewarm letter of recommendation.

EXERCISE 7   Choose the right form of *sit* or *set*, *lie* or *lay*.

1. The folders *sat/set* on the desk while we were *sitting/setting* up a new filing system.
2. Her uncle *set/sat* a record for flagpole *sitting/setting*.
3. This time of year, the tourists *lie/lay* in the sun, while the natives *sit/set* in the shade.
4. Broken columns were *lying/laying* on the ground; some fragments had been *laid/lain* end to end.
5. Thick dust *lie/lay* on the artifacts that for centuries had *lain/laid* in the tomb undisturbed.

EXERCISE 8   Choose among *was*, *were*, or *be*, using the *subjunctive* where appropriate.

1. If *Alice in Wonderland* _____ being written today, Alice would use words like *awesome* and *totally cool*.
2. If neither parent _____ a Catholic, she must be a convert.
3. The measure proposed that utility companies _____ barred from producing nuclear waste within the state.
4. Brian's aunt always acted as if she _____ his mother.
5. Journalists and ministers urged that the sentence _____ commuted.

---

4   AGREEMENT

Most nouns and pronouns have different forms for one of a kind (**singular**) and more than one (**plural**): *key/keys, prize/prizes, woman/women, child/children.* Verbs often offer us a similar choice: one *goes*/several *go*; one *is* gone/several *are* gone; one *has* arrived/several *have* arrived. When we match the right forms, the subject and its verb **agree** in number:

SINGULAR: The clock *ticks*. The listener *was* bored. She *writes* often.
PLURAL: The clocks *tick*. The listeners *were* bored. They *write* often.

Note: For nouns, the -s ending is a plural signal: *boys, cars, tickets, houses, promotions.* But for verbs, the -s is a signal for singular: He *talks,* she *writes,* it *leaks.*

SINGULAR OR PLURAL

Sort out confusing singulars and plurals.

Recognize unfamiliar plurals, and know how to handle agreement when form seems to point one way and meaning the other.

(1) Know the irregular plurals of borrowed words. Most English nouns use the -s plural (cars, buildings, trees, books, petitions). But some words borrowed from Greek and Latin have kept irregular plural forms:

SINGULAR	PLURAL	SINGULAR	PLURAL
crisis	crises	criterion	criteria
thesis	theses	phenomenon	phenomena
analysis	analyses	medium	media
hypothesis	hypotheses	stimulus	stimuli
curriculum	curricula	nucleus	nuclei

SINGULAR:	The artist's favorite *medium was* acrylic paint.
PLURAL:	The *media were* turning the trial into a circus.
SINGULAR:	*This phenomenon has* been discovered only recently.
PLURAL:	*These phenomena have* been extensively studied.

Note: Acceptable anglicized plurals are ind*exes* (rather than ind*ices*) and formu*las* (rather than formul*ae*). But use *data* as a plural to be safe (data *are* items of information).

(2) Know pronouns that seem plural in meaning but are singular in form. Treat as singular *each, either, neither, everybody,* and *everyone.* Though they point to more than one, look at them *one at a time:*

SINGULAR: Each of the plans *has* its flaws. Either of the candidates *seems* weak. Everybody *approves* of your decision.

(3) Know nouns that look plural but are treated as singulars. Words ending in -*ics*—*aeronautics, mathematics, physics, aerobics*—are often singular names for a field or activity: Modern physics *allows* for uncertainty. Some words ending in *-ics* can go either way:

SINGULAR: Politics *bores* me. Statistics *attracts* math majors.
PLURAL: Her politics *have* changed. These statistics *are* suspect.

Collective nouns like *audience, committee, family, police, group, jury,* or *team* are singular when we think of the whole group. They are plural when we think of the *members* of the group:

SINGULAR: The nuclear family *is* the exception, not the rule.
PLURAL: The family *were* gathered around the table.

(4) Expressions showing the whole amount may be singular even when plural in form. They are singular when they point to the sum or total:

SINGULAR: Thirteen dollars *seems* excessive for a small cutlet and two carrots.
One third of the world is rich, and two thirds *is* poor.

Number of is singular when it stands for a total: *The number of* joggers *has* declined. It is plural when it stands for "several": *A number of* joggers *were* still on the trail.

---

agr   **4b**   # COMPOUND SUBJECTS

Check agreement when there is more than one subject.

When the word *and* joins several subjects, the resulting **compound subject** is normally plural. But the word *or* may merely give us a choice between two singular subjects:

PLURAL: Rafting and canoeing *clear* the smog from the lungs and the fumes from the brain.
SINGULAR: Either the surgeon or the anesthesiologist *is* to blame.

Sometimes, however, two words joined by *and* point to the same thing or person: Corned beef and cabbage *is* good to eat. The President and chief executive *is* one single person.

Note: Expressions like *as well as, together with,* and *in addition to* do not add one subject to another. (Instead they introduce a prepositional phrase.)

SINGULAR: The mayor's *office,* together with other agencies, *is* sponsoring the event.
The *memo,* as well as the other documents, *has* been shredded.

agr   **4c** | **BLIND AGREEMENT**

Make subject and verb agree even when they are separated by other material.

Avoid **blind agreement:** Do not make the verb agree with a word close to it that is *not* its subject.

(1) Check agreement when a plural noun comes between a singular subject and its verb. Disregard any wedge between subject and verb:

SINGULAR: An ad [in these small local papers] *produces* results.
Understanding [the opponent's motives] *is* important.

(2) Check agreement when the subject follows the verb. Do not make the verb agree with a stray noun that stands in front of it:

PLURAL: Inside the yellowed envelope *were* several large bills.
(What was inside? *Bills* were inside.)

(3) Check for agreement in sentences starting with *there is, there are, and the like.* After *there,* the verb agrees with the **postponed subject**—with whatever is "there":

SINGULAR: There *was* polite *applause* from the better seats.
PLURAL: There *were* scattered *boos* from the balcony.

In formal usage, the plural verb is required even when followed by a compound subject of which each part is singular:

PLURAL: There *were* a bed and a chair for each patient.

(4) Make a linking verb agree with its subject, not the completer. In the following sentence, *problem* is the subject; *parts* is the completer (or complement): "Our chief *problem* is (not *are*) defective parts."

agr   **4d** | **LOGICAL AGREEMENT**

If necessary, carry agreement beyond subject and verb.

Where the meaning requires it, extend agreement beyond the subject and verb of a sentence.

(1) Check for agreement after relative pronouns. *Who, which,* or *that* may point back to one (a guest who *leaves*) or to several (guests who *leave*). Watch for agreement in combinations like "one of those who *believe*":

PLURAL: Jean is *one of those students who go* to classes after work.   (Many students *go* to classes after work.)

SINGULAR: Jean is *the only one* of those students *who goes* to classes after work.   (Only one student *goes* to classes after work.)

(2) If necessary, carry agreement through to other elements of the sentence. Revise for **logical agreement** in sentences like the following:

ILLOGICAL: Many advertisers now beam their messages at *women* who are a *wife, mother, and executive* at the same time.

REVISED: Many advertisers now beam their messages at *women* who are *wives, mothers, and executives* at the same time.

EXERCISE 9   In each sentence, solve an *agreement problem* by replacing a single word (usually the verb or first auxiliary). Write the changed word after the number of the sentence.

1.   Each of these candidates are equally unqualified.
2.   Much feinting, chutzpah, and false humility is required in a successful job interview.
3.   For American tourists who eat at the Paris McDonald's, the weeks spent studying European culture has been wasted time.
4.   The description of his appearance and manners hint at turbulent hidden emotions.
5.   As we enter the post-modern period, the styles of the office towers subtly change.
6.   For every miracle drug, there is unexpected side effects and tremendous variations in individual response.
7.   The deep thinkers heard on talk shows solve all the world's problems by the use of their powerful mind.
8.   The weak chemical bonds among oxygen atoms in ozone allows the molecules to break apart.
9.   Many crime shows make the viewers feel tough by association and boosts their egos.
10.   Computer monitoring of coffee breaks and phone calls are turning offices into electronic sweatshops.

EXERCISE 10   Choose the right forms, paying special attention to common sources of *faulty agreement*.

1.   Complaints about poor quality *has/have* hurt American efforts to capture overseas markets.

2. The steps that American companies have taken to improve quality control *is/are* producing only limited results.
3. Ford Motor Company as well as other leading manufacturers *has/have* recalled large numbers of cars and trucks.
4. Having to admit that the front seats tend to shake loose *does/do* little for the image of a new car.
5. True, few customers wind up with one of those cars that *spends/spend* more time in the shop than on the road.
6. But a buyer may discover that there *is/are* an electronically controlled door that doesn't open and a windshield wiper motor that has shorted out.
7. According to some foreign customers, computer chips made in America *tends/tend* to be chipped.
8. Gauges in a new jumbo aircraft *was/were* crosswired so that a fire in one engine showed on the gauge for another.
9. Fire suppression nozzles in the cargo hold *was/were* spraying fire retardant in the wrong direction.
10. The ability to turn out high-quality products *is/are* essential if American industry wants to compete around the world.

---

5   PRONOUN REFERENCE

When you use a pronoun like *he* or *this,* it should be clear who *he* is or what *this* points to. A pronoun has to refer clearly to its **antecedent—** what "went before."

ref   5a

VAGUE OR AMBIGUOUS PRONOUN

Make a pronoun point clearly to its antecedent.

Pronouns easily sow confusion when we mention several people in the same breath: *"Linda* disliked *Ann* because *she* was very competitive." Which of the two was competitive? Reshuffle the material in such a sentence:

CLEAR: Because *Linda* was very competitive, *she* disliked Ann.
Because *Ann* was very competitive, Linda disliked *her.*

If a *they* follows two plural nouns, you might point it at the right one by making the other singular. (Similarly, you might change one of two singular nouns to a plural.)

AMBIGUOUS: *Students* like *science teachers* because *they* are realistic and practical.

CLEAR: A *student* usually likes *science teachers* because *they* are realistic and practical.   (*They* can no longer be mistakenly referred to *students*.)

(1) Revise awkward reference to modifiers: "James worked in an *asbestos plant,* and *it* got into his lungs" (the plant?); "I reached for *the horse's saddle,* but *it* shied away" (the saddle?)

CLEAR: James worked in an asbestos plant, and *the asbestos* got into his lungs.
As I reached for *its* saddle, *the horse* shied away.

(2) Revise vague idea reference. Revise a vague *this* or *which* pointing back to an earlier idea:

AMBIGUOUS: The police knew the employees were stealing, but management was not aware of *this.*   (of the stealing, or of the police knowing?)

CLEAR: The police knew the employees were stealing, but management did not realize *word had got out.*

We can often make a vague *this* more specific: "this *assumption,*" "this *practice.*" A vague *which* is more difficult to improve:

AMBIGUOUS: I have received only one letter, *which* frightens me.

CLEAR: *Receiving* only one letter frightened me.
The letter (the only one I received) frightened me.

(3) Spell out implied antecedents. In informal conversation, we often make a pronoun point to something that we have not actually mentioned. In writing, spell out the implied antecedent:

IMPLIED: In Nebraska, *they* grow mostly wheat.
CLEAR: In Nebraska, *the farmers* grow mostly wheat.

IMPLIED: My mother was a musician; therefore, I have also chosen *it* as my profession.
(The *it* stands not for *musician* but for *music.*)
CLEAR: My mother was a *musician;* therefore, I have also chosen *music* as my profession.

---

ref   5b | AGREEMENT OF PRONOUN |

Make pronouns agree with their antecedents.

To make a pronoun point to what it stands for, make pronoun and antecedent agree in *number:*

WRONG: *Abortions* should not be outlawed because *it* is often required for medical reasons.
RIGHT: *Abortions* should not be outlawed because *they* are often required for medical reasons.

(1) Make a singular pronoun point to one representative person. Treat as singular *a person, an individual, the typical student,* or *an average American—one* person that represents many:

WRONG: *The typical male* today is expected to assume a larger share of parenting, but *they* are often poorly prepared for this task.

RIGHT: *The typical male* today is expected to assume a larger share of parenting, but *he is* often poorly prepared for this task.

(2) Use a singular pronoun to refer to expressions like *everybody* and *someone*. These **indefinite pronouns** do not point to a particular person: *everybody (everyone), somebody (someone), nobody (no one), anybody (anyone), one.* Although they may seem to point to many different people, use them as if you were looking at *one person at a time:*

RIGHT: *Everybody* on the team did *her* best.
Nobody should meddle in affairs that are none of *his or her* business.

None started as the equivalent of "no one," but today either singular or plural forms after it are acceptable to most readers:

BOTH RIGHT: *None* of the women had to interrupt *her* schooling (or "*their* schooling").

(3) Deal with the pronoun dilemma. Informal English uses the plural pronoun in sentences like "Everybody received *their* copy of the test." Handbooks used to prescribe the singular *he (his, him):* "Everybody received *his* copy of the test." This **generic** *he,* meant to refer to both men and women, is now widely shunned. For a mixed group, use *he or she (his or her).*

NONSEXIST: Today's executive has a computer by *his or her* desk.

If several uses of *he or she* (and perhaps *himself and herself*) would slow down a sentence, convert the whole sentence to the plural:

INFORMAL: *Everyone* I knew was increasing *their* insurance to protect *themselves* against lawsuits.
FORMAL: *All my friends* were increasing *their* insurance to protect *themselves* against lawsuits.

(For more on gender-biased pronouns, see "Avoiding Sexist Language" in Chapter 15.)

EXERCISE 11   In each of the following, replace one pronoun in order to solve a problem of *pronoun reference.* Write the changed pronouns after the number of each sentence.

1. Each member had their own private excuse for joining the fraternity.
2. Universities often prove mixed blessings to the towns surrounding it.

3. The bear feeds primarily on roots; to attack livestock, they would have to be desperate.
4. The actress had played roles as a sassy, randy young girl; it had led to her being stereotyped as a hussy.
5. Most medical students are still white males, although admission policies are now less biased in his favor.
6. Nonsmokers are refusing to patronize a restaurant because of the smoke he might inhale.
7. A woman who spends years preparing for a career in the theater might find themselves acting in mattress commercials.
8. Each person runs differently, depending on their body size.
9. The Founding Fathers intended that someone's religion should be their own responsibility.
10. England consistently had a much lower homicide rate because they enforced strict gun control laws.

EXERCISE 12   Rewrite each sentence to revise ambiguous or unsatisfactory pronoun reference.

1. A five-year-old boy was shot by a police officer mistaking his toy gun for a real weapon.
2. The book's title sounded interesting, but when I read it I found it boring.
3. The average individual respects the wishes of the group because they hate to be considered odd.
4. My father is extremely intelligent, though he does not always express it in a verbal form.
5. Prisons are run by undertrained and underpaid individuals, not to mention that they are hopelessly overcrowded.
6. Many voters know little about Central America, which makes it difficult for the President to gain popular support for his policies.

6   PRONOUN CASE

Some pronouns have alternate forms: *I* and *he* are **subject forms,** identifying the person that the predicate says something about. *Me* and *him* are **object forms,** identifying the object of a verb or preposition. Only half a dozen pronouns have separate object forms: *I—me, we—us, he—him, she—her, they—them, who—whom.* These differences are called differences in **case.**

SUBJECT	OBJECT	OBJECT OF PREPOSITION
I snubbed	*him.*	
He recommended	*me*	to *them.*
They prejudiced	*her*	against *me.*

ca   **6a**   ## SUBJECT AND OBJECT

Use the right pronoun forms for subject and object.

Formal use of these forms differs from what we hear in informal and nonstandard speech.

(1) Choose the standard form when a pronoun is one of several subjects or objects. To find the right pronoun for a compound subject or compound object, try the parts one at a time:

SUBJECT: The supervisor and *I* [not: *Me* and the supervisor] worked hand in hand.
(*Who* worked? *I* worked.)

OBJECT: She asked my brother and *me* [not: my brother and *I*] to lower the volume.
(*Whom* did she ask? She asked *me.*)

(2) Be careful with pronoun-noun combinations. Choose between *we girls—us girls* or *we Americans—us Americans:*

SUBJECT: *We scouts* are always eager to help.   (*We* are eager.)
OBJECT: He told *us scouts* to keep up the good work.   (He told *us.*)

(3) Use object forms after prepositions: *with* **her,** *because of* **him,** *for* **me.** Use the object form for a pronoun that is the second or third object in a prepositional phrase:

OBJECT: This kind of thing can happen to you and *me* [not "to you and *I*"].
I knew there was something between you and *her* [not "between you and *she*"].
She had bought tickets for Jim, Laura, and *me* [not "for Jim, Laura, and *I*"].

(4) Use the right pronoun after *as* **and** *than.* In shortened comparisons, fill in enough of what is missing to discover whether the pronoun would be subject or object:

SUBJECT: He is as tall as *I* (am).
His sister earned more than *he* (did).

OBJECT: I owe you as much as (I owe) *them.*
They liked the other candidate better than (they liked) *me.*

(5) In formal usage, use subject forms after linking verbs. These introduce not an object of an action but a description of the subject:

FORMAL:　The only ones absent were *she* and a girl with measles.
　　　　　(*She* and the other girl were absent.)
　　　　　It was *he* who had initiated the proposal.

　　　Note: Conservative editors object to **reflexive pronouns** (*myself, himself*) as substitutes for the plain subject form or object forms:

FORMAL:　My friend and *I* [not "and *myself*"] were the last ones to leave.
　　　　　I asked both his friend and *him* [not "and *himself*"] to come over after dinner.

---

ca　　**6b**　　## *WHO* AND *WHOM*

Know how to use *who* and *whom.*

Who is increasingly replacing *whom* in speech. Know when to use *whom* in your writing.

(1) Choose *who* or *whom* at the beginning of a question. *Who* asks a question about the subject. *Whom* asks a question about an object:

SUBJECT:　*Who* took the message? *He* did.
OBJECT:　*Whom* did you notify? I notified *him.*
　　　　　To *whom* should I write? To *him.*

In more complicated questions, it may not be obvious whether a *who* asks about a subject or about an object. However, the *he/him* or *she/her* test will always work:

SUBJECT:　*Who* do you think will win?　(I think *she* will win.)
OBJECT:　*Whom* did you expect to come?　(I expected *her* to come.)

(2) Choose *who* or *whom* at the beginning of a dependent clause. To apply the *he/him* or *she/her* test to a dependent clause, cut it from the rest of the sentence. In the following examples, *who* (or *whoever*) is the subject of a verb:

SUBJECT:　Ask her / *who* typed the letter.　(*He* did.)
　　　　　We approached the customer / *who* was waiting.　(*She* was.)
　　　　　Here is a dollar for / *whoever* gets there first.　(*He* gets there.)

In the following examples, *whom* is the object of a verb or of a preposition:

OBJECT:　*Whom* we should invite / is a difficult question.　(We should invite *her.*)
　　　　　She knew my brother, / *whom* I rarely see.　(I rarely see *him.*)
　　　　　He knew few people / on *whom* he could rely.　(He could rely on *them.*)

EXERCISE 13   In each of the following sentences, change *one pronoun* to the form that is right for written English. Write the changed form after the number of the sentence.

1. Jane's lawyer brought bad news for she and her mother.
2. I recognized the man's face; it was him who had thrown the pie.
3. This information should remain strictly between you and I.
4. The new ruler surrounded himself with subordinates on who he could rely.
5. Visitors from outer space might laugh at the technology that us Earthlings possess.
6. People who are asked to "play themselves" in a movie often find that a good actor can portray their type more effectively than them.
7. My brother and me had no respect for the people with whom we worked, and soon we had no respect for ourselves.
8. Rumors abounded about a rift between the board and I.
9. People who we had not seen for months or whom we knew very slightly telephoned and offered to board the cat.
10. People who cannot suffer can never grow up or discover whom they are.

---

7   MODIFIERS

Modifiers help us build up bare-bones sentences. Modifiers range from single words to long prepositional or verbal phrases:

ADJECTIVES:	The *dutiful* son obeyed his *angry* parents.
ADVERBS:	Jean will *probably* leave *early*.
PREP. PHRASE:	A woman *in overalls* was standing *on a ladder*.
VERBAL PHRASE:	The man *waiting in the dark doorway* was an old friend.

adv   7a | ADJECTIVES AND ADVERBS

Use the distinctive adverb form.

Adjectives modify nouns, telling us which one or what kind: the *sad* song, an *easy* answer, a *careful* driver, *high* praise, an *immediate* reply. **Adverbs** modify verbs. They tell us how (also when or where) something is done: speak *sadly*, won *easily*, drive *carefully*, praised him *highly*, reply *immediately*.

(1) Use the adverb form to modify a verb. Often, we convert adjective to adverb by activating the *-ly* ending: *bright—brightly, cheerful—cheerfully, considerable—considerably, happy—happily*. Choose the distinctive adverb form to tell the reader *how*—how something was done or how something happened:

ADVERB: The inspectors examined every part *carefully*.
We have changed the original design *considerably*.
No one took the new policy *seriously*.

Note: Some words ending in *-ly* are not adverbs but adjectives: a *friendly* talk, a *lonely* life, a *leisurely* drive. And for words like *fast, much*, and *early*, the adjective and the adverb are the same:

ADJECTIVE: The *early* bird gets the worm.
ADVERB: The worm should not get up *early*.

(2) Avoid the informal adverbs of casual talk. Use *well* and *badly* as adverbs instead of *good* and *bad*. Change "I don't hear *good*" to "I don't hear *well*"; "I write pretty *bad*" to "I write *badly*."

WRONG: This morning, the motor was running *good*.
RIGHT: This morning, the motor was running *well*.

Replace informal adverbs like *slow, quick,* and *loud*: drive *slowly*, react *quickly*, speak *loudly*.

(3) Use adverbs to modify other modifiers. Use the adverb form to modify either an adjective or another adverb:

ADVERB **+** ADJECTIVE: It was a *surprisingly beautiful* bird.
ADVERB **+** ADVERB: You sang *admirably well*.

Edit out informal expressions like *real popular, awful expensive,* and *pretty good*. Use *very* in such combinations or a distinctive adverb form like *really, fairly,* or *extremely*: Punk rock was *extremely popular*. The crowd was *fairly well-behaved*.

Note: Adjectives instead of adverbs follow linking verbs. After a **linking verb,** an adjective points back to the subject; it pins a label on the subject: The *bottles* are *empty* (empty bottles). The most common linking verb is *be* (*am, is, are, was, were, has been,* and so on). Others are *become, remain,* and similar words (become *poor*, remain *calm*, grow *rich*, turn *pale*). Additional linking verbs stand for perceptions of the five senses (look *fine*, sound *scary*, taste *flat*, smell *sweet*, feel *bad*).

DM, MM   7b | # MISPLACED MODIFIERS |

Make modifiers point clearly to what they modify.

Moving a modifier will often change the meaning of a sentence:

ADVERB:	Riots *almost* broke out at every game. (but they never quite did)
	Riots broke out at *almost* every game. (they did frequently)
PREP. PHRASE:	The man *with the parrot* started a conversation.
	The man started a conversation *with the parrot*.
VERBAL:	Manuel watered the plants *wilting in the heat*.
	Wilting in the heat, Manuel watered the plants.

(1) Shift a misplaced modifier to the right position. If necessary, rewrite the whole sentence:

MISPLACED:	The manager looked at the room we had painted *with ill-concealed disgust*. (painted with disgust?)
REVISED:	*With ill-concealed disgust,* the manager looked at the room we had painted.
MISPLACED:	*Made of defective material,* the builder had to redo the sagging ceiling.
REVISED:	*Since it was made of defective material,* the builder had to redo the sagging ceiling.

(2) Link a dangling modifier to what was left out of the sentence. Look for danglers like the following:

DANGLING:	*To become a computer specialist,* an early start is essential.
	(Who wants to become a computer specialist?)
REVISED:	To become a computer specialist, *a student* needs an early start.
DANGLING:	Having watched *Dallas* and *Dynasty,* real people will seem dull.
REVISED:	Having watched *Dallas* and *Dynasty,* viewers will find real people dull.

(3) Keep a squinting modifier from pointing two ways at once:

SQUINTING:	I feel *subconsciously* Hamlet wanted to die.
	(Are we talking about *your* subconscious feelings—or Hamlet's?)
REVISED:	I feel that Hamlet *subconsciously* wanted to die.

Note: Some verbal phrases are not meant to modify any one part of the main sentence. These are called **absolute constructions.** The most common ones clarify the attitude or intention of the speaker:

RIGHT:	*Generally speaking,* traffic is getting worse.
	They had numerous children—seven, *to be exact.*

EXERCISE 14   In each of the following sentences, change one word to the distinctive *adverb form*. Write the changed word after the number of the sentence.

1.   When the witness testified, she spoke nervously and very defensive.
2.   He was tired and unable to think logical.
3.   I read the questions as careful as panic allowed.
4.   Toward the end of the story, the events unfold very sudden, as they sometimes do in real life.
5.   My father regarded life more philosophical than most plumbers do.
6.   Macbeth interpreted the prophecies of the weird sisters very literal.
7.   During the time Judy spent in France, her horizon widened considerable.
8.   Computers solve math problems faster and more efficient than the fastest human mathematician.
9.   An experienced cryptographer can decipher a simple code very easy.
10.   Sebastian went in for arm wrestling because he didn't do good in other sports.

EXERCISE 15   Rewrite each of the following sentences to eliminate unsatisfactory *position of modifiers*.

1.   Having run for an hour, the carrot juice tasted great.
2.   The car was towed away by John, having exploded on Interstate 59.
3.   Unsure of my future, the navy was waiting for me.
4.   After ringing for fifteen minutes, the bellboy answered the phone.
5.   He was hit by a rotten egg walking back to the dorm.
6.   After graduating from high school, my stepfather asked me to vacate the premises.
7.   When traveling during the night without sufficient lighting, other motorists will have difficulty seeing the vehicle.
8.   These magazines appeal to immature readers with torrid love affairs.
9.   I watched a television show with my aunt on a weekend that ended with the murderer throwing himself from the top of a skyscraper.
10.   I just wrote to my family for the first time since I came here on the back of a postcard.

8   CONFUSED SENTENCES

Straighten out confused sentences by asking, "Who does what? What is compared to what? What caused what?"

st   8a | OMISSION AND DUPLICATION |

Check for omitted or duplicated elements.

Revise omission or duplication that results from hasty writing, inaccurate copying, or careless typing.

(1) Supply sentence parts that you have left out. Fill in the missing *a, the, has, be, we,* or *they:*

INCOMPLETE: Our astronauts walked on the moon but have faltered since.   (*Who* faltered?)
COMPLETE: Our astronauts walked on the moon, but *we* have faltered since.

(2) Delete duplicated words. Check especially for doubling up of words like *of* and *that:*

DUPLICATED: They had built a replica of the Eiffel Tower *of* which they were very proud *of.*
REVISED: They had built a replica of the Eiffel Tower *of* which they were very proud.
DUPLICATED: Economists claim *that* because of political pressures in an election year *that* the deficit will grow.
REVISED: Economists claim *that* because of political pressures in an election year the deficit will grow.

mx   8b | MIXED CONSTRUCTION |

Do not mix two ways of expressing the same idea.

We sometimes start a sentence one way and finish it another. To revise such a sentence, retrace your steps. Disentangle the two ways of saying what you had in mind:

MIXED: My mother *married* at the age of nineteen, as *were* most of her friends.
REVISED: My mother *married* at the age of nineteen, as *did* most of her friends.
   My mother *was* married at the age of nineteen, as *were* most of her friends.

MIXED: *In case of* serious flaws in design *should have been reported* to the regulatory agency.
REVISED: *Serious flaws* in design *should have been reported* to the regulatory agency.
   In case of serious flaws in design, *the regulatory agency* should have been notified.

Note: Avoid the "Because . . . does not mean" sentence, where the adverbial clause starting with *because* appears as if it were the subject of a verb. Use a noun clause starting with *that:*

MIXED: *Because* we listened to his proposal *does not mean* we approve.
REVISED: *That* we listened to his proposal *does not mean* that we approve.

FAULTY PREDICATION

Make sure what the predicate says applies logically to the subject.

The subject of a sentence calls our attention to something. The predicate then makes a statement about the subject: "The choice (subject) *was difficult* (predicate)." Make sure the statement made by the predicate can apply logically to the subject:

ILLOGICAL: *The choice* of the new site *was selected* by the mayor.
(What was selected? The site, not the choice)
LOGICAL: *The new site was selected* by the mayor.

ILLOGICAL: *The participation* at her séances *is always overcrowded*.
(What is overcrowded? The séances, not the participation)
LOGICAL: Her séances *are always overcrowded.*

Check for special cases of faulty predication:

(1) Revise equations when they link two labels that do not stand for the same thing. In *"Dinosaurs* were *giant reptiles,"* the dinosaurs are reptiles, and the reptiles are dinosaurs. But in *"Her job* was *a mail carrier,"* the mail carrier is not really a job but a person: "She *worked* as a mail carrier." (Or "Her job was *that of* a mail carrier.")

ILLOGICAL: *A student* with a part-time job *is a common cause of* poor grades.
(A student is not a cause.)
LOGICAL: A student's *part-time* job is a common cause of poor grades.

(2) Revise faulty equation caused by *is-when* or *was-when* sentences. Avoid sentences like "Conservation is *when* we try to save energy." Conservation is not a time when something happens but a practice or a goal.

ILLOGICAL: Parole *is when* a prisoner is set free on condition of good behavior.
LOGICAL: Parole *is the practice* of setting prisoners free on condition of good behavior.

FAULTY APPOSITIVES

Make sure appositives apply logically to the nouns they follow.

An **appositive** is a noun that tells us more about another noun: "Ferraro, *the vice-presidential candidate,* had served in Congress." Here, Ferraro and the candidate are the same person. Revise sentences when the second label does not logically fit:

ILLOGICAL: They had only one *vacancy, the assistant manager.*
                     (The manager is not vacant; the position is.)

LOGICAL: They had only one *vacancy, the position* of assistant manager.

EXERCISE 16   Revise each of the following *confused sentences.*

1. Usually it takes a minimum of brain power to watch *Dallas* than it does to read a book.
2. She tried to promote peace among each individual.
3. Young people smoke because it makes them feel sophisticated or perhaps a rebellion against adults.
4. While attending college and working at the same time makes it hard to shine as a scholar.
5. Typical playground equipment fails to keep in mind the needs of the tot.
6. A woman is more likely to understand another woman's anger better than a man.
7. The players up for the team were about even in ability and was a hard decision to make.
8. A person who fails in various things might give him an inferior feeling.
9. Radical opinions are too biased and will not accept realistic compromise.
10. Assimilation is when we try to make every Spock a clone of Captain Kirk.
11. In an era of dwindling resources, we will all have to give up conveniences to which we are used to.
12. Because little of the pledged money actually came in does not mean we have to abandon the project.
13. Scientists know how to distill drinking water from salt water, but the cost of such a project is too unprofitable.
14. By cutting the number of jurors in half greatly reduces the time used in selecting a jury.
15. The legislators were flooded with angry letters, mostly members of the NRA.

---

9   **INCOMPLETE CONSTRUCTIONS**

In written English, we avoid shortcuts common in informal speech. Check constructions like the following for logical completeness.

INCOMPLETE COMPARISON

Complete incomplete comparisons.

Normally, *more, better,* and *whiter,* the **comparative** forms, help us compare two elements:

COMPARATIVE: The company seemed to employ more *tax lawyers* than *engineers.*

Most, best, and *whitest,* the **superlative** forms, help us compare three elements or more:

SUPERLATIVE: The annual classic at Le Mans is the most dangerous *automobile race in Europe.*

(1) Spell out what is being compared. Revise incomplete comparisons using *more* and *the most:* "That girl has *more* luck" (than who or than what?). "I had *the most* wonderful experience" (of the day? of a lifetime?).

INCOMPLETE: The author turned the life of Mozart into *the most exciting play.*
COMPLETE: The author turned the life of Mozart into *the most exciting play of the season.*

(2) Compare things that are really comparable. Revise sentences like the following: "The *fur* was as soft as a *kitten.*" The fur was as soft as a *kitten's* (fur), or as soft as *that* of a kitten.

ILLOGICAL: *Her personality* was unlike *most other people* I have known.
LOGICAL: *Her personality* was unlike *that of* most other people I have known.

(3) Clarify three-cornered comparisons. When you mention three comparable items, which two are being compared?

CONFUSING: We distrusted the *oil companies* more than the *local governments.*
CLEAR: We distrusted the oil companies more than *we did* the local governments.
              We distrusted the oil companies more than the local governments *did.*

(4) Correct overlapping comparisons. Comparisons like the following are blurred: "The forward was faster than *any player on her team.*" The forward is part of the team and cannot be faster than *any player* on the team, including herself.

RIGHT: The forward was faster than *any other player* on the team.

INCOMPLETE COORDINATION

Check coordinate elements for excessive shortcuts.

When items of the same kind are coordinated by *and, or,* or *but,* leave out only those forms that would cause unnecessary duplication.

(1) Check for completeness when shortening one of several similar verbs. Leave out only words that would be exactly identical: "It can [*be done*] and will *be done*."

INCOMPLETE: The bear *was given* an injection and the instruments *made* ready.

COMPLETE: The bear *was given* an injection, and the instruments *were made* ready.

(2) Revise shortcuts of the "as-good-if-not-better" type: "Korean cars turned out to be *as good if not better than* ours." The complete forms would be *as good as* and *not better than*:

REVISED: Korean cars turned out to be *as good as, if not better than,* ours.

BETTER: Korean cars turned out to be *as good as* ours, *if not better.*

(3) Check several linked prepositional phrases. Keep prepositions that are not identical but merely express a similar relationship.

WRONG: I have great *respect and faith in* our leadership.

RIGHT: I have great *respect for* and *faith in* our leadership.

I have great *admiration and respect for* our leadership.

EXERCISE 17   Make each of the following *incomplete sentences* more complete by rewriting the italicized part. Write the rewritten part after the number of the sentence.

1. People today live longer and eat up more resources *than the previous century.*
2. *Juries have always and will always be swayed* by the grandstanding of a lawyer.
3. An older person's need for love is *as big as a child.*
4. Taxpayers are already *familiar and hostile to the usual explanations.*
5. The population of China is already *bigger than any country.*
6. *The club had in the past and was still barring* "undesirables" from membership.
7. The Sears Building in Chicago is *as tall or taller than any building in New York City.*
8. People in show business *seem to have more bad luck.*
9. The statistics for rape are much less complete *than robbed banks or stolen bicycles.*
10. Few of my friends were *preoccupied or even interested in the love lives of celebrities.*
11. In much of Europe, American films are *more popular than any other country.*
12. Children understand other children *better than adults.*
13. The impact of American books, magazines, and comics in Great Britain is *much greater than British publications in the United States.*

14.   The liberal arts are excellent preparation *for such practical professions as engineers and lawyers.*

15.   Critics of our schools must realize that *they can and are doing great harm by indiscriminate attacks.*

---

10   # CONSISTENCY

Like a road with unexpected twists and turns, sentences that lack consistency slow down the reader.

sf   **10a**   ## SHIFTS IN TENSE

Revise confusing shifts in time.

Verbs have a built-in reference to time: We *agree* (now). We *agreed* (then). When describing a situation or telling a story, be aware of the **tense** forms you are using to show time.

(1) Avoid shifting from past to present. Do not switch to the present when something becomes so real that it seems to be happening before your eyes:

SHIFT: *We were waiting* for the elevator when suddenly all lights *go* out.
REVISED: *We were waiting* for the elevator when suddenly all lights *went* out.

(2) Show differences in time to avoid confusion:

SHIFT: Linda *was* only a messenger, but she *was* now the supervisor of the whole floor.
CONSISTENT: Linda *had been* only a messenger, but she *was* now the supervisor of the whole floor.
(Working as a messenger came before promotion.)

SHIFT: My uncle always *talked* about how farming *has changed.*
CONSISTENT: My uncle always *talked* about how farming *had changed.*
(about how it had changed up to the time when he talked)

(3) Be consistent when dealing with possibilities. Note the difference between factual reference to a possibility and the **conditional,** which makes the possibility seem less probable, more remote:

SHIFT: If they *come* to this country, the government *would* offer them asylum.
FACTUAL: If they *come* to this country, the government *will* offer them asylum.
CONDITIONAL: If they *came* to this country, the government *would* offer them asylum.

FACTUAL: If terrorists *threaten* to use an atomic weapon, what *will* we do?

CONDITIONAL: If terrorists *threatened* to use an atomic weapon, what *would* we do?

(4) Adjust tense forms in indirect quotation. What the speaker felt or observed at the time would be in the present tense in direct quotation: He said, "I *feel* elated." It would be in the past tense in indirect quotation: He said that he *felt* elated.

DIRECT: Roosevelt said, "We *have* nothing to fear but fear itself."

INDIRECT: Roosevent said that the nation *had* nothing to fear but fear itself.

Failure to adjust the tenses in indirect quotations can lead to sentences like the following:

SHIFT: The president of Austria admitted that he *was* [should be "*had been*"] an intelligence officer in the German army.

---

sf **10b** | SHIFTS IN REFERENCE

Revise confusing shifts in reference.

The pronoun you use to refer to yourself is *I, me,* or *my* (**first person singular**). Writers who want to speak directly to their readers can call them *you* (**second person singular** and **plural**). However, *you* also appears as an informal equivalent of *one* or *a person,* referring to people in general. In formal writing, use *you* only to mean "you, the reader":

INFORMAL: Sailing to the colonies, *you* had to worry about pirates. (The reader wasn't there.)

FORMAL: Sailing to the colonies, *travelers* had to worry about pirates.

(1) Avoid shifts to the indefinite, generalized *you*. Revise sentences that shift to *you* after the person involved has already been identified:

SHIFT: *I* would not want to be a celebrity, with people always knowing what *you* are doing.

CONSISTENT: *I* would not want to be a celebrity, with people always knowing what *I* am doing.

(2) Avoid shifts to the request form. Giving directions or instructions, we naturally use the form for requests or commands (**imperative**): *Dice* the carrots. *Remove* the hubcaps. But avoid shifting to the request form when giving more general advice:

SHIFT: Managers *should stop* tallying every move of the employee and every trip to the restroom. *Build* employee morale and *stimulate* group loyalty, as the Japanese do.

CONSISTENT: Managers *should stop* tallying every move of the employee and every trip to the restroom. *They should build* employee morale and *stimulate* group loyalty, as the Japanese do.

sf   **10c** | **SHIFTS TO THE PASSIVE** |

Do not shift to the passive when the same person is still active in the sentence.

Do not confuse your readers by shifting from an **active** construction ("She *remodeled* her own house") to a **passive** one ("The roof *was put on by* her").

SHIFT: He *retyped* his résumé, and it *was mailed* the same day. (by whom?)
REVISED: He *retyped* his résumé and *mailed* it the same day.

¶P or //   **10d** | **FAULTY PARALLELISM** |

Use parallel structure for repeated sentence parts

Sentence parts joined by *and, or,* and *but* should be *parallel,* fitting into the same grammatical category. If you put an *and* after *body,* readers expect another noun: "body and *mind,* "body and *soul.*" The same principle applies to other sentence parts:

INFINITIVES: Two things that a successful advertisement must accomplish are *to be noticed* and *to be remembered.*

CLAUSES: The young people *who brood* in their rooms, *who forget* to come down to the dining hall, and *who burst out* in fits of irrationality are not worrying about who will win the great game.

Faulty parallelism results when the added part does not fit the expected pattern. For instance, "*ignorant* and *a miser*" is off balance because it joins an adjective and a noun. You could change *ignorant* to a noun ("He was an *ignoramus* and a miser") or *miser* to an adjective ("He was ignorant and *miserly*").

FAULTY: They loved *the wilderness* and *to backpack to solitary lakes.*
PARALLEL: They loved *to explore* the wilderness and *to backpack* to solitary lakes.

FAULTY: She told me of *her plans* and *that she was leaving.*
PARALLEL: She *informed* me of her plans and *told* me that she was leaving.

(1) Avoid mixing a noun and an adjective as modifiers:

FAULTY: The schools must serve *personal and society* needs as they evolve.
PARALLEL: The schools must serve *personal and social* needs as they evolve.

(2) Check for parallelism when using paired connectives (correlative conjunctions): *either . . . or, neither . . . nor, not only . . . but also,* and *whether . . . or:*

FAULTY: I used to find him either *in the spa* or *chatting with his friends.*
PARALLEL: I used to find him either *soaking in the spa* or *chatting with his friends.*

FAULTY: Reporters wondered whether *to believe* him or *should* they try to verify his story.
PARALLEL: Reporters wondered whether they should *believe* him or *try* to verify his story.

(3) Avoid faulty parallelism in a series of three or more elements. The **series** that concludes the following sentence has three parallel parts:

PARALLEL: Computer programs now check student papers for *spelling errors, awkward sentences,* and *sexist phrases.*

But sometimes we read what looks like a series, only to have the last element snap out of the expected pattern:

FAULTY: He loved to *talk, drink* wine, and *good food.*
PARALLEL: He loved *conversation,* good *wine,* and good *food.*

If the elements in a series are not really parallel in meaning, your revision might break up the series altogether:

FAULTY: The new manager was *ambitious, hard-driving,* and *an MBA from Harvard.*
REVISED: The new manager, *an MBA from Harvard,* was ambitious and hard-driving.

EXERCISE 18   Rewrite the following sentences to eliminate *shifts in perspective* and *faulty parallelism.*

1. Robots with artificial vision will not only lift and weld but also putting in car windows and installing taillights.
2. Teenagers armed with rags and towels swarmed around the still dripping car, and quickly the outside was wiped dry and the chrome polished.
3. The affluent American has a large income, a nice house, and lives in the nice part of town.
4. Parents must take an active interest in what their children are doing. Coach a ball team or be a counselor to a scout troup.
5. Office workers discovered that computers monitored the time you took to staple memos or open envelopes.
6. As I walk by the shop, the owner, not having anything to do, followed me with his eyes.
7. The boy described how he was beaten by his masters, taken advantage of by the older servants, and the meager meals of bread and porridge he received.

8. The success of a television program depends on how well the program has been advertised, the actors taking part, and is it comedy or serious drama.

9. As a legal secretary, I had to prepare wills, depositions, and basically run the office.

10. The police were warning us that if the crowd did not calm down, arrests will be made.

11. Only when one faces the decision of whether to have an abortion can you really feel what a tough issue it is.

12. Stricter gun control laws would be difficult to enforce, resented by many citizens, and only a doubtful method of preventing crime.

13. The television news always includes stories about a sniper with a rifle or someone murdered a relative.

14. My favorite television program was already in progress. Right in the middle of a dramatic scene, the station goes off the air.

15. As the world grew dark, he dreams of a place he will never see.

---

11   END PUNCTUATION

End punctuation brings what we are saying to a complete stop. We use it to separate complete sentences—units that can stand by themselves. Here are three kinds of complete sentences:

STATEMENTS: We hear much about solar energy.
Space probes have landed on Venus.

QUESTIONS: Do our big cities have a future?
Why has your policy changed?

REQUESTS/COMMANDS: Send in your coupon now!
Sell real estate in your spare time!

(1) Use the period to mark off complete sentences. (See **1a** on how to revise **sentence fragments**.)

FRAGMENT: They had calculated the cost of coffee breaks. *At 53 cents a minute.*

REVISED: They had calculated the cost of coffee breaks at 53 cents a minute.

(2) Use the question mark to mark direct questions. These appear exactly as you would ask them of another person. ("Who shredded the documents?") Do you remember to use question marks at the end of questions that are long or involved?

QUESTION: Are our needs shaped by advertisers, or do advertisers cater to our needs?

PUNCTUATION MARKS: REFERENCE CHART

Comma

before coordinators *(and, but, or)*	12b
with nonrestrictive adverbial clauses	12d
after introductory adverbial clauses	12d
with nonrestrictive relative clauses	12e
with nonrestrictive modifiers	13b
after introductory modifiers	13c
with conjunctive adverbs *(therefore, however)*	12c
with *especially, namely, for example*	14e
with *after all, of course*	13c
between items in a series	14a
in a series of parallel clauses	1c
between coordinate adjectives	14b
with dates, addresses, and measurements	14c
with parenthetic elements	15c
between repeated or contrasted elements	14d
with direct quotations	16a, 16b

Semicolon

between paired sentences	12a, 1c
before adverbial connectives	12c, 1c
before coordinators between clauses containing commas	12b
in a series with items containing commas	14a
outside a quotation	16b

Colon

to introduce a list or an explanation	14e, 1a
to introduce a formal quotation	16a

Period

at end of sentence	1a, 11
for ellipsis	16c
with abbreviations	23a

Dash

to show a break in thought	15a
before summary at end of sentence	15a
to set off modifier with commas	13b, 15a

Quotation Marks

with direct quotations	16a
for quotation within quotation	16a
with terminal marks	16b
with technical terms	16e
to set off titles	16f

Exclamation Mark	11
Question Mark	11, 16b
Parentheses	15b
Slash	16a

(3) Use the exclamation mark (rarely!) for emphasis. Use it to mark an order or a shout, to signal indignation or surprise. Note that the exclamation mark appears rarely in ordinary prose.

EMPHASIS: Win a trip to Tahiti!
              The jury found him not guilty!

EXERCISE 19   Check the following for rhetorical questions (with the right answer already built in) and questions that are long or involved. Mark them *Q* to show that they should end with a question mark. Mark the other examples *S* (for ordinary statement).

1. What good does it do to kill a person for taking someone else's life.
2. Early in Presidential campaigns, old political warhorses go foraging among the grass roots before they support a candidate.
3. Can voters be persuaded to vote for a candidate that does not have simple answers for difficult questions.
4. Why does a campaign have to be a demolition derby won by the last battered survivor.
5. What used to be a chance to arouse local voters is now little more than a photo opportunity.

---

12   LINKING PUNCTUATION

When several short statements become part of a larger whole, we call each subsentence in the new combined sentence a **clause**. Independent clauses are self-contained; they could easily be separated again by a period. Dependent clauses have been welded together more permanently, so that (like this example) they cannot easily be pulled apart.

CS or /;   12a   **SEMICOLON ONLY**

Use a semicolon between two paired statements.

Often two statements go together as related information; they are part of the same story. When a semicolon replaces the period, the first word of the second statement is *not* capitalized:

SEMICOLON: The thin look was in; yogurt sales soared.
               We constantly coin new words: Governments spread *disinformation*; executives are protected by *golden parachutes*.

Do not use a comma alone to join two independent clauses. A **comma splice** runs on from one independent clause to the next with only a comma between them. (See **1c**.)

COMMA SPLICE: Carol is twenty-eight years old, she might go back to school.
REVISED: Carol is twenty-eight years old; she might go back to school.

---

p or /,   **12b**   # COORDINATORS

Use a comma when a coordinator links two clauses.

Use a comma before a **coordinating conjunction** (coordinator, for short): *and, but, for, so, or, nor,* and *yet.* Put a comma before—but not after—the *and, but,* or *so:*

COMMA: The lights dimmed, *and* a roar went up from the crowd.
She remembered the face, *but* she forgot the name.
The picnic fizzled, *for* it started to rain.
The star was late, *so* the warmup band played forever.
We had better apologize, *or* we will never be invited again.
Her parents did not approve of divorce, *nor* did her spouse.
Reporters knew the truth, *yet* no one dared to print it.

(1) Do not use the comma when the coordinator merely joins words or phrases:

NO COMMA: Farmbelt legislators clamored for tariffs on imports *and* for subsidies for their constituents.

(2) If it is needed for clarity, use a semicolon between clauses with internal commas:

SEMICOLONS: Now in the Big Bend the river encounters mountains in a new and extraordinary way; *for* they lie, chain after chain of them, directly across its way.   Paul Horgan

---

p or /;   **12c**   # CONJUNCTIVE ADVERBS

Use a semicolon with conjunctive adverbs.

Conjunctive adverbs are adverbs used as connectives: *therefore, however, nevertheless, furthermore, consequently, moreover, accordingly, besides,* as well as *hence, thus, indeed,* and *in fact.* A period could replace the semicolon; however, a comma would cause a comma splice.

COMMA SPLICE:	The weather turned ugly, *therefore* the launch was postponed.
RIGHT:	The weather turned ugly; *therefore*, the launch was postponed.
ALSO RIGHT:	The weather turned ugly. *Therefore*, the launch was postponed.

Put the semicolon where the two clauses join, even if the connective follows later. Like other adverbs, conjunctive adverbs can shift their position in a sentence:

Demand had dropped off; *nevertheless*, prices remained high.
Demand had dropped off; prices, *nevertheless*, remained high.
Demand had dropped off; prices remained high, *nevertheless*.

We often pause slightly for conjunctive adverbs; commas, therefore, often set them off from the rest of the second statement. Formal writing usually requires the added punctuation; however much popular writing does without it.

FORMAL:	We liked the area; rents, *however*, were impossible.
INFORMAL:	We liked the area; rents *however* were impossible.

_p or /,_   **12d** | ## SUBORDINATORS

Use a comma or no punctuation with subordinators.

Subordinating conjunctions (subordinators for short) start **adverbial clauses**—clauses that, like adverbs, tell us when, where, why, or how:

TIME AND PLACE:	when, whenever, while, before, after, since, until, as long as, where, wherever
REASON/CONDITION:	because, if, unless, provided
COMPARISON:	as, as though
CONTRAST:	though, although, whereas, no matter how

An *if* or a *because* changes a self-sufficient, independent clause into a **dependent clause,** which normally cannot stand by itself. "If I were in charge" does not become a complete sentence until you answer the question "If you were in charge, *then what?*" ("If I were in charge, elevator music would be banned.") Beware of dependent clauses added to a main statement as an afterthought:

FRAGMENT:	He failed the test. *Because he ran out of time.*
REVISED:	He failed the test *because he ran out of time.*

(1) Use no comma when a restrictive clause comes last. A **restrictive** clause limits the scope of the main clause, narrowing the possibilities, imposing essential conditions. "I will raise wages" sounds like an unqualified promise. "I will raise wages *after we strike oil*" puts a restriction on the offer. Such restrictive clauses are essential to the meaning of the whole sentence. We do not set them off *when they follow the main clause*.

RESTRICTIVE: Hundreds will perish *if the dam breaks.*
                 Gold prices rise *when the dollar falls.*
                 They would not treat the patient *unless we signed a release.*

   (2) Set off a nonrestrictive clause. Use a comma before *though, although,* and *whereas.* These introduce **nonrestrictive** material, which does not impose essential restrictions or conditions. Rather, they set up a contrast; both statements are separately true. Similarly, *whether or not* and *no matter how* show that the main statement is true regardless:

NONRESTRICTIVE: Hundreds applied for the job, *although the salary was low.*
                 Reactors produce nuclear wastes, *whereas coal leaves only inert ash.*
                 The figures were wrong, *no matter what the computer said.*

   Note that a word like *when* or *where* may merely introduce extra information when the time or place has already been specified—and stays the same:

NONRESTRICTIVE: She never went back *to Georgia, where she was born.*

   (3) Set off any adverbial clause that comes first. When a subordinator joins two clauses, you can reverse their order: Vote for me *if you trust me. If you trust me,* vote for me. When the dependent clause comes first (restrictive or not), use a comma to show where the main clause starts:

COMMA: *If the dam breaks,* hundreds will perish.
                 After we noticed the police car, we drove more slowly.

   Note special uses of some connectives: *though* used as a conjunctive adverb (with a semicolon); *however* used as a subordinator (with a comma):

   Henry Ford II went to Yale; *he didn't graduate, though.*
   His underlings could not please him, *however hard they tried.*

---

p or /,   12e | **RELATIVE CLAUSES**

Use commas or no punctuation with relative clauses.

   Relative clauses are clauses that start with a **relative pronoun:** *who (whose, whom), which,* or *that.* Such clauses add information about one of the nouns (or pronouns) in the main part of the sentence. They may, therefore, appear at different points in the sentence, interrupting rather than following the main clause:

The odds favored candidates *who applied early.*
Those *who know how to talk* can buy on credit.   Creole proverb

(1) Do not set off restrictive relative clauses. They are **restrictive** when we need them to know "Which one?" or "What kind?" ("A mole is a spy *who burrows into the enemy's bureaucracy.*") Such relative clauses narrow the possibilities. They help us identify; they single out one person or group: the runner *who tripped;* drugs *that kill pain.*

NO COMMA: People *who live in glass houses* should not throw stones.   (only those)
Call the woman *whose name appears on this card.*   (only her)

Note: The pronoun *that* almost always introduces a restrictive clause. Shortened relative clauses with a pronoun like *that* or *whom* left out are always restrictive:

NO COMMA: The forms *[that] we sent* were lost in the mail.
The lawyer *[whom] she recommended* charged large fees.

(2) Set off nonrestrictive relative clauses. A **nonrestrictive** clause does not limit the scope of the main clause; it does not single out one from a group or one group among many. We know which one or what kind; we merely learn more about something already identified: Beethoven, *who was deaf;* aspirin, *which kills pain.*

COMMA: Sharks differ from *whales, which surface to breathe.*   (all do)
We drove down *Pennsylvania Avenue, which leads past the White House.*

Use *two* commas when the nonrestrictive clause interrupts the main clause:

TWO COMMAS: Computers, *which perform amazing feats,* do break down.

NOUN CLAUSES

Do not set off noun clauses.

Use no punctuation when the place of a noun is taken by a clause within a clause. Clauses that take the place of a noun are called **noun clauses:**

NOUN: The mayor announced *her plans.*
NOUN CLAUSE: The mayor announced *that she would retire.*

NOUN: The *Post* first revealed *his identity.*
NOUN CLAUSE: The *Post* first revealed *who had leaked the news.*

NOUN: *The writer* knew your name.
NOUN CLAUSE: *Whoever wrote it* knew your name.

EXERCISE 20   Punctuate the following combined sentences. For each blank space, choose one of the following: *C* for comma, *SC* for semicolon, or *No* for no punctuation:

1. We need regulations to ensure safe working conditions _____ however, some regulations infringe on individual rights.
2. She wasn't a big-time photographer _____ but she had enough work to keep up her studio.
3. Students who needed financial aid _____ were grilled like suspects in a bank robbery.
4. Space exploration is astronomically expensive _____ therefore, only the richest nations take part.
5. The new law aimed at ex-convicts _____ who carry guns.
6. If a marriage becomes unglued _____ the partners tend to blame each other.
7. Lawmakers must stop computer crime _____ before it reaches epidemic proportions.
8. When meteors hit the surface _____ they form craters like those made by volcanoes.
9. Her parents tolerated her friends _____ though one was a body builder with a shaved head.
10. The plaintiff was never told _____ why the application was denied.
11. Freedom of speech includes freedom for those _____ whose views make us ill.
12. Jobs were scarce and insecure _____ so my parents left town.
13. The sun, which is the final source of most of our energy _____ is a gigantic nuclear furnace.
14. The furniture was all glass and steel _____ and the walls were a bright red.
15. Human beings could not survive on other planets _____ unless they created an artificial earthlike environment.

---

13   PUNCTUATING MODIFIERS

Often nouns and verbs carry along material that develops or modifies their meaning. How we punctuate such modifiers depends on the role they play in the sentence.

UNNECESSARY COMMAS: A SUMMARY

- between subject and verb:

   The needle on the dial⌒*swung* erratically.

- before an ordinary prepositional phrase:

   She had first flown a plane⌒*in Ohio* in 1972.

- with restrictive modifiers and clauses:

   The hunt was on for migrants⌒*entering the country illegally.*

   American diplomats⌒*who speak Chinese*⌒are rare indeed.

- with coordinators joining words or phrases:

   The Vikings reached Greenland⌒*and the coast of North America.*

- after coordinators:

   WRONG: He promised to call *but*⌒he never did.

   RIGHT: He promised to call, *but he never did.*

- before coordinators joining two dependent clauses:

   He told the court *that* the building had been only partially insured⌒*and that* the policy had lapsed.

- before noun clauses:

   We already know⌒*what the future holds* for the poor of the world.

- after *such as:*

   The new plan called for more teaching of basics, *such as*⌒English and algebra.

- between adjective and noun:

   Clint Eastwood movies are known for their *crude, brutal*⌒*violence.*

- after last items in a series:

   Natives, tourists, *and pickpockets*⌒mingled in the city square.

NOTE: Other elements *added* to a sentence may require commas in situations similar to those above.

UNNECESSARY COMMAS

Do not use commas between basic sentence elements.

Do not use a comma between the subject and its verb, or between the verb and one or more objects. In the following sentence, there should be no comma between the **compound** (or double) **subject** and the verb:

SUPERFLUOUS COMMA: *Information and common sense, do* not always *prevent* the irresponsible use of mind-altering substances.

In addition, do *not* set off the many modifiers that blend into a simple sentence without a break. These include many single-word modifiers: adjectives and adverbs. They also include most prepositional phrases:

WRONG: Forms *with unanswered questions,* will be returned.
RIGHT: Forms *with unanswered questions* will be returned.

WRONG: The next Olympic Games were to be held, *in 1992.*
RIGHT: The next Olympic Games were to be held *in 1992.*

---

p or /,   **13b** | RESTRICTIVE AND NONRESTRICTIVE |

Know when to use commas with modifiers.

Restrictive modifiers are "musts"; they are needed to narrow the possibilities or single out one among several. They are essential to the sentence and are not set off. We use them to narrow the field, to limit a term that otherwise would apply too broadly: cars *built in Japan* (only those); students *eligible for aid* (only those).

Nonrestrictive modifiers are "extras"; they merely add information about something already identified. They are set off by a comma, or *two* commas if they interrupt the sentence. They leave the term they follow unrestricted or generally applicable: the sparrow, *a pesky bird* (applies to all of them); soap operas, *watched by millions* (applies to the whole type).

RESTRICTIVE: A student *showing a valid I.D.* will enter free.
(Other students pay.)
NONRESTRICTIVE: My friends, *showing valid I.D.s,* entered free.
(No friends were excluded.)

(1) Set off most appositives. An **appositive** is a second noun that modifies the first. Most appositives are nonrestrictive. They do not winnow one possibility from among several; they answer questions like "*What else* about the person?" or "*What else* about the place?" ("Her aunt, *a lawyer*, lived in Boston, *my favorite city*.") A proper name is usually adequate identification, and the appositive that follows it is set off:

COMMA: She joined the Actors' Theater, *a repertory company.*
COMMAS: H. J. Heinz, *the Pittsburgh pickle packer*, keeps moving up in the food-processing industry.

Occasionally, however, a restrictive appositive helps us tell apart two people of the same name:

NO COMMAS: I find it hard to distinguish between Holmes *the author* and Holmes *the Supreme Court Justice.*

(2) Set off nonrestrictive verbals and verbal phrases. A **verbal phrase** modifying a noun usually starts with a form like *running, explaining, starting* or like *dressed, sold, taken.* Such phrases are restrictive when used to narrow down a general term or single out one among several:

NO COMMAS: The person *running the place* talked like a drill sergeant.
The restaurant excluded guests *dressed in togas.*

Verbal phrases are nonrestrictive when they merely *tell us more* about something we have already identified:

COMMAS: Our singing telegram, *smiling broadly*, stood in the doorway.
We saw the bride, *dressed in white.*

(3) Set off nonrestrictive adjective phrases. An **adjective phrase** is made up of several adjectives, or of an adjective and other material:

RESTRICTIVE: We collected containers *suitable for recycling.*   (only those)
NONRESTRICTIVE: The climbers, *weary but happy*, started down.   (all did)

(4) Use dashes to set off a modifier that already contains one or more commas. The dashes then signal the major breaks:

DASHES: Her sister—*a stubborn, hard-driving competitor*—won many prizes.

SENTENCE MODIFIERS

Set sentence modifiers off by commas.

Modifiers may modify sentence elements other than nouns. They may also modify the sentence as a whole rather than any part.

(1) Know when to set off verbals and verbal phrases modifying a verb. They may be either restrictive or nonrestrictive. Notice the comma showing the difference:

RESTRICTIVE: He always rushed into the office *reading from fan letters just received.*
(contains main point)
NONRESTRICTIVE: Deadline newspaper writing is rapid because it cheats, *depending heavily on clichés and stock phrases.*
(elaborates main point)

(2) Always set off verbal phrases modifying the sentence as a whole. Such phrases are often called **absolute constructions**:

COMMA: *To tell you the truth*, I don't even recall his name.
The business outlook being rosy, he invested his savings in stocks.
Our new manager has done well, *considering her lack of experience.*

(3) Set off long introductory modifiers. Use a comma to show where the main sentence starts. Use this comma after prepositional phrases of three words or more:

COMMA: *Like many good reporters,* they deplored the low status of most journalists.
In the etiquette books of colonial times, females were instructed in the art of passivity.

Set off *introductory verbals* and *verbal phrases* even when they are short:

COMMA: *Smiling,* the officer tore up the ticket.
To start the motor, turn the ignition key.

(4) If you wish, use the optional commas with transitional expressions. Expressions like *after all, of course, unfortunately, on the whole, as a rule,* and *certainly* often help us go on from one sentence to another. Depending on the amount of emphasis you would give such a modifier when reading, make it stand out from the rest of the sentence by a comma:

COMMA: *After all,* we are in business for profit.
On the other hand, the records may never be found.
You will submit the usual reports, *of course.*

Sentence modifiers that are set off require *two* commas if they do not come first or last in the sentence:

COMMAS: Institutions do not, *as a rule,* welcome dissent.
A great many things, *to be sure,* could be said for him.

EXERCISE 21   Punctuate the following sentences. For each blank, write *C* for comma, *NC* for no comma, or *D* for dash.

1. In spite of repeated promises _____ the shipment never arrived.
2. The agency collected debts _____ from delinquent customers.
3. Whipped by the wind _____ five-foot swells splash over the deck.
4. The book told the story of Amelia Earhart _____ a true pioneer.
5. An engraved receipt was promised to listeners _____ sending in large donations.
6. I looked with amazement at the pots _____ filled with large snapping Dungeness crabs.
7. Working on the pitching and rolling deck _____ we hauled up the heavy nets.
8. The owner, a large woman with mean eyes _____ watched us the whole time.

9. Back at the wharf _____ we sipped hot coffee, trying to get warm.
10. The city, on the other hand _____ has shown no interest in the proposed arena.
11. The mechanics working on a competitor's car _____ are racing against the clock.
12. The wooden benches, bolted to the planks _____ were torn loose by the waves.
13. My uncle—a jovial, fast-talking man _____ sold earthquake insurance.
14. Their performance has been unsatisfactory _____ to say the least.
15. A blizzard of invoices _____ marked "Past Due" is designed to frighten the customer.

---

14   **COORDINATION**

When we coordinate parts of a sentence, we make similar or related elements work together. Use the comma (or other marks) with several elements of the same kind.

p or /,   **14a** | **SERIES**

Use commas between items in a series.

A **series** is a set of three or more parts of the same kind: *red, white,* and *blue; single, married,* or *divorced; life, liberty,* and the *pursuit* of happiness. Separate the elements in a set of three by commas, with the last comma followed by an *and* or *or* that ties the whole group together:

VERBS: On the trail, *we talked, laughed,* and *sang.*
ADJECTIVES: The hills were bright with *red, white,* and *brown* poppies.
NOUNS: Only 18 percent of this country's 56 million families are conventionally "nuclear," with *breadwinning fathers, homemaking mothers,* and *resident children.*   Jane Howard

(1) The basic *A, B,* and *C* pattern can be stretched to four elements or more:

COMMAS: The stand sold *nuts, raisins, apples,* and *every other kind* of organic lunch.
The repertory of the humpback whales includes *groans, chirps, clicks, bugles,* and *roars.*

(2) Groups of words that form a series may already contain commas. To prevent misreading, use semicolons to show the major breaks:

SEMICOLONS: Three people were left out of her will: *John, her greedy brother*; *Martin, her no-account nephew*; and *Helen, her one-time friend*.

(3) The *and* or the *or* tying the series together may have been left out. The following set of four uses commas only:

COMMAS ONLY: The idea was to pool all the needs of all those who had in one way or another been bested by their environment—*the handicapped, the sick, the hungry, the ragged*.

Note: In informal or journalistic writing, the last comma is often left out, but most teachers require it. Use it to be safe:

LAST COMMA: Computer programs can now check student papers for *spelling errors, awkward sentences,* and *sexist phrases*.

---

p or /,   **14b**   ## COORDINATE ADJECTIVES

Use a comma between coordinate adjectives.

Coordinate adjectives work together to modify the same noun: a *tall, handsome* stranger. They are interchangeable adjectives; use a comma between them when you can reverse their order: *slanted, sensational* reporting or *sensational, slanted* reporting.

COMMA: The *snoopy, brash* new magazine pilloried the most *annoying, appalling* people in New York and the nation.

Use the comma only when an *and* could take the place of the comma:

RIGHT: a *hypocritical, cliché-ridden* speech   (hypocritical *and* cliché-ridden)
WRONG: a *dedicated, public* servant   (not: dedicated *and* public)

---

p or /,   **14c**   ## DATES AND ADDRESSES

Use commas with information in several parts.

Dates, addresses, page references, and the like often come in several parts, kept separate from each other by a comma. The last item is followed by a comma if the sentence continues:

DATE: The date was *Tuesday, January 5, 1988*.

ADDRESS: Please send my mail to *113 Robin Street*, *Birdsville*, *Alabama*, starting the first of the month.

REFERENCE: The quotation is from *Chapter 5*, *page 43*, *line 7*, of the second volume.

Remember the comma that separates city and state:

At the *Lordstown*, *Ohio*, and *South Gate*, *California*, plants, laser-equipped robots measure car bodies to make sure they meet exact specifications.

Commas also separate the parts of *measurements* employing more than one unit of measurement. Here the last item is usually *not* separated from the rest of the sentence:

MEASURE: The boy is now *five feet*, *seven inches* tall.
Nine pounds*, *three ounces* is an unusual weight for this fish.

Note: The comma is usually left out if the day of the month precedes rather than follows the month: "12 November 1989."

---

p or /,   **14d** | **REPETITION AND CONTRAST**

Use commas to signal repetition or contrast.

Use commas between expressions that repeat the same idea:

REPETITION: *Produce, produce!* This is the law among artists.
RESTATEMENT: We were there in the nine days before Christmas, *the Navidad*.

Use commas also to set up a *contrast*:

CONTRAST: Many entering freshmen and their parents seek an education that leads to *job security*, *not critical and independent thinking.*   Adele Simmons

---

: or /,   **14e** | **ENUMERATION**

Use a colon or a comma to introduce examples and explanations.

We often need punctuation when we continue a sentence to illustrate (give examples) or to enumerate (list several items).

(1) Use the colon to introduce an explanation or a more detailed list for something already mentioned. The colon then means "as follows":

EXPLANATION: Marcia had a single wish: *a home computer.*
LIST: Military life abounds with examples of regimentation: *fixed hours, a rigid meal schedule, the dress code.*

Unless introducing elaborate lists or charts, avoid a colon after a verb:

WRONG: My two major interests are: *jogging and swimming.*

RIGHT: My two major interests are jogging and swimming.

(2) Use a comma when explanation or illustration follows transitional expressions. Use the comma before *such as* or *especially:*

COMMA: The article described computer languages, *such as* Fortran.

TWO COMMAS: Recent immigrants, *especially* Vietnamese, now live downtown.

Use a comma before and after *namely, for example, for instance,* and *that is:*

TWO COMMAS: American colleges neglect major world languages, *for example,* Chinese and Russian.

EXERCISE 22   Check the following sentences for punctuation of *coordinate* or *closely related elements.* After the number of each sentence, put *S* (for satisfactory), or *U* (for unsatisfactory). Be prepared to explain how you would revise unsatisfactory sentences.

1. It was economics that altered the condition of slavery, not *Uncle Tom's Cabin.*
2. Advertising helps sell goods, services candidates and ideas.
3. In the world of tabloids, nuclear tension, homelessness, the national debt, and ecological disaster do not exist.
4. My cousin was always flying off to places like Chattanooga Tennessee or Missoula Montana.
5. The editorial offices were at 235 East 45th Street, New York, New York.
6. Aaron thought of himself as a noble, dedicated person persecuted by callous, materialistic employers.
7. Lee was known as a strategist not as a tactician.
8. Before long, most of the population of Mexico will live in cities like Guadalajara, Monterrey, Puebla, and Mexico City.
9. The new electronic message center can store incoming calls, signal waiting messages, distribute the same message to many recipients, and route outgoing calls on the least expensive lines.
10. After a while, the messenger arrives with the cholesterol special: a triple order of bacon; two fried eggs, over easy; and bagels, split and buttered.

EXERCISE 23   What should be the punctuation at the blank space in each of the following sentences? Put *C* (for comma) or *NC* (for no comma) after the number of the sentence.

1. Bumper stickers _____ graffiti, and buttons give inarticulate people a chance to express themselves.
2. The company had moved its offices to Atlanta _____ Georgia.
3. Young journalists dream of exposing corrupt _____ public officials.
4. Seven feet, two inches _____ was unusual even for a basketball player.
5. The final clue appeared in Chapter 8 _____ page 148.
6. They had started their shop as a hobby _____ not as a business.
7. Kidnappings _____ bombings, and armed attacks had become commonplace.
8. Jonathan had come to Jamestown, Virginia _____ from Liverpool, England.
9. He loved Italian opera, such as _____ *Madame Butterfly.*
10. She used the new software to conduct a quick _____ thorough search for articles on tax reform.

---

15   PARENTHETIC ELEMENTS

Use dashes, parentheses, or commas to set off parenthetic elements—elements that interrupt the normal flow of thought.

/—   15a   DASHES

Use the dash—sparingly—to signal a sharp break.

Use dashes to do the following:

(1) Make a word or phrase stand out for dramatic effect:

DRAMATIC BREAK: Every time we look at one of the marvels of modern technology, we find a by-product—*unintended, unpredictable, and often lethal.*

It seems possible that more than two billion people—*almost half of the human beings on earth*—would be destroyed in the immediate aftermath of a global thermonuclear war.   Carl Sagan

(2) Set off a complete sentence that interrupts another sentence:

INSERTED POINT: Americans have an intense—*perhaps the right word is obsessive*—interest in weight.

(3) Set off modifiers that would normally require commas but that already contain internal commas. Dashes then signal the stronger breaks:

COMMAS IN MODIFIER: The old-style family—*large,* *closely knit,* *firmly ruled by the parents*—is becoming rare.

(4) Set off a list that interrupts rather than follows a clause:

INSERTED LIST: The group sponsored performers—*dancers, poets, musicians*—from around the world.

(5) After an introductory list, show where the sentence starts over with a summarizing *all, these,* or *those*:

LIST FIRST: *Arabs, Japanese, Vietnamese, South Americans*—all these are a familiar part of the campus scene.

15b PARENTHESES

Put parentheses around less important material (or mere asides).

Parentheses signal facts or ideas mentioned in passing:

ASIDE: The University of Mexico was founded in 1553 (almost a century before Harvard).

Use parentheses around dates, addresses, page references, chemical formulas, and similar information if it might interest some readers but is not an essential part of the text: *(p. 34) (first published in 1910) (now called Market Street).*
Caution: When a sentence in parentheses begins *after* end punctuation, end punctuation is required inside the final parenthesis:

Select your purchases with care. (*No refunds are permitted.*)

15c COMMAS

Use a comma, or commas, to signal slight interruptions.

Use commas with parenthetic elements that blend into a sentence with only a slight break.

(1) Use commas when you address the reader or comment on what you are saying:

DIRECT ADDRESS: Few remember, *dear reader,* the crash of 1929.
COMMENT: A good divorce, *you must remember,* will last you a lifetime.
Romance, *it seems,* is not the same as a relationship.

(2) Use commas to set off introductory tags and tag questions. Set off introductory greetings and exclamations, an introductory *yes* or *no,* and echo questions at the end of a sentence:

TAG OPENING: *Why*, 'tis a loving and a fair reply.   *Hamlet*
                Yes, beggars can't be choosers.
TAG QUESTION: They signed the agreement, *didn't they?*

(3) Use commas for slight breaks caused by unusual word order:

UNUSUAL ORDER: The Spaniards, *at the height of their power*, were great builders of towns.

EXERCISE 24   Check the following passages for punctuation of *parenthetic elements*. After the number of each passage, write *S* (for satisfactory) or *U* (for unsatisfactory). Explain why satisfactory passages were punctuated the way they were.

1. Well, Your Honor, that is only one version of the incident. Other witnesses, you realize, have told a different story.
2. Nuclear power though first heralded as a boon to humanity, has become a huge headache for utility companies.
3. Hard as it is for many of us to believe, women are not really superior to men in intelligence or humanity—they are only equal.   Anne Roiphe
4. Most of the energy we use—whether from coal, oil, or water—ultimately derives from the sun.
5. Why if I were you I would return the whole shipment to the company.
6. Geothermal power in one's backyard, unless there is a geyser on the property, is just not feasible.
7. Most energy (as leaders of the ecology movement have told us for years) comes from fossil fuels.
8. Nuclear fuel would create an enormous waste problem (as indeed there is already with our existing uranium plants.
9. Many people would agree, offhand, that every creature lives its life and then dies. This might, indeed, be called a truism. But, like some other truisms, it is not true. The lowest forms of life, such as the amoebae, normally (that is, barring accidents) do not die.   Susanne K. Langer
10. Fashions (especially adolescent fashions) do not, as a rule outlast their generation.

EXERCISE 25   Copy the following sentences, adding all punctuation needed for *parenthetic elements.*

1. Why this town my friends has weathered far worse storms.

657

2. My aunt headstrong quick-witted and deeply religious ruled the family with an iron hand.
3. To change the rules all the time we revised them twice last year does not make sense does it?
4. Well this theory it seems to me was rejected long ago.
5. Pride in the immigrant past loyalty to family and compassion for the unfortunate these it appeared were the themes of her campaign.

---

16 | QUOTATION

When we use **direct quotation,** we quote word for word what someone else has said. When we use **indirect quotation,** we put the ideas into our own words:

FULL QUOTATION: Mark Twain said: "One man's comma is another man's colon."
PARTIAL QUOTATION: One engineer called the company's drug-testing program "a paranoid overreaction."
INDIRECT QUOTATION: The National Academy of Sciences reports that the cholesterol we were supposed to give up may not be bad for us after all.

/"   **16a** | DIRECT QUOTATION

Use quotation marks whenever you repeat someone's exact words.

Use quotation marks to enclose material you quote directly, word for word. Use a comma to separate the quotation from the **credit tag**—the statement that identifies the source. Use a colon for a somewhat more formal or emphatic introduction:

COMMA: The Irish essayist Robert Lynd once said, "The last person in the world whose opinion I would take on what to eat would be a doctor."
"News stories deal with food as if it were a foreign agent," the article said.
COLON: The rule says: "No tools will be taken from this building."

(1) Check punctuation if the credit tag interrupts a quotation. Use commas before and after if the credit tag splits one complete sentence:

COMMAS: "Both marijuana and alcohol," *Dr. Jones reports,* "slow reaction times on a whole spectrum of tasks."

Use a comma before and a period (or semicolon) after if the credit tag splits two complete sentences. Avoid a comma splice:

COMMA SPLICE: "Language habits are changing," the article said, "a lover is now a significant other."

PERIOD: "Language habits are changing," the article said. "Love is now a relationship."

SEMICOLON: "Language habits are changing," the article said; "forming close ties is now called bonding."

Note: No comma is required when the credit tag follows a question or exclamation:

NO COMMA: "To rest is to rust!" the poster said.

(2) Use no comma with partial quotations. Use no comma when you quote only part of a sentence, or when a very short quoted sentence becomes part of a larger statement:

NO COMMA: Goodman said that food should not be considered a potential poison; it "should be eaten and enjoyed."

"The small family lives better" was the official slogan of the campaign to curb population growth.

(3) Use single quotation marks when you shift to a quotation within a quotation:

SINGLE MARKS: He said, "People who say 'Let me be honest with you' seldom are."

As Goodman says, "The urge to take charge of our lives has led us headlong into the arms of the 'experts.'"

(4) Type long quotations as block quotations. Set off quotations of more than four typed lines—*no* quotation marks, indented *ten* spaces. Set off lines of poetry the same way, but center them on the page (indent fewer than ten spaces if necessary):

SET OFF: Plath had an uncanny gift for setting up ironic contrasts, as in the opening lines of her poem "The Water Rat":

> Droll, vegetarian, the water rat
> Saws down a reed and swims from his limber grove,
> While the students stroll or sit,
> Hands laced, in a moony indolence of love . . .

Note: You may run in one or two lines of poetry with your continuous text. A **slash** then shows where a new line begins:

RUN-IN: With her usual gift for upsetting conventional expectations, Plath makes the rat seem amusing and harmless: "Droll, vegetarian, the water rat / Saws down a reed . . ."

END MARKS

End quotations correctly.

Remember to use quotation marks to *end* your quotation and know where to place them in relation to other marks.

(1) Keep commas inside, semicolons outside a quotation:

COMMA: As he said, "Don't worry about me," the boat pulled away.
SEMICOLON: You said, "I don't need sympathy"; therefore, I didn't offer any.

(2) Keep end punctuation inside the quotation except in special situations. Make sure a period comes before a final quotation mark:

PERIOD: The letter said: "You have been selected to receive a valuable gift."

Usually, a question mark or exclamation mark will also come before the final quotation mark. However, keep it *outside* the quotation if you are asking a question or exclaiming about the quotation:

QUOTED QUESTION: He asked, "Where are they now?"
QUESTIONED QUOTE: Who said, "To err is human"?

QUOTED SHOUT: She shouted: "The dam broke!"
SHOUTED QUOTE: He actually said: "You don't count"!

(3) Do not normally duplicate a terminal mark at the end of a quotation. Use only one question mark when you ask a question about a question:

Did you ever ask, "What can I do to help?"

INSERTIONS AND OMISSIONS

Use special marks to show changes you have made in the original text.

Signal insertions and omissions:

(1) Identify comments of your own. Put them in **square brackets**:

ADDITION: The note read: "Left Camp B Wednesday, April 3 [actually April 4]. Are trying to reach Camp C before we run out of supplies."

(2) Show that you have left out unnecessary or irrelevant material. Indicate the omission by three spaced periods (called an **ellipsis**).

If the omission occurs after a complete statement in the original text, use a sentence period and then add the ellipsis. (Use four spaced periods if you leave out a whole sentence.)

OMISSION:　The report concluded on an optimistic note: "All three patients . . . are making remarkable progress toward recovery."

"To be a bird is to be alive more intensely than any other living creature, man included. . . . They live in a world that is always present, mostly full of joy." So wrote N. J. Berrill, Professor of Zoology at McGill University.

---

p　　**16d**　|　# INDIRECT QUOTATION

Do not use quotation marks when you put someone else's ideas into your own words.

Indirectly quoted statements are often noun clauses introduced by *that*. Indirectly quoted questions are often noun clauses introduced by words like *whether, why, how,* and *which*. Remember: *No* introductory comma or colon, *no* quotation marks.

DIRECT:　　The mayor replied, "I doubt the wisdom of such a move."
INDIRECT:　The mayor replied *that she doubted the wisdom of such a move.*

DIRECT:　　The artist asked, "Which of the drawings do you like best?"
INDIRECT:　The artist asked *which of the drawings I liked best.*

Note: Even in an indirect quotation, you may want to keep part of the original wording. Use quotation marks to show you are repeating selected words or phrases exactly as they were used:

QUOTED PHRASE:　Like Thackeray's daughters, I read *Jane Eyre* in childhood, carried away "as by a whirlwind."　　Adrienne Rich

---

"/ or ital　**16e**　|　# WORDS SET OFF

Use quotation marks or italics for words outside your normal vocabulary.

Set off the following:

(1) Use quotation marks to show that an expression is not your own:

IRONIC:　At a New York restaurant, lone diners share companionship over pasta at a special "friendship table."

However, avoid apologetic quotation marks for slang or offensive language:

APOLOGETIC: Many highly skilled positions have been "infiltrated" by women.
BETTER: Many highly skilled positions have been filled by women.

(2) Use quotation marks or italics for technical words or words discussed as words. Italics are shown by underlining in a typed manuscript.

TECHNICAL: She described the "Skinner box," a device used by behaviorist psychologists.
WORD AS WORD: The word *comet* comes from the Greek *aster kometes,* meaning long-haired star.

(3) Use italics to identify foreign words. Italicize words borrowed from foreign languages and not yet fully assimilated, including many legal and scientific terms:

FOREIGN: For a Bolivian *campesino,* the pay for a bird for the illegal parrot trade is not bad.
LEGAL TERM: A writ of *certiorari* is used by a superior court to obtain judicial records from an inferior court or a quasi-judicial agency.

"/or ital 16f ┃ **TITLES OR NAMES SET OFF**

Use quotation marks or italics to set off titles or names.

Look for the following:

(1) Distinguish between whole publications and their parts. Put quotation marks around the titles of poems, articles, songs, and other pieces that would normally be *part* of a larger publication ("The Tiger"). Italicize (underline in typing) the title of a *complete* publication—a magazine, newspaper, or book (*The Poems of William Blake*).

PUBLICATION: The index to the *New York Times* devoted three column inches to the heading "Sex" in 1952.
Joan Didion's "Notes of a Native Daughter" was reprinted in *Slouching Towards Bethlehem.*

Note: Do *not* use italics when naming the Bible or its parts (or other sacred writing: Talmud, Koran).

SCRIPTURE: She opened the Bible and read from the Book of Job.

(2) Italicize the titles of works of art or entertainment. Italicize (underline) the titles of plays, major musical works including operas and ballets, movies, television and radio programs, and such works of art as paintings and sculptures:

ENTERTAINMENT: My aunt wanted us to watch *Romeo and Juliet* or *Swan Lake* rather than *I Love Lucy* or *The Price Is Right*.

ART: Every summer, an army of tourists troops past the *Mona Lisa*.

(3) Italicize the names of ships and aircraft. Italicize (underline) the names of ships and other craft, including space vehicles, planes, or trains: the *Queen Mary, Apollo IX*, the *Hindenburg*.

SHIPS: The ill-fated *Titanic* became one of the best-known ships of all time.

TRAINS: The *California Zephyr* and the other great trains will live only in legend.

EXERCISE 26   Study ways of punctuating quoted material that are illustrated in the following sentences. Explain why each sentence was punctuated the way it was.

1. A recent article in *Smithsonian* magazine was titled: "With Tabloids, 'Zip! You're in Another World!'"
2. The world of tabloids is what science fiction writers call a "parallel universe."
3. In the words of the *Smithsonian* author, "It's like ours, but with more gusto!"
4. "Cave Explorers Find Alien Mummy!" proclaimed one screaming headline.
5. The article claimed that a Turkish scientist had found a human-like creature with green skin and wings in a glass coffin that dates back to the Ice Age.
6. "With a creature such as this," the scientist said, "I'm not at all certain it really is dead."
7. "300-lb. Mom Swaps Twins for Cookies," said another recent heading.
8. Perhaps this was the same mom who "dyes twins red and green so she can tell them apart!"
9. Favorite topics are homicidal spouses ("Ghoulish Husband Turns Wife into Goulash") and the lifestyle of royalty ("Fergie Pregnant—With Sextuplets?").
10. Who could pass up another recent classic, "Woman Eaten by Pigs"?

EXERCISE 27   What punctuation, if any, is missing at the blank space in each of the following passages? Write it after the number of the passage. Write *No* if no punctuation is necessary. (Make no changes in capitalization.)

1. The psychologist said _____ The accidents will be simulated."
2. The lead actor had what *Time* magazine calls "shirt-ad looks _____
3. Where does it say, "No minors are allowed _____

663

4. According to Rachel Carson, "Sir James Clark Ross set out from England in command of two ships 'bound for the utmost limits of the navigable globe _____

5. The first wheelchair races in the history of the Olympic Games marked an "emotional milestone _____ for disabled spectators and athletes.

6. "The main problem," the commission said _____ is insufficient training of personnel."

7. "The main problem is not mechanical defects," the report said _____ it is human error."

8. "What do you mean—'deep pockets _____ the governor asked.

9. He just mumbled _____ Excuse me" and staggered on.

10. She explained _____ why the regulations had not been followed.

---

17   PROOFREADING FOR SPELLING

Poor spelling, like static, comes between you and the audience. It undercuts what you have to say. As a courtesy to your reader and as a favor to yourself, allow time for careful, word-by-word proofreading of a final draft. If possible, wait a few hours (or a day) after you finish typing.

sp   **17a**   **SPELLING PROBLEMS**

Solve familiar spelling problems.

Many word processing programs and electronic typewriters have a built-in spelling check that flags predictable problems. Learn to flag predictable spelling problems by studying the words in high-risk categories:

(1) Check for the true unforgivables. A handful of common words again and again trip up poor spellers. No matter how capable you are, misspelling one of these will make you look ignorant. Copy them, read them over, spell them out—until the correct spelling becomes second nature:

accept	definite	occurred	probably
all right	environment	occurrence	receive
a lot	believe	perform	similar
athlete	conscience	preferred	studying

surprise	used to	writing	would have
truly	villain	could have	should have

(2) Watch for differences between speech and writing. Watch for silent letters or words not clearly heard in informal speech:

SILENT LETTERS:

condemn	debt	mortgage
foreign	doubt	sovereign

OFTEN NOT HEARD:

accidentally	candidate	library
basically	government	probably
February	incidentally	quantity

Watch for vowels in unstressed positions. The vowels *a*, *e*, and *i* blur in endings like -*ate* and -*ite*, -*able* and -*ible*, -*ant* and -*ent*. As a memory aid, link the word with a close cousin: *definite* (finish, definition); *separate* (separation); *ultimate* (ultimatum); *indispensable* (dispensary).

> *a:* acceptable, acceptance, advisable, attendance, attendant, brilliant, performance
>
> *e:* consistent, excellence, excellent, existence, experience, independent, persistent, tendency
>
> *i:* irresistible, plausible, possible, susceptible

(3) Watch for different spellings of the same root. The root -*cede* is spelled with a single *e* in *secede* (from the union), *recede* (like a swelling), *precede* (and causing a *precedent*), *concede* (making a concession), and *intercede* (stepping in). However, *exceed* and *proceed* have a double *e*. Then the double *e* disappears again in *procedure*.

till/until:	*till* dark	but	*until* dark
four/forty:	*four* and *fourteen*	but	*forty* thieves
nine/ninth:	*nine* and *ninety*	but	the *Ninth* Symphony

The spelling of a noun may be different from that of a related verb or adjective:

absorb—absorption	dissent—dissension
advise (v.)—advice (n.)	generous—generosity
conscience—conscientious	genius—ingenious
courteous—courtesy	proceed—procedure
curious—curiosity	pronounce—pronunciation

(4) Watch out when spelling changes because of a change in grammatical form. For instance, we "choose" and "lead" in the present, but we "chose" and "led" in the past. Some plurals trip up the unwary: one *man* but several *men*, one *woman* but several *women*.

SINGULAR:	hero	Negro	potato	tomato	wife
PLURAL:	hero*es*	Negro*es*	potato*es*	tomato*es*	wi*ves*

SINGULAR:	freshman	Irishman	life	veto	calf
PLURAL:	freshm*en*	Irishm*en*	li*ves*	veto*es*	cal*ves*

Be sure to add the *-ed* **for** *past tense* **or** *past participle* **in words like the following:**

used to:	He use*d* to sell used cars.
supposed to:	She was suppose*d* to be opposed.
prejudiced:	They were prejudice*d* (biase*d*) against me.

1p   **17b** | ## CONFUSING PAIRS

Master words that sound similar or alike.

Distinguish between sound-alikes or near sound-alikes:

accept/except	*accept* responsibility (take it on); make an *exception* (take it out)
Capitol/capital	the *Capitol* (buildings) is in the *capital* (the whole city)
conscious/conscience	we are *conscious* (aware); we have a *conscience* (moral sense)
effect/affect	it has *effects* (results); it *affects* (alters) my grade
lose/loose	win or *lose;* fast and *loose*
personal/personnel	a *personal* (private) matter; a *personnel* (staff) matter
presents/presence	bring *presents* (gifts); *presence* or absence
principal/principle	the *principal's* office; against my *principles*
quite/quiet	*quite* (entirely) true; peace and *quiet*
than/then	bigger *than* life (comparison); now and *then* (time)
there/their	here and *there;* they and *their* friends
to/too	back *to* Georgia (direction); *too* much *too* soon (degree); you *too* (also)
whether/weather	*whether* or not (choice); foul *weather* (climate)

EXERCISE 28   Which choice fits the context?

1. The governor *accepted/excepted* the resignation of two top aides.
2. China *use/used* to experience large-scale famines.
3. The decision *affected/effected* thousands of commuters.
4. The townspeople were *prejudice/prejudiced* against the new immigrants.
5. Macbeth was tormented by a guilty *conscious/conscience*.
6. Marcel was *to/too* tall to play Napoleon.
7. We recognized the voices of several of the *woman/women*.
8. Your friend should *of/have* tried out for the part.
9. Brokers know dozens of ways to *lose/loose* money.
10. Basques invoked the *principal/principle* of self-determination.

EXERCISE 29   Insert the missing letter or letters in each of the following words:

accept____nce, attend_____nce, brilli_____nt, consist____ncy, curi____sity, defin____te, excell_____nt, exist____nce, experi____nce, independ ____nt, indispens____ble, occurr_____nce, irresist____ble, perform_____nce, persist____nt, prec____ding, proc____dure, pron____nciation, separ_____te, tend____ncy.

EXERCISE 30   Test your knowledge of words often misspelled. Have someone dictate these sentences to you. Make a list of the words that give you trouble.

1. *Amateurs benefited* more than other *athletes*.
2. The *committee* heard every *conceivable opinion*.
3. *Manufacturers developed* a new *device*.
4. We kept all *business decisions confidential*.
5. Her *appearance* was *definitely a surprise*.
6. She *accused* her *opponent* of *hypocrisy*.
7. The *absence* of *controls* proved *disastrous*.
8. We met a *prominent professor* of *psychology*.
9. Their *marriage succeeded exceptionally* well.
10. These *privileges* are *undoubtedly unnecessary*.
11. The *sponsor* was *dissatisfied* with the *performance*.
12. Their *approach* was *strictly practical*.
13. *Companies* can seldom just *eliminate* the *competition*.
14. A *repetition* of the *tragedy* is *inevitable*.
15. This *subtle difference* is *irrelevant*.

667

Spelling rules help you memorize words that follow a common pattern. Let a few simple spelling rules help you with high-frequency errors:

(1) Put *i* before e except after c. The combinations *ie* and *ei* often stand for the same sound. (*Relieved* rhymes with *received*.) Use *i* before *e* except after *c*:

> *ie:* achieve, believe, chief, grief, niece, piece (of pie), relieve

> *cei:* ceiling, conceited, conceive, perceive, receive, receipt

Exceptions: *either, leisure, neither, seize, weird; financier, species*

(2) Know when to double a final consonant. Often, a single final consonant is doubled before an ending (or **suffix**) that begins with a vowel: *-ed, -er, -est, -ing.* The word *plan* has a single final *n;* we double the *n* in *planned, planning,* and *planner.* The word *big* has a single final *g;* we double the *g* in *bigger* and *biggest.* Two conditions:

☐ *Double only after a short or single vowel.* There is no doubling after a long or double vowel: *ai, oo, oa, ea, ee,* or *ou* (boat/boating, read/reading). Some long vowels are shown by a silent final *e* (bite/biting, hope/hoping, bare/baring):

DOUBLING	NO DOUBLING
stop—stopping	stoop—stooping
wrap—wrapped	rape—raped
red—redder	raid—raider

☐ *Double only at the end of stressed syllable.* There is no doubling when the stress shifts *away* from the final syllable:

DOUBLING	NO DOUBLING
ad*mit*, admitted, admittance	*ed*it, edited, editing
for*get*, forgetting, forgettable	*ben*efit, benefited
be*gin*, beginning, beginner	*har*den, hardened
re*gret*, regretted, regrettable	pro*hib*it, prohibited, prohibitive
over*lap*, overlapping	de*vel*op, developing
pre*fer*, preferred, preferring	*pref*erence, preferable
re*fer*, referred, referring	*ref*erence

Note: Words that used to be exceptions (doubling at the end of *un*stressed syllable) now usually follow the rule:

BOTH RIGHT: worshiped (worshipped), traveled (travelled), programed (programmed)

(3) Change *y* to *ie* before *s*. As a single final vowel, *y* changes to *ie* before *s* (one city—several cit*ies*; the sixt*ies*, the eight*ies*). It changes to *i* before all other endings except *-ing* (*dried* but *drying*, *burial* but *burying*).

ie: family—families, fly—flies, study—studies, try—tries, quantity—quantities

i: beauty—beautiful, bury—burial, busy—business, copy—copied, dry—drier, lively—livelihood, noisy—noisily

y: burying, copying, studying, trying, worrying

When it follows another vowel, *y* is usually preserved: *delays, joys, played, valleys*. Exceptions: *day—daily, gay—gaily, lay—laid, pay—paid, say—said*.

(4) Drop a silent *e* before an added vowel. Keep it before an ending that begins with a consonant:

	DROPPED *e*	KEPT *e*
bore	boring	boredom
hate	hating	hateful
like	liking, likable	likely
love	loving, lovable	lovely

Remember the following exceptions:

DROPPED *e*: (argue) argument, (due) duly, (true) truly, (whole) wholly, (judge) judgment, (acknowledge) acknowledgment

KEPT *e*: (mile) mileage, (dye) dyeing (tinting or coloring as against *die—dying*)

Note: A final *e* may signal the difference in the final sound of *rag* and *rage*, or *plastic* and *notice*. Keep such a final *e* not only before a consonant but also before *a* or *o*:

ge: advantage—advantageous, change—changeable, courage—courageous, outrage—outrageous

ce: notice—noticeable, peace—peaceable

EXERCISE 31   Insert *ei* or *ie*:

ach____vement, bel____ver, dec____tful, f____ld,
inconc____vable, misch____f, perc____ve, rec____ving,
rel____f, s____ze, w____rd, y____ld.

EXERCISE 32   Combine the following words with the suggested endings:

accompany_____ed, advantage_____ous, argue_____ing, benefit_____ed, carry_____s, come_____ing, confide_____ing, differ_____ing, excite_____able, friendly_____ness, lively_____hood, occur_____ing, prefer_____ed, remit_____ance, sad_____er, satisfy_____ed, shine_____ing, sole_____ly, study_____ing, tragedy_____s, try_____s, use_____ing, valley_____s, whole_____ly, write_____ing.

EXERCISE 33   For each blank space, what would be the right form of the word in parentheses? Put the right form after the number of the sentence.

1. (family) Several _____ were having a picnic.
2. (plan) The holdup had been _____ by experts.
3. (study) My friends were _____ in the library.
4. (regret) I have always _____ this oversight.
5. (pay) They had already _____ the bill.
6. (love) They never stopped hating and _____ each other.
7. (quantity) Great _____ of food had been consumed.
8. (occur) The thought had _____ to us.
9. (begin) My patience was _____ to wear thin.
10. (copy) He had _____ the whole paragraph.
11. (refer) Your doctor should have _____ you to a specialist.
12. (lay) We had _____ the tile ourselves.
13. (admit) Marcia had _____ her mistake.
14. (refer) She was _____ to a famous incident.
15. (apply) Sue had _____ to several colleges.

19   APOSTROPHES

The apostrophe, which can't be heard, is the typist's nemesis.

ap   19a   CONTRACTIONS

Use the apostrophe in informal shortened forms.

Use the apostrophe to show that part of a word has been left out: *o'clock, ma'am, class of '85.* Avoid common misspellings:

(1) Include the apostrophe in contractions. In particular, you can't afford to misspell a combination with a shortened form of *not (can't, won't, doesn't)*:

(we *are* ready)	*we're* ready
(she *is* a friend)	*she's* a friend
(he *will* be back)	*he'll* be back
(you *are* right)	*you're* right
(let *us* ask)	*let's* ask
(we *cannot* leave)	we *can't* leave
(she *will not* say)	she *won't* say
(he *could not* stay)	he *couldn't* stay
(you *are not* safe)	you *aren't* safe
(it *is not* true)	it *isn't* true

Make sure not to misspell *don't* and *doesn't*. These are shortened forms of *do not* and *does not*:

do not: We *don't* usually hire in the summer.

does not: The new converter *doesn't* work.

(2) Know familiar confusing pairs. Use *it's* (= it is) only when it's really an abbreviation. Otherwise use *its*—the possessive pronoun that shows where something belongs: a nation and *its* leaders (tells us *whose* leaders); the bird beat *its* wings (tells us *whose* wings).

it's (it *is*, it *has*):	*it's* true, *it's* raining, *it's* a shame; *it's* been cold
its (of it):	took *its* course, lost *its* value, heavy for *its* size
who's (who *is* or *has*):	*Who's* to blame? *Who's* seen him? the one *who's* guilty
whose (of whom):	*Whose* turn is it? friends *whose* help counts
they're (they are):	*they're* late, *they're* glad, if *they're* here
their (of them):	*their* belongings, *their* friends, they and *their* parents

ap   **19b**   ## POSSESSIVES

Use the apostrophe for the possessive of nouns.

The **possessive** form of nouns shows who owns something (*Macy's*) or to whom something belongs (*the driver's seat*). We usually produce the possessive by adding an apostrophe plus *s* to the plain form:

WHOSE? my *sister's* car | Mr. *Smith's* garage
        her *aunt's* house | the *student's* name
        the *family's* debts | one *person's* opinion
        our *mayor's* office | the *mind's* eye

Besides ownership, the possessive signals other relationships that tell us "whose?": the *senator's* enemies, the *defendant's* innocence, a *crook's* exposure, the *committee's* activities. Usually the possessive comes before another noun, but sometimes it's been cut loose from it:

WHOSE? For once the fault was not the *governor's*.   (not the *governor's* fault)
        It's either the owner's car or her *son's*.   (her *son's* car)

(1) Distinguish between singular and plural possessives. If a plural noun already ends in *-s*, we add only the apostrophe—not a second *s*: a *lovers'* quarrel, the *slaves'* revolt.

SINGULAR: the *twin's* bicycle, a *parent's* duties, one *family's* home
PLURAL: the *twins'* birthdays, both *parents'* duties, both *families'* homes

Use the regular possessive when a plural noun does not have a plural *-s*: *children's* toys, *women's* rights, *men's* wear, *people's* feelings. Both kinds of plurals appear in the following sentence:

PLURAL: *Judges'* gowns now come in *men's* and *women's* sizes.

Caution: Do not start using the apostrophe with nouns that are *not* possessives.

WRONG: The *player's* went on strike.
RIGHT: The *players* went on strike.   (Who?)
        The *player's* jersey had ripped.   (Whose?)

(2) Use the apostrophe in expressions dealing with time or value: *today's* paper, a *moment's* notice, a *dime's* worth, a *day's* work. Distinguish between singular and plural:

SINGULAR	PLURAL
a *week's* pay	two *weeks'* pay
an *hour's* drive	three *hours'* drive
a *dollar's* worth	two *dollars'* worth
a *month's* salary	three *months'* salary

(3) Use the apostrophe with the possessive forms of indefinite pronouns: *everyone (everybody), someone (somebody), anyone (anybody), no one (nobody),* and *one:*

to *everybody's* surprise	*anyone's* guess
at *someone's* suggestion	*nobody's* fault
(also: at someone *else's* house)	*one's* best friends

Caution: Do *not* use the apostrophe with **possessive pronouns:** *its, hers, ours, yours, theirs.* Remember *its* as a major exception to the use of apostrophes with possessives (the movie and *its* sequel, the college and *its* faculty). Use *it's* only to mean *it is:* "*It's* too late."

NO APOSTROPHE: both *its* ears   it was *hers*   this is *yours*

(4) Follow your preference when the singular noun already has a final -s. With some words, the additional syllable seems clearly required: the *boss's* office, the *waitress's* tip. We usually do *not* add the extra syllable to the word *Jesus* or to Greek names: for *Jesus'* sake, in *Sophocles'* plays. But with many other proper names, either form would be right:

BOTH RIGHT:	*Dolores'* trip	*Dolores's* trip
	Jones' raise	*Jones's* raise
	Dickens' novel	*Dickens's* novel

Note: Many combinations form the possessive as if they were single words: the *commander in chief's* orders, a *father-in-law's* hopes (plural: her *brothers-in-law's* store, my *in-laws'* support), *Simon & Schuster's* spring list. But sometimes we want to show that something belongs to several people: *a mother's and father's* worries, *Simon's and Adele's* marriage.

ap   19c

PLURALS OF LETTERS AND SYMBOLS

Use the apostrophe for plurals of letters, symbols, abbreviations, and words named as words.

Use the apostrophe before you add the plural *-s* to the name of a letter or symbol, to a number, to an abbreviation, or to a word named as a word: the early 1900's; average I.Q.'s.

LETTERS:	Teachers were giving more C's and D's, fewer A's.
NUMBERS:	The phone number started with three 3's and ended with four 7's.
ABBREVIATIONS:	People with Ph.D.'s were driving cabs.
WORDS:	Her replies were full of if's and but's.

Letters of the alphabet and words discussed as vocabulary items should be italicized—underlined in typing (see **16e**). Do not italicize the plural -s:

She spelled her name with two e's and two s's.
She punctuated her advice with many *Honey's* and *Darling's*.

Note: Except with letters of the alphabet and abbreviations using a period, the apostrophe is now often left out: the 1900s; several 3s; ifs and buts.

EXERCISE 34   Change each of the following to the possessive form. Examples: pay for a month—a *month's* pay; the wedding of my brother—my *brother's* wedding.

1. the budget of the President
2. wages for two weeks
3. the friends of her family
4. the homes of many families
5. the future of America
6. the locker room for girls
7. the worth of a dollar
8. the employment record of a person
9. the fringe benefits of the employees
10. the vote for women

EXERCISE 35   Choose the right spelling in each of the following pairs:

1. The *judge's/judges* ruling made necessary some quick changes in both *lawyer's/lawyers'* strategies.
2. Since the *mayor's/mayors* resignation, many *voter's/voters* have been worrying about *whose/who's* going to succeed her.
3. *Mens/Men's* and *womens/women's* cycling found enthusiastic *spectators'/spectators* when introduced as new Olympic sports.
4. In *today's/todays* competitive world of sports, a *gymnast's/gymnasts* training takes up many hours every day.
5. My *friend's/friends'* face fell, as if she were looking at an empty mailbox on *Valentines/Valentine's* Day.
6. *It's/Its* not easy for *parent's/parents* to let a child find *it's/its* own answers.
7. *Lets/Let's* borrow *someones/someone's* car and go for an *hour's/hours'* drive.
8. *Charles/Charles's* father murmured that the *relatives/relative's* had consumed twenty *dollars/dollars'* worth of food.

---

20 CAPITALS

We capitalize the first word of each sentence and—immodestly—the pronoun *I*. In addition, we use capitals for proper names and for words in titles.

cap 20a | **PROPER NAMES**

Capitalize proper names.

Capitalize names—of people, places, regions, countries, languages, periods, ships and other craft, days of the week, months (but not seasons), organizations, institutions, and religions: *Daniel Boone, Kalamazoo,* the *Everglades, Zimbabwe, Arabic,* the *Middle Ages,* the *Challenger, Saturday, July* (but *summer*), the *Salvation Army, Harvard, Islam.*

(1) Capitalize words derived from proper names. Capitalize words that use the name of a country, place, or religion. In particular, capitalize the names of languages and nationalities:

CAPITALS: Imports from *Japan* replaced *German* cameras, *Swiss* cuckoo clocks, *British* motorcycles, and *American* cars.
Marxist intellectuals criticized the role of *Christian* missionaries and *Buddhist* monks.
Few *Americans* study *Arabic, Chinese,* or *Japanese.*

In some words, the original proper name has been lost sight of, and we now use a lowercase letter: *pasteurized* milk, *guinea* pig, *india* rubber.

(2) Capitalize words that become part of a name. When it combines with a proper name, capitalize the general label for a title, family relationship, institution, or geographic feature: *Sergeant Bilko, Grandma Moses, Nuclear Energy Commission, Silicon Valley.* Some titles point to one person only and are capitalized like a proper name: the *Pope,* the *Queen* (of England), our *President* (of the United States).

(3) Capitalize a general word put to special use as a proper name. A general label may double as a proper name for one person, institution, organization, or place. Historically, republicans (lowercase) hated kings and preferred a republic; in the United States, Republicans (capitalized) are members of one major party.

GENERAL WORD	PROPER NAME
democratic (many institutions)	Democratic (name of the party)
orthodox (many attitudes)	Orthodox (name of the church)
history (general subject)	History 31 (specific course)
west (general direction)	Middle West (the specific area)
my mother (common relationship)	Mother (name you call the person)

TITLES OF PUBLICATIONS

Capitalize major words in titles.

A capital letter marks the first and last words and all major words in the title of a book, other publication, or work of art. Words not counting as major are articles (*a, an,* and *the*) and also prepositions (*at, in, on, from, with*) or conjunctions (*and, but, if, when*). Even these are usually capitalized when they have five or more letters (*Through, Because*).

Observe these conventions in writing headlines (*Man Revives During Autopsy*) and the titles of your papers:

Raising the Mirth Rate

Travels with a Camel Through Arid Country

How I Quit Drugs and Learned to Love the Police

The same conventions apply to titles cited in a sentence:

TITLES: *New York Times Magazine*'s "About Men" column is the weekly counterpart of the older "Hers" column; *Esquire* has published numerous articles on subjects like "Men, Babies, and the Male Clock" or "The Pain of the Divorced Father."

Lange, who titled her book *An American Exodus,* was becoming famous for photographs like "Ditched, Stalled, and Stranded" and "Ex-Slave."

EXERCISE 36   Which of the words in the following sentences should be capitalized? After the number of each sentence, write down and capitalize all such words.

1. Players from brazil and argentina have played for france and italy in the world cup.

2. The authenticity of some of rembrandt's most popular paintings—*the man with the golden helmet* and *polish rider*—has been challenged.

3. Pistol shots crackled in dearborn, the detroit suburb that was home to the ford motor company's sprawling river rouge plant.

4. In october, a huge and very ugly statue of sir winston churchill was unveiled in parliament square, london.

5. As he was helped aboard, egyptian mohammed aly clutched a small blue-bound koran that had been given to him by the arab mayor of hebron.

6. The sprawling city of canton, 110 miles by rail from hong kong, has for centuries been china's principal gathering place for asian and european traders.

7. Delegates met in manhattan to celebrate the centennial of the union of american hebrew congregations, founded in cincinnati by rabbi isaac wise.

8. At columbia and barnard, at atlanta's morehouse college and the university of virginia, economics was the subject to take.

9. Seven novels by mickey spillane are among the thirty best-selling novels of all time, along with *gone with the wind, peyton place, lady chatterley's lover,* and *in his steps,* by charles monroe sheldon, 1897.

10. Like other newspapers, the *new york journal-american* had learned the art of catering to irish catholics.

---

21 HYPHENS

The easy-to-miss **hyphen** provides an example of slow-moving, long-term change. A pair of words may start as two words (*baby boom*), pick up a hyphen (*baby-sitter*), and finally become one word (*crybaby*). When in doubt, use the most recent edition of a good dictionary as your guide.

hy 21a COMPOUND WORDS

Know which compound words require a hyphen.

Some **compound words** differ from ordinary combinations in both speech and writing: "a wild LIFE" but "our WILDlife"; "a strong MAN" but "a STRONGman"; "a dark ROOM" but "a DARKroom." Such unmistakable compounds are *headache, highway,* and *stepmother.* In many similar pairs, however, the parts are kept separate: *high school, labor union.* Still other compound words conventionally require the hyphen: *cave-in, great-grandfather, mother-in-law.*

ONE WORD:	bridesmaid, stepfather, checklist, highlight, headquarters, blackout, bittersweet
TWO OR MORE WORDS:	commander in chief, goose flesh, vice versa, off year, high command
HYPHEN:	able-bodied, bull's-eye, drive-in, court-martial, merry-go-round, six-pack, in-laws, vice-president, Spanish-American, one-sided, off-season, in-group, President-elect

(1) Learn to recognize common types of hyphenated words:

☐   in-laws, off-season, drive-in, sit-in, off-duty, take-off, trade-off

☐   ten-speed, six-pack, one-sided, three-cornered, second-rate, one-way, two-dimensional

☐   Polish-American, Asian-American, Anglo-Saxon, Graeco-Roman

☐   law-abiding, Spanish-speaking, cancer-causing, award-winning, money-losing

☐   dark-haired, Washington-based, air-conditioned, computer-aided, career-oriented, middle-aged, foreign-born, college-bound

☐   fuel-efficient, cost-effective, water-repellent, image-conscious, toll-free, gender-neutral

☐   self-conscious, ex-husband, all-purpose, great-grandfather, co-star, pro-Arab, non-Catholic

☐   south-southeast, north-northwest

☐   two-by-four, cash-and-carry, fly-by-night, father-in-law

(2) Hyphenate compound numbers from *twenty-one* to *ninety-nine*. Also hyphenate fractions used as modifiers:

NUMBERS:	There were *twenty*-six survivors.
	The plane was *one*-third empty.
	The tank was *three*-quarters full.

Practice varies for other uses of fractions:

FRACTIONS:	*Two thirds* (or *Two-Thirds*) remained poor.

Caution: Be sure to spell correctly combinations that are often misspelled:

ONE WORD:	today, tomorrow, nevertheless, nowadays
TWO WORDS:	all right, a lot (of time), be able, no one

---

hy   **21b** | **PREFIXES** |

Know which prefixes require a hyphen.

Many hyphenated compounds combine a word and its prefix. A **prefix** can be attached at the beginning of many different words.

(1) Use a hyphen with *all-, ex-* (in the sense of "former"), *quasi-, self-,* and sometimes *co-:* *all-knowing, ex-husband, quasi-judicial, self-contained, co-worker.*

all-:	all-powerful, all-American, all-male, all-star
ex-:	ex-champion, ex-convict, ex-wife, ex-governor
self-:	self-confident, self-conscious, self-image, self-destruct

(2) Use a hyphen with all prefixes before words beginning with a capital letter. Hyphenate *anti-American, pro-British, un-American, non-Catholic, Pan-Arabic.*

(3) Use a hyphen to prevent the meeting of two identical vowels or three identical consonants. Hyphenate *anti-intellectual, semi-independent, fall-like.*

Note: Sometimes, a hyphen distinguishes an unfamiliar use of a prefix from a familiar one: *recover—re-cover* (make a new cover), *recreation—re-creation* (creating again or anew).

---

hy   21c | **GROUP MODIFIERS**

Use the hyphen with group modifiers.

Hyphenate words that work together like a single modifier before a noun (a *thirty-page* report):

HYPHENS:	a *middle-of-the-road* policy	*off-the-cuff* remarks
	a *low-income* neighborhood	*wall-to-wall* carpeting
	an *in-depth* interview	a *down-to-the-wire* race
	after-school activities	a *step-by-step* account

HYPHENS: San Francisco has always been a happy hunting ground for painters producing *seagull-and-cable-car* kitsch.   *Time*

Use no hyphens when the same combinations serve some other function in a sentence: tend toward the *middle of the road;* explain a process *step by step.*

HYPHENS: Gradually, the drug user's *twice-a-week* habit changes to a *four-times-a-week* need.
NO HYPHENS: Gradually, we reduced the frequency of treatment from *four times a week* to *twice a week.*

Note: No hyphen is used when a modifier before a noun is in turn modified by an adverb ending in *-ly:* a *fast-rising* executive but a *rapidly growing* city; a *well-balanced* account but a *carefully documented* study.

EXERCISE 37   After the number of each sentence, write all combinations that should be hyphenated or written as one word.

1. This is the story of a flabby middle aged two pack a day smoker who transformed himself into a 160 pound marathon runner.
2. The room was only about two thirds full, with seventy five people in attendance.
3. Though at times her son in law seemed self conscious, he never the less had a well balanced personality.
4. The self righteous law and order candidate promised to crack down on ex convicts.
5. Several players from Italian American families had gone on to become all Americans.
6. Those who denounced the parking privileges for out of town students were obviously not from out of town.
7. The ex ambassador complained about anti Soviet demonstrations by pro Israeli citizens.
8. The Connecticut based subsidiary produces computer aided high performance robots for state of the art factories.
9. Now a days few self respecting candidates conduct old fashioned campaigns taking them to out of the way places.
10. Jane Andrew and her co author have written a well documented account of the un democratic procedures followed by quasi judicial agencies.

22   MANUSCRIPT MECHANICS

The outward appearance of your manuscript sends a message—preferably, that you care about your readers' convenience and respect their standards.

22a   PENMANSHIP AND TYPING

ms

Prepare a legible and attractive manuscript.

A paper scribbled on a page torn from a notebook, a smudged and heavily erased typescript on see-through paper, a pale printout—all of these create reader's block, a reluctance to read and a tendency to block out your message. Write legibly, pruning your handwriting of excessive loops and curlicues. (Do not print or leave every other line blank unless instructed to do so.) Type on unlined paper of standard size and weight, double-spacing all material. When in doubt about the quality of the print-out delivered by a word processor, show a sample to your instructor.

(1) Observe conventional spacing. Leave one space after most punctuation marks (comma, semicolon) but *two* spaces after end punctuation. After a colon, leave one space if the colon appears before the end of the sentence. Leave two spaces if it appears at the end.

ONE SPACE:	`We saw new construction: offices and hotels.`
TWO SPACES:	`The news was out:  The test had failed.`

Use two hyphens—with no space on either side—to make a **dash**:

`Use two hyphens--with no space on either side.`

Note: Leave no space after a period that occurs *within* an abbreviation—but leave one space each if several initials are part of a person's name:

`The U.S. Supreme Court    T. S. Eliot`

(2) Leave adequate margins. Leave about an inch and a half on the left and at the top, an inch on the right and at the bottom. *Indent* the first line of a paragraph—about an inch in longhand, or five spaces in typed copy.

(3) Make necessary final corrections. Always make time for final proofreading. If necessary, make handwritten last-minute corrections. Draw a line through a word to delete it or to write the corrected word in the space above. (Use a snaking line to reverse the order of two transposed letters.)

`Film critics have found` ~~profound~~ *deep* `maening in` `in Laurel and`
`Hardy.`

To separate two words, draw a vertical line; to close up a space, use two curved lines. Insert a **caret** (∧) to show where a missing word is to go:

`Film|critics have in` ^`vestigated` *the* `symbolism of King Kong.`

To start a new paragraph, insert the symbol ¶; to take out a paragraph break, insert "no ¶" in the margin.

| **DIVIDING WORDS**

Observe conventional syllabication.

Use a hyphen to divide words at the end of a line. Dictionaries generally use centered dots to indicate where a word may conventionally be divided:

ad•dress   af•fec•ta•tion   en•vi•ron•ment   mal•ice

(1) Recognize recurrent patterns. For instance, divide words before the *-ing* ending, but keep the added consonant with the ending when you have doubled a final consonant:

play•ing	sell•ing	edit•ing
plan•ning	hum•ming	submit•ting

Divide between two consonants when they go with two separate syllables in slow pronunciation:

op•tics *but* neu•tral | fac•tor *but* su•preme

(2) Do not divide proper names and combinations that in the reader's mind form a single unit. Avoid dividing names (*Kiplinger, Washington*). Do not divide contractions (*doesn't, wouldn't*) and abbreviations (*NATO, UNESCO, UCLA*). Do not split sums (*$1,175,000*) or expressions using abbreviations like *a.m.* and *B.C.*

(3) Do not set off single letters. Do not divide words like *about, alone,* and *enough* or like *many* and *via.* Similarly, do not set off the ending *-ed* in words like *complained* or *renewed.* (Do not divide one-syllable words: *strength, through.*)

(4) Divide hyphenated words at the original hyphen. Do not break up the *American* in "un-American" or the *sister* in "sister-in-law."

(5) Do not divide the last word on a page.

| **ITALICS**

Use italics to set off special words and phrases.

Italics (or slanted type) are signaled in handwritten and most typed manuscript by underlining.

(1) Italicize for emphasis. Use **italics** (underlining) to call attention to important words or to words that will prevent misunderstanding. (Use italics and other attention-getters *sparingly.*)

EMPHASIS: The group was a professional *association,* not a union.

(2) Italicize words discussed as words or words still considered foreign.

WORD AS WORD: Dictionaries lag behind, only slowly beginning to include *hot tub, prime time, gulag, preppie,* and *putdown.*

FOREIGN: He developed a taste for *tostadas* and the music of the *mariachis.*

(3) Italicize titles of whole publications. Italicize or underline titles of books (*Veil: The Secret Wars of the CIA*), magazines (*Popular Mechanics*), newspapers (*Chicago Tribune*), and other complete publications. Put in quotation marks the titles of articles, poems, short stories, songs, and other items that are normally *part* of a larger publication: "The Love Song of J. Alfred Prufrock"; "The Lottery"; "I Got You, Babe."

WHOLE: Her latest book, *A Distant Mirror,* was reviewed in *Time, Newsweek,* and *Saturday Review.*

PART: The earliest essays had titles like "California Dreaming" and "Marrying Absurd."

Note: The name of the Bible and the names of its parts (Genesis, Book of Job) are usually *not* italicized.

(4) Italicize the names of works of art, music, and entertainment. Use italics (underlining) for the names of paintings, ballets, operas, major orchestral works, plays, movies, radio and television shows. (See also **16f.**)

ART: He dreamed of seeing Michelangelo's *David* in Florence or listening to *Lohengrin* in Bayreuth.

ENTERTAINMENT: From *The War of the Worlds* to *Star Wars,* some of the greatest successes of popular entertainment have been works of science fiction.

(5) Italicize the names of trains, aircraft, ships, and other vessels. (See also **16f.**)

VESSELS: Legendary ships from the *Mayflower* and the *Titanic* to the *Hindenburg* and *Apollo IX* have been symbols of human hopes and fears.

---

23 ABBREVIATIONS AND NUMBERS

Avoid the overuse of abbreviations.

Abbreviations save time and space. Here as in other matters, however, avoid excessive shortcuts.

ab 23a | ABBREVIATIONS

Spell out inappropriate abbreviations.

Some abbreviations (*Mr.*, *CIA*, *a.m.*) are generally acceptable in ordinary prose. Others (*lb.*, *Ave.*, *NY*) are appropriate only in invoices, reports, addresses, and other special contexts.

(1) Use the acceptable abbreviations for titles and degrees. Before and after names, use the titles *Mr.*, *Mrs.*, *Ms.*, *Dr.*, and *St.* (Saint), and the abbreviations *Jr.* (Junior) and *Sr.* (Senior). Use standard abbreviations for degrees: *M.D.*, *Ph.D.* Use *Prof.* only before the full name.

TITLES: Mr. John J. Smith, Jr.
Dr. Alice Joyce *or* Alice Joyce, M.D.
Prof. Shelby F. Jones *but* Professor Jones

(2) Use familiar initials for organizations. Use initials or **acronyms** for agencies, organizations, firms, technical processes, chemical compounds, and the like when the full name is awkward or unfamiliar:

INITIALS: IBM, AFL-CIO, FBI, CIA, UNESCO, PTA, FM radio

Note: Use the **ampersand** (&) and abbreviations like *Inc.* and *Bros.* only when organizations use them in their official titles: *Smith & Company, Inc.*

(3) Use familiar abbreviations related to time and number. Before or after numerals, use *A.D.* and *B.C.*, *a.m.* and *p.m.* (also *A.M.* and *P.M.*), *no.* (also *No.*):

YEARS: Augustus reigned from 27 *B.C.* to *A.D.* 14.
HOURS: Planes leave at 11 *a.m.* and 2:30 *p.m.*
NUMBER: This issue was Volume 7, *no.* 2.

(4) Spell out addresses and geographic names. Use abbreviations like *NY* or *CA* only when writing an address for a letter or the like. (Exceptions: *USSR*; *Washington, D.C.*; and *U.S.* in combinations like *U.S. Navy.*)

WRONG: When in the *U.S.*, she lived on *Grant Ave.* in San Francisco, *Calif.*
RIGHT: When in the United States, she lived on Grant Avenue in San Francisco, California.

(5) Spell out most measurements. In ordinary prose, *lb.* (pound), *oz.* (ounce), *ft.* (foot), and *in.* (inch) are usually spelled out. Some units of measurement are more unwieldy and are abbreviated, provided they are used with figures: *45 mph, 1500 rpm.* Spell out % (percent) and ¢ (cent), but use $ for exact figures: $287.55.

MEASUREMENTS: He used to weigh 305 *pounds,* which made him a bit sluggish in competition.

num   **23b** | NUMBERS |

Use figures in accordance with standard practice.

Figures are generally appropriate in references to the day of the month (*May 13*), the year (*1917*), street numbers (*1014 Union Avenue*), and page numbers (*Chapter 7, page 18*). For other uses of numbers, the following conventions are widely observed:

(1) Spell out round numbers. Numbers from one to ten, and round numbers requiring no more than two words, are usually spelled out: *three dollars a seat, five hundred years later, ten thousand copies, about seventy-five reservations.*

WORDS: My aunt came from Ireland a *hundred* years ago, when she was *seven* years old.
FIGURES: The church was *250* years old and had withstood a major earthquake *84* years ago.

(2) Use numerals for exact figures. Use numerals for exact counts, exact sums, technical measurements, decimals, numbers with fractions and percentages:

FIGURES: 500,867 inhabitants $3.86   65 mph   4.3 miles   3½ hours   92% (or 92 percent)

Use numerals also for references to time using *a.m.* or *p.m.*

TIME: 2:30 p.m. (*but* three o'clock, half past twelve)

(3) Avoid numerals at the beginning of a sentence. Write "Fifteen out of 28 replied" or "When questioned, 15 out of 28 replied." Except in special situations like this one, avoid changes from figures to words (and vice versa) in a series of numbers.

(4) Hyphenate compound numbers. When spelled out, compound numbers from 21 to 99 are hyphenated: *twenty-five, one hundred and forty-six.*

gl   **24**   **GLOSSARY OF USAGE**

The following glossary reviews the status of words, word forms, and constructions that are frequently criticized.

a, an Use *a* only before words that begin with a consonant when pronounced: *a desk, a chair, a house, a year, a C, a university.* Use *an* before words that begin with a vowel when pronounced (though, in writing, the first letter may be a consonant): *an eye, an answer, an honest mistake, an A, an M, an uninformed reader*. The *a* before a vowel is nonstandard:

WRONG: *a* ear, *a* accident, *a* automobile, *a* athlete
RIGHT: *an* ear, *an* accident, *an* automobile, *an* athlete

ain't Nonstandard for *am not, isn't, aren't,* or *hasn't* (she *ain't* been seen since).

all right Spell as two words. (Although *alright* appears in some dictionaries, most readers will consider it a misspelling.)

allusion, illusion An *allusion* is a brief mention that reminds us of a story or an event (the speaker's *allusion* to Watergate). An *illusion* is a deceptive appearance or false hope (the Vietnam war destroyed many *illusions*.)

a lot Always spell as two words. "*A lot* of money" is informal; "*lots* of money" is slang:

FORMAL: She owed us a large amount of money.

amount, number Use *amount* only when thinking about bulk or a sum (the total *amount* of the debt). Use *number* when thinking about countable items (the *number* of whooping cranes).

RIGHT: A large *number* (not *amount*) of people were waiting.
          The *number* (not *amount*) of unsold cars on dealers' lots was growing steadily.

and and *but* **at the beginning of a sentence** A traditional rule banned *and* and *but* at the beginning of a sentence. But many modern writers start sentences with *and* or *but* merely to avoid heavier, more formal links like *moreover, furthermore, however,* and *nevertheless.*

and/or And/or is sometimes necessary in commercial or official documents. Avoid it in ordinary writing.

anyone, anybody Anyone and *anybody* stand for "any person at all." *Any one* singles out: "Take any *one* of those three." *Any body* refers to the physical body.

anyways, anywheres, anyplace In writing, use *anyway* or *anywhere.*

as As is nonstandard as a substitute for *that* or *whether* ("I don't know as I can come"). It is also nonstandard as a substitute for *who* ("Those *as* knew her avoided her"). As a substitute for *because* or *while, as* is often criticized as weak or ambiguous:

As (better: "because") we had no money, we gave him a check.

attribute, contribute Attribute means "to trace to a cause" or "to credit to a source." *Contribute* means "to give one's share" or "to have a share" in something.

RIGHT: She *attributed* her success to perseverance.

bad, badly Use the adjective *bad* after the linking verb *feel,* which shows a condition: "His resignation made everyone feel *bad."* Use the adverb *badly* to show how something is done: "She handled the assignment *badly."*

being as, being that Nonstandard as substitutes for *because* or *since* ("being *that* I was ill").

between, among Use *between* in references to two of a kind (distinguish *between* right and wrong). Use *among* in references to more than two (distinguish *among* different shades of color). *Between* is also appropriate when more than two things can be considered in pairs of two:

RIGHT: Bilateral trade agreements exist *between* many countries.

burst, bursted, bust, busted *Bursted* is a nonstandard form of *burst:* "The tank *burst* (not *bursted*) and killed two of the workers." *Bust* as a verb meaning "break" or "arrest" is slang.

can and may Formal English uses *can* in the sense of "be able to." It uses *may* to show permission. The use of *can* to show permission, common in speech and writing, is often considered informal:

FORMAL: Visitors *may* (are permitted to) enter the country only if they *can* (are able to) prove their identity.

cannot help but Use either *cannot help* or *cannot but:*

RIGHT: I *cannot help* wishing that I had never met you.
I *cannot but* wish that I had never met you.

complement, compliment The first word means "complete" or "supplement." The second word means "say nice things, flatter." *Complementary* findings round out or complete a picture. *Complimentary* remarks flatter. (*Complimentary* tickets are given free of charge to create a good impression.)

couple of In formal writing, *couple* refers to two of a kind, a pair. Used in the sense of "several" or "a few," it is informal. Used before a plural noun without a connecting *of,* it is nonstandard:

INFORMAL: We had to wait a *couple of* minutes.
NONSTANDARD: We had only a *couple* dollars left.

different than *Different from* used to be expected in formal English. *Different than,* widely used in speech, is becoming acceptable in writing.

ECONOMICAL: We tried a different method *than* we had used last year.
LESS ECONOMICAL: We tried a different method *from the one* we had used last year.

disinterested, uninterested In formal English, *disinterested* means "not swayed by personal, selfish interest" or "impartial." *Disinterested* used in the sense of "uninterested" or "indifferent" is objectionable to many readers:

RIGHT: We were sure she would be a *disinterested* judge.
He seemed *uninterested* in our problems.

double comparative, double superlative Short adjectives usually form the comparative by adding the suffix *-er (cheaper)*, the superlative by adding the suffix *-est (cheapest)*. Long adjectives, and adverbs ending in *-ly*, usually employ the intensifiers *more* and *most* instead *(more expensive, most expensive; more carefully, most carefully)*. Forms using both the suffix and the intensifier are nonstandard *(more cheaper, most cheapest)*.

double negative Double negatives say no twice. The use of additional negative words to reinforce a negation already expressed is nonstandard: "I *didn't* do *nothing*"; "*Nobody* comes to see me *no more*."

RIGHT: I *didn't* do *anything*.
Nobody comes to see me *anymore*.

Similar to double negatives are expressions like *couldn't hardly* or *couldn't scarcely*:

RIGHT: I *could hardly* keep my eyes open during the talk.

***due to* as a preposition** Use *due to* as an adjective: "His absence was *due to* ill health." "His absence, *due to* ill health, upset our schedule." (In these examples, you could substitute another adjective: "His absence was *traceable* to ill health.") Avoid *due to* as a preposition meaning "because of":

OBJECTIONABLE: Computer chips fail *due to* poor quality control.
SAFE: Computer chips fail *because of* poor quality control.

each other, one another Conservative writers distinguish between *each other* (referring to two persons or things) and *one another* (referring to more than two):

Bride and groom had known *each other* since childhood.
The members of his family supported *one another*.

etc. Etc., the Latin abbreviation for "and so on," often serves as a vague substitute for additional examples or illustrations. Furthermore, *ect.* is a common misspelling. "And etc." and "such as . . . etc." are redundant. To avoid trouble, steer clear of *etc.* altogether.

farther, further; all the farther A traditional rule requires *farther* in references to space and distance ("We traveled *farther* than we had expected"). It requires *further* in references to degree and quantity ("We discussed it *further* at our next meeting") and in the sense of "additional" ("without *further* delay"). *All the farther* in the sense of "as far as" ("This is *all the farther* we go") is informal or dialectal.

flaunt, flout We *flaunt* (show off) wealth or possessions. We *flout* (defy or ignore) laws.

get, got, gotten In American English, *have gotten* is an acceptable alternative to *have got* in the sense of "have obtained" or "have become." For example: "Her grandparents had *got* (or *gotten*) wealthy after the Civil War."

hadn't ought to In formal English, *ought,* unlike some other auxiliaries, has no form for the past tense. *Hadn't ought* is informal, *had ought* is nonstandard:

INFORMAL:	You *hadn't ought* to ask him.
FORMAL:	You *ought not to have* asked him.

hopefully When used instead of "I hope" or "let us hope," *hopefully* is widely considered illogical:

INFORMAL:	*Hopefully,* the forms will be ready by Monday.
FORMAL:	*I hope* the forms will be ready by Monday.

if, whether *If* is sometimes criticized when used to express doubt or uncertainty after such verbs as *ask, don't know, wonder, doubt.* The more formal subordinator is *whether:* "I doubt *whether* his support would do much good."

in, into Formal writing often requires *into* rather than *in* to indicate direction: "He came *into* (not *in*) the room."

in terms of A vague all-purpose connective frequent in jargon: "What have you seen lately *in terms of* new plays?"

JARGON:	What did she expect *in terms of* salary?
BETTER:	What salary did she expect?

infer, imply Use *imply* to mean "hint or suggest a conclusion." Use *infer* to mean "draw a conclusion on the basis of what has been hinted or suggested." A speaker implies something; the audience infers what is meant from the speaker's hints.

irregardless Use *regardless. Irregardless,* sometimes heard in educated speech, is widely considered illogical and nonstandard.

it's me, it is I Grammarians require *it is I* on the grounds that the linking verb *is* equates the pronoun *I* with the subject *it* and thus makes necessary the use of the subject form. *It's me* is now freely used in informal speech. Avoid it and parallel uses of other pronouns *(us, him, her)* in your writing:

INFORMAL:	I thought it was *him.* It could have been *us.*
FORMAL:	It was *she* who paid the bills.

judicial, judicious A judicial decision is reached by a judge or by a court. A judicious decision shows sound judgment.

learn, teach In standard English, the teacher *teaches* (rather than *learns*) the learner. The learner is *taught* (rather than *learned*) by the teacher.

STANDARD: They *taught* (not *learned*) us everything we know.

leave, let In formal usage, *leave* does not mean "allow" or "permit." You do not "leave" somebody do something. Nor does *leave* take the place of *let* in suggestions like "Let us call a meeting."

less, fewer To be safe, use *less* in references to extent, amount, degree (*less* friction, *less* money, *less* heat). Do not use it in references to things you can count: *fewer* people, *fewer* homes, *fewer* requirements.

like as a conjunction In informal speech, *like* is widely used as a subordinator replacing *as* or *as if* at the beginning of a clause. Avoid this informal *like* in your writing:

INFORMAL: Do *like* I tell you.
FORMAL: Do *as* I tell you.

INFORMAL: The patient felt *like* he had slept for days.
FORMAL: The patient felt *as if* (or *as though*) he had slept for days.

In formal usage, *like* is acceptable as a preposition, followed by an object: *like* a bird, *like* a cloud. It is not acceptable as a connective that starts a clause, with its own subject and verb: *like* a bird flies, *like* a cloud had passed.

most, almost *Most* is informal when used in the sense of "almost" or "nearly": "*Most* everybody was there." "Jones considers herself an authority on *most* any subject." Use "*almost* everybody," "*almost* any subject."

nohow, nowheres, nowhere near *Nohow* and *nowheres* are nonstandard for *in no way* and *nowhere*. *Nowhere near* is informal for *not nearly*: "They were not nearly as clever as they thought."

off of Nonstandard for *off* or *from:*

STANDARD: Take it *off* (not *off of*) the table.
She deducted two dollars *from* (not *off of*) the price.

on account of Nonstandard as a substitute for *because:*

NONSTANDARD: When promoted, people may stop trying *on account of* (should be "because") they have reached their goal.

plus *Plus* is acceptable in writing when used about figures, sums, and the like. Avoid using it as an informal substitute for *and* or *also:* "He dresses shabbily, *and* (not *plus*) he smells."

possessives with verbal nouns A traditional rule requires that a verbal noun (**gerund**) be preceded by a possessive in sentences like the following:

FORMAL: He mentioned *John's winning* a scholarship.
            I am looking forward to *your mother's staying* with us.

In informal English, the plain form is common:

INFORMAL: Imagine *John winning* a scholarship!

A combination of a pronoun and a verbal with the *-ing* ending may express two different relationships. In the sentence "I saw *him returning* from the library," you actually saw *him*. In the sentence "I object to *his using* my toothbrush," you are not objecting to *him* but merely to one of *his* actions. Use the possessive pronoun (*my, our, his, their*) when the object of a verb or of a preposition is not the person but one of his or her actions, traits, or experiences:

RIGHT: We investigated the chances of *his* being elected.
           There is no excuse for *their* not writing sooner.

predominate *Predominate* is a verb: "Shirt sleeves and overalls *predominated* in the crowd." *Predominant* is the adjective: "Antiwar feeling was *predominant*." "Democrats were the *predominant* party."

preposition at the end of a sentence The preposition that ends a sentence is idiomatic, natural English, though more frequent in informal than in formal use:

INFORMAL: I don't remember what we talked *about*.
FORMAL: Let us not betray the ideals *for* which these men died.

prepositions often criticized *Inside of* (for *inside*), *outside of* (for *outside*), and *at about* (for *about*) are redundant.

Back of for *behind* (*back of* the house), *inside of* for *within* (*inside* of three hours), *outside of* for *besides* or *except* (no one *outside* of my friends), and *over with* for *over* (it's *over with*) are colloquial.

As to, as regards, and *in regard to* often seem heavy-handed and bureaucratic:

AWKWARD: I questioned him *as to* the nature of his injury.
PREFERABLE: I questioned him *about* his injury.

As to whether, in terms of, and *on the basis of* flourish in all varieties of jargon.

Per (a dollar *per* day), *as per* (*as per* your request), and *plus* (quality *plus* service) are common in business and newspaper English but inappropriate in a noncommercial context.

provided, provided that, providing Provided, *provided that*, and *providing* are interchangeable in a sentence like "He will withdraw his complaint, *provided* you apologize." However, only *provided* has escaped criticism and is therefore the safest form to use.

reason is because The reason . . . *is because* is often criticized as redundant, since *because* repeats the idea of cause already expressed in the word *reason*.

INFORMAL: *The reason that the majority rules is because it is strongest.*
FORMAL: *The reason that the majority rules is that it is strongest.*

shall, will In current American usage, *will* usually indicates simply that something is going to happen. (I will ask him tomorrow.) The more emphatic *shall* often shows determination, obligation, or command:

We *shall* do our best.
Wages of common laborers *shall* not exceed twenty dollars a day.

   Shall is also common in questions that invite the listener's approval or consent:

Shall I wait for you?
Shall we dance?

   Handbooks no longer require *shall* for simple future in the first person: "I *shall* see him tomorrow."

so **and** *such* Informal English often uses *so* or *such* without going on to the *so . . . what?* "They were *so* frightened" (that what?). "There was *such* an uproar" (that what?). Substitute "They were *extremely* frightened" or add the *so . . . what?*

RIGHT: They were so frightened *that they were unable to speak.*
There was such an uproar *that the judge banged the gavel in vain.*

split infinitives Occasionally, a modifier breaks up an infinitive, that is, a verbal formed with *to* (*to come, to promise, to have written*). The resulting split infinitive occurs in the work of distinguished writers, and the traditional rule against it has been widely abandoned. However, a split infinitive can be awkward if the modifier that splits the infinitive is more than one word:

AWKWARD: He ordered us *to* with all possible speed *return* to our stations.
BETTER: He ordered us *to return* to our stations with all possible speed.

superlative in reference to two In informal speech and writing, the superlative rather than the comparative frequently occurs in comparisons between only two things. This use of the superlative is often considered illogical:

INFORMAL: Which of the two candidates is the *best* speaker?
FORMAL: Which of the two candidates is the *better* speaker?

these kind Avoid "*these kind* of cars" and "*those kind* of cars." Agreement requires "*this kind* of car" (both singular) or "*these kinds* of fish" (both plural).

titles: *Dr., Prof., Reverend* In references to holders of academic degrees or titles, *Dr. Smith* and *Professor Brown* are courteous and correct. *Professor* is sometimes abbreviated in addresses when it precedes the full name: *Prof. Martha F. Brown.* In references to clergy, *Reverend* is usually preceded by *the* and followed by the first name, by initials, or by *Mr.* (*the Reverend William Carper; the Reverend W. F. Carper; the Reverend Mr. Carper*).

type, type of, -type Omitting the *of* in expressions like "this *type* of plane" is colloquial. Avoid *type* used as a suffix to turn nouns into adjectives: "an *escape-type* novel," "a *drama-type* program." Use "an *escape* novel," "a *dramatic* program."

unique It is often argued that one thing cannot be *more unique* than another. Either it is unique (one of a kind) or it isn't. Formal English therefore often substitutes *more nearly unique.*

used to, didn't use to, used to could *Used to* in questions or negative statements with *did* is informal. Avoid it in writing:

INFORMAL: She *didn't use to* smoke.
FORMAL: She *used not to* smoke.

Used to could is nonstandard for *used to be able.*

where, where at, where to In formal English, *where* takes the place of *where to* ("*Where* was it sent?") and *where at* ("*Where* is he?") *Where* used instead of *that* ("I read in the paper *where* a boy was killed") is informal.

who, which, and *that* *Who* and *whom* refer to persons ("the man *whom* I asked"). *Which* refers to ideas and things ("my son's car, *which* I bought"). A *who, whom,* or *which* introducing a restrictive clause may be replaced by *that.* In such situations, conservative usage keeps *who (whom)* but prefers *that* to *which.*

RESTRICTIVE: The people *whom* I asked liked the car *that* I bought.

Of which and *in which* can easily make a sentence awkward. *Whose* is therefore widely accepted in reference to ideas and things: "the Shank-

Painter Swamp, *whose* expressive name . . . gave it importance in our eyes" (Thoreau).

-*wise* People often change a noun into an adverb by tacking on *-wise;* this practice is common in business or advertising jargon:

JARGON: The delay was advantageous *tax-wise.*
BETTER: The delay was advantageous *for tax purposes.*

without *Without* is nonstandard when used as a conjunction (subordinator) introducing a clause:

NONSTANDARD: The owner won't let me stay *without* I pay the rent.
STANDARD: The owner won't let me stay *unless* I pay the rent.

you with indefinite reference Formal writing limits *you* to the meaning of "you, the reader." Much informal writing uses *you* with indefinite reference to refer to people in general; formal writing would substitute *one:*

INFORMAL: In ancient Rome, *you* had to be a patrician to be able to vote.
FORMAL: In ancient Rome, *one* had to be a patrician to be able to vote.

---

25   LETTERS

Make your business letters suggest competence and efficiency.

Correspondence creates special problems of manuscript form. Know how to write the kind of letter that you may have to write to a teacher, to a college official, or to a future employer.

25a   FORMAT OF BUSINESS LETTERS

Follow conventional letter form.

Study the samples of business correspondence on the following pages. Use them as models for spacing, indentation, punctuation, and the like.

(1) Return address. When you are not using the letterhead of a firm or an organization, type your return address above the date, as follows. Place it on the right side of the page:

```
                                        138 South Third Street
                                        San Jose, CA 95126
                                        January 12, 1989


Ms. Patricia Sobell
Personnel Manager
San Rafael Gazette
2074 Washington Avenue
San Rafael, CA 94902


Dear Ms. Sobell:
```

The sample letters on pages 696–698 illustrate a modern unindented **block format** and the more traditional indented format, as well as a streamlined, simplified alternative. Sample letters and advice in this section are adapted in part from Walter Wells, *Communications in Business*, and William C. Himstreet and Wayne Murlin Baty, *Business Communications: Principles and Methods*.

(2) **Inside address.** Write the complete address of the recipient. Use a courtesy title like *Mr.* or *Ms.* (the latter now widely replacing the traditional *Mrs.* and *Miss*). A woman may show her preference for one of the possible choices in the signature line of her own correspondence:

```
Sincerely                          Sincerely,

Kate Gordon                        Helen Freid

(Mrs.) Kate Gordon                 (Ms.) Helen Freid
```

(3) **Salutation.** Whenever you can, address your letter to a specific individual and name the person in your salutation: "Dear Dr. Carosso:"

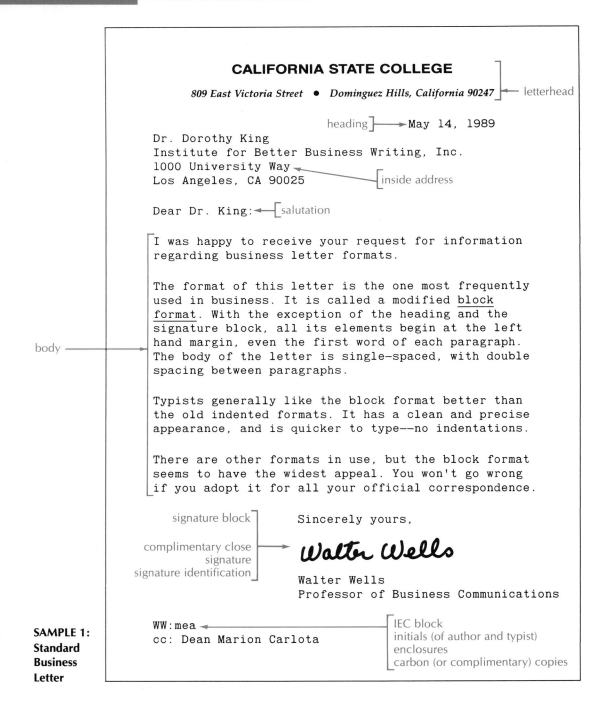

The Ironworks

2520 Eastern Avenue
Las Vegas, NE 89109

May 7, 1989

Mr. Perry Sneed, Manager
Green Thumb Nursery
3619 Kyrene Road
Tempe, AZ 85282

Dear Mr. Sneed:

Your order for three dozen wrought iron
potracks was shipped today.

We appreciate receiving Green Thumb Nursery as
a new account. Thank you for your initial order, and
we look forward to a pleasant business relationship.

Sincerely,

Loraine Holloway

Loraine Holloway
Sales Manager

fb

postscript—
last-minute
addition to
letter

P.S. We have just learned that some of our
shipments have been delayed briefly en route because
of a handlers' strike. We apologize for any
inconvenience.

**SAMPLE 2:
Short Letter;
Indented
Format**

CALIFORNIA STATE COLLEGE

809 East Victoria Street ● Dominguez Hills, California 90247

May 21, 1989

Institute for Better Writing, Inc.
1000 Commercial Way
Houston, TX 70747

THE SIMPLIFIED FORMAT IN BUSINESS LETTERS

As a follow-up to my letter of May 14, I'm writing
this letter to illustrate the simplified format in
action.

The simplified format, with its subject line in place
of a salutation, makes it easy for the reader to
identify the subject. But if that subject is
negative, the writer may want to find some phrasing
that avoids a negative impression at the outset.

Some teachers now teach the simplified format
exclusively. Others are holding out for one or the
other of the more traditional forms. As usual, all
the alternatives have their advantages and their
drawbacks.

Walter Wells

Walter Wells

WW:mea

SAMPLE 3:
Alternate
Simplified
Style

When you write to an office or organization, the traditional "Gentlemen:" or "Dear Sir:" is out. As more women hold responsible positions, the traditional greetings have become inaccurate and offensive. Look at different ways of handling (or sidestepping) the gender issue:

INDIVIDUAL:
```
Ms. Jane Day, President
The Waxo Company
225 East Elm Street
Walls, KS 76674


Dear Ms. Day:
```

OFFICE:
```
Personnel Director          or    Personnel Director
Wilson Chemical Company           Wilson Chemical Company
Hartville, KY 41052               Hartville, KY 41052


Dear Sir or Madam:                Dear Director:
```

ORGANIZATION:
```
The Jackson Manufacturing Company
1334 West Devonshire Road
Bolivar, MO 65613

Ladies and Gentlemen:
```

To sidestep the gender issue, you may want to use "Dear Reader:", "Dear Customer:", "Dear Participant:", or similar alternatives. Many writers, using a simplified format, now avoid the salutation altogether and use a **subject line** instead:

```
Alumni Club
2876 Dearborn Avenue
Las Vegas, NV 89109


SUBJECT: Your Lifetime Membership Offer
```

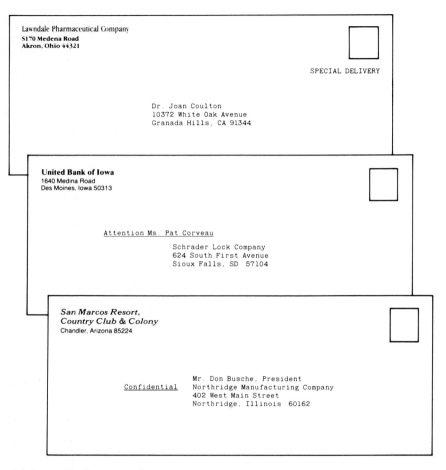

SAMPLE 4: Business Envelopes
(Here are some examples of well-typed business envelopes. Remember:
Accurate names and addresses are essential. Neatness counts.)

25b   ## THE LETTER OF APPLICATION

Write letters of application that will put you ahead of other applicants.

Employers look for applicants who will prove an asset to their organizations. Make your letter suggest initiative—willingness to do more than the minimum; curiosity—willingness to learn about the job or the organization; adaptability—willingness to meet the requirements of a new situation. Employers shy away from applicants who seem to promise problems, grievances, or an overinflated ego.

(1) If you can, be specific about the position for which you apply. Mention the advertisement or the person that alerted you to the vacancy. (But do not mention leads that smack of the grapevine.)

(2) Find a way in. If at all possible, show some knowledge of the company or the institution; show that the future employer already means something to you. For instance, mention an open house you attended at the company's research facility, a tour of a manufacturing plant, or a newspaper article about the company's plan for a new product or technique.

(3) Present your academic qualifications to advantage. Mention selected key courses that might relate to the employer's needs; stress what you got out of them.

(4) Stress previous experience. Make the most of part-time work. If at all appropriate, mention volunteer work, fund-raising efforts, campaign organizing, and the like. Stress what you learned from such experiences—for instance, learning to handle people's special needs by working with disabled students, or learning to budget resources by being in charge of equipment in a youth camp.

(5) If you want to list references, first get permission from those whose names you want to use. Quietly drop from your list the names of teachers or former employers who show little enthusiasm when you tell them about your plans.

(6) Consider preparing a separate résumé. If the account of your qualifications is extensive, put it on a separate data sheet.

EXERCISE 38   Find a project or recent development that merits *publicity or support*. Write a letter about it to the editors of a newspaper or magazine, to a legislator, or to a responsible official. Observe conventional letter form.

EXERCISE 39   Write a *letter of inquiry or request* in connection with some project in which you are currently interested. Observe conventional letter form.

EXERCISE 40   Write a *letter of application* for a position in which you have at one time or another taken an interest. State the qualifications that you might have by the time you are ready to apply for the position in earnest.

Dear Ms. Gabriel:

In answer to your advertisement, I wish to apply for a post as general reporter. My credentials are that I am a journalism major, and I have had some practical experience of working for a newspaper.

On February 1, I will graduate from San Jose State University. While getting a degree, I have taken a broad range of courses, representing all areas of editing and reporting. One course of special value to me has been a two-semester sequence of photojournalism that focused on the respective roles of word and image in news reporting.

I have been a general reporter for the Spartan Daily for two years and a feature editor for one year. Last summer I worked for thirteen weeks on the Santa Clara Journal, as an intern sponsored by the Journalism Department of my college. My special assignment was coverage of minority affairs with emphasis on multiethnic cultural events and bilingual education.

The following people have agreed to supply references:

          Dr. Mary Jane Cahill
          Department of Journalism
          San Jose State University
          San Jose, CA 95116

          Mr. Thomas Bigelow, General Manager
          Santa Clara Journal
          23 Roosevelt Avenue
          Santa Clara, CA 95052

          Mr. Richard H. James, Editor
          Los Angeles Examiner
          481 Elvira St.
          Los Angeles, CA 90037

I am prepared to be interviewed when you find it convenient.

          Yours truly,

          Pat C. Romeros

          Pat C. Romeros

JEAN LAPORTE

Demmler Hall   Age: 23
Valhalla University   Ht: 6-1 Wt: 170
Kent, Ohio 26780   Willing to relocate
(613) 538-7600

Education

B.S. in Industrial Engineering, Valhalla University, June
    1987; top 10% of class, with special course work in
    statistics, motivational psychology, business law, and
    communications.

Won U.S. Paint Company Scholarship 1986
Member of Industrial Relations Club
Elected Secretary of the Student Council
On Dean's Honor Roll since 1984

Also attended Colfax College, Colfax, Indiana, 1982-1985

Experience

    Staff Supervisor, Cleveland Summer Camp, Kiowa, Ohio,
        summer 1986; responsible for housing, activities
        scheduling and occasional discipline of fourteen
        counselors and 110 campers.

    Camp Counselor, Cleveland Summer Camp, Kiowa, Ohio,
        summers of 1983 and 1984.

Personal Interests

    Politics, world affairs, camping, chess, junior chamber
        of commerce member, and volunteer hospital worker

References

    Will gladly be provided upon request.

SAMPLE RÉSUMÉ

703

INDEX

Note: Boldfaced numbers preceding page numbers refer to the numerical handbook key. Page numbers followed by (gl) refer to an entry in the Glossary of Usage.

WRITING SAMPLE SOURCES

Isaac Asimov, "The 'Threat' of Creationism," *The New York Times*, June 14, 1981. Used with permission of Isaac Asimov.

Joan Beck, "Equality Approaches," *Chicago Tribune*, December 1977. Used with permission of the *Chicago Tribune*.

Rachel Carson, *Silent Spring*. Copyright © 1962 by Rachel Carson. Used with permission of Houghton Mifflin Company.

Marya Mannes, "Television: The Splitting Image," *Saturday Review*, November 14, 1970. Copyright © 1971 by Marya Mannes. Used with permission of the author's representative, David J. Blow.

Tracy Kidder, "Touble in the Stratosphere," *Atlantic*, November 1982. Used with permission of Tracy Kidder.

Jeffrey L. Pasley, "The Idiocy of Rural Life," *The New Republic*, December 8, 1986. © 1986 The New Republic, Inc. Used with permission of *The New Republic*.

Jonathan Raban, *Old Glory*. Copyright © 1981 by Jonathan Raban. Used with permission of Simon & Schuster, Inc.

Vincent S. Romano, "The Godfather Image Persists," *NEA Today*, October 1982. Used with permission of Vincent S. Romano.

Jon Swan, "The Opening," *The New Yorker*, April 2, 1960. © 1960, 1988 The New Yorker Magazine, Inc. Used with permisssion of *The New Yorker*.

May Swenson, "Question." Copyright © 1954, renewed © 1982 by May Swenson. Used with permission of May Swenson.

Barbara Tuchman, "Mankind's Better Moments," *The American Scholar*, Autumn 1980. Copyright © 1980 by Barbara W. Tuchman. Originally delivered as a Jefferson Lecture, Washington, D.C., April 1980. Used with permission of the author's agent, Russell & Volkening, Inc.